Gender and U.S. Immigration

Gender and U.S. Immigration

Contemporary Trends

EDITED BY

Pierrette Hondagneu-Sotelo

UNIVERSITY OF CALIFORNIA PRESS

Berkeley   Los Angeles   London

The following chapters were originally published in *American Behavioral Scientist* 42, no. 4 (Jan. 1999), © 1999 by Sage Publications, and are reprinted here by permission of Sage Publications, Inc.:

Chapter 2, "Engendering Migration Studies: The Case of New Immigrants in the United States," by Patricia R. Pessar, pp. 577–600

Chapter 4, "The Global Context of Gendered Labor Migration from the Philippines to the United States," by James A. Tyner, pp. 671–689

Chapter 5, "Gender and Labor in Asian Immigrant Families," by Yen Le Espiritu, pp. 628–647

Chapter 6, "The Intersection of Work and Gender: Central American Immigrant Women and Employment in California," by Cecilia Menjívar, pp. 601–627

Chapter 8, "Gendered Ethnicity: Creating a Hindu Indian Identity in the United States," by Prema Kurien, pp. 648–670

Chapter 14, "Engendering Transnational Migration: A Case Study of Salvadorans," by Sarah J. Mahler, pp. 690–719

The following chapter was originally published in *Signs* 26, no. 2 (2001), © 2001 by the University of Chicago Press, and is reprinted here by permission of the University of Chicago Press:

Chapter 13, "'We Don't Sleep Around Like White Girls Do': Family, Culture, and Gender in Filipina American Lives," by Yen Le Espiritu, pp. 415–440

The following chapter was originally published in *Gender & Society* 11 (1997).

Chapter 15, "'I'm Here, but I'm There': The Meanings of Latina Transnational Motherhood," by Pierrette Hondagneu-Sotelo and Ernestine Avila, pp. 317–340.

University of California Press
Berkeley and Los Angeles, California

University of California Press, Ltd.
London, England

© 2003 by the Regents of the University of California

Library of Congress Cataloging-in-Publication Data

Gender and U.S. immigration : contemporary trends / edited by Pierrette Hondagneu-Sotelo.
    p. cm.
    Some chapters were previously published in various sources.
    Includes bibliographical references and index.
    ISBN 0-520-22561-9 (cloth : alk. paper) — ISBN 0-520-23739-0 (pbk. : alk. paper)
    1. Women immigrants—United States.   2. United States—Emigration and immigration.   I. Hondagneu-Sotelo, Pierrette.

JV6602 .G457   2003
304.8'73'0082—dc21   2002043198

For Mike, with love and appreciation

CONTENTS

ACKNOWLEDGMENTS

This book brings together research by a diverse array of social science scholars seeking to understand new developments in gender and U.S. immigration. The volume began when I was invited by a journal to serve as guest editor for a special issue on gender and migration to the United States; six of the articles that originally appeared in the *American Behavioral Scientist* (January 1999) are reproduced here. I subsequently invited other scholars working in diverse communities at the intersections of gender and immigration to contribute to this book. I thank this talented group of social scientists for their hard work, their commitment to this project, their close attention to detail in the revision process, and for their patience. Although we never came together in a conference format to discuss our respective projects, our ideas and words have migrated across space and time. We are a community bound by similar interests, and I hope the dialogue will continue and expand to include others.

I am also grateful to my students at the University of Southern California for their inspiration and interests in many of the themes discussed in this volume. In particular, I wish to acknowledge Fajima Bedran, Belinda Lum, and Akiko Yasuike, graduate students who participated in a directed reading group where we read and discussed many of the initial drafts that appear here. Belinda Lum deserves special thanks. At the tail end of this project, she helped keep me on track with her incredible organizational skills and computer wizardry. She's amazing!

Pierrette Hondagneu-Sotelo

PART ONE

Introduction

CHAPTER I

Gender and Immigration

A Retrospective and Introduction

Pierrette Hondagneu-Sotelo

The intent of this volume is both modest and ambitious. High-caliber social science research has emerged on gender and U.S.-bound immigration in recent years, and this book simply draws together some of the best new work in the field. The book includes essays by pioneers who have logged nearly two decades in the field of gender and immigration, and new empirical work by both young scholars and well-established social scientists who bring their substantial talents to this topic for the first time. More ambitiously, this volume seeks to alert scholars and students to some of the gender consequences emerging from the last three decades of resurgent U.S. immigration. This immigration is changing life as we know it, in the United States and elsewhere, in many ways. One important change concerns the place of women and men in society.

I felt a need to put together this book because of the continued silence on gender in the contemporary social science literature on U.S. immigration. A glance at the main journals and at recent edited volumes on American immigration and international migration reveals that basic concepts such as sex, gender, power, privilege, and sexual discrimination only rarely enter the vocabulary or research design of immigration research. This is puzzling. Gender is one of the fundamental social relations anchoring and shaping immigration patterns, and immigration is one of the most powerful forces disrupting and realigning everyday life. It is my hope that the chapters in this volume will earn the recognition they deserve, spur a wider conversation about immigration and how it is changing social life for women and men, and prompt immigration scholars to design research that acknowledges the gendered social world in which we live.

THE EMERGENCE OF IMMIGRATION SCHOLARSHIP
AND GENDER STUDIES

During the 1980s and 1990s, the social sciences experienced major transformations. Among the most notable were two separate developments: the growth in feminist-oriented scholarship and immigration research. The establishment of women's studies programs and research derived from the second-wave feminist movement, which emerged in the 1970s to advocate equality for women. Feminist research called attention to the unequal power relations between women and men in society and illuminated and analyzed how women's and men's actions, positions, and relative privileges in society are socially constructed in ways that tend to favor men. Since then, we have witnessed a shift away from the premise of a unitary notion of "women" or "men" to an increasingly accepted perspective that acknowledges how the multiplicities of masculinities and femininities are interconnected, relational, and, most important, enmeshed in relations of class, race, and nation. Globalization, immigration, and transnationalism are significant sites for contemporary inquiries of gender.

The growth in immigration research derived not from a social movement like feminism, but from the massive increase in literal human movement across borders during the late 20th century. Today, it is estimated that as many as 150 million people live in nations other than those in which they were born. Only a small portion of these millions have come to the United States, although many Americans believe that the whole world has descended on their country. U.S. immigrants *have* reached unprecedented numbers—about 28 million according to the 2000 census—but this constitutes only about 10% of the total U.S. population, a smaller percentage than we saw earlier in the 20th century. Immigration is certainly nothing new for the United States—it is, after all, foundational to the national narrative—but the resurgence of immigration during the last three decades has taken many Americans by surprise. Prompted by global restructuring and post–World War II U.S. military, political, and economic involvement throughout Asia, the Caribbean, and Latin America, and facilitated by the 1965 amendment to the McCarran-Walter Immigration Act, which erased national origin quotas that had previously excluded Asians, U.S. immigration picked up in the 1970s and shows few signs of diminishing.

In the 1980s and 1990s, immigration to the United States from Asia, Latin America, and the Caribbean increased dramatically. These contemporary immigrants are a diverse lot. Among them are refugees and preliterate peasants as well as urbane, highly educated professionals and entrepreneurs. Although a fairly constant barrage of restrictionist, nativist, and blatantly xenophobic campaigns and legislation has raised tremendous obstacles to these newcomers, the number of legal permanent residents—those who can be legally admitted to live and work in the United States—has steadily increased in the 1990s. Nearly one million immigrants are now granted legal permanent residency status each year. Immigrants and their children today constitute about one fifth of the U.S. population, and the percentages are much higher in cities such as Los Angeles, New York, and Miami, where immigrants concentrate.

Different dimensions of immigrant social life are threaded by the dynamics of gender, and this volume exposes some of the complex ways in which these threads are woven. The chapters cover a range of topics, including the way gender informs the sexual practices and values among immigrant parents and their adolescent daughters, transnational political group participation, household divisions of labor, naturalization, and even our definition of childhood. Readers of this volume will gain insight into the lives of immigrants as diverse as affluent, cosmopolitan Indian Hindu professionals and relatively poor, undocumented, and modestly schooled manual workers from El Salvador and Mexico. All of the contributors to these chapters recognize that gender does not exist in a vacuum but emerges together with particular matrices of race relations, nation, occupational incorporation, and socioeconomic class locations, and the analyses reflect nuances of intersectionality.

Distinct approaches and areas of concern, which correspond to different stages of development, have characterized the gender and immigration scholarship. While the periodization is not nearly as linear as I present it below, glancing back at these legacies will allow us to better situate the contemporary research on gender and immigration.

FIRST STAGE: REMEDYING THE EXCLUSION OF WOMEN IN RESEARCH

The first stage of feminist scholarship emerged in the 1970s and early 1980s, and might be labeled "women and migration." This early phase of research sought to remedy the exclusion of women subjects from immigration research and to counter sexist as well as androcentric biases. It seems inconceivable to us today, but several very highly regarded immigration studies had relied entirely on survey or interview responses from men, and yet, based on this research, had made claims purported to represent the entire immigrant population. In some instances, men were asked to report for their wives and female kin. In other projects, women were unproblematically assumed to automatically follow male migrants as "associational" or dependent migrants and were often portrayed as somehow detached or irrelevant to the labor force. These premises were usually unfounded.[1] The first stage of research thus set about the task of actually taking women into account. As modest as this first-stage project seems to us today, it was met in many corners with casual indifference and in some instances, with hostile, defensive reception.[2]

Given the long-standing omission of women from migration studies, an important first step involved designing and writing women into the research picture. In retrospect, this stage is sometimes seen as consisting of a simplistic "add and stir" approach, whereby women were "added" as a variable and measured with regard to, say, education and labor market participation, and then simply compared with migrant men's patterns. This approach worked well in quantitative studies that sought to compare, say, immigrant women's and men's earnings. This type of approach, however, fails to acknowledge that gender is fundamentally about power. Gender informs different sets of social relations that organize immigration and social institutions (e.g., family, labor markets) in both immigrants' place of origin and place of destination.

Other research projects of this era focused exclusively on migrant women. This prompted several problems, among them the tendency to produce skewed "women only" portraits of immigration experiences. This approach characterized many historical monographs. Commenting on this trend in the introduction to an edited volume of multidisciplinary essays on immigrant women, historian Donna Gabaccia observed that "the numbers of volumes exploring immigrant women separately from men now exceeds the volumes that successfully integrate women into general accounts" (Gabaccia, 1992, p. xv). Paradoxically, this approach further marginalized immigrant women into a segregated subfield, separate from major social dynamics of immigration.

Equally problematic, as Cynthia Cranford and I have pointed out elsewhere (1999), both "add and stir" and "women only" efforts were often mired in some variant of sex-role theory. In this view, women's migration is explained with respect to "sex-role constraint," generally understood to be a set of stable, freestanding institutional practices and values rather than a fluid and mutable system that intersects with other social institutions. In the sex-role paradigm, separate spheres of public and private reign and men's and women's activities are seen as complementary and functional, while the manner in which these are relational, contested and negotiated, and imbued with power, privilege, and subordination is glossed over.

In retrospect, we can see that the immigrant "women only" and "add and stir" approaches limit our understanding of how gender as a social system shapes immigration processes for all immigrants, men and women. Only women, not migrant men, are marked as "gendered," and institutions with which they interact—family, education, and employment, etc.—are presumed to be gender neutral. The preoccupation with writing women into migration research and theory stifled theorizing about the ways in which constructions of femininities and masculinities organize migration and migration outcomes.

A different and exciting body of feminist migration research appeared in the early to mid-1980s, and although not centered on U.S.-bound migration, it has left a significant impact on the field. It focused on the recruitment of poor, young, mostly unmarried women from peasant or agrarian backgrounds for wage work in the new export processing plants owned by multinational firms in the Caribbean, along the U.S.-Mexico border, and Asia. These studies alerted us to the linkages between deindustrialization in the United States and the emergence of a new "feminized" global assembly line. Case studies from around the globe explored the relationship between young women workers' migration, the shifting gender and generational dynamics in their family relations, and their incorporation into new regimes of production and consumption (see Arizpe & Aranda, 1981; Fernández-Kelly, 1983; Wolf, 1992).

In a key article published in a 1984 special issue of the *International Migration Review* on women and migration, Saskia Sassen posited a relationship between internal rural-urban migration of young women to work in export manufacturing and agriculture in the Third World, and the increasing labor migration of women from these countries to the United States. Both types of female migration, Sassen suggests, are driven by the dynamics of corporate globalization: the intensification of profit and the reliance on low-wage work performed by disenfranchised Third World women. This moment marks a significant switch from a "women only" and "sex-role constraints" individualistic approach to one that looks more broadly at how gender is incorporated into corporate globalization strategies.

SECOND STAGE: FROM "WOMEN AND MIGRATION" TO "GENDER AND MIGRATION"

A distinctive second phase of research emerged in the late 1980s and early 1990s, displacing an exclusive focus on women with recognition of gender as a set of social practices shaping and shaped by immigration. Prompted in part by the disruption of the universal category "women" in feminist scholarship, by heightened awareness of the intersectionality of race, class, and gender relations, by the observation that men possess, display, and enact a variety of masculinities, and by the recognition of the fluidity of gender relations, this research focused on two aspects: the gendering of migration patterns *and* how migration reconfigures new systems of gender inequality for women and men.

Among this crop of gender and migration studies are Sherri Grasmuck and Patricia Pessar's study of Dominican migration to New York City, much of which is reported in the book *Between Two Islands: Dominican International Migration* (1991), Nazli Kibria's *Family Tightrope: The Changing Lives of Vietnamese Americans* (1993), and my own research on undocumented Mexican migration to California, reported in *Gendered Transitions: Mexican Experiences of Immigration* (1994). All of these studies take as their launching point a critique of "household strategies," a model explicitly and implicitly used by many migration studies of that period. The critiques put forth in these three books, informed and driven by feminist insights, particularly those from Third World contexts, counter the image of a unitary household undivided by gender and generational hierarchies of power, authority, and resources. Families and immigrant social networks, these studies underscore, are highly gendered institutions. This body of research highlights conflict in gender relations, the result of a strong feminist lens on the lookout for evidence of patriarchy and male domination *and* of methodological reliance on interviews and ethnography. These methods, as both Prema Kurien and Patricia Pessar note in their essays in this volume, tend to throw into relief gender conflicts and negotiations that might appear uncontested when survey methods are used.

The second-stage research is also notable for drawing attention to the ways in which men's lives are constrained and enabled by gender and also the ways in which immigrant gender relations become more egalitarian through the processes of migration. This constitutes the "migration and emancipation" studies that Pessar soberly reassesses in chapter 2 of this volume. Equally as problematic as some of the issues that Pessar points to is the extent to which these empowerment studies were anchored by the idea that immigrant women's wages and jobs necessarily lead to gender equality in families and households. Several of the essays in this volume (Menjívar, Kurien, Espiritu) continue this focus on the family-work nexus, but they bring considerably more sophistication and attention to dimensions besides wages and family.

Identifying and naming distinctively gendered orientations to settlement—that is, how immigrant women and men feel about staying in the United States and how these preferences derive from alterations to immigrant gender relations—is another accomplishment of second-stage research. Immigrant women's enhanced social status (won variously through jobs, social network resources, or new interactions with social institutions) often goes hand in hand with immigrant men's loss of public and domestic status. In the United States, immigrant men may for the first time in their lives occupy subordinate positions in class, racial, and citizenship hierarchies. This prompts many of them to express nostalgia and a desire to return to their country of origin. Several of the essays in this volume use this analysis of gendered settlement outcomes and orientations to explain new terrain, including gendered arenas as diverse as naturalization strategies (Singer and Gilbertson), participation in transnational political associations (Goldring), and family-work intersections among Jewish immigrants from different nation-states (Gold).

One of the weaknesses of the way many of the second-stage research projects were conducted is the implication that gender resides almost exclusively in mesolevel social institutions, such as family, households, community institutions, or social networks. In retrospect, this meso-focused approach seems myopic and faulty, and my own work exemplifies this oversight. In *Gendered Transitions,* I underlined the extent to which Mexican migration is gendered by focusing on family relations and networks. The book argues that while the origins of undocumented Mexican migration lie in the political and economic transformations within the United States and Mexico and especially in the linkages established between the two countries, it is gender operating at the family and community levels that shapes distinctively gendered patterns of migration. In some families, for example, daughters and wives may not be accorded permission or family resources with which to migrate, but they sometimes find ways to circumvent or alter these "patriarchal constraints."

The problem with this perspective is that not only families and communities but also other institutions are gendered, including both informal and programmatic labor recruitment efforts, as Terry Repak (1995) has emphasized. We live in a society where occupational sex segregation stubbornly prevails in the labor force and consequently shapes labor demand and migration. This is particularly urgent to-day, as immigrant women from around the world migrate to many postindustrial societies for work as nurses, nannies, cleaners, and sex workers. Particular types of societies create particularly gendered labor demands. This is an important issue to consider, but work and employment were generally only considered by second-stage researchers insofar as women's earnings or job schedules affected gender relations in families and households. Just because we can "see" gender most saliently in face-to-face institutions such as families and households does not mean that it is not critical to the constitution of other institutions and processes.

In our haste to analyze how everyday relationships and institutions enable or constrain migration, we gave other arenas short shrift. Among these are the gen-dered and racialized nature of labor markets in the nations of origin and destina-tion, and the ways these are conditioned by globalization, cultural change, and eco-nomic restructuring. Similarly, the privileging of men, marriage, and normative heterosexuality in immigration legislation has scarcely received scholarly attention. Racial formation, Michael Omi and Howard Winant's (1994) conceptualization of how race relations are simultaneously shaped by historical and social processes *and* built into social institutions, has invigorated race relations research. Similarly, we may begin to think of this next stage of research as gender formation.

To reiterate, a primary weakness of the second-stage research is that it allocated too much attention to the level of family and household, suggesting that gender is somehow enclosed within the domestic arena. Consequently, many other impor-tant arenas and institutions—jobs, workplaces, labor demand, notions of citizen-ship and changing immigration policy, public opinion, immigration and refugee policies, state agencies, sites of consumption, media, and the Border Patrol, to name a few—were ignored by feminist research and appeared then as though they were devoid of gender.

THIRD STAGE: GENDER AS A CONSTITUTIVE ELEMENT OF IMMIGRATION

The third stage of feminist scholarship in immigration research is now emerging, and here the emphasis is on looking at gender as a key constitutive element of im-migration. In this current phase, research is beginning to look at the extent to which gender permeates a variety of practices, identities, and institutions implicated in immigration. Here, patterns of labor incorporation, globalization, religious prac-tice and values, ethnic enclave businesses, citizenship, sexuality, and ethnic iden-tity are interrogated in ways that reveal how gender is incorporated into a myriad of daily operations and institutional political and economic structures. As this col-lection of essays shows, gender organizes a number of immigrant practices, beliefs, and institutions.

While most of the gender-inflected research continues to be produced by female scholars, men are making important contributions as well, as the chapters in this volume by Tyner and Gold show. Among the studies looking at community political mobilization by immigrants is research conducted by Michael Jones-Correa. Focusing on Latino immigrant political identity and practice in New York City and building on the research of earlier feminist inquiries that suggests that immigrant men shift their orientation to their home countries and to the prospect of return migration as they lose status in the United States, Jones-Correa (1998) reveals that immigrant women are more likely than immigrant men to participate in community organizations that interface with U.S. institutions. Looking at the other side of this coin, researcher Luin Goldring (this volume) has studied the recently emergent and now quite powerful transnational Mexican hometown associations, organizations formed by Mexican immigrants in the United States that typically raise funds in the United States to assist with community development projects "back home." These can be read, Goldring persuasively suggests, as efforts that allow immigrant men to claim social status denied to them in the new society. In these transmigrant organizations, which span nation-state borders, men find a privileged arena of action, enhancing their gender status. Women participate in these associations as beauty pageant contestants or as men's helpers, and although they remain absent from active leadership or decision-making roles in the transnational associations, they practice what Goldring calls "substantive social citizenship" in community organizations in the United States.

LOCATING GENDER AND IMMIGRATION

Chapters 2 and 3 are written, respectively, by two of the most renowned pioneers in the gender and immigration field. In chapter 2, Patricia Pessar reviews in detail and with tremendous insights how the field has relied on analyses of households and social networks. She calls for greater awareness of how relations of class, race, and nation shape immigrant women's incorporation, and she suggests that looking at different levels of analysis will lead us to see that immigrant women's gains have always been uneven and often contradictory, a conclusion that certainly resonates with several chapters in this volume.

The chapter by globalization theorist Saskia Sassen pushes the analysis of gender to the macro scale. Sassen suggests that a new "counter-geography of globalization" is under way and that it is constituted in part by the cross-national, unauthorized movements of women as diverse as mail-order brides, enslaved and trafficked sex workers, and undocumented immigrant factory and service workers. Sassen's provocative work is always stimulating, and we can certainly think of a myriad of occupations in postindustrial urban societies now almost wholly dependent on the deliberate recruitment of foreign-born women. In our postindustrial service economies, work that native-born women once performed for free is now purchased in the global marketplace. This prompts us to think about how realignments in gender arrangements in host countries have in fact generated labor demand for immigrant women. Domestic workers, sex workers, cleaners, and nurses are some examples of this occupational explosion.

Sassen emphasizes the connections between these international labor migrations, Structural Adjustment Policies that have undermined poor women's economic survival throughout parts of Asia, Latin America, and the Caribbean, and the growing importance of remittances for countries such as El Salvador and the Philippines. Today it is estimated that immigrant workers annually send to Mexico, El Salvador, and the Philippines, respectively, $8 billion, $3.5 billion, and $7 billion. Migrant remittances keep these economies afloat. The emotional connections that immigrant workers maintain with their families back home fuel the extensive remittances that today account for a significant source of foreign exchange for these countries. Sassen's specification begins to connect some of the dots in the big global picture and allows us to better understand the specificity of gendered immigration to the United States.

GENDER AND EMPLOYMENT

The study of work continues to occupy a good deal of space in immigration studies—work is, after all, the primary reason immigrants come to the United States—and the following clusters of chapters tackle familiar questions of gender and employment. They do so, however, with an eclectic bag of approaches. Using insights from political geography, James Tyner analyzes Filipino international migration to the United States. The Philippine government channels the movement of Filipino women and men to multiple sites around the world. Filipinos, Tyner informs us, now go to a whopping 130 countries, *and nearly all of these flows reveal a distinctive sex composition.* Filipino men have been recruited primarily for construction jobs in the Middle East ("men's jobs") while Filipina women have been routed into "women's jobs" as nurses and domestic workers throughout Asia, the Middle East, Europe, Canada, and the United States.

What remains particularly striking is that post-1965 U.S.-bound Filipino migration appears to be, comparatively speaking, an anomaly. It occurs outside the institutionalized labor contract system, it consists primarily of skilled technicians and nurses rather than manual laborers, and it includes women *and* men, unlike many of the other more sex-segregated Filipino migration flows. The United States does not solicit sex-segregated Filipino migration, due to the diversity of U.S. labor demand and the liberalization of immigration policies, which have emphasized since 1965 family reunification and skilled professional status as criteria for legal permanent residence.

Asian immigrant women have recorded the highest labor force participation rates among women in the United States, and Yen Le Espiritu addresses the familiar question of how this has affected gender relations in immigrant families. Her starting premise is that occupational and socioeconomic heterogeneity, together with racial subordination, determines outcomes. Espiritu situates her analysis in a triadic taxonomy of Asian immigrant occupational structure: salaried profession-als, self-employed entrepreneurs, and wage laborers. Through an exhaustive review of the literature, Espiritu finds that each occupational group exhibits distinctive gender dynamics. Among Asian immigrant professionals, there seems to be evi-dence that immigrant women's occupational status as professionals is more trans-ferable to the United States than is men's. In fact, in some instances women's job status as professionals has allowed them to petition for their husbands and families to legally immigrate to the United States. The men are thus dependent on their wives to obtain legal permanent residency status. These resources—legal status and professional job status—seem to translate into more equality in the home for these women. The situation is very different for Asian immigrant women who may be equally class privileged but who remain locked in family businesses, where they may work in isolation and remain mired in dependency. Espiritu's work reminds us of the importance of nuanced analyses of class and occupation.

Asking similar questions about a diverse group of Salvadoran and Guatemalan immigrant women in California, Cecilia Menjívar observes that California's urban and suburban labor markets tend to favor Central American women over men. Central American women find jobs faster, work more hours, and appear to earn, on average, more than their Central American male partners do in California. Yet contrary to what we might expect using a relative resources gauge, this apparent labor market advantage does not automatically or uniformly lead to more egali-tarian relations in the family. In fact, women's employment advantage may inflame rather than quell family tensions and household inequalities.

Going beyond simple wage differentials to pursue her analysis, Menjívar finds that cultural-ethnic legacies and ideals about gender and family, marriage patterns, and the sex-segregated venues of employment shape gender outcomes. The ap-proach in previous studies has usually treated gender relations in the home coun-try as monolithic, but Menjívar acknowledges important distinctions, in this case between mestizo and indigenous cultures. Not content to simply acknowledge em-ployment, Menjívar considers how the context of employment shapes new gender ideals and practices. While many of the Central American women, for example, work in private domestic work and bring home new ideals of husbands and wives sharing cooking and child rearing, the men tend to work with other Latino men and find support for maintaining their old ways of life. New ideals of companion-ate marriage and household divisions of labor may emerge together.[3]

In the final chapter in this section, sociologist Steve Gold engages the literature on gendered settlement preferences. He emphasizes the importance of comparing immigrants' status and employment opportunities in the United States with what they might conceivably return to in their countries of origin. He compares two groups of well-educated White middle-class immigrants: Israeli Jewish and Russian Jewish immigrants. While both groups are fairly secular, their religious-ethnic iden-tity as Jews remains an important one to them. Here, the intersection of nation, gender, and ethnicity is key, as Russian Jews had their religious and cultural identity suppressed and disparaged in the former USSR, while the Israeli Jews' ethnic identity was openly celebrated as key to the nation of Israel. When they come to the United States, Israeli Jewish men find that they are no longer integral to the nation, but they seem willing to accept a demoted ethnic status in return for enhanced economic opportunities in the United States. By contrast, Israeli Jewish women often wish to return because they miss access to women's networks and the stronger welfare state resources. What these immigrant women and men left back home proves to be crucial in their assessments of life in the United States.

ENGENDERING RACIAL AND ETHNIC IDENTITIES

Most of the recent immigration research has focused on immigrant groups that are socioeconomically disadvantaged, those who have entered as labor migrants or political refugees. Consequently, we know little about gender relations among highly educated professional and entrepreneurial immigrants who came to the United States in significant numbers in the 1970s and 1980s. The scholarship of Prema Kurien fills this lacuna and underlines the mutually constitutive features of ethnicity, religion, and gender among Hindu Indian immigrant professionals in Southern California.

Hindu Indian immigrants generally live in suburban locations, and many of them have formed new Hindu religious associations. Kurien assesses gender relations among these groups, but, not content to confine her analysis to the household or family level, she also assesses gender in these newly invented Hindu congregations and in larger pan-Indian immigrant organizations. At the level of family and congregations, Kurien finds that Indian immigrant women make tremendous strides toward equality: husbands do more housework than they did in India, and in the congregations women actively reshape the culture in ways that reflect their own enhanced status. These forward strides, however, are reduced to backward steps in the large pan-Indian organizations, where men occupy the leadership positions and, under racist and assimilationist pressures, seek to present a model-minority countenance to Americans. At this level, women may find themselves placed in more retrograde positions than they did in India. Kurien reminds us that in the reconfiguration of gender relations, diverse levels of analysis and ethnicity are intertwined with distinct outcomes.

Nancy Lopez moves down the generational scale to consider the educational and occupational outcomes for second-generation Caribbean young adults. Research activity on the new second generation has flourished as a cottage industry, and the concept of "segmented assimilation," introduced by Alejandro Portes and Min Zhou (1993), emphasizes that there is no singular outcome. Many scholars have recently grappled with the finding that across the board immigrant girls, like girls in general, are obtaining higher levels of education than their brothers. Several commentators have suggested these outcomes reflect "gendered pathways" (Waldinger

& Perlmann, 1998, p. 12). The idea here is that patriarchal notions that girls require greater protection, greater constraints on spatial mobility, and stricter curfews in order to maintain virtue, virginity, and reputation meshes with educational systems that reward compliance and obedience, traits associated with femininity. Meanwhile, immigrant parents often give boys freer reign, and, for immigrant boys of color, experiences of racism may fuel a masculinist "oppositional culture" in which street values, rather than school values, predominate (Foner, 2000; Waters, 1999).

In her chapter, Lopez identifies distinctively gendered experiences with racism, particularly in the world of work. Rather than seeing oppositional culture as the key culprit of poor educational outcomes among young second-generation youth, she examines everyday experiences with racism in mostly sex-segregated occupations. Brilliantly reversing the traditional school-work trajectory, she shows that employment experiences, inflected by race and gender, wind up either motivating or de-motivating students to pursue higher education. For some Caribbean second-generation youth, particularly the young men phenotypically identified as Black, the consequences are particularly harsh, and they are thus most likely to suffer second-generation decline. Young women are not spared some of the most insidious forms of racial exclusion and stereotyping; indeed, they endure grotesque sexist and racist comments made directly to them in their jobs. But the office jobs where they are likely to be incorporated offer them greater opportunities and financial returns for education. Hence, they are more motivated to pursue education beyond high school. The consequences of racial oppression and employment thus appear to most severely disadvantage and demoralize young men, particularly those perceived as Black.

In the subsequent chapter, Maura Toro-Morn and Marixsa Alicea also focus on young adults through their interview research with the children and grandchildren of Puerto Ricans who came to Chicago and New York City. Puerto Ricans are not classic immigrants, as their nation and culture have been formally colonized by the United States since 1898. The labor migration of Puerto Ricans to the U.S. mainland occurs in this context, and, inspired by cultural studies, Toro-Morn and Alicea explore how Puerto Ricans born and raised in the United States see themselves in relation to Puerto Rico. When the authors asked these young Puerto Ricans born and raised in the United States how they imagine "home," the responses indicated that their learned notions of home have deeply shaped gender and identities. Puerto Rican parents disciplined their children in the United States by constantly invoking the idea that Puerto Rico is a fixed, static, pristine cultural space, one with different rules for boys and girls. For adolescent girls, adhering to this notion of authenticity accentuates gender oppression.

GENDER, GENERATION, AND IMMIGRATION

Many new immigrants perceive the United States to be a dangerous and undesirable place to raise a family, one where their children will be exposed to drugs, violence, excessive consumerism, and social norms that contest parental authority. The innovative chapters in this section focus on generational relations between immigrant parents and their children, examining how parents and their children negotiate new social challenges with cultural integrity. This section includes one chapter on gendered and changing notions of childhood in transnational contexts, and two others that explore, respectively, how two deeply Catholic immigrant groups, Mexicans and Filipinos, approach sexuality—which some of them perceive as an intensified "danger"—among their adolescent daughters. Sexuality is fundamental to structuring gender inequality, but the gender and migration literature, with few exceptions, has shied away from this topic.

In the first chapter, Gloria González-López uses sociological insights and her background working as a family therapist to explore the content of what Mexican immigrant mothers teach their daughters about virginity and sexuality in Los Angeles. Contrary to what she had expected to find in her interviews with twenty women from Mexico City and twenty from the rural state of Jalisco, Mexico, Mexican immigrant women do not blindly follow the Catholic Church's well-known sexually repressive teachings, which mandate premarital sexual abstinence and virginity for their daughters. More important in informing their views than Catholicism, which the Mexican immigrant women tended to see as separate from their private lives, were their immigration experiences and the regional cultures from which they originate. Mexican immigrant women from cosmopolitan, urban Mexico City were more open to teaching their daughters about birth control and sexual intimacy than were immigrant women from the heart of rural Jalisco, a western state widely known in Mexico for its unremitting masculinist culture of *charros* (rodeo cowboys), tequila, and bride kidnapping. The regional patriarchies, or *machismos regionales,* that prevail in these two locales are not, however, the only influences informing Mexican immigrant women's sexual values and practices. Mexican mothers want their daughters to remain virgins only to the extent that it enhances their daughters' life opportunities; they soon realize that virginity has less salient currency in Los Angeles than it did in Mexico.

The following chapter in this section, based on team research in multiple immigrant communities conducted by Barrie Thorne, Marjorie Faulstich Orellana, Wan Shun Eva Lam, and Anna Chee, moves further down the age ladder to where scholars of contemporary immigration have never tread. In this pathbreaking work, the authors examine immigrant children—more correctly, constructions of childhood—in various transnational contexts, analyzing how culture, age, and gender mesh. The field research for this chapter examines the diverse experiences of Central American and Korean children who mostly reside in the Pico Union and Korea Town neighborhoods of Los Angeles, and Cantonese, Laotian, and Yemeni children in Oakland. I say "mostly reside" because many of these children travel back to their home countries, some to be disciplined, some to learn the home culture, and others to simply visit relatives. Even those children who are not physically moving across nation-states and cultures may be exposed to radically different social fields.

Thorne and her colleagues underline for us that basic concepts such as "growing up" and "raising children" imply movement to adulthood and involve a set of practices that must be applied *to* children to transform them into adults. What happens, they ask, when parents are raising children in transnational contexts and must negotiate conflicting ideals? There are no uniform patterns, but two central guiding principles, sure to inspire and frame future research, are offered: legal constructions of childhood and adulthood vary, and transnational families must negotiate these; and gendered constructions of boyhood and girlhood vary within transnational sites. As the authors note, some immigrant parents have expectations (adultlike responsibilities, including work in family businesses or caring for younger siblings) that conflict with late 20th-century American notions of childhood, which tend to emphasize sentimentality, play, and educational development. These too are gendered.

The final chapter in this section, by Yen Le Espiritu focuses on the regulation of young women's sexuality. Based on interviews conducted with Filipino American parents and children, she finds that Filipino immigrant parents do impose strong expectations and restrictions on their adolescent daughters' sexuality and dating practices. In doing so, she argues, they are not acting out some scripted cultural legacy, but rather reacting to the experience of colonialism, the Americanization of their nation, and their experience of racism in the United States. "Racialized immigrants," Espiritu argues, "claim through gender the power denied them through racism." Policing their daughters' bodies and restricting their spatial mobility is one of the few venues through which racially subordinated groups can reconstruct White Americans as inferior and themselves as superior. Espiritu shows that immigrant parents do this not by invoking the simplistic madonna/whore dichotomy, but rather by invoking notions of cultural-ethnic and national authenticity. Filipinas, the parents tell their daughters, do not act with the sexual freedom and autonomy of White American girls. This exacts a deep emotional cost on the daughters, for whom sexual transgressions or even modest outings with friends signify not only gender and generational contestations, but larger betrayals of race, nation, and culture.

GENDER, CITIZENSHIP, AND THE TRANSNATIONAL

Transnationalism, which emphasizes the ongoing attachments that immigrants maintain with people and institutions in their places of origin, has seriously challenged conventional ideas about immigrants and immigration. Rather than viewing immigration as a linear, one-way process that requires new immigrants to sever all connections with the old country, scholars inspired by transnational approaches examine how people stay connected and often form a cohesive community across nation-state borders. This final section of the book brings together four essays that consider the place of gender in transnational practices and institutions.

In the first chapter, Sarah Mahler draws on years of research in Salvadoran immigrant communities in suburban Long Island to ask how a particular rural area of El Salvador has been affected by out-migration and the creation of new transnational communities. Gender relations are malleable to all kinds of processes, and Mahler shows how local, national, and transnational processes intersect to shape immigrant social networks and gender ideals for children and youth. At the other end of the generational spectrum, Mahler investigates the relatively new and quintessentially transnational occupation of cross-border couriers. These are self-employed entrepreneurs who travel back and forth across international borders to deliver remittances (the largest source of foreign exchange for El Salvador), letters, parcels, and appliances. While the work is risky, older women are preferred in this occupation because they are seen as trustworthy and capable of easing people's worries. In this instance, conceptions of womanhood that hark back to Victorian ideals of women's moral superiority seem to give women an edge.

In the next chapter, Ernestine Avila and I examine how the exigencies of domestic work, financial scarcity, and precarious legal status have forced many immigrant women to leave their children behind in their countries of origin. While they care for other people's children in the United States, immigrant domestic workers may encounter long separations of time and space from their own children. Our analysis underscores the emergence of new international inequalities of social reproductive work and focuses on how these women are forging new meanings of motherhood that we call "transnational motherhood." Particular migration and employment patterns bring about new meanings of family life and new definitions of what constitutes a "good mother," but these are generally accompanied by ambivalences and great costs.

Ties and loyalties to the "old country" are an enduring feature of immigration, but immigrant women and men may express these loyalties in different ways. Immigrants from countries such as the Dominican Republic, Colombia, and Mexico have formed thousands of hometown associations in the United States. These are social and civic clubs that allow migrants living in the United States to sponsor parties, engage in collective fund-raising for public works projects in their town of origin, and sometimes to influence political campaigns in the country of origin. Based on an examination of Mexican hometown associations in Los Angeles, California, that are tied to towns in Zacatecas, Mexico, Luin Goldring discovers that it is primarily men who prevail in all of the leadership positions. In a provocative and compelling argument, Goldring argues that the Mexican hometown associations constitute a unique site for a "masculine gendered project," one that allows Mexican immigrant men—particularly those with sufficient resources—to recoup the status and privilege they lost through migration.

In the final chapter, Audrey Singer and Greta Gilbertson interrogate a little-researched but key legal passage for many immigrants, naturalization. The pursuit of U.S. citizenship intensified among many Latino immigrant groups during the highly xenophobic climate of the 1990s. Contrary to the image of naturalization as the ultimate form of assimilation, many immigrants in California were simply scared into becoming U.S. citizens by California's 1994 passage of Proposition 187—which promised to deny public health care and public education to the children of undocumented immigrants. While that proposition ultimately proved unconstitutional, it opened the doors to far more draconian federal legislation. The 1996 Illegal Immigrant Refugee and Immigration Responsibility Act (IIRIRA)—a complex piece of legislation dubbed the most draconian immigration law passed in late 20th-century United States—severely disenfranchised legal permanent residents, and was signed into effect the same year as the Personal Responsibility and Work Opportunity Reconciliation Act. In their chapter, Singer and Gilbertson explore how Dominican immigrant women and men responded to these pressures. Sensitive to life-course stages, they provide a close-up examination of multiple orientations in one Dominican transnational family that spans five generations and sixty-five members. Some of the men, they find, see acquisition of U.S. citizenship as a way to advance their return to the Dominican Republic, thereby uncoupling residency and state citizenship, while many of the women pursue naturalization to further the project of settlement and connection with their children and grandchildren.

All of the chapters in this book clearly move far beyond "add and stir" or immigrant "women only" approaches. They also stretch us well beyond the earlier "empowerment studies," which tended to couch gender changes in either-or terms, and they direct the analysis beyond household and family to consider other institutions. The list of new themes interrogated in this book—including transnational hometown associations, responses to immigration laws, childhood, and sexuality—show that there is a vast frontier waiting for analysis of gender and immigration. No one can predict what life will be like in the 21st century, but both the dimensions of U.S.-bound immigration and the rapid-fire changes and contestations over what is deemed appropriate for women and men suggest that there is no shortage of material for students and scholars of gender and immigration.

NOTES

1. The idea that women are necessarily migrant followers is informed largely by the history of the guest worker programs in Europe and the Bracero contract labor program in the United States. Women's agency was assumed to be absent. In both instances, the intention was to recruit male immigrant labor for a finite, temporary period of time, but instead permanent family settlement came about after women kin migrated.

2. As modest as this first-stage project seems to us today, some commentators responded with blatant, vitriolic hostility. British anthropologist Anthony Leeds (1976), for example, opined that "the category of 'women' seems to me a rhetorical one, not one which has (or can be proved to have) generic scientific utility," and he decried this focus as "individualistic, reductionist, and motivational." Leeds argued that focusing on migrant women would deflect scholarly attention away from structural processes of capitalist labor exploitation. That in itself is telling, as it encodes the assumption that women do not act in economic or structural contexts and are somehow cloistered and sheltered from capitalist institutions.

3. The rise of new ideals of companionate marriage and marital intimacy among Mexican immigrants has been documented by Jennifer Hirsch (2000).

REFERENCES

Arizpe, Lourdes, & Aranda, Josefina. (1981). The "comparative advantages" of women's disadvantages: Women workers in the strawberry export agribusiness in Mexico. *Signs: Journal of Women in Culture and Society, 7,* 453–473.

Fernández-Kelly, María Patricia. (1983). *For we are sold, I and my people: Women and industrialization in Mexico's frontier.* Albany: State University of New York Press.

Foner, Nancy. (2000). *From Ellis Island to JFK: New York's two great waves of immigration.* New Haven, CT: Yale University Press.

Gabaccia, Donna. (1992). Introduction. In Donna Gabaccia (Ed.), *Seeking common ground: Multidisciplinary studies of immigrant women in the U.S.* (pp. xi–xxvi). Westport, CT: Praeger.

Grasmuck, Sherri, & Pessar, Patricia. (1991). *Between two islands: Dominican international migration.* Berkeley & Los Angeles: University of California Press.

Hirsch, Jennifer S. (2000). *En el norte la mujer manda:* Gender, generation, and geography in a Mexican transnational community. In Nancy Foner, Rubén G. Rumbaut, & Steven J. Gold (Eds.), *Immigration research for a new century: Multidisciplinary perspectives* (pp. 369–389). New York: Russell Sage Foundation.

Hondagneu-Sotelo, Pierrette. (1994). *Gendered transitions: Mexican experiences of immigration.* Berkeley & Los Angeles: University of California Press.

Hondagneu-Sotelo, Pierrette, & Cranford, Cynthia. (1999). Gender and migration. In Janet Saltzman Chafetz (Ed.), *Handbook of the sociology of gender* (pp. 105–126). New York: Kluwer Academic/Plenum Publishers.

Jones-Correa, Michael. (1998). *Between two nations: The political predicament of Latinos in New York City.* Ithaca, NY: Cornell University Press.

Kibria, Nazli. (1993). *Family tightrope: The changing lives of Vietnamese Americans.* Princeton, NJ: Princeton University Press.

Leeds, Anthony. (1976). Women in the migratory process: A reductionist outlook. *Anthropological Quarterly, 49*(1), 69–76.

Omi, Michael, & Winant, Howard. (1994). *Racial formation in the United States: From the 1960s to the 1990s.* New York: Routledge.

Portes, Alejandro, & Zhou, Min. (1993, November). The new second generation: Segmented assimilation and its variants among post-1965 immigrant youth. *Annals of the American Academy of Political and Social Science, 530,* 74–98.

Repak, Terry. (1995). *Waiting on Washington: Central American workers in the nation's capital.* Philadelphia: Temple University Press.

Sassen-Koob, Saskia. (1984). Notes on the incorporation of Third World women into wage-labor through immigration and off-shore production. *International Migration Review, 18*(4), 1144–1167.

Waldinger, Roger, & Perlmann, Joel. (1998). Second generations: Past, present, future. *Journal of Ethnic and Migration Studies, 24,* 5–24.

Waters, Mary C. (1999). *Black identities: West Indian immigrant dreams and American realities.* Cambridge, MA: Harvard University Press.

Wolf, Diane. (1992). *Factory daughters: Gender, household dynamics, and rural industrialization in Java.* Berkeley & Los Angeles: University of California Press.

CHAPTER 2

Engendering Migration Studies
The Case of New Immigrants in the United States

Patricia R. Pessar

This review highlights contributions made by scholars who have treated gender as a central organizing principle in migration, and it suggests some promising lines for future inquiry. When gender is brought to the foreground in migration studies, a host of significant topics emerge. These include how and why women and men experience migration differently and how this contrast affects such processes as settlement, return, and transmigration. A gendered perspective demands a scholarly reengagement with those institutions and ideologies immigrants create and encounter in the "home" and "host" countries in order to determine how patriarchy organizes family life, work, community associations, law and public policy, and so on. It also encourages an examination of the ways in which migration simultaneously reinforces and challenges patriarchy in its multiple forms.[1]

New immigration research is developing a more sophisticated understanding of gender and patriarchy. It avoids the common fallacy of equating gender only with women, and it acknowledges the "transgressive" fact that non-White immigrant males may be stripped of patriarchal status and privilege by White men and women (Espiritu, 1997). Consequently, a new wave of migration scholarship challenges feminists who insist on the primacy of gender, thereby marginalizing racism and other structures of oppression. In place of theories that treat structures such as gender and race as mutually exclusive, this recent work urges us to develop theories and design research that capture the simultaneity of gender, class, race, and ethnic exploitation. The payoff is explanatory models that account for outcomes that have largely eluded those who employ more unitary frameworks. For example, by acknowledging and theorizing the interpenetrating class, racial, legal, and gender oppressions characterizing immigrant women's lives, we are best prepared to interpret their modest challenges to patriarchal privilege and exploitative family practices, despite the fact that migration tends to narrow the material and social foundations for gender inequities.

THE MIGRANT AS MALE

More than a decade ago I wrote,

> Until recently the term "migrant" suffered from the same gender stereotyping found
> in the riddles about the big indian and the little indian, the surgeon and the son. In
> each case the term carried a masculine connotation, unless otherwise specified. While
> this perception makes for amusing riddles, the assumption that the "true" migrant is
> male has limited the possibility for generalization from empirical research and pro-
> duced misleading theoretical premises. (Pessar, 1986, p. 273)

To appreciate why women were largely absent from empirical research and writings produced in the 1950s, 1960s, and early 1970s, it is useful to consider the theoretical assumptions guiding much of the migration scholarship of that period.
Most scholars were influenced by neoclassical theory, and according to one popular variant, those individuals with the ability to project themselves into the role of
"Western man" headed off to the cities where the benefits of modern life could be
attained (Lewis, 1959; Redfield, 1955). And it was males, indeed, who they alleged
were more apt to be risk takers and achievers, whereas women were portrayed as
guardians of community tradition and stability. Hence, in Everett Lee's (1966) sem-
inal "push-pull" theory of migration, we learn that "children are carried along by
their parents, willy-nilly, and wives accompany their husbands though it tears them
away from the environment they love" (p. 51).

Migration research of this period also suffered from the more general tendency to
disregard women's contributions to economic, political, and social life. As June Nash
(1986) writes, "Whether investigators were influenced by neoclassical, Marxist, dependency or developmentalist paradigms, they tended to stop short of an analysis of
women's condition in any but the most stereotyped roles in the family and biological
reproduction" (p. 3). The same ideological template operated as labor-importing nations, such as France, chose to enumerate immigrant women alongside children as dependents rather than workers in official immigration statistics (Morokvasic, 1984).

Not surprisingly, researchers of the day designed studies of immigrant populations that included only male subjects. Thus, in the introduction to their 1975 book
on migrant workers in Europe, John Berger and Jean Mohr write,

> Among the migrant workers in Europe there are probably two million women. Some
> work in factories, many work in domestic service. To write of their experience ade-
> quately would require a book itself. We hope this will be done. Ours is limited to the
> experience of the male migrant worker. (p. 8)

And in 1985, we find Alejandro Portes explaining that the surveys he conducted
over the course of the 1970s with Mexicans and Cubans in the United States had
to be restricted to male family heads because they

> felt at the time that an exploratory study, directed at comparison of two immigrant
> groups over time, would become excessively complex were it to encompass all cate-

gories of immigrants. In subsequent interviews, however, respondents were also used as informants about major characteristics of other family members, in particular, their wives. (Portes & Bach, 1985, p. 95)

A male bias also existed in the works of many immigration historians of the period who either assumed that only male immigrants' lives were worthy of official documentation and scrutiny (Handlin, 1951; Howe, 1976) or that the history of male migrants was gender neutral, thus making it unnecessary to treat women at all, except perhaps in a few pages on the family (Bodnar, Weber, & Simon, 1982).

SCHOLARSHIP ON IMMIGRANT WOMEN

Once feminist scholarship gained a foothold in migration studies, it progressed through a series of stages common to the broader engagement between feminism and the social sciences. In the 1970s and 1980s, researchers attempted to fill in the gaps that resulted from decades of research based predominantly on male immigrants. In their rush to fill this void, the more empirically minded migration scholars tended to treat gender as a mere variable rather than as a central theoretical concept. For example, in Douglas Gurak and Mary Kritz's (1982) writings on Dominican and Colombian immigrants in New York City, we learn of high rates of female labor force participation—far exceeding rates prior to emigration. Yet, these empirical findings are never contextualized in a larger discussion of gender segmentation within the sending and receiving labor markets (see Gabaccia, 1994; Sassen-Koob, 1984) nor extended through an examination of the impact women's wage labor has had on gender relations within these immigrant families and the wider communities (see Pessar, 1986, 1988).

Although there is now a sizable body of empirical studies on women immigrants, which is aimed at redressing a tradition of male bias, we are only beginning to take the next step in reformulating migration theory in light of the anomalous and unexpected findings revealed in this body of work. The remainder of this essay reviews the key components needed to more fully engender migration studies. I note where advances have been made and suggest where future theorizing and research should proceed.

ENGENDERING MIGRATION THEORY AND RESEARCH

Researchers have only recently begun to explore how changing politico-economic conditions in labor-exporting and labor-importing societies differentially affect men and women and how this, in turn, may provide them with contrasting incentives and constraints on movement and foreign settlement.[2] Hondagneu-Sotelo (1994), for example, notes that the Bracero Program provided opportunities for male laborers and that these individuals went on to create informal social networks that recruited additional men. It was not until the 1970s that equally effective women-to-women networks consolidated (Kossoudji & Ranney, 1984). In contrast, Irish migration in the 19th and early 20th centuries was female dominated. As Hasia Diner (1983) and Pauline Jackson (1984) explain, the larger continent-wide transition from an agrarian, feudal mode to an industrial, capitalist one was exacerbated in Ireland by the local norms of single inheritance and single dowry. These changes affected women more heavily than men, leading increasing numbers of women to conclude that their best chances for employment (overwhelmingly in domestic service) and eventual marriage could be found by emigrating to the United States. It was women who created and maintained the migration chains that linked female kin and friends and that produced a pattern of migration that was basically a female mass movement.[3]

Researchers argue that export-led production in Third World countries carries different implications for female and male workers, although in both instances it is migration-inducing (Fernández-Kelly, 1983; Sassen-Koob, 1984). Offshore production promotes displacement and international migration by creating goods that compete with local commodities, by feminizing the workforce without providing equivalent factory-based employment for the large stock of under- and unemployed males, and by socializing women for industrial work and modern consumption without providing needed job stability over the course of the women's working lives.

For several decades, the United States has attracted proportionally more female migrants than other labor-importing countries have, and women constitute the majority among U.S. immigrants from Asia, Central and South America, the Caribbean, and Europe (Donato, 1992). This dominance reflects economic restructuring in the United States and the subsequent growth of female-intensive industries, particularly in service, health care, microelectronics, and apparel manufacturing. According to Yen Le Espiritu (1997), immigrant women, as feminized and racialized labor, are more employable in these labor-intensive industries than their male counterparts due to "the patriarchal and racist assumptions that women can afford to work for less, do not mind dead-end jobs, and are more suited physiologically to certain kinds of detailed and routine work" (p. 74). She illustrates with a quote from a White male production manager and hiring supervisor in a California Silicon Valley assembly shop:

> Just three things I look for in hiring [entry-level, high-tech manufacturing operatives]: small, foreign, and female. You find those three things and you're pretty much automatically guaranteed the right kind of workforce. These little foreign gals are grateful to be hired—very, very grateful—no matter what. (Hossfeld, 1994, p. 65, as cited in Espiritu, 1997)

Revisionist scholarship on immigrant enclaves provides a further example of the power of engendered inquiry. The earliest writing on the Cuban enclave in Miami praised it as a mode of economic incorporation that, unlike the secondary sector, provided immigrants with significant returns to education and previous job experience as well as opportunities for training and comparatively higher wages (Portes & Bach, 1985). More recent research on the Cuban enclave (Portes & Jensen,

1989) and the Chinese enclave in New York City (Zhou, 1992; Zhou & Logan, 1991), which control for gender, reveals a far different pattern, however, with women receiving few, if any, of the advantages their male counterparts enjoy. In the case of the New York City enclave, Min Zhou (1992) writes, "Better-paying jobs in the enclave economy tend to be reserved for men because male supremacy that dominates the Chinese culture (and the Western culture) reinforces gender discrimination in the enclave labor market" (p. 182). Greta Gilbertson (1995), too, concludes in her study of Dominican and Colombian immigrants employed in Hispanic firms in New York that rather than conferring benefits to women, enclave employment is highly exploitative. Indeed, she claims that some of the success of immigrant small-business owners and their male workers comes at the expense of subordinated immigrant women.

Finally, in a sobering piece on U.S. immigrants' "progress" over the decade of the 1980s, Roger Waldinger and Greta Gilbertson (1994) find that although male immigrants from select countries (e.g., India, Iran, Japan) were better able to convert their education into higher occupational status rankings than were native-born Whites of native parentage, none of their female counterparts were able to do the same. For example, relatively few females were able to convert high levels of education into prestigious jobs as managers, professionals, or business owners. If the social erasure of immigrant women caused assimilationists to dwell on and celebrate the progress of immigrant men alone, Waldinger and Gilbertson's research shows that "making it" in America may sadly, yet, be a story about men despite the inclusion of women (p. 440).

Migration studies have not only benefited from an appreciation of the ways in which gender operates within the processes of economic displacement and the demand for immigrant labor. A gendered optic is also essential to appreciate the role played by mediating institutions, such as households and social networks, in international migration.

RETHINKING HOUSEHOLDS AND SOCIAL NETWORKS

There is general agreement that the inclusion of the household and social networks has helped elucidate the factors that precipitate and sustain migration as well as condition its effects. Simultaneously, however, there have been calls to refine the ways in which these analytical constructs have been conceptualized and operationalized.

Criticism has been primarily directed at formulations of the household. Inspired by feminist scholarship, critics have objected to the notion that migrant households are organized solely on principles of reciprocity, consensus, and altruism. They have countered that although household members' orientations and actions may sometimes be guided by norms of solidarity, they may equally be informed by hierarchies of power along gender and generational lines; thus, the tension, dissention, and coalition building these hierarchies produce within the migration process also must be examined (Grasmuck & Pessar, 1991). A particularly graphic example of a lack of consensus among household members is provided by Pierrette Hondagneu-Sotelo (1994), who describes a young Mexican wife whose fear of abandonment by her migrant husband leads her to pray that he will be apprehended by the Border Patrol and sent back home to her and her young children (p. 43). In the sociologist's words, "Once we actually listen to the voices of Mexican immigrants . . . the notion that migration is driven by collective calculations or household-wide strategies becomes increasingly difficult to sustain" (p. 55).

There is also a problem with the new economists' relatively narrow view of the nature of migrant households' cost-benefit analyses (Stark, 1991). It fails to acknowledge that the calculations involve not only a consideration of the market economy, but the household political economy as well. For example, when unmarried Dominican women urge their parents to allow them to emigrate alone, parents weigh the threat to the family's reputation posed by the daughter's sexual freedom and possible promiscuity against the very real economic benefits her emigration will bring. Similarly, in assessing the benefits of return migration, many Dominican immigrant women assess the personal gains that settlement and blue-collar employment in the United States have brought them against the expectation of "forced retirement" back on the island (Pessar, 1995b).

Scholars who adopt what may be called a moral economy perspective tend to view households as essentially passive units whose members are collectively victimized by the larger market economy. We see this vision in the pioneering work of Claude Meillassoux (1981) on African migrant households and domestic communities. He recognized that the domestic and productive activities of the migrant wives who remained in rural communities were essential for the social reproduction of male migrant labor on a seasonal and generational basis. Although Meillassoux acknowledged that women who engage in noncapitalist activities within the household and migrant community are in a contradictory and exploited relationship vis-à-vis the capitalist economy, this observation did not lead him to analyze the equally exploitative social and economic relations within migrant households. With such a model of passive and unitary households, we are totally unprepared to account for such "transgressive" practices as the decisions of many Kikuyu women to migrate alone to a nearby city rather than accept the onerous burden of maintaining homes and lands over the duration of their migrant husbands' and fathers' prolonged absences. Nici Nelson (1978) describes these exploited women as "voting with their feet" (p. 89).

Now, more than 15 years after the publication of Meillassoux's (1981) work, we continue to compile additional case studies documenting the social reproduction of migrant labor by labor-exporting households (Dandler & Medeiros, 1988; Griffith, 1985; Soto, 1987). What is in far shorter supply, however, are treatments of the strains and limitations on the perpetuation of a labor reserve. For example, we need comparative research on whether and how the "enforced" immobility of migrant wives and sisters is contested by women responding to the increased demand for female labor both in export-oriented industries at home and in immigrant-dominated sectors abroad (Grasmuck & Pessar, 1991). Along these lines, we require more research on how images, meanings, and values associated with gender, consumption, modernity, and the family circulate within the global cultural economy (Appadurai, 1990) and how these "ideoscapes" and "mediascapes" are interpreted and appropriated in varied sites by different household members in ways that either promote or constrain mobility (Mills, 1997). Finally, there is also a paucity of literature on the limits to grandmothers' and other kin's willingness and capacities to care for the children left behind and to "resocialize" rebellious youth sent "home" by their distraught migrant parents (Basch, Schiller, & Szanton Blanc, 1994; Guarnizo, 1997).

The common claim that the immigrant family in the United States is an adaptive social form requires rethinking. This proposition assumes an immigrant household already firmly in place (Pérez, 1986). It diverts our attention from the important task of analyzing legislation and government policies that effectively block or limit the formation, unification, and material well-being of immigrant families (Espiritu, 1997; Garrison & Weiss, 1979; Hondagneu-Sotelo, 1995; Hondagneu-Sotelo & Avila, 1997; Mohanty, 1991). We also need to turn a critical gaze on the accompanying rhetoric that makes these initiatives thinkable and credible. For example, work on the Chinese Exclusion Act points to its racist and sexist precepts; beginning with the 1875 Page Law, all would-be Chinese immigrant women were suspected of being prostitutes who would bring in "especially virulent strains of venereal diseases, introduce opium addiction, and entice young white boys to a life of sin" (Chan, 1991, p. 138).

Finally, households have assumed an important place within transnational migration theory as well. Researchers stress that household members often develop economic strategies that transcend national labor markets and pursue social reproduction strategies that may similarly stretch across national divides, as, for example, when immigrant women work abroad as nannies/housekeepers while their children remain in their countries of origin (Hondagneu-Sotelo & Avila, 1997). Recent work on the related phenomena of "transnational mothering" and "the new employable mothers" (Chang, 1994) has raised important questions about the meanings, variations, and inequities of motherhood in the late 20th century.

Research on migration and social networks has not received as concerted a critique and retooling as has the scholarship on migrant households. Back in 1989, Monica Boyd observed that much of the research on social networks remained indifferent to gender. Fortunately, since then there has been some progress in exploring the multiple ways in which gender configures and organizes immigrants' social networks. For example, Christine Ho (1993) maintains that kinship lies at the center of Caribbean social life both at home and transnationally, and it is women who give these networks shape and substance. Feminist scholarship has also challenged the popular assumption that immigrants' social networks are socially inclusive. As Hondagneu-Sotelo (1994) writes, "Immigrant social networks are highly contested social resources, and they are not always shared, even in the same family" (p. 189). In fact, she found that migrant networks were traditionally available to Mexican males; now that women have developed independent female networks, it is not uncommon for family and household members to use entirely different social networks (p. 95).

The new scholarship on the gendered dimensions of the supply and demand for immigrant labor and of the role of migrant households and social networks in the migration process has inspired a complementary line of research that explores the relationship between migration and women's emancipation.

MIGRATION AND EMANCIPATION

Many scholars have examined the impact immigrant women's regular wage work has on gendered relations. A review of this literature points to the fact that despite gender inequities in the labor market and workplace, immigrant women employed in the United States generally gain greater personal autonomy and independence, whereas men lose ground (e.g., Grasmuck & Pessar, 1991; Guendelman & Pérez-Itriaga, 1987; Hondagneu-Sotelo, 1994; Kibria, 1993; Lamphere, 1987; Pedraza, 1991). For example, women's regular access to wages and their greater contribution to household sustenance frequently lead to more control over budgeting and other realms of domestic decision making. It also provides them with greater leverage in appeals for male assistance in daily household chores. There is some indication that the smaller the wage gap between partners' earnings, the greater the man's willingness to participate in domestic work (Espiritu, 1997; Lamphere, Zavella, & Gonzales, 1993; Pessar, 1995b). Immigrant women's spatial mobility and their access to valuable social and economic resources beyond the domestic sphere also expand (Hondagneu-Sotelo, 1994; Pessar, 1995b). In the words of immigrant men and women can be found further evidence that migration and settlement bring changes in traditional patriarchal arrangements. In what Nazli Kibria (1993) describes as a tongue-in-cheek description of gender transformations, several Vietnamese immigrant men told her, "In Vietnam the man of the house is king. Below him the children, then the pets of the home, and then the women. Here, the woman is the king and the man holds a position below the pets" (p. 108). Conversely, a Mexican female returnee told her interviewers, "In California my husband was like a mariposa (meaning a sensitive, soft, responsive butterfly). Back here in Mexico he acts like a distant macho" (Guendelman & Pérez-Itriaga, 1987, p. 268).

The pioneering work on women and migration tended to couch its concerns in stark, either-or terms: Was migration emancipatory or subjugating for women? Most soon concluded that immigrant women did not equally or consistently improve their status in the home, workplace, or community (Morokvasic, 1984). For individual immigrants, like many of my Dominican informants, gains have been most pronounced in one domain (e.g., the household), whereas gender subordination continues in other arenas such as the workplace and ethnic associations (Grasmuck & Pessar, 1991). For other immigrant women, "gains" within a specific sphere, like the household, are frequently accompanied by strains and contradictions. This fact is clearly manifested in Hondagneu-Sotelo and Avila's (1997) research on transnational mothering. Although many Mexican and Central American immigrant nannies and housekeepers take pride in their paid reproductive work, especially in caring for other people's children, and in stretching the definition of motherhood to encompass breadwinning, there are substantial costs. According to the authors, in separating in space and time from their communities of origin, homes, children, and sometimes husbands, these women must "cope with stigma, guilt, and criticism from others" (p. 7). There are also signs of generational conflicts within immigrant households, which incline some women, such as the Vietnamese immigrants Kibria (1993) studied, to recommit themselves even more forcefully to patriarchal family systems "because of the power it [gives] them, as mothers, over [transgressive] children" (p. 143).[4] To account for these seeming inconsistencies and contradictions in immigrant women's lives, it is useful to recall Myra Ferree's (1990) observation that many of our feminist models founder because they have sought consistency in working women's lives where no such consistency exists.

Although there is now broad consensus that immigrant women attain some limited, albeit uneven and sometimes contradictory, benefits from migration and settlement, we await the next wave of scholarship. This would consolidate and then deconstruct the available literature to determine those gendered domains in which the greatest and least gains for women have been made. And it would both isolate and interrelate those factors that condition these outcomes. These would include migrants' age, education, employment history (prior and subsequent to emigration), race, ethnicity, sexual preference, social class, and legal status as well as family structures and gender ideologies (prior to and subsequent to emigration). As we proceed in such a venture, it will be necessary to deconstruct excessively inclusive terms such as *racial-ethnic* women and *racialized subjects*. Promising work lies ahead as we explore how the evolving processes of racialization and social stratification within and between "Asian," "Latino," "Caribbean," and "European" populations (Omi & Winant, 1994) affect the gendered identities and experiences of specific immigrant populations. Finally, to assess those factors that facilitate or impede gender parity, it would be wise to systematically reengage those accounts that qualify or dispute the claim that migration improves women's status (Castro, 1986; Zhou, 1992). For example, we are likely to find less change among immigrant populations such as the rural Portuguese whose premigration gender ideologies already assign wives to essential duties in both the domestic and productive spheres (Lamphere, 1986).

Although I do not intend to minimize the importance of those factors that may mitigate challenges to patriarchal practices, I want to suggest that differences among researchers regarding the emancipatory nature of migration may originate, at least in part, in the actual research strategies pursued. In a formal research setting, such as one in which surveys or structured interviews are administered, an immigrant woman's decision to cloak her own and her family's experiences in a discourse of unity, female sacrifice, and the woman's subordination to the patriarch represents a safe, respectful, and respectable "text." As I look back on my own work, this is the female voice that usually emerged from my attempts at survey research. By contrast, my ethnographic collection of discourses that reveal family tensions and struggles emerged far more frequently out of encounters when my presence was incidental, that is, not the defining purpose for the ensuing dialogue, or after many months of participant observation had substantially reduced the initial formality and suspicion (see Pessar, 1995a). In light of our increased appreciation for the dialogical nature of the research encounter, I am hardly surprised that the fieldworker who has presented some of the richest and most compelling case material on women's circumvention or contestation of patriarchal authority assumed the roles of both activist and researcher and was no doubt perceived by many of her informants as a transgressive female herself (Hondagneu-Sotelo, 1994, p. xiii). Neither am I surprised that the chronicler of by far the best histories of divergent migration projects spent more than 2 years studying a limited number of immigrant families in both Mexico and Northern California and chose to feature in his writings only one family with whom he lived and socialized (Rouse, 1987, 1989).

SETTLEMENT, RETURN, AND TRANSNATIONALITY

A gendered approach is essential to account for men's and women's orientations to settlement, return, and transmigration. Indeed, gender-free models of migrant settlement and return (e.g., Piore, 1979) are hard to defend in light of informants' statements such as the one cited above by the Mexican return migrant who saw her "butterfly" turn back into a distant macho and the joking remark of a Laotian refugee, "When we get on the plane back to Laos, the first thing we will do is beat up the women" (Donnelly, 1994, p. 74). Research shows consistently that gains in gender equity are central to women's desires to settle, more or less permanently, to protect their advances (Chavez, 1991; Georges, 1990; Goldring, 1992; Hagan, 1994; Hondagneu-Sotelo, 1994). In contrast, many men seek to return home rapidly to regain the status and privileges that migration itself has challenged. In my own work, I document how many Dominican women spend large amounts of money on expensive durable goods, such as major appliances and home furnishings, which serve to root the family more securely in the United States and deplete the funds necessary to orchestrate a successful reentry back into Dominican society and economy. Conversely, men often favor a far more frugal and austere pattern of consumption that is consistent with their claim that "five dollars spent today meant five more years of postponing the return to the Dominican Republic" (Pessar, 1986, p. 284).

Further strides in our understanding of how immigrant women consolidate settlement have been made by Hondagneu-Sotelo (1994), who observes that, as traditional family patriarchy weakens, immigrant women assume more active public and social roles—actions that at once reinforce their improved status in the household and ultimately advance their families' integration in the United States. She identifies three arenas in which this consolidation takes place: the labor market in which women seek permanent, nonseasonal employment; institutions for public and private assistance; and the immigrant/ethnic community. Hondagneu-Sotelo and others have shown that women are particularly adept at locating and using financial and social services available in the new society (Chavira, 1988; Kibria, 1993) and in using social-networking skills for community building (O'Connor, 1990).

As researchers continue to explore community building and community activism among new immigrants, they would be wise to take a leaf from immigration historians who have noted that women's sense of community often differs substantially from that of men, who tend to gravitate to formal institutions such as political parties and labor unions (Hyman, 1980; Weinberg, 1992). Moreover, it should be borne in mind that women are positioned differently than men with regard to both the broader economy and the state. As women, they are socially assigned responsibility for the daily and generational sustenance of household members, even when, as is the case for many immigrants, family wages are wholly insufficient. Research is badly needed to determine whether and how immigrant women manage to overcome very real concerns over legal vulnerability to confront the state over family and community welfare issues (Hondagneu-Sotelo, 1995; Sacks, 1989; Susser, 1982; Torruellas, Benmayor, & Juarbe, 1997; Zavella, 1987).

Recent work on migrants' transnational identities, practices, and institutions alerts us that permanent settlement or permanent return are merely two of the possible outcomes; lives constructed across national boundaries is another. As several scholars have noted, gender remains marginalized within transnational migration theory and research (Hondagneu-Sotelo & Avila, 1997; Kearney, 1995; Mahler, n.d.). Based on the few studies that do consider gender, we are left with the impression that men are the major players in transnational social fields (Graham, 1997; Ong, 1993). Sarah Mahler (n.d.) astutely questions the implicit message that women are more passive and argues that when the research focus is shifted from public domains, such as international investment and hometown associations, to more private ones, such as the management of transnational migrant households, a different representation emerges (see also Ho, 1993; Hondagneu-Sotelo & Avila, 1997; Soto, 1987). On this score, Sandhya Shukla (1997) observes that South Asian women have organized across the diaspora and subcontinent around the problem of domestic violence. She notes that through these transnational activities, "the South Asian woman" is being constituted as a political subject. As such, some of these women have come to contest the more mainstream, patriarchal narratives of ethnic identity and solidarity that are emerging in diverse diaspora communities. These mainstream narratives, she claims, are vigorously and romantically nationalist rather than embracing the women's pan-ethnic identity of South Asian. And they "are steeped in images of the traditional nuclear family with its specified gender roles as a metaphor for distinctly cultural values in the face of Western change" (p. 270). Shukla's work alerts us to an important dialectic that has received insufficient scholarly attention: the mutually constituting projects of racial and ethnic "othering" of immigrants and ethnics carried out by members of host countries and the creation of nationalist, often fundamentalist, counternarratives produced by these othered subjects. What are the roles of men and women in either supporting or challenging these projects? And in what ways are the symbols of nation, diaspora, and belonging imbued with notions of gender and sexuality? Surely, much more research is needed to determine how transnational migration identities, practices, and experiences are gendered and whether patriarchal ideologies and roles are reaffirmed, tempered, or both within transnational social spaces. We also need to situate gender within the current historical moment—one in which researchers note the contradiction between economic globalization and the renationalizing of politics (Harris, 1995; Sassen, 1996). One extremely unfortunate byproduct of this contradiction is the recent tendency for U.S. policy makers to characterize immigrant women and children as dangerous others whose rapacious demands on the public coffers thwart the state's ability to fulfill its social contract with the "authentic" and truly "deserving" members of the nation (Chavez, 1996; Hondagneu-Sotelo, 1995; Naples, 1997).

A REENCOUNTER WITH FEMINIST STUDIES

In my earliest work on Dominican migration, I was quite adamant about the gains I believed Dominican immigrant women had made (Pessar, 1986). My enthusiasm originated from several sources: a flush of early feminist optimism (see Pessar, 1995a), my observations based on fieldwork in both the Dominican Republic and the United States of changes in gender practices (Grasmuck & Pessar, 1991), and a desire to communicate my female informants' pleasure at what they viewed as far more equitable gender relations. Yet, as I have come to both follow the lives of several of these women over the years and critically engage the comparative literature on immigration and patriarchy, I have tempered my enthusiasm. I now conclude that, in general, immigrant women's gains have been modest. In retrospect, I believe many of us anticipated a far greater degree of emancipation for immigrant women because our theoretical guideposts were firmly planted in early feminist theory. To understand why most immigrant women have only nibbled at the margins of patriarchy, we must abandon the notion that gender hierarchy is the most determinative structure in their lives. This leaves us with the far more daunting task of examining how women's and men's lives are affected by multiple and interrelated forms of oppression linked to gender, class, race, ethnicity, and foreign status.

Many U.S. feminists were encouraged by economic trends in the 1970s and 1980s. There was a marked increase in the proportion of dual-wage-earning families, and escalating rates of male unemployment served to underscore the centrality of women's contributions to household budgets. Predictions of profound changes in U.S. gender relations and family structures followed. Heidi Hartmann (1987), for example, disputed the claim that the recent increase in female-headed households was by definition deleterious for women and their families. She wrote, "To the extent that there is a family crisis, it is by and large a healthy one, particularly for women" (p. 49). This was the case, she maintained, because increased economic opportunities for women had, in her words, allowed women "to choose" to head their own households rather than to live with men. Along similar lines, Alice Kessler-Harris and Karen Brodkin Sacks (1987) observed that women's improved access to wages allowed them either to resist gender and generational subordination within the family or to "avoid family situations altogether" (p. 70).

A review of the literature on immigrant families unearths scant evidence of a radical revamping of gender ideology and lines of authority or of an emancipatory abandonment of conjugal units, despite rates of employment for immigrant women that rival those of native-born Americans. We learn of Vietnamese immigrant women who defend their own "traditional" family forms against what they perceive to be individualistic and unregulated American family practices (Kibria, 1993), and of Latina nannies who endorse motherhood as a full-time vocation when financial resources permit (Hondagneu-Sotelo & Avila, 1997). We encounter a Dominican woman who describes her divorce as "one of the saddest days in my life. Not only did I lose the respect I once had as a married woman, but my children and I lost the material support [my husband] was able to provide" (Pessar, 1995a, p. 41). Many researchers report that immigrant women view their employment as an extension of their obligations as wives and mothers (Pedraza, 1991; Segura, 1994). With the caveat that they are merely "helping their husbands"—a refrain that immigrant women frequently repeat to researchers (Chavira, 1988; Pessar, 1995a)— these women manage to keep the fires of patriarchy burning by minimizing long hours in the workplace and substantial contributions to the household budget. Why have these immigrant women been less inclined than their White, North American counterparts to level assaults on patriarchal domestic ideologies and practices?

IMMIGRANT FAMILIES AS BASTIONS OF RESISTANCE

There are multiple external forces that buffet immigrant families. Legislation informed by racist and sexist discourse has in the past and present severely challenged the survival and well-being of immigrant families (Hondagneu-Sotelo, 1995; Mohanty, 1991). Immigrant men are increasingly frustrated and scapegoated; they expect, and are expected, to be the breadwinners. Yet they face structural impediments that block the fulfillment of this role. As Patricia Fernández-Kelly and Anna García (1990) remind us, "For poor men and women the issue is not so much the presence of the sexual division of labor or the persistence of patriarchal ideologies but the difficulties of upholding either" (p. 148). Owing to an all too common tendency to conflate male dominance with patriarchy, many social scientists have been slow, or reluctant, to appreciate their informants' unwillingness to lose the benefits derived from some patriarchal marital unions (Nash, 1988).[5] Whether through choice or necessity, large numbers of immigrant women have also assumed wage-earning responsibilities. Their pursuit of employment is far more often the result of severe economic need and an expression of vulnerability than an indication of their strength within the home and marketplace (Fernández-Kelly & García, 1990). As noted above, it is often because they are "small, foreign, female" and non-White that they enjoy the dubious advantage of being the preferred category of labor for the lowest paid and most insecure segment of the economy. In light of these multiple assaults, it would be patronizing to interpret immigrant women's struggles to maintain intact families as acquiescence to traditional patriarchy. Rather, in many cases, these struggles represent acts of resistance against those forces within the dominant society that threaten the existence of poor, minority families (see Collins, 1990; Zinn, Weber Cannon, Higginbotham, & Thornton Dill, 1986). This does not mean, as Evelyn Glenn (1986) reminds us, that immigrant women do not simultaneously experience the family as an instrument of gender subordination. Indeed, their attempts to use wages as leverage for greater gender parity in certain arenas of domestic life attest to this fact. The dilemma confronting many immigrant women, it would seem, is to defend and hold together the family while attempting to reform the norms and practices that subordinate the women (Glenn, 1986, p. 193).

The importance of keeping multiple-wage-earning families intact is underscored by statistics revealing far higher incidents of poverty among female-headed immigrant households than among similar conjugal units (Bean & Tienda, 1988; Pessar, 1995b; Rosenberg & Gilbertson, 1995). Maxine Zinn (1987) provides a more adequate depiction of these female-headed units than that proposed by Hartmann (1987):

> Conditions associated with female-headed families among racial-ethnics are different and should be interpreted differently. Because white families headed by women have much higher average incomes than minority families in the same situation, we must not confuse an overall improvement with what is in fact an improvement for women in certain social categories, while other women are left at the bottom in even worse conditions. (p. 167)

In spite of the many social and material disincentives militating against the disbanding of unions and the formation of female-headed households, there are, nonetheless, several immigrant populations, such as Dominicans, with extremely high rates of female headedness. Research is needed to account for the factors contributing to differing rates of marital instability and female headedness within and among immigrant populations in the United States (Bean, Berg, & Van Hook, 1996). We also require more in-depth investigations to document the survival strategies of poor immigrant families (Menjívar, 1995). Several researchers have pointed to the importance of household extension, that is, the incorporation of adults other than the husband and wife into the household. These coresident adults provide additional income to compensate for low earnings or sporadic unemployment and facilitate the labor force participation of married and single mothers (Angel & Tienda, 1982; Kibria, 1993; Rosenberg & Gilbertson, 1995).

Although poor immigrant families may experience difficulties in upholding a patriarchal division of labor and often suffer socially and materially as a consequence of men's unemployment, upwardly mobile couples may confront the opposite challenge. They must confront the contradiction that dual wage earning poses for households that have achieved, by their standards, a middle-class standing. In certain Dominican and Cuban immigrant families, for example, women's "retirement" to the domestic sphere is a favored practice for marking the household's collective social advancement (Fernández-Kelly & García, 1990; Pessar, 1995a). Many of the Dominican women I knew who agreed to leave wage employment clearly viewed their alternatives as being improved social status for the entire family through female retirement, on one hand, versus improved gender relations for the wife through continued wage work, on the other. In leaving the workforce, many of the most conflicted women chose to place immigrant ideology, with its stress on social mobility, and traditional family domestic ideology, with its emphasis on both patriarchy and collective interests, before personal struggle and gains. Such actions, of course, contradict the feminist tenet that women's interests are best served by positioning themselves in both the household and workplace (Ferree, 1990). Yet, some of my informants saw themselves struggling on another front to challenge the distorted and denigrating cultural stereotypes about Latino immigrants held by many members of the majority culture. As the following quote from one of my female informants illustrates, Dominican women resisted these negative stereotypes by symbolizing the household's respectability and elevated social and economic status in a fashion common to the traditional Dominican middle class: they removed themselves from the visible productive sphere.

> When we had finally purchased our home and our business, Roque insisted that I stop working. He said it would be good for the children and good for all of us. At first I protested, because I never again wanted to be totally dependent upon a man. . . . But then I began to think about how much I have suffered in this country to make something for my family. And I thought, even though we own a home and a business, most Americans think the worst of us. They think we all sell drugs, have too many babies, take away their jobs, or are living off the government (i.e., receiving welfare). I decided, I'm going to show them that I am as good as they are, that my husband is so successful that I don't have to work at all.

This woman's words echo a broader claim advanced by Espiritu (1997) and others: in a hostile environment, "some women of color, in contrast to their white counterparts, view unpaid domestic work—having children and maintaining families—more as a form of resistance to racist oppression than as a form of exploitation by men" (p. 6).

Other Dominican women accounted for their departure from the workforce in terms similar to those of Cuban women interviewed by Fernández-Kelly and García (1990). They had envisioned their employment alongside their husbands as a temporary venture necessary until the family could achieve its goal of social advancement. Once this goal was attained, women's employment apparently contradicted a more enduring and apparently valued notion of the family and the sexes that features the successful man as the sole breadwinner and the successful woman as the guardian of a unified household. These cases reveal that a unilinear and unproblematic progression from patriarchy to parity is by no means assured. They also point out the need for continuing research on class differences not only between immigrant and native-born women but among immigrant women as well.

Relatively few studies address the question of whether migration promotes or hampers a feminist consciousness (Shukla, 1997). Most of these report, not surprisingly, that the majority of the immigrant women studied do not tend to identify as feminists or participate in feminist organizations (Foner, 1986; Hondagneu-Sotelo, 1995; Pessar, 1984). Immigrant women, we are told, are more likely to base their dissatisfactions and complaints about life in the United States on injustices linked to class, race, ethnicity, and legal-status discrimination rather than to gender. For example, according to Nancy Foner (1986), her Jamaican female informants experienced racial and class inequalities more acutely than gender-based inequalities, and this sense of injustice gave them a basis for unity with Jamaican men. Moreover, the many domestic workers in their ranks felt no sense of sisterhood with their upper-middle-class White employers, whose "liberation" these immigrant women facilitated by providing inexpensive child care so that their female employers could compete in the male occupational world (Foner, 1986). Nonetheless, Hondagneu-Sotelo's (1994) point is well taken when she concludes that although none of the Mexican immigrant women she interviewed

> identified "gender subordination" as a primary problem, rearrangements induced by migration do result in the diminution of familial patriarchy, and these transformations may enable immigrant women to better confront problems derived from class, racial/ethnic, and legal-status subordination. Their endeavors may prompt more receptiveness to feminist ideology and organizations in the future. (p. 197)

Clearly, more comparative research is needed on the local and global factors and processes leading both to the development of feminist consciousness and organization and to its suppression.[6]

The materials presented in this section highlight the inadequacy of studying gender removed from other interpenetrating structures of difference, such as race and social class. Another related body of scholarship that merits serious attention consists of works emerging out of cultural studies and ethnic studies. This scholarship addresses how representations of majority White American men and women and those of immigrants and ethnics of color are mutually constituting. This scholarship makes the important point that ideological representations of gender and sexuality are central in the exercise and perpetuation of patriarchal, racial, and class domination (Espiritu, 1997). For example, it has been claimed that the representation of Asian men as both hypersexual and asexual and of Asian women as both superfeminine and masculine exists to define, maintain, and legitimate White male virility and supremacy (Espiritu, 1997; Kim, 1990).

CONCLUSION

Migration scholars have made great advances in moving beyond an earlier male bias in theory and research. And the days when gender was treated as merely one of several equally significant variables, such as education and marital status, are mostly behind us. We are now moving toward a more fully engendered understanding of the migration process. This article has noted several key advances and has signaled the way to future developments in theory and research. We are starting to accumulate case studies documenting how men and women experience migration differently, how they create and encounter patriarchal ideologies and institutions across transnational migration circuits, and how patriarchy is reaffirmed, reconfigured, or both as a consequence of migration. The time is ripe to build on and move beyond these rich individual case studies toward a more comparative framework of migration and patriarchy. In doing so, it will be necessary to discard the notion that gender oppression transcends all divisions among men and women. Rather, we must develop theories and analytical frameworks that allow us to capture and compare the simultaneity of the impact of gender, race, ethnicity, nationality, class, and legal status on the lives of immigrants and native-born men and women. Thus, we await the next wave of research that is at once committed to comparative studies among immigrants yet refuses to stop there. We should resist disciplinary precedents that tempt us to ghettoize the gendered study of immigrants within migration studies. We are all far better served by taking the next step to relate our investigations of the representations, identities, and social conditions of immigrant men and women to those prevailing among members of the majority White and minority "brown" segments of U.S. society as well.

NOTES

1. I restrict myself here to a discussion of research on transnational migration to and between the United States and its labor-exporting partners. Review essays and edited volumes on women and international migration include Phizacklea (1983), Morokvasic (1984), Simon and Brettell (1986), Pedraza (1991), Tienda and Booth (1991), Gabaccia (1992), and Buijs (1993).

2. Of the limited scholarship that does exist on the factors contributing to displacement, far more attention has been paid to what is conventionally thought of as labor immigration than refugee displacement. In my view, this imbalance needs redressing; recent scholarship

that examines rape and genital mutilation as human rights violations generally targeted at women is a step in the right direction (Hoskin, 1981; Saadawi, 1980). Another promising line of scholarship challenges the assumption that women, in particular, are subordinated and "silenced" in refugee camps (Billings, 1995).

3. For research on female-led Salvadoran migration to Washington, D.C., see Cohen (1977) and Repak (1995).

4. Although Kibria (1993) stresses Vietnamese immigrant mothers' use of patriarchal privilege to maintain authority over children who emulate elements of American youth culture, Vicki Ruiz (1992) describes Mexican immigrant mothers who find themselves not pitted between two worlds "but navigating multiple terrains at home, at work, and at play" (p. 151). Following on Ruiz's observations, I suspect that immigrant women may sometimes find themselves as captivated by transgressive elements of U.S. popular culture as are their children (though perhaps for differing motives) and may accordingly join forces with their progeny to challenge features of traditional family ideology and patriarchal practices. And at other times, women may find that their own attempts to nibble at patriarchal structures make it difficult for them to fully oppose their children's related challenges. For example, Dominican women's desires to anchor their families in the United States by expending income on expensive commodities likely compromises their opposition to their children's use of their own income to participate in commercial youth culture. More work needs to be done to identify and explore the subjectivities, social practices, and social sites around which immigrant mothers (and parents) enforce children's adherence to preemigration patterns and those around which new coalitions for change are emerging.

5. I thank June Nash for pointing this out to me.

6. A topic that merits further study is national and global initiatives taken by immigrant and refugee women to engender the universalist conception of human rights (see Afkhami, 1994; Smith, 1994).

REFERENCES

Afkhami, M. (1994). *Women in exile.* Charlotteville: University Press of Virginia.

Angel, R., & Tienda, M. (1982). Determinants of extended household structure: Cultural pattern or economic need? *American Journal of Sociology, 87*(6), 1360–1383.

Appadurai, A. (1990). Disjuncture and difference in the global economy. *Public Culture, 2*(2), 1–24.

Basch, L., Schiller, N. G., & Szanton Blanc, C. (1994). *Nations unbound: Transnationalized projects and the deterritorialized nation-state.* New York: Gordon & Breach.

Bean, F., Berg, R., & Van Hook. J. (1996). Socioeconomic and cultural incorporation among Mexican Americans. *Social Forces, 75*(2), 593–618.

Bean, F., & Tienda, M. (1988). *The Hispanic population in the United States* [Monograph]. New York: Russell Sage.

Berger, J., & Mohr, J. (1975). *A seventh man: The story of a migrant worker in Europe.* Harmondsworth, UK: Penguin.

Billings, D. (1995). *Identities, consciousness, and organization in exile: Guatemalan women in the camps of southern Mexico.* Unpublished doctoral dissertation, University of Michigan, Ann Arbor.

Bodnar, J., Weber, M., & Simon, R. (1982). *Lives of their own: Blacks, Italians, and Poles in Pittsburgh, 1900–1960.* Urbana: University of Illinois Press.

Boyd. M. (1989). Family and personal networks in international migration: Recent developments and new agendas. *International Migration Review, 23*(3), 638–670.

Buijs, G. (1993). Migrant women: Crossing boundaries and changing identities. Oxford, UK: Berg.

Castro, M. (1986). Work versus life: Colombian women in New York. In J. Nash & H. Safa (Eds.), *Women and change in Latin America* (pp. 231–255). South Hadley, MA: Bergin & Garvey.

Chan, S. (1991). The exclusion of Chinese women. In S. Chan (Ed.), *Entry denied: Exclusion and the Chinese community in America, 1882–1943* (pp. 94–146). Philadelphia: Temple University Press.

Chang, G. (1994). Undocumented Latinas: The new "employable mothers." In E. N. Glenn, G. Chang, & L. R. Forcey (Eds.), *Mothering* (pp. 259–285). New York: Routledge.

Chavez, L. (1991). Outside the imagined community: Undocumented settlers and experiences of incorporation. *American Ethnologist, 18*(2), 257–278.

Chavez, L. (1996). *Nativism and immigration reform.* Paper prepared for the SSRC Committee on Immigration, Sanibel, Florida.

Chavira, A. (1988). Tienes que ser valiente: Mexican migrants in a Midwestern farm labor camp. In M. Melville (Ed.), *Mexicans at work in the United States* (pp. 64–73). Houston, TX: Mexican American Studies Program, University of Houston.

Cohen, L. (1977). The female factor in resettlement. *Society, 14*(6), 27–30.

Collins, P. (1990). *Black feminist thought.* Boston: Hyman.

Dandler. J., & Medeiros, C. (1988). Temporary migration from Cochabamba, Bolivia to Argentina: Patterns and impact in sending areas. In P. Pessar (Ed.), *When borders don't divide: Labor migration and refugee movements in the Americas* (pp. 8–41). New York: Center for Migration Studies.

Diner, H. (1983). *Erin's daughters in America: Irish immigrant women in the nineteenth century.* Baltimore: Johns Hopkins University Press.

Donato, K. M.(1992). Understanding U.S. immigration: Why some countries send women and other countries send men. In D. Gabaccia (Ed.), *Seeking common ground: Multidisciplinary studies of immigrant women in the United States* (pp. 159–184). Westport, CT: Greenwood.

Donnelly, N. (1994). *Changing lives of Hmong refugee women.* Seattle: University of Washington Press.

Espiritu, Yen Le. (1997). *Asian American women and men: Labor, laws, and love.* Thousand Oaks, CA: Sage.

Fernández-Kelly, M. P. (1983). *For we are sold, I and my people: Women and industry in Mexico's frontier.* Albany: State University of New York Press.

Fernández-Kelly, M. P., & García, A. (1990). Power surrendered, power restored: The politics of home and work among Hispanic women in Southern California and southern Florida. In L. Tilly & P. Guerin (Eds.), *Women, politics, and change* (pp. 130–149). New York: Russell Sage Foundation.

Ferree, M. (1990). Between two worlds: German feminist approaches to working-class women and work. In J. Nielsen (Ed.), *Feminist research methods* (pp. 174–192). Boulder, CO: Westview.

Foner, N. (1986). Sex roles and sensibilities: Jamaican women in New York and London. In R. Simon & C. Brettell (Eds.), *International migration: The female experience* (pp. 133–249). Totawa, NJ: Rowman & Allanheld.

Gabaccia, D. (1992). Introduction. In D. Gabaccia (Ed.), *Seeking common ground: Multidisciplinary studies of immigrant women in the United States* (pp. xi–xxvi). Westport, CT: Greenwood.

Gabaccia, D. (1994). *From the other side: Women, gender, and immigrant life in the U.S. 1820–1990.* Bloomington: Indiana University Press.

Garrison, V., & Weiss, C. (1979). Dominican family networks and United States immigration policy: A case study. *International Migration Review, 12*(2), 264–283.

Georges, E. (1990). *The making of a transnational community: Migration, development, and cultural change in the Dominican Republic.* New York: Columbia University Press.

Gilbertson, G. (1995). Women's labor and enclave employment: The case of Dominican and Colombian women in New York City. *International Migration Review, 29*(3), 657–671.

Glenn, E. N. (1986). *Issei, Nisei, war bride: Three generations of Japanese-American women in domestic service.* Philadelphia: Temple University Press.

Goldring, L. (1992). La migración Mexico-EUA y la transnacionalización de espacio político y social: Perspectivas desde el México rural. [Mexican-U.S. migration and the transnationalization of political and social space: Perspectives from rural Mexico]. *Estudios Sociológicos, 10*(29), 315–340.

Graham, P. (1997). *Re-imagining the nation and defining the district: The simultaneous political incorporation of Dominican transnational migrants.* Unpublished doctoral dissertation, University of North Carolina, Chapel Hill.

Grasmuck, S., & Pessar, P. (1991). *Between two islands: Dominican international migration.* Berkeley & Los Angeles: University of California Press.

Griffith, D. (1985). Women, remittances and reproduction. *American Ethnologist, 12*(4), 676–690.

Guarnizo, L. (1997). "Going home": Class, gender, and household transformation among Dominican return migrants. In P. Pessar (Ed.), *Caribbean circuits: New directions in the study of Caribbean migration* (pp. 13–60). New York: Center for Migration Studies.

Guendelman, S., & Pérez-Itriaga, A. (1987). Double lives: The changing role of women in seasonal migration. *Women's Studies, 13*(3), 249–271.

Gurak, D., & Kritz, M. (1982). Dominican and Colombian women in New York City: Household structure and employment patterns. *Migration Today, 10*(3/4), 249–271.

Hagan, J. (1994). *Deciding to be legal.* Philadelphia: Temple University Press.

Handlin, O. (1951). *The uprooted,* Boston: Little, Brown.

Harris, N. (1995). *The new untouchables.* New York: Penguin.

Hartmann, H. (1987). Changes in women's economic and family roles in post–World War II United States. In L. Beneria & C. Stimpson (Eds.), *Women, households, and the economy* (pp. 33–64). New Brunswick, NJ: Rutgers University Press.

Ho, C. (1993). The internationalization of kinship and the feminization of Caribbean Migration: The case of Afro-Trinidadian immigrants in Los Angeles. *Human Organization, 25*(1), 32–40.

Hondagneu-Sotelo, P. (1994). *Gendered transitions: Mexican experiences of immigration.* Berkeley & Los Angeles: University of California Press.

Hondagneu-Sotelo, P. (1995). Women and children first. *Socialist Review, 25,* 169–190.

Hondagneu-Sotelo, P., & Avila, E. (1997). "I'm here, but I'm there": The meanings of Latina transnational motherhood. *Gender and Society, 11*(5), 548–571.

Hoskin, F. (1981, Summer). Female genital mutilation and human rights. *Feminist Issues,* pp. 3–23.

Hossfeld, K. (1994). Hiring immigrant women: Silicon Valley's "simple formula." In M. Baca Zinn & B. T. Dill (Eds.), *Women of color in U.S. society* (pp. 65–93). Philadelphia: Temple University Press.

Howe, I. (1976). *World of our fathers.* New York: Simon & Schuster.

Hyman, P. (1980). Immigrant women and consumer protest: The New York City kosher meat boycott of 1902. *American Jewish History, 71*(1), 91–105.

Jackson, P. (1984). Women in 19th century Irish emigration. *International Migration Review, 18*(4), 1004–1020.

Kibria, N. (1993). *Family tightrope: The changing lives of Vietnamese-Americans.* Princeton, NJ: Princeton University Press.

Kearney, M. (1995). The local and the global: The anthropology of globalization and transnationalism. *Annual Review of Anthropology, 24,* 547–565.

Kessler-Harris, A., & Brodkin Sacks, K. (1987). The demise of domesticity in America. In L. Beneria & C. Stimpson (Eds.), *Women, households, and the economy* (pp. 65–84). New Brunswick, NJ: Rutgers University Press.

Kim, E. (1990). "Such opposite creatures": Men and women in Asian American literature. *Michigan Quarterly Review, 29*(1), 68–93.

Kossoudji, S., & Ranney, S. (1984). The labor market experience of female migrants: The case of temporary Mexican migration to the U.S. *International Migration Review, 18*(4), 120–143.

Lamphere, L. (1986). From working daughters to working mothers: Production and reproduction in an industrial community. *American Ethnologist, 13*(1), 118–130.

Lamphere, L. (1987). *From working daughters to working mothers: Immigrant women in a New England community.* Ithaca, NY: Cornell University Press.

Lamphere, L., Zavella P., & Gonzales, F. (with Evans, P.). (1993). *Sunbelt working mothers.* Ithaca, NY: Cornell University Press.

Lee, E. (1966). A theory of migration. *Demography, 3*(1), 47–57.

Lewis, O. (1959). *Five families: Mexican case studies in the culture of poverty.* New York: Basic Books.

Mahler, S. (1996). *Bringing gender to a transnational focus: Theoretical and empirical ideas.* Unpublished manuscript, Department of Anthropology, University of Vermont, Burlington.

Meillassoux, C. (1981). *Maidens, meal, and money: Capitalism and the domestic community.* Cambridge, UK: Cambridge University Press.

Menjívar, C. (1995). Kinship networks among immigrants: Lessons from a qualitative comparative approach. *International Journal of Comparative Sociology, 36*(3/4), 219–232.

Mills, M. (1997). Contesting the margins of modernity: Women, migration, and consumption in Thailand. *American Ethnologist, 24*(1), 37–61.

Mohanty, C. (1991). Cartographies of struggle: Third World women and the politics of struggle. In C. T. Mohanty et al. (Eds.), *Third World women and the politics of feminism* (pp. 1–47). Bloomington: University of Indiana Press.

Morokvasic, M. (1984). Birds of passage are also women. *International Migration Review, 18*(4), 886–907.

Naples, N. (1997). The "new consensus" on the gendered "social contract": The 1987–1988 U.S. congressional hearings on welfare reform. *Signs, 22*(4), 907–945.

Nash, J. (1986). A decade of research on women in Latin America. In J. Nash & H. Safa (Eds.), *Women and change in Latin America* (pp. 3–21). South Hadley, MA: Bergin & Garvey.

Nash, J. (1988). Cultural parameters of sexism and racism in the international division of labor. In J. Smith, J. Collins, T. Hopkins, & A. Muhammad (Eds.), *Racism, sexism, and the world-system* (pp. 11–36). Westport, CT: Greenwood.

Nelson, N. (1978). Female centered families: Changing patterns of marriage and family among Buzaa Brewers of Mathare Valley. *African Urban Studies, 3,* 85–104.

O'Connor, M. (1990). Women's networks and the social needs of Mexican immigrants. *Urban Anthropology, 19*(1), 81–98.

Omi, M., & Winant, H. (1994). *Racial formation in the United States: From the 1960s to the 1990s.* New York: Routledge.

Ong, A. (1993). On the edge of empires: Flexible citizenship among Chinese in diaspora. *Positions, 1*(3), 745–778.

Pedraza, S. (1991). Women and migration: The social consequences of gender. *Annual Review of Sociology, 17,* 303–325.

Pérez, L. (1986). Immigrant economic adjustment and family organization: The Cuban success story reexamined. *International Migration Review, 20* (1), 4–20.

Pessar, P. (1984). The linkage between the household and workplace in the experience of Dominican immigrant women in the United States. *International Migration Review, 18,* 1188–1211.

Pessar, P. (1986). The role of gender in Dominican settlement in the United States. In J. Nash & H. Safa (Eds.), *Women and change in Latin America* (pp. 273–294). South Hadley, MA: Bergin & Garvey.

Pessar, P. (1988). The constraints on and release of female labor power: Dominican migration to the United States. In D. Dwyer (Ed.), *A home divided: Women and income in the Third World* (pp. 195–215). Stanford, CA: Stanford University Press.

Pessar, P. (1995a). On the homefront and in the workplace: Integrating immigrant women into feminist discourse. *Anthropological Quarterly, 68*(1), 37–47.

Pessar, P. (1995b). *A visa for a dream: Dominicans in the United States.* New York: Allyn & Bacon.

Phizacklea, A. (Ed.). (1983). *One way ticket: Migration and female labour.* Boston: Routledge & Kegan Paul.

Piore, M. (1979). *Birds of passage: Migrant labor in industrial society.* New York: Cambridge University Press.

Portes, A., & Bach, R. (1985). *Latin journey: Cuban and Mexican immigrants in the United States.* Berkeley & Los Angeles: University of California Press.

Portes, A., & Jensen, L. (1989). The enclave and the entrants: Patterns of ethnic enterprise in Miami before and after Mariel. *American Sociological Review, 54*(6), 929–949.

Redfield, R. (1955). *The little community.* Chicago: University of Chicago Press.

Repak, T. (1995). *Waiting on Washington: Central American workers in the nation's capital.* Philadelphia: Temple University Press.

Rosenberg, E., & Gilbertson, G. (1995). Mother's labor force participation in New York City: A reappraisal of the influence of household extension. *Journal of Marriage and the Family, 57,* 243–249.

Rouse, R. (1987). *Migration and the politics of family life: Divergent projects and rhetorical strategies in a Mexican transnational community.* Paper presented at the Center for U.S.-Mexican Studies, University of California, San Diego.

Rouse, R. (1989). *Mexican migration to the United States: Family relations in the development of a transnational migrant circuit.* Unpublished doctoral dissertation, Stanford University, Stanford, CA.

Ruiz, V. (1992). The flapper and the chaperone: Historical memory among Mexican-American women. In D. Gabaccia (Ed.), *Seeking common ground* (pp. 141–158). Westport, CT: Greenwood.

Saadawi, N. (1980). *The hidden face of Eve*. London: Zed Books.

Sacks, K. (1989). Toward a unified theory of class, race, and gender. *American Ethnologist, 16*(3), 534–550.

Sassen, S. (1996). *Losing control*. New York: Columbia University Press.

Sassen-Koob, S. (1984). Notes on the incorporation of Third World women into wage-labor through immigration and off-shore production. *International Migration Review, 18*(4), 1144–1167.

Segura, D. (1994). Working at motherhood: Chicana and Mexican immigrant mothers and employment. In E. N. Glenn, G. Chang, & L. R. Forcey (Eds.), *Mothering* (pp. 211–233). New York: Routledge.

Shukla, S. (1997). Feminisms of the diaspora both local and global: The politics of South Asian women against domestic violence. In C. Cohen, K. Jones, & J. Tronto (Eds.), *Women transforming politics: An alternative reader* (pp. 269–283). New York: New York University Press.

Simon, R., & Brettell, C. (Eds.). (1986). *International migration: The female experience*. Totowa, NJ: Rowman & Allanheld.

Smith, P. (1994). Can you imagine? Transnational migration and the globalization of grass-roots politics. *Social Text, 39*(15), 15–33.

Soto, I. (1987). West Indian child fostering: Its role in migrant exchanges. In C. Sutton & E. Chaney (Eds.), *Caribbean life in New York City—Sociocultural dimensions* (pp. 131–149). Staten Island, NY: Center for Migration Studies.

Stark, O. (1991). *The migration of labor*. Cambridge, UK: Basil Blackwell.

Susser, I. (1982). *Norman street*. New York: Oxford University Press.

Tienda. M., & Booth, K. (1991). Gender, migration, and social change. *International Sociology, 6*(1), 138–148.

Torruellas, R., Benmayor, R., & Juarbe, A. (1997). Negotiating gender, work, and welfare: Familia as productive labor among Puerto Rican women in New York City. In A. Ortiz (Ed.), *Puerto Rican women and work: Bridges in transnational labor* (pp. 184–208). Philadelphia: Temple University Press.

Waldinger, R., & Gilbertson, G. (1994). Immigrants' progress: Ethnic and gender differences among U.S. immigrants in the 1980s. *Sociological Perspectives, 37*(3), 431–444.

Weinberg, S. S. (1992). The treatment of women in immigration history: A call for change. In D. Gabaccia (Ed.), *Seeking common ground: Multidisciplinary studies of immigrant women in the United States*. Westport, CT: Greenwood.

Zavella, P. (1987). *Women's work and Chicano families*. Ithaca, NY: Cornell University Press.

Zhou, M. (1992). *Chinatown*. Philadelphia: Temple University Press.

Zhou, M., & Logan, J. (1991). Returns on human capital in ethnic enclaves: New York City's Chinatown. *American Sociological Review, 54*(5), 809–820.

Zinn, M. (1987). Structural transformations and minority families. In L. Beneria & C. Stimpson (Eds.), *Women, households, and the economy* (pp. 155–172). New Brunswick, NJ: Rutgers University Press.

Zinn, M., Weber Cannon, L., Higginbotham, E., & Thornton Dill, B. (1986). The exclusionary practices in women's studies. *Signs, 11*(2), 290–303.

CHAPTER 3

Strategic Instantiations of Gendering in the Global Economy

Saskia Sassen

Economic globalization has multiple localizations, many of which typically go unrecognized. One such localization is constituted by the set of global circuits focused on in this essay. These are cross-border circuits in which the role of women, and especially the condition of being a foreign woman, is crucial. These circuits include illegal trafficking in women and children for the sex industry; the mostly illegal trafficking in migrant workers that is a growing source of profit for both legal and illegal contractors; and, more generally, emigration that has become an important source of hard currency for governments in home countries. The employment and/or use of foreign-born women covers an increasingly broad range of economic sectors, from prostitution, which is illegal in many countries, to highly regulated occupations such as nursing. The key actors giving shape to these processes are the individuals themselves in search of work and, increasingly, illegal traffickers and contractors, as well as the governments of home countries.

In the first section I conceptualize these alternative circuits to situate them in the global economic system. This should help in the analytic shift from detecting the presence of women to understanding the gender dynamics that might be operating in the global economy. The second section seeks to ground these theorized circuits in the empirical conditions in developing countries that are associated with economic globalization, such as growing unemployment, the closure of a large number of typically small and medium-sized enterprises oriented to national rather than export markets, and large and often increasing government debt. My purpose is to establish the existence of systemic links between these conditions and the growth of these alternative circuits for survival, for profit making, and for securing government revenue. While these economies are frequently grouped under the label *developing*, they are in some cases struggling or stagnant and even shrinking. For the sake of brevity I will use *developing* as shorthand for this variety of situations. In fact, the poorest countries are not the ones likely to have even the minimal resources necessary for setting up the alternative circuits examined in this essay. The third section interprets this combination of conditions as the feminizing of survival for a growing share of households and for a range of illegal traffickers, and the feminizing of particular forms of government revenue enhancement.

THEORIZING GENDER IN THE GLOBAL ECONOMY

What are the strategic sites where the gender dynamics of current processes of globalization can be detected, studied, and theorized? This is an important and difficult analytical task. As happened with earlier phases of economic internationalization, the current scholarship on the global economy largely ignores the facts and modalities of gender dynamics.

It took a pioneering effort to begin to redress this omission for earlier phases of economic internationalization (Boserup, 1970; Deere, 1976). The resulting scholarship shows us that in export-oriented agriculture gendering organizes the nexus between subsistence economies and capitalist enterprise. In the internationalization of manufacturing production gendering organizes the nexus between the dismantling of an established, largely male "labor aristocracy" in major industries with shadow effects on an increasing sector of developed economies and the formation of an offshore, largely female proletariat in new and old growth sectors. Offshoring and feminizing this proletariat (which is, after all, employed in what are growth industries) has kept it from becoming an empowered "labor aristocracy" with actual union power. This also prevents existing largely male "labor aristocracies" from becoming stronger. Introducing a gendered understanding of economic processes lays bare these connections.

Among the strategic sites in today's global economy are those linked to the new organization of politico-economic power and the formation of global cities.[1] Among other features, global cities are key sites for the specialized servicing, financing, and management of global economic processes. These cities are also a site for the incorporation of large numbers of women and immigrants in activities that service the strategic sectors. This mode of incorporation renders these workers invisible, thereby breaking the nexus between being workers in leading industries and having the opportunity to become—as had been historically the case in industrialized economies—a "labor aristocracy" or its contemporary equivalent. In this sense "women and immigrants" in the global city emerge as the systemic equivalent of the offshore proletariat. Further, the demands placed on the top-level professional and managerial workforce in global cities are such that the usual modes of handling household tasks and lifestyle become inadequate. This type of household could be described as the "professional household without a 'wife,'" regardless of the fact that it may consist of a man and woman or man and man or woman and woman, so long as they are both in demanding jobs. As a consequence, we are seeing the return in all the global cities around the world of the so-called serving classes, made up largely of immigrant and migrant women (Chang, 1998; Hondagneu-Sotelo, 2001; Parreñas, 2001; Sassen, 2001, chap. 9).

But the master images in the currently dominant account of economic globalization in media and policy circles, as well as in much economic analysis, basically do not deal with these types of conditions. The emphasis is on hypermobility, global communications, the neutralization of place and distance, and the highly educated, human-capital-intensive worker. This account privileges the capability for global transmission over the material infrastructure that makes transmission possible; information outputs over the workers who produce those outputs, from specialists to secretaries; and the new transnational corporate culture over the multiplicity of work cultures, including immigrant cultures, within which many of the "other" jobs of the global information economy take place.

Detecting gender dynamics requires a shift in focus to the *practices* that constitute what we call economic globalization and global control: the top-level firms and the top-level households in charge of the work of producing and reproducing the organization and management of a global production system and a global marketplace for finance, as well as the vast infrastructure of low-wage jobs and low-profit activities that service the former.

A focus on practices draws the categories of place and work process into the analysis of economic globalization and allows us to recapture people, workers, communities, and, more specifically, the many different work cultures, besides the corporate culture, involved in the work of globalization. There is considerable articulation of firms, sectors, and workers who may appear as though they have little connection to an urban economy dominated by finance and specialized services, but in fact fulfill a series of functions that are an integral part of that economy. They do so, however, under conditions of sharp social, earnings, and, often, sex and racial/ethnic segmentation. The global city can be seen as one strategic research site for the study of these processes.

In the day-to-day work of the leading services complex dominated by finance in the case of a city like New York, a large share of the jobs are low paid and manual, many held by women and immigrants. Although these types of workers and jobs are never represented as part of the global economy, they are in fact part of the infrastructure of jobs involved in running and implementing the global economic system, including such an advanced form as international finance. The top end of the corporate economy—the corporate towers that project engineering expertise, precision, *techne*—is far easier to mark as necessary for an advanced economic system than are truckers and other industrial service workers, even though these are a necessary ingredient.[2]

At work here is a series of processes that valorize and overvalorize certain types of outputs, workers, firms, and sectors, and devalorize others. We cannot take devalorization as a given: devalorization is a produced outcome. In my reading, the forms of devalorization of certain types of workers and work cultures described here are partly embedded in the demographic transformations evident in large cities. The growing presence of women, immigrants, and people of color in large cities, along with a declining middle class, has facilitated devalorization processes. The fact of gendering—for example, the devaluing of female-typed jobs—facilitates the devalorization of a broad range of jobs performed by the growing and mostly female "serving classes" in global cities.[3] This is significant for an analysis of globalization because these cities are strategic sites for the materialization of global processes and for the valorization of the new forms of global corporate capital (Sassen, 2001).

The alternative global circuits that are the focus of this essay are yet another instantiation of gendering in the global economy, but from the perspective of disadvantaged locations rather than from the perspective of global cities. These disadvantaged locations can be both illegal, as in the trafficking of women and children for the sex industry, or they can be fully legal, as in the growing dependence of many governments in poorer countries on the remittances sent by their low-wage emigrants. The analysis of globalization contained in the global city model incorporates the presence of disadvantaged locations (workers, urban neighborhoods, firms) inside the global city, and in the invisibility of their articulation with dominant dynamics because of their demographic embeddedness in immigrant and minority women. The decentering of the analysis of globalization developed in this essay is grounded in the presence of alternative global circuits that connect sites in different countries—survival economics and global cities can be located on the same global circuits.

These alternative circuits can be interpreted as constituting a countergeography of globalization. They are deeply imbricated with some of the major dynamics constitutive of globalization: the formation of global markets, the intensifying of transnational and translocal networks, and the development of communication technologies that easily escape conventional surveillance practices. The strengthening and, in some of these cases, the formation of new global circuits is embedded or made possible by the existence of a global economic system and its various associated institutional supports for cross-border money flows and markets, a condition that reaches its most formalized version in the proliferation of free-trade agreements and in the overall structure of the World Trade Organization (WTO).[4] Positing this embeddedness has been an important element in my research on globalization: that is, the notion that once there is an institutional infrastructure for globalization, processes that have basically operated at the national level can scale up to the global level even when this is not necessary for their operation. This would contrast with processes that are by their very features global, such as the network of financial centers underlying the formation of a global capital market.

Besides being enabled by the existing infrastructure of globalization, these alternative global circuits may well be a systemic outcome that is partly constitutive of globalization. Of interest here is the fact that the WTO and major regional free-trade agreements contain specific provisions concerning the cross-border mobility of specialized professional workers in finance, telecommunications, and a broad range of highly specialized services (Sassen, 1998, chap. 2). The North American Free Trade Agreement contains such provisions even though it was negotiated as an agreement that explicitly had nothing to do with cross-border flows of workers. These provisions amount to a specialized regime for the circulation of service workers that is an integral part of the liberalization of international trade and investment in services. These provisions concern a largely privileged male workforce; many of the women in this category of workers are likely to function as male subjects. In contrast, the alternative circuits concern an increasingly feminized and exploited workforce. Yet some of these alternative circuits may also be an increasingly necessary component of the global economy—the search for new survival, profit-making, and government-revenue-securing strategies in the global south that increasingly function on the backs of poor women. We can see here the elements of a dynamic of gendering.

As with the analysis of the global city, understanding the gender dynamics involved is a more difficult task than detecting the presence of women in these alternative global circuits. Although the evidence for these conditions is incomplete and partial, there is a growing consensus among experts that they are expanding and that women are often a majority, including in situations that used to be made up of mostly males. These are, in many ways, old conditions. What is different today is their rapid growth and their rapid internationalization. The fact of gendering is easier to see in the case of trafficking for the sex industry than in the more generalized condition of profit making and government revenue enhancement through migration for work. In my analysis the intermediation here is to be found, on the one hand, in the systemic linkages between the negative impacts of globalization on male employment and government revenue based on what were predominantly male waged-employment-based economies, and on the other hand, in the associated growing pressures on women to ensure household survival and to offer alternative modes for profit making and government revenue. These alternative circuits are dynamic and changing in their locational features: to some extent they are part of the shadow economy, but it is also clear that they use some of the institutional infrastructure of the regular economy.

NEO-LIBERALISM AND DEVELOPING COUNTRIES: GENDERED OUTCOMES

Some of the major dynamics linked to economic globalization have had significant impacts on developing economies. The latter have had to implement a bundle of new policies and accommodate new conditions associated with globalization: Structural Adjustment Programs, the opening up of these economies to foreign firms either through free-trade agreements or the provisions of the WTO, the elimination of multiple state subsidies, and, it would seem almost inevitably, financial crises and the prevailing types of programmatic solutions put forth by the International

TABLE 3.1. External Debt and Debt Service in Developing Countries, 1991 to 1999, Selected Years (in U.S.$)

	1991	*1995*	*1998*	*1999*
External Debt	1,269.8	1,714.4	1,965.2	1,969.6
Net Credit	22.2	29.9	58.9	64.5
Net Debit	1,247.6	1,684.5	1,906.3	1,905.1
by Official Lenders	234.5	286.8	292.9	300.3
by Private Lenders	674.1	990.8	1,166.6	1,162.5
by Diverse Lenders	338.9	406.9	446.8	442.2
Debt Service	150.1	242.9	316.1	331.8
Net Credit	1.8	7.1	8.5	8.6
by Official Lenders	16.5	25.8	22.7	16.8
by Private Lenders	99.5	165.2	213.5	240.9
by Diverse Lenders	32.2	44.8	71.4	65.5

SOURCE: *World Economic Outlook* and staff studies for the *World Economic Outlook,* 1992–1999, IMF.
NOTE: Developing countries include countries in Africa, Asia, the Middle East, and Eastern and Western Europe.

Monetary Fund (IMF). It is now clear that in most of the countries involved, whether Mexico or South Korea, these conditions have created enormous costs for certain sectors of the economy and of the population, and have not fundamentally reduced government debt.

Among these costs are, prominently, the growth in unemployment, the closure of a large number of firms in often fairly traditional sectors oriented to the local or national market, the promotion of export-oriented cash crops that have increasingly replaced survival agriculture and food production for local or national markets, and, finally, the ongoing and mostly heavy burden of government debt in most of these economies.

Debt and debt-servicing problems have become a systemic feature of the developing world since the 1980s. Generally, most countries that became deeply indebted in the 1980s have not been able to solve this problem. And in the 1990s we have seen a whole new set of countries become deeply indebted. Over these two decades many innovations were launched, most importantly by the IMF and the World Bank through their Structural Adjustment Programs and Structural Adjustment Loans, respectively. The latter were tied to economic policy reform rather than the funding of a particular project. The purpose of such programs is to make states more "competitive," which typically means sharp cuts in various social programs.

Structural Adjustment Programs became a new norm for the World Bank and the IMF on grounds that they were a promising way to secure long-term growth and sound government policy. Yet all of these countries have remained deeply indebted, with 41 of them now considered as Highly Indebted Poor Countries (HIPC). (UNDP, 2000; see also Tables 3.1–3.3). Furthermore, the actual structure

TABLE 3.2. Budget Allocation to Basic Social Services
and Debt Service in Selected Countries

Country	Year	Total Basic Social Services (%)	Debt Service (%)
		Asia	
Nepal	1997	13.6	14.9
Philippines	1992	7.7	30.7
Sri Lanka	1996	12.7	21.5
Thailand	1997	14.6	1.3
		Africa	
Benin	1997	9.5	10.8
Burkina Faso	1997	19.5	10.2
Cameroon	1996–97	4.0	36.0
Côte d'Ivoire	1994–96	11.4	35.0
Kenya	1995	12.6	40.0
Namibia	1996–97	19.1	3.0
Niger	1995	20.4	33.0
South Africa	1996–97	14.0	8.0
Tanzania (mainland)	1994–95	15.0	46.0
Uganda	1994–95	21.0	9.4
Zambia	1997	6.7	40.0
		Latin America and the Caribbean	
Belize	1996	20.3	5.7
Bolivia	1997	16.7	9.8
Brazil	1995	8.9	20.0
Chile	1996	10.6	2.7
Colombia	1997	16.8	7.9
Costa Rica	1996	13.1	13.0
Dominican Republic	1997	8.7	10.0
El Salvador	1996	13.0	27.0
Honduras	1992	12.5	21.0
Jamaica	1996	10.2	31.2
Nicaragua	1996	9.2	14.1
Peru	1997	19.3	30.0

SOURCES: UNDP, 2000.

TABLE 3.3. Public Expenditure on Health, Malnutrition, and Life Expectancy in Selected Highly Indebted Countries

	Public Expenditure on Health— % GDP	Prevalence of Malnutrition—% Children Under Age 5	Life Expectancy at Birth— % Change
	1990–1998	1992–1997	1990–1997
Angola	3.9	35	0
Botswana	2.7	27	n/a
Côte d'Ivoire	4.0	24	−3.1
Ethiopia	1.7	48	−1.7
Haiti	1.3	28	n/a
Kenya	2.2	23	−5.0
Mozambique	2.1	26	n/a
Nigeria	0.2	39	5
Tanzania	1.3	31	−2.1
Uganda	1.8	26	−4.3
Vietnam	0.4	n/a	1.6
Zambia	2.3	n/a	−6.0
Zimbabwe	3.1	16	n/a

SOURCES: World Development Report, 1999/2000; World Development Indicators, 1999/2000.

*n/a = not available.

of these debts, their servicing, and how they fit into the economies of the debtor countries suggest that most of these countries will, under current conditions, be unable to pay this debt in full.[5] Structural Adjustment Programs seem to have made this even more likely by demanding economic reforms that have added to unemployment and the bankruptcy of many smaller, national-market-oriented firms.

Debt service to GNP ratios in most HIPC countries exceed sustainable limits (OXFAM, 1999); these ratios are far more extreme than what were considered unmanageable levels in the Latin American debt crisis of the 1980s. Debt to GNP ratios are especially high in Africa, where they stood at 123%, compared with 42% in Latin America and 28% in Asia (Cheru, 1999). Many of these countries pay over 50% of their government revenues toward debt service or 20–25% of their export earnings (Ambrogi, 1999). Thirty-three of the 41 Highly Indebted Countries paid $3 in debt service payments to the North for every $1 in development assistance. This debt burden inevitably has large repercussions on the composition of state spending.

It is in this context of a systemic condition marked by high unemployment, poverty, bankruptcy of a large number of firms, and shrinking resources in states to meet social needs that alternative, increasingly feminized circuits for survival emerge and can be seen as articulated with those conditions. The formation of these alternative circuits for survival, however, is dependent on certain conditions, such as the existence of an infrastructure that facilitates the cross-border flows described in the preceding section and more specific linkages between particular countries, including ethnic networks. The formation of these circuits is also mediated by other conditions. Important among these are the existence of older traditions of trafficking and organized crime, government initiatives to develop special programs for exporting workers, and patriarchal households that devalue women. These conditions can activate the fact of unemployment and shrinking options for profit making and for securing revenue into the search for alternatives.

FEMINIZING SURVIVAL

Are there systemic links between these two sets of developments—the rise in unemployment and debt in these economies and the growing presence of women from developing economies in the alternative global circuits discussed in the first section of this article? One way of articulating this in substantive terms is to posit that the shrinking opportunities for male employment in many of these countries, the shrinking opportunities for more traditional forms of profit making in these same countries as they increasingly accept foreign firms in a widening range of economic sectors and are pressured to develop export industries, and, finally, the fall in revenues for the governments in many of these countries, partly linked to these conditions and to the burden of debt servicing, have all contributed to raise the importance of alternative ways of making a living, making a profit, and securing government revenue.

There is a research literature on women and the debt, focused on the implementation of a first generation of Structural Adjustment Programs in several developing countries, linked to the growing debt of governments in the 1980s; this literature has documented the disproportionate burden these programs put on women.[6] And now there is a new literature on a second generation of such programs, programs that are more directly linked to the implementation of the global economy in the 1990s.[7]

These programs have detrimental effects on government spending for women and children, notably education and health care—investments clearly necessary to ensure a better future (Alarcon-Gonzalez & McKinley, 1999; Buchmann, 1996). Further, the increased unemployment typically associated with the austerity and adjustment programs implemented by international agencies to address government debt also have adverse effects on women (Chossudovsky, 1997; Elson, 1995; Rahman, 1999; Standing, 1999). Unemployment, both among women and also more generally among the men in their households, has added to the pressure on women to find ways to ensure household survival. Subsistence food production, informal work, emigration, and prostitution have all grown as survival options for women.[8]

Heavy government debt and high unemployment have resulted in a search for survival alternatives; and a shrinking of regular economic opportunities has resulted in expanded illegal profit-making by enterprises and organizations. In this regard, heavy debt burdens play an important role in the formation of alternative global circuits for survival, profit making, and government revenue enhancement. Economic globalization has to some extent added to the rapid increase in certain components of this debt, and it has provided an institutional infrastructure for cross-border flows and global markets. We can see economic globalization as facilitating the operation of these alternative circuits at a global scale.

Prostitution and labor migration are growing in importance as ways of making a living; illegal trafficking in women and children for the sex industry and in migrant laborers is growing in importance as a way to make a profit. The remittances sent by emigrants, as well as the organized export of workers, are increasingly important sources of revenues for some of these governments (see, e.g., Altink, 1995; Heyzer, 1994; Lim, 1998; Shannon, 1999). Women are by far the majority group in prostitution and in trafficking for the sex industry, and they are becoming a majority group in migration for labor.

Trafficking in women for the sex industry is highly profitable for those running the trade (CIA, 2000).[9] The United Nations estimates that 4 million people were trafficked in 1998, producing a profit of U.S.$7 billion to criminal groups.[10] These funds include remittances from prostitutes' earnings and payments to organizers and facilitators in these countries. It is estimated that in recent years several million women and girls have been trafficked within and out of Asia and the former Soviet Union, two major trafficking areas. Growth in both these areas can be linked to women being pushed into poverty or sold to brokers because of the poverty of their households or parents. Women also can be the ones initiating the transaction.

Trafficking in migrants is also a profitable business. According to a UN report, criminal organizations in the 1990s generated an estimated U.S.$3.5 billion per year in profits from trafficking migrants generally (not just women) (OIM, 1996). The entry of organized crime into migrant trafficking is a recent development. Before, the trafficking was more often the work of petty criminals. There are also reports that organized crime groups are creating intercontinental strategic alliances through networks of coethnics throughout several countries; this facilitates transport, local contact and distribution, provision of false documents, and so on. The Global Survival Network reported on these practices after a two-year investigation in which a dummy company was established to enter the illegal trade (1997). Such networks also facilitate the organized circulation of trafficked women among third countries—not only from sending to receiving countries. Traffickers may move women from Burma, Laos, Vietnam, and China to Thailand, while Thai women may be moved to Japan and the United States.[11]

Some of the features of immigration policy and enforcement may well contribute to make women who are victims of trafficking even more vulnerable and give them little recourse to the law. If they are undocumented, which is likely, they will not be treated as victims of abuse but as violators of the law insofar as they have violated entry, residence, and work laws.[12] Addressing undocumented immi-

gration and trafficking through greater border controls over entry raises the likelihood that women will use traffickers to cross the border, and some of these may
turn out to belong to criminal organizations linked to the sex industry.

While some women know that they are being trafficked for prostitution and some
consider it a job, for many others the conditions of their recruitment and the extent of abuse and bondage become evident only after they arrive in the receiving
country. The conditions of confinement are often extreme, akin to slavery, and so
are the conditions of abuse, including rape and other forms of sexual violence and
physical punishments. They are severely underpaid, and wages are often withheld.
They are not allowed to use methods to protect against AIDS, and typically have
no right to medical treatment. If they seek police help, they may be taken into detention because they are in violation of immigration laws; if they have been provided with false documents, there are criminal charges.[13]

As tourism has grown sharply over the last decade and become a major development strategy for cities, regions, and whole countries, the entertainment sector has
seen a parallel growth and been recognized as a key development strategy (Judd &
Fainstein, 1999; Wonders & Michalowski, 2001). In many places, the sex trade is part
of the entertainment industry and has similarly grown (see, e.g., Bishop & Robinson,
1998; Booth, 1999; Wonders & Michalowski, 2001). At some point it becomes clear
that the sex trade itself can become a development strategy in areas with high unemployment and poverty and for governments desperate for revenue and foreign
exchange reserves. When local manufacturing and agriculture can no longer function as sources of employment, profits, and government revenue, what was once a
marginal source of earnings, profits, and revenues becomes a far more important one.
The increased importance of these sectors in development generates growing tie-ins.
For instance, when the IMF and the World Bank see tourism as a solution to some
of the development impasses in many poor countries and provide loans for its development, they may well be contributing to a broader institutional setting for the expansion of the entertainment industry and indirectly of the sex trade. This tie-in with
development strategies signals that trafficking in women may expand sharply.

The entry of organized crime into the sex trades, the formation of cross-
border ethnic networks, and the growing transnationalization in so many aspects
of tourism suggests that we are likely to see further development of a global sex
industry. This could mean greater attempts to enter into more and more "markets"
and a general expansion of the industry. It is a worrisome possibility, especially in
the context of growing numbers of women with few if any employment options.
Such growing numbers are to be expected given high unemployment and poverty,
the shrinking of a world of work opportunities embedded in the more traditional
sectors of these economies, and the growing debt burden of governments that renders them incapable of providing social services and support to the poor.

Women in the sex industry become—in certain kinds of economies—a crucial
link supporting the expansion of the entertainment industry and, through that,
tourism as a development strategy, with tourism in turn becoming a source of gov-

ernment revenue. These tie-ins are structural, not a function of conspiracies. Their weight in an economy will be raised by the absence or limitations of other sources for securing a livelihood, profits, and revenues for workers, enterprises, and governments.

Women, and migrants generally, enter the macrolevel of development strategies through yet another channel: the sending of remittances, which in many countries are a major source of foreign exchange reserves for the government. While the flows of remittances may be minor compared with the massive daily capital flows in various financial markets, they are often very significant for developing or struggling economies.

In 1998 global remittances sent by immigrants to their home countries reached over U.S.$70 billion. To understand the significance of this figure, it should be related to the GDP and foreign currency reserves in the specific countries involved, rather than compared with the global flow of capital. For instance, in the Philippines, a key sender of migrants generally and of women for the entertainment industry in several countries, remittances have been the third largest source of foreign exchange over the last several years. In Bangladesh, another country with significant numbers of its workers in the Middle East, Japan, and several European countries, remittances represent about a third of foreign exchange.

Exporting workers and remittances are ways for governments to cope with unemployment and foreign debt. There are two ways in which governments have secured benefits through these strategies. One of these is highly formalized; the other is simply a by-product of the migration process itself. The Philippine government formalized the export of its citizens as a way of dealing with unemployment and securing needed foreign exchange reserves through their remittances. The government played an important role in the emigration of Filipino women to the United States, the Middle East, and Japan through the Philippine Overseas Employment Administration (POEA) (Tyner, 1999).[14] Established in 1982, the POEA organized and oversaw the export of nurses and maids to high-demand areas in the world. In the last few years Filipino overseas workers have sent home on average almost U.S.$1 billion. Confronted with a sharp shortage of nurses, a profession that demands years of training yet garners rather low wages and little prestige or recognition, the United States passed the Immigration Nursing Relief Act of 1989, which allowed for the import of nurses.[15]

An estimated 200 mail-order bride companies arrange 2,000 to 5,000 marriages in the United States a year (Yamamoto, 2000). The Philippines and Russia are currently the main source countries for contract brides to the United States. The Philippine government also passed regulations that permitted mail-order bride agencies to recruit young Filipinas to marry foreign men as a matter of contractual agreement (Philippines Information Service, 1999). The rapid increase in this trade was centrally due to the organized effort by the government. Among the major clients were the United States and Japan. There are many stories of abuse by foreign husbands. In the United States the Immigration and Naturalization Service has recently reported that domestic violence toward mail-order wives has become acute.

While the Philippines has perhaps the most developed program, it is not the only country to have explored these strategies. After the 1997–1998 financial crisis, Thailand started a campaign in 1998 to promote the migration for work of Thai workers and their recruitment by firms overseas. The government sought to export workers to the Middle East, the United States, Great Britain, Germany, Australia, and Greece. Sri Lanka's government has tried to export another 200,000 workers in addition to the one million it already has overseas; Sri Lankan women remitted U.S.$880 million in 1998, mostly from their earnings as maids in the Middle East and Far East (Anon, 1999). Bangladesh organized extensive labor export programs to the OPEC countries of the Middle East as early as the 1970s. This has continued, and along with the individual migration to these countries and to various other countries, notably the United States and Great Britain, organized labor export is a significant source of foreign exchange. Its workers remitted $U.S.1.4 billion in each of the last few years (David, 1999).

Increasingly, these forms of making a living, making a profit, and securing government revenue are realized on the backs of women. Thus in using the notion of feminization of survival I am not only referring to the fact that households and indeed whole communities are increasingly dependent on women for their survival. I want to emphasize that governments, too, are dependent on women's earnings in these various circuits, and so are types of enterprises whose forms of profit making exist at the margins of the "licit" economy. In this sense, these circuits indicate the growing feminization of survival. Systemic connections are uncovered between, on the one hand, the mostly poor and low-wage women often represented as a burden rather than a resource, and, on the other hand, what are emerging as significant sources for profit making, especially in the shadow economy, and for government revenue enhancement. To this we can add the savings achieved by governments through severe cuts in health care and education. These cuts are often part of the effort of making the state more competitive as demanded by Structural Adjustment Programs and other policies linked to the current phase of globalization. These types of cuts are generally recognized as hitting women particularly hard insofar as women are responsible for the health and education of household members.

CONCLUSION

We are seeing the growth of a variety of alternative global circuits for making a living, making a profit, and securing government revenue. These circuits incorporate increasing numbers of women. Among the most important of these global circuits are the invisible trafficking in women for prostitution as well as for regular work, organized exports of women as brides, nurses, and domestic servants, and the remmitances sent back to their home countries by an increasingly female emigrant workforce. Some of these circuits operate partly or wholly in the shadow economy.

The emergence of these circuits and/or their global scale is linked to major dynamics of economic globalization in both the highly developed and developing economies. The global city is one type of site that makes visible the formation/expansion of a demand for what these circuits deliver and hence the (relative) profitability of these circuits. In the developing countries, key indicators of conditions promoting the supply of workers and the formation of these circuits are the heavy and rising burden of government debt, the growth in unemployment, sharp cuts in government social expenditures, the closure of a large number of firms in often fairly traditional sectors oriented to the local or national market, and the promotion of export-oriented growth. The growth of a global economy has brought with it an institutional infrastructure that facilitates cross-border flows and represents, in that regard, an enabling environment for these alternative circuits.

I call these "alternative circuits of globalization" because they are (1) directly or indirectly associated with some of the key programs and conditions that are at the heart of the global economy, but (2) are circuits not typically represented as connected to globalization, and often actually operate outside of and in violation of laws and treaties, yet are not exclusively embedded in criminal operations as is the case with the illegal drug trade. Linking these alternative circuits to programs and conditions at the heart of the global economy also helps us understand how gendering enters into their formation and viability.

NOTES

This essay is based on the author's larger, multiyear project Governance and Accountability in the Global Economy (Department of Sociology, University of Chicago). It is a revised version of an article published in *Journal of International Affairs*, 53(2), 503–524. We thank the journal for permission to publish it.

1. The rest of this discussion up to page [51] is based on Sassen, 1998, chap. 5.

2. This is illustrated by the following event: When the first acute stock market crisis happened in 1987 after years of enormous growth, there were numerous press reports about the sudden and massive unemployment crisis among high-income professionals on Wall Street. The other unemployment crises on Wall Street, affecting secretaries and blue-collar workers, was never noticed or reported upon, in spite of the fact that the stock market crash created a very concentrated unemployment crisis, for instance, in the Dominican immigrant community in northern Manhattan where a lot of the Wall Street cleaners live.

3. The rapid growth of industries with strong concentrations of high- and low-income jobs has assumed distinct forms in the consumption structure, which in turn has a feedback effect on the organization of work and the types of jobs being created. The expansion of the high-income workforce in conjunction with the emergence of new cultural forms has led to a process of high-income gentrification that rests, in the last analysis, on the availability of a vast supply of low-wage workers. This has reintroduced—to an extent not seen in a very long time—the whole notion of the "serving classes" in contemporary high-income

households. The immigrant woman serving the White middle-class professional woman has replaced the traditional image of the Black female servant serving the White master.

4. I have argued this for the case of international labor migrations (e.g., Sassen, 1998, chaps. 2, 3, and 4, 1999).

5. In 1998 the debt was held as follows: Multilateral institutions (IMF, World Bank, and regional development banks) hold 45% of the debt; bilateral institutions (individual countries and the Paris group) hold 45% of the debt; and private commercial institutions hold 10% (UNDP, 1999; Ambrogi, 1999; see also tables in Sassen, 2001, chap. 4).

6. This is by now a large literature in many different languages; it also includes a vast number of limited-circulation items produced by various activist and support organizations. For overviews, see, for example, Beneria & Feldman, 1992; Bose & Acosta-Belen, 1995; Bradshaw, Noonan, Gash, & Buchmann, 1993; Moser, 1989; Tinker, 1990; Ward, 1990.

7. See, for example, Alarcon-Gonzalez & McKinley, 1999; Buchmann, 1996; Cagatay & Ozler, 1995; Chossudovsky, 1997; Elson, 1995; Jones, 1999; Rahman, 1999; Safa, 1995; Standing, 1999. For an excellent overview of the literature on the impact of the debt on women, see Ward, 1990, and Ward & Pyle, 1995.

8. On these various issues see, for example, Alarcon-Gonzalez & McKinley, 1999; Buchmann, 1996; Cagatay & Ozler, 1995; Chant, 1992; Jones, 1999; Safa, 1995.

9. Trafficking involves the forced recruitment and/or transportation of people within and across states for work or services through a variety of forms all involving coercion. Trafficking is a violation of several distinct types of rights: human, civil, political. Trafficking is related to the sex market, to labor markets, to illegal migration. Much legislative work has been done to address trafficking: international treaties and charters, UN resolutions, and legislation by various bodies and commissions (see, e.g., Chuang, 1998; for a critical analysis of legislative measures adopted by the United States, see Dayan, 1999). NGOs are also playing an increasingly important role. For instance, the Coalition Against Trafficking in Women has centers and representatives in Australia, Bangladesh, Europe, Latin America, North America, Africa, and Asia Pacific. The Women's Rights Advocacy Program has established the Initiative Against Trafficking in Persons to combat the global trade in persons.

10. See, generally, the Foundation Against Trafficking in Women (STV) and the Global Alliance Against Traffic in Women (GAATW). For regularly updated sources of information on trafficking, see http://www.hrlawgroup.org/site/programs/traffic.html. See, generally, Altink, 1995; Kempadoo & Doezema, 1998; Lim, 1998; Lin & Marjan, 1997; Shannon, 1999.

11. There are various reports on the particular cross-border movements in trafficking. Malay brokers sell Malay women into prostitution in Australia. East European women from Albania and Kosovo have been trafficked by gangs into prostitution in London (Hamzic & Sheehan, 1999). European teens from Paris and other cities have been sold to Arab and African customers (Shannon, 1999). In the United States the police broke up an international Asian ring that imported women from China, Thailand, Korea, Malaysia, and Vietnam (Booth, 1999). The women were charged between U.S.$30,000 and U.S.$40,000 in contracts to be paid through their work in the sex trade or needle trade. The women in the sex trade were shuttled around several states in the United States to bring continuing variety to the clients.

12. See, generally, Castles & Miller, 1998; Castro, 1999; Mahler, 1995.

13. A fact sheet by the Coalition to Abolish Slavery and Trafficking reports that one survey of Asian sex workers found that rape often preceded their being sold into prostitution and that about one third had been falsely led into prostitution.

14. The largest number of Filipinas going through these channels work overseas as maids, particularly in other Asian countries. The second largest group, and the fastest growing, is "entertainers," who largely go to major cities in Japan (Sassen, 2001, chap. 9).

15. About 80% of the nurses brought in under the new act were from the Philippines.

REFERENCES

Alarcon-Gonzalez, Diana, & McKinley, Terry. (1999). The adverse effects of structural adjustment on working women in Mexico. *Latin American Perspectives, 26*(3), 103–117.

Altink, Sietske. (1995). *Stolen lives: Trading women into sex and slavery.* New York: Harrington Park Press; London: Scarlet Press.

Ambrogi, Thomas. (1999, July). Jubilee 2000 and the campaign for debt cancellation. *National Catholic Reporter.*

Beneria, Lourdes, & Feldman, Shelley (Eds). (1992). *Unequal burden: Economic crises, persistent poverty, and women's work.* Boulder, CO: Westview.

Bishop, Ryan, & Robinson, Lillian. (1998). *Night market: Sexual cultures and the Thai economic miracle.* New York: Routledge.

Booth, William. (1999, August 21). Thirteen charged in gang importing prostitutes. *Washington Post.*

Bose, Christine E., & Acosta-Belen, Edna (Eds.). (1995). *Women in the Latin American development process: From structural subordination to empowerment.* Philadelphia: Temple University Press.

Boserup, E. (1970). *Woman's role in economic development.* New York: St. Martin's Press.

Bradshaw, York, Noonan, Rita, Gash, Laura, & Buchmann, Claudia. (1993). Borrowing against the future: Children and third world indebtedness. *Social Forces, 71*(3), 629–656.

Buchmann, Claudia. (1996). The debt crisis, structural adjustment, and women's education. *International Journal of Comparative Studies, 37*(1–2), 5–30.

Cagatay, Nilufer, & Ozler, Sule. (1995). Feminization of the labor force: The effects of long-term development and structural adjustment. *World Development, 23*(11), 1883–1894.

Castles, Stephen, & Miller, Mark J. (1998). *The age of migration: International population movements in the modern world* (2nd ed.). New York: Macmillan.

Castro, Max (Ed.). (1999). *Free markets, open societies, closed borders?* Coral Gables, FL: North-South Center Press.

Chang, Grace. (1998). Undocumented Latinas: The new "employable mothers." In M. Andersen & Patricia Hill Collins (Eds.), *Race, class, and gender* (3rd ed., pp. 311–319). Belmont, CA: Wadsworth.

Chant, Sylvia (Ed.). (1992). *Gender and migration in developing countries.* London: Belhaven Press.

Chossudovsky, Michel. (1997). *The globalisation of poverty.* London: Zed/TWN.

Chuang, Janie. (1998, Winter). Redirecting the debate over trafficking in women: Definitions, paradigms, and contexts. *Harvard Human Rights Journal, 10.*

CIA (Central Intelligence Agency). (2000). *International trafficking in women to the United States: A contemporary manifestation of slavery and organized crime.* Prepared by Amy O'Neill Richard. Washington, DC: Center for the Study of Intelligence. Available: http://www.cia.gov/csi/monograph/women/trafficking/pdf (May 2001).

David, Natacha. (1998, January 8). Migrants made the scapegoats of the crisis. *ICFTU On-Line* (International Confederation of Free Trade Unions) [On-line]. Available: http://www.hartford-hwp.com/archives/50/012.html (Jan. 1999).

Dayan, Hilla. (1999). *Policy initiatives in the U.S. against the illegal trafficking of women for the sex industry.* Unpublished manuscript, Department of Sociology, University of Chicago.

Deere, C. D. (1976). Rural women's subsistence production in the capitalist periphery. *Review of Radical Political Economy 8*(1), 9–17.

Elson, Diane. (1995). *Male bias in the development process* (2nd ed.). Manchester, England: Manchester University Press.

Global Survival Network. (1997, November). Crime and servitude: An exposé of the traffic in women for prostitution from the newly independent states [On-line]. Available: http://www.globalsurvival.net/femaletrade.html (Jan. 1999).

Hamzic, Edin, & Sheehan, Maeve. Kosovo sex slaves held in Soho flats (1999, July 4). *Sunday Times,* London, pp.

Heyzer, Noeleen. (1994). *The trade in domestic workers.* London: Zed.

Hondagneu-Sotelo, Pierrette. (2001). *Domestica: Immigrant workers cleaning and caring in the shadow of affluence.* Berkeley & Los Angeles: University of California Press.

International Organization for Migration (various years). *Trafficking in Migrants.* Quarterly bulletin. Geneva: International Organization for Migration.

Jones, Erika. (1999). The gendered toll of global debt crisis. *Sojourner, 25*(3), 20–38.

Judd, Dennis, & Fainstein, Susan. (1999). *The tourist city.* New Haven, CT: Yale University Press.

Kempadoo, Kamala, & Doezema, Jo. (1998). *Global sex workers: Rights, resistance, and redefinition.* London: Routledge.

Lim, Lin. (1998). *The sex sector: The economic and social bases of prostitution in Southeast Asia.* Geneva, Switzerland: International Labor Office.

Lin, Lap-Chew, & Marjans, Wijers. (1997). *Trafficking in women, forced labour, and slavery-like practices in marriage, domestic labour, and prostitution.* Utrecht: Foundation Against Trafficking in Women (STV); Bangkok: Global Alliance Against Traffic in Women (GAATW).

Mahler, Sarah J. (1995). *American dreaming: Immigrant life on the margins.* Princeton, NJ: Princeton University Press.

Moser, Carolyn. (1989). The impact of recession and structural adjustment policies at the micro-level: Low-income women and their households in Guayaquil, Ecuador. In *The Invisible Adjustment: Poor Women and the Economic Crisis.* Santiago, Chile: UNICEF.

OXFAM. (1999, April). *International submission to the HIPC debt review* [On-line]. Available: http://www.caa.org/au/oxfam/advocacy/debt/hipcreview.html (Jan. 1999).

Parreñas, Rhacel Salazar. (2001). *Servants of globalization: Women, migration, and domestic work.* Stanford, CA: Stanford University Press.

Pessar, Patricia. 1995. On the homefront and in the workplace: Integrating immigrant women into feminist discourse. *Anthropological Quarterly, 68*(1), 37–47.

Philippines Information Service. (1999). Filipina brides [On-line]. Available: http://www.pis.or.jp/data/tothug.htm (Jan. 1999).

Rahman, Aminur. (1999). Micro-credit initiatives for equitable and sustainable development: Who pays? *World Development, 27*(1), 67–82.

Safa, Helen. (1995). *The myth of the male breadwinner: Women and industrialization in the Caribbean.* Boulder, CO: Westview Press.

Sassen, Saskia. (1988). *The mobility of labor and capital.* Cambridge, England: Cambridge University Press.

Sassen, Saskia. (1998). *Globalization and its discontents: Essays on the mobility of people and money.* New York: New Press.

Sassen, Saskia. (2001). *The global city: New York, London, Tokyo* (2nd ed.). Princeton, NJ: Princeton University Press.

Singh, Someshwar. (1999, August). Making the world safe for TNCs. Available: http://www.twnside.org.sg/souths/twn/title/safe-cn.htm. Fantu Cherus's report to UN Sub-Commission on the Promotion and Protection of Human Rights in Geneva [online] (Jan. 2001).

Shannon, Susan. (1999, May). The global sex trade: Humans as the ultimate commodity. *Crime and Justice International*, 5–25.

S. Lankan migrant workers remit Rs. 60 billion in 1998. (1999, February 12). Xinhua News Agency.

Standing, Guy. (1999). Global feminization through flexible labor: A theme revisited. *World Development, 27*(3), 583–602.

Tinker, Irene (Ed.). (1990). *Persistent inequalities: Women and world development.* New York: Oxford University Press.

Toussaint, E. (1999). Poor countries pay more under debt reduction scheme? [on-line]. Available: http://www.twnside.org.sg/souths/twn/title/1921-cn.htm (Jan. 2001).

Tyner, James. (1999). The global context of gendered labor emigration from the Philippines to the United States. *American Behavioral Scientist, 42*(40), 671–694. [Also this volume]

Ward, Kathryn. (1990). *Women workers and global restructuring.* Ithaca, NY: Cornell University Press.

Ward, Kathryn. (1990, September). As the debt crisis turns: Does finance have a gender? Paper presented at "Women and Employment: Linking local and global" conference, Women's Studies Program, Illinois State University, Bloomington, IL.

Ward, Kathryn, & Pyle, Jean. (1995). Gender, industrialization, and development. In Christine E. Bose & Edna Acosta-Belen (Eds.), *Women in the Latin American development process: From structural subordination to empowerment* (pp. 37–64). Philadelphia: Temple University Press.

Wonders, Nancy A., & Michalowski, Raymond. (2001). Bodies, borders, and sex tourism in a globalized world: A tale of two cities—Amsterdam and Havana. *Social Problems, 48*(4), 545–571.

Yamamoto, Satomi. (2000). *The incorporation of women workers into a global city: A case study of Filipina nurses in the metropolitan Chicago area.* Unpublished manuscript, on file with author.

PART TWO

Gender and Employment

The Global Context of Gendered Labor Migration from the Philippines to the United States

James A. Tyner

Throughout the 20th century, international labor migration from the Philippines has exhibited a shift both in global points of destination and in gender composition. Large-scale emigration from the Philippines began in response to labor shortages on U.S.-owned sugar plantations in Hawaii. Between 1907 and 1929, more than 102,000 Filipinos were recruited to work on these plantations: approximately 87% of these migrants were men (Teodoro, 1981). During the 1920s and 1930s, additional migratory flows developed as a response to labor shortages throughout the western portion of the continental United States, and this migratory system was likewise dominated by male laborers.[1]

During the late 1960s and early 1970s, Philippine institutions[2] played an important role in shaping the international migration of Filipinos. The global dispersion of Filipinos increased considerably, with migrants living and working in more than 130 countries and territories by the early 1990s. The United States became and remains a prime destination, although the contract labor migration between the United States and the Philippines, and the role of Philippine institutions, is relatively insignificant compared with other destinations. Indeed, larger flows of Philippine labor migrants are directed toward the Middle East and East Asia. These new patterns also reflect distinct sex differences in composition. Philippine labor flows toward the Middle East, Africa, and Oceania are male dominated, whereas flows toward Asia, western Europe, and North America are female dominated.

How are we to understand this global shift in Philippine international labor migration? How is gender implicated in this shift? This essay situates gendered labor migration from the Philippines to the United States within a global context. I argue that the migration of Filipinos to the United States and to the rest of the world must be seen as part of an institutional response to a changing global economy. Significantly, however, a state's position in the global economy translates into different institutional pursuits. As developed in this essay, the United States is in many respects unique among labor-importing states. The combination of a liberal immigration policy and the proximity of alternative cheap labor supplies means that the participation of the United States in the global labor market is fundamentally different from the receiving countries of the Middle East and Asia. Second, the institutional control of international migration is highly gendered; conceptions of masculinity and femininity figure prominently in the organization, regulation, and management of labor flows. Since the 1960s, the Philippines has expanded its political relations beyond the confines of the United States. Consequently, the Philippines has become more fully incorporated within the global economy. Labor export emerged in this era as a development strategy, and this was shaped by the Philippine institutional response to a shifting, gendered, global labor market.

GENDERED MIGRATION RESEARCH

The study of gender and migration has matured beyond infancy into a period of adolescence. Previous work sought primarily to identify sex differences in migration systems, and these efforts reflect, in part, changing patterns of international labor migration (e.g., Tyree & Donato, 1986). Consider, for example, that of the approximately 130,000 Sri Lankan labor migrants (circa 1990), roughly 80% are women; likewise, of the 140,000 Indonesian labor migrants, approximately 70% are women. Observations such as these have led some researchers to speak of a feminization of international migration (Boyd & Taylor, 1986). More recent scholarship, building on the significant advances of this earlier work, has attempted to place the gendered dimensions of international migration within broader explanatory frameworks (cf. Chant, 1992), a trend that reflects a greater integration of feminist scholarship into the social sciences in general.

It is imperative, at this juncture, to clarify the distinction between *gendered* migration and the *sex differences* of migration systems. Gender refers to the ways that society regulates human interaction and allocates resources differentially, based on socially constructed norms of masculinity and femininity. Strictly speaking, a study of gendered migration would seek to explain observed sex differences in migration flows through the incorporation of historically and geographically specific socially created ideals of masculinity and femininity. Studies of sex differences, conversely, examine different patterns of male and female migrants, irrespective of social processes and relations. Gendered migration research must also guard against female exclusivity. There is a tendency in gender research to focus exclusively on women, as if gender were synonymous with "female." At a certain level, this bias is understandable—and perhaps justified—considering the neglect of women within previous migration studies. Nevertheless, an overemphasis on women to the exclusion of men reifies an already existing segregation of research and risks missing important gendered dimensions of the migratory process. More significant is that a focus on women implies that problems, and solutions, are confined to women (Kabeer, 1994, p. 65). To speak only of the feminization of international migration is to discount the thousands of male migrants. Rather, we should uncover the relevant processes that contribute both to the feminization and masculinization of migration.

THE GENDERED GLOBAL LABOR MARKET

International labor migration, in all its myriad forms, represents a flexible response to labor shortages. Through the importation of workers—documented or undocumented, forced or voluntary—recipient countries are able to satisfy both absolute or relative labor shortages (Sassen, 1988). Moreover, the importation of labor is highly selective, as labor-importing countries are able to derive four significant benefits from a flexible workforce. First, labor importers are able to hire specialized labor forces for specified periods of time. In periods of economic hardship, or when labor becomes redundant, immigrant workers may be repatriated (Balderrama & Rodriguez, 1995). Second, the reproductive costs of labor (e.g., education, job training) are generally borne by labor-exporting countries (Zolberg, 1991). Third, employers may be able to selectively hire workers from areas of surplus, thereby paying lower wages and saving on direct labor costs (Woodward, 1988). Finally, certain labor-related benefits, such as health care, may not be provided, thus saving on indirect labor costs (Heer, 1996).

The transfer of labor from areas of surplus to areas of shortage is neither a simple nor inevitable process. Government and private institutions, located in both labor-exporting and labor-importing societies, organize, regulate, and manage the international mobility of labor (Abella, 1992, 1993; Huguet, 1992; Shah & Arnold, 1986). It is within this selective transfer of labor that patterns of gendered labor migration are produced. International labor migration must be seen as a socially constituted process, composed of numerous participants—including foreign employers, labor recruiters, politicians, and potential migrants—attempting to satisfy their own agendas as they simultaneously affect the global parameters of labor migration (Goss & Lindquist, 1995; Tyner, 1994, 1996a, 1996b).

Throughout this article, the global labor market is seen as the dominant area of inquiry. It is within this sphere that gender is initially manifest in establishing the structural parameters of labor exchange and population mobility. As Zolberg (1991) and others (Calavita, 1992; Smith, 1993) have argued, international migration—and the selective enforcement of national boundaries, visa requirements, and overall immigration legislation—imparts a level of institutional control that must be acknowledged prior to (or at the very minimum, in conjunction with) understanding individual migrant decision making. This organization, regulation, and management of international migration, as demonstrated in this article, is not gender neutral.

The functioning of the global labor market is similar to the social processes embedded within local labor markets (cf. Peck, 1996). Capitalists seek to hire productive labor forces. However, as Peck (1996) identifies,

> the process of assessing a person for a job goes ... beyond whether they are capable of operating the technology in the required way, but also involves consideration of inherently unpredictable factors such as reliability, creativity, sociability [sic], deference to authority, and adaptability. These traits, and their unpredictability, follow from the fact that labor is not a commodity but a set of capacities borne by people. (p. 34)

Hiring risks are compounded when face-to-face interviews between potential employers and employees are not possible—as is generally the case with international labor exchanges. Existing research indicates that employers use various strategies to reduce the risks involved in the hiring process (Ehrenberg & Smith, 1997; Peck, 1996; Woodward, 1988). One such strategy is to continue to hire workers from the same intermediary or labor recruitment agency. This process contributes to channelized migration flows. Another similar strategy is to hire friends and relatives of current employees. In this case, the social network of actual migrants assumes primacy in the continuation of channelized migration flows. When these strategies are insufficient, employers may use statistical prejudgments—stereotypes—in an attempt to minimize hiring risks (Ehrenberg & Smith, 1997). It is within this process that people, places, and occupations come to be labeled masculine or feminine, and patterns of gendered labor migration may result. When statistical prejudgments are based on ethnic or nationality differences, racialized labor migration results.

Historically, sexual stereotypes have been institutionalized within labor markets (Acker & Van Houten, 1974; Adkins, 1995; Kanter, 1977). Indeed, one of the most distinctive and persistent features of the capitalist labor market has been the sex-based segregation of occupations (Lim, 1983). This results, in part, from the social construction of domestic (sexual) divisions of labor and the segmentation of daily activities into *productive* tasks and *reproductive* tasks (cf. Sayer & Walker, 1992). Those activities within the productive sphere are postulated as contributing to the material well-being of individuals, households, and societies. Reproductive tasks are those that provide for the upbringing of the next generation of laborers, and include cooking, cleaning, and child care.

Socialization processes have produced and reproduced these sexual divisions of labor. Direct socialization occurs when children are taught that different standards, values, and behaviors exist for boys and girls. These attitudes may be reinforced through government-sponsored education and training programs. Postsecondary education, for example, may not be an option for women on the assumption that they are either incapable of learning advanced skills or that this knowledge is not necessary for them in their daily household chores. Indirect socialization also occurs, as when television shows or films reinforce stereotyped images of women and men. Particular occupations may be expected for women but not for men (and vice versa). Norms have evolved to maintain these separations, many of which have constricted the daily activities of women, and research has documented how these have likewise affected the spatial mobility of women in many different cultures (Pittin,

1984; Pryer, 1992). These norms, attitudes, and assumptions may be subsumed under the concept of patriarchy, whereby the subordinate position of women within households, labor markets, and society at large is based on ascribed characteristics of supposed biological differences between women and men.

Capitalism did not create the patriarchal relations of society. It has, however, benefited from the incorporation of these sexually discriminatory norms, ideals, and attitudes (Lim, 1983; Peck, 1996; Sayer & Walker, 1992). In the job market, employers may benefit from the reduction in labor costs through the employment of women by capitalizing on patriarchal attitudes, social relations, and stereotypes. Employers, for example, may assume that a woman's income is supplementary to the maintenance of a household, thereby justifying lower wages. Women's work is often seen as an extension of household activities; thus, women are consigned to caregiving and service occupations such as domestic work, nursing, teaching, and clerical work. Many employment opportunities open to women are classified as nonskilled or semiskilled, thus dictating lower wages. In addition, women are often assumed to be docile and more easily controlled in the workplace (A. Ong, 1987).

Just as capitalism did not create patriarchy, neither did institutions within the international exchange of labor create patriarchy. Labor recruitment-related institutions do, however, take advantage of these sexual divisions of labor. Tyner (1996b) has proposed an institutional-based framework to examine the manifestation of gender within the international exchange of labor. According to this framework, the production of formal contract labor migration consists of three circuits of social organization: *contract procurement, labor recruitment,* and *worker deployment.* These circuits effectively bind origins and destinations. Underlying these circuits of social organization are various unwritten rules, assumptions, and principles of interaction that, collectively, lead to the social constitution of international labor migration (Tyner, 1994, 1996b). Patriarchy forms the dominant principle of the contemporary global labor market.

The first circuit, contract procurement, consists of negotiations and bargaining between labor recruiters, foreign employers, and government officials. It is within this circuit that labor-importing firms (e.g., hospitals, multinational corporations) request foreign workforces. Labor-exporting institutions, conversely, attempt to solicit the most attractive employment opportunities in an attempt to deploy migrant workers. Parallel processes are found within local labor markets, whereby intermediaries (employment agencies) attempt to match the specific demands of employers with existing supplies of labor. As research for a variety of locations has indicated, the use of statistical prejudgments, including gendered ideologies, is prevalent within the specific demands of foreign employers (for Sri Lanka, see Eelens & Speckmann, 1990; for the Philippines, see Tyner, 1996b).

The second circuit, labor recruitment, operates mostly within labor-exporting countries. This circuit consists mostly of labor recruiters, government officials, and worker-applicants. To a considerable degree, labor recruiters acquiesce to the demands of foreign employers when developing recruitment strategies (Tyner, 1996b).

Thus, although the specific requests of foreign employers during the circuit of contract procurement lead to the initial gendering of labor flows, the second circuit of organization reinforces these patterns. A similar process, again, is found within local labor markets (Bakan & Stasiulis, 1994, 1995).

Worker deployment, the third circuit of organization, occurs when potential migrants gain access to an employment opportunity and must decide whether to take the offer. Considerable research, based on household strategies perspectives, has examined the manifestation of gender within this decision-making process (cf. the collections in Chant, 1992). Throughout this article, I focus exclusively on the first circuit of organization.

THE GEOGRAPHIES OF PHILIPPINE GENDERED LABOR MIGRATION

Labor markets are systematically structured by institutional action and power relations (Peck, 1996, p. 5). Within the global labor market, these actions and relations are a reflection of a country's level of development and position within the global economy (Sassen, 1988). In the following section, I interpret the changing gendered patterns of Philippine international labor migration. I contend that these patterns reflect the emergence of a labor-export development strategy as a response to global economic restructuring. Moreover, the United States, as a former colonizer of the Philippines, as well as a hegemonic participant in the world economy, has played a special—albeit indirect—role in the development of Philippine labor export and the subsequent gendering of Philippine international labor migration.

Postindependence: The Context

After 350 years of colonization, Philippine political independence came in 1946. As a newly independent country, the Philippines structured its economy around a strategy of import-substitution industrialization, a scheme based on capital-intensive, large-scale manufacturing of products earmarked for domestic consumption. A rising tide of nationalism accompanied the protective tariffs, which were established to nurture domestic industries. By the late 1960s, however, this economic strategy had failed to meet the growing demands placed on economic development (Jayasuriya, 1987; Jose, 1991). Most of the older, established manufacturing industries were unable to expand beyond the protected home market, and industrial growth could not absorb the expanding labor force—estimated at 700,000 new workers per year (Jose, 1991; Villegas, 1986).

Politicians could not agree on how to redirect the economy. Local supporters of foreign business interests, multinational corporations, and international monetary agencies such as the World Bank and the International Monetary Fund sought to dismantle the protective barriers, whereas Philippine nationalists were adamantly opposed to any form of increased foreign intervention (Bello, Kinley, & Elinson, 1982;

Wurfel, 1988). Compounding the political and economic tensions, the social climate of the Philippines also deteriorated. Demonstrations by landless peasants, students, and workers were escalating to apparently dangerous levels (Bello et al., 1982, p. 138). Terrorist acts throughout the country—supposedly by communist insurgents—and threats of revolution further heightened the anxiety of the late 1960s and early 1970s.

By 1972, events in the Philippines reached crisis proportions. Numerous actors, all operating under the guise of political stability and economic development, attempted to gain control of the Philippines. The convergence of three growing conflicts—(a) power-holding elites and the increasingly discontented landless peasants, (b) foreign investors and economic nationalists, and (c) President Ferdinand Marcos and his political opponents—came to a climax in September 1972 with the implementation of martial law.

The U.S. Immigration Act of 1965

The U.S. Immigration and Nationality Act of October 3, 1965, represents the most significant and unexpected change in the history of U.S. immigration legislation. The chief thrust of the act was to eliminate the racist national-origins quotas (established in 1921 and 1924) and replace these with an emphasis on family reunification. Even so, the immigration of Asian peoples was not expected to increase significantly (Hing, 1993).

To many scholars, an emphasis on family reunification signified that labor market aspects were not of primary importance. Yet the 1965 act did precipitate the large-scale recruitment of technicians and professionals, many of them from the Philippines. Changes in U.S. immigration legislation occurred during a period of profound changes within the Philippines. As discussed above, political and economic conditions had worsened during the late 1960s and early 1970s, and Philippine industrialization could not absorb the increasing number of students in many professional sectors, such as engineering. The educational system eventually came to be seen as a stepping-stone for overseas employment (Gupta, 1973, p. 183). The liberalization of immigration laws in the United States and in other countries (e.g., Canada, Australia) intensified Philippine migration. The number of Philippine entrants to the United States, for example, rose tenfold between 1964 and 1970, increasing from 3,000 immigrants per year to more than 30,000.

After the passage of the 1965 act, Philippine immigrants to the United States were concentrated in particular occupational categories. Between 1970 and 1974, slightly more than half of the 100,700 Philippine immigrants who were subject to numerical limitations entered under the third and sixth preference categories. The percentage of immigrant professionals to total immigration from the Philippines more than doubled in the years following the 1965 act—from about 12% between 1961 and 1965 to 28% for the 1966–1970 period (Cariño, 1987, pp. 307–308).

Women arriving from the Philippines outnumbered their male counterparts. During the 1960s, two thirds of all Philippine immigrants to the United States were women. According to Pido (1992), this reflected changing structural conditions in both the Philippines and the United States. Women in the Philippines had obtained educational and occupational credentials in "preferred" sectors (e.g., health-rated fields) and were able to take advantage of the third and sixth preference categories. These immigrants were assisted by private recruitment agencies in collaboration with travel agencies, both in the United States and in the Philippines (L. Ong & Azores, 1994; Pido, 1992; Shockey, 1989). Direct recruitment also selectively channeled Filipinas into hospitals, health organizations, and nursing homes (L. Ong & Azores, 1994; Pido, 1992). The incorporation of Philippine women into the U.S. labor market was a response to structural changes in the overall provision of health management (cf. L. Ong & Azores, 1994). Native-born U.S. workers were either ill prepared or less willing to satisfy labor demands. Government reductions in educational spending created a shortage of trained personnel (especially within health-related sectors), and the lack of decent wages in many of these sectors—including nursing—induced many qualified American women and men to shun these jobs. Additionally, native-born American workers were less motivated to work in the increasing number of part-time, low-paying jobs available. The continued use of foreign workers in the health-related sectors of the U.S. economy also offered more flexible control over the supply of physicians rather than the continued expansion of medical schools (L. Ong & Lui, 1994, pp. 60–61). At no (or minimal) cost to the United States, Philippine-based medical schools were able to provide a plethora of highly skilled workers.

That these new entrants into the U.S. health labor market were predominantly women is a reflection of women's segmentation into nursing professions in both the Philippines and the United States. As Morrow (1988) notes, essential care functions are sex-role stereotyped as female; society assumes that feminine characteristics and traits are required to carry out these functions (p. 22). It is thus not surprising that in the Philippines young women are encouraged to partake in health-related educational opportunities and that in the United States hospitals and nursing homes prefer to recruit these women over their male counterparts.

The Emergence of Philippine Labor Export

During the 1970s, the Philippine government, under the control of Marcos, attempted to stabilize the Philippine economy. Expansion in agribusiness and in export-oriented industrialization benefited Marcos and his cronies, but the effects on the Philippine economy were less favorable. As Sassen (1988) has argued, these "modernization" policies are extremely destabilizing to populations. Agribusiness is capital intensive and requires large tracts of land; consequently, the number of landless peasants tends to increase, with a subsequent increase in migration from rural to urban areas. Export-oriented industrialization is also destabilizing as it incorporates new segments of the population (mostly young women) into the paid labor force. High employee turnover, as a cost-reducing practice, is often encouraged in these factories. Thus, export-oriented industrialization can also lead to greater levels of rural-to-urban migration and a concomitant rise in urban unemployment.

A third economic strategy was the emergence of labor export in 1974. Although the Philippine government had initiated foreign employment programs as early as the 1950s, government involvement was minimal. This was partially due to the very real possibility (particularly following martial law) of losing too many qualified individuals—the brain-drain phenomenon. Although the export of labor was allowed, it was far from encouraged.

By the early 1970s, however, the Philippine government reversed its position and actively supported a policy of labor export. The Philippine government wished to simultaneously reduce internal tension and take advantage of changing global employment opportunities. Internally, labor export was expected to reduce levels of unemployment and underemployment (especially of the educated, professional surplus population), to improve the stock of human capital as workers returned with skills acquired from abroad, and to promote Philippine development and alleviate the balance of payment problems through mandatory remittances.

Globally, the Philippines attempted to strengthen ties with the changing world economy. In particular, the Philippine government realized that it could not remain completely dependent on a single country—the United States. In the wake of the American defeat in Vietnam, an effort was made by the Philippine government to diversify its foreign relations, even to include China and the socialist bloc (Timberman, 1991, p. 91). Marcos sought to use the international economy, through foreign policy, to contribute to domestic economic growth (Wurfel, 1988); labor export was one such means.

The Philippines capitalized on newly emerging employment opportunities throughout the Middle East and Asia. The 1973 oil embargo led to a quadrupling of oil prices. With increased revenues, many Middle Eastern states (e.g., Saudi Arabia, Kuwait, United Arab Emirates, Bahrain) initiated massive infrastructure projects. Faced with acute labor shortages, governments turned to the import of labor. Asia, likewise, was industrializing. In Singapore and Hong Kong, export-oriented industrialization benefited from the increased labor force participation of female workers.

By the mid-1970s, the Philippine government, along with numerous Philippine private employment agencies, was able to tap effectively into these dynamic, and rapidly growing, labor markets (see Table 4.1). Between 1975 and 1982, the total number of workers processed for foreign employment increased by 1,900%, going from 12,501 processed applicants to 250,115.[3] The increase in labor out-migration can be linked to the growing government involvement and its working relationship with the private sector. In 1974, two agencies were created: the Overseas Employment Development Board (OEDB) and the National Seaman Board (NSB). Combined, these two agencies were responsible for activities within the first circuit of organization, contract procurement. The Bureau of Employment Services (BES) functioned as a transitory government-run employment agency while regu-

TABLE 4.1. Processed Land-Based Philippine
Contract Workers by Region, 1975–1987

Year	Africa	Asia	Europe	Middle East	Americas	Other	Total
1975	342	4,217	3,160	1,552	2,285	945	12,501
1976	473	5,399	2,902	7,813	2,165	469	19,221
1977	515	5,290	2,482	25,721	2,265	872	36,676
1978	1,305	9,994	1,268	34,441	3,369	584	50,961
1979	1,134	12,604	673	73,210	3,738	1,152	92,519
1980	1,612	17,708	846	132,044	3,706	1,478	157,394
1981	2,144	20,322	1,126	183,582	2,363	1,399	210,936
1982	1,098	31,011	1,463	211,003	3,782	1,758	250,115
1983	2,353	40,814	2,878	323,414	5,654	5,150	380,263
1984	2,146	43,385	3,724	311,517	5,832	4,461	371,065
1985	2,054	54,411	3,675	266,617	6,890	4,107	337,754
1986	2,072	76,650	4,225	262,758	6,595	5,387	357,687
1987	2,125	96,018	6,610	306,757	7,562	6,809	425,881
TOTAL	19,373	417,823	35,032	2,140,429	56,206	34,110	2,702,973

SOURCE: Philippine Overseas Employment Administration, 1987.

lating private labor recruiters (Alegado, 1992), thereby assuming many of the functions of the second circuit of organization, labor recruitment.

The growth in labor export was highly gendered (see Table 4.2). Occupational demand in the Middle East was construed as masculine, with workers recruited to the construction and production sectors. Female workers, fewer in total numbers, were recruited as clerical assistants. The changing Asian labor market sought women to replace the Chinese women who had entered other sectors of the labor force. By the 1970s, Chinese women rejected paid domestic work. Yet as more Chinese women sought entry into higher paying, higher status factory work and clerical jobs, their movement from the home to the workplace created greater demand for paid domestic workers (Constable, 1997). As incomes rose in many countries, including Singapore and Hong Kong, the ability to hire a foreign domestic worker also became, in many social circles, a status symbol (Eviota, 1992; Tan & Devasahayam, 1987). Sexual and racial preferences aligned so that women, and especially the lighter skinned, English-speaking women from the Philippines, were perceived as the ideal domestic workers.

In both the Middle East and Asia, many employers used gendered and racialized statistical prejudgments in their labor requests. As evidenced by help-wanted advertisements in newspapers and letters of intent directed toward labor recruiters, potential employers were often very specific in their solicitations for workers (Tyner, 1994). Typical requests printed in Hong Kong newspapers read: "Cheerful, live-in Filipina maid/cook wanted" or "Temporary Filipina maid wanted . . . clean, tidy appearance" (Mission for Filipino Migrant Workers, 1983). In the Saudi labor market, Filipinos were perceived as being more productive than other workers (e.g., Bangladeshis) and also were found to exhibit better English-speaking abilities and better appreciation for U.S. technology and administration (Woodward, 1988, p. 48).

Philippine immigration to the United States also remained highly gendered, although statistical evidence suggests a change in the migratory process. During the late 1970s, many Filipinos came to the United States as entrants in family preference categories, and relatively fewer came as occupational-based entrants. This is commonly explained by factors in the United States, such as labor agitation, union complaints, and general anti-immigrant sentiment associated with the economic recession following the 1973 oil crisis. The proportional rise in family preference categories to the decline in occupational categories in this period, however, is not completely explained by a tightening economy. Despite the recession, a demand for immigrant workers still existed; other channels of entry were simply more accessible to Philippine immigrants (L. Ong & Azores, 1994).

Throughout the 1970s, the U.S. economy was affected by increased Asian imports and a concomitant period of deindustrialization (Bluestone & Harrison, 1982; Sassen, 1988). U.S.-based firms responded by relocating their factories to sites with cheaper labor and fewer union activities. Administrative headquarters remained in key urban areas (e.g., New York, Los Angeles). The U.S. labor market, in response, has become more polarized, marked by the expansion of high-wage, high-skilled occupations and low-wage, low-skilled jobs. Philippine immigrants (and other Asian immigrant groups) were able to satisfy much of the demand within the professional sectors. The large number of Philippine-based educational and training programs ensured a continual supply of workers.

The Philippine Overseas Employment Administration

As economic conditions in the Philippines worsened in the early 1980s, the importance of labor export as a development policy increased in scale and scope. To increase efficiency and to address the increased competition of other labor-exporting countries (e.g., Sri Lanka and Pakistan), the OEDB, NSB, and BES merged in 1982 to form the Philippine Overseas Employment Administration (POEA).

A primary task of the POEA has been the active encouragement of diversifying geographic destinations and occupations. Although the majority of destinations remain in the Middle East and Asia, the overall number of destinations increased from 74 countries and territories in 1975 to 130 in 1987.

The occupational profile of Philippine labor migrants likewise reveals greater diversity. Although numerically dominated by male workers in the production and construction sectors, Philippine labor migrants have increasingly entered the service sector. This includes the phenomenal growth of female migrants deployed to Taiwan, following its liberalization of foreign-worker policies, as well as an overall

TABLE 4.2. Deployment of Philippine Contract Workers by Occupation, Sex, and Selected Region, 1987

Occupation	Africa		Asia	
	Number of Workers	Percentage Female	Number of Workers	Percentage Female
Professional, technical	414	20.3	1,646	19.1
Entertainers	1	100.0	33,607	93.4
Administrative, management	29	3.5	119	20.2
Clerical	45	17.8	223	40.8
Sales	0	0.0	189	79.9
Services	82	23.2	52,471	98.3
Agriculture	0	0.0	2	0.0
Production, construction	1,285	0.1	2,177	1.3
TOTAL	1,856	6.1	90,434	92.4

SOURCE: Philippine Overseas Employment Administration, 1987.

commodification of domestic economies and the increased demand for domestic workers in places experiencing economic growth, such as Singapore, Hong Kong, Saudi Arabia, and Jordan (Constable, 1997; Humphrey, 1991). The overall diversity of occupations and the feminization of current Philippine international labor migration, however, is explained primarily by a shift occurring within the Middle Eastern labor market. By the mid- to late 1980s, the oil-rich Gulf states had completed massive infrastructural projects (e.g., airports, hospitals, hotels), and they no longer needed male migrant workers for production and construction. The gendered demand for Philippine migrant workers then switched to the female workers who would maintain and service the infrastructure.

Statistically, the United States remains an insignificant market for contract labor migration, as indicated by numbers processed by the POEA. In 1993, for example, the POEA registered only 3,049 deployed contract workers to the United States, representing just 0.4% of all deployed Philippine contract workers. For the entire period of 1975 to 1987, only 32,572 Philippine labor migrants were processed for the United States compared with more than 1.6 million workers processed for Saudi Arabia during the same period.

These numbers downplay, however, the importance of the United States as a prime destination for labor migrants. Labor migration appears insignificant because flows are hidden in other forms. Indeed, the United States participation in the global labor market is fundamentally different from the receiving countries of the Middle East and Asia. Two key institutional factors set the United States apart. First, whereas the majority of other labor-importing countries rely almost exclusively on government-sponsored contract labor to satisfy their needs, the United States is able to satisfy its labor needs through a liberal immigration policy. In effect, the role of government and private institutions in the first circuit of labor organi-

Europe		Middle East		Americas	
Number of Workers	Percentage Female	Number of Workers	Percentage Female	Number of Workers	Percentage Female
292	74.7	65,031	42.2	3,343	88.8
172	80.8	106	47.2	5	20.0
3	0.0	1,066	5.9	10	20.0
49	59.2	13,203	26.9	12	66.7
3	100.0	3,512	51.0	1	0.0
4,738	89.7	68,424	70.5	1,832	95.0
0	0.0	1,911	0.5	5	20.0
386	4.1	118,795	3.9	413	26.6
5,643	82.5	272,038	31.5	5,621	85.9

zation is circumvented through an emphasis on family reunification and kin-based social networks. When we examine flows of settlement migration, the United States emerges as a prime destination for employment. During the same period, 1975 to 1987, more than 500,000 Philippine settlement migrants entered the United States, in addition to thousands of other immigrants on tourist and student visas. As L. Ong and Azores (1994) correctly identify, immigrants arriving under the family preference categories should still be seen as part of the labor market process because they are indeed working on arrival (p. 176). "Third World" countries—such as the Philippines—with relatively well-advanced educational systems but a lack of domestic employment opportunities are able to supply the United States with an inexpensive cadre of trained labor.

Second, the geographic situation of the United States relative to other "developing" countries ensures a steady supply of labor through unofficial channels (e.g., undocumented workers from Central and South America). More proximate and impoverished countries, particularly throughout Central America and the Caribbean, provide the United States with a supply of low-wage, low-skilled workers. These institutional factors are clearly visible in the subsequent sex-based occupational distribution of Philippine immigrants (see Tables 4.3 and 4.4). In general, a larger proportion of Philippine immigrants in the United States—male and female—find employment in higher status and higher skilled occupations; conversely, Philippine contract workers in most other countries are predominantly employed as low-skilled and menial laborers. Moreover, female Philippine immigrants in the United States are decidedly more concentrated within professional sectors, unlike their counterparts in the Middle East and Asia. Thus, even though there is a large demand for household workers in the United States, similar to the Middle East and Asia, U.S.-based employers are able to meet their needs through the incorporation of Cen-

TABLE 4.3. Occupation of Foreign-Born Filipinos[a]
in the United States by Sex, 1980

Occupation	Total	Female (%)
Managerial and professional	78,743	46,653 (59.0)
Technical, sales, and administrative	93,182	59,933 (64.3)
Services	47,070	25,562 (54.3)
Farming, forestry, fishing	8,067	1,946 (24.1)
Precision production	21,022	5,589 (26.6)
Operators and general laborers	38,615	17,559 (45.5)
TOTAL	286,699	157,242 (54.8)

SOURCE: U.S. Department of Commerce, 1980, Table 27.

[a] Employed persons 16 years and older.

tral American and Caribbean immigrants rather than importing Filipinas. In total, the differences in the sex-based occupational structure of U.S.-bound Philippine immigrants and Philippine contract workers suggest that for the U.S. labor market there is less institutional channeling, or segmentation, of the migratory process. As such, the overall status of immigrant legislation—whether liberal or restrictive—will greatly influence the parameters of government and private institutions in the organization, management, and regulation of labor migration.

SUMMARY AND IMPLICATIONS

To appreciate fully the changing gendered dimensions of Philippine immigration to the United States we must situate it within the shifting geographies of a gendered global labor market. In this essay, I have argued that the gendering of Philippine international labor migration to the United States and other destinations reflects an institutional response to global economic restructuring. Philippine government and private institutions organize, manage, and regulate gendered patterns of labor migration as they pursue a labor-export policy that fits into a global economy. Institutional behavior, however, must operate within the boundaries established by immigration legislation. The more liberal basis of U.S. immigration policy translates into a less institutionalized occupational segregation by sex.

In retrospect, we can see the rise of government-sponsored Philippine labor export as a panacea for decades of economic development problems and political corruption. The Philippines has more fully integrated itself into the global economy as it seeks out employment opportunities for its unemployed and underemployed labor force. Indeed, the growth and regulation of the government's labor export program has been a function of market growth (Alegado, 1992), so much so that currently more than 500,000 Filipinos—men and women—leave their coun-

TABLE 4.4. Occupation of Philippine Contract Workers by Sex, 1987

Occupation	Total	Female (%)
Professional, technical	71,614	31,221 (43.6)
Entertainers	33,924	31,579 (93.1)
Administrative, management	1,503	131 (8.7)
Clerical	13,694	3,806 (27.8)
Sales	3,722	1,949 (52.4)
Services	128,704	106,800 (83.0)
Agriculture	2,215	13 (0.6)
Production, construction	126,853	4,942 (3.9)
TOTAL	382,229	180,441 (47.2)

SOURCE: Philippine Overseas Employment Administration, 1987.

try each year, usually on temporary visas, to work in more than 130 countries and territories. From Argentina to Zambia, they find employment as doctors, nurses, and engineers or as janitors, gardeners, and maids.

The Philippine government's attempt at economic growth and development is hindered by its (semi-) peripheral position in the world system. Although labor-exporting countries such as the Philippines retain a considerable amount of flexibility and control in the global exchange of labor (Abella, 1992, 1993), we should not lose sight that international labor migration, and international migration in general, is more a reflection of specific demands within immigrant-receiving societies (Zolberg, 1991). As Hondagneu-Sotelo (1994) argues,

> It is not the influx of immigrants that has created the concentration of immigrant workers in certain jobs, firms, and industries; rather the processes of national and global economic restructuring have transformed the occupational structure that sustains and encourages immigration. (p. 28)

Thus, the changing structural conditions in the United States and elsewhere will significantly influence the procurement of contracts and the recruitment of labor. Moreover, we should also recognize that the Philippine government and its attendant private institutions have created neither the capitalist economic order nor the segmented, gendered, global labor market. The Philippine government does, however, in an attempt to achieve economic growth and development, operate within these gendered parameters of labor demand (i.e., in its contract procurement and labor recruitment policies and practices) and, as such, does reinforce existing patterns and processes of sex segregation within the global labor market (Tyner, 1996b). Ultimately, studies of gendered labor migration—and subsequent policy formulation—must be cognizant of how institutions affect the simultaneous geographies of gender and migration.

NOTES

1. In 1934, the Philippines fell under restrictive U.S. immigration legislation. With few exceptions, Philippine international migration between 1934 and 1965 remained insignificant, constrained by the Philippines' colonial and, later, postcolonial relations with the United States.

2. The term *institution* as used in this article refers to both private and government organizations that affect policy change.

3. Data on Philippine contract workers is separated into processed workers and deployed workers: the former includes all applicants who are processed by the Philippine Overseas Employment Administration (POEA), whereas the latter consist of workers who actually leave the Philippines. Although data collection began in 1975 on processed workers, it was not until 1982 that the POEA began monitoring deployed workers. As such, analysis of historical trends is generally based on processed workers.

REFERENCES

Abella, M. (1992). Contemporary labour migration from Asia: Policies and perspectives of sending countries. In M. M. Kritz, L. L. Lim, & H. Zlotnik (Eds.), *International migration systems: A global approach* (pp. 263–278). Oxford, UK: Clarendon.

Abella, M. (1993). Role of formal labour schemes in the development of Third World countries. *International Migration, 31*(2/3), 389–402.

Acker, J., & Van Houten, D. R. (1974). Differential recruitment and control: The sex structuring of organizations. *Administrative Science Quarterly, 19*, 152–163.

Adkins, L. (1995). *Gendered work: Sexuality, family and the labour market.* Philadelphia: Open University Press.

Alegado, D. T. (1992). *The political economy of international labor migration from the Philippines.* Unpublished doctoral dissertation, University of Hawaii at Manoa.

Bakan, A. B., & Stasiulis, D. (1994). Foreign domestic worker policy in Canada and the social boundaries of modern citizenship. *Science and Society, 58*(1), 7–33.

Bakan, A. B., & Stasiulis, D. (1995). Making the match: Domestic placement agencies and the racialization of women's household work. *Signs: Journal of Women in Culture and Society, 20*(2), 303–335.

Balderrama, F. E., & Rodriguez, R. (1995) *Decade of betrayal: Mexican repatriation in the 1930s.* Albuquerque: University of New Mexico Press.

Bello, W., Kinley, D., & Elinson, E. (1982). *Development debacle: The World Bank in the Philippines.* San Francisco: Institute for Food and Development Policy, Philippine Solidarity Network.

Bluestone, B., & Harrison, B. (1982). *The deindustrialization of America: Plant closings, community abandonment, and the dismantling of basic industry.* New York: Basic Books.

Boyd, M., & Taylor, C. (1986). The feminization of temporary workers: The Canadian case. *International Migration, 24*(4), 717–733.

Calavita, K. (1992). *Inside the state: The Bracero Program, immigration and the INS.* New York: Routledge.

Cariño, B. V. (1987). The Philippines and Southeast Asia: Historical roots and contemporary linkages. In J. T. Fawcett & B. V. Cariño (Eds.), *Pacific bridges: The new immigration from Asia and the Pacific Islands* (pp. 305–325). New York: Center for Migration Studies.

Chant, S. (Ed.). (1992). *Gender and migration in developing countries.* New York: Belhaven.

Constable, N. (1997). *Maid to order in Hong Kong: Stories of Filipina workers.* New York: Cornell University Press.

Eelens, F., & Speckmann, J. D. (1990). Recruitment of labor migrants for the Middle East: The Sri Lankan case. *International Migration Review, 24*(2), 297–322.

Ehrenberg, R. G., & Smith, R. S. (1997). *Modern labor economics: Theory and public policy.* New York: Addison-Wesley.

Eviota, E. U. (1992). *The political economy of gender: Women and the sexual division of labour in the Philippines.* Atlantic Highlands, NJ: Zed Books.

Goss, J., & Lindquist, B. (1995). Conceptualizing international labor migration: A structuration perspective. *International Migration Review, 29*(2), 317–351.

Gupta, M. L. (1973). Outflow of high-level manpower from the Philippines. *International Labor Review, 8,* 167–191.

Heer, D. (1996). *Immigration in America's future: Social science findings and the policy debate.* Boulder, CO: Westview.

Hing, B. O. (1993). *Making and remaking Asian America through immigration policy, 1850–1990.* Stanford, CA: Stanford University Press.

Hondagneu-Sotelo, P. (1994). *Gendered transitions: Mexican experiences of immigration.* Berkeley & Los Angeles: University of California Press.

Huguet, J. W. (1992). The future of international migration within Asia. *Asian and Pacific Migration Journal, 1*(2), 250–277.

Humphrey, M. (1991). Asian women workers in the Middle East: Domestic servants in Jordan. *Asian Migrant, 4*(2), 53–60.

Jayasuriya, S. K. (1987). The politics of economic policy in the Philippines during the Marcos era. In R. Robinson, K. Hewison, & R. Higgott, R. (Eds.), *Southeast Asia in the 1980s: The politics of economic crisis* (pp. 80–112). London: Allen & Unwin.

Jose, V. R. (1991). Philippine external debt problem: The Marcos years. *Journal of Contemporary Asia, 21*(2), 222–245.

Kabeer, N. (1994). *Reversed realities: Gender hierarchies in development thought.* New York: Verso.

Kanter, R. M. (1977). *Men and women of the corporation.* New York: Basic Books.

Lim, L.Y.C. (1983). Capitalism, imperialism, and patriarchy: The dilemma of Third-World women workers in multinational factories. In J. Nash & M. P. Fernández Kelly (Eds.), *Women, men, and the international division of labor* (pp. 70–91). Albany: State University of New York Press.

Mission for Filipino Migrant Workers. (1983). *A situationer on Filipino migrant workers.* Unpublished manuscript.

Morrow, H. (1988). Nurses, nursing and women. *International Nursing Review, 35*(1), 22–25.

Ong, A. (1987). *Spirits of resistance and capitalist discipline: Factory women in Malaysia.* Albany: State University of New York Press.

Ong, L., & Azores, T. (1994). The migration and incorporation of Filipino nurses. In P. Ong, E. Bonacich, & L. Cheng (Eds.), *The new Asian immigration in Los Angeles and global restructuring* (pp. 164–195). Philadelphia: Temple University Press.

Ong, L., & Liu, J. M. (1994). U.S. immigration policies and Asian migration. In P. Ong, E. Bonacich, & L. Cheng (Eds.), *The new Asian immigration in Los Angeles and global restructuring* (pp. 45–73). Philadelphia: Temple University Press.

Peck, J. (1996). *Work-place: The social regulation of labor markets.* New York: Guilford.

Philippine Overseas Employment Administration (POEA). (1987). *Statistical yearbook.* Manila: Author.

Pido, A. J. A. (1992). *The Pilipinos in America: Macro/micro dimensions of immigration and integration*. New York: Center for Migration Studies.

Pittin, R. (1984). Migration of women in Nigeria: The Hausa case. *International Migration Review, 18*(4), 1293–1314.

Pryer, J. (1992). Purdah, patriarchy and population movement: Perspectives from Bangladesh. In S. Chant (Ed.), *Gender and migration in developing countries* (pp. 139–153). New York: Belhaven.

Sassen, S. (1988). *The mobility of labor and capital: A study in international investment and labor flow*. Cambridge, UK: University of Cambridge Press.

Sayer, A., & Walker, R. (1992). *The new social economy: Reworking the division of labor*. Cambridge, UK: Blackwell.

Shah, N., & Arnold, F. (1986). Government policies and programs regulating labor migration. In F. Arnold & N. Shah (Eds.), *Asian labor migration: Pipeline to the Middle East*. Boulder, CO: Westview.

Shockey, B. L. (1989). Foreign nurse recruitment and authorization for employment in the United States. In T. Moore & E. Simendinger (Eds.), *Managing the nursing shortage* (pp. 252–263). Rockville, MD: Aspen.

Smith, S. J. (1993). Immigration and nation-building in Canada and the United Kingdom. In P. Jackson & J. Penrose (Eds.), *Constructions of race, place and nation* (pp. 50–77). Minneapolis: University of Minnesota Press.

Tan, T.T.W., & Devasahayam, T. W. (1987). Opposition and interdependence: The dialectics of maid and employer relationships in Singapore. *Philippine Sociological Review, 35*(3/4), 34–41.

Teodoro, L. V. (Ed.). (1981). *Out of this struggle: The Filipinos in Hawaii*. Honolulu: University Press of Hawaii.

Timberman, D. G. (1991). *A changeless land: Continuity and change in Philippine politics*. New York: M.E. Sharpe.

Tyner, J. A. (1994). The social construction of gendered migration from the Philippines. *Asian and Pacific Migration Journal, 3*(4), 589–617.

Tyner, J. A. (1996a). Constructions of Filipina migrant entertainers. *Gender, Place and Culture: A Journal of Feminist Geography, 3*(1), 77–93.

Tyner, J. A. (1996b). The gendering of Philippine international labor migration. *Professional Geographer, 48*(4), 405–416.

Tyree, A., & Donato, K. M. (1986). A demographic overview of the international migration of women. In R. J. Simon & C. B. Brettel (Eds.), *International migration: The female experience* (pp. 21–41). Totowa, NJ: Rowman & Allanheld.

U.S. Department of Commerce, Bureau of the Census. (1980). *Asian and Pacific Islander Population in the United States: 1980*. Washington, DC: U.S. Government Printing Office.

Villegas, B. (1986). The economic crisis. In J. Bresnan (Ed.), *Crisis in the Philippines: The Marcos era and beyond* (pp. 145–175). Princeton, NJ: Princeton University Press.

Woodward, P. N. (1988). *Oil and labor in the Middle East: Soudi Arabia and the oil boom*. New York: Pracger.

Wurfel, D. (1988). *Filipino politics: Development and decay*. New York: Cornell University Press.

Zolberg, A. R. (1991). The future of international migrations. In S. Diaz-Briquets & S. Weintraub (Eds.), *Determinants of emigration from Mexico, Central America, and the Caribbean* (pp. 319–351). Boulder, CO: Westview.

CHAPTER 5

Gender and Labor in
Asian Immigrant Families

Yen Le Espiritu

Through the process of migration and settlement, patriarchal relations undergo continual negotiation as women and men rebuild their lives in the new country. An important task in the study of immigration has been to examine this reconfiguration of gender relations. Central to the reconfiguration of gender hierarchies is the change in immigrant women's and men's relative positions of power and status in the country of settlement. Theoretically, migration may improve women's social position if it leads to increased participation in wage employment, more control over earnings, and greater participation in family decision making (Pessar, 1984). Alternatively, migration may leave gender asymmetries largely unchanged even though certain dimensions of gender inequalities are modified (Curtis, 1986). The existing literature on migration and changing gender relations suggests contradictory outcomes whereby the position of immigrant women is improved in some domains even as it is eroded in others (Hondagneu-Sotelo, 1994; Morokvasic, 1984; Tienda & Booth, 1991).

This essay is a first attempt to survey the field of contemporary Asian immigrants and the effects of employment patterns on gender relations. My review indicates that the growth of female-intensive industries in the United States—and the corresponding preference for racialized and female labor—has enhanced the employability of some Asian immigrant women over that of their male counterparts and positioned them as coproviders, if not primary providers, for their families. The existing data also suggest that gender relations are experienced differently in different structural occupational locations. In contrast with the largely unskilled immigrant population of the pre–World War II period, today's Asian immigrants include not only low-wage service sector workers but also significant numbers of white-collar professionals. A large number of immigrants have also turned to self-employment (Ong & Hee, 1994). Given this occupational diversity, I divide the following discussion into three occupational categories and examine gender issues within each group: the salaried professionals, the self-employed entrepreneurs, and the wage laborers.[1] Although changes in gender relations have been slow and uneven in each of these three groups, the existing data indicate that men's dependence on the economic and social resources of women is most pronounced among the wage laborers. In all three groups, however, Asian women's ability to transform patriarchal family relations is often constrained by their social position as racially subordinated women in U.S. society.

As a review of existing works, this article reflects the gaps in the field. Overall, most studies of contemporary Asian immigrants have focused more on the issues of economic adaptation than on the effects of employment patterns on gender relations. Because there is still little information on the connections between work and home life—particularly among the salaried professionals—the following discussion on gender relations among contemporary Asian immigrants is at times necessarily exploratory.

IMMIGRATION LAWS, LABOR NEEDS, AND CHANGING GENDER COMPOSITION

Asian Americans' lives have been fundamentally shaped by the legal exclusions of 1882, 1917, 1924, and 1934, and by the liberalization laws of 1965.[2] Exclusion laws restricted Asian immigration to the United States, skewed the sex ratio of the early communities so that men were disproportionately represented, and truncated the development of conjugal families. The 1965 Immigration Act equalized immigration rights for all nationalities. No longer constrained by exclusion laws, Asian immigrants began coming in much larger numbers than ever before. In the period from 1971 to 1990, approximately 855,500 Filipinos, 610,800 Koreans, and 576,100 Chinese entered the United States (U.S. Bureau of the Census, 1992). Moreover, with the collapse of U.S.-backed governments in South Vietnam, Laos, and Cambodia in 1975, more than one million refugees from these countries have resettled in the United States. As a consequence, in the 1980s, Asia was the largest source of U.S. legal immigrants, accounting for 40% to 47% of the total influx (Min, 1995b, p. 12).[3] In 1990, 66% of Asians in the United States were foreign born (U.S. Bureau of the Census, 1993, Figure 3).

Whereas pre–World War II immigration from Asia was composed mostly of men, the contemporary flow is dominated by women. Women make up the clear majority among U.S. immigrants from nations in Asia but also from those in Central and South America, the Caribbean, and Europe (Donato, 1992). Between 1975 and 1980, women (20 years and older) constituted more than 50% of the immigrants from China, Burma, Indonesia, Taiwan, Hong Kong, Malaysia, the Philippines, Korea, Japan, and Thailand (Donato, 1992). The dual goals of the 1965 Immigration Act—to facilitate family reunification and, secondarily, to admit workers with special job skills—have produced a female-dominated flow. Since 1965, most visas have been allocated to relatives of U.S. residents. Women who came as wives, daughters, or mothers of U.S. permanent residents and citizens make up the primary component of change (Donato, 1992, p. 164). The dominance of women immigrants also reflects the growth of female-intensive industries in the United States, particularly in the service, health care, microelectronics, and apparel-manufacturing industries (Clement & Myles, 1994, p. 26). Of all women in the United States, Asian immigrant women have recorded the highest rate of labor force participation (Gardner, Robey, & Smith, 1985). In 1980, among married immigrant women between 25 and 64 years of age, 61% of Korean women, 65% of Chinese women, and 83% of Filipino women were in the labor force (Duleep & Sanders, 1993). In 1990, Asian women had a slightly higher labor force participation rate than all women, 60% as opposed to 57% (U.S. Bureau of the Census, 1993, Figure 6).

ECONOMIC DIVERSITY AMONG CONTEMPORARY ASIAN IMMIGRANTS

Relative to earlier historical periods, the employment pattern of today's Asian Americans is considerably more varied, a result of both immigration and a changing structure of opportunity. During the first half of the 20th century, Asians were concentrated at the bottom of the economic ladder—restricted to retailing, food service, menial service, and agricultural occupations. After World War II, economic opportunities improved but not sufficiently for educated Asian Americans to achieve parity. In the post-1965 era, the economic status of Asian Americans has bifurcated, showing some great improvements but also persistent problems. The 1965 Immigration Act and a restructuring of the economy brought a large number of low-skilled and highly educated Asians to this country, creating a bimodalism (Ong & Hee, 1994). As indicated in Table 5.1, Asian Americans were overrepresented in the well-paid, educated, white-collar sector of the workforce and in the lower paying service and manufacturing jobs. This bimodalism is most evident among Chinese men: although 24% of Chinese men were professionals in 1990, another 19% were in service jobs.

Asian professional immigrants are overrepresented as scientists, engineers, and health care professionals in the United States. In 1990, Asians were 3% of the U.S. total population but accounted for close to 7% of the scientist and engineer workforce. Their greatest presence was among engineers with doctorate degrees, constituting more than one fifth of this group in 1980 and in 1990 (Ong & Blumenberg, 1994, p. 169). Although Asian immigrant men dominated the fields of engineering, mathematics, and computer science, Asian immigrant women were also overrepresented in these traditionally male-dominated professions. In 1990, Asian women accounted for 5% of all female college graduates in the U.S. labor force but 10% to 15% of engineers and architects, computer scientists, and researchers in the hard sciences (Rong & Preissle, 1997, pp. 279–280).

In the field of health care, two thirds of foreign nurses and 60% of foreign doctors admitted to the United States during the fiscal years 1988 to 1990 were from

TABLE 5.1. Occupational Distribution by Gender and Ethnicity,
1990 (in Percentages)

Occupation	All	Chinese	Japanese	Filipino	Korean	Vietnamese
			Men			
Managerial	13	15	20	10	15	5
Professional	12	24	20	12	16	13
Technical, sales	15	18	17	15	29	18
Administrative support	7	8	9	16	6	8
Service	10	19	9	16	10	12
Fish, forestry	4	<1	4	2	1	2
Production, craft	19	8	12	12	12	19
Operators	20	9	8	15	12	22
			Women			
Managerial	11	15	14	10	9	7
Professional	17	17	19	20	11	9
Technical, sales	16	17	16	16	25	17
Administrative support	28	21	28	25	14	18
Service	17	14	14	17	20	19
Fish, forestry	1	<1	1	1	<1	<1
Production, craft	2	3	3	3	6	10
Operators	8	13	5	7	14	20

SOURCE: Mar & Kim, 1994, p. 25, Table 3. Reprinted with permission.

Asia (Kanjanapan, 1995, p. 18). Today, Asian immigrants represent nearly a quarter of the health care providers in public hospitals in major U.S. metropolitan areas (Ong & Azores, 1994a, p. 139). Of the 55,400 Asian American nurses registered in 1990, 90% were foreign born (Rong & Preissle, 1997, pp. 279–280). The Philippines is the largest supplier of health professionals to the United States, sending nearly 25,000 nurses to this country between 1966 and 1985 and another 10,000 between 1989 and 1991 (Ong & Azores, 1994a, p. 154). Due to the dominance of nurses, Filipinas are more likely than other women and than Filipino men to be in professional jobs. Table 5.1 indicates that in 1990, 20% of Filipino women but only 12% of Filipino men had professional occupations.

Responding to limited job opportunities, particularly for the highly educated, a large number of Asian Americans have also turned to self-employment. Asian immigrants are much more likely than their native-born counterparts to be entrepreneurs: In 1990, 85% of the Asian American self-employed population were immigrants (Ong & Hee, 1994, p. 51). Korean immigrants have the highest self-employment rate of any minority and immigrant group (Light & Bonacich, 1986). A 1986 survey showed that 45% of Korean immigrants in Los Angeles and

Orange counties were self-employed. A survey conducted in New York City revealed an even higher self-employment rate of more than 50% (Min, 1996, p. 48). Because another 30% of Korean immigrants work in the Korean ethnic market, the vast majority of the Korean workforce—three out of four Korean workers—are segregated in the Korean ethnic economy either as business owners or as employees of coethnic businesses (Min, 1998, p. 17). The problems of underemployment, misemployment, and discrimination in the U.S. labor market have turned many educated and professional Korean immigrants toward self-employment (Min, 1995a, p. 209). Based on a 1988 survey, nearly half of the Korean male entrepreneurs had completed college (Fawcett & Gardner, 1994, p. 220).

Although some Asian immigrants constitute "brain drain" workers and self-employed entrepreneurs, others labor in peripheral and labor-intensive industries. The typical pattern of a dual-worker family is a husband who works as a waiter, cook, janitor, or store helper and a wife who is employed in a garment shop or on an assembly line. In a study conducted by the Asian Immigrant Women Advocates (AIWA), 93% of the 166 seamstresses surveyed in the San Francisco Bay–Oakland area listed their husbands' jobs as unskilled or semiskilled, including waiter, busboy, gardener, day laborer, and the like (Louie, 1992, p. 9). Most disadvantaged male immigrants can get jobs only in ethnic businesses in which wages are low but only simple English is required (Chen, 1992, p. 103). On the other hand, since the late 1960s, the United States has generated a significant number of informal sector service occupations—paid domestic work, child care, garment and electronic assembly—that rely primarily on female immigrant workers (Hondagneu-Sotelo, 1994, pp. 186–187). Due to the perceived vulnerability of their class, gender, ethnicity, and immigration status, Asian immigrant women—and other immigrant women of color—have been heavily recruited to toil in these low-wage industries. As indicated in Table 5.1, Asian women of all ethnic groups were much more likely than Asian men to be in administrative support and service jobs.

GENDER RELATIONS AMONG SALARIED PROFESSIONALS

Although the large presence of Asian professional workers is now well documented, we still have little information on the connections between work and home life—between the public and private spheres—of this population. The available case studies suggest greater male involvement in household labor in these families. In a study of Taiwan immigrants in New York, Hsiang-Shui Chen (1992) reports that the degree of husbands' participation in household labor varied considerably along class lines, with men in the professional class doing a greater share than men in the working and small-business classes (p. 77). Although women still performed most of the household labor, men helped with vacuuming, disposing of garbage, laundry, dishwashing, and bathroom cleaning. In a survey of Korean immigrant families in New York, Pyong Gap Min (1998) found a similar pattern: younger, professional husbands undertook more housework than did men in other occupational categories, although their wives still did the lion's share (pp. 42–43). Professional couples of other racial-ethnic groups also seem to enjoy more gender equality. For example, Beatriz M. Pesquera (1993) reports that Chicano "professional men married to professional women did a greater share than most other men" (p. 194). This more equitable household division of labor can be attributed to the lack of a substantial earning gap between professional men and women, the demands of the women's careers, and the women's ability to pressure their husbands into doing their share of the household chores (Hondagneu-Sotelo, 1994; Hood, 1983; Kibria, 1993; Pesquera, 1993). On the other hand, Chen (1992), Min (1998), and Pesquera (1993) all conclude that women in professional families still perform more of the household labor than their husbands do. Moreover, Pesquera reports that, for the most part, the only way women have altered the distribution of household labor has been through conflict and confrontation, suggesting that ideologically most men continue to view housework as women's work (p. 185). These three case studies remind us that professional women, like most other working women, have to juggle full-time work outside the home with the responsibilities of child care and housework. This burden is magnified for professional women because most tend to live in largely White, suburban neighborhoods where they have little or no access to the women's social networks that exist in highly connected ethnic communities (Glenn, 1983, p. 41; Kibria, 1993).

Given the shortage of medical personnel in the United States, particularly in the inner cities and in rural areas, Asian women health professionals may be in a relatively strong position to modify traditional patriarchy. First, as a much sought after group among U.S. immigrants, Asian women health professionals can enter the United States as the principal immigrants (Espiritu, 1995, p. 21). This means that unmarried women can immigrate on their own accord, and married women can enter as the primary immigrants, with their husbands and children following as dependents. My field research of Filipino American families in San Diego suggests that a female-first migration stream, especially when the women are married, has enormous ramifications for both family relations and domestic roles. For example, when Joey Laguda's mother, a Filipina medical technologist, entered the country in 1965, she carried the primary immigrant status and sponsored Joey's father and two other sons as her dependents. Joey describes the downward occupational shift that his father experienced on immigrating to the United States: "My father had graduated in the Philippines with a bachelor's degree in criminology but couldn't get a job as a police officer here because he was not a U.S. citizen. So he only worked blue-collar jobs" (Espiritu, 1995, p. 181). The experience of Joey's father suggests that Asian men who immigrate as their wives' dependents often experience downward occupational mobility in the United States, while their wives maintain their professional status. The same pattern exists among Korean immigrant families in New York: While Korean nurses hold stable jobs, many of their educated husbands are unemployed or underemployed (Min, 1998, p. 52).

Moreover, given the long hours and the graveyard shifts that typify a nurse's work schedule, many husbands have had to assume more child care and other household responsibilities in their wives' absences. A survey of Filipino nurses in Los Angeles County reveals that these women, to increase their incomes, tend to work double shifts or in the higher paying evening and night shifts (Ong & Azores, 1994b, pp. 183–184). In her research on shift work and dual-earner spouses with children, Harriet Pressner (1988) finds that the husbands of night-shift workers do a significant part of child care; in all cases, it was the husbands who supervised the oft-rushed morning routines of getting their children up and off to school or to child care. Finally, unlike most other women professionals, Asian American nurses often work among their coethnics and thus benefit from these social support systems. According to Paul Ong and Tania Azores (1994b), there are "visible clusterings of Filipino nurses" in many hospitals in large metropolitan areas (p. 187). These women's social networks can provide the emotional and material support needed to challenge male dominance.

Despite their high levels of education,[4] racism in the workplace threatens the employment security and class status of Asian immigrant professional men and women. Even when these women and men have superior levels of education, they still receive economic returns lower than those of their White counterparts and are more likely to remain marginalized in their work organizations, to encounter a glass ceiling, and to be underemployed (Chai, 1987; Ong & Hee, 1994, pp. 40–41; Yamanaka & McClelland, 1994, p. 86). As racialized women, Asian professional women also suffer greater sexual harassment than do their Western counterparts due to racialized ascription that depicts them as politically passive and sexually exotic and submissive. In her research on racialized sexual harassment in institutions of higher education, Sumi Cho (1997) argues that Asian American women faculty are especially susceptible to hostile-environment forms of harassment. This hostile environment may partly explain why Asian American women faculty continue to have the lowest tenure and promotion rate of all groups (Hune & Chan, 1997). Racism in the workplace can put undue stress on the family. Singh, a mechanical engineer who immigrated to the United States from India in 1972, became discouraged when he was not advancing at the same rate as his colleagues and attributed his difficulties to job discrimination based on national and racial origins. Singh's wife, Kaur, describes how racism affected her husband and her family: "It became harder and harder for my husband to put up with the discrimination at work. He was always stressed out. This affected the whole family" (Dhaliwal, 1995, p. 78). Among Korean immigrant families in New York, the husbands' losses in occupational status led to marital conflicts, violence, and ultimately divorce. Some Korean men turned to excessive drinking and gambling, which contributed to marital difficulties (Min, 1998, pp. 52, 55). A Korean wife attributes their marital problems to her husband's frustration over his low economic status:

> Five years ago, he left home after a little argument with me and came back two weeks later. He wanted to get respect from me. But a real source of the problem was not me but his frustration over low status.   (Min, 1998, p. 54)

Constrained by racial and gender discrimination, Asian professional women, on the other hand, may accept certain components of the traditional patriarchal system because they need their husbands' incomes and because they desire a strong and intact family—an important bastion of resistance to oppression.

GENDER RELATIONS AMONG
SELF-EMPLOYED ENTREPRENEURS

Ethnic entrepreneurship is often seen as proof of the benefits of the enterprise system: If people are ambitious and willing to work hard, they can succeed in the United States. In reality, few Asian immigrant business owners manage to achieve upward mobility through entrepreneurship. The majority of the businesses have very low gross earnings and run a high risk of failure. Because of limited capital and skills, Asian immigrant entrepreneurs congregate in highly competitive, marginally profitable, and labor-intensive businesses such as small markets, clothing subcontracting, and restaurants (Ong, 1984, p. 46). In an analysis of the 1990 census data, Ong and Hee (1994) show that the median annual income of self-employed Asian Americans is $23,000, which is slightly higher than that of Whites ($20,000) (p. 47). But there is a great deal of variation in earnings: A quarter earn $10,400 or less, another quarter earn at least $47,000, and 1% earn more than $200,000 (Ong & Hee, 1994, p. 55, note 17). The chances for business failure appear particularly high for Southeast Asian immigrants; for every 20 businesses started by them each month, 18 fail during the first year (May, 1987).

Given the labor-intensive and competitive nature of small businesses, women's participation makes possible the development and viability of family enterprises. Initially, women contribute to capital accumulation by engaging in wage work to provide the additional capital needed to launch a business (Kim & Hurh, 1985). In a study of professional and educated Korean couples in Hawaii, Alice Chai (1987) found that Korean immigrant women resisted both class and domestic oppression by struggling to develop small family businesses where they work in partnership with their husbands. Operating a family business removes them from the racist and sexist labor market and increases their interdependence with their husbands. Women also keep down labor costs by working without pay in the family enterprise (Kim & Hurh, 1988, p. 154). Often, unpaid female labor enables the family store to stay open as many as 14 hours a day, and on weekends, without having to hire additional workers (Bonacich, Hossain, & Park, 1987, p. 237). According to Ong and Hee (1994), three quarters of Asian immigrant businesses do not have a single outside employee—the typical store is run by a single person or by a family (p. 52).[5] Their profits come directly from their labor, the labor of their families, and from staying open long hours (Gold, 1994). According to Ong and Hee (1994), approximately 42% of Asian American business owners work 50 hours or more per week, and 26% work 60 hours or more per week (p. 47). Finally, the grandmothers who watch the children while the mothers labor at the family stores form an additional layer of unpaid family labor that also supports these stores (Bonacich et al., 1987, p. 237).

Because of their crucial contributions to the family enterprise, wives are an economically valuable commodity. A 1996–1997 survey of Koreans in New York City indicates that 38% of the working women worked together with their husbands in the same businesses (Min, 1998, pp. 38–39). A study of Korean immigrants in Elmhurst, Illinois, indicates that "a man cannot even think of establishing his own business without a wife to support and work with" (Park, 1989, p. 144). Yoon (1997) reports a similar finding among Korean businesses in Chicago and Los Angeles: Wives are the most important source of family labor (p. 157). Corresponding changes in conjugal relationships, however, have been slow and uneven. Unlike paid employment, work in a family business seldom gives women economic independence from their husbands. She is co-owner of the small business, working for herself and for her family, but she is also unpaid family labor, working as an unpaid employee of her husband. It is conceivable that, for many immigrant women in small businesses, the latter role predominates. Min (1998) reports that in almost all cases, when a Korean husband and wife run a business, the husband is the legal owner and controls the money and personnel management of the business. Even when the wife plays a dominant role and the husband a marginal role in operating and managing the family business, the husband is still considered the owner by the family and by the larger Korean immigrant community (Min, 1998, pp. 45–46). In such instances, the husbands could be the women's "most immediate and harshest employers" (Bonacich et al., 1987, p. 237).

Even though the family business, in some ways, is the antithesis of the separate gender spheres (men's public world of work and women's private world of domesticity), it can exacerbate dependency. Like housework, managing stores fosters alienation and isolation because it "affords little time and opportunity for women who run them to develop other skills or to establish close friendships" (Mazumdar, 1989, p. 17). Also, living and working in isolation, immigrant entrepreneurs may not be as influenced by the more flexible gender roles of U.S. middle-class couples and thus seem to be slower than other immigrant groups to discard rigid gender role divisions (Min, 1992). In most instances, women's labor in family businesses is defined as an extension of their domestic responsibilities. Kaur, a South Asian immigrant women who manages the family grocery store, describes the blurred boundaries between home and work:

> I have a desk at home where I do my paperwork. This way I can be home when my daughters get home from school, and when my husband gets home from work I can serve him dinner right away . . . . I bought a stove for the store on which I cook meals for my husband and children during the hours when business is slow at the store. . . . I try to combine my housework with the store work such as grocery shopping. When I go shopping I buy stuff for home and the store. (Dhaliwal, 1995, p. 80)

The family's construction of Kaur's work as an extension of her domestic responsibilities stabilizes patriarchal ideology because it reconciles the new gender arrangement (Kaur's participation in the public sphere) with previous gender expectations and ideologies. Similarly, Min (1998) reports that in most Korean produce, grocery, and liquor stores that stay open long hours, wives are expected to perform domestic functions at work such as cooking for their husbands and, often, other employees (p. 49).

When these small businesses employ coethnics, wages are low and working conditions dismal. Ong and Umemoto (1994) list some of the unfair labor practices endured by workers in ethnic businesses: unpaid wages and unpaid workers' compensation, violation of worker health and safety regulations, and violation of minimum wage laws (p. 100). The exploitation of coethnic workers, specifically of women workers, is rampant in the clothing subcontracting business. Asian immigrant women make up a significant proportion of garment workers. Asian immigrant men also toil in the garment industry but mostly as contractors—small-business owners who subcontract from manufacturers to do the cutting and sewing of garments from the manufacturers' designs and textiles. Because they directly employ labor, garment contractors are in a sense labor contractors who mobilize, employ, and control labor for the rest of the industry (Bonacich, 1994).

As middlemen between the manufacturers and the garment workers, these contractors struggle as marginally secure entrepreneurs on the very fringes of the garment industry (Wong, 1983, p. 365). The precarious nature of the business is indicated by the high number of garment factories that close each year (Ong, 1984, p. 48; Wong, 1983, p. 370).[6] Given the stiff business competition, Asian male contractors have had to exploit the labor of immigrant women to survive. The steady influx of female limited-English-speaking immigrants puts the sweatshop owner in an extremely powerful position. Because these women have few alternative job opportunities, the owners can virtually dictate the terms of employment: They can pay low wages, ignore overtime work, provide poor working conditions, and fire anyone who is dissatisfied or considered to be a troublemaker (Wong, 1983, p. 370). In retaliation, various unionization and employment organizations such as AIWA have worked for the empowerment of immigrant Asian women workers in the garment industry as well as in the hotel and electronics industries (Lowe, 1997, p. 275). It is important to stress that the problem of exploitation is not primarily gender or ethnic based but also inherent in the organization of the garment industry. Embedded in a larger, hierarchically organized structure, Asian immigrant contractors both victimize the workers they employ and are victimized by those higher up in the hierarchy. The contracting system insulates the industry's principal beneficiaries—the manufacturers, retailers, and bankers—from the grim realities of the sweatshops and the workers' hostility (Bonacich, 1994). Against these more dominant forces, Asian American men and women have, occasionally, formed a shared sense of ethnic and class solidarity that can, at times, blunt some of the antagonism in the contractor-worker relationship (Bonacich, 1994, p. 150; Wong, 1983, p. 370).

In sum, the burgeoning Asian immigrant small-business sector is being built, in part, on the racist, patriarchal, and class exploitation of Asian (and other) immigrant women. Barred from decent-paying jobs in the general labor market, Asian immigrant women labor long and hard for the benefit of men who are either their husbands or their employers or both—and in many cases, for the benefit of corporate America (Bonacich et al., 1987, p. 238). The ethnic business confers quite different economic and social rewards on men and women (Zhou & Logan 1989). Whereas men benefit economically and socially from the unpaid or underpaid female labor, women bear the added burden of the double workday. Thus, it is critical to recognize that the ethnic economy is both a thriving center and a source of hardship and exploitation for Asian immigrant women.

GENDER RELATIONS AMONG THE WAGE LABORERS

Among the three occupational groups reviewed in this article, gender role reversals—wives' increased economic role and husbands' reduced economic role—seem to be most pronounced among the wage laborers. In part, these changes reflect the growth of female-intensive industries in the United States, particularly in the garment and microelectronics industries, and the corresponding decline of male-dominated industries specializing in the production and distribution of goods (Clement & Myles, 1994, p. 26). As a consequence, Asian immigrant women with limited education, skills, and English fluency have more employment options than do their male counterparts. Since the late 1960s, a significant number of U.S. informal sector occupations have recruited primarily female immigrant workers. The garment industry is a top employer of immigrant women from Asia and Latin America. The growth of U.S. apparel production, especially in the large cities, has been largely driven by the influx of low-wage labor from these two regions (Blumenberg & Ong, 1994, p. 325). In Los Angeles, Latin American immigrants (mainly from Mexico) and Asian immigrants (from China, Vietnam, Korea, Thailand, and Cambodia) make up the majority of the garment industry workforce; in New York, Chinese and Dominican workers predominate; and in San Francisco, Chinese and other Asians prevail (Loucky, Soldatenko, Scott, & Bonacich, 1994, p. 345). The microelectronics industry also draws heavily on immigrant women workers from Asia (mainly Vietnam, the Philippines, South Korea, and Taiwan) and from Latin America (mainly Mexico) for its low-paid manufacturing assembly work (Green, 1980; Katz & Kemnitzer, 1984; Snow, 1986). Of the more than 200,000 people employed in California's Silicon Valley microelectronics industry in 1980, approximately 50% (100,000 employees) were in production-related jobs; half of these production-related workers (50,000–70,000) worked in semiskilled operative jobs (Siegel & Borock, 1982). In a study of Silicon Valley's semiconductor manufacturing industry, Karen Hossfeld (1994) reports that the industry's division of labor is highly skewed by gender and race. At each of the 15 subcontracting firms (which specialize in unskilled and semiskilled assembly work) that Hossfeld observed, between

80% and 100% of workers were Third World immigrants, the majority of whom were women (p. 72). Based on interviews with employers and workers at these firms, Hossfeld concludes that "the lower the skill and pay level of the job, the greater the proportion of Third World immigrant women tends to be" (p. 73).

In labor-intensive industries such as garment and microelectronics, employers prefer to hire immigrant women, as compared with immigrant men, because they believe that women can afford to work for less, do not mind dead-end jobs, and are more suited physiologically to certain kinds of detailed and routine work. The following comment from a male manager at a microelectronics subcontracting assembly plant typifies this "gender logic": "The relatively small size [of many Asian and Mexican women] makes it easier for them to sit quietly for long periods of time, doing small detail work that would drive a large person like [him] crazy" (Hossfeld, 1994, p. 74). As Linda Lim (1983) observes, it is the "*comparative disadvantage* of women in the wage-labor market that gives them a comparative advantage vis-à-vis men in the occupations and industries where they are concentrated—so-called female ghettoes of employment" (p. 78). A White male production manager and hiring supervisor in a Silicon Valley assembly shop discusses his formula for hiring:

> Just three things I look for in hiring [entry-level, high-tech manufacturing operatives]: small, foreign, and female. You find those three things and you're pretty much automatically guaranteed the right kind of workforce. These little foreign gals are grateful to be hired—very, very grateful—no matter what.   (Hossfeld, 1994, p. 65)

In Hawaii, Korean immigrant women likewise had an easier time securing employment than men did because of their domestic skills and because of the demand for service workers in restaurants, hotels, hospitals, and factories (Chai, 1987). These examples illustrate the interconnections of race, class, and gender. On one hand, patriarchal and racist ideologies consign women to a secondary and inferior position in the capitalist wage-labor market. On the other hand, their very disadvantage enhances women's employability over that of men in certain industries, thus affording them an opportunity to sharpen their claims against patriarchal authority in their homes.

The shifts in women's and men's access to economic and social resources is most acute among disadvantaged Southeast Asian refugees (Donnelly, 1994; Kibria, 1993). The lives of the Cambodian refugees in Stockton, California, provide an example (Ui, 1991). In Stockton, an agricultural town in which the agricultural jobs have already been taken by Mexican workers, the unemployment rate for Cambodian men is estimated to be between 80% and 90%. Unemployed for long periods of time, these men gather at the corners of the enclaves to drink and gamble. In contrast, Cambodian women have transformed their traditional roles and skills—as providers of food and clothing for family and community members and as small traders—into informal economic activities that contribute cash to family incomes. Women have also benefited more than men from government-funded language and job-training programs. Because traditionally male jobs are scarce in

Stockton, these programs have focused on the education of the more employable refugee women (Ui, 1991, pp. 166–167). In particular, refugee women are trained to work in social service agencies serving their coethnics primarily in secretarial, clerical, and interpreter positions. In a refugee community with limited economic opportunities, social service programs—even though they are usually part-time, ethnic specific, and highly susceptible to budget cuts—provide one of the few new job opportunities for this population, and in this case, most of these jobs go to the women. Relying on gender stereotypes, social service agency executives have preferred women over men, claiming that women are ideal workers because they are more patient and easier to work with than men (Ui, 1991, p. 169). Thus, in the Cambodian community of Stockton, it is often women, and not men, who have relatively greater economic opportunities and who become the primary breadwinners in their families. On the other hand, stripped of opportunities for employment, men often lose their "place to be" in the new society (Ui, 1991, pp. 170–171).

The shifts in the resources of immigrant men and women have challenged the patriarchal authority of Asian men. Men's loss of status and power—not only in the public but also in the domestic arena—places severe pressure on their sense of well-being, leading in some instances to spousal abuse and divorce (Luu, 1989, p. 68). A Korean immigrant man describes his frustrations over changing gender roles and expectations:

> In Korea [my wife] used to have breakfast ready for me. . . . She didn't do it anymore because she said she was too busy getting ready to go to work. If I complained she talked back at me, telling me to fix my own breakfast. . . . I was very frustrated about her, started fighting and hit her. (Yim, 1978, as cited in Mazumdar, 1989, p. 18)

According to a 1979 survey, marital conflict was one of the top four problems of Vietnamese refugees in the United States (Davidson, 1979, as cited in Luu, 1989, p. 69). A Vietnamese man, recently divorced after 10 years of marriage, blamed his wife's new role and newfound freedom for their breakup:

> Back in the country, my role was only to bring home money from work, and my wife would take care of the household. Now everything has changed. My wife had to work as hard as I did to support the family. Soon after, she demanded more power at home. In other words, she wanted equal partnership. I am so disappointed! I realized that things are different now, but I could not help feeling the way I do. It is hard to get rid of or change my principles and beliefs which are deeply rooted in me. (Luu, 1989, p. 69)

Loss of status and power has similarly led to depression and anxieties in Hmong males. In particular, the women's ability—and the men's inability—to earn money for households "has undermined severely male omnipotence" (Irby & Pon, 1988, p. 112). Male unhappiness and helplessness can be detected in the following joke told at a family picnic: "When we get on the plane to go back to Laos, the first thing we will do is beat up the women!" The joke—which generated laughter by both men and women—drew upon a combination of "the men's unemployability, the sudden economic value placed on women's work, and men's fear of losing power in their families" (Donnelly, 1994, pp. 74–75).

The shifts in the resources of men and women have created an opportunity for women to contest the traditional hierarchies of family life (Chai, 1987; Kibria, 1993; Williams, 1989, p. 157). Existing data indicate, however, that working-class Asian immigrant women have not used their new resources to radically restructure the old family system but only to redefine it in a more satisfying manner (Kibria, 1993). Some cultural conceptions, such as the belief that the male should be the head of the household, remain despite the economic contributions of women. Nancy Donnelly (1994) reports that although Hmong women contribute the profits of their needle-work sales to the family economy, the traditional construction of Hmong women as "creators of beauty, skilled in devotion to their families, and embedded in a social order dominated by men" has not changed (p. 185). In the following quotation, a Cambodian wife describes her reluctance to upset her husband's authority:

> If we lived in Cambodia I would have behaved differently toward my husband. Over there we have to always try to be nice to the husband. Wives don't talk back, but sometimes I do that here a little bit, because I have more freedom to say what I think here. However, I am careful not to speak too disrespectfully to him, and in that way, I think I am different from the Americans. (Welaratna, 1993, p. 233)

The traditional division of household labor also remains relatively intact. In a study of Chinatown women, Loo and Ong (1982) found that despite their employment outside the home, three fourths of the working mothers were solely responsible for all household chores. In her study of Vietnamese American families, Kibria (1993) argues that Vietnamese American women (and children) walk an "ideological tightrope"—struggling both to preserve the traditional Vietnamese family system and to enhance their power within the context of this system. According to Kibria, the traditional family system is valuable to Vietnamese American women because it offers them economic protection and gives them authority, as mothers, over the younger generation.

For the wage laborers then, the family—and the traditional patriarchy within it—becomes simultaneously a bastion of resistance to race and class oppression and an instrument for gender subordination (Glenn, 1986, p. 193). Women also preserve the traditional family system—albeit in a tempered form—because they value the promise of male economic protection. Although migration may have equalized or reversed the economic resources of working-class men and women, women's earnings continue to be too meager to sustain their economic independence from men. Because the wage each earns is low, only by pooling incomes can a husband and wife earn enough to support a family. Finally, like many ethnic, immigrant, poor, and working-class women, working-class Asian women view work as an opportunity to raise the family's living standards and not only as a path to self-fulfillment or even upward mobility as idealized by the White feminist movement. As such, employment is defined as an extension of their family obligations—of their roles as mothers and wives (Kim & Hurh, 1988, p. 162; Pedraza, 1991; Romero, 1992).

CONCLUSION

My review of the existing literature on Asian immigrant salaried professionals, self-employed entrepreneurs, and wage laborers suggests that economic constraints (and opportunities) have reconfigured gender relations within contemporary Asian America society. The patriarchal authority of Asian immigrant men, particularly those of the working class, has been challenged due to the social and economic losses that they suffered in their transition to the status of men of color in the United States. On the other hand, the recent growth of female-intensive industries—and the racist and sexist "preference" for the labor of immigrant women—has enhanced women's employability over that of men and has changed their role to that of a coprovider, if not primary provider, for their families. These shifts in immigrant men's and women's access to economic and social resources have not occurred without friction. Men's loss of status in both public and private arenas has placed severe pressures on the traditional family, leading at times to resentment, spousal abuse, and divorce. For the women's part, Asian women's ability to restructure the traditional patriarchy system is often constrained by their social-structural location—as racially subordinated immigrant women—in the dominant society. In the best scenario, responding to the structural barriers in the larger society, both husbands and wives become more interdependent and equal as they are forced to rely on each other, and on the traditional family and immigrant community, for economic security and emotional support. On the other hand, to the extent that the traditional division of labor and male privilege persists, wage work adds to the women's overall workload. The existing research indicates that both of these tendencies exist, though the increased burdens for women are more obvious.

NOTES

1. Certainly, these three categories are neither mutually exclusive nor exhaustive. They are also linked in the sense that there is mobility between them, particularly from professional to small-business employment (Chen, 1992, p. 142). Nevertheless, they represent perhaps the most important sociological groupings within the contemporary Asian immigrant community (Ong & Hee, 1994, p. 31).

2. The Chinese Exclusion Act of 1882 suspended immigration of laborers for 10 years. The 1917 Immigration Act delineated a "barred zone" from whence no immigrants could come. The 1924 Immigration Act denied entry to virtually all Asians. The 1934 Tydings-McDuffie Act reduced Filipino immigration to 50 persons a year. The 1965 Immigration Act abolished "national origins" as a basis for allocating immigration quotas to various countries—Asian countries were finally placed on equal footing.

3. After Mexico, the Philippines and South Korea were the second- and third-largest source countries of immigrants, respectively. Three other Asian countries—China, India, and Vietnam—were among the 10 major source countries of U.S. immigrants in the 1980s (Min, 1995b, p. 12).

4. According to the 1990 U.S. Census, 43% of Asian men and 32% of Asian women 25 years of age and older had at least a bachelor's degree, compared with 23% and 17%, re-

spectively, of the total U.S. population (U.S. Bureau of the Census, 1993, p. 4). Moreover, the proportion of Asians with graduate or professional degrees was higher than that of Whites: 14% versus 8% (Ong & Hee, 1994). Immigrants account for about two thirds to three quarters of the highly educated population (Ong & Hee, 1994, pp. 38–39).

5. For example, in Southern California, many Cambodian-owned doughnut shops are open 24 hours a day, with the husbands typically baking all night, while wives and teenage children work the counter by day (Akast, 1993).

6. In New York City, more than a quarter of Chinatown garment shops went out of business between 1980 and 1981. Similarly, of the nearly 200 Chinatown garment shops that registered with California's Department of Employment in 1978, 23% were sold or closed by 1982 and another 8% were inactive (Ong, 1984, p. 48).

REFERENCES

Akast, D. (1993, March 9). Cruller fates: Cambodians find slim profit in doughnuts. *Los Angeles Times*, p. D1.

Blumenberg, E., & Ong, P. (1994). Labor squeeze and ethnic/racial composition in the U.S. apparel industry. In E. Bonacich, L. Cheng, N. Chinchilla, N. Hamilton, & P. Ong (Eds.), *Global production: The apparel industry in the Pacific Rim* (pp. 309–327). Philadelphia: Temple University Press.

Bonacich, E. (1994). Asians in the Los Angeles garment industry. In P. Ong, E. Bonacich, & L. Cheng (Eds.), *The new Asian immigration in Los Angeles and global restructuring* (pp. 137–163). Berkeley and Los Angeles: University of California Press.

Bonacich, E., Hossain, M., & Park, J. (1987). Korean immigrant working women in the early 1980s. In E. Yu & E. H. Philipps (Eds.), *Korean women in transition: At home and abroad* (pp. 219–247). Los Angeles: California State University, Center for Korean-American and Korean Studies.

Chai, A. Y. (1987). Freed from the elders but locked into labor: Korean immigrant women in Hawaii. *Women's Studies, 13*, 223–234.

Chen, H. S. (1992). *Chinatown no more: Taiwan immigrants in contemporary New York*. Ithaca, NY: Cornell University Press.

Cho, S. (1997). Asian Pacific American women and racialized sexual harassment. In E. Kim, L. Villanueva, & Asian Women United of California (Eds.), *Making more waves: New writing by Asian American women* (pp. 164–173). Boston: Beacon.

Clement, W., & Myles, J. (1994). *Relations of ruling: Class and gender in postindustrial societies*. Montreal, Canada: McGill-Queen's University Press.

Curtis, R. (1986). Household and family in theory on equality. *American Sociological Review, 51*, 168–183.

Dhaliwal, A. K. (1995). Gender at work: The renegotiation of middle-class womanhood in a South Asian-owned business. In W. L. Ng, S.-Y. Chin, J. S. Moy, & G. Y. Okihiro (Eds.), *Reviewing Asian America: Locating diversity* (pp. 75–85). Pullman: Washington State University Press.

Donato, K. M. (1992). Understanding U.S. immigration: Why some countries send women and others send men. In D. Gabaccia (Ed.), *Seeking common ground: Multidisciplinary studies of immigrant women in the United States* (pp. 159–184). Westport, CT: Greenwood.

Donnelly, N. D. (1994). *Changing lives of refugee Hmong women.* Seattle: Washington University Press.

Duleep, H., & Sanders, S. (1993). Discrimination at the top: American-born Asian and White men. *Industrial Relations, 31,* 416–432.

Espiritu, Y. L. (1995). *Filipino American lives.* Philadelphia: Temple University Press.

Fawcett, J. T., & Gardner, R. W. (1994). Asian immigrant entrepreneurs and non-entrepreneurs: A comparative study of recent Korean and Filipino immigrants. *Population and Environment, 15,* 211–238.

Gardner, R., Robey, B., & Smith, P. C. (Eds.). (1985). Asian Americans: Growth, change, and diversity [Special issue]. *Population Bulletin, 40*(4).

Glenn, E. N. (1983). Split household, small producer and dual wage earner: An analysis of Chinese-American family strategies. *Journal of Marriage and the Family, 45,* 35–46.

Glenn, E. N. (1986). *Issei, Nisei, war bride: Three generations of Japanese American women at domestic service.* Philadelphia: Temple University Press.

Gold, S. (1994). Chinese-Vietnamese entrepreneurs in California. In P. Ong, E. Bonacich, & L. Cheng (Eds.), *The new Asian immigration in Los Angeles and global restructuring* (pp. 196–226). Philadelphia: Temple University Press.

Green, S. (1980). *Silicon Valley's women workers: A theoretical analysis of sex-segregation in the electronics industry labor market.* Honolulu, HI: Impact of Transnational Interactions Project, Cultural Learning Institute, East-West Center.

Hondagneu-Sotelo, P. (1994). *Gendered transition: Mexican experiences in immigration.* Berkeley and Los Angeles: University of California Press.

Hood, J. G. (1983). *Becoming a two job family.* New York: Praeger.

Hossfeld, K. (1994). Hiring immigrant women: Silicon Valley's "simple formula." In M. Baca Zinn & B. T. Dills (Eds.), *Women of color in U.S. society* (pp. 65–93). Philadelphia: Temple University Press.

Hune, S., & Chan, K. (1997). Special focus: Asian Pacific American demographic and educational trends. In D. Carter & R. Wilson (Eds.), *Minorities in education* (Report No. 15). Washington, DC: American Council on Education.

Irby, C., & Pon, E. M. (1988). Confronting new mountains: Mental health problems among male Hmong and Mien refugees. *Amerasia Journal, 14,* 109–118.

Kanjanapan, W. (1995). The immigration of Asian professionals to the United States: 1988–1990. *International Migration Review, 29,* 7–32.

Katz, N., & Kemnitzer, D. (1984). Women and work in Silicon Valley: Options and futures. In K. B. Sacks & D. Remy (Eds.), *My troubles are going to have trouble with me: Everyday trials and triumphs of women workers.* New Brunswick, NJ: Rutgers University Press.

Kibria, N. (1993). *Family tightrope: The changing lives of Vietnamese Americans.* Princeton, NJ: Princeton University Press.

Kim, K. C., & Hurh, W. M. (1985). Ethnic resource utilization of Korean immigrant entrepreneurs in the Chicago minority area. *International Migration Review, 19,* 82–111.

Kim, K. C., & Hurh, W. M. (1988). The burden of double roles: Korean wives in the U.S.A. *Ethnic and Racial Studies, 11,* 151–167.

Light, I., & Bonacich, E. (1986). *Immigrant entrepreneurs: Koreans in Los Angeles, 1965–1982.* Berkeley and Los Angeles: University of California Press.

Lim, L.Y.C. (1983). Capitalism, imperialism, and patriarchy: The dilemma of Third-World women workers in multinational factories. In J. Nash & M. P. Fernández Kelly (Eds.),

Women, men, and the international division of labor (pp. 70–91). Albany: State University of New York Press.

Loo, C., & Ong, P. (1982). Slaying demons with a sewing needle: Feminist issues for Chinatown's women. *Berkeley Journal of Sociology, 27,* 77–88.

Loucky, J., Soldatenko, M., Scott, G., & Bonacich, E. (1994). Immigrant enterprise and labor in the Los Angeles garment industry. In E. Bonacich, L. Cheng, N. Chinchilla, N. Hamilton, & P. Ong (Eds.), *Global production: The apparel industry in the Pacific Rim* (pp. 345–361). Philadelphia: Temple University Press.

Louie, M. C. (1992). Immigrant Asian women in Bay Area garment shops: "After sewing, laundry, cleaning and cooking, I have no breath left to sing." *Amerasia Journal, 18,* 1–26.

Lowe, L. (1997). Work, immigration, gender: Asian "American" women. In E. Kim, L. Villanueva, & Asian Women United of California (Eds.), *Making more waves: New writing by Asian American women* (pp. 269–277). Boston: Beacon.

Luu, V. (1989). The hardship of escape for Vietnamese women. In Asian Women United of California (Ed.), *Making waves: An anthology of writings by and about Asian American women* (pp. 60–72). Boston: Beacon.

Mar, D., & Kim, M. (1994). Historical trends. In P. Ong (Ed.), *The state of Asian Pacific America: Economic diversity, issues, and policies* (pp. 13–30). Los Angeles: LEAP Asian Pacific American Public Policy Institute and University of California at Los Angeles Asian American Studies Center.

May, L. (1987, February 2). Asians looking to broaden horizons: Immigrants prosper but hope to venture outside the "business ghetto." *Los Angeles Times.*

Mazumdar, S. (1989). General introduction: A woman-centered perspective on Asian American history. In Asian Women United of California (Ed.), *Making waves: An anthology of writings by and about Asian American women* (pp. 1–22). Boston: Beacon.

Min, P. G. (1992). Korean immigrant wives' overwork. *Korea Journal of Population and Development, 21,* 23–36.

Min, P. G. (1995a). Korean Americans. In P. G. Min (Ed.), *Asian Americans: Contemporary trends and issues* (pp. 199–231). Thousand Oaks, CA: Sage.

Min, P. G. (1995b). An overview of Asian Americans. In P. G. Min (Ed.), *Asian Americans: Contemporary trends and issues* (pp. 10–37). Thousand Oaks, CA: Sage.

Min, P. G. (1996). *Caught in the middle: Korean communities in New York and Los Angeles.* Berkeley and Los Angeles: University of California Press.

Min, P. G. (1998). *Changes and conflicts: Korean immigrant families in New York.* Needham Heights, MA: Allyn & Bacon.

Morokvasic, M. (1984). Birds of passage are also women. *International Migration Review, 18,* 886–907.

Ong, P. (1984). Chinatown unemployment and the ethnic labor market. *Amerasia Journal, 11,* 35–54.

Ong, P., & Azores, T. (1994a). Health professionals on the front line. In P. Ong (Ed.), *The state of Asian Pacific America: Economic diversity, issues, and policies* (pp. 139–163). Los Angeles: LEAP Asian Pacific American Public Policy Institute and University of California at Los Angeles Asian American Studies Center.

Ong, P., & Azores, T. (1994b). The migration and incorporation of Filipino nurses. In P. Ong, E. Bonacich, & L. Cheng (Eds.), *The new Asian immigration in Los Angeles and global restructuring* (pp. 164–195). Philadelphia: Temple University Press.

Ong, P., & Blumenberg, E. (1994). Scientists and engineers. In P. Ong (Ed.), *The state of Asian Pacific America: Economic diversity, issues, and policies* (pp. 165–189). Los Angeles: LEAP Asian Pacific American Public Policy Institute and University of California at Los Angeles Asian American Studies Center.

Ong, P., & Hee, S. (1994). Economic diversity. In P. Ong (Ed.), *The state of Asian Pacific America: Economic diversity, issues, and policies* (pp. 31–56). Los Angeles: LEAP Asian Pacific American Public Policy Institute and University of California at Los Angeles Asian American Studies Center.

Ong, P., & Umemoto, K. (1994). Life and work in the inner-city. In P. Ong (Ed.), *The state of Asian Pacific America: Economic diversity, issues, and policies* (pp. 87–112). Los Angeles: LEAP Asian Pacific American Public Policy Institute and University of California at Los Angeles Asian American Studies Center.

Park, K. (1989). Impact of new productive activities on the organization of domestic life: A case study of the Korean American community. In G. Nomura, R. Endo, S. Sumida, & R. Leong (Eds.), *Frontiers of Asian American studies* (pp. 140–150). Pullman: Washington State University Press.

Pedraza, S. (1991). Women and migration: The social consequences of gender. *Annual Review of Sociology, 17,* 303–325.

Pesquera, B. M. (1993). "In the beginning he wouldn't lift a spoon": The division of household labor. In A. de la Torre & B. M. Pesquera (Eds.), *Building with our hands: New directions in Chicana studies* (pp. 181–195). Berkeley and Los Angeles: University of California Press.

Pessar, P. R. (1984). The Linkage Between the Household and the Workplace in the Experience of Dominican Immigrant Women in the U.S., *International Migration Review,* 18,1188–1211.

Pressner, H. (1988). Shift work and child care among young dual-earner American parents. *Journal of Marriage and the Family, 50,* 133–148.

Romero, M. (1992). *Maid in the U.S.A.* New York: Routledge.

Rong, X. L., & Preissle, J. (1997). The continuing decline in Asian American teachers. *American Educational Research Journal, 34,* 267–293.

Siegel, L., & Borock, H. (1982). *Background report on Silicon Valley* (Prepared for the U.S. Commission on Civil Rights). Mountain View, CA: Pacific Studies Center.

Snow, R. (1986). The new international division of labor and the U.S. workforce: The case of the electronics industry. In J. Nash and M. P. Fernández Kelly (Eds.), *Women, men, and the international division of labor.* Albany: State University of New York Press.

Tienda, M., & Booth, K. (1991). Gender, migration, and social change. *International Sociology, 6,* 51–72.

Ui, S. (1991). "Unlikely heroes": The evolution of female leadership in a Cambodian ethnic enclave. In M. Burawoy (Ed.), *Ethnography unbound* (pp. 161–177). Berkeley & Los Angeles: University of California Press.

U.S. Bureau of the Census. (1992). *Statistical abstract of the United States* (112th ed.). Washington, DC: U.S. Government Printing Office.

U.S. Bureau of the Census. (1993). *We the American Asians.* Washington, DC: U.S. Government Printing Office.

Welaratna, U. (1993). *Beyond the killing fields: Voices of nine Cambodian survivors in America.* Stanford, CA: Stanford University Press.

Williams, M. (1989). Ladies on the line: Punjabi cannery workers in central California. In Asian Women United of California (Ed.), *Making waves: An anthology of writings by and about Asian American women* (pp. 148–159). Boston: Beacon.

Wong, M. (1983). Chinese sweatshops in the United States: A look at the garment industry. *Research in Sociology of Work: Peripheral Workers, 2,* 357–379.

Yamanaka, K., & McClelland, K. (1994). Earning the model-minority image: Diverse strategies of economic adaptation by Asian-American women. *Ethnic and Racial Studies, 17,* 79–114.

Yoon, I. J. (1997). *On my own: Korean businesses and race relations in America.* Chicago: Chicago University Press.

Zhou, M., & Logan, J. R. (1989). Returns on human capital in ethnic enclaves: New York City's Chinatown. *American Sociological Review, 54,* 809–820.

CHAPTER 6

The Intersection of Work and Gender

Central American Immigrant Women and Employment in California

Cecilia Menjívar

This essay examines the effects of immigration on gender relations among Central American women. I focus on these women's experiences in relation to the immigrant men's situations and assess how immigration affects their gendered perceptions of work. Building on the work of others (Glenn, 1986; Zavella, 1987), I examine the differential effect of U.S. employment for Central American men and women and how this, in turn, affects these immigrants' perceptions of work. This approach allows for a more complex examination of how gender relations are transformed or affirmed through contemporary immigration, as sociocultural patterns and broader forces are configured differently across time and locales. Clearly, changes that occur in gender relations as a result of the immigrants' entry into paid work can no longer be seen as simple or unidirectional. Nor are these changes simply the result of earning a wage. There are important social processes of U.S. employment that alter gender relations between men and women.

Empirically, this article is based on the experiences of recent Salvadoran and (indigenous and *ladina*)[1] Guatemalan immigrant women in California. The 1980s brought about the greatest population movements in contemporary Central American history (Torres-Rivas & Jiménez, 1985). These movements occurred as the politico-economic stability of the region was shaken when the regimes of some countries—particularly those of El Salvador, Guatemala, and Nicaragua—engaged in military confrontations. During this time, many Central Americans migrated to neighboring countries, Mexico, and the United States. Despite the political turmoil prevailing in their homelands, Central American immigrants were not treated as political refugees by the U.S. government, a contradiction focused on by some researchers of Central American migration (Jones, 1989; Stanley, 1987; Ward, 1987). Other researchers examined the psychosocial trauma among these immigrants (Aron, Corne, Fursland, & Zelwer, 1991; Guarnaccia & Farias, 1988), their participation in the labor force (Repak, 1995), and the social processes of community building (Hagan, 1994; Mahler, 1995; Menjívar, 1997; Rodríguez & Hagan, 1992). But, in spite of the predominance of women in Central American migration, their specific experiences have not been placed at the center of analyses (for a few exceptions, see Hagan, 1996, and also studies with a sociopsychological bent such as Aron et al., 1991; Guarnaccia & Farias, 1988).

The study participants discussed in this article migrated recently from Guatemala to Los Angeles and from El Salvador to San Francisco. On their arrival, both groups encountered similarly disadvantaged contexts of reception—hostile immigration policies, stiff competition in the labor market, and local communities with few resources. The context of reception is vital, as it shapes the structure of opportunity for men and women in different ways. Also important is an analysis of how these immigrants' diverse backgrounds—including specific sociocultural aspirations and ideologies—contribute to transform or affirm gender relations as these immigrant women enter paid work in the United States.

The majority of these women worked for an income in their own countries before migrating to the United States; so earning a living is not new for them. What is novel is their entrance into U.S. paid work in a new and different social, economic, political, and cultural context brought about by their migration. I argue that these new conditions carry great potential for gender relations—either transforming or affirming them. I seek to examine these women's perceptions of how, through migration, their lives as income earners within the broader context of gender relations may have changed. These results do not depend solely on the women's abilities to earn incomes but on the social processes of working outside the home as conditioned by the new context. This study may help isolate analytically the effects of immigration on gender relations without conflating migratory effects with entry into paid work. This research will add to the body of research that examines immigrant women with premigration paid-work experience (see Georges, 1990; Grasmuck & Pessar, 1991). With the increasing feminization of the workforce around the world, insights gained from these studies may enhance our understanding of a growing immigrant population.

Furthermore, even though I analyze the experiences of Central American women—Guatemalan and Salvadoran—it must be emphasized that this is not a homogeneous category. The differences between these groups and between the ladina and indigenous among the Guatemalans preclude a universalization of experiences for these women. Thus, because the "social location" (Zavella, 1991) of these informants is diverse, examining their experiences allows us to tease out elements that pertain to gender, class, nationality, or ethnicity. The social location of families (i.e., where they are situated in relation to social institutions that allocate resources) results in different family characteristics such as gender and marriage patterns (Zinn, 1996, p. 175). Differences in social location are important to discern because they often get fused with issues pertaining to gender, particularly when immigrant women are characterized as a homogeneous and unified group. Situating these identities within a broader context—politics of reception, local labor market conditions, and the organization of the receiving community—helps to convey the dynamic and fluid nature of gender relations. Broader politico-economic and sociocultural factors are patterned differently across time and locale and, as such, generate a multiplicity of experiences. And, although patriarchal ideologies are more general and may even be universal, their local expression varies according to the social characteristics of the immigrants and historical specificities of their migration. Thus, each immigrant group is confronted with its own dilemmas in gender relations and their reconfiguration.

Evaluating the gains and losses of immigration for these women represents a highly subjective enterprise. To minimize an outsider's bias, I will present their experiences and assessments of their predicaments in their own voices. Situations that an observer might deem oppressive may actually represent forms of liberation for the women involved, and vice versa. Bachu (1986) and Foner (1986) in their studies of Ugandan Indians in London and of Jamaican women in New York, respectively, point out that immigrant women evaluate their current situations in comparison with what they left behind, a point also echoed by Morokvasic (1984, p. 894). Moreover, immigration brings about changes in gender relations that have complex and uneven effects; it presents women with opportunities and, at the same time, imposes constraints (Morokvasic, 1984; Tienda & Booth, 1991). Often, a gain in one sphere results in a loss in another (Kibria, 1990), making it difficult for women to provide unambiguous assessments of their new predicaments. In this regard, Pessar (1995) reminds us that "respecting and acknowledging the subjects' multiple and sometimes contradictory voices gives us license to explore the inconsistencies and ambivalence in their words and actions" (p. 45). Thus, although this approach adds complexity to our observations, it captures the immigrants' social worlds more accurately.

Even though the work I present here focuses on the experiences of the immigrants in their places of destination, to make sense of what happens there, it will be useful to examine events that occurred prior to the immigrants' arrival. After discussing the data sources and the methodology employed, I provide a brief overview of the contexts of both exit and reception, followed by the immigrants' accounts organized around two main areas: these immigrants' perceptions of U.S. employment and their consequences for gender relations in families.

DATA AND METHOD

The data used in this study come from intensive interviews done in Spanish with 26 Salvadoran immigrant women in San Francisco and with 25 Guatemalan immigrant women in Los Angeles, complemented with participant observation in both locations. These immigrants were "recently arrived"; that is, they had been in the United States for no longer than 5 years when I first interviewed them. Fieldwork in San Francisco took place from approximately 1990 to 1994, and in Los Angeles from 1994 to 1995. Even though the focus of the study is on the women's stories, I also interviewed and spoke informally with many men during the course of the fieldwork. I conversed informally with these immigrant women's friends, neighbors, family members, and on a few occasions their employers, too. I met with community leaders and workers, including Catholic priests and evangelical pastors who complemented greatly my informants' own stories.

I contacted my informants through language schools, clinics, community organizations, and churches located in various neighborhoods with high concentrations of Central American immigrants. These places also provided me with an opportunity to gather important observations because I spent many hours in these locations. During this time, I helped my informants with translations, car rides, filling out forms, or with any information or advice I could provide. Some reciprocated these small favors with kind invitations to eat special meals at their homes or to celebrations such as birthdays, baptisms, or weddings. This allowed me to gain an in-depth look at the social world of my informants and provided me with invaluable opportunities to ask about their perceptions of their lives. Although I took steps to ensure that my informants would represent different sectors of the Salvadoran and Guatemalan populations by contacting them in diverse places, the small number of informants in this study and their characteristics are not meant to be representative in a strict statistical sense. Thus, it would be inappropriate to attempt to generalize directly from these observations to all Guatemalans or Salvadorans in the United States, much less to all immigrants.

The 26 Salvadoran women had a mean age of 31, and 9 years of education. Half of them mentioned some knowledge of English, although none were fluent speakers. Almost half were either in consensual unions or legally married. The class backgrounds of these immigrants were varied: Some were students in El Salvador; others were teachers, clerks, factory workers, and secretaries; and one was a housekeeper and another a street vendor. All the Salvadoran women had been working full-time or part-time prior to their migration.[2] They came from all regions of the country, many from the capital city where they had migrated prior to leaving for the United States. In San Francisco, they lived in and around the Mission District, the predominantly Latino section of the city.

The 25 Guatemalans include two sociodemographically and culturally different groups—14 ladinas and 11 indigenous women.[3] The mean age for the ladinas was 30 years, and 33 for the indigenous women. Two thirds of the Guatemalan women—almost equal proportions of ladinas and indigenous—were either married or in consensual unions. On average, the ladinas had 8 years of education, whereas the indigenous women had only 4 years. A quarter of the Guatemalans mentioned some knowledge of English, but none spoke English fluently. Compared with the Salvadorans, both groups of Guatemalans were less urban. The ladinas came from towns and cities in eastern Guatemala, and the indigenous women came from the western highlands, mostly from the Kaqchikel region, but some were from El Quiché. All the indigenous women and two thirds of the ladinas had earned incomes in Guatemala. Their class backgrounds, while varied, were not as diverse as those of the Salvadorans. The indigenous women mostly worked weaving merchandise to sell, and the ladinas worked as clerks, housekeepers, and owners of small businesses. There were a couple of former students among the ladinas, but none among the indigenous women. All the indigenous women were bilingual in Spanish and either Kaqchikel or K'iche.[4] The ladinas lived primarily in Hollywood and south-central Los Angeles, and the indigenous were concentrated around Pico Union and Westlake, both areas immediately west of downtown Los Angeles.

CONTEXT OF EXIT AND JOURNEY

Many Central Americans have brought with them memories and traumatic experiences stemming from the political upheaval in their countries, making the context and circumstances of their exit of particular importance in shaping their lives. The politico-military crisis in Central America received more international attention than the socioeconomic reverberations that affected all sectors of those societies with different degrees of intensity. Within an environment of generalized violence, however, women become particularly vulnerable as victims of assaults, rapes, and kidnappings (Martin-Forbes, 1992; Menjívar, 1993; Seller, 1981).

The crises of the 1980s can be generally traced back to the early years of independent history in Central America and, more specifically, to the developmental years of the 1950s. Governments and local elites attempted to transform these mainly agro-exporting societies into industrialized ones through policies of import substitution in a vacuum of broader structural reforms (Menjívar, 1993). The resulting economic boom benefited only a small group, further impoverishing the urban and rural poor. This polarization magnified the already marked class differences. The number of dissatisfied groups that had been adversely affected by or altogether excluded from the development process increased over the years, and by the 1980s this culminated in an armed conflict fueled by outside intervention and institutionalized violence. These events drove thousands of Central Americans from all sectors of society to abandon their usual places of residence. It has been estimated that up to one third of El Salvador's inhabitants were displaced by the 12-year war, many of whom migrated to the United States. Estimates range from 8% of the country's population (Lopez, Popkin, & Telles, 1996) to close to 20% (Montes & García, 1988).

The Guatemalan armed conflict started much earlier and extended approximately 30 years. In addition to generalized social change and accompanying conflict in the region, indigenous communities in Guatemala went through profound transformations in the 1970s, most notably as progressive forms of organization were instituted and ideologies disseminated (i.e., cooperatives, unions, theology of liberation, etc.) (Stepputat, 1994). The government army responded with repression and engaged in counterinsurgency campaigns, mainly in the indigenous-populated western highlands where it believed forces promoting social change had sympathizers. The result of this campaign was the destruction of many villages and the displacement of between a half million and a million people (Manz, 1988). Many of them fled as refugees to neighboring areas such as southern Mexico, but a significant number made their way to the United States. These U.S.-bound, indigenous Guatemalans were joined by nonindigenous migrants who were not only motivated by the economic dislocations during the crisis but also by their direct suffering from the rampant violence during that period.

Because most of these immigrants undertake their journeys without either a Mexican or a U.S. visa and, therefore, are forced to travel by land, the trip from either Guatemala or El Salvador to the United States is plagued by vicissitudes and the uncertainty of an eventual arrival. Most of the men and women with whom I spoke commented on the perils of the trip: the abuses on the part of immigration officials in Mexico and, in many cases, the unscrupulous coyotes (smugglers) whom they hired to bring them into the United States. Many of these immigrants' harrowing experiences during their journeys left them with more or equally severe trauma than the violence in their countries had caused. This trip is particularly dangerous for women who, in addition to extortion and robberies, are exposed to gender-specific crimes such as sexual assault and intimidation. Sometimes, however, women are able to negotiate better treatment by using their vulnerability as women to appeal to compassionate persons.

CONTEXT OF ARRIVAL

Several factors of the Central Americans' arrival impinge greatly on the lives of both male and female immigrants, ultimately shaping the ways they relate to each other. Government reception policies, local labor market opportunities, and the receiving community's organization combine to mold the structure of opportunities available to immigrants. As Portes and Rumbaut (1996) note, the context of reception channels immigrants in differing directions, often altering the link between individual skills and expected rewards. As we shall see, the receiving context has a powerful homogenizing effect on these Central American immigrants. Even though their class backgrounds are diverse, their insertion in U.S. society is similar. Furthermore, the context of reception affects men and women in different ways.

Although Salvadorans and Guatemalans were fleeing violence in their countries, they were not accorded refugee status by the U.S. government, who instead treated them as economic (mostly undocumented) immigrants. U.S. policies on Central America had more to do with these immigrants' treatment than their motivations and conditions of exit. Once on U.S. soil, Salvadorans and Guatemalans could apply for asylum, but fewer than 3% were actually granted such a status (National Asylum Study Project, 1992). Relatively few of these immigrants qualified for amnesty through the Immigration and Reform Control Act of 1986 because the bulk of them migrated after the 1982 cutoff date. In practice, this meant that many Salvadorans and Guatemalans were ineligible for assistance for their resettlement regardless of the conditions of their exit.

During the time I was conducting fieldwork, some Salvadorans were granted temporary protected status (TPS), guaranteeing them the right to work; however, this temporary status had to be renewed every 18 months and expired in December 1994. Those who had been denied asylum earlier and those who had been granted TPS became eligible to resubmit asylum applications. The Immigration and Naturalization Service (INS) considers these applications on a case-by-case basis, and it is expected that fewer than 10% will be granted asylum. Immigration policy toward Salvadorans seems more ambiguous than ever because the INS announced that, although there will be no massive deportations, a blanket amnesty will not be granted. Of the Salvadoran women in this study, only 11 had documents—either permanent residence or TPS. The majority were undocumented, with few prospects for obtaining legal status; this was also the case with the Guatemalans. Only 5 of the Guatemalan women in this study had documents. In both groups, however, more men than women had documents.[5] Guatemalans were not granted TPS; they were only allowed to resubmit asylum applications. The legal status of these immigrants considerably narrows their employment opportunities and the availability of resources. This, in turn, strongly affects their social relations and has important repercussions on gender relations and expectations.

In efforts to fill the vacuum of official resettlement aid, community members (mostly middle-class, White, politically active U.S. citizens and newcomer Central Americans themselves) set up community organizations to address the needs of newly arrived Central Americans. This organized response focused on emergency assistance, food and shelter, free clinics, job search strategies, and legal services. These organizations depend on private donations for the most part; and, as their financial difficulties have grown in the midst of an economic crisis, they are not able to provide services at the same rate as they have in the past.

As the local labor markets of both San Francisco and Los Angeles experienced a boom in the 1970s and 1980s, the Central American immigrants found opportunities in low-wage services. These labor markets were segmented by gender, as Central American women procured jobs mainly as domestic workers or as janitors in new hotels and office buildings. In Los Angeles, women found low-paying factory jobs as well. In both cities, men found jobs as janitors, as gardeners for increasingly affluent professionals, as busboys in the booming restaurant business, or as construction workers. However, as this boom gave way to the recession of the early 1990s (compounded by the 1989 Loma Prieta earthquake in San Francisco and the 1992 riots in Los Angeles), even these low-paying jobs became scarce. The result has been increased job competition among newcomer immigrants and, for immigrant men, a shift toward day labor from low-paying formal jobs (Chinchilla & Hamilton, 1992, p. 87).

All the participants in this study were either looking for work or employed. Those who worked held low-paying temporary or part-time (usually both) service jobs, and many worked without documents. Interestingly, more women than men were employed.[6] This situation may be indicative of the demand for domestic jobs that, as

Repak (1995) observed, are available even in recessionary times (p. 103), or it may reflect how gender ideologies play out in the local labor markets (Menjívar, 1997, p. 110). Men do not work in domestic jobs. Their work in gardening, construction, and restaurants requires them to be more visible than if they worked inside a home as most women do. In a tight labor market, when the employers are supposed to be held accountable by the INS, it is easier to fill domestic jobs with undocumented women because that type of employment is harder to regulate. Although women may work more hours and may even earn more than men do, the lack of control inherent in domestic work often translates into job instability. Besides, when both men and women work, men earn more than women do. However, as we will see in the following section, this situation carries significant consequences for gender relations.

EFFECTS OF U.S. EMPLOYMENT

Employment has been seen as a source of women's increased bargaining power and control over resources, which, in turn, is believed to be the basis for personal liberty and more egalitarian relationships within the home (Benería & Roldán, 1987; Safa, 1995). However, a close examination of the cases in this study suggests that the situation is more complex. For these immigrant women, entry into paid work in the United States is not an unqualified indication of empowerment and improved status within the family.

In general, for these women, particularly for the ladina Guatemalans and Salvadorans, earning an income in the United States has had uneven consequences. Patriarchal gender notions have been somewhat relaxed primarily because of the precarious conditions in which these immigrants live. Some ladinas mentioned that they feel "stronger" in the United States; however, most of the women's evaluations of their new situations do not reveal a straightforward correlation between work and emancipation. For example, Esperanza, a ladina, explained,

> Here we are all equal, we both work [for an income], so we both have to do stuff at home, there's no way around it. But I can't really say that it's better here or there, because there I didn't work [outside the home] this much. Here I earn more, but there I worked less.

Some found that U.S. employment has improved their self-esteem, if not their social status. Rosa, a Salvadoran, explained,

> We are all humans so we all change a little in another country. . . . Maybe it's the lifestyle. Here, the man and the woman, both have to work to be able to pay the rent, the food, the clothes, a lot of expenses. Probably that . . . makes us, the women, a little freer in the United States . . . the ones who work. Because maybe yes, in El Salvador I didn't feel as secure as I feel here. In this country if you are courageous and have strength, you can get ahead by yourself, with or without him [a husband]. There are more opportunities for the person who wants to get ahead . . . no matter if it's a

man or a woman. Then, possibly, I would say that's why here the woman doesn't follow the man more.

In contrast, indigenous Guatemalans tended to be less ambivalent and commented on the fact that the new environment provided different possibilities for
both men and women. As Miriam, a K'iche, put it,

> I have earned a living since I was 9, so work is part of me, and here it's the same. But
> other things are different here. In Guatemala everything is harder for us . . . maybe
> because we are poor or because . . . we are different. . . . People think that because we
> wear *traje* [traditional indigenous clothing] we can't think or something. But here no,
> it's different. Here you can do something with your work, there are possibilities, op-
> portunities for us. Here I feel more equal to everyone [nonindigenous]. . . . This is bet-
> ter for both men and women, I would say.

Miriam's viewpoint may be related to gender relations that are relatively more egalitarian among indigenous Guatemalans than are those among ladino Guatemalans
or Salvadorans. Comparisons of gender relations between ladino and indigenous
Guatemalans have emphasized the greater male dominance among ladino men,
whereas indigenous gender relations have been characterized as more egalitarian
(Bossen, 1984; Loucky, 1988; Maynard, 1974; Wolf, 1959, 1966). Also, because
Miriam perceived better opportunities in the United States in comparison with
what she faced in Guatemala as an indigenous person, the gender component of
her experience took second stage.

"Here One Earns Almost to Support One's Husband": Women as Main Earners and Its Consequences

As indicated earlier, an important aspect in the experiences of these immigrants is
that women often work longer hours than men do and, thus, may earn more than
the men even though the women are paid less for their work. Oftentimes, women
are the major contributors, or even the sole earners, in a household. It must be
emphasized that the important fact here is that some women work while their husbands or partners do not. This situation, where the men's authority is reduced as
a consequence of the women's increased economic contributions, has been observed in other groups (Kibria, 1994; Kudat, 1982; Lamphere, 1987), and it has been
noted that this may lead to conflict. Similarly, in this study, I argue that when women
become the main providers they do not gain more authority automatically, and it
often brings serious, negative consequences for them. Many times, men turn to
drinking out of frustration at failing to fulfill their socially expected role. This creates conditions ripe for domestic violence. In the words of Lolita, a Salvadoran,

> The Salvadoran man continues to be macho here. . . . The man becomes dependent
> on the woman. The woman goes to work, not the man. But men bring machismo
> with them, and the woman takes on more responsibility. . . . When men see themselves

like that, they drink and that only brings a lot of problems home. . . . The women end up suffering a lot because the men let their frustrations out by beating the women. I have not seen a family that is in good shape yet.

When these women assess their predicaments, they often do so in ambiguous ways. The case of Amparo, a self-described housewife in rural El Salvador who used to make tortillas and raise chickens for sale, exemplifies this pattern. In her words,

There [in El Salvador] one earns to help one's husband, here one earns almost to support one's husband. The men don't like this because they can't order around the house anymore. For women it would be better if they [the husbands] worked more because that's why they become very irresponsible here. There they have to earn because it's their obligation. Here they think "oh she can [earn] so I don't have to." So there are positives and negatives, everything has advantages and disadvantages.[7]

However, ethnicity introduces an important qualification in this respect. Perhaps because indigenous Guatemalans start out from a more egalitarian point, indigenous men do not appear as threatened as the ladino Guatemalans or Salvadorans do when the women are the main, or even sole, earners. In some cases, indigenous men even encourage the women to get ahead. The case of Hermelinda, a Kaqchikel, exemplifies this point. Her husband Jacobo, a day laborer, has not been successful in finding a steady job even though he goes to stand at the "corner"—the place where day laborers congregate to wait for prospective employers—every single day. Hermelinda, on the other hand, has been baby-sitting almost since she arrived and, thus, has been financially responsible for the household. In fact, 2 days after Hermelinda gave birth, she had to resume baby-sitting two children because this was the only source of stable income they had. She also does embroidery to sell when the children she baby-sits are gone. Jacobo confided that he is personally worried about this situation and would like her to stop working, not because his "reputation as a man is at risk," but because he wants something different for both. Recognizing the value of her work, he explained,

I want her to stop baby-sitting, not because I don't want her to work . . . she's always worked, but because I don't want to get stuck. There are many opportunities here and she is smart in business and she can learn English quickly. Only if she learns English can she find a better job, and we can get ahead. It upsets me to find her at home all the time, when she could be doing something better.

Whereas the women's increased ability to procure jobs became an affront for some ladino Guatemalan and Salvadoran men, indigenous men saw it as an opportunity for both to get ahead.

Social Class, Aspirations, and the Meaning of Work

Many ladina Guatemalans and Salvadorans, particularly those with middle-class aspirations, see paid employment as an economic necessity, as a temporary strategy to get ahead. This point underscores Fernández-Kelly and García's (1990) observation of the Cuban women who saw their garment jobs as transitory in order to recover or attain a middle-class status. With few exceptions, these Central American women mentioned that the only reason they work is that they could not live on the husband's income alone; with a more comfortable life, they would opt not to work. Their husbands agreed and expressed their frustration at not being able to be the sole providers (in some cases, for not providing at all) for their families. In the words of Julio, a Salvadoran,

> Believe me, I feel as if my hands are tied, and my head ready to explode from the tension and disappointment. I don't want to be a *mantenido* [supported] by the wife. I don't feel like a man, I feel like a lady, and excuse me, but that's really terrible, insulting, for a man who's used to providing for his family.

Some of the women who worked as housekeepers mentioned that they could not understand why some of their female employers, in spite of "having money," continued to work. Alicia, a Guatemalan, commented,

> If I were Mrs. Brooks, I would spend my days sitting at home reading, *paseando* [going places], waking up late. No, instead of that, no, she goes out to work every single day. These Americans have customs that one never understands.

The point here is that these women do not see their work in a liberating light but only as a way to meet the survival requirements of their families. Clearly, these women's entry into paid work is predicated on their husbands' or companions' lack of adequate earnings; once the economic status of the men is reconstituted, the women wish to withdraw from employment.

For indigenous women, on the other hand, even though work is an economic necessity as well, historico-cultural factors prompt them to see it in a different light. Rosa, a K'iche, said,

> Work is a part of life for both [men and women] here or in Guatemala. . . . Well, for us [indigenous people], it is. The man always has things to do, and the woman, too. In Guate[mala] I wove and sold my textiles and he worked the land. Here he works in different things, and I make food for sale and baby-sit. A woman always has to be busy, always has to work. She is more appreciated if she works hard. There's even a saying that the idle woman gets the devil in her head.

In contrast with ladina Guatemalans and Salvadorans, indigenous Guatemalan women's entry into employment does not depend on the economic vulnerability of men. Thus, they do not desire to withdraw from employment once the men regain their economic positions because these women have a different sociocultural perception of work. They do not have the same ethnic- and class-specific perceptions of work and aspirations as the women in the other two groups.

I had the opportunity to observe how earning an income gives some women a measure of independence with regard to spending. They dispose of it in ways that reinforce middle-class (and, to some extent, ethnic-specific) gender ideologies that many women aspire to and consider ideal. Some of my ladina Guatemalan informants invited me to a crystal party (similar to a Tupperware party) one Sunday afternoon. The Salvadoran woman who was selling expensive pieces of crystal emphasized how beautiful these pieces would look in their houses. The women, most of whom bought small pieces (for which they had to pay in installments), pointed out that they may not have beautiful homes in which to display the pieces now, but that it felt good to use them to adorn their humble dwellings either in Los Angeles or back in Guatemala. These women, all ladina Guatemalans of modest origins, joked about an unspecified time in the future when they could be "housewives" and spend time decorating their homes in the style of their employers' homes instead of going to work. In the course of the conversation, it was revealed that the money they would use to purchase the crystal was from their own earnings. Apparently, their husbands—all were recent immigrants, and all but one were working temporary jobs at no more than the minimum wage—considered these "women's things." The husbands either did not understand why the women purchased the crystal or thought of it as an outright waste of money. For the women, on the other hand, these expensive pieces of crystal might symbolize a desire for middle-class status, particularly in the absence of middle-class financial resources.

"But We Really Have Three Families to Support":
Migration Patterns and the Separation of Earnings

There are other cases where paid work in the United States may signify greater freedom for women in terms of spending money, but at the same time may carry negative consequences. Such situations are linked not merely to earning wages and being able to spend them but to a specific migration pattern. As with other immigrants, many Guatemalans and Salvadorans were separated for several years from their partners by the migration of one of them before the other. During their time apart, it was not uncommon for these immigrants to form new unions in the United States, chiefly *acompañándose* (cohabiting) with partners who already had children from previous unions.[8] These U.S.-established unions were significant for my informants. Among the Salvadoran and ladina Guatemalan women who were in unions (whether legally married or acompañadas), slightly fewer than half were or had been in U.S.-established unions. Although there may be indigenous women who established these unions, I did not come across any. Nonetheless, among ladina Guatemalans and Salvadorans, it is a significant pattern that deserves attention, particularly in relation to notions of the family and gender relations. Also, this practice is slightly more common among people who were in consensual unions in their countries than among the legally married, and it must be noted that it did not emerge first in the United States. Historically, among rural, poor (mostly landless) men in El Salvador who made a living as seasonal workers, it was not uncommon to form new unions in the places where they went to work because it was difficult to move their entire families (Menjívar, 1992).[9]

According to informants in these unions, given the difficulty of both migrating from those countries and regularly visiting their families back home, it only made sense to find new partners in the United States. It is noteworthy that the women and men in the U.S.-established unions often have separate financial objectives. Many are responsible for their own families in their countries of origin or in the United States and, therefore, are much more likely to keep their earnings and expenditures separate. In these cases, the women feel that it is imperative to earn their own incomes in order to spend them as they please, especially when they support families back home. Estela, a ladina Guatemalan who works 7 days a week cleaning houses, explained that she will keep on working at this rate due to her responsibilities for her children back home. In her words,

> I can't stop working even if my husband works because, if he supports me, I won't be able to send money to my children. Besides, he can't give me enough money because he has his own family to support. If both of us work, both of us can dispose of money and do with it whatever one pleases. It'd be different if we only had one family, but we really have three families to support . . . and because we're poor, we need to work more.

Maintaining separate finances, however, may actually worsen the women's burden, particularly for ladina Guatemalans and Salvadorans. Some of the men, already feeling constrained by their own inability to command adequate earnings and realizing the women's potential to support the households, have responded by evading their own financial responsibilities. Ethnic differences need to be drawn here again, as this pattern is more common among ladina Guatemalans and Salvadorans than among indigenous Guatemalans. And, although this pattern has encountered fertile soil in the United States given the inability of men to fulfill their socially ascribed role, it predates migration. For instance, Maynard (1974) analyzes two types of patriarchy in Guatemala: a "responsible patriarchy" among indigenous groups and an "irresponsible patriarchy" among ladino Guatemalans. Although men are seen as dominant in both groups, indigenous men are more likely to provide regular support for their families, whereas ladino Guatemalan men seemed less reliable. For the Salvadoran case, Adams (1959/1976) found that women headed approximately 33% of urban and 20% of rural households in the late 1950s in El Salvador. Recent estimates of the national rate of female-headed households in El Salvador range from 27% (García & Gomáriz, 1989) to a high of 40% (Carter, Insko, Loeb, & Tobias, 1989), compared with only 15% in Guatemala. Unlike with the Guatemalans, the Salvadoran rate was high before the conflict began. And, even in the most conservative estimate, the Salvadoran rate is the highest in the region (García & Gomáriz, 1989),[10] due primarily to the previously mentioned historical pattern of seasonal migration among landless, or nearly landless, men.

The case of a Salvadoran couple, Chentía and her husband Don David, demonstrates this pattern.[11] Chentía works for a janitorial company where she is able to make $11 per hour, a high wage by the standards of Salvadoran immigrants, plus a substantial insurance package that covers her entire family. Don David is the manager of the building where they live rent free in addition to his monthly salary of $600, though Chentía was not sure exactly how much Don David was paid. When I first met them, they both mentioned that they shared the household's expenses equally, and Don David boasted of his responsibility, even though he noted that he earned less than she did. However, when I met alone with Chentía a few weeks later, she confided that Don David does not contribute a cent to the household expenses. In her words, "I am supporting him entirely, he doesn't even give me money to buy soap. He puts all his money in the bank, and I have to support him. But I won't do this for long. I don't need him." Chentía's situation might have been further complicated by the fact that she only married Don David in hopes of obtaining a green card, which Don David knew. She pointed out that Don David might not have been contributing to the household in order to make her "pay" for the marriage. As soon as Chentía obtained TPS with help from a community organization, she left Don David.

Similarly, Irma, a ladina Guatemalan, mentioned that she was tired of her consensual partner's excuses for not contributing to the household expenses. Although Irma's partner did not have a steady job, Irma thought he could contribute from the money he had earned from a few odd jobs he had in the previous months. She had been thinking about leaving him to go live with a female cousin who shares an apartment with another woman and her children. In this case, the eventual formation of this female-headed household was probably linked to the increased potential of the women to support their households, but more directly, it had to do with the men's economic instability. This point underscores findings that household formations among U.S. minorities are more affected by the economic vulnerability of men than by the economic well-being of women (Fernández-Kelly & García, 1990; Pessar, 1995).

Division of Labor within the Household

The effects of women's employment on the household division of labor are varied.[12] Some studies have documented a reaffirmation in household gender relations (Goldring, 1996); others have demonstrated greater participation in household chores by husbands or partners (Foner, 1978; Guendelman & Perez-Itriaga, 1987); and still others, notably by Hondagneu-Sotelo (1994), present a complex picture linking negotiations in household work to different types of migration. This study does not offer a simple, straightforward answer, for these arrangements are linked in various ways to broader institutions and to the social position of the immigrants and, as such, present a multiplicity of experiences. The attitudes of the husbands toward women's paid employment are not uniform either. Some, evidently, are opposed to the wife working outside the home because it has the potential to diminish household services; it also serves as a reminder that the husband cannot be the sole provider. Others appreciate the financial contribution from their wives because it allows for both to survive in the United States and, importantly, to send money back home. And still others are ambivalent about the women's entry into paid work in the United States, as this has often meant more than simply a chance to earn money, and the men find it difficult to weigh the pros and cons. Although it is difficult to ascertain exactly what may contribute to the variation in the men's responses, my observations indicate that ethnicity and class may affect these attitudes. Ambivalence or opposition to a working wife seemed to be a particularly important issue among the ladino Guatemalans with aspirations for middle-class status, for whom it was a matter of prestige to support their wives.

The case of Mayra and Ricardo, a Salvadoran couple, serves as an illustration of a transformation in the household division of labor that can be interpreted as resulting directly from Mayra's employment in the United States and how she and her husband perceive it. Mayra worked full-time as a primary-school teacher in San Salvador before she migrated; however, she always saw her income as "complementary" to Ricardo's. In the United States, they both work full-time, but their views have changed—perhaps due to the social perception of her work in El Salvador and the financial challenges in the United States of trying to sustain a family on one income. Ricardo explains,

> Here we both work equally, we both work full-time, and we both have responsibilities at work. If she is asked to stay at work late, I have to stay with the children, feed them, care for them. In El Salvador it was different. I never touched a broom there [laughing] so don't tell anyone you saw me here like this.... There, everyone knows that if a woman is married, she has family responsibilities, and that comes first. So if she needs to quit working because of her family, OK, nobody suffers too much. Here, no. If she quits, we don't eat. That's the truth. Everything is so expensive here: rents, food, hospitals.... We don't have insurance so you can imagine. So she has to work like me, I don't help her [financially], and she doesn't help me. It's equal.

In this case, this new perception has translated into real gains for Mayra in terms of the household division of labor. As Mayra explains,

> Now he washes clothes, cleans, sweeps, and even feeds the girls if I'm not home. I am surprised because in El Salvador he never entered the kitchen. But this is another country. Sometimes I laugh when I see him, but I don't tell him anything so that he won't be embarrassed.

Mayra's cousin Rosa María is not so convinced of the changes in Salvadoran men's attitudes and offered this explanation:

> I believe men help because it's so easy here. Back [in El Salvador] I had to sweep and mop, here it's only the vacuum. There I had to wash by hand, then iron even the sheets. Here, no, you have washing and drying machines. So it's not the same when one says that men do household chores here. Here it is like playing.

The case of Margarita, a ladina Guatemalan, further exemplifies changes in the household division of labor. In her case, however, she relates it to her new position as a wage earner, as she did not work outside the home in Guatemala. She told me that "he [her husband] was the one who worked in Guatemala. I was the house-wife. He used to decide everything . . . and I would do everything, but everything, at home. But things changed here." When I asked her why, she replied,

> Because I think that in this country one [the woman] has to work like the man. Over there he used to tell me not to work, but here I have to, otherwise we can't survive. So the man and the woman change. . . . They have to. So now he takes care of the children, even gives them a bath. You may think this is little, but this is a great trans-formation for him. . . . In Guatemala he would not even get up to get a glass of wa-ter, I had to do it for him. Here he even cooks for himself sometimes! The change is like night and day.[13]

But the change, or its perception, is, of course, rooted in what happened in the past. Thus, according to my indigenous Guatemalan informants, the men's atti-tudes had not changed very much. It is not that indigenous men regularly engaged in household chores in Guatemala, but that "they accommodate to the conditions," as Hermelinda, a Kaqchikel, put it. In her case, her husband would help out at home in Guatemala when Hermelinda could not do everything on her own. So the fact that in the United States he washes dishes, does the laundry, cooks, or irons even after getting home from work (or looking for work), does not surprise Her-melinda. In her words,

> Sometimes he gets home and wants to wash the dishes, and I tell him no, you're tired. But he says that I'm tired because I have been home taking care of the children that I baby-sit. The truth is that we're both tired, so we try to lighten each other's burden a little. . . . So this is the same, here or there [in Guatemala]. What's different is the [actual] work that needs to be done.

Working Women's Balancing Acts

Women's access to regular employment may lead to greater leverage in negotiat-ing assistance with household chores. But when the woman is the sole earner as a result of the man's inability to earn regular wages, it often has the opposite effect, particularly for ladina Guatemalans. Although it may happen among indigenous Guatemalans, I did not observe it in any of the cases in this study. But as the case of Hermelinda, above, suggests, perhaps because indigenous Guatemalans start out from a more egalitarian point, the fact that the woman works when the man cannot does not tend to have the negative consequences that it has in the other groups. Contrary to what one might expect, among the ladina Guatemalans (less so among the Salvadorans) when women are the sole providers for the household, they often have to do all the household chores as well. In these situations, entry into paid work in the United States reaffirms gender relations—either ideologically or practically—and both the men and the women become active agents in this process. In a way, this serves to assure the men, conceivably threatened by the women's improved economic opportunities, that they still hold authority.

The case of Nora, a ladina Guatemalan, exemplifies this point. Nora takes care of an elderly Mexican American woman who has allowed Nora and her family to live with her. Nora finds this extremely taxing because it is a 24-hour, 7-days-a-week job. In addition, she does all the household chores; only when she is exhausted does she ask her children to help her out. She seldom leaves the house—not even to attend mass on Sunday—and feels her life is *esclavizada* (enslaved). Her husband lost his job as a construction worker when he demanded to be hired legally after he became a permanent resident. Although he has been unemployed for more than 6 months, he almost never lends a hand with household chores. Nora seems convinced that it is her duty to do all the housework because, in Guatemala, she used to be a housewife, and thus, she was used to that. Her husband, however, instead of taking steps to increase his participation in household chores, is seeking a solution more in line with his views. He explained, "I am thinking of moving to Reno. I have heard that there are plenty of jobs for men there, so Nora won't have to work and will only take care of the children, as it should be." Nora smiled in approval of her husband's statement.

Other women made a conscious effort to avoid making their husbands or partners feel inadequate, as mentioned by Antonieta, a ladina Guatemalan. Antonieta works from 3 P.M. to midnight as a waitress in a downtown Los Angeles cafeteria. Although she usually stays after the place closes to clean up, she does not get paid overtime for it. Her partner tries hard to find regular employment but has found only temporary jobs. Before Antonieta leaves for work, she prepares her partner's dinner and makes sure the house is clean. Apparently, he does not like reheated dishes and prefers Guatemalan-style meals, so she must cook every day because he will not accept a sandwich or a ready-made meal. Sometimes, when Antonieta returns home, she washes the dishes from her partner's dinner, though often she leaves them for the next day. Even though Antonieta recognizes the superhuman character of her efforts, she does it all because

> it's the way it should be. The woman has to take care of the house. . . . If I work, that's because I have to. But I don't want to make him feel as if I'm the man of the house. . . . It's not right. . . . It creates problems . . . because it's not normal.

This point parallels the balancing act that Kudat (1982) discusses in her study of Turkish women.

In these cases I have presented, both Nora and Antonieta see their position as main or sole earners as temporary—and somewhat aberrant at that. Thus, they do not upset what is perceived as normative, that is, orthodox arrangements in the household division of labor, even if they are cognizant of the great burden that their double shifts represent. Still, for other women who are aware of their double shifts, particularly legally married women, the objective is different. Carmen, a Salvadoran, explained,

> I kill myself working all day and come home to keep on working, it's very tiring. . . .
> But when one is married, has children, I say to myself, one has to see that the household doesn't disintegrate, that we stay united.

Carmen's words echo a statement by a Dominican informant in Pessar's (1995) study that Pessar interprets as an illustration of the struggle working-class women face (pp. 43–44). Moreover, efforts such as Carmen's to maintain the conjugal unit are related not only to the women's fears that they will be left financially incapacitated if they separate from their husbands but also to the social meaning of a marital union. In the case of many Central Americans, the conjugal unit is an idealized family pattern—a symbol associated with middle-class standing and a luxury that cannot be shared by all. Female-headed households, on the other hand, are commonly associated with lower-class background (Bossen, 1984, pp. 161, 289; Ferrán, 1974).

Employment and Gender Ideology

From my observations, the potential effects of paid work in the United States on gender relations for the women in this study cannot be discussed in purely economic terms. Possible advantages do not seem to stem directly from the economic gains of employment but from the particular social process that accompanies it. For many women, it is not the sole act of working and earning wages that brings changes to their worlds but the social organization of their work. The lives of most of these immigrants are structured so that they do not actively interact with the wider society; instead they live, shop, and socialize mainly with other Latinos. However, the organization of women's and men's work differs, and it exposes them to dissimilar worlds where they observe behaviors and practices and take in new ideas. The work women perform allows them to observe practices and behaviors beyond their immediate groups, which they may selectively incorporate in their own routines. Besides, women are typically more enthusiastic about embracing values that would enhance their position (Foner, 1997). This is not a crude form of assimilation, for these women do not claim to abandon practices they bring with them and become "Americanized," but a more subtle social process that takes place as they come into contact with the world of their employers.

Baby-sitting, cleaning, and caring for the elderly are tasks that are accomplished individually, presenting isolating experiences that keep these women away from other Latinas. Women are not isolated from one another as they gain access to jobs through networks with fellow Latina women, but they spend many hours laboring alone.[14] However, at work, these women—particularly live-in domestics—are more exposed to their employers' middle-class patterns of behavior (particularly within the household). Whereas the social organization of work exposes women to progressive changes in gender relations, work serves to reaffirm for the men the gender orthodoxy brought from home. The work men tend to do—gardening, construction, restaurant services—brings them in close contact primarily with other Latino men and, thus, does not so readily allow them to observe novel gender relations. This is particularly the case among the more educated ladina Guatemalans and the Salvadorans, who may see it as socially feasible to adopt some of their employers' behaviors. According to Lolita, a Salvadoran with a college degree who was a labor organizer in her country,

> We have to reeducate the people, in various ways, starting with the men. Imagine, I work with a couple, caring for their baby. She's Jewish and he's Irish. I like the way they are with each other, very understanding. He helps in the house, and they seem happy. She and I talk about these things. I ask how she did it, and she laughs. But just to see how they live, it's exemplary, and it shows the happy side of being married. Why can't Salvadoran men learn from this?

The case of Ana Ruth and Mauricio, a Salvadoran couple, further exemplifies the ladina Guatemalans' and Salvadorans' desire to adopt U.S. gender relations that they witness in their workplaces. Ana Ruth has been cleaning houses for three Anglo families for 2 years and reports that she sees a lot of what she would like Mauricio and her to "imitate because it's good." For instance, she recalls how the husband of one of the families minds the baby and cooks dinner because the wife routinely stays at work late. "Americans have good customs. . . . I see it a lot in the houses where I work, and it'd be nice if we could live like them." Mauricio does not quite see it that way and laughs whenever Ana Ruth brings up the topic. He jokes that Ana Ruth "gets her head full of things because she watches too much TV," and he teases her by suggesting that she "is trying to imitate her employers, she thinks she'll become a gringa. . . . It's foolish." Ana Ruth does not give up and adds,

> Little by little he'll see other things, like I did. When I came here I had other ideas, but I have seen other things around me. One learns good things here. The problem is that Mauricio hangs out with our people, and you know how macho they are, the Salvadorans, Nicaraguans, and Mexicans, and they fill his head with garbage.

Similar to the Dominican women in Grasmuck and Pessar's study (1991), these women were attempting to pattern more egalitarian relationships with their partners based on what they perceived as the American model. But, once again, ethnicity introduces an important qualification here. Indigenous Guatemalans (and perhaps others with similarly disadvantaged backgrounds) may perceive their social worlds as too distant from those of their employers and, thus, may not consider incorporating some of those behaviors into their own. Besides, as has been widely documented (Bossen, 1984; Loucky, 1988; Maynard, 1974; Wolf, 1959), indigenous women already experience relatively more egalitarian gender relations and, thus, may not see the need to incorporate many changes into their families.[15]

The future, as well as the present, does not hold clear answers regarding the consequences of migration for gender relations. Some women see a definite advantage in remaining in the United States. They see the benefit as not so much improving their own social position in the household but as providing opportunities for their children. Others, particularly those trying to attain or reclaim a middle-class status, believe that it is more feasible to attain this goal in their own countries if they are able to return with enough savings. And still others, given the uncertainty of their legal status and its consequences for their overall economic prospects in the United States, believe that the best course to take would be to return home, in spite of perceived gains in the United States. Although no one I interviewed was actually planning to return home, several men and women were paying off mortgages for houses or plots of land they had bought in El Salvador and Guatemala, as they thought such investments ensured future security.

CONCLUDING REMARKS

My intention in this study was to understand the intersection of U.S. paid work and gender relations in the family lives of Central American immigrant women. Earning an income in the United States has had ambivalent consequences for the social status of Central American women; they have experienced both benefits and losses. It appears that immigration has contributed both to reaffirm and to transform gender relations. In my view, a partial explanation for this ambiguity can be found in the dissimilar, albeit severely constrained, structure of opportunities that Central American men and women encounter in the United States. The structure of opportunity for these immigrants is shaped by restrictive immigration policies that deny them security of residence and rights to work and by the dynamics of the local economy. Within this general framework, however, men and women face dissimilar conditions. Gender ideologies and the local labor markets in San Francisco and Los Angeles place the mostly undocumented women in a relatively favorable position with respect to access to paid work, whereas their male peers do not fare so well.

The dynamics of the local labor market, therefore, have facilitated these immigrant women's opportunities for work; they often work more hours and even earn more than men do. The consequences of this situation, however, reflect the women's vulnerability rather than their independence; it does not automatically benefit women and sometimes ends up reinforcing gender subordination in families. Gender ideologies rooted in social and cultural prescriptions qualify the link between women's employment and a potential increase in their status within the family. If the men feel threatened because they cannot fulfill the socially ascribed role of the breadwinner, the women experience losses. These men often respond by diminishing their own responsibilities, thereby creating great burdens—physically and financially—for the women at home. Furthermore, the social organization of the work to which these men and women have access exposes them to dissimilar practices and ideologies. Employment as domestic workers gives women the opportunity to witness relatively more egalitarian gender behaviors that they perceive as beneficial and wish to incorporate in their own lives. For men, employment in gardening, construction, or restaurants serves to reproduce orthodox gender ideologies because it brings them close to peers with such views. This differential exposure affects the women's and men's perceptions of gender relations in families. Thus, the effects of immigrant women's employment do not depend mechanistically on the ability of the women to earn wages. It is the social process of employment that alters gender relations among men and women.

Macrostructural forces affect relations within a family or a household. These forces, however, manifest themselves differently as they interact with the social position—determined by class, ethnicity, and nationality—of the immigrants, as it differentiates benefits and rewards available to them. The cases in this study indicate that the social position of the immigrants does make a difference with respect to how immigrant women's paid work in the United States is perceived and how household arrangements are negotiated. Ladino Guatemalan and Salvadoran immigrants often value orthodox middle-class gender ideals such as stable and legal unions where the men are the financial providers and the women guard a unified family and domesticity. Yet, they often live in unstable situations and in poverty that preclude them from realizing such ideals. In these cases, the material conditions in their lives undermine what otherwise would be ideal—the upholding of patriarchal family roles. For indigenous Guatemalan immigrants who hold relatively more egalitarian notions about gender relations, the potential benefits of immigration for women may not be materialized. They have restricted access to institutional resources and must toil in unregulated jobs that pay little and offer few opportunities for social mobility.

This study has explored only a few aspects of the immigrants' social positions, and it has offered only a glimpse of the complexity in gender relations. The intersection of other social characteristics and dissimilar contexts is likely to generate a variety of experiences at different points of time and place, even for the same immigrant group. A lesson to be learned might be that this plurality of experiences precludes a universal answer applicable to all immigrant women. However, these explorations may prove fruitful avenues for research, as they may offer more nuanced assessments of the effects of immigration on gender relations and, thus, reflect more accurately the immigrants' social worlds.

NOTES

1. The term *ladina* or *ladino* denotes the nonindigenous Guatemalans, mostly mestizos (but also some European descendants) who have been culturally Hispanicized. The indigenous population of Guatemala makes up more than half of the total population of the country.

2. Salvadoran women have a long tradition of labor force participation (Carter, Insko, Loeb, & Tobias, 1989; Garcia & Gomáriz, 1989; Ministerio Público de El Salvador, 1983;

Nieves, 1979). The rate of employment in formal activities reached 37% in 1988 (Garcia & Gomáriz, 1989, p. 115), and it might have been up to 40% by 1990. Their participation in the informal sector is also substantial and, in some cases, surpasses that of men. Among non-indigenous Guatemalan women, the labor force participation rate has been reported at 27.6%, whereas among indigenous women it is close to 20%. This lower reported rate for indigenous women is due to the underreporting of their employment in agricultural and artisanal activities (García & Gomáriz, 1989, p. 198).

3. In addition to marked demographic differences, these groups differ in sociocultural characteristics, including, as we will see later, important aspects of gender relations. In fact, ladino Guatemalans and Salvadorans share similar patterns of gender relations that differ from those among indigenous Guatemalans.

4. These names are usually spelled in the literature as *Cackchiquel* and *Quiché*. The spellings I use are those used by the Guatemalan Ministry of Education and indigenous groups themselves in Guatemala.

5. Of the Salvadorans I interviewed (including the 24 Salvadoran men not in this study) who had some form of documents, more than half were men. I did not interview Guatemalan men independent from the women in this study (I only interviewed those that were related to my female informants), but in the lives of these women almost twice the number of men had documents.

6. It becomes difficult to evaluate this difference quantitatively because during my fieldwork (which lasted close to 4 years among the Salvadorans and about 1 year among the Guatemalans) only a handful of my informants were able to keep their jobs for long. The great majority (of both men and women) worked temporarily, which does not allow me to provide an exact number of how many more women than men worked because, so often, both would be out of a job. However, the women consistently were able to find jobs more quickly than the men were. And because of the nature of women's jobs (e.g., caring for the young and the elderly), they seemed to be able to hold on to their jobs longer than the men could.

7. Even though in Amparo's experience men become irresponsible in the United States, one must not forget the fact that this is also a problem that many women in El Salvador face, particularly single and divorced mothers (see Baires, Marroquín, Murguialday, Polanco, & Vásquez, 1996).

8. Some studies have found that migration increases the chances for union dissolution. Landale and Ogena (1995) discuss the prevalence of marital dissolution among Puerto Rican women who have migrated to the U.S. mainland.

9. Unfortunately, there is very scant information on family formations and formal and consensual unions in El Salvador, particularly prior to the conflict; thus, direct comparisons with the U.S. situation cannot be made.

10. In Central America, as in other regions, the type of marriage is related to class background, with most middle- or upper-middle class people marrying legally, and the poor in both urban and rural areas remaining in consensual unions. Bossen (1984) found that 90% of marriages in a middle-class suburb in Guatemala City were legally contracted, as opposed to approximately 40% in poorer locations, with both indigenous and ladino Guatemalan populations (pp. 161, 289).

11. There is a reason why I do not refer to them equally. Don David was in his 70s, so like everyone else, I called him Don David out of respect. At first, I started addressing Chentía with either *Niña* (the colloquial Salvadoran word to convey respect for a woman of any age) or *Doña*. But she did not want me to use these forms of address because she said that

she was young, "not old like him." As their relationship deteriorated, she emphasized their 24-year age difference more and more. Often, she would use the age difference to get back at him, and it was an area where Chentía could "win." Don David, for his part, made snide remarks about her "youth." This got much worse for Don David when Chentía left him and married a man much younger than herself.

12. Even though it is very difficult to assess what goes on with the household division of labor, even with participant observation, I will discuss it because it was an area that my informants invariably brought up in our conversations about changes in gender relations.

13. Even though Margarita's life in Guatemala may appear to have been under the control of her husband, she was the one who took the initiative and made all the arrangements to migrate (with help from her brothers who were already in the United States). After 11 months, she sent money for her husband to join her. The point here is to reiterate that gender relations are uneven and complex, and even if one area of these women's lives may reflect a strict patriarchal ideology, another one may reveal more egalitarian grounds.

14. Hagan (1996) finds that the networks of live-in domestics are limited in their assistance potential and that many of these women end up isolated from the rest of the community.

15. Another factor that may be operating here is that a strong value in Guatemalan indigenous culture is the preservation of a distinct sociocultural identity. The indigenous Guatemalans have been resisting cultural encroachment by other groups for five centuries, and thus, they may be more equipped to resist the easy incorporation of U.S. customs and ideologies. The ladino Guatemalans and Salvadorans, on the other hand, may be less resistant because their cultural identities in their countries have not been threatened, and consequently, they have less experience resisting cultural encroachment.

REFERENCES

Adams, R. N. (1976). *Cultural surveys of Panama, Nicaragua, Guatemala, El Salvador, & Honduras* (Pan American Sanitary Bureau, World Health Organization). Detroit, MI: Ethridge. (Original work published 1959)

Aron, A., Corne, S., Fursland, A., & Zelwer, B. (1991). The gender-specific terror of El Salvador and Guatemala. *Women's Studies International Forum, 14,* 37–47.

Bachu, P. (1986). Work, dowry, and marriage among East African Sikh women in the United Kingdom. In R. J. Simon & C. Brettell (Eds.), *International migration: The female experience* (pp. 229–240). Totowa, NJ: Rowman & Allanheld.

Baires, S., Marroquín, D., Murguialday, C., Polanco, R., & Vásquez, N. (1996). Mami, mami, demanda la quota . . . la necesitamos: Un análisis feminista sobre la demanda de cuota alimenticia a la Procuraduría [Mommy, mommy, ask for the dues . . . A feminist analysis of the demand of the food dues from the General Attorney's Office for the Poor]. (Mujeres por la Dignidad y la Vida—Las Dignas). San Salvador, El Salvador: Algier's Impresores.

Benería, L., & Roldán, M. (1987). *The crossroads of class and gender: Industrial homework, subcontracting, and household dynamics in Mexico City.* Chicago: University of Chicago Press.

Bossen, L. H. (1984). *The redivision of labor: Women and economic choice in four Guatemalan communities.* Albany: State University of New York Press.

Carter, B., Insko, K., Loeb, D., & Tobias, M. (1989). *A dream compels us: Voices of Salvadoran women.* Boston: South End.

Chinchilla, N. S., & Hamilton, N. (1992). Seeking refuge in the city of angels. In G. Riposa & C. Deusch (Eds.), *City of angels* (pp. 84–100). Dubuque, IA: Kendall/Hunt.

Fernández-Kelly, M. P., & García, A. M. (1990). Power surrendered, power restored: The politics of work and family among Hispanic garment workers in California and Florida. In L. A. Tilly & P. Gurin (Eds.), *Women, politics, and change* (pp. 130–149). New York: Russell Sage Foundation.

Ferrán, F. (1974). La "familia nuclear" de la subcultura de la pobreza Dominicana [The "nuclear family" of the subculture of Dominican poverty]. *Estudios Sociales, 27*, 137–185.

Foner, N. (1978). *Jamaica farewell: Jamaican migrants in London.* Berkeley & Los Angeles: University of California Press.

Foner, N. (1986). Sex roles and sensibilities: Jamaican women in New York City. In R. J. Simon & C. Brettell (Eds.), *International migration: The female experience* (pp. 133–151). Totowa, NJ: Rowman & Allanheld.

Foner, N. (1997). The immigrant family: Cultural legacies and cultural changes. *International Migration Review, 31*, 961–974.

Garcia, A. I., & Gomáriz, E. (1989). *Mujeres Centroamericanas: Ante la crísis, la guerra y el proceso de paz: Tomo I. Tendencias Estructurales* [Central American women: Confronting the crisis, the war, and the peace process: Vol. 1. Structural factors]. San José, Costa Rica: FLACSO.

Georges, E. (1990). *The making of a transnational community: Migration, development, and cultural change in the Dominican Republic.* New York: Columbia University Press.

Glenn, E. N. (1986). *Issei, Nisei, war bride: Three generations of Japanese American women in domestic service.* Philadelphia: Temple University Press.

Goldring, L. (1996). Gendered memory: Constructions of rurality among Mexican transnational migrants. In E. M. Dupuis & P. Vandergeest (Eds.), *Creating the countryside: The politics of rural and environmental discourse* (pp. 301–329). Philadelphia: Temple University Press.

Grasmuck, S., & Pessar, P. R. (1991). *Between two islands: Dominican international migration.* Berkeley & Los Angeles: University of California Press.

Guarnaccia, P. J., & Farias, P. (1988). The social meanings of nervios: A case study of a Central American woman. *Social Science Medicine, 26*, 1223–1231.

Guendelman, S., & Perez-Itriaga, A. (1987). Double lives: The changing role of women in seasonal migration. *Women's Studies, 13*, 249–271.

Hagan, J. M. (1994). *Deciding to be legal: A Mayan community in Houston.* Philadelphia: Temple University Press.

Hagan, J. M. (1996). *Social networks, gender, and immigrant settlement: Resource and constraint* (WPS 96-8r). Houston: University of Houston, Center for Immigration Research.

Hondagneu-Sotelo, P. (1994). *Gendered transitions: Mexican experiences of immigration.* Berkeley & Los Angeles: University of California Press.

Jones, R. C. (1989). Causes of Salvadorean migration to the United States. *Geographical Review, 79*(2), 183–194.

Kibria, N. (1990). Power, patriarchy, and gender conflict in the Vietnamese community. *Gender and Society, 4*, 9–24.

Kibria, N. (1994). Household structure and family ideologies: The dynamics of immigrant economic adaptation among Vietnamese refugees. *Social Problems, 41*, 81–96.

Kudat, A. (1982). Personal, familial and societal impacts of Turkish women's migration to Europe. In *Living in two cultures: The socio-cultural situation of migrant workers and their families* (pp. 291–305). New York: Gower Publishing & UNESCO Press.

Lamphere, L. (1987). *From working daughters to working mothers: Immigrant women in a New England industrial community.* Ithaca, NY: Cornell University Press.

Landale, N. S., & Ogena, N. B. (1995). Migration and union dissolution among Puerto Rican women. *International Migration Review, 29,* 671–692.

Lopez, D. E., Popkin, E., & Telles, E. (1996). Central Americans: At the bottom, struggling to get ahead. In R. Waldinger & M. Bozorgmehr (Eds.), *Ethnic Los Angeles* (pp. 279–304). New York: Russell Sage.

Loucky, J. (1988). *Children's work and family survival in highland Guatemala.* Unpublished doctoral dissertation, Department of Anthropology, University of California, Los Angeles.

Mahler, S. (1995). *American dreaming: Immigrant life on the margins.* Princeton, NJ: Princeton University Press.

Manz, B. (1988). *Refugees of a hidden war: The aftermath of counterinsurgency.* Albany: State University of New York Press.

Martin-Forbes, S. (1992). *Refugee women.* London: Zed Books.

Maynard, E. (1974). Guatemalan women: Life under two types of patriarchy. In C. Matthiasson (Ed.), *Many sisters* (pp. 77–98). New York: Free Press.

Menjívar, C. (1992). *Salvadoran migration to the United States: The dynamics of social networks in international migration.* Unpublished doctoral dissertation, Department of Sociology, University of California, Davis.

Menjívar, C. (1993). History, economy, and politics: Macro and micro-level factors in recent Salvadorean migration to the U.S. *Journal of Refugee Studies, 6,* 350–371.

Menjívar, C. (1997). Immigrant kinship networks and the impact of the receiving context: Salvadorans in San Francisco in the early 1990s. *Social Problems, 44,* 104–123.

Ministerio Público de El Salvador. (1983). *Procuraduría general de pobres, Oficina de la mujer. Primera jornada de trabajo de la oficina de la mujer, tema: El empleo* [General Attorney's Office for the Poor, Office of the Woman. First workshop of the Office of the Woman, topic: Employment]. San Salvador, El Salvador: Author.

Montes, S., & García, J. J. (1988). *Salvadoran migration to the United States: An exploratory study.* Washington, DC: Center for Immigration Policy and Refugee Assistance, Hemispheric Migration Project, Georgetown University.

Morokvasic, M. (1984). Birds of passage are also women. *International Migration Review, 18,* 886–907.

National Asylum Study Project. (1992). *An interim assessment of the asylum process of the Immigration and Naturalization Service* (Immigration and Refugee Program, Program of the Legal Profession, Harvard Law School). Cambridge, MA: Harvard University.

Nieves, I. (1979). Household arrangements and multiple jobs in San Salvador. *Signs, 5,* 134–142.

Pessar, P. (1995). On the homefront and in the workplace: Integrating immigrant women into feminist discourse. *Anthropological Quarterly, 68,* 37–47.

Portes, A., & Rumbaut, R. G. (1996). *Immigrant America: A portrait* (2nd ed.). Berkeley & Los Angeles: University of California Press.

Repak, T. A. (1995). *Waiting on Washington: Central American workers in the nation's capital.* Philadelphia: Temple University Press.

Rodriguez, N. P., & Hagan, J. M. (1992). Apartment reconstructing and Latino immigrants: A case study. *Comparative Urban and Community Research, 4,* 164–180.

Safa, H. I. (1995). *The myth of the male breadwinner: Women and industrialization in the Caribbean.* Boulder, CO: Westview.

Seller, M. S. (Ed.). (1981). *Immigrant women.* Philadelphia: Temple University Press.

Stanley, W. (1987). Economic migrants or refugees from violence? A time-series analysis of Salvadorean migration to the United States. *Latin American Research Review, 22,* 132–154.

Stepputat, F. (1994). Repatriation and the politics of space: The case of the Mayan diaspora and return movement. *Journal of Refugee Studies, 7,* 175–185.

Tienda, M., & Booth, K. (1991). Gender, migration, and social change. *International Sociology, 6,* 51–72.

Torres-Rivas, E., & Jiménez, D. (1985). Informe sobre el estado de las migraciones en Centro América [Report on the state of migration within Central America]. *Anuario de Estudios Centroamericanos, 11,* 25–66.

Ward, T. (1987). *Price of fear: Salvadorean refugees in the city of angels.* Unpublished doctoral dissertation, Social Work, University of California, Los Angeles.

Wolf, E. (1959). *Sons of the shaking earth.* Chicago: University of Chicago Press.

Wolf, E. (1966). *Peasants.* Englewood Cliffs, NJ: Prentice Hall.

Zavella, P. (1987). *Women's work and Chicano families: Cannery workers of the Santa Clara Valley.* Ithaca, NY: Cornell University Press.

Zavella, P. (1991). Mujeres in factories: Race and class perspectives on women, work, and family. In M. di Leonardo (Ed.), *Gender at the crossroads of knowledge* (pp. 312–336). Berkeley & Los Angeles: University of California Press.

Zinn, M. Baca (1996). Family, feminism, and race in America. In E. Ngan-Ling Chow, D. Wilkinson, & M. Baca Zinn (Eds.), *Race, class, and gender: Common bonds, different voices* (pp. 169–183). Thousand Oaks, CA: Sage.

CHAPTER 7

Israeli and Russian Jews

Gendered Perspectives on Settlement and Return Migration

Steven J. Gold

INTRODUCTION

The study of gendered settlement decisions offers a valuable corrective to models of migration that either ignore gender or understand migrant gender relations in terms of idealized cooperative family arrangements. By examining how women and men adapt to host societies and evaluate plans to stay on or return, scholars demonstrate that a group's presence in a new national setting causes women and men to encounter distinct structures of opportunity and consequently transforms their relations with each other (Grasmuck & Pessar, 1991; Hirsch, 1999; Hondagneu-Sotelo, 1994, 1995; Kibria, 1993; Pessar, 1999).

Studies of Latina and Asian immigrant women reveal that while women must shoulder new responsibilities in host settings, at the same time, through paid work, they also gain access to levels of income and power that were unavailable in the country of origin. Consequently, they plan to stay on. In contrast, co-national men generally find the new setting to be less congenial, due to their newly subordinated racial status, lack of legal standing, limited earnings, and lessened prestige. In reaction, they seek to return home (Gilbertson, 1995; Grasmuck & Pessar, 1991; Pedraza, 1991; Waters, 2000). In a now classic statement, Patricia Pessar (1986, p. 276) asserts that women migrants are generally immune to the tension between "the household in the host society and the home community" that imperils migrant men: "In contrast to men, migration does not rupture the social sphere in which women are self-actualized. On the contrary, migration reinforces women's attachment to the household because it emerges as a more valued institution and becomes a social field for women to achieve greater autonomy and equity with their male partners."

While this body of literature has contributed much to our understanding of gender in migration, its ability to characterize the full range of migrant populations is hindered for three reasons. First, nearly all of this research has been conducted among immigrants of color, often undocumented working-class labor migrants entering the United States from weak nation-states in Latin America, the Caribbean, and Asia. While there are sound reasons to study these groups, in limiting our scholarly gaze to them we restrict our ability to generate a more comprehensive theory that can address the experience of women from a more inclusive set of national, class, cultural, and racial origins and contexts of settlement (Espiritu, 1997; Lessinger, 1995). For example, it is difficult to specify the impact of racialization or undocumented status on women migrants without considering the experience of groups who are privileged in terms of race and legal status (Gabaccia, 1994; Gold, 2000; Light & Gold, 2000, chap. 6).[1]

In fact, several reports suggest that women from relatively resource-rich migrant groups sometimes gain less through migration relative to co-national men than is the case among the women of proletarian groups (Dallalfar, 1994; Lev-Ari, 2000; Min, 1998). This is because affluent and/or educated migrant men often deploy social, economic, cultural, and religious resources to retain positions of patriarchal status and control in host societies. Despite their economic resources and their significant contributions to family businesses and community building, middle-class migrant women from Soviet Central Asia, Israel, Iran, Korea, and Vietnam are subject to social isolation, confinement to domestic roles, and even physical threats, undergirded by coethnic men's social, economic, and human capital in places of settlement (Bui, 1998; Dallalfar, 1994; Gold, 1995b; Min, 1998; Orleck, 1999).

A second flaw in existing research on gender and settlement is that it assumes migrating populations originate from societies that are uniformly more patriarchal than the United States. However, migrant men's and women's positions in countries of origin vary considerably. While the polices and social environments of some countries—such as the Dominican Republic or Mexico—tend to reward males, other societies, including Israel, present arrangements that women prize (Coleman, 1988; Gold, 1995b; Goldring, 1999; Pessar, 1986; Sabar, 2000). Other source countries, ranging from Cuba and the former Soviet Union to the Philippines, offer women benefits, such as professional training, at rates that approach or even exceed those of the United States (Barkan, 1996; Simon, 1985). Further, various national regimes maintain policies of taxation and military service that penalize men who return more heavily than they do women (Sobel, 1986).

Finally, much literature on gender and settlement focuses solely on labor migrants. In other words, it assumes that migration is primarily motivated by economic needs. However, a considerable number of contemporary migrant populations—including Vietnamese, Cubans, Soviet Jews, and Armenians, overseas Chinese, Iranians, Somalis, Kurds, Gypsies, and Salvadorans—are de facto or de jure refugees who are reviled in their countries of origin due to their race, religion, ethnicity, ideology, or other factors (Castles & Miller, 1998; Faist, 2000; Gold, 1994d; Haines, 1996; Portes & Rumbaut, 1996; Reimers, 1985;). Among these groups, the degree of social marginalization confronted in the country of origin may exceed that encountered in the host society. Such circumstances mean that neither the men

nor the women of exiled groups can consider a permanent return to the country
of origin in the same manner as voluntary immigrants (Dallalfar, 1994; Kibria,
1993).

Women evaluate adaptation, settlement, and remigration differently than men,
generally in light of a wide range of factors (status, national identity, access to networks, family unification and settlement, quality of life) that impinge on the well-
being of their entire household. In contrast, men generally focus on economic factors alone (Collins, 1991; Goldring, 1999; Guarnizo, 1997; Tran & Nguyen, 1994).
Accordingly, assessment of settlement or return in view of conditions in the country of origin is a matter of special concern for women migrants, one worthy of
greater investigation.

In order to extend our understanding of the gendered process of migrant adjustment in the United States, this essay explores the settlement preferences of two
groups of women migrants—Soviet Jews and Israelis—whose social characteristics
and relations to the country of origin are distinct from the subjects of existing research on gender and settlement decisions. Constituting the two largest contemporary groups of Jewish migrants in the United States, Jews from the former Soviet Union and Israelis are well educated, largely middle class, and have legal status.
Both groups are White. However, as Jews, they are also ethno-religious minorities.

While the two groups of women share racial, religious, class, and legal positions in the United States, they are characterized by markedly different social standing in their countries of origin. In the former USSR, Jews are a stigmatized minority group who have encountered discrimination and persecution from the time
of the czars to the present (Orleck, 1999). In contrast, Israeli Jews are members of
the ethnic, religious, and linguistic majority of their homeland—the only country
on earth where Jews do not constitute a minority group.

In coming to the United States, Russian Jewish women escape minority status
and enter a social context that enables them and their families to enjoy a more stable and secure way of life than that available in the country of origin (Gold, 1995a;
Simon, 1985). Their behavior is consistent with the conclusions about gender and
migration summarized by Pessar (1986) and other scholars: The host society is good
for the household, and they plan to remain.

In contrast, Israeli women are troubled by their status as ethnic minorities in the
United States and miss the supportive familial and informal networks and government services available in Israel that yield a high quality of life. While their husbands would prefer to remain in the United States, where economic opportunities
are more accessible, Israeli women seek to return home precisely because the country of origin offers conditions of greater benefit to their household than those available in the United States (Gold, 1995b). Pessar's assertion about women migrants'
dedication to their households is verified in the Israeli case. However, her assumptions about their lack of orientation toward the community of origin are not. Because Soviet Jewish and Israeli women occupy similar positions in U.S. society, yet
evaluate settlement so distinctly, a comparison of these groups offers a unique op-

portunity to examine how differing gender patterns and contrasting relationships with countries of origin shape women's experience of migration. Gender relations are especially important to these groups' patterns of adaptation. However, gender influences their settlement decisions in a manner distinct from that suggested in existing research. In large measure, these Jewish migrant women consider settlement and return by comparing conditions and opportunities in the United States with those available in their countries of origin.

SOVIET JEWS AND ISRAELIS IN THE UNITED STATES

Since the early 1970s, over half a million Jewish immigrants have come to the United States from the former Soviet Union[2] (about 350,000) and Israel (approximately 200,000) (Gold, 1994b; Gold & Phillips, 1996). Now accounting for about 10% of the American Jewish population, both groups are well educated, urbanized, and tend to settle in the same municipalities—especially in the older Jewish neighborhoods of New York, Los Angeles, and other major cities. Both groups achieve high levels of earnings in the United States, are well represented among the self-employed and as professionals, and share high rates of naturalization (Gold, 1999).

Despite their commonalities, these groups are also marked by significant differences. Soviet Jews enter the United States as refugees, due to their experience of discrimination in the country of origin. This makes them eligible for resettlement services and legal resident status from the U.S. government, and a wide range of outreach programs are available from the American Jewish community, who accept the role of proximal host and sponsor. During the cold war era (prior to 1990) travel back to the country of origin was all but impossible (Gold, 1992, 1994b). In contrast, Israelis come to the United States voluntarily, and most can travel freely between the two countries. Israelis live, work, and marry with American Jews. However, as a group, American Jews have been less welcoming to Israelis, in large part because they endorse Zionism, which calls for the world's Jews to move from the Diaspora to Israel, rather than the other way around (Goldstein, 1995; Zerubavel, 1995).

METHODS

Data for this chapter were collected through ethnographic study of Soviet Jewish and Israeli immigrant communities. With both groups, interviews and participant observation focused on premigration life, motives for emigration, patterns of social and economic adaptation, religious, ethnic, and national identity, and plans with regard to settlement/return. I devoted special attention to gender differences in examining all of these topics. Research on Soviet Jews was conducted between 1982 and 1994, primarily in the San Francisco Bay area and Los Angeles. I conducted in-depth interviews with 68 émigrés and 25 nonrefugee service providers. I also did extensive participant observation as a volunteer English teacher in émigré homes, businesses, and other settings. Finally, I worked for two years as a resettlement worker and several years as a board member in agencies that served Soviet Jewish immigrants (Gold, 1992, 1995b).

To learn about the experience of Israeli immigrants, I worked in conjunction with five Hebrew-speaking women research assistants to collect several forms of data between June 1991 and October 1999. A major source was 99 in-depth interviews (conducted in both Hebrew and English) with Israeli immigrants and others knowledgeable about their community (45 women and 54 men, including both the wife and husband of 10 couples). While most of the research took place in Los Angeles, additional interviews were conducted in suburban Detroit, London, Paris, and with returned emigrants in Israel, as part of an ongoing study on the Israeli Diaspora (Sheffer, 1998).

Referrals to Israeli respondents were obtained from a variety of sources, including Jewish communal agencies, the Israeli Consulate, representatives of various Israeli associations, research assistants' acquaintances, and snowball referrals (whereby the people we interviewed directed us to additional respondents from their social networks). To facilitate rapport and openness, we did not use a formal interview schedule. However, questions were selected from prepared lists of interview issues (Gold, 1994b). In addition to in-depth interviews, we also conducted participant observation research at a variety of religious and secular community activities and other Israeli settings such as parties, restaurants, shops, communal celebrations (such as Israeli Independence Day), and at the pool of a San Fernando Valley apartment complex where many Israelis rent apartments. Field observations were recorded in written field notes and photography (Gold, 1994b).

Interview quotes are presented directly from interview transcripts (with grammatical errors intact) in order to reflect the speech patterns of respondents. Pseudonyms are used throughout to protect respondents' identities. We sought to contact respondents who would represent various social groups—in terms of class, education, occupation, ethnicity, age, gender, ideology, and religion—within both emigrant populations.[3] Descriptive statistics about Soviet Jews and Israelis were derived from the 5% Public Use Microsample (PUMS) of the 1990 census for New York City and Los Angeles County SMSAs (Standard Metropolitan Statistical Area)—these groups' two largest settlements in the United States—as well as from various published studies.

JEWISH WOMEN AND WORK

Jews have a long tradition of women contributing to family earnings through factory labor, home work, and entrepreneurship. Nearly all Jewish women who would eventually make their way to the United States from the former Soviet Union as well as over half of those from Israel trace their family origins to eastern Europe, which was the center of the Jewish population prior to World War II (Goldstein, 1995). As Nancy Foner (1999, p. 97) notes, during the 19th and early 20th century, "women's work throughout the world of Eastern European Jews was considered necessary and respectable." Jewish customs encouraged women's involvement in paid labor or entrepreneurship to support their husbands' immersion in religious study and to make ends meet (Glenn, 1990). While Jewish women failed to gain full political or religious equality through their work, they did become skilled and sometimes independent economic actors.

Two important historical events, the Russian Revolution in 1917 and the migration of Jews to Palestine (leading to the creation of the State of Israel in 1948), required physical and mental labor that women were able to provide. Both the USSR and Israel adhered to socialist-inspired egalitarian ideology that called for women's involvement in the paid labor force (Goldscheider, 1996; Orleck, 1999; Remennick, 1999a). Further, because many men in both the former Soviet Union and Israel were immersed in military service (World War II in the USSR, several wars and a high level of military preparedness in Israel), women's labor was especially in demand. Finally, in Israel, high rates of inflation mandated multiple-earner households (Bernstein, 1993). Accordingly, prior to their entering the United States, Soviet Jewish and Israeli Jewish women were accustomed to working outside of the home for income. Both the former Soviet Union and Israel have higher rates of female labor force participation than the United States (Gold, 1995b; Simon, 1985).

Premigration Life for Soviet Jewish Women

Despite women's relative economic equality, "traditional Russian patriarchy continued to flourish under socialism, albeit in disguised and mutant forms" (Remennick, 1999a, p. 352). Women had little representation at the top of the professional pyramid, or in political posts, and the few women who held administrative ranks had little input into decision making (Khotkina, 1994; Voronina, 1994). Due to cultural norms and the limited availability of social services, domestic work and care for sick relatives (even during extended hospital stays) were the responsibility of female family members—wives, daughters, and daughters-in-law—not paid staff. (Remennick, 1999b).

As an oppressed minority group in the former Soviet Union, Jewish women relied on informal networking to help them acquire health care and various services in a hostile environment (Remennick, 1999a, p. 354). They obtained as much education as possible, built a wide variety of informal connections to procure goods and services (from food to a child's education), and limited their fertility to about one child in order to maximize available resources and to cope with the ubiquitous housing shortage (Shlapentokh, 1984; Simon, 1985). Knowing that they had limited career options and would have to both earn income and provide domestic care for their families, educated Soviet women also adopted a pragmatic attitude toward marriage. While few chose to be alone, given the shortage of men (a result of World War II deaths and rampant alcoholism) and the limited domestic assistance available from them, divorce and single parenthood were relatively common (Markowitz, 1993; Remennick, 1999a; Shlapentokh, 1984).

Premigration Life for Israeli Women

Like the former Soviet Union, Israel is marked by gender patterns that appear to be at once more liberated *and* more restrictive than those to which American women are accustomed. For example, Israel has mandatory military service for women and had a powerful woman head of state during the 1970s (Golda Meir). Hanna Senesh, a Nazi-fighting martyr, is celebrated along with many male heroes as a founder of the country. On the other hand, the government-sanctioned Jewish religious establishment in Israel reinforces "the disadvantaged position of women as decision makers" and discourages the legal incorporation of women's full equality, while privileging men (Goldscheider, 1996, p. 161). These contrasting images of gender can be traced to two traditions—egalitarian, humanitarian political beliefs, on the one hand, and Orthodox Jewish theology, on the other—that are manifested in Israel's national identity, as well as in many of its political, ideological, and ethnic conflicts (Azmon & Izraeli, 1993).

Because Israeli society is less individualistic and more collectivistic than U.S. society, it is generally assumed that women will both work and have a family in order to benefit the larger society. Israel never developed a cult of motherhood that assigns the care of the child exclusively to the mother or views extrafamilial partners in this task as harmful. Consequently, there is a general reliance on day-care and preschool services that are seen as beneficial to children's development. This encourages women's employment, both by providing employment that involves caring for children and by deflecting the criticism and feelings of guilt experienced by American mothers who separate from their small children during paid work (Azmon & Izraeli, 1993, p. 10; Lieblich, 1993).

At the same time, because of the society's pervasive familism, which emphasizes women's domestic and child-rearing duties, Israeli women are generally discouraged "from investing in high-commitment careers" and rarely hold high-ranking positions (Azmon & Izraeli, 1993, p. 1).[4] Many feel that they have few options with regard to marriage, career, and children (Lieblich, 1993, p. 199). Finally, the relatively small fraction of women who pursue lives without men (those who are unmarried, divorced, and single parents) are stigmatized.

ECONOMIC ADAPTATION IN THE UNITED STATES

Jewish migrants from the former USSR and Israel are, as a rule, highly educated and skilled and have access to coethnic networks and American Jewish communal services. Consequently, they tend to prosper. According to the 1990 census, over 50% of both USSR and Israel-born persons in New York and Los Angeles, age 24–65, had one or more years of college, and over 30% of both nationality groups were college graduates.[5] Thus, Jewish migrants are much better educated than the U.S. population at large, which has a 20% rate of college graduation.

Reflecting their high levels of education, recent Jewish immigrants experience rapid economic mobility. According to the 1990 census, the incomes of established,[6] employed Soviet- and Israel-born men and women residing in New York City and Los Angeles approximately equaled the average for employed White men and women in those cities. One third of former Soviets and just under half of Israelis work as professionals, managers, administrators, or technical specialists, and many others are in white-collar and craft occupations. Soviet and Israeli men and women have among the highest rates of self-employment of all nationality groups in the United States (Gold, 1999; Yoon, 1997).

One economic asset of Soviet Jewish and Israeli immigrants over natives and other immigrant groups is the substantial number of women with professional and technical skills. According to the 1990 census, 29% of Soviet émigré women in New York City and 21% of Soviet émigré women in Los Angeles County work as professionals, while the rate for Israeli women is 41% in New York and 33% in LA. In both cities, a smaller proportion of Jewish immigrant men are employed in these occupations. Soviet Jewish women are often able to access especially high incomes because a relatively large fraction are in nontraditional occupations for women, including engineers, dentists, doctors, and computer programmers. This occupational profile is a consequence of the former USSR's willingness to train women for technical professions, together with Russian Jewish women's efforts to enter occupations devoid of ideological content, since non-Russians were seen as politically suspect (Simon, 1997).[7]

Despite Soviet Jewish women's high earning potential, according to the 1990 census they still make only about 60% of Soviet Jewish men's income, and additionally feel less happy with work conditions than do coethnic men (Gold, 1994a, p. 24; Simon, Shelly, & Schneiderman, 1986, p. 89). While Israeli women have an even greater rate of professional employment in the United States than Russians, they are disproportionately employed in Jewish communal occupations, notably as Hebrew teachers, which are less well paid than the technical, scientific, and business fields in which Soviet Jewish women concentrate.

One difference between the two populations is that Soviet Jewish women have substantially higher labor force participation rates in the United States than Israeli women. Israeli men and established Soviet Jewish men (those in the United States more than 3 years) had identical labor force participation rates of 88–89% in New York and Los Angeles in 1990. In contrast, Israeli women in LA and New York had labor force participation rates of 59% and 50% respectively, between 12% and 18% lower than those of former Soviet Jewish women in these cities (Los Angeles 71% and New York 68%). The difference in levels of women's labor force participation is due to several factors, including Russian women's near-universal employment prior to migration, former Soviets' greater need for income, and Israeli women's immersion in unpaid efforts to create a congenial environment for their families in the United States. Like Cuban and Sikh immigrant women, Israeli mothers often plan their involvement in education and work according to personal and family needs for caregiving and income (Fernández-Kelly & García, 1990; Gibson, 1988; Light & Gold, 2000).

CONTEXTS OF INCORPORATION

Migrants' reactions to America are shaped by the reception they receive from Americans in general and American coethnics in particular. However, it is also important to consider immigrants' status and opportunity structure in the host society versus what is available in the country of origin.

Soviet Jews' Outlooks

The initial reactions of Soviet émigrés are often a mixture of awe at the opulence of American society and concern over its lack of order, commercialism, and low cultural standards. While Jews from the former Soviet Union feel ambivalent about American culture and social practices, few express a desire to return or to move to Israel. A 1981 survey of 900 Soviet Jews in 14 U.S. cities found that if given the chance, 86% would migrate to the United States again, 5% would return to the USSR, and 6% would go to Israel (Simon, 1985, p. 31). Émigrés from the former Soviet Union build their own communities in the United States where they can maintain a comfortable social life (Gold, 1995a; Markowitz, 1993). A Soviet Jewish woman who has lived in the San Francisco Bay area for 10 years comments on how her community copes with their feelings of distance from Americans:

> From the beginning, everybody wants to be assimilated, to get out of this ghetto and nobody wants to accept it that they are in a ghetto in the Richmond District, Sunset District. But after that, people get out and a lot of them probably didn't fill up their expectation and they had a problem socializing with American (Jews) and this is not their language. And after a while, they get back together and about 25% of the community still wanted to get out and 75% completely satisfied with what they have.

In general, Jewish women from the former USSR feel that they gain a great deal in settling in the United States. Most believe that they are escaping a society that was at worst openly hostile and at the very least marked by disorganization and declining opportunity (Siegel, 1998). Many contend that they lose cultural capital in coming to the United States because they are unfamiliar with the language, culture, and way of life. However, few claim that the system in the former USSR is better than that of the United States or that their general status was better there.[8]

Many migrant populations encounter racialization as they adjust to the United States (Basch, Schiller, & Szanton Blanc, 1994; Waters, 2000). In contrast, Soviet Jews find themselves among the upper echelon of all migrants due to their largely European origins, high levels of education, legal status, connections to established coethnics, and white skin. In fact, Soviet Jewish immigrants observe that their social status is higher in the United States than it was in the country of origin. One émigré commented on this. "Here I feel less a Jew than in Russia. . . . I live calmly and nobody bothers me. . . . Nobody tells me I'm Jewish" (Gold, 1995a; Markowitz, 1988; Ritterband, 1997, p. 332).

Having already adopted a practical and pragmatic approach to family and career prior to migration, the Soviet émigré women I observed were generally more adaptable than coethnic men in the States. Men often mourned the careers they lost through migration, and spent months or even years in an effort to secure an equivalent position, leaving their wives to both care for children and support the family (Gold, 1992). In contrast, women more often resolved to do what was necessary to care for children (and often, parents) while making a living in the States. Among those I interviewed was a concert pianist who worked as a respiratory therapist, a history professor who had become a bookkeeper, and a doctor who worked in a garment factory. Further, Russian women often mastered English and became competent in American culture sooner than coethnic men.

Paulina Furman, a resettlement worker who is herself a Jewish immigrant from Poland, described Soviet women's adaptability:

> You see, I admire Russian women much more than I admire Russian men. They do heroic things. They keep the family together, they cook the goddamn dinners, they clean up. They do it here and they did it there. They keep the family stability and the burden of immigration is on their shoulders. I even think that the women from Eastern Europe are tremendous.
>
> They don't have this ambiguity of American women who don't know who they are, boys or girls. They are proud of having their hand kissed and having a seat given to them on the bus. They can do both things, they really can. American women are so unsure of their role.

Paradoxically, by being flexible and pragmatic in the United States (in contrast with men who remain captivated with finding a high-status job like the one they held prior to emigration), women often develop better careers than men in the United States. Their flexibility, earnings, and cultural/linguistic competence increased their status and power over that which they could deploy in the USSR. At least in the economic realm, Soviet Jewish women's premigration survival techniques appear to work well in the United States, leaving them with a feeling of security and a degree of optimism about their own and their children's futures.

As a consequence, Soviet Jewish women generally find the task of raising children and caring for their families to be easier in the United States than in the country of origin. Such was the case for recently widowed Zoya, who asserted that the United States offered an opportunity for a single parent like herself to support her children in a manner inconceivable in the former USSR. "In Russia, my husband was very sick for more than two years. All the last year of his life, I supported the family. It was real hard, almost impossible. But in this country, one working person can support their family." Similarly, Zenya, a former factory accountant who arrived in California prior to the fall of the USSR, claimed:

In Russia, everything is bad, nothing is good. Everything now is very expensive. Food—you can't find nothing in the stores. To buy something is terrible trouble. It's a good country but lots of problems. They spoiled all the country—environment, everything is spoiled. It's the wrong system, the basis is wrong. No idealism now, the kids 5–6 years old are pragmatic, they don't believe anything. So America makes life easier for me and my family. (Gold, 1992, p. 39).

Israeli Migrants' Views

For most Israeli women, the decision to migrate to the United States was made by their husbands (Lipner, 1987; Sabar, 2000). Migration to the United States increases opportunities for career advancement, education, and earnings. America's economic advantages include lower levels of tax and regulation on business operations, a greater availability of credit and loans, lower inflation, higher salaries, no annual military reserve duty, greater opportunities for professional advancement, a much larger scale of economic activity, and easier admission to higher education (DellaPegola, 1992; Elizur, 1980; Sobel, 1986). However, such economic and social benefits are most directly enjoyed by Israeli men (Gold, 1995a; Lipner, 1987). In the words of Rachel, an Israeli woman living in the San Fernando Valley:

For most of the people that came here, the men came and the women came after them. Like when I came, my husband came for a job. I had to leave my job and I had to find a new job and it was very painful. I think now there are women coming on their own, but if you look at most cases, it is the men coming after jobs and it means that the women are the ones that have to take care of finding an apartment, finding schools for kids. As a result, they get depressed, very badly depressed.

Yael, who returned to Israel after she and her husband worked in high-tech companies for four years in the United States, offers a similar account. She enjoyed the material benefits of life in the United States, and hopes to find work with an American company in Israel. However, her feelings of estrangement and family concerns ultimately brought about her reemigration.

Yael: In the States they have the good life. (Laughter) And easy life. You don't have to work very hard. Easy money. You can make and buy and do whatever you like much easier than here. But I don't miss anything more than this material thing.
    Investigator: Why did you return to Israel?
    Yael: First, because we thought we want to be with our family and to us, our children [should be] here in Israel. And even if there is a lot of opportunity in USA to make money, we decided we want to live here because this is our country and here we don't feel strange and this is our home anyway.

Although they derive financial and educational benefits from their presence in the United States, Israeli women almost universally consider Israel to be a better place for raising children. It is safer, has fewer social problems, and does not impose the manifold generational conflicts Israelis confront when raising children in the United States. Further, in Israel, Jews are the culturally and religiously dominant group. The institutions of the larger society teach children Hebrew and instruct them about basic national, ethnic, and religious identity as well as Jewish history.

In the United States, Israelis become a religious minority group, a status that is seen in Israeli society as incompatible with a virtuous and self-defined existence. In Israel, it is widely believed that "Diaspora Jews (those living outside of Israel) are plagued by a 'galut' (exilic) mentality that precludes them from freely expressing themselves as proud, self-confident, and self-respecting Jews" (Cohen, 1991, p. 122). Israeli emigrant women often fear that their children will lose their Jewish and Israeli identity as a result of living in an unfamiliar, Christian society.

While Israeli society is becoming increasingly individualistic, it is still far more collectivist in ways that enhance family life than is U.S. society (Etzioni-Halevy, 1998). In coming to the United States, Israeli women lose communal networks based upon family, friendship, and neighborhood that provided a social life and assistance in raising children. Married Israeli women generally make up for lost social capital for both their own families and the entire co-national community. The practice of burdening women with communal and domestic duties is common among Israeli immigrants in the United States and is reflected in their relatively low rates of labor force participation in the United States (Gold, 1995b). Hanna describes how she is in charge of decisions affecting the children in her family: "My husband trusts me with the children. He knows that what I choose, I choose good from the day they were born. I choose every school that they went to." Israeli women find their domestic and communal tasks to be arduous in the United States. This increase in difficulty in women's tasks is contrasted with the various advantages U.S. presence often yields for their husbands' involvement in the economic sphere. Michal described this:

> I am convinced from all my friends that the quality of life in Israel is better than the quality here and the problem for Israeli women, whether they have a career or they don't have a career, is that they have to tend to the children and those worries here are tremendous.
>
> Where do you send your kids to school? You use the public system if you cannot afford to send [them] to private school. You have to deal with all those things, and they fall on the woman. They don't fall on the man. The man comes home and he hopefully brings the bread. That's all he does.

Because they are responsible for child rearing and many of the family's domestic and social activities, Israeli women are the family members who most directly confront alien social norms and cultural practices. For example, Israeli women frequently commented on their aversion to American norms regarding child rearing, friendship, and leisure activities (Lipner, 1987). This contrasts with men's more positive interactions with education and work (Kimhi, 1990).

Faced with a poor communal climate, but economically supported by their husbands' earnings, many Israeli women attempt to re-create a supportive social en-

vironment. (Working women also seek communal ties.) Because of their own feelings of isolation, Israeli women are often extremely generous in helping recently
arrived friends, relatives, and other co-nationals. As Shoshana commented, by
building networks in the United States, "friends become like family."

> Shoshana: Some of my American friends are always amazed that I always have peo-
> ple over. People come from Israel and stay with me and they [American friends] don't
> understand how can I live like that and ... well sometimes it's tough. But that's the
> Israeli way. We don't want to disconnect. ... I think the Israelis long for other Israelis,
> they long for that.
> Investigator: Americans want to have their own private space, their private life.
> You know, we get together once a month.
> Shoshana: Well, we want it too. It's not that you don't want it, it's just that, peo-
> ple expect from you, and when you go to Israel it's the same. Nobody in Israel will
> tell you "I don't have space for you," or something like that. They always have food
> for you, or a place to sleep, even though they have only two bedrooms. So, that's the
> way ... that's, I think, the difference.

Within the Israeli community of Los Angeles, we found a pattern of women
performing central and even dominant roles in establishing informal networks,
formal organizations, and social and cultural activities, ranging from friendship
networks and home-based child-care centers to Hebrew schools, counseling services, Hebrew-language publications, and philanthropic organizations (Gold,
1994c, 1995b). Initially contrived by immigrant women to satisfy immediate needs
and overcome feelings of isolation, many of these organizations have become important community institutions, providing benefits for many Israelis and facilitating ties between migrants and host Jewish communities as well as the State of
Israel.

Despite their communal activism and the financial benefits they derive from living outside of the Jewish state, Israeli women, especially those with husbands and
children, are much more interested in returning to the country of origin than are
their partners.

> Investigator: How would you compare the feelings of the Israeli men versus women
> who come to America?
> Michal: Frustration for some women. I am frustrated because I had a career in
> Israel and I have none here. And do you know what the cost is? The only rewards go
> to the man—the economic advances. Both spiritually and fulfillment-wise, it is a lot
> more important for the woman to be in Israel.

Conflicts between husbands and wives over settlement plans place stress on Israeli migrants' marriages. However, divorce and single parenthood remain highly
stigmatized in both the country of origin and in the Israeli American community.
According to a Los Angeles–based Israeli social worker with a coethnic practice,
Israeli immigrant women often have little choice but to remain in these unhappy
unions.

For single mothers, the immigrant community is very much like the Israeli society. So it might be that the woman would want to get divorced, but she would not do it because it would put her in a situation of great, great, great stress, and at risk.

For an Israeli woman to get divorced, especially if she is not highly educated, she will have to be tremendously strong and stable economically so that she can rely on herself. You can count them on your fingers.

INDUCEMENTS TO RETURN

According to Luis Guarnizo (1997, p. 15), "no matter how settled, migrants still dream that one day they will return to their homeland." Our interviews revealed that Soviet Jewish and Israeli women treat such dreams quite differently. In large part, these differences in outlook can be attributed to the very different messages they receive from their countries of origin with regard to returning.

Soviet Jewish Women Reject Returning

As refugees, Soviet Jews view the former Soviet Union as a hostile environment. Those who left during the Soviet era were deprived of their citizenship, subjected to considerable harassment, and labeled traitors (Gold, 1992; Simon, 1985). Since that time, a substantial proportion of the Soviet Jewish population has fled, not only for the United States but to Israel, Canada, and Western Europe (Gold, 1994b; Siegel, 1998). The current climate in the former USSR—one characterized by impending economic crisis, social disorder, a revival of intolerant churches, and the rise of ultra-nationalism—appears to be a textbook example of a setting ripe for anti-Semitic outbreaks (Gold, 1994b; Siegel, 1998).

Further, since about 1990, several Soviet-era policies that did benefit women— including opportunities for education and work, and public safety—have withered away. Women have lost a disproportionate number of high-status jobs since the end of the Soviet period (Mezentseva, 1994). In addition, a far more limiting mythology of womanhood has come to dominate the media in the post-Communist period—one that idealizes docile, seductive, and home-focused females. "Women are now afraid to display independence and self confidence in any way for fear of being linked to this stereotype" of the "conservative, rigid, fanatical Communist and Stalinist who attacks all forms of liberalism, from economic reforms to sexual freedom" (Lipovskaya, 1994, p. 124). As a consequence of these economic, political, and cultural developments, Jewish women from the former Soviet Union who have relocated to the United States and other countries plan to stay. For example, a Ukrainian-born structural engineer who has lived in Southern California for 5 years expressed her feelings of national identification:

You know, what I think helps me is that I cut my ties to Russia. When my mama and papa sometime say "at home it was so and so," I say, "No, your home is here." They cannot forget about it. But I made myself forget. No Russia anymore. I never was Russian.

In addition to repudiating the country of origin, some émigré women take their participation in American society quite seriously. Recoiling from her cynicism toward the former USSR, Helena describes her desire to engage American society in a "good way":

> Adjustment is difficult in a different country. And some people, they don't even want to adjust in a good way. But if you want to be a good member of society, I mean a working member, I don't mean with a job, I mean just thinking and everything, and giving everything, which is the most important point, not only to take but to give. It's important. For me it was difficult.
>
> It wasn't difficult to find a car or buy an apartment, no. But language and understanding and reading the papers and realizing at least what's going on and how this country is built and everything, I think for me to live here my whole life doesn't give me enough experience.

Israeli Women and Re-Aliyah *(Reemigration to the Promised Land)*

Israeli women feel a much greater pull—formally and informally—from their country of origin than do Soviet Jewish women. Israelis are socialized to experience a strong connection to their nation-state. Many value their service in the Israeli Defense Forces as a life-shaping experience. Women especially prize their military duty, since it is less dangerous and shorter than that required of men. In fact, it is not uncommon for young Israeli women living abroad to return home for their stint in the army.

Seeking to develop its economic, political, and demographic viability, the government of Israel remains interested in its citizens abroad. Retracting the negative statements that officials made about emigrants in the 1970s (which were initially expressed to discourage emigration), since the late 1980s the Israeli government has actively encouraged its consular officials to initiate the development of relations between Israeli immigrants and American Jewish institutions. According to a recent report, "it was agreed that the Jewish State could no longer afford to ignore these citizens abroad" (Rosen, 1993). In 1991, Prime Minister Yitzhak Rabin recanted his famous condemnation of Israeli emigrants in the United States and elsewhere, asserting "What I said then doesn't apply today . . . the Israelis living abroad are an integral part of the Jewish community and there is no point in talking about ostracism" (Rosen, 1993, p. 3).

Israelis who have become U.S. citizens—and even their American-born children who have never set foot in the Jewish state—are still considered to be Israeli citizens. Israeli embassies in many cities maintain a series of programs and speakers (called Israeli Houses) intended to retain connection with Israelis abroad. Finally, "because of the importance it attaches to the re-emigration of Israelis to Israel," since 1992 the Israeli government has offered expatriates a package of benefits, including cash assistance, low-cost airfare, suspension of import duties, education, and assistance in finding jobs and housing, to encourage their return (*For Those Returning Home,* 1995).

In addition to the attraction of these government programs, Israeli émigrés frequently report that family members and friends often encourage their return. For example, in the following quote, Batya, who has returned to Israel following several years in Denver, describes her family's reasons for coming back.

> I wanted to raise my kids in Israel and obviously my parents really wanted us to come back. I think more about this all the time, because family is really important for me, especially with kids. Every time that we came to Israel or my parents used to come to Denver, I really saw how great it is for my kids to have grandparents.

CONCLUSIONS

Despite their many similarities, Soviet Jewish and Israeli women feel differently about their presence in the United States. The gender arrangements of both groups and the conditions that women would face upon returning home are important in shaping these groups' styles of adaptation. Russian women feel relatively complacent about their presence in the United States. Although they retain cultural and linguistic patterns associated with their country of origin, and enjoy interacting in coethnic settings, they are content to fit into the widely accepted pattern of "hyphenated American" ethnic membership. Their white skin, legal status, and high educational profile grants them a privileged status in the new setting, which contrasts quite favorably with the centuries of ethnic oppression they endured in the country of origin. Thus, Soviet Jewish women find less discrimination and more family-benefiting security in the United States. Further, most discover that the family-based patterns of child-focused involvement and support that urban women developed to deal with challenges in the former USSR work well in the American context (Gold, 1995b; Markowitz, 1993; Shlapentokh, 1984). Following this pragmatic approach, they are often more adaptable than coethnic men and, as a consequence, often relatively content. Few consider returning to the former USSR.

In contrast, despite the Caucasian appearance and middle-class status that Israeli women share with the former Soviets, they are much less comfortable with their presence in the States. They feel directly connected to the nation-building process of their country of origin, where they were members of the dominant religious and linguistic group. Expressing distress over their standing as a minority group in the Diaspora, Israeli women believe that the U.S. environment is inferior to that of the country of origin as a setting for family life. This concern is most strongly felt by married women who are heavily involved in domestic and communal efforts intended to replace the congenial environment and networks they enjoyed at home. In contrast, Israeli men who are immersed in work often prefer life in the United States. Accordingly, Israeli women retain ties to the home country, which they visit frequently and to which they sometimes return, bringing their families with them. Even when they lack explicit plans to repatriate, most define their U.S. presence as a temporary stay.

These findings indicate that settlement decisions—and issues of migration more generally—should be examined in a broad context. Women migrants from divergent origins are characterized by a variety of social characteristics, ranging from privileged and resource rich to severely disadvantaged. They go abroad as refugees as well as labor migrants. Moreover, countries of origin present returning women and men with a diverse array of benefits and liabilities, linked to their gender, race, ethnicity, and social status. Accordingly, migrant women evaluate settlement from the perspective of the diverse opportunities and costs associated with both the place of settlement and the country of origin. Often, the gendered process of comparing the host society with the country of origin is as important a determinant of action as is the opportunity structure of the point of settlement. In conclusion, our greater understanding of gender and migration will only benefit from the study of a full diversity of groups and contexts, reflecting an inclusive range of social, racial, economic, religious, legal, political, familial, and other characteristics.

NOTES

1. The literature describes transnationalism as a strategy by which disadvantaged groups "resist incorporation into the bottom of the racial order in the United States" or elude other social obstacles, such as undocumented status (Schiller et al., 1992, p. 3). However, several studies reveal that the use of transnational family arrangements is not limited to poor, racialized, and undocumented migrants (Gold, 1997; Lessinger, 1995; Min, 1998; Wong, 1998). Through such comparison, we might conclude that while a group's undocumented status and low rank in the American racial hierarchy can contribute to its preservation of extra-national identities, the maintenance of transnational ties by relatively privileged groups shows that other factors are involved as well.

2. Throughout the article, I use the terms "Soviet Jews," "Russian Jews," and "Jews from the former Soviet Union" interchangeably.

3. As a nation of immigrants (from Europe, the Americas, North Africa, and Asia), the Israeli population—and the Israeli emigrant community in the United States—reflects considerable ethnic, linguistic, cultural, and racial diversity (Goldscheider, 1996).

4. Middle-class Israel-born and European-origin Israeli women tend to have greater autonomy and better opportunities for education and professional employment than working-class Israeli women from North Africa or the Middle East (Goldscheider, 1996). Several studies suggest that Israeli emigrants in the United States are disproportionately drawn from the former group—the most Westernized and educated sectors of Israeli society. Accordingly, these emigrants are well prepared to profit from opportunities for education, work, and religious expression that are presented by the U.S. culture, economy, and more pluralistic Jewish community (Goldscheider, 1996; Rosenthal & Auerbach, 1992; Sobel, 1986; Toren, 1980).

5. All census data are derived from the 1990 5% PUMS and refer to New York City and Los Angeles County SMSAs.

6. This figure refers to Soviets who had been in the United States at least 9 years.

7. While their families have lived in Russia for centuries, Jews' official documents in the former USSR labeled their nationality as "Jewish" rather than Russian or Ukrainian. Consequently, they were (and still are) considered to be foreigners.

8. Some professionals, academics, artists, engineers, doctors, and musicians described their loss of standing in coming to the United States.

REFERENCES

Azmon, Yael, & Izraeli, Dafna. (1993). Introduction: Women in Israel—A sociological overview. In Yael Azmon & Dafna Izraeli (Eds.), *Women in Israel* (pp. 1–21). New Brunswick, NJ: Transaction.

Barkan, Elliot R. (1996). *And still they come: Immigrants and American society: 1920 to the 1990s.* Wheeling, IL: Harland Davidson.

Basch, Linda, Schiller, Nina Glick, & Szanton Blanc, Cristina. (1994). *Nations unbound: Transnational projects, postcolonial predicaments, and deterritorialized nation-states.* Basel, Switzerland: Gordon & Breach.

Bernstein, Deborah. (1993). Economic growth and female labour: The case of Israel. In Yael Azmon & Dafna Izraeli (Eds.), *Women in Israel* (pp. 67–96). New Brunswick, NJ: Transaction.

Bui, Hoan N. (1998, October). *Gendered transitions and family violence among Vietnamese immigrants.* Paper presented at the annual meeting of the Michigan Sociology Association, Flint, MI.

Castles, Stephen, & Miller, Mark J. (1998). *The age of migration* (2nd ed.). New York: Guilford.

Cohen, Steven M. (1991). Israel in the Jewish identity of American Jews: A study in dualities and contrasts. In David M. Gordis & Yoav Ben-Horin (Eds.), *Jewish identity in America* (pp. 119–135). Los Angeles: Wilstein.

Coleman, James. (1988). Social capital in the creation of human capital. *American Journal of Sociology, 94*(Suppl.), S95–S120.

Collins, Randall. (1991). Women and men in the class structure. In Rae Lesser Blumberg (Ed.), *Gender, family, and economy: The triple overlap* (pp. 52–73). Newbury Park, CA: Sage.

Dallalfar, Arlene. (1994). Iranian women as immigrant entrepreneurs. *Gender and Society, 8*(4), 541–561.

DellaPergola, Sergio. (1992). Israel and world Jewish population: A core-periphery perspective. In Calvin Goldscheider (Ed.), *Population and social change in Israel* (pp. 39–63). Boulder, CO: Westview.

Elizur, Dov. (1980). Israelis in the U.S. *American Jewish Yearbook, 80,* 53–67.

Espiritu, Yen. (1997). *Asian American women and men.* Thousand Oaks, CA: Sage.

Etzioni-Halevy, Eva. (1998). Collective Jewish identity in Israel: Towards an irrevocable split? In Ernest Krausz & Gitta Tulea (Eds.), *Jewish survival: The identity problem at the close of the twentieth century* (pp. 65–76). New Brunswick, NJ: Transaction.

Faist, Thomas. (2000). *The volume and dynamics of international migration and transnational social spaces.* Oxford, England: Oxford University Press.

Fernández-Kelly, M. Patricia, & García, Anna M. (1990). Power surrendered, power restored: The politics of work and family among Hispanic garment workers in California and Florida. In Louise A. Tilly & Patricia Gurin (Eds.), *Women, politics, and change* (pp. 130–149). New York: Russell Sage Foundation.

Foner, Nancy. (1999). Immigrant women and work in New York City, then and now. *Journal of American Ethnic History, 18*(3), 95–113.

For Those Returning Home. (1995). [Hebrew] Supplement to *Yisrael Shelanu.*

Gabaccia, Donna. (1994). *From the other side: Women, gender, and immigrant life in the U.S., 1820–1990.* Bloomington: Indiana University Press.

Gibson, Margaret A. (1988). Punjabi orchard farmers: An immigrant enclave in rural California. *International Migration Review, 22*(1), 28–50.

Gilbertson, Greta A. (1995). Women's labor and enclave employment: The case of Dominican and Colombian women in NYC. *International Migration Review, 29*(3), 657–670.

Glenn, Susan. (1990). *Daughters of the shtetl.* Ithaca, NY: Cornell University Press.

Gold, Steven J. (1992). *Refugee communities: A comparative field study.* Newbury Park, CA: Sage.

Gold, Steven J. (1994a). Patterns of economic cooperation among Israeli immigrants in Los Angeles. *International Migration Review, 28*(105), 114–135.

Gold, Steven J. (1994b). Soviet Jews in the United States. *American Jewish Yearbook, 94,* 3–57.

Gold, Steven J. (1994c). Israeli immigrants in the U.S.: The question of community. *Qualitative Sociology, 17*(4), 325–363.

Gold, Steven J. (1994d). Chinese-Vietnamese entrepreneurs in California. In Paul Ong, Edna Bonacich, & Lucy Cheng (Eds.), *The new Asian immigration in Los Angeles and global restructuring* (pp. 196–226). Philadelphia: Temple University Press.

Gold, Steven J. (1995a). Gender and social capital among Israeli immigrants in Los Angeles. *Diaspora, 4*(3), 267–301.

Gold, Steven J. (1995b). *From the workers' state to the golden state: Jews from the former Soviet Union in California.* Boston: Allyn & Bacon.

Gold, Steven J. (1997). Transnationalism and vocabularies of motive in international migration: The case of Israelis in the U.S. *Sociological Perspectives, 40*(3), 409–426.

Gold, Steven J. (1999, Spring). From "The Jazz Singer" to "What a Country!" A comparison of Jewish migration to the U.S., 1880 to 1930 and 1965 to 1998. *Journal of American Ethnic History, 18*(3), 114–141.

Gold, Steven J. (2000). Transnational communities: Examining migration in a globally integrated world. In Preet S. Aulakh & Michael G. Schechter (Eds.), *Rethinking globalization(s): From corporate transnationalism to local intervention* (pp. 73–90). London: Macmillan.

Gold, Steven J., & Phillips, Bruce A. (1996). Israelis in the United States. *American Jewish Yearbook,* 51–101.

Goldring, Luin. (1999, August 10). *The gender and geography of citizenship practices in Mexico-U.S. transnational spaces.* Paper presented at the annual meeting of the American Sociological Association, Chicago.

Goldscheider, Calvin. (1996). *Israeli's changing society: Population, ethnicity, and development.* Boulder, CO: Westview Press.

Goldstein, Joseph. (1995). *Jewish history in modern times.* Brighton, England: Sussex Academic Press.

Grasmuck, Sherri, & Pessar, Patricia. (1991). *Between two islands: Dominican international migration.* Berkeley & Los Angeles: University of California Press.

Guarnizo, Luis Eduardo. (1997). "Going home": Class, gender, and household transformation among Dominican return migrants. In Patricia R. Pessar (Ed.), *Caribbean circuits: New directions in the study of Caribbean migration* (pp. 13–60). Staten Island, NY: Center for Migration Studies.

Haines, David (Ed.). (1996). *Refugees in the 1990s: A reference handbook.* Westport, CT: Greenwood.

Hirsch, Jennifer S. (1999). En el norte la mujer manda: Gender, generation, and geography in a Mexican transnational community. *American Behavioral Scientist, 42*(9), 1332–1349.

Hondagneu-Sotelo, Pierrette. (1994). *Gendered transitions: Mexican experiences of immigration.* Berkeley & Los Angeles: University of California Press.

Hondagneu-Sotelo, Pierrette. (1995). Beyond "the longer they stay" (and say they will stay): Women and Mexican immigrant settlement. *Qualitative Sociology, 18*(1), 21–43.

Khotkina, Zoya. (1994). Women in the labour market: Yesterday, today, and tomorrow. In Anastasia Posadskaya (Ed.), *Women in Russia: A new era in Russian feminism* (pp. 85–108). New York: Verso.

Kibria, Nazli. (1993). *Family tightrope: The changing lives of Vietnamese Americans.* Princeton, NJ: Princeton University Press.

Kimhi, Shaol. (1990). *Perceived change of self-concept, values, well-being, and intention to return among Kibbutz people who migrated from Israel to America.* Unpublished doctoral dissertation, Pacific Graduate School of Psychology, Palo Alto, CA.

Lessinger, Johanna. (1995). *From the Ganges to the Hudson.* Boston: Allyn & Bacon.

Lev-Ari, Lilach. (2000, March 23–26). *Who gains, who loses? Gender and ethnic position differences among Israeli immigrants to the United States.* Paper presented at the annual meeting of the Pacific Sociological Association, San Diego, CA.

Lieblich, Amia. (1993). Preliminary comparison of Israeli and American successful career women at mid-life. In Yael Azmon & Dafna Izraeli (Eds.), *Women in Israel* (pp. 195–208). New Brunswick, NJ: Transaction.

Light, Ivan, & Gold, Steven J. (2000). *Ethnic economies.* San Diego, CA: Academic Press.

Lipner, Nira H. (1987). *The subjective experience of Israeli immigrant women: An interpretive approach.* Unpublished doctoral dissertation, George Washington University, Washington, DC.

Lipovskaya, Olga. (1994). The mythology of womanhood in contemporary "Soviet" culture. In Anastasia Posadskaya (Ed.), *Women in Russia: A new era in Russian feminism* (pp. 123–134). New York: Verso.

Markowitz, Fran. (1988). Jewish in the USSR, Russian in the USA. In Walter P. Zenner (Ed.), *Persistence and flexibility: Anthropological perspectives on the American Jewish experience* (pp. 79–95). Albany, NY: SUNY Press.

Markowitz, Fran. (1993). *A community in spite of itself: Soviet Jewish émigrés in New York.* Washington, DC: Smithsonian Institution Press.

Mezentseva, Yelena. (1994). What does the future hold? (Some thoughts on the prospects for women's employment). In Anastasia Posadskaya (Ed.), *Women in Russia: A new era in Russian feminism* (pp. 74–84). New York: Verso.

Min, Pyong Gap. (1998). *Changes and conflicts: Korean immigrant families in New York.* Boston: Allyn & Bacon.

Orleck, Annalise. (1999). *The Soviet Jewish Americans.* Westport, CT: Greenwood.

Pedraza, Silvia. (1991). Women and migration: The social consequences of gender. *Annual Review of Sociology, 17*, 303–325.

Pessar, Patricia R. (1986). The role of gender in Dominican settlement in the U.S. In June Nash & Helen Safa (Eds.), *Women and change in Latin America* (pp. 273–294). South Hadley, MA: Bergin & Garvey.

Pessar, Patricia R. (1999). Engendering migration studies: The case of new immigrants in the United States. *American Behavioral Scientist, 42*(4), 577–600.

Portes, Alejandro, & Rumbaut, Rubén G. (1996). *Immigrant America: A portrait* (2nd ed.). Berkeley & Los Angeles: University of California Press.

Reimers, David M. (1985). *Still the golden door: The Third World comes to America.* New York: Columbia University Press.

Remennick, Larissa I. (1999a). Women of the "sandwich" generation and multiple roles: The case of Russian immigrants of the 1990s in Israel. *Sex Roles: A Journal of Research, 40*(5/6), 347–378.

Remennick, Larissa I. (1999b). Gender implications of immigration: The case of Russian-speaking women in Israel. In Gregory A. Kelson & Debra L. DeLaet (Eds.), *Gender and immigration* (pp. 163–185). London: Macmillan.

Ritterband, Paul. (1997). Jewish identity among Russian immigrants in the U.S. In Noah Lewin-Epstein, Yaacov Ro'i, & Paul Ritterband (Eds.), *Russian Jews on three continents: Migration and resettlement* (pp. 325–342). London: Frank Cass.

Rosen, Sherry. (1993). *The Israeli corner of the American Jewish community* (Issue Series #3). New York: Institute on American Jewish-Israeli Relations, American Jewish Committee.

Rosenthal, Mira, & Auerbach, Charles. (1992). Cultural and social assimilation of Israeli immigrants in the United States. *International Migration Review, 99*(26), 982–991.

Sabar, Naama. (2000). *Kibbutzniks in the diaspora.* Albany, NY: SUNY Press.

Schiller, Nina Glick, Basch, Linda, & Blanc-Szanton, Cristina. (1992). Transnationalism: A new analytic framework for understanding migration. In Nina Glick Schiller, Linda Basch, & Cristina Blanc-Szanton (Eds.), *Towards a transnational perspective on migration: Race, class, ethnicity, and nationalism reconsidered* (pp. 1–24). New York: New York Academy of Sciences.

Sheffer, Gabriel. (1998). The Israeli diaspora yordim (Emigrants are the authentic diaspora). In S. Massil (Ed.), *The Jewish year book* (pp. xix–xxxi). London: Valentine Mitchell.

Shlapentokh, Vladimir. (1984). *Love, marriage, and friendship in the Soviet Union: Ideals and practices.* New York: Praeger.

Siegel, Dina. (1998). *The great immigration: Russian Jews in Israel.* New York: Berghahn Books.

Simon, Rita J. (1985). *New lives: The adjustment of Soviet Jewish immigrants in the United States and Israel.* Lexington, MA: Lexington Books.

Simon, Rita J. (1997). *In the golden land: A century of Russian and Soviet Jewish immigration in America.* Westport, CT: Praeger.

Simon, Rita J., Shelly, Louise, & Schneiderman, Paul. (1986). Social and economic adjustment of Soviet Jewish women in the United States. In Rita James Simon & Caroline B. Brettell (Eds.), *International migration: The female experience* (pp. 76–94). Totowa, NJ: Rowman & Littlefield.

Sobel, Zvi. (1986). *Migrants from the promised land.* New Brunswick, NJ: Transaction.

Toren, Nina. (1980). Return to Zion: Characteristics and motivations of returning emigrants. In Ernest Krausz (Ed.), *Studies of Israeli society: Vol. 1. Migration, ethnicity, and community* (pp. 39–50). New Brunswick, NJ: Transaction.

Tran, Thanh V., & Nguyen, Thang D. (1994). Gender and satisfaction with the host society among Indochinese refugees. *International Migration Review 28*(2), 323–337.

U.S. Bureau of the Census. (1990). Census of Population, 5% Public Use Microsample. Washington, DC: U.S. Bureau of the Census.

Voronina, Olga. (1994). The mythology of women's emancipation in the USSR as the foundation for a policy of discrimination. In Anastasia Posadskaya (Ed.), *Women in Russia: A new era in Russian feminism* (pp. 37–56). New York: Verso.

Waters, Mary. (2000). *Black identities: West Indian immigrant dreams and American realities.* Cambridge, MA: Harvard University Press.

Wong, Bernard. (1998). *Ethnicity and entrepreneurship: The new Chinese immigrants in the San Francisco Bay area.* Boston: Allyn & Bacon

Yoon, In-Jin. (1997). *On my own: Korean businesses and race relations in America.* Chicago: University of Chicago Press.

Zerubavel, Yael. (1995). *Recovered roots: Collective memory and the making of Israeli national tradition.* Chicago: University of Chicago Press.

PART THREE

Engendering Racial and Ethnic Identities

CHAPTER 8

Gendered Ethnicity

Creating a Hindu Indian Identity in the United States

Prema Kurien

This essay examines the central role played by gender in the creation of ethnic communities and cultures among Hindu Indian immigrants. Gender relations and constructs are reworked during the course of immigration and settlement and are crucial to the Hindu American ethnicity developed in the United States. There is a contradiction in the literature on gender and migration among Indian Americans. One body of literature describes the settlement process as leading to women's empowerment and to greater gender equality (Bhutani, 1994; Rangaswamy, 1996; Rayaprol, 1997). However, another body of literature argues that in the process of creating an Indian ethnicity in this country, Hindu immigrants have institutionalized a more inegalitarian and restrictive model of Indian womanhood than that prevalent in India, one that suppresses feminist critique and awareness of gender abuse (Bhattacharjee, 1992; DasGupta & Dasgupta, 1996; Shaikh & Abraham, 1997).

My research, based on a study of three Hindu Indian religio-cultural organizations whose members live in and around a metropolitan area in California, shows that there is evidence to support both perspectives. As I will go on to demonstrate, there are several factors involved in the process of migration, settlement, and ethnic formation, some of which have contradictory effects on gender relationships and the construction of gender ideology. This being said, however, the opposing viewpoints in the two bodies of literature are primarily due to the difference in the approach and type of evidence used by the two groups of writers. Although all of the studies were conducted by female Indian American scholars who were part of and involved in Indian American communities, the first body of literature was produced by academics whose conclusions were based on in-depth interviews with a snowball sample of Indian American women. In contrast, the second body of literature was written by feminist activists who were involved with South Asian women's organizations dealing with domestic violence. Thus, the conclusions of this group were based on conversations with victims of domestic abuse and on the opposition they as activists faced from community leaders when they attempted to obtain social support and financial assistance for the women's organizations. Why these differences should lead to opposing conclusions will become clear below.

In this article, I demonstrate that although both perspectives are valid, each is partial because it looks only at one aspect of the settlement process. My argument is that migration and settlement result in an interrelated but distinct sequence of gendered processes at three analytical levels—the household, the local ethnic community, and the pan-Indian umbrella organizations. The processes occurring at the three levels intermesh in a complicated and contradictory dynamic. The contradictions are manifested in the construction of gendered ethnicity and in gender practice, particularly at the organizational level.

Religion plays a central role in ethnic construction in immigrant contexts because it generally serves as a vehicle for the transmission of culture and also provides the institutional framework for community formation (Burghart, 1987; Kelly, 1991; Mearns, 1995; Vertovec, 1995; Williams, 1988). According to Warner (1993), this is particularly the case in the United States because Americans view religion as the most acceptable and nonthreatening basis for community formation and expression (p. 1058). Individuals from a Hindu background form the largest group of Indian immigrants in the United States.[1] In another publication (Kurien, 1998), I argued that for this group, developing a Hindu American community and identity had facilitated the transition from being sojourners in the United States to becoming residents and citizens. In this essay, I extend the analysis by demonstrating that differential gender participation and the recasting of gender identities are integral parts of this transition and the creation of an "American Hinduism."

Briefly, my argument is that as a consequence of the gendered and class-based patterns of migration and settlement, the more conventional and male-led group of professional migrants form the religio-cultural associations officially recognized by the Indian American leadership as comprising the local units of the Indian American community. Because these associations are self-selective with direct and indirect mechanisms to restrict membership to those with similar interests and backgrounds (Kurien, 1998), migration reinforces patriarchy and elitism within this group. However, the settlement process also leads to women's empowerment because they play a critical role in the economic, social, and religio-cultural life of the household and local community. A majority of Indian women in the United States enter the workforce, and women's socialization function and their role as cultural custodians are also greatly increased as a consequence of immigration (see also Andezian, 1986; Leonard, 1993; Leonardo, 1984). In India, children "breathe in the values of Hindu life" (Fenton, 1988, p. 127) and of "Indianness," but in the immigrant situation, the meaning and content of religion and culture have to be explicitly articulated and explained. Much of this task is performed by women (Rayaprol, 1997). The idealized family based on traditional gender images from Hindu religion is a central icon in the construction of an American Hinduism. Because women are the primary transmitters of religious and cultural traditions within the household and local associations, at these levels they are also able to re-interpret the patriarchal images more in their favor and construct a model of gender that emphasizes the importance of male responsibilities.

However, it is the pan-Indian umbrella organizations (both secular and religious) that present the public face of Indian Americans and that most explicitly codify an Indian American ethnicity. In keeping with the patriarchal and elitist nature of the local religio-cultural associations, the umbrella organizations representing them are dominated by wealthy Indian males. Few women obtain leadership positions in such organizations. Faced with the pressures of racism and assimilation, Indian immigrants construct an "exemplary public face" to locate themselves as a "model minority" group (Bhattacharjee, 1992, p. 32; DasGupta & Dasgupta, 1996, p. 384). Gender and class are central to this construction. The diversity of gender models within Hinduism and Indian society are homogenized, and the Hindu Indian woman is constructed as a virtuous and self-sacrificing homemaker, enabling the professional success of her husband and the academic achievements of her children through her unselfish actions on their behalf. Simultaneously, however, Hindu Indian culture is characterized as being gender egalitarian. The high educational levels of Indian American women and the large number of professionals in this group are cited as proof. The costs of this idealization and contradiction are borne by the women and girls of the community who have to meet these exacting and unrealistic standards. Due to the emphasis on living up to the model minority image, the dissent, diversity, and gender abuse that exist within the Indian American society are suppressed. Thus, the opposing conclusions of the two groups of scholars on the effects of migration on female Indian immigrants are due to the fact that women who experience domestic violence in the United States are very unlikely to reveal this, particularly to a researcher, and feminists who publicize such problems are seen as "traitors to the community" (DasGupta & Dasgupta, 1996, p. 385).

Following a brief description of the three religious organizations that were the focus of my research and a description of Hinduism in America, I discuss the way in which gender selectivity in migration works to reinforce gender inequalities among those who form subcultural Indian American communities (based on religion and region of origin in India). In the next section, I look at the nature of the settlement process and how various factors result in changes in gender relations toward greater egalitarianism. Finally, I examine gender ideology and unequal gender work and discuss the way the contradictions embedded in the above two processes are manifested in the construction of ethnicity.

THE THREE ORGANIZATIONS

Most of the local Indian American associations, particularly in areas where there are a large proportion of Indian immigrants, form on the basis of religion and linguistic background. Such associations also tend to be fairly homogeneous in terms of caste and class background. Because the division of states in India has generally been on the basis of language, there is an overlap between linguistic background and region of origin in India. I conducted research on two such associations whose members were from the South Indian states of Kerala and Tamil Nadu—the Kerala Hindu Organization (KHO) and a Tamil *bala vihar* (child development). (The names of the associations and of the members have been changed in this article.) I also studied a pan-Hindu umbrella organization based in California—the Federation of Hindu Associations (FHA).

The KHO is a religio-cultural organization of about 50 to 75 Malayalee Hindu families (Hindus speaking Malayalam, the language of Kerala) that was established in 1991. Members meet on the second Saturday of the month in different locations (mostly member homes) for a 2-1/2-hour *pooja* (worship) consisting of prayers and *bhajan* (devotional hymns) singing. In addition to the monthly meetings, the KHO also celebrates the major Kerala Hindu festivals with religious and cultural programs. Organizations like the KHO have generically been called *satsangs* (congregations of truth).

The second group that I studied consisted of 12 Tamil Hindu families (Hindus speaking Tamil from the state of Tamil Nadu in South India) who meet on the third Sunday of the month for a bala vihar meeting. The Tamil bala vihar (with a changing group of families) has been in existence for 14 years. The bala vihar consists of a 3-1/2-hour session divided into several short class periods, each dealing with a specific topic. Children learn bhajans and *slokams* (chants), discuss Hindu philosophy, and are told stories from the Hindu epics. There is also a Tamil language class. The parents (mostly the mothers) are the teachers of the bala vihar.

The FHA was formed in 1993 and launched its major activities in 1995. The FHA is a regional organization, but its leadership has close ties with like-minded individuals and organizations around the country. Most of its activists and leaders are wealthy, middle-aged, upper-caste, North Indian business men. The goal of the organization is to unify Hindu Americans to "specifically pursue Hindu political interests."[2] They are strong supporters of the *Hindutva* (Hinduness) movement calling for the establishment of a Hindu state in India. This movement has become a powerful force in contemporary Indian politics.

DESCRIPTION OF RESEARCH

My fieldwork provided me with information about gendered processes at the household, local community, and pan-Indian organizational levels. I conducted an ethnographic study of the KHO between 1994 and 1996. In addition to attending monthly meetings, I visited the homes of many of the members and conducted semistructured interviews with them. In all, I interviewed one or both partners of 18 married couples. In all but one of these cases, I was able to interview the women in detail—either alone or with their husbands—but I was able to have detailed interviews with only 14 of the 18 husbands. I also talked more informally with many more women and men as I participated in several activities with the members in the group. My own position as a Malayalee immigrant and a professional helped me considerably. However, my Christian background created some discomfort on both sides. Delicate situations occurred, particularly when I was introduced to new members, because my last name clearly identifies my background. My being non-Hindu most certainly affected many of the statements members made to me regarding their ideas and feelings about religion. My status as a young, unmarried (at the time) woman had both benefits and disadvantages. On one hand, it meant that I was able to have easy access and a good rapport with the women of the group. However, although never voiced directly, it was clear to me that my youth and gender only increased the unease of members regarding my expertise to do a study of a "sensitive" issue such as religion. Despite their concerns, most members were warm, welcoming, and hospitable.

I studied the Tamil bala vihar for a year (between 1995 and 1996), and here, my fieldwork consisted primarily of attending the monthly meetings and some other public events at which group members participated. I talked to members at the meetings but did not do detailed interviews with them. Although I am a Malayalee by ancestry, I grew up in Tamil Nadu and studied Tamil in school and am therefore familiar with the language and culture. However, as a Christian and non-Tamil single woman, my outsider status was even more conspicuous in this setting. The friendship extended to me by a group member—Mrs. Lakshmi Narayan, a university researcher who could relate to my project—was crucial in easing my entrée into the group. Despite this, however, I was never able to overcome the outsider barrier fully and was therefore not able to develop an easy rapport with members of this group.

I chose to study these two groups because of my own linguistic and regional background. However, for several reasons, the members of the two groups may not be representative of the average Indian immigrant in the United States because most Indian immigrants to the United States are from northern India.[3] Because there are distinct social, cultural, and historical differences between the northern and southern regions, the two South Indian groups in my study have a lot in common but are not likely to represent North Indian immigrant groups in some ways. A key variation is in the degree of education, particularly of women. In general, women in South India are more educated than their northern Indian counterparts. There is also a divergence between Kerala and Tamil Nadu in this regard, with Kerala having higher rates of education in general, and female education in particular, than Tamil Nadu (and the rest of India). Despite these differences, there are still many similarities between my research findings and those of others who have done studies of Indian American women.

My study of the FHA was conducted over a period of a year through in-depth interviews with the leaders,[4] through an examination of their own publications and the accounts of their activities published by Indian American newspapers, and finally, through attending some of their meetings and functions.

AN AMERICAN HINDUISM

Migration and relocation challenge many of the givens of life, such as culture and identity. Stephen Warner and other commentators have indicated that the disruptions and existential questions raised by migration and resettlement in a new environment result in a "theologizing experience" (Smith, 1978, p. 1175, as cited in Warner 1993, p. 1062; see also Saran, 1985; Williams, 1988). Many of the Indian immigrants I have spoken to mentioned that they had become more religious after coming to this country, where for the first time they had to think about the meaning of their religion and religious identity, something they could take for granted in India. According to Saran (1985), Indian immigrants with children are particularly likely to turn to religion and religious practices "since they see this as a way of raising Indian consciousness among their children" (p. 42). Thus, satsang groups like the KHO and bala vihars like that of the Tamil group described earlier have proliferated among the immigrant Indian community in the United States. They represent two different strategies adopted by Indian immigrants to re-create a Hindu Indian environment and community on foreign soil. Satsangs largely target adults and celebrate and reenact religious practices. Bala vihars are directed at children and aim to teach them about the religion. Women play key roles in both types of organizations.

In the process of institutionalization in the United States, however, Hinduism is also reinvented to fit in with the American milieu. Both satsangs and bala vihars are forms of religious practice that do not typically exist in India. Group religious activity does not exist in traditional Hinduism. In India, Hindus worship largely as families or individuals in their homes or in the temple.

One of the primary reasons for the development of "congregational forms of worship" (Warner, 1993, p. 1054) is the need for community. This need is acutely felt by Indian immigrants in the United States as they are the most spatially dispersed immigrant group in the United States (Portes & Rumbaut, 1990, p. 39). Unlike Mexican immigrants or Vietnamese refugees who typically settle in low-income barrios or ethnic residential enclaves, Asian Indians are mainly dispersed in the suburbs. Thus, the satsangs and bala vihars of Indian Americans are often the only times when they meet other Indians. In addition to changes in organizational structure, there are also changes in the content and practice of Hinduism in the United States. These reformulations are made so that Hinduism can be understood in and relevant to the American cultural context. Reformulations of gender ideology are a very important part of this process.

Despite the fact that associations like the KHO and the Tamil bala vihar are based on language and subcultural origin within India, a certain amount of uniformity is developing in the Hinduism practiced by the various Indian American subgroups. Scholars such as Raymond Williams (1988) have noted that in the United States, Hinduism is being transformed into what has been variously called an "American Hinduism" or "Ecumenical Hinduism," whereby a pan-Indian "Great Tradition" is created (pp. 238–240). Temples and Hindu organizations like the FHA attempt to unify Hindu Indian Americans on this basis.

The mobilization of a Hindu identity as the axis around which community, ethnic pride, and individual identity revolve has provided a receptive soil for the rise of the Hindutva movement among Indian Americans. Ironically, Hindutva has achieved more acceptability and support among Hindus in this country than among Hindus in India (Kurien, 2001; Rajagopal, 1995), and investigations both in India and the United States have established that much of the financial resources and support for the movement comes from Hindu Indian Americans.[5] Although the American and Indian Hindutva movements are closely linked, there are also differences in the particular issues emphasized by each. One difference is in the area of gender relations. Gender is generally not an important issue in the ideology of Indian Hindutva, but the idealization of gender relations in Hindu culture and the corresponding negative characterization of gender relations in Western and Islamic cultures forms a central component of and justification for the American Hindutva movement.

GENDER AND MIGRANT SELECTIVITY

Most members of the KHO and the Tamil bala vihar, both male and female, are professionals—mainly doctors, engineers, scientists, and accountants who have been in the United States for between 20 and 30 years. In the case of 14 of the 18 married couples in the KHO whom I interviewed, one or both spouses had come to the United States as graduate students. Typically, they arrived with the intention of returning home after their studies but then found work and stayed in the country.

The literature on contemporary Asian immigration has described Asian immigrants as coming to the United States on immigrant visas, primarily through either the special skills or the family reunification provisions of the 1965 Immigration Act. However, education has been the primary entry route for a significant proportion of Indian Americans (Nimbark, 1980).

Migration is a selective process in many ways, and therefore the immigrant population rarely represents the diversity of the original society. In this section, I discuss how gender ideology shaped the selection of Indians arriving in the United States and the implications of this selectivity for ethnic formation. I will begin with the case of Indian students. In 11 of the 14 cases of married couples of the KHO mentioned above, it was the man who was the primary visa holder.[6] In most of the cases, the male students had been unmarried when they started graduate studies in this country and had returned to India to have an arranged marriage. The wives had subsequently joined them.

Indians who arrived as students in the 1960s and 1970s were overwhelmingly male. Estimates of the proportions of males among Indian students vary from a high of 97% in the 1950s and 1960s (Helweg & Helweg, 1990, p. 101) to a low of about 70% for the late 1970s (Nimbark, 1980, p. 253). Most of the men came to do graduate work in the sciences or in business-related areas (Nimbark, 1980, p. 260). From the 1980s onward, however, larger numbers of women students arrived, and they were also much more diversified in terms of academic disciplines. Many students from India also came to do their undergraduate studies.

Despite the fact that by this period the proportions of men and women Indian students had become more equal, they did not marry each other. "The men were looking to get married and the women were looking to get married, but they rarely connected," said Malini, an Indian graduate student, describing the situation at a university she had attended. She explained that this was because "the Indian men defined the women students here as unmarriageable. They wanted and married brides straight from India." The women, on their part, tend to view many of the Indian men here as "sexist," "traditional," and "boorish." Consequently, male and female Indian students generally exhibit very different marriage patterns. Many of the Indian women students marry Americans or non-Indians that they meet here. Many Indian men go home to marry women from the same caste and linguistic background, selected for them by their families (see also DasGupta & Dasgupta, 1996, p. 382). There are, of course, some number of marriages that take place between Indian men and women who meet here. In such cases, they are most often from different linguistic and caste backgrounds.

In an earlier paper in which I discussed this issue at more length, I argued that the differences in the marriage patterns of male and female Indian students could be explained by the way in which gender shapes migration (Kurien, 1996). Indian gender norms that emphasize the importance of virginity in women generally discourage the migration of young, single women because the permissive sexual atmosphere in countries such as the United States is viewed as a threat to women's purity. Thus, the women who arrive here for graduate study are by definition a very self-selective group, generally also hailing from relatively nonconformist families that were willing to go against the prevailing norms. On the other hand, Indian gender norms encourage men to go into professional programs and to migrate to Western countries for education and jobs. Thus, men pursuing prestigious professional programs such as engineering, medicine, or business in India and then arriving in the United States for graduate study are more likely to be those who value conformity, making them as a group very different from the female Indian students in the United States (Kurien, 1996).

What is of importance to the argument here is that these differences play a crucial role in community building and in shaping the nature of the ethnic community and identity that develops in the United States. Men who come here to study and then stay on, by virtue of their more conformist dispositions and marriages to women from the same linguistic, caste, and religious backgrounds, are more likely to form or join subcultural Indian communities (which, as mentioned, are constructed on the basis of common language and religion). Indian women with non-Indian spouses or Indian spouses with a different subcultural background are generally not too comfortable (and are frequently not welcomed) in subcultural associations.[7] A significant proportion of the Indian women who arrive as single graduate students and then become immigrants tend toward liberal activism in support of feminist and human rights causes (see also DasGupta & Dasgupta, 1996, p. 382) and form communities and friendships on the basis of these shared values rather than on the basis of ascriptive characteristics. In short, my argument is that those individuals who join the subcultural community are not representative of all Indian immigrants in the United States but are likely to be among the more conventional.

Not surprisingly, Indian gender norms also shape the migration patterns of those Indians who enter the United States as immigrants. A study of Indian American women in Chicago found that all the women who had been married at the time of immigration "came to the United States through marriage, either along with their husbands or later" (Rangaswamy, 1996, p. 426). Most cases of Indian family immigration to the United States tend to be male led, with the man arriving in search of better professional or business opportunities. Sometimes the family arrives along with him. In other cases, the man sends for the family after he establishes himself.[8] Such families also tend to join subcultural Indian American associations.

In this section, I have shown how gendered migration patterns work to reinforce patriarchy among those who attend the meetings and programs of Indian American associations like the KHO and the Tamil bala vihar on a regular basis. Because it is these groups that largely define and construct Indianness in the United States, this selectivity also affects the nature and content of the American ethnic identity that is developed.

SETTLEMENT AND GENDER—THE HOUSEHOLD LEVEL

Although migration occurs within a patriarchal framework, the settlement process results in changes in gender relations toward greater egalitarianism (see also Eastmond, 1993; Hondagneu-Sotelo, 1994). In this section, I discuss how the social isolation of the family and women's entry into the paid labor force result in women's empowerment.

Isolation

First, migration generally results in the isolation of the family from relatives and friends. This can be particularly difficult for women who do not work outside the home. In a study of Indian immigrant women living in the Delaware and New York region, Bhutani (1994) indicates that "without exception, all the women in my sample spoke about loneliness . . . in the U.S. and identified 'family' and 'support networks' as the one thing they missed most on leaving India" (p. 38; see also Rangaswamy, 1996, p. 426).

Many of the women I spoke to also described the loneliness and the anguish they experienced in their early years in this country. Meena, a woman in her late

40s and a member of the KHO, described how desperately unhappy she had been in the first few months.

> Arvind [her husband] would go off to work and the children to school and then I would be all by myself in the apartment. I have never been so alone. I did not know anyone around—I had no relatives or friends nearby. I cried a lot during this period but I kept my intense unhappiness from my husband. And when I met other Indians who were smiling and laughing, I would ask them, how can you laugh and smile.

The isolation is also experienced by Indian men. In a discussion about the initial period of migration, Ravi, a male member of the KHO, mentioned that he and his wife "were so lonely and depressed—it almost drove us out of our minds at times. We looked through the phone book for Indian-sounding names and called them but many of the Indians we reached were not very friendly."

In India, men and women generally have separate social networks and thus receive most of their social support from members of their own sex. The loss of this social network forces Indian immigrant couples to depend much more on each other for companionship and emotional intimacy than they would have in India. This is particularly the case in the immediate postmigration period when couples generally have no one else to turn to but each other to process the new experiences they confront. Ambika told me that one outcome of the difficult early period of migration was that she and her husband developed a closer relationship and "really started talking to each other." Another positive outcome for women is the freedom they obtain in the United States from the social constraints of in-laws and relatives. One of Bhutani's (1994) respondents sums this up very well when she says, "No one interferes in my life here, I can come and go as I want, I can dress as I want, and I don't have to worry constantly about whether my behavior is appropriate or not" (p. 70).

Women's Employment

Figures from the census indicate that a majority of Indian American women work outside the home. In 1990, 59.6% of foreign-born Indian American women older than 16 years of age were in the labor force. Because a majority of females between 16 and 21 are likely to be full-time students[9] and many more Indian Americans go in for postgraduate study, the number of married women who are employed is probably much higher. All of the women in the KHO (except one who was studying at the time of my research and another who had been a well-known actress in India and had quit acting after her marriage) were working outside the home at the time of my study. All had professional or white-collar positions and worked as doctors (the most common profession), scientists, and accountants and as employees in banks, the computer industry, and government offices. Although almost all of the women had at least a bachelor's degree at the time of marriage, several would probably not have worked had they stayed in India (see Leonard, 1993, p. 169). A combination of factors was responsible for propelling them into the paid labor force. In addition to the isolation that housewives felt, household chores were less time consuming here due to the availability of processed food and gadgets and the modification of many of the time-consuming traditional cooking practices, leaving women with more time on their hands. There were also more opportunities for education and more flexibility in the times courses were offered, allowing women to schedule their studies around their household responsibilities by going to school part-time and by attending evening and weekend classes. Even in cases in which the husbands had initially resisted, the financial contribution provided by the jobs served to overcome their resistance. In India, family wealth helps individuals launch their married lives and to purchase housing. Due to foreign exchange restrictions and the low value of the rupee in dollar terms, Indian immigrants generally do not have this source of financial support. Thus, a second income becomes more necessary in the United States.

Another very important reason for the larger proportion of working Indian women in the United States is the redefinition of male and female honor that takes place as a consequence of the social independence and economic need experienced by immigrant families. Several women, including Meena, told me that the reason they had not worked outside the home in India was because their husbands feared that it would be seen as dishonorable by relatives and friends. Many of these Indian men eventually yielded to their wives' requests in the United States because it was much more acceptable and even normative within the Indian American society that now functioned as their reference group. Vidhya's comment, "Oh, he [her husband] finally said I could work as long as it did not interfere with my household responsibilities," was echoed by many of the women. In another study, a respondent reported that her in-laws in India had initially questioned her decision to work and that she and her husband "had to convince them that since in America everyone works, it was really quite okay and didn't reflect negatively on his [her husband's] ability to support us financially" (Bhutani, 1994, p. 51).

All of the employed women I spoke to reported that despite the long hours they worked and the problems involved in juggling their household responsibilities and their jobs, their careers gave them a sense of achievement and self-fulfillment. Meena's husband had recently quit his job in a government agency to start his own business at home. When I asked Meena (who had been complaining about her long commute) whether she would also join her husband in the business, she replied quickly, "Oh no. I need my independence." Indira, a woman in her mid-40s, who had taken evening classes and completed her certified public accountant degree and who was a very successful financial consultant, described the exhilaration she experienced when top company executives called her at home to ask for advice or listened to her deferentially at "high-power" meetings. Other studies also refer to the importance Indian American women accord to their careers (Bhutani, 1994, p. 51; Rangaswamy, 1996, p. 426).

In the context of women's employment, the absence of servants, and the redefinition of honor, women were often able to get their husbands to help with housework to at least some degree. Madhu, a young Indian woman, told me how she and her husband Ram talked about returning to India. She said she had mixed feelings because she felt that once he was there, the "masculinity thing" would become increasingly important and they would lose some of the companionship they now enjoyed. At this point, Ram entered the room. Turning to him Madhu said to me, "I asked him whether he would do all this for me [take out the garbage, wash the dishes, help with the groceries] if we were in India." Ram replied as if on cue, "No, definitely not," and then added, "But there you will have servants to help you."

Indian women generally have more independence and spatial mobility in the United States (see also Rayaprol, 1997, p. 99). As Lakshmi pointed out, "Here you can just get into the car and go where you want to. In India, people don't like women going out alone, so you are always dependent on someone else to take you out." Meena told me that around once a year, she and a few of her female friends would go to a neighboring city, rent a room in a hotel, and spend a weekend sightseeing, relaxing, and talking together. This would be much less likely to happen in India.

In short, I have argued in this section that over time, gender relations between immigrant Indian men and women tend to change in the United States, mostly to the benefit of women. After a discussion of how the relationship between her husband and herself had undergone a transformation after coming to this country, Padma, an office bearer of the KHO, summed it up saying, "Now we are almost equal." That men may not be altogether pleased by these developments is indicated by what Shanti, another Malayalee woman in her mid-40s, told me. She mentioned that her husband, who had gone to India after a space of several years, had remarked rather woefully on his return that "women there treat their husbands so nicely!" Other studies of Indian American women support the conclusion that a greater egalitarianism develops in gender relations (Bhutani, 1994; Leonard, 1993; Rangaswamy, 1996; Rayaprol, 1997).[10]

However, there is another side of Indian American family life that has not been captured by my research or by any of the other studies on Indian American women mentioned above. Those who work with South Asian women's social service agencies around the country argue that the incidence of marital violence within South Asian households is much higher in the United States than in India. According to one estimate, such violence takes place in one out of five South Asian American families (Shaikh & Abraham, 1997). The isolation from family, friends, and relatives who would probably have intervened in spousal conflict and played a mediatory role in India and the stresses of immigrant life are cited as being the factors responsible for this increase. Shaikh and Abraham also mention that, in most cases, South Asian women do not disclose their experiences to others and that those women who approach agencies do so only if they feel confident they will be guaranteed confidentiality. Thus, it is not surprising that the topic of domestic violence did not come up in my study or in the other studies of Indian American women (see also Bhutani, 1994, p. 71) that were not specifically focused on this issue.

SETTLEMENT AND GENDER—THE COMMUNITY LEVEL

An important factor that facilitates the improvement of women's status is the development of associations like the KHO and the Tamil bala vihar, as they allow women to strengthen their position in the immigrant community. The friendships formed during the monthly meetings of the KHO and the Tamil bala vihar constitute a support group for women and compensate for the social networks left behind in India. I will narrate two incidents to illustrate this.

Generally, women got together in little groups during the potluck dinner that followed the meetings of both associations to catch up on the month's news. A good part of the time was spent comparing notes on husbands, in-laws, and children. A husband about whom a woman complained was sometimes chided publicly by the rest of her friends. I witnessed one such incident at the Thanksgiving potluck meal organized by the KHO. Malini told the others that her husband Gopi had not wanted to come (because it was a long distance) and had only reluctantly agreed after a lot of persuasion. Apparently, the man had continued to grumble during the entire length of the drive. When Gopi came to pick up his wife at the end of the evening, Malini's friends scolded him for his unwillingness to attend the event and also told him not to complain again on the return drive. Gopi backed away muttering about how much "less aggressive, more modest, and more cultivated" Tamil women were (he said he was friendly with a Tamil group). There was an immediate outcry from the women (who interestingly only seemed to object to Gopi's characterization of Tamil women as "more cultivated"), who proceeded to tell him that Tamilians were "not cultivated" because they ostracized divorced and widowed women. They mentioned that two such women had turned to KHO and had been taken in as members.

During the break in one of the Tamil bala vihar meetings, Latha came up to her friends and said she had been dying to tell them about a couple she and her husband had as house guests. Apparently, the wife had done everything for the man, including tying his shoelaces. Latha's friends reacted with amazement, scorn, and amusement to this account. The husbands who were also there said nothing. After the round of exclamations had died down, one of the women said with a laugh, "Well, we have taught our husbands how to do things for themselves, and we take pride in the fact that they can now tie their shoelaces on their own!" Clearly, this message was also directed at the men standing within earshot.

To conclude this section, most women in both the KHO and the Tamil bala vihar were professionals. In many cases, husband and wife had similar positions (e.g., as doctors or researchers). In a few cases, the women had better jobs (in terms of income and status) than their husbands had. Some of the women had already been working in India before marriage. However, in many cases, the women had obtained their training in this country and then started working. In the previous section, I have mentioned some of the reasons for this development and discussed how this factor combined with others led to changes in gender relations and ideology.

GENDER AND ETHNICITY—THE LOCAL COMMUNITY

In this section, I will show how the contradictory effect of immigration on gender relations is reflected in the construction of ethnicity. As I have indicated, in immigrant contexts, it is mostly women's work that re-creates ethnicity. In the case of the two Indian groups that I studied, it was largely women and girls who wore the clothes, cooked the food, bought (or made) the cultural artifacts for the household, grew the flowers and vegetables, and learned, taught, and performed the music and dances that embodied material culture (see also Rayaprol, 1997). Again, it was the women who observed religious and cultural codes of conduct such as fasting and the rules about pollution and purity, including menstrual taboos and food prohibitions.[11] Thus, women are the primary masons of ethnic identity. However, through their roles as teachers and transmitters of tradition, women also play an important part in conceptualizing the shape of that ethnic identity.

Although both the associations—the KHO and the Tamil bala vihar—were headed by men, women played dominant roles within them. The pooja performed as part of the monthly KHO meeting was conducted by a man, Mr. Ramakrishna Iyer, an engineer and businessman by profession and the lay priest of the group, but the bhajan singing that occupied most of the evening was primarily led by women. Toward the end of my fieldwork, a "Gita discussion" period was introduced toward the end of the worship where two verses of the *Bhagavad Gita* were translated, explained, and discussed by Mrs. Kumari Menon, a university professor. In the bala vihar, most of the class sessions were taught by women. While one person was designated as the official teacher of each class session, the rest of the parents were encouraged to distribute themselves between the various classes to help the designated teacher with the task at hand. Most of the women did this, but none of the men except the designated teachers attended the class sessions. The men would generally go off in small groups to different rooms to talk and would only come back at the end when the whole group reconvened.

Because of the dominant role that women played as cultural and religious producers, they were also able to reinterpret traditional gender images and constructs. Because most of the women were professionals with independent careers (it was mostly such women who took the lead in the two organizations) and because they were presenting Hinduism and Indian culture to children growing up in America, the interpretations tended to emphasize more egalitarian gender ideologies and relationships. I will give three different examples.

As part of a Father's Day surprise, the older children in the bala vihar's language class were practicing a skit written and directed Mrs. Venkatraman, a physician and one of the parents. They were enacting the bedlam in a Tamil Brahmin household (in India) consisting of a busy professional couple, three irrepressible children, and a harum-scarum servant. The husband in the skit was loving and solicitous of his wife. On several occasions while directing the boy playing the part of the husband, Mrs. Venkatraman emphasized to the group of teenagers (and the other

women who were also in the room) what she considered to be appropriate husbandly behavior "which would go a long way in maintaining the harmony of the
household." So the boy was directed to be attentive to his "wife" when she came
back tired after a long workday, to tell the children to be considerate of their mother,
and to be willing to take the family out to dinner if there was no food prepared.
Thus, besides improving their language skills, the children who participated in the
skit were exposed to directives on appropriate gender and intergenerational behavior. Because it was to be performed for the men of the group, the message of
the skit was clearly also directed at them.

The story time toward the end of the bala vihar, when the whole group reconvened together in one room, was a much-awaited monthly event—both by the children and parents. The stories were taken from the Hindu epics and Mrs. Krishnan, the storyteller, was a gifted narrator. A good number of the stories dealt with
the importance of family relationships and obligations. Undoubtedly, this concern
stemmed from being within the American setting because the contrast was always
implicitly or explicitly with the American family. Many of the stories dealt with phi-
landering men and the punishments they faced. Others dealt with assertive women
and the ways in which they were able to influence or direct the course of events.
Although the stories were directed primarily at the children, all the adults were generally present at this time, so the import and implications of the message were
hardly missed by them. The presentation and interpretation of the story of the
pativrata, or the ideal wife, is a good example of the way in which Mrs. Krishnan
was able to recast a central concept in Hindu culture to fit the American context.
The story was about a devoted wife, who, through her devotion to her husband,
was able to amass greater spiritual power than a mendicant who had fasted and
meditated for many years. The moral of the story was that the earthly duty of
women toward their husbands was more important and fundamental than their
spiritual obligations and that this devotion alone could procure them supernatural
powers. Mrs. Krishnan concluded triumphantly that, therefore, "Women actually
have a better deal since men do not have this power." She hastened to add, "But
this is not because women are seen as dumb or passive but precisely because they
are capable." Mrs. Krishnan went on to emphasize that this duty was not just one
sided, because men had the obligation to look after their wives and to take care of
their needs too. It also did not mean that women should be submissive. She gave
several examples from the Hindu epics of loving husbands and of assertive women
to illustrate her arguments. She concluded,

> All these stories were written to show that the family was seen as the fundamental unit
> of society and to provide rules to keep the family together. If this requires patience
> and forbearance from the woman, so be it. If the woman is always saying "what's in
> it for me," the family can never survive.

This presentation and interpretation of the story and its moral is considerably different from that traditionally given to the concept of pativrata, according to which

the ideal wife is one who worships her husband as God, puts his interest above hers in all situations, and does everything she can to fulfill his every desire.

Finally, my third example has to do with the role of women in the production of diasporic culture. Like most other Indian American cultural programs, the annual Onam cultural program of the KHO was dominated by women.[12] Women and girls were on stage as singers, dancers, narrators, and comperes. Women as producers of culture also have some ability to mold the culture. Thus, for one Onam function of the KHO, a leading dance teacher and exponent in the region had her students present a series of dances based on the work of a contemporary Kerala poet Sugathakumari, who has dealt with the position of women and environmental concerns in her poems. Thus, dance teachers in the United States are able to present unconventional works and to reinterpret conventional dance themes to suit their interests (see also Leonard, 1993, p. 173).

The above three examples show the more egalitarian interpretation given to Hinduism and Indian culture in the United States. I have argued that there are two primary reasons for this development. First, women play a much more crucial role in the United States in defining and transmitting culture and ethnicity. Thus, the nature of the settlement process that brought about changes in gender relations in turn shapes and modifies traditional Hindu Indian gender images. Second, these changes are brought about so that Indian gender concepts fit in with the American culture and are thus more relevant to the lives of the first- and second-generation Indian Americans. Rayaprol (1997) explains, "When immigrants begin to live in a new society and imbibe that society's values and norms through acculturation, the dominant ideology carried from their countries of origin undergoes a transformation" (p. 108).

Despite the fact that the women in groups like the KHO and the Tamil bala vihar play a much more active role in the construction of ethnicity and Indianness and can therefore reinterpret gender ideology and practices in their favor; as a consequence of their position as dependent immigrants, they are generally limited to operating within a male model of a "patriarchal bargain" (Kandiyoti, 1988). Women's agency within the context of the Indian American religio-cultural associations is largely confined to reinterpreting the conventional patriarchal images of womanhood in such a way that instead of a one-sided duty imposed on women (e.g., the Indian version of pativrata), men are also urged to uphold their share of the bargain by being responsible and considerate husbands and fathers. This is seen clearly in the first and second examples. Both Mrs. Venkatraman in her rendering of appropriate husbandly behavior and Mrs. Krishnan's version of the pativrata story emphasized men's obligations toward their wives.

However, Hinduism and Indian culture are pluralistic, and therefore the patriarchal model of gender is not the only model in India. Although there are a multiplicity of gender models available, as DasGupta and Dasgupta (1996, p. 390) point out, there are two central and widely recognized images of womanhood within Hinduism. The first is the conventional image of the obedient, wifely goddess.

However, there is also another image—that of the powerful, independent, and aggressive warrior goddess. Although the first is the preferred and dominant model, the second model is also respected. Unlike in the American context, where the "characterological qualities" (Kopytoff, 1990, p. 88) of femininity are greatly elaborated and imposed on all women (hence the difficulty of women in politics, for instance), in India, class, caste, education, and extraordinary familial or personal qualities can outweigh or at least counterbalance gender. Thus, women who do not want to conform to the conventional model of the submissive, selfless "superwife" have some freedom to chose other models, and exceptional women and women from elite backgrounds in India have always been able to draw on the second model. This explains the seeming paradox of a traditional, patriarchal society producing a woman prime minister and other top female politicians and professionals (see also Kopytoff, 1990). The two models of womanhood will be discussed further in the next section in the context of the construction of an Indian American ethnicity.

In short, in this section I have argued that women's greatly enlarged responsibilities as cultural custodians in the immigrant context can be empowering but can also be limiting because this model only views women as wives and mothers (see also Rayaprol, 1997, p. 108).

GENDER AND ETHNICITY—THE PAN-INDIAN ORGANIZATIONS

Although women play an important part in religio-cultural associations that operate at the community level and can therefore shape the construction of ethnicity and identity within such associations, their position as ethnic architects is informal because their influence is largely confined to the household and community. It is the leaders of pan-Indian ethnic organizations, both religious and secular, who have the formal and officially recognized task of codifying and communicating what Indian culture and Indian religion stand for (see also Bhattacharjee, 1992, p. 23). They speak at large public functions, and their speeches and publications are carried by both ethnic and nonethnic media and thus obtain wide circulation. The organizations are dominated by upper-class, upper-caste males, and these characteristics also go a long way in shaping the content of the ethnicity they develop (Bhattacharjee, 1992; DasGupta & Dasgupta, 1996).

It is important to understand the background within which these ethnic constructions are undertaken. In addition to the dislocation that all immigrants experience, as Third World immigrants, Indians in the United States also face racism[13] and ethnocentrism. Hindus are particularly sensitive to the fact that their religion is misunderstood and stigmatized by most Americans. Faced with the pressures of racism and assimilation, Hindu Americans strive to present a model-minority image of themselves and their culture. The upper-class male architects make class and gender central elements of this construction. The figure of the chaste, nurturing, and self-sacrificing Indian woman becomes the linchpin of the family values and work ethic that Indians deem as being responsible for their professional success in the United States (see also Bhattacharjee, 1992; DasGupta & Dasgupta, 1996). According to this construction, it is the unconditional faithfulness, the homemaking and child-rearing talents, and the uncomplaining and self-sacrificing nature of Indian women that allow Indian men to invest all their energy in their professional careers, work long hours, and become successful. Acutely sensitive to the negative perception of the status of Indian women among Americans, the ethnic architects also emphasize that Hindu culture treats women with honor and respect and that Hindu culture is gender egalitarian. The large proportion of Indian American women professionals is cited as proof of this assertion.

The FHA provides a good case study of the above. The idealization of Indian womanhood and gender relations is one of the central indicators within the American Hindutva discourse used to signify that Hindu Indian culture presents the ideal middle ground between "Western" culture (which is criticized for its high divorce rates and promiscuous sexual relations) on one hand and "Islamic" culture (criticized for polygamy and the repression of women) on the other. Thus, the FHA characterizes Hindu culture as placing "a high premium on character and chastity in marriage. One-wife-one-husband is the banner of Hinduism." They go on to argue that in terms of

> religious, cultural, social and individual aspects, a woman has the same rights as man in Hindu society. "Where women are honored, gods are pleased" declare Hindu scriptures. Hindus have elevated women to the level of Divinity. Only Hindus worship God in the form of [the] Divine Mother. ("Hindu Philosophy," 1995, p. 6)

A fundamental part of the Hindutva ideology is the belief that ancient Hindu India embodied the ideal society whose essence was sullied by the invasion of Muslims, the British, and the postcolonial domination of "pseudosecular" Indians. Thus, the Hindutva movement calls for a restoration of the ancient glory of Hinduism through the establishment of a Hindu state in India. The centrality of gender is made clear in a page entitled "Proud to be a Hindu Woman," where the FHA indicates that in "no nation of antiquity were women held in so much esteem as amongst the Hindus. The position of women thus supplies a good test of the civilization of the great Hindus" (FHA, 1995, p. 48). The restrictive image of womanhood in the Hindutva discourse is illustrated by the FHA's characterization of Hindu women. Despite their claim that women and men have the same rights in Hinduism, the first sentence of the section titled "Proud to be a Hindu Woman" describes Hindu women as the "embodiment of patience, ... virtue, love, life, self-control" and as "chaste" and "giving" (FHA, 1995, p. 48).

As DasGupta and Dasgupta (1996) point out, in the process of institutionalizing Hinduism in this country, the preferred model of womanhood in India (as chaste, selfless, and obedient wives) has become the sole model. "The role of the *virangana* [brave warrior woman struggling against injustice] while alive and well in subcontinental cultures has been wiped out in Indian American communities" and thus immigrants have "failed to bring over these traditional spaces for Indian women's strength" (p. 390). According to the authors, social activism is seen as being Western within this framework even though there is a long-established tradition of women's activism and power within Indian history and mythology, and thus, "feminists and other activists are systematically marginalized from the Indian American hegemonic construction of community" (p. 385; see also Bhattacharjee, 1992).[14]

DasGupta and Dasgupta (1996) assert that because "immigrant patriarchy has rested the validity of the entire community upon the submissiveness of the community's women, ... the 'proper' behavior of both first- and second-generation Indian women in America has become a litmus test of community solidarity" (p. 384). According to them, these two groups therefore experience "significantly higher levels of anxiety" than Indian American men do (Dasgupta & DasGupta, 1996, p. 239). Due to the idealization of gender relations within the Indian culture, problems that occur, such as domestic violence, are not acknowledged. This in turn increases the likelihood that such abuse occurs and further worsens the situation of the victims. Women who do not conform to the ideal of submissive womanhood are deemed "un-Indian" and are marginalized.

The "daughters of the community" are also "disproportionately burdened with the preservation of culture" (DasGupta & Dasgupta, 1996, p. 386). In an eloquent narration at the South Asian Women's conference, which left several young women in the audience in tears, Kauser Ahmed (1997) spoke about the "pain and loss" experienced by her adolescent female South Asian American respondents. Their parents had completely unrealistic expectations of how they as young girls should behave in American society. Conforming to those expectations alienated them from their peers, and, at the same time, not conforming forced them to live "double and fractured lives" where they presented one facade at home and another at school. Ahmed's respondents lamented their inability to have the kind of open and honest relationships that many of their peers were able to have with their parents.

CONCLUSION

Thus, immigration is a mixed blessing for Indian immigrant women. On one hand, it is empowering because women take on several additional responsibilities as wives and mothers in the immigrant context. On the other hand, these expanded responsibilities themselves can be burdening and restricting because they limit women's options to wifehood and motherhood.

My research also shows just how complicated the process of settlement and ethnic formation can be. I have argued that to understand the contradictions involved in this process, we should study the types of forces operating at the household, community, and organizational levels. Different factors come to play at each level, precluding any simple prediction or characterization of the outcome. Perhaps all one can say with certainty is that gender negotiations will constitute an important determinant.

NOTES

1. Hindus also form more than 80% of the population of India.

2. This statement was made by the president of the organization at a banquet function (Saberwal, 1995, p. D SW 6).

3. According to a study of Indian Americans based on the 1980 census, immigrants with Malayalee and Tamil backgrounds constituted only 5.7% and 5.2%, respectively, of the total Indian immigrant population (Xenos, Barringer, & Levin, 1989, p. 10).

4. Some of these were conducted by a research assistant who taped and transcribed the discussions for me.

5. Biju Mathew, a scholar based on the East Coast, estimates that between January 1992 and December 1993 a minimum of $350,000 was sent by Indians in the United States to support the Hindutva movement in India (Prashad, 1997, p. 9).

6. In two cases, the man and woman had arrived in the country independently and had married later. Only in one case did the woman come first as a medical student and then subsequently sponsor her husband.

7. The same is true (though to a much lesser extent) in the cases of men who married non-Indian women or Indian women from a different subcultural background.

8. The significant exception to this pattern is in the cases of the immigration of nurses from India. As a consequence of Indian gender norms, most individuals who work in such professions tend to be women. Due to the interaction of ethnicity and gender, a significant proportion of Indian nurses (both in India and overseas) are Christians from Kerala state. The shortage of nursing professionals in the United States served as the stimulus for the immigration of the group, who subsequently sponsored their husbands (see George, 1998; Joseph, 1992).

9. Foreign-born Indian women have the highest rates of education of any group in the United States. According to the 1990 census, 48.7% have at least a bachelor's degree compared with 17.6% of the general American population.

10. Two studies, both based on interviews with Bengali-speaking Indian women in New Jersey, found that the respondents felt that the effect of migration on their lives had mostly been negative due to the loss of their "female world" that provided emotional intimacy and social support in India (S. S. Dasgupta, 1989, p. 159; Ganguly, 1992, p. 42).

11. Rayaprol (1997) documents that women have played important roles in the establishment and running of the Sri Venkateshwara temple in Pittsburgh. The language and religious education classes at the temple youth camps were also frequently conducted by women (pp. 91–96). Leonard (1993) similarly notes that in the Malibu temple near Los Angeles, it is the women who sit at the doorway and give out pamphlets and who explain Hindu beliefs and rituals to casual visitors (p. 172).

12. Significantly, the only time when there were men on the stage was during the speeches of the Kerala Hindu Organization president and the chief guest of the function, both of whom were men.

13. DasGupta and Dasgupta (1996) point out that racism is also gendered and that the stereotype of Asian Americans contains within it an image of Asian women as "hyperfeminine" and Asian men as not "fully male" (p. 393).

14. Madhu Kishwar, editor of the feminist Indian magazine *Manushi*, reported being "flabbergasted" by the hostility that she faced within the male immigrant community in the United States, as she had received a great deal of support from men in India (cited in Das-

Gupta & Dasgupta, 1996, p. 394). Again, Mallika Sarabhai, one of the foremost Indian dancers, has also talked about the fact that expatriate reactions to her feminist work are "more extreme and conservative than those in India" (Sarabhai & Mathur, 1995, p. 225).

REFERENCES

Ahmed, K. (1997, September). *South-Asian American adolescent girls: Integrating identities and cultures.* Paper presented at the South Asian Women's Conference, Los Angeles.

Andezian, S. (1986). Women's roles in organizing symbolic life: Algerian female immigrants in France. In R. J. Simon & C. B. Brettell (Eds.), *International migration: The female experience* (pp. 254–265). Totowa, NJ: Rowman & Allanheld.

Bhattacharjee, A. (1992). The habit of ex-nomination: Nation, woman and the Indian immigrant bourgeoisie. *Public Culture, 5*(1), 19–44.

Bhutani, S. D. (1994). *A study of Asian Indian women in the U.S.: The reconceptualization of self.* Unpublished doctoral dissertation, Department of Education, University of Pennsylvania.

Burghart, R. (1987). The perpetuation of Hinduism in an alien cultural milieu. In R. Burghart (Ed.), *Hinduism in Great Britain: The perpetuation of religion in an alien cultural milieu* (pp. 224–251). London: Tavistock.

DasGupta, S., & Dasgupta, S. D. (1996). Women in exile: Gender relations in the Asian Indian community in the U.S. In S. Maira & R. Srikanth (Eds.), *Contours of the heart: South Asians map North America* (pp. 381–400). New York: Asian American Writers Workshop.

Dasgupta, S. D., & DasGupta, S. (1996). Public face, private space: Asian Indian women and sexuality. In N. B. Maglin & D. Perry (Eds.), *"Bad girls,"/"good girls": Women, sex, and power in the nineties* (pp. 226–243). New Brunswick, NJ: Rutgers University Press.

Dasgupta, S. S. (1989) *On the trail of an uncertain dream: Indian immigrant experience in America.* New York: AMS Press.

Eastmond, M. (1993). Reconstructing life: Chilean refugee women and the dilemmas of exile. In G. Buijs (Ed.), *Migrant women: Crossing boundaries and changing identities* (pp. 35–53). Oxford, UK: Berg.

Federation of Hindu Associations. (1995). *Directory of temples and associations of Southern California and everything you wanted to know about Hinduism.* Artesia, CA: No Press.

Fenton, J. Y. (1988). *Transplanting religious traditions: Asian Indians in America.* New York: Praeger.

Ganguly, K. (1992). Migrant identities: Personal memory and the construction of selfhood. *Cultural Studies, 6,* 27–50.

George, S. (1998). Caroling with the Keralites: The negotiation of gendered space in an Indian immigrant church. In R. S. Warner & J. G. Wittner (Eds.), *Gatherings in diaspora: Religious communities and the new immigration* (pp. 265–294). Philadelphia: Temple University Press.

Helweg, A. W., & Helweg, U. M. (1990). *An immigrant success story: East Indians in America.* Philadelphia: University of Pennsylvania Press.

Hindu philosophy has no place for caste system, says FHA. (1995, March 17). *India Post,* p. 6.

Hondagneu-Sotelo, P. (1994). *Gendered transitions: Mexican experiences of immigration.* Berkeley & Los Angeles: University of California Press.

Joseph, R. B. (1992). *Perceived change of immigrants in the United States: A study of Kerala (Asian Indian) immigrant couples in greater Chicago.* Unpublished doctoral dissertation, Department of Sociology and Anthropology, Loyola University of Chicago.

Kandiyoti, D. (1988). Bargaining with patriarchy. *Gender and Society, 2*(3), 274–290.

Kelly, J. D. (1991). *A politics of virtue: Hinduism, sexuality, and countercolonial discourse in Fiji.* Chicago: University of Chicago Press.

Kopytoff, I. (1990). Women's roles and existential identities. In P. R. Sanday & R. G. Goodenough (Eds.), *Beyond the second sex: New directions in the anthropology of gender* (pp. 75–98). Philadelphia: University of Pennsylvania Press.

Kurien, P. A. (1996, October). *Gendering ethnicity: Creating a Hindu Indian identity in the United States.* Paper presented at the 25th annual conference on South Asia, Madison, WI.

Kurien, P. A. (1998). Becoming American by becoming Hindu: Indian Americans take their place at the multi-cultural table. In R. S. Warner & J. G. Wittner (Eds.), *Gatherings in diaspora: Religious communities and the new immigration* (pp. 37–70). Philadelphia: Temple University Press.

Kurien, P. A. (2001). Constructing 'Indianness' in the United States and India: The role of Hindu and Muslim Indian immigrants. In M. López-Garza & D. R. Diaz (Eds.), *Asian and Latino immigrants in a restructuring economy: The metamorphosis of Southern California.* Palo Alto, CA: Stanford University Press.

Leonard, K. (1993). Ethnic identity and gender: South Asians in the United States. In M. Israel & N. K. Wagle (Eds.), *Ethnicity, identity, migration: The South Asian context* (pp. 165–180). Toronto, Canada: Center for South Asian Studies, University of Toronto.

Leonardo, M. di. (1984). *The varieties of ethnic experience: Kinship, class, and gender among California Italian-Americans.* Ithaca, NY: Cornell University Press.

Mearns, D. J. (1995). *Shiva's other children: Religion and social identity amongst overseas Indians.* New Delhi: Sage.

Nimbark, A. (1980). Some observations on Asian Indians in an American educational setting. In P. Saran & E. Eames (Eds.), *The new ethnics: Asian Indians in the United States* (pp. 247–271). New York: Praeger.

Portes, A., & Rumbaut, R. G. (1990). *Immigrant America: A portrait.* Berkeley & Los Angeles: University of California Press.

Prashad, V. (1997, February). Culture vultures. *Communalism Combat,* No. 30, p. 9.

Rajagopal, A. (1995). *Better Hindu than Black? Narratives of Asian Indian identity.* Paper presented at the annual meeting of the Society for the Scientific Study of Religion and Religious Research Association, St. Louis, MO.

Rangaswamy, P. I. (1996). *The imperatives of choice and change: Post 1965 immigrants from India in metropolitan Chicago.* Unpublished doctoral dissertation, Department of History, University of Illinois, Chicago.

Rayaprol, A. (1997). *Negotiating identities: Women in the Indian diaspora.* Delhi, India: Oxford University Press.

Saberwal, S. (1995, July 28). FHA unity banquet raises $20,000 for Norwalk temple, support emphasized at Sangeet Sandhya. *India Post,* pp. D SW 6.

Sarabhai, M., & Mathur, C. (1995, Summer). "I do not have the luxury of being apolitical": A conversation with Mallika Sarabhai by Chandana Mathur. *Samar (South Asian Magazine for Action and Reflection), 5,* 23–29.

Saran, P. (1985). *The Asian Indian experience in the United States.* Cambridge, MA: Schenkman.

Shaikh, S. I., & Abraham, M. (1997, September). *Domestic violence in the South Asian community.* Paper presented at the South Asian Women's Conference, Los Angeles.

Smith, T. (1978). Religion and ethnicity in America. *American Historical Review, 83,* 1155–1185.

Vertovec, S. (1995). Hindus in Trinidad and Britain: Ethnic religion, reification, and the politics of public space. In P. van der Veer (Ed.), *Nation and migration: The politics of space in the South Asian diaspora* (pp. 132–156). Philadelphia: University of Philadelphia Press.

Warner, S. (1993). Work in progress toward a new paradigm for the sociological study of religion in the United States. *American Journal of Sociology, 98,* 1044–1193.

Williams, R. B. (1988). *Religions of immigrants from India and Pakistan: New threads in the American tapestry.* Cambridge, UK: Cambridge University Press.

Xenos, P., Barringer, H., & Levin, M. J. (1989, July). *Asian Indians in the United States: A 1980 census profile* (No. 111). Honolulu, HI: Papers of the East-West Population Institute.

CHAPTER 9

Disentangling Race-Gender Work Experiences

Second-Generation Caribbean Young Adults in New York City

Nancy Lopez

INTRODUCTION

I think that if I'm applying for a job and there's a White person, the job would be given to him because he's White. And that has happened to me in a job that I applied for. It was a job in a lawyer's office. I remember that I applied and then I just kept calling them and calling them and calling them, until one day, they told me the job was taken. And I knew something was up. They sounded kind of fishy to me. I know it probably had to do with my race because they looked at me funny.
(PETER, 23-year-old Dominican man)

At the beginning of the 21st century, an unusual gender gap in educational attainment has emerged in the United States. Women from all racial and ethnic groups attain higher levels of schooling than men (*Reaching the Top*, 1999). Some predict that by 2007 the gender gap will reach 2.3 million, with 9.2 million women enrolled in college and only 6.9 million men (Lewin, 1998). Although this phenomenon is relatively new among groups that have been racial(ized) as Whites, women from groups that have been defined as racial minorities have historically reached higher levels of education than their male counterparts.[1] In the 1990s, African American women were twice as likely to obtain a college degree as African American men (Hawkins, 1996). In the Boston public high school graduating class of 1998, there were only 100 Black and Hispanic males going to a four-year college for every 180 Black and Hispanic females going (Sum, Kroshko, Fogg, & Palma, 2000). In New York City public schools, where the majority of students are Black and Latino, women graduates outnumber men. Even at the City University of New York, women constitute the majority of enrolled Black and Latino undergraduates—up to 70% in graduate programs (*CUNY Student Data Book*, 1996).

This gender gap is already discernible among the new second generation—the children of post-1965 immigrants from Latin America, the Caribbean, and Asia. A longitudinal survey of second-generation youth from various racial and ethnic backgrounds in California and Florida found that young women outperform young men in terms of educational attainment, grade point averages, and educational aspirations (Rumbaut, 1998). Although Caribbean immigrants constitute the largest number of recent immigrants in New York City, no studies have investigated the gender gap among second-generation Caribbean New Yorkers.[2]

This study examines how the *actual work experiences* of second-generation Dominican, Anglophone West Indian, and Haitian young adults living in New York City influence their outlooks on the role of education in their lives. The chapter begins with a discussion of segmented assimilation theory and racial formation theory. The *race-gender experience theory* is proposed as an alternative conceptual framework for understanding the *racial(ized)* and *gender(ed) experiences* of the second generation in contemporary U.S. society and how these episodes affect youth outlooks toward education. Next, the work experiences of second-generation Caribbean men and women are described against the backdrop of a changing New York economy. An examination of the life histories of the second generation revealed that men and women had quite different experiences in the labor market, which significantly shaped their views on education.

Segmented Assimilation Theory and Racial Formation Theory

Operating largely within the ethnicity paradigm, segmented assimilation theory is the prevailing theory for examining the second generation. Portes and Zhou (1993) posit that the type of assimilation the second generation undergoes is segmented and depends largely on four factors: (1) mode of incorporation, (2) social networks and the cultural capital of its respective ethnic community, (3) place of residence, and (4) color. Acknowledging that assimilation may mean upward or downward mobility, segmented assimilation theorists postulate that the second generation may follow one of three employment trajectories (Portes, 1996). It may repeat the work patterns of early European immigrants who experienced upward social mobility by assimilating into the mainstream economy. Alternatively, the second generation may assimilate into the racially stigmatized lower classes and reject the low-status jobs their immigrant parents accepted.[4] The third possibility is that close-knit immigrant communities possess dense social networks within an ethnic economy, which may serve as a springboard for upward mobility.

While segmented assimilation theory focuses on what sector of U.S. society a given ethnic group is assimilating into, racial formation theories are concerned with how a given immigrant group is assigned racial meaning. Omi and Winant's (1994) racial formation theory places racialization processes at the center of the analysis; racial formation is "a process of historically situated *projects* in which human bodies and social structures are represented and organized" (Omi & Winant, 1994, p. 55). As explained by Omi and Winant, "racial projects can take place not only at the macro-level of racial policy-making, state activity, and collective action, but also at the micro-level of everyday experience" (1994, p. 58).

Toward a Race-Gender Experience Theory

The proposed race-gender experience theory is an attempt to unearth the ways in which men's and women's views about education and social mobility are shaped by their lived experiences, as racial(ized) *and* gender(ed) bodies.[5] A guiding premise of the study is that race and gender are intersecting, socially constructed processes that are historically variable, overlapping, intertwined, and inseparable (see Omi & Winant, 1994). A second assumption is that race and gender can be understood as *lived experience* (see Feagin & Sikes, 1994). The proposed race-gender experience theory includes two major concepts: *race-gender experiences* and *race-gender outlooks.* Race-gender experiences are the episodes in which men and women undergo racial(izing) and gender(ing) processes in a variety of social spaces, such as in public space, school, work, and family life. Over time, these repeated experiences have a cumulative effect on their race-gender outlooks—life perspectives on education and social mobility.

METHODOLOGY

The primary data are life history interviews conducted during 1996 and 1997 (see Lopez, 2002). These data were part of a larger study on second-generation youth in metropolitan New York.[6] The sampling approach was door-to-door solicitation in block-level census tracts with high and low concentrations of Dominicans, West Indians, and Haitians. In total, 66 second-generation Caribbean young adults, ages 18 to 30, were surveyed: 31 women and 35 men. Respondents included 27 Dominicans, 22 West Indians, and 17 Haitians.[7] Participants were from low-income households; none of the participants had two parents with college degrees. Of the 66 participants, only 4 women earned four-year college degrees. Although none of the men held college degrees, 63% of them had pursued educational training beyond high school, compared with 77% of the women.[8]

Women were concentrated in traditional service sector pink-collar work, such as clerical jobs (33%) and sales (30%). A cluster of women worked in public sector jobs (27%), such as health care services. Over half of the men (52%) had worked in the service sector and were concentrated in traditional male-dominated work, such as security and stock personnel (37%), with a smaller concentration in sales (15%). Less than one fifth of men (18%) had worked in the public sector, compared with almost a third of the women. Four times as many men as women had worked in the informal economy (12% compared with 3%).

Follow-up life history interviews were conducted to explore the racializ(ing) and gender(ing) processes second-generation Caribbean youth undergo during job searches and while working.[9] In total, 41 of the 66 participants were re-interviewed.[10] Participants were selected with a view to striking a balance between age and gender. An effort was made to interview people with varied educational attainment and different employment status. Respondents included 10 Dominican men, 11 Dominican women, 6 West Indian men, 6 West Indian women, 5 Haitian men, and 3 Haitian women.

The participants had complexions of varying darkness. According to the U.S. one-drop rule, all of the participants could have been racially categorized as "Black," whereby any trace of African ancestry defines one as Black. Participants reported that other people sometimes thought they were African Americans. None of the lighter-skinned Dominicans, Haitians, and West Indians reported that strangers mistook them for Whites. However, a few of the lighter-skinned participants said that other people thought that they were Puerto Rican. Before turning to the excerpts from the transcribed in-depth interviews, it is important to mention some of the major changes in the economy.

COLOR(ING) AND GENDER(ING) URBAN RESTRUCTURING

Since 1965 over 15 million immigrants have entered the United States. After Mexico, the Caribbean produced the most immigrants during the 1980s.[11] New York City, as a main entry point, has attracted about one fifth of all immigrant arrivals in recent decades. The single largest number of immigrants in the New York City area during the 1980s came from the Caribbean Basin.[12]

The first cohorts of Caribbean immigrants were concentrated in manufacturing. However, in the 1980s and 1990s the vast majority of first-generation Dominicans, Haitians, and West Indians were concentrated in secondary sector jobs. This reality was evidenced in the types of jobs held by the parents of the second-generation youth who participated in the study. Overall, the parents were concentrated in low-wage, dead-end jobs. The mothers worked primarily as factory workers or in the health care industries as home attendants (29%). Another segment worked in the informal economy (18%) as child-care providers or in food preparation. The fathers of the participants held a variety of jobs, including superintendent of buildings and general maintenance (15%), taxi services (13%), electrical work (11%), factory work (11%), and auto repair (11%).[13]

Although there has been some speculation about how the employment trajectories of the second generation will differ from those of their parents, it is clear that there are two major differences in the employment scenarios of the new second generation. Whereas the children of turn-of-the-century European immigrants entered an expanding post–World War II manufacturing economy, the children of post-1965 immigrants are faced with a two-tiered hourglass economy that is largely reliant on services (Gans, 1992). Moreover, the entry of the second generation into the labor market coincides with the increasing feminization of the workforce.

MEN'S MARGINALIZATION
Color(ing) and Gender(ing) Job Searches

Against the backdrop of a restructured urban economy, men spoke at length about their vulnerability as stigmatized racial minorities. Richard, a 24-year-old Haitian man who grew up in Prospect Heights, Brooklyn, had worked in an assortment of odd jobs, including retail stores, school cafeterias, and a gas company. At the time of the interview Richard was between jobs and offered his thoughts on the "color" of job searches:

> Employers tell you "Oh yes, we were hiring last week, we're not hiring anymore. We'll keep your application on file. When we have an opening, we'll let you know." Yeah, right! I've thought about this and I've spoken to a few people about this. You go to certain job interviews and they turn you down. After you get turned down six or seven times, everywhere you go, all you hear is "oh yeah, we'll keep your application on file." Some people get so frustrated they don't even want to go back out there to deal with this BS.

While acknowledging that he had more employment opportunities in the United States than in Haiti, Richard said that times were hard for him because, as a member of a stigmatized racial group, he faced discrimination even when applying for minimum-wage, entry-level jobs.

In addition to the discrimination faced by all immigrants and people who are not of European phenotype, there is an internal hierarchy with respect to people of color. People of any discernible African phenotype are generally ranked lower than Asians or lighter skinned Latinos. Since overall, Dominicans are more likely to be of African phenotype than other Latinos, they may face more discrimination based on skin color (Torres & Bonilla, 1995). One morning when Peter, the young Dominican man quoted in the introduction, applied for work, he was reminded that his "color" was a source of suspicion:

> I will never forget. I went to the Department of Labor and there was a White man who was helping me. And he looked at me and really quickly asked me: "Can I see your green card? Can I see your green card?" And I looked at him and I said, "I was born in the United States." And then he didn't apologize or anything and I didn't like that.

Peter was asked for his immigration status because the Immigration Reform and Control Act of 1986 created sanctions for employers who knowingly hire undocumented immigrants and established requirements to prove work eligibility before starting a job.[14] These incidents lead men to doubt that opportunities are open to them or that they can experience upward mobility, as their dark skin precludes them from ever "looking American," regardless of their place of birth or ethnic identification.

Complicating the dynamic of racial hierarchies in the labor market, researchers have pointed to the fact that employers draw sharp distinctions between women and men employees, especially among those from stigmatized racial groups. One African American respondent in Kirchenman's Chicago-based study of employer discrimination offered his explanation:

> Whites are not afraid of Black women because Black women have been part of their households for a long time—as the white man's mistress, as the mother of his children, as domestics, as cooks in restaurants and as office cleaners. (1997, p. 218)

In the United States, the "symbolic taint" attached to men of dark skin casts them as unstable, uncooperative, dishonest, uneducated, and generally unreliable workers, while their female counterparts are viewed as more exploitable (see Kasinitz & Rosenberg, 1996, and Kirchenman & Neckerman, 1993). Whereas potential employers may fear hiring minority men because they have been racialized as problematic workers, they may not have the same reservations about minority women.[15]

The rejection of dark-skinned men in the labor market appears to be a global phenomenon. Model's (1997) cross-national study of West Indian immigrants living in the United States, Canada, and England found that Caribbean men had lower occupational status than women. Similarly, Hurtado and colleagues (1992) found that the same dynamic affects Latino communities. Census data show that Latino male employment and earnings are lower than those of White males with the same education, but the racial gap is less pronounced between White women and Latina women, as well as between Black and White women (see Smith, 1995).

Experiencing the "Hoodlum" Narrative at Work

The racialization of men of African phenotype as "hoodlums" who are potential criminals and drug dealers was the quintessential racial project of the "war on drugs" of the 1980s and 1990s. Men experienced the "hoodlum" narrative, not only through the difficulties they encountered looking for work, but also while working. José, a 24-year-old Dominican man who grew up in Washington Heights, Manhattan, had held an assortment of jobs. José bitterly recalled the negative experiences he had while working as a stockboy for a major electronics store in midtown Manhattan:

> Three days ago, I went to the main store at the electronic franchise where I work to get something for my boss because he needed a piece for a television set. And as soon as I entered, the employees at the main store did not know I was from the same store. So, everybody just came up to me looking at me strange, looking at me like I was going to steal something!

Other men reported even more blatant forms of racial harassment at work. During high school, Steven, a Brooklyn-born 23-year-old West Indian man, worked off the books in an Italian-owned ice cream parlor. Steven painfully recalled that his boss sometimes hurled racial epithets at him:

> One time I didn't put enough sugar in the ice machine and that's the main ingredient. . . . And my boss screamed at me and called me all types of words. They always call you the negro, nigger word.

Experiences such as these reminded José and Steven of their stigmatized status in the White/Black racial pyramid. These episodes deeply affect men's thinking about the "color" of social mobility in contemporary U.S. society.

Since minority men are placed at the end of the hiring queue, they are largely confined to the most exploitative jobs. Joaquín, a 20-year-old Dominican man who grew up in Inwood, had worked as a jack-of-all-trades at an elite social club in Manhattan. When asked why he left, Joaquín explained:

> I got back spasms and I figured out that anybody was going to get back spasms lifting 200-pound folding tables by himself, while working without a carry belt. One day I fell down and I hurt my back. I couldn't pay the ambulance. My boss didn't want to call an ambulance, so I had to call my cousin to pick me up. That's why I left. I don't know how I didn't get a hernia!

Without health insurance or disability coverage, Joaquín was forced to leave his job because the unsafe working conditions left him maimed. Joaquín had tried to obtain unionized blue-collar work in sanitation and construction, but union jobs, which provided a steady source of employment for early poor and working-class European immigrants, have withered in the new economic landscape.[16] Consequently, the men in this study had very checkered work histories in low-level blue-collar jobs, which were not only unstable but hazardous.

The proliferation of income-generating activities outside the sphere of public regulation is an integral part of the postindustrial city. Subcontracting, part-time work, and personal services and working "under the table" are the linchpins of restructured urban labor markets. Low-wage service workers, such as messengers and part-time clerical workers, are the immigrant sweatshop employees of the late 20th century. Consequently, during the 1980s, the real wages of the average worker declined by 10%, while poverty rates continued to climb (see Fine & Weis, 1998). In many ways, then, the labor market experiences of second-generation Caribbean men echoed those of their parents, many of whom are locked into the most exploitative dead-end jobs in the lowest echelons of the labor market.

Social Critique and Worried Outlooks

It has been widely argued that second-generation Caribbean youths will experience "second generation decline" because they have adopted a "native minority oppositional" anti-school attitude and lack the work ethic to sustain steady employment (see Grasmuck & Pessar, 1996; Ogbu & Simons, 1998). Allegedly, unlike their parents who accepted exploitative jobs, second-generation youths reject minimum-wage menial jobs and lack the skills to pursue professional jobs. Our findings challenge this analysis. Rather than expressing contempt for servile work, the men in this study said they would accept any job that paid the minimum wage. When asked about the lowest wage he would accept, Paul, an 18-year-old Haitian man who grew up in East Flatbush, Brooklyn, said he had only been able to find short-term work as a paper delivery boy. Paul's reflections echoed the sentiments of other men: "It doesn't matter to me because I really want to get a job. As long as I am getting paid, I'll accept any kind of job." In a study of poor and working-class fast-food workers in Harlem, Newman and Ellis (1999) also found that Black and Latino youth did not disdain low-status jobs.

The more prevalent problem for youth that society defines as racially stigmatized minorities, particularly men, is that it is hard for them to secure any kind of paid work. Despite the gains in education, the employment of Black men has worsened, especially among the younger cohorts. During the 1980s, the unemployment rate for Blacks ages 16 to 19 was 36%, while the rate for Hispanics was 33% (see Griffins, 1994). In contrast, the unemployment rate for Whites was less than half that of Blacks and Hispanics. These figures leave out the unknown number of discouraged workers who have traditionally been excluded from the calculation of unemployment rates. Men who are racially stigmatized have borne the brunt of economic restructuring and continued racial discrimination; increasingly, they constitute a reserve labor force not able to find stable employment.

The cumulative effects of dealing with social rejection in the labor market lead men to worry about the relevance of educational credentials in a society that continually discriminates against them. Men noted that some of their male friends and family members with college degrees had been unable to find employment commensurate with their educational levels. Rodrigo, a Dominican man who grew up on the Lower East Side of Manhattan, recalled that one of his male friends had earned a Bachelor of Arts degree in computer technology but was unable to find work and resorted to working as a mechanic with his father. Not surprisingly, Rodrigo concluded:

> I think that in this day and age, you need people in high places. Because imagine, the people from Yale, Princeton, Columbia, all those rich people! They had their mom and dad pay for their education and they had contacts with people in the business world. All the parents had to do was say "do me a favor," and they're set. And us, for us, it will be much harder. You have to have people in high places in order to get the connections.

As Rodrigo pointed out, it is extremely difficult for minority and immigrant youth, especially men, who are residentially segregated and educated in substandard schools, to develop their academic skills and engage in supportive relations with institutional agents outside their immediate kinship unit. Stanton-Salazar posits that "school success, and economic and social integration in society, depends upon regular and unobstructed opportunities for constructing instrumental relationships with institutional agents across key social spheres and institutional domains dispersed throughout society" (1997, p. 6).

Even young men who were fortunate enough to tap into established institutional links within an expanding sector of the economy still faced institutionalized discrimination. Paven, a 19-year-old West Indian man who grew up in Bushwick, Brooklyn, worried that he might face the same difficulties his older cousin encountered:

> My cousin, who has a BA in accounting, was working as an intern for the number two firm in the City, but out of the ten interns, two were already chosen. Right now he's not working. He quit a job at some bank because they had him photocopying and that

really pissed him off. He jokes about it, but I know that deep down inside he feels an-
gry. He tells me, "You know what I think about school, what's my philosophy on school
now?" I was like, "Forget school because what has it gotten you in four years? Look
what you're doing. You're doing nothing!" That's the answer to it!

In spite of the rising educational levels in minority communities, racial discrimination continues to affect the underrepresentation of Blacks in the high-paying
growth sectors. The legacy of racism has historically meant that education has
less of a payoff for stigmatized minorities than for Whites. During the 1990s, Black
men with college degrees earned $798 for every $1,000 earned by White men (see
Hacker, 1992).[17] Moreover, Black and Latino men who entered semiprofessional
careers were concentrated in the lowest rungs of their career ladders (see Robinson, 1993). In light of these trends, Feagin and Sikes (1994) have concluded that
whereas Whites have careers, Blacks and Latinos have jobs. However, in spite of
Paven's social critique of racial job ceilings in the workplace, he was still pursuing
an associate's degree at a local community college.

As they continued to experience problems in the labor market, men showed vac-
illating views about the role of education in their lives. Reflecting on his parents'
advice, Richard agreed that education was necessary for upward mobility, but he
also had reservations:

> In a way . . . I agree with my mom about the importance of an education. But when
> I see people who can't get jobs, I kind of gave up on that. But, then again, it was
> good to go to school and get a degree and let it sit there. At least you know you have
> it, you don't have to go back and do it over. It was good to let it sit there and when
> opportunities open you can go for it. Eventually, you can be the lucky one.

In a similar vein, Steven, the West Indian man who grew up in East Flatbush,
Brooklyn, had interrupted his undergraduate studies because of academic troubles, as well as financial hardships, but he still planned to return someday to earn
a Bachelor of Arts degree:

> I know I have to go back to school . . . so that I can get my college education. You get
> a little more respect when you have that paper—the college diploma. You use your
> mind when you get the paper. But, it's just a bragging right. That's all it is. I think that
> there will always be discrimination.

Steven did not oppose education and planned to return to college, but he worried
that regardless of the level of education he reached, he would be discriminated
against in the workplace.[18] Fine and Weis's 1998 study of the social critique ema-
nating from poor and working-class White, Black, and Latino communities also
found that men were generally concerned that educational credentials would not
pay off in the future. For Fine and Weis, this ambivalence must be understood as
"an accurate portrayal of the economic prospects of poor and working-class young

adults in American in the 1990s" (1998, p. 234). However, Fine and Weis also found that women appear more hopeful about their occupational prospects.

WOMEN'S GHETTOIZATION

The dramatic loss of manufacturing jobs, traditionally a mobility ladder for less-skilled men, and the simultaneous expansion of low-level white-collar jobs, which increasingly employ women, has important implications for the way men and women regard education. "Of the ten occupations that will require the largest number of new workers, two—registered nurses and primary school teachers—require college degrees. All the others—janitors, cashiers, truck drivers, and the like—involve skills that can be picked up on the job with little if any schoolroom knowledge" (see Waldinger, 1996). Moreover, the jobs that require college degrees are occupations traditionally considered women's work, while those that require minimal training are typically considered men's work.

Growing industries such as finance and law rely heavily on a peripheral support staff composed mostly of women. To be exact, in the 1980s, four out of five people who worked in offices and processed information for businesses and government were women (see Epstein & Duncombe, 1991). However, despite women's continued entry into traditionally male-dominated work, the sex segregation of occupations has continued. Eighty percent of clerical workers were female in 1980, compared with 60% in 1950 (Epstein & Duncombe, 1991).

Networked into Pink-Collar Work

Partly because the feminization of the workplace has created more opportunities in the service sector, the women in this study reported far fewer problems in finding work. Women reported fewer difficulties than men in finding employment because they have better networks for potential job opportunities.[19] When asked how they found their work, women frequently mentioned ties to community-based organizations, churches, and their family members. Women reported working through the Summer Youth Employment Program (SYEP) and subsequently being offered part-time work during the academic year. Twenty-five percent of the women surveyed had entered the labor market through SYEP, compared with only 8% of the men.[20]

Good relationships with teachers sometimes materialized into employment opportunities for women. Janet, a 26-year-old Dominican woman who grew up in Washington Heights, Manhattan, and earned a Bachelor of Arts degree in psychology, reminisced:

> I got my current job as the director of fund-raising at my former Catholic high school through my principal, who happened to be my eighth-grade teacher and thought I

was capable. The job that I had prior to this, actually all the jobs that I've ever held, have been through people who know me and know that I was probably capable of it—my first job being with my aunt. Then, one of my roommates, when I lived on Long Island, got me the job at the college, in the Bursar's Office. And now this job. So for me, that's how it has been.

Studies suggest that teacher links to jobs are of particular importance to Black and Latino youths. In a study of high-school-to-work links in Chicago, Rosenbaum and Binder concluded that teachers "provide a good channel of access for students, and in inner city schools these students' best chance of getting a job is through their teachers" (1997, p. 79). Rosenbaum, Roy, and Kariya (1995) also found that women were far more likely than men to have established supportive relationships with people, such as teachers, who are networked to job opportunities.

Family members, particularly other women, such as aunts, sisters, and cousins, also provided women entry into growing sectors of the economy. Yvonne, a 23-year-old Dominican woman who grew up in Williamsburg, Brooklyn, credited her aunts with giving her a valuable "jump start" in the labor market:

> I started working as a research assistant at an investment firm because my aunt worked there. She actually spoke for me. My aunt once told me, "You know what, the first job you get, try for it to be a good job and something that can take you somewhere." I never really thought about it, but it's true. My first job was at the brokerage firm and my friend's job was at our local supermarket. My friend is still at the supermarket! We're the same age, went to the same high school and college, had the same upbringing and she's still a cashier at that supermarket! I'm sure that if my aunts didn't have those kinds of jobs I would have been a cashier too, because I didn't know where to start or where to go.

Although Yvonne entered a low-level pink-collar job, she, like many other women, "got her foot in the door" to an expanding economic sector. Yvonne planned to become an investment banker, in part because her experiences as a research assistant at an investment firm gave her a panoramic view of potential career trajectories in a growing sector of the economy—an experience many of the men lacked.

Since women generally obtained more work experience in the formal labor market than men, they had better qualifications for future employment. Maryse, a 23-year-old Haitian woman who grew up in Crown Heights, was looking for work at the time of the interview, but she was confident that her office skills and references would help her find administrative work. Maryse's employment trajectory mirrored that of the other women:

> It was an internship program through the school. . . . It was basically administrative work like typing and filing. It was a great experience for me, definitely a learning experience. I was working for an architect. My boss actually constructed my school. I really enjoyed working there.
>
> [During high school I worked in the summer] . . . for three years. It was administrative work. It was a program through my mother's union that they constructed for

the summer for kids whose parents were working through the union. I also worked as a child-care provider through the Summer Youth Employment Program.

Through their job experiences in the service sector, women acquired many of the "soft skills," such as familiarity with professional demeanor and dress. Hence, by the time they graduated high school, men and women had accumulated resumes, references, work experiences, and contacts that were quite different.

Color(ing) and Gender(ing) the Glass Ceiling

The feminization of the workforce has had mixed results for Black and Latina women. Occupational shifts have produced vacancies in white-collar work for Black and Latina women who were formerly confined to domestic services and factory work; however, these women continue to work in ghettoized jobs and do not receive a salary commensurate with their educational credentials (see Bound & Dresser, 1999; Wrigley, 1992). Even "Black women with four years of college who work full time, on average, earn the equivalent of a White male high school dropout who works full time. 'Equal' education does not translate across racial/ethnic and gender into equal 'income'" (see Fine & Weis, 1998). Jahaira, a Dominican woman who grew up in Bushwick, Brooklyn, and worked as a research assistant at an investment firm, explained that the glass ceiling was quite different from that faced by women who were not defined as racial "others":

> They expect you to do much more work than your White counterpart. Same exact job but they expect you to do so much more for less money. I didn't think that existed but it does. It really, really does. I was getting paid . . . $23,000 a year and this White woman who just started, came in with the same credentials. I'm a college graduate. The only thing that she had that I didn't have was something called a Series 7, which you have to get to be a broker. It's a licensing thing. Okay, so that's why she was making $35,000 already. So, when I heard her talking on the phone she was making $40,000 a year, I raised hell and I got a lot of raises quickly!

Ironically, the painful incidents women had had with discrimination reminded them of the importance of pursuing education. Instead of being discouraged by the racial and gender discrimination she experienced at work, Jahaira fought back by "raising hell" and not accepting her ghettoization. Significantly, Jahaira aspired to become an investment manager and planned to obtain a master's degree in business administration.

Cassandra, a Dominican woman who grew up in Washington Heights, Manhattan, also had a social critique of the race-gender stratification she experienced at work. Cassandra explained that she experienced a multifaceted glass ceiling at work:

> I worked in corporate America for six years, at a major commercial bank. And believe me, yes it was very good when you're bilingual, but they use it against you when it comes to promotion time. Oh yeah, they love to have a bilingual person. I had a

Spanish-speaking clientele that was from Argentina and Israel and they wouldn't ask for anybody else but me. But when it comes to being an assistant manager, which I was already doing the job and I knew everything, somehow it never got to me. I was always the next in line, but they always skipped the line to the next White person.

Cassandra's experience was not simply the addition of gender, racial, class, or language discrimination but a complex entanglement and interaction of all of these processes. After her negative experiences in the private sector, Cassandra sought employment in the public sector and at the time of the interview was working in housing management for city government. Research points to how Black women are considerably more likely than White women to believe that they need to pursue postgraduate work in order to advance their careers. Higginbotham's and Weber's (1999) study of Black and White professional women found that while White women were content with their work situations, Black women anticipated moving to a new firm in order to achieve occupational mobility.

A more insidious form of discrimination in the workplace reported by the interviewees was episodes of racialized sexual harassment. Racialized sexual harassment is "a particular set of injuries resulting from the unique complex of power relations facing ... women of color in the workplace" (Cho, 1997). Cassandra recalled how she also grappled with the "mamasita" stereotype at work:

> It's a very shocking thing. It's a constant. They have a stereotype of Dominican and Latina women as mamasitas. I have even had guys ask me, "Are Dominican women as hot as they say they are?" And I say, "Why don't you do me a favor. Take a hot pepper and stick it up yours and see how hot it is!"

Cassandra added that at times her male coworkers insisted they knew that Dominican "ladies" liked to be called "mamasita."[21] The stereotype of Latina women as "mamasitas"—sexually available, immoral, and "cheap" women—is akin to the jezebel stereotype of African American women. This narrative is part of the race-gender-sexual exoticization and "symbolic taint" of the urban ghetto and its inhabitants. Collins (1990) explains that these "controlling images" are used to justify the exploitation of women who are deemed racially inferior.[22]

Optimistic Outlooks

Although women maintained a social critique of racial and gender discrimination in the labor market, they also remained hopeful about the role of education in contesting negative stereotypes about them as "mamasitas" (Fine & Weis, 1998). This was in part because they have had more work experiences in the formal labor market. This allowed them to see the relevance of educational credentials in a postindustrial economy.[23] In a study of racial identity among second-generation Haitian and West Indian youth, Waters (1996) found that women believed there were more work opportunities for them than for men. Similarly, Dunn (1998) also found that

African American women completed higher levels of education because they believed there were more jobs for them than for their male counterparts.

Women constantly pointed to examples of other women who had been successful through pursuing an education. Marie, a 19-year-old Haitian woman who grew up in Crown Heights, Brooklyn, was struggling with academic problems in college but was still firmly committed to education:

> I think that if you work hard in school it will pay off. I truly think that . . . like my aunt, right now. She wanted to be a registered nurse so bad. She was a nurse's aide. She went to school, she just studied, she was in the library every day, and she went back to college. Now she's a registered nurse and she's really happy.

Even those women who were ghettoized into the lowest service sector jobs and those who were temporary workers maintained an optimistic outlook about the importance of education. Tina, a 21-year-old West Indian woman who grew up in South Ozone Park, Queens, and worked as a nurse's assistant while attending college, echoed the sentiments of the women:

> Education is very, very important. I see people stuck. . . . I'm not going to stay there. But, for them that's their family support. . . . In my opinion, people can make it by getting a good education and then finding a good job. It takes a while to get where you're going. But, eventually you get there. It's better than just sitting home and staying stagnant and not doing anything. Even if you get your bachelor's, from there you go on, you do another two or three years, or four years for a doctorate degree. But you still get there.

Although Tina was working in a low-level job, she expected to finish a graduate degree and become a child psychologist. It was shocking that while many of the women knew about a PhD, none of the men mentioned this as a possibility.

Women always linked the importance of obtaining an education to their status as women. According to Maryse, the Haitian woman who grew up in Crown Heights, Brooklyn, and was attending a paralegal school and planned to become a lawyer:

> You can be successful through education, hard work, and persistence. That's how you can make it in the business world. You have to be educated because you are competing against men.

Although the women in this study expressed interest in traditionally female-dominated fields, such as nursing and teaching, it is significant that they aspired to professional jobs within those fields.[24] Whereas men struggled to name a specific career they wanted to pursue, women articulated clear career goals, such as psychologist, teacher, investment manager, and registered nurse. This was in part because women saw possibilities for work in these expanding sectors of the economy, while men, lacking this type of work experience, did not even have a clear sense of where they fit in the new postindustrial economy.

CONCLUSION

The synergy of deindustrialization, the emergence of a postindustrial economy, the feminization of the workforce, and continued institutionalized discrimination along racial and gender lines have produced rather different employment scenarios for second-generation men and women who are racially stigmatized in U.S. society. Second-generation Caribbean men, like other men of African phenotype, such as African Americans, experience great difficulty finding work because employers see them as potential criminals and untrustworthy employees. Part-time work and temporary jobs, such as unloading trucks and making deliveries for "pocket money," were often the only type of jobs available to them because they are viewed primarily as hoodlums. Continually encountering negative experiences during their job searches and while at work, men increasingly perceived a *job ceiling* working against them. In due course, men formulated *worried outlooks* about their employment possibilities. It is important to note that men did not oppose education as a route for social mobility. Men did express doubts that education would protect them from the virulent racial discrimination they encountered even when looking for entry-level work. The multiple problems men experienced in the labor market are not due to any "oppositional identity" they harbored, but rather reflect the reality that they are continually placed at the bottom of the hiring queue.

Women generally reported fewer difficulties in finding work. Although women's positions were often in pink-collar ghettos, such positions did provide women with a window to potential career paths in growth sectors of the economy, such as education, health, and finance. Given that many of these positions require educational credentials, women linked social mobility with education. Despite the negative race, gender, and sexual incidents they confronted in the workplace, they formulated optimistic outlooks about the importance of education for them as women defined as racial minorities. Men's and women's disparate outlooks relate to the distinct and cumulative race-gender experiences they were subjected to in their everyday lived experiences during their youth and young adulthood in the workplace.

What are the implications of these findings for contemporary research on the children of immigrants? While segmented assimilation is a very valuable framework for understanding ethnic identity, its focus on the resources and vulnerabilities of different ethnic groups may miss more dynamic processes, namely the salience of race and gender processes in the lived experiences of the second generation.[25] Reducing race and gender to elements of the assimilation process is problematic because it deflects attention from "the ubiquity of racial [and gender] meanings and dynamics" in everyday life experiences, as well as in institutional practices (Omi & Winant, 1994).

The proposed race-gender experience theory attempts to bring race and gender processes from the margins of analysis to the center of the analysis; it unearths how the lived experiences of the second generation are framed by the racialized and gendered narratives in the larger U.S. landscape. Employers do not see and treat the second generation as "genderless ethnics," but rather as racial(ized) and gender(ed) bodies. Given that the very networks and resources that are open to the second generation are structured along racial and gender lines, it is important that future studies of the second generation place race and gender processes at the forefront of the analysis. In this way, the racial and gender differences in the education and work trajectories of the second generation will no longer appear to be the "natural" fates of different "ethnic" groups that possess different resources. Rather, they can be understood as socially constructed processes that need to be unraveled and interrupted.

NOTES

1. Note that the use of the suffix "(ing)" in terms such as "gender(ing)," "race(ing)," and "color(ing)" is meant to highlight the social construction of race and gender processes. The author's preference for this terminology stems from an effort to stress that race and gender are not biological facts or unchangeable "essences," but rather represent historically variable socially constructed processes that can be described at the microlevel of social interaction and at the macrolevel of institutional practices. (See Hondagneu-Sotelo, 1999.)

2. Studies of the second generation have focused on examinations of their ethnic identity. (See Waters, 1996.)

3. For a discussion of segmented assimilation theory, see Portes, 1996.

4. Since they lack the education and work skills to obtain more prestigious work, this "second generation decline" would mean long-term poverty, disadvantage, and downward mobility for the children of immigrants. (See Grasmuck & Pessar, 1996.)

5. For a sampling of critical race theory, critical race feminist theory, and Latino critical race theory, see Crenshaw et al., 1996; Delgado, 1995; Fine and Weis, 1998; Haney-López, 1996; Hurtado, 1996.

6. The principal investigators for The Second Generation in Metropolitan New York, sponsored by the Center for Urban Research, Graduate School, and University Center, City University of New York, are John Mollenkopf, Philip Kasinitz, and Mary Waters.

7. Second-generation youth are defined as U.S.-born children of immigrant parents or youth who had most of their schooling in the United States. The following is a gender breakdown of the youth interviewed: For Dominicans there were 12 men and 15 women; among West Indians there were 15 men and 7 women; and for Haitians there were 8 men and 9 women.

8. This percentage included college, vocational institutions, the military, and the police academy.

9. It is important to conduct qualitative studies of racialization processes because the terms "Latino" and "Black," which are used in survey research, may obfuscate concrete differences in their lived experiences. These terms refer to a great variety of people with different phenotypes, genders, sexual orientation, and so on.

10. I conducted all but three of the in-depth interviews with Caribbean participants.

11. The Dominican Republic yielded over half a million immigrants (580,225), followed by Cuba (456,997), Jamaica (417,652), Haiti (275,581), Guyana (179,627), and Trinidad and Tobago (129,618). (See *Statistical Yearbook 1994*, pp. 28–31, quoted in Parillo, 1999, p. 426. See also Hernández, 2002; Hernández & Rivera-Batiz, 1997; Torres-Saillant & Hernández, 1998.)

12. Overall, a third of immigrants in New York were born in the Caribbean. (See Waldinger, 1996, p. 50.)

13. While some participants reported that their family had operated a small business, such as a bodega (grocery store), typically these businesses had failed and therefore could not serve as a job safety net for them.

14. Given that in the collective consciousness of the United States, the "color" of undocumented immigrants is dark, second-generation Caribbean youth may be subjected to more racial discrimination in the labor market.

15. Even Black employers' hiring queues appear to disadvantage men. (See Kirchenman, 1997.)

16. Although in the 1990s some immigrant groups were able to make inroads into the construction industry, European immigrants and their coethnics have largely controlled it. (See Waldinger, 1996.)

17. Wealth disparities are even more blatant. Blacks with Bachelor of Arts degrees possess 23 cents for every dollar owned by Whites. (See Oliver & Shapiro, 1995, p. 110.)

18. These findings diverged sharply with MacLeod's (1995) ethnographic study of White, Black, and Latino young men living in a New York City housing project. MacLeod found that Blacks and Latinos believed that being a racial minority was an asset in the labor market because racial minorities were advantaged in comparison with Whites through affirmative action programs.

19. First-generation Latina women have better job networks than their male counterparts. (See Hagan, 1998.)

20. This may be in part because the types of jobs offered through this program were traditionally pink-collar jobs, such as child care and administrative assistant.

21. Jahaira, who also worked in finance, recalled a White male colleague who always wanted to know where she was "really" from. At other times this colleague made derogatory comments about Haitians because he thought Jahaira was from Haiti. Even at the company Christmas party, Jahaira's White coworkers asked her if she was feeling okay, because she was not dancing or talking loudly. In their view, all women from the Caribbean were naturally wild and colorful partygoers. These racial(ized) and gender(ed) stereotypes are rooted in the historically unequal power relations, military interventions, and exploitation in the Third World. (See Cho, 1997.)

22. Given the ways in which the racialization of minority women is tied to racially stigmatized notions of their sexuality, it is imperative that particular attention be paid to the "color" of the sexual harassment in the workplace. As explained by Cho (1997, p. 204): "the Law's current dichotomous categorization of racial discrimination and sexual harassment as separate spheres of injury is inadequate to respond to racialized sexual harassment." In this regard, the sexual harassment that minority women are exposed to must be understood as intersecting with racial discrimination.

23. Women who had obtained jobs as administrative assistants at law firms or social service agencies learned about high-level white-collar professional positions, such as in social work, law, and education.

24. These findings contrasted sharply with Weis's (1990) study of the effect of deindustrialization among White working-class youth, where women articulated career goals that were pinned to traditional pink-collar ghettoized work. Weis found that most women still selected secretary as their career goal.

25. It is important to highlight that race-gender experience theory emphasizes that there are no "essential" differences between men and women. Rather, differing race-gender outlooks arise because of differences in experiences, not biology. These experiential differences

are the outcome of social interactions and structural relationships; as such, race and gender are not only categories of identity, but embody social relations and social organizations. It is the differing race-gender experiences men and women had in the domain of work, not their racial identity, that shaped their attitudes toward education and social mobility.

REFERENCES

Bound, John, & Dresser, Laura. (1999). Losing ground: The erosion of the relative earnings of African American women during the 1980s. In Irene Browne (Ed.), *Latinas and African American women at work: Race, gender, and economic inequality.* New York: Russell Sage Foundation.

Cho, Sumi. (1997). Converging stereotypes in racialized sexual harassment: Where the model minority meets Suzie Wong. In Adrien Katherine Wing (Ed.), *Critical race feminism: A reader.* New York: New York University Press.

Collins, Patricia Hill. (1990). *Black feminist thought: Knowledge, consciousness, and the politics of empowerment.* Boston: Unwin Hyman.

Crenshaw, Kimberlé, Gotanda, Neil, Peller, Garry, & Thomas, Kendall (Eds.) (1996). *Critical race theory: The key writings that formed the movement.* New York: New Press.

CUNY student data book. (1996, Fall). (Vol. 1). New York: City University of New York.

Delgado, Richard. (Ed.). (1995). *Critical race theory: The cutting edge.* Philadelphia: Temple University Press.

Dunn, James. (1998). The shortage of black male students in the college classroom: Consequences and causes. *Western Journal of Black Studies, 12*(2), 73–76.

Epstein, Cynthia Fuchs, & Duncombe, Stephen. (1991). Women clerical workers. In John Mollenkopf & Manuel Castells (Eds.), *Dual city: Restructuring New York.* New York: Russell Sage Foundation.

Feagin, Joe, & Sikes, Melvin. (1994). *Living with racism: The black middle class experience.* New York: Routledge.

Fine, Michelle, & Weis, Lois. (1998). *The unknown city: Lives of poor and working-class young adults.* Boston: Beacon Press.

Gans, Herbert. (1992). Second-generation decline: Scenarios for the economic and ethnic futures of the post-1965 American immigrants. *Ethnic and Racial Studies, 15*(2), 173–193.

Grasmuck, Sherri, & Pessar, Patricia. (1996). First and second generation settlement of Dominicans in the United States: 1960–1990. In Silvia Pedraza & Rubén Rumbaut (Eds.), *Origins and destinies: Immigration, race, and ethnicity in America.* Belmont, CA: Wadsworth.

Griffins, M. L. (1994). *Critical choices: Education and employment among New York City youth.* New York: Community Services Society.

Hacker, Andrew. (1992). *Two nations: Black and white, separate, hostile, unequal.* New York: Random House.

Hagan, Jacqueline. (1998). Social networks, gender, and immigrant incorporation. *American Sociological Review, 63*(1), 55–67.

Haney-López, Ian. (1996). *White by law: The legal construction of race.* New York: New York University Press.

Hawkins, Denise. (1996). Gender gap: Black females outpace male counterparts at three degree levels. *Black Issues in Higher Education,* 20–22.

Hernández, Ramona. (2002). *The mobility of labor under advanced capitalism: Dominican migration to the United States.* New York: Columbia University Press.

Hernández, Ramona, & Rivera-Batiz, Francisco. (1997). *Dominican New Yorkers: A socioeconomic profile, 1990.* New York: Dominican Studies Institute, City University of New York.

Higginbotham, Elizabeth, & Weber, Lynn. (1999). Perceptions of workplace discrimination among black and white professional-managerial women. In Irene Browne (Ed.), *Latinas and African American women at work: Race, gender, and economic inequality.* New York: Russell Sage Foundation.

Hondagneu-Sotelo, Pierrette. (1999). Gender and contemporary U.S. immigration. *American Behavioral Scientist, 42*(4), 565–576.

Hurtado, Aída. (1996). *The color of privilege: Three blasphemies on race and feminism.* Ann Arbor, MI: University of Michigan.

Hurtado, Aída, Hayes-Bautista, David E., Valdez, R. Burciaga, & Hernández, Anthony C. R. (1992). *Redefining California: Latino social engagement in a multicultural society.* Los Angeles: UCLA Chicano Studies Research Center.

Kasinitz, Philip, & Rosenberg, Jan. (1996). Missing the connection: Social isolation and empowerment on the Brooklyn waterfront. *Social Problems, 43*(2), 180–196.

Kirchenman, Joleen. (1997). African American employers' attitudes toward African American workers. In Steven Tuch & Jack Martin (Eds.), *Racial attitudes in the 1990s: Continuity and change.* Westport, CT: Praeger.

Kirchenman, Joleen, & Neckerman, Kathryn. (1993). We'd love to hire them, but ... : The meaning of race for employers. In Michael Katz (Ed.), *The "underclass" debate: View from history.* Princeton, NJ: Princeton University Press.

Lewin, Tamar. (1998, December 6). American colleges begin to ask, Where have all the men gone? *New York Times,* p. A1.

Lopez, Nancy. (2002). *Hopeful girls, troubled boys: Race and gender disparity in urban education.* New York: Routledge.

MacLeod, Jay. (1995). *Ain't any makin' it: Aspirations and attainment in a low-income neighborhood.* San Francisco: Westview Press, 1995.

Model, Suzanne. (1997). An occupational tale of two cities: Minorities in London and New York. *Demography, 34*(4), 539–550.

Newman, Katherine, & Ellis, Catherine. (1999). "There's no shame in my game": Status and stigma among Harlem's working poor. In Michael Lamont (Ed.), *The cultural territories of race: Black and white boundaries.* Chicago: University of Chicago.

Ogbu, John, & Simons, Herbert. (1998). Voluntary and involuntary minorities: A cultural-ecological theory of school performance with some implications for education. *Anthropology and Education Quarterly, 29*(2), 155–188.

Oliver, Melvin, & Shapiro, Thomas. (1995). *Black wealth/white wealth: A new perspective on racial inequality.* New York: Routledge.

Omi, Michael, & Winant, Howard. (1994). *Racial formation in the United States: From 1960s to 1990s.* New York: Routledge.

Parillo, Vincent. (1999). *Strangers to these shores: Race and ethnic relations in the United States.* Boston: Allyn & Bacon.

Portes, Alejandro (Ed.). (1996). *The new second generation.* New York: Russell Sage Foundation.

Portes, Alejandro, & Zhou, Min. (1993). The new second generation: Segmented assimilation and its variants. *Annals of the American Academy of Political and Social Science, 530,* 74–96.

Reaching the top: A report on the National Task Force on Minority High Achievement. (1999). New York: College Board Publications.

Robinson, William. (1993). The global economy and the Latino populations in the United States: A world systems approach. *Critical Sociology, 19*(2), 29–59.

Rosenbaum, James, & Binder, Amy. (1997). Do employers really need more educated youth? *Sociology of Education, 70*, 68–85.

Rosenbaum, James, Roy, Kevin, & Kariya, Takehico. (1995). *Do high school students help some students enter the labor market?* Paper presented at the annual meeting of the American Sociological Association, Washington, DC.

Rumbaut, Rubén. (1998). *Transformations: The post-immigrant generation in an age of diversity.* Paper presented at the annual meeting of the Eastern Sociological Society, Philadelphia.

Smith, Thomas M. (1995). *The educational progress of immigrant students: Findings from the conditions of education* (NCES 95-767). Washington, DC: National Center for Educational Statistics.

Stanton-Salazar, Ricardo. (1997). A social capital framework for understanding the socialization of racial minority children and youths. *Harvard Educational Review, 67*(1), 1–40.

Statistical Yearbook 1994. (1995). Washington, DC: U.S. Government Printing Office.

Sum, Andrew, Kronshko, J., Fogg, N., & Palma, S. (2000). *The college enrollment and employment outcomes for the class of 1998 Boston Public High School graduates: Key findings of the 1999 follow-up surveys.* Boston: Center for Labor Market Studies, Northeastern University.

Torres, Andres, & Bonilla, Frank. (1995). Decline within decline. In Rebecca Morales & Frank Bonilla (Eds.), *Latinos in a changing United States economy: Comparative perspectives on growing inequality.* London: Sage.

Torres-Saillant, Silvio, & Hernández, Ramona. (1998). *The Dominican Americans.* Westport, CT: Greenwood.

Waldinger, Roger. (1996). *Still the promised cities: African-American and new immigrants in a postindustrial New York.* Cambridge, MA: Harvard University Press.

Waters, Mary. (1996). The intersections of gender, race, and ethnicity in identity development of Caribbean American teens. In Bonnie Leadbeater & Niobe Way (Eds.), *Urban girls: Resisting stereotypes, creating identities.* New York: New York University.

Weis, Lois. (1990). High school girls in a de-industrializing economy. In Lois Weis (Ed.), *Class, race, and gender in American education.* Albany: State University of New York Press, 1990.

Wrigley, Julia. (1992). Gender, education, and the welfare state. In Julia Wrigley (Ed.), *Education and gender equality.* New York: Falmer Press.

CHAPTER 10

Gendered Geographies of Home

Mapping Second- and Third-Generation Puerto Ricans' Sense of Home

Maura I. Toro-Morn and Marixsa Alicea

INTRODUCTION

The idea for this essay developed over a series of conversations we had about what "home" means to us given our different personal stories. Maura was born and raised in Puerto Rico and migrated to the Midwest in the early 1980s, whereas Marixsa was born and raised in Chicago and lived on the island for only several months at a time. In sharing stories about our upbringing, we noted the complexities and contradictions that made up our notions of "home."[1] In the face of the racism, classism, and otherness that we felt in U.S. society and in the academy, home and family informed how we defined ourselves racially, ethnically, and culturally, offered personal nurturance and support, and defined our professional work and our passions. Yet, we were also aware that our "homes" were fraught with many contradictions, complexities, tensions, and ambiguities. Our homes, both in Puerto Rico and in U.S. Puerto Rican communities, rather than offering us solace from gender oppression, were themselves sites of this form of subjugation.

Thus, we became interested in how Puerto Ricans who had been born and raised in the United States think of and imagine the concept of home. As Puerto Rican women, we were also interested in the gendered aspects of these processes. How is "home" connected to our racial and gendered identities as Puerto Ricans? What do visits to Puerto Rico mean? What are some of the complexities and contradictions that make up our notions of home? To help answer these questions, we conducted interviews with second- and third-generation Puerto Ricans in Chicago.

Our research shows that for second- and third-generation Puerto Ricans notions of home are complex and diverse. Although second- and third-generation Puerto Ricans grew up hearing stories about Puerto Rico, their relationship to the island and their communities of origin defies easy categorization. These stories shaped not only racial/ethnic and gendered identities, but also understandings of Puerto Rico and Puerto Rican communities in the United States as home.

This essay explores those aspects that make negotiating multiple identities and life on the borderlands difficult. Although recently life on the borderlands has been defined as a source of creation and celebration, in our research we found that life on the margins can be difficult because there are few road maps or frameworks for constructing identities that are transnational. Second- and third-generation Puerto Ricans struggle with living in two cultures. Like many of us, they grew up to believe they should belong to one place or another, and that allegiance to one place precludes allegiance to another. With respect to gender issues, we found that Puerto Rican parents constructed their U.S. homes as "authentic" cultural spaces and expected their children to conform to traditional gender roles and values. Sons and daughters sometimes experienced the double standard between their parents' gender ideologies and actual practices. For example, daughters described how they admired their mothers' struggle to juggle work and family responsibilities, but resented their parents' overprotectiveness and gender expectations concerning their sexuality. Sons, on the other hand, sought to reconcile the conflicts, ambiguities, and tensions of their masculine identities. Despite these struggles, the second and third generation seek solace from the multiple forms of oppression they confront as colonized people in the United States by invoking romanticized images of the homeland.

LITERATURE REVIEW AND BACKGROUND

Much of the literature concerning second-generation immigrants has focused on the degree to which this generation is assimilating, both culturally and structurally, into U.S. society (see, e.g., Portes, 1996; Rumbaut, 1996; Zhou, 1997). When confronted with the persistence of ethnic identities across generations, studies have sought to explain why second-generation groups did not follow the conventional paths toward Americanization (Zhou, 1997). According to Portes's and Zhou's (1993) model of segmented assimilation, factors such as the place of settlement, opportunity structures, and race, as well as the degree of assistance that an immigrant group receives from both coethnic and U.S. institutions, help explain the process of assimilation. In addition, other scholars have sought to understand the conflicts that occur when first-generation immigrant parents try to instill within their children homeland cultural values but are faced with second-generation children who reject the homeland culture (Rumbaut, 1996; Zhou, 1997). While this literature has generated important insights about the adaptation processes of the new second generation, gender remains almost entirely neglected in such studies.

In contrast with assimilationist perspectives, the transnational migration literature shows how immigrants maintain ties to homeland communities as a reference point for defining their identity and their place in U.S. society (Duany, 1999, 2000). Scholars argue that families in racial-ethnic communities provide a haven from the racist world and that immigrants maintain ties to home communities in an effort to resist disadvantaged class conditions and race oppression. In addition, recent studies of immigrant groups have argued that "remembered place . . . serve[s] as symbolic anchors of community for dispersed people" (Gupta & Ferguson, 1992, p. 11). This literature, however, has not sufficiently addressed the contradictory nature of U.S. homes and homeland communities for women (Rouse, 1992; Wiltshire, 1992). The metaphoric use of homeland and U.S. homes as an anchor highlights solidarity, yet it dissolves separations and the hierarchical relations of inequality among family members (Brow, 1990). This depiction obscures the race, class, and gender tensions and ambiguities that are a part of second- and third-generation Puerto Rican immigrants' experiences and notions of U.S. homes and homeland communities.

Recent attempts to capture the gendered aspects of the second-generation experience can be found in the work of Espiritu (1999, this volume), DasGupta (1997), and Perez (1998). These studies found that while first-generation immigrant groups maintain connections with homeland and U.S. ethnic communities as a way to resist race and class oppression, they do so at the expense of perpetuating gender oppression within U.S. home communities. This new work highlights how immigrants attempt to construct U.S. homes as "authentic" cultural spaces. Yet, part of constructing "authentic" cultural spaces requires many parents to uphold traditional gender roles and expect their children to do likewise. Espiritu's (1999) study of Filipinos, for example, suggests how parents invoke idealized notions of home that are meant to keep second-generation young women within subordinate gender roles. In particular, Espiritu (1999) explores how second-generation daughters are expected to "maintain (uphold) traditional gender roles in the name of the community's culture survival and nationalism, acting as emblems of cultural authenticity" and purity. Immigrant families and communities assert the moral superiority of their culture by attempting to control young women's autonomy, mobility, and personal decision making. In addition, DasGupta's (1997) study of Indian immigrants in New York observes that immigrant parents try to control their daughters and maintain their labor and sexuality by emphasizing the importance of family honor and female virginity in the attempt to resist disadvantaged race and class positions. This interpretation of home "facilitated a stark contrast against their stereotypes of 'American' culture, which by their definition was degenerate" (Das-Gupta, 1997). This strategy, however, comes at a high cost for women.

We build on this work to show that second- and third-generation Puerto Ricans use Puerto Rico and U.S. Puerto Rican homes as a reference point to affirm racial and class identity. Young women, however, recognize that the real and imagined notions of homeland cannot fully serve as a place to define all the aspects of their gendered identities. That is, they are aware that while they can embrace some aspects of home, they must reject others. They embrace the homeland as an important reference for racial and ethnic identity, yet they challenge traditional gender expectations. Given their history as a colonized people who have also had to endure neocolonial positions within U.S. society, second- and third-generation Puerto Ricans find themselves in a "world traversed with intersecting lines of power and resistance," a world that we must come to understand "in terms of its destructive divisions of gender, color, class, sexuality, and nation" (Mohanty, 1991, p. 2). It is a world of asymmetrical power relations where gendered power relations are reconstituted from home societies to U.S. societies.

Finally, exploring the experiences of second- and third-generation Puerto Rican immigrants also adds to the growing and diverse literature on Puerto Rican migration and settlement in the United States (see, e.g., History Task Force, 1979; Ortiz, 1996; Padilla, 1987; Rodriguez, 1989; Whalen, 1998). Studies of the Puerto Rican migration experience have explored the migration of Puerto Ricans to New York and other East Coast communities (Sánchez Korrol, 1983, 1986; Whalen, 1998). In addition, studies have also analyzed the labor market experiences of Puerto Rican workers (Cintron-Velez, 1999; Daponte, 1996; Falcon, Gurak, & Powers, 1990; Santana-Cooney & Ortiz, 1983; Santana-Cooney & Colón-Warren, 1979) and the social problems that they have confronted as immigrants in the process of settlement (Bourgois, 1996; Colberg & Burgos, 1988; Roschelle, 1997). We have also seen the development of studies that explore the experiences of Puerto Rican women outside New York (Alicea, 1997; Padilla, 1987; Padilla & Santiago, 1993; Peterman, 1998; Toro-Morn, 1995; Whalen, 1998). A smaller number of studies have examined the experiences of second- and third-generation Puerto Ricans in the East Coast Puerto Rican communities, but most of this literature has tended to focus on their assimilation process (Canino, 1994; Gurak & Kritz, 1985; Rogler & Santana-Cooney, 1984; Rogler & Santana-Cooney, 1994). Our explorations of the second and third generation in Chicago reflect our intellectual and personal desire to add to the growing literature on Puerto Ricans in the United States and to theorize about this neglected area of the Puerto Rican diaspora.

METHODOLOGY

In an attempt to capture the complexities of how second and third generations reconstructed home, we incorporated a range of data-gathering techniques. We began with the data we had each generated during our dissertation research, since this data contained some interviews with second-generation Puerto Ricans in Chicago, New York, and Puerto Rico. We used these interviews as preliminary explorations that allowed us to generate new questions for a second wave of interviews. We conducted twelve interviews with second and third generations in Chicago and central Illinois. The interviews lasted between 1 and 3 hours, were conducted in English, Spanish, and Spanglish, and were fully transcribed and analyzed by both of us.

We use the term *second generation* to refer to the children of Puerto Rican immigrants who were born or reared in the United States. *Third generation* refers to the children of second-generation Puerto Ricans. While most of our sample consists of second- and third-generation Puerto Ricans who were born and raised in Chicago, we also included four interviews with second-generation Puerto Ricans who were born in New York but are currently residing in Illinois. Most of the second-generation Puerto Ricans were born in the 1960s and came of age in the 1970s, while the third generation were born in the 1980s and came of age in the 1990s. This meant that second- and third-generation Puerto Ricans were growing up at a time of increasing racial and ethnic diversity in the large urban centers of Chicago and New York in which they lived. In Chicago, second- and third-generation Puerto Ricans experienced firsthand the process of community concentration into what has been known, until recently, as Chicago's Puerto Rican community, along Division Street. More recently, the process of gentrification has moved Chicago Puerto Ricans westward.

PUERTO RICAN MIGRATION TO CHICAGO

The migration of Puerto Ricans to the United States has been a continuous process since the military invasion of the island in 1898. The U.S. invasion and the subsequent economic, political, and cultural colonization that accompanied it propelled Puerto Rican workers into a complex global network of migrations. By the turn of the 20th century, Puerto Rican men and women had become part of the international flow of labor to areas in the United States in need of cheap labor.

The most significant movement of Puerto Ricans to the United States took place at the end of World War II (Dietz, 1986; Falcon, Gurak, & Powers, 1990; Pantojas García, 1990). In the late 1940s, the impact of U.S. investment and modernization of the economy transformed Puerto Rico from a predominantly agricultural to an industrial economy. Operation Bootstrap, as the development model became popularly known in Puerto Rico, attracted labor-intensive light manufacturing industries like textiles and apparel to Puerto Rico by offering tax incentives, cheap labor, and easy access to U.S. markets (Dietz, 1986; Pantojas García, 1990). These changes in Puerto Rico's economy had profound consequences for Puerto Rican families. The development model was unable to create enough jobs, and working-class Puerto Ricans began to leave the island, heading for familiar places like New York City and new places like Chicago.

Today, it is difficult to find a Puerto Rican family that has not been touched by migration, either directly or indirectly. It is not uncommon to find three generations of one family who had migrated between the United States and Puerto Rico (Alicea, 1990, p. 92). Initially, migration to Chicago was a working-class phenomenon, a response to the changes in the economy introduced by the new colonial power at different times. Eventually middle-class and educated Puerto Ricans joined working-class Puerto Ricans in the migration process. Educated and professional Puerto Ricans have dealt with the changes in the political economy in Puerto Rico by migrating to the United States (Toro-Morn, 1995).

Gender has shaped the migration of Puerto Ricans to Chicago in many ways. For example, Puerto Rican women migrated to Chicago as part of an organized recruitment effort to provide cheap labor for the growing industrial sector and to resolve the shortage of domestic workers in the city in the 1950s (Toro-Morn, 1999). Government officials rationalized the migration of young single women as domestic workers by maintaining that Puerto Rican women were inherently well suited for domestic work. Alicea (1997) found that migration to Chicago was also a form of resistance to gender oppression in Puerto Rico. Once in Chicago, Puerto Rican women contributed to the formation of a transnational community through kinship work and caring work. Women organized family gatherings, weddings, and anniversaries involving family members both in Puerto Rico and Chicago. This kinship and caring work, though highly demanding and labor intensive, allowed women to resist racial and class discrimination and find opportunities for self-expression, satisfaction, and recognition.

Chicago has been the home of Puerto Ricans for nearly half a century, and is today home to the largest Puerto Rican community in the Midwest. Puerto Ricans have worked very hard to establish an ethnic community as a way to resist institutionalized discrimination. In the early stages of community development, civic organizations and hometown clubs provided the first wave of migrants with a sense of community. In the 1960s and 1970s, alongside hometown clubs, grassroots organizations developed to deal with the social problems Puerto Ricans encountered as newly arrived migrants in the city of Chicago. Puerto Ricans were subject to racial discrimination by the police and the political establishment. By the 1990s, however, the Puerto Rican community of Chicago had become an important player in the city's politics and ethno-cultural landscape, an important sign of a matured ethnic community.

REAL AND IMAGINED HOMES:
RESISTING RACIAL OPPRESSION

Many of the second- and third-generation Puerto Ricans told us that their immigrant parents and grandparents had shared with them jokes, stories, and songs offering vivid images of the island's landscape. These stories provided concrete, physical anchoring points for their experiences as Puerto Ricans. In the stories, the island emerged as a secure, romanticized place that provided nurturance. Like many other immigrants, first-generation Puerto Rican parents showed an unrelenting desire for home, for stability, for protection in the face of continual racial/ethnic and class exploitation. A first-generation migrant woman described how her sister holds on to memories of home and their mother: "Yes [the house is there] and we have remodeled it. My sister, the youngest one, doesn't want to get rid of it. Every time she goes, she goes there and it's like she sees our mother." The stories parents told became an important part of how the second and third generations came to learn and construct both real and imagined notions of Puerto Rico, regardless of whether they had visited Puerto Rico. They became important for resisting belittling definitions of their race and class and for defining a sense of place both in Puerto Rico and the United States. Celia, a third-generation Puerto Rican raised in the Bronx who has never visited the island, described her connection to Puerto Rico as a familial one: "I feel connected through my lineage. For me it's my mom and my grandparents that connects me to Puerto Rico."

Although the Puerto Rican parents migrated to Chicago at a time that Puerto Rico was undergoing a massive industrialization and urbanization program, they tended to remember Puerto Rico as a pristine rural paradise where there was a natural flow of life and connection to the land (Perez, 1998, 2000). These depictions also tended to highlight communal intensity and extended family networks. Eduardo's mother, for example, constructed a view of Puerto Rico as a tropical paradise.

> My mom used to tell me stories about when she lived on the island. They used to live on a farm and they had all these animals: cows, sheep, stuff like that. She used to have all these nice trees, they used to have an avocado tree, a coconut tree, and a mango tree. She really likes mangos, so I remember her talking about that. And I remember her talking about when somebody would die, they would always have a procession through the street. What else . . . she used to build this raft every year and she'd go down the little creek in the raft. That was really cool.

For some second- and third-generation Puerto Ricans who have never been to the island, these stories awaken a desire to visit. We asked Eduardo how he felt about these stories and he replied: "They're kinda cool in a way. You sit there and you're like, wow, because this is where I'm from. . . . I always want to go, I haven't been there myself."

Celia had traveled all over the world, yet she had never visited Puerto Rico. We asked her what motivated her to go now? She replied: "I want to know my roots. I'm going to Puerto Rico, even if I have to go by myself to see where my family came from." Rosa too wanted to "know her roots":

> All of the sudden I wanted to know about my roots. I wanted to know where I came from. I made my dad take me to Puerto Rico. . . . I think it is a time in everybody's life that you want to know your roots. I was about 18. . . . So I told my father I want to go to Puerto Rico. My father hated airplanes, but he went with me. I was there about a month. I liked what I saw. . . . That's why I went back for a month. I was able to go around, the people were friendly, the air was clean. To me it was one big playground. People were so simple. Clean.

Traveling to Puerto Rico helped second- and third-generation immigrants gain a sense of relief from the racism and discrimination they experienced in the United States. It alleviated the general sense of alienation and "otherness" many of them experienced daily. Ironically, in recounting their stories of visits home, these second- and third-generation Puerto Ricans seemed to be unaware of the racial tensions that have always existed in their homeland. Rico was 26 years old when he first traveled to Puerto Rico. He explained his visit by saying, "I wanted to feel complete. I wanted to smell the air." Several respondents, in their descriptions of visiting the island, talked about letting their "shield" down. Here is how Rico described it.

> It's automatic! . . . Every time I leave this country and return I put on my shield. My invisible shield! [Shield? Shield you from what?] You have to be cautious! [You didn't have a shield in Puerto Rico?] Naaa! I took it off! You don't think about it. It automatically happens. Like a covering, like you were saying, it's a cover. In Puerto Rico, it's our nation. This is our land.

Esperanza described the same sense of relief expressed by Rico. While she was aware that in Puerto Rico she might be considered "other" or different because she was born and raised in the United States and did not speak Spanish fluently, during her visit she felt accepted and that she belonged.

> I was scared because I have heard that they are not going to accept you because my Spanish was really not that great. . . . My family lives in Yauco, so we had to take the expressway and then you passed all the mountains and then I just started crying, I was . . . it was so beautiful. . . . But hearing the coquís at night and just, you know, looking out at stars, it was intense. It was really intense. . . . In a grocery store, I stopped and I looked around and it was like, oh, my God this is the first time that I am in a place where everyone around me is same thing and they are not looking at me like I am going to steal something, like I don't belong here, whatever. I'm home. Even though I have never been there and even though I didn't know about it until I got older. I'm home.

Others described it as relief from having to explain themselves and "what they were." Sylvia explains:

> It was more peaceful there—no one was looking at me or judging me, in any way. I was just like family when I was there. . . . [What do you mean that no one was judging you?] Because here in the United States—you are Puerto Rican and you have the African American, you have the White, you have the Asian, you have all these races and they look at you like you're different. . . . And then you feel like you have to explain what your side of the culture is for them to understand and they won't understand. I felt more comfortable in Puerto Rico because they all knew me. That was home there.

Images of the homeland as a haven and of communal intensity, in fact, permeate Puerto Rican literary work. In her narrative work, Judith Ortiz Cofer echoes these sentiments in speaking about her grandmother's house in Puerto Rico.

> My grandmother's house is like a chambered nautilus; it has many rooms, yet it is not a mansion. Its proportions are small and its design simple. It is a house that has grown organically, according to the needs of its inhabitants. To all of us in the family it is known as la casa de mama. It is the place of our origin, the stage for our memories and dream of island life. (1990, p. 23)

Second- and third-generation immigrants portrayed their U.S. Puerto Rican communities in this same way. Rico, for example, embraces the idea of Chicago as his home because of the familial and geographic ties to his identity.

Chicago will always be home. [Home in what sense?] Home in the, eh, sense that . . . that's my history. You know Humboldt Park, it's just my history!!! Home . . . that . . . that is memory. Every time I drive down a certain street I oh yeah I remember I grew up around here. My childhood experience. Home in the sense that all my family are in Chicago basically. My grandparents, my aunts, my uncles, my cousins.

Mainland Puerto Rican writers echo the sentiments of the second- and third-generation immigrants we interviewed. In Nicholasa Mohr's coming-of-age novel, *Nilda,* home is represented as a refuge from the hostile, alien Anglo world outside the barrio and represents as well the preservation of culture and stability essential to the protagonist's development. Home is constructed as a very private space of Puerto Ricanness, in contrast with the strange and public space of Anglo life. Among the Puerto Rican migrants we spoke to, there is a desire for sameness and a secure place that provides nurturance. Puerto Rican men's and women's stories demonstrate what Martin and Mohanty refer to as "unrelenting . . . desire for home, for stability, for protection—and not only the desire for them, but the expectation of a right to these things" (1986, p. 206).

GENDERED NOTIONS OF HOME AND
SOCIALIZATION OF CHILDREN

Puerto Rican immigrant parents constructed homeland communities as pristine and pure as a way to resist belittling definitions of their race and class. This project also included efforts to reconstitute Puerto Rican cultural values in the United States. Similar to the Filipina and Indian immigrants that Espiritu (this volume) and DasGupta (1997) studied, Puerto Rican parents attempted to reconstitute homeland communities and values in the United States as "authentic" cultural and gendered spaces. This meant that parents expected children to uphold traditional notions of gender. Young women, for example, were to act as symbols of cultural authenticity and purity.

Puerto Rican immigrants' homes served as the primary space where children were socialized into traditional Puerto Rican ways of living. It was the site where "traditions," distinct from "American" ways, were produced. Consequently, parents subscribed to the traditional gender division of labor in which men function as providers and women are relegated to being caretakers of the home and children. Underlying this gender division of labor is a patriarchal ideology, machismo, emphasizing men's sexual freedom, virility, and aggressiveness and women's sexual repression and submission (Acosta-Belen, 1986). Machismo represents the male ideal and plays an important role in maintaining sexual restrictions and the subordination of women. According to Cofresí,

In their roles as heads of households, men are expected to manage family finances and make decisions that affect all family members. For instance, men may decide what women can or cannot do outside of the immediate vicinity of home. Men are responsible for chores such as house and car repairs, but they are not expected to do any housework. Similarly, men are seen as having superior authority over their children, but they are not expected to be involved in their day-to-day care. Men are required to be good providers, are responsible for the economic well-being of their families, and are entrusted to protect the sexual honor of the women in their families. (1999, p. 162)

This ideology rationalizes a double standard where a woman can be seen as *una mujer buena o de la casa* (a good woman, or a woman of the house) or as *una mujer mala o de la calle* (a bad woman, or a woman of the streets). Men have to show that *el lleva los pantalones en la casa* (he is the one who wears the pants in the family) and are free to *echar una canita al aire* (literally, blow a gray hair to the wind; culturally, it means to have an affair). In Puerto Rico, the masculine ideology stresses sexuality. According to Rafael Ramírez, Puerto Rican men are taught to enjoy their sexuality, declare it, boast about it, and feel proud of it.

The macho seduces, conquers, and takes and uses his sexual power in keeping with an old saying: *Yo suelto mi gallo, los demas que recogan sus gallinas* (I'm letting my cock loose, you'd better hide your hens). (1993, pp. 44–45)

The counterpart of machismo is *marianismo*, in which the Virgin Mary is seen as the model for women (Sanchez-Ayendez, 1986). Within this context, a woman's sexual purity and virginity is a cultural imperative. Motherhood, in Puerto Rican culture, lies at the center of such ideology. A woman is defined by her self-abnegation and by placing family and community above her own needs (Cofresí, 1999).

In Chicago, parents tried to socialize girls and boys according to these two codes of sexual behavior. Immigrant parents constructed notions of Puerto Rico as a culturally pure and authentic place and urban life in Chicago as dangerous for their children (Perez, 1998). In particular, parents worried that young women would be tempted to lose their virginity and explore their sexuality and that young men would fall into crime and gang violence. For example, Carmen was sent to Puerto Rico when she was a teenager to, as she put it, *"para que no se dañara"* ("so that I wouldn't be spoiled") (Perez, 1998, p. 14). She adds: "we young girls always come back and get in worse trouble than when we left." Now, as a mother herself, she spends a great deal of her time trying to prevent her daughters from *"meter las patas"* (getting pregnant). Ironically, teenage pregnancy and gang activity have also become major social problems in Puerto Rico (Perez, 1998).

In the hierarchical gendered world of immigrant family relations, a great deal of emphasis was placed on the behavior of daughters. Puerto Rican parents were protective of daughters' sexuality. Daughters were encouraged to value their virginity, family, motherhood. For example, in the following passage, Irene captures how her mother socialized her.

My mother raised me to be very traditional Latino—very traditional. I know how to cook. I know how to clean. She wanted me to get married, wear white, never to have sex before I got married. And so she tried to instill a lot of the cultural values within me.

Irene's brother, on the other hand, was exempted from this kind of traditionalism. As she saw it, "my brother was exempted from doing chores and he pretty much did whatever he wanted to do."

In our work, we also found that Puerto Rican mothers expected their daughters to take on household and child-rearing responsibilities as soon as they reached preadolescent years. When Claudia reached 9 years, she acquired household responsibilities. She was given keys to the apartment, and after school she was expected to clean the kitchen, pick up around the house, and start dinner. Similarly, Diana states that her mother "had us trained." She adds "after school we went back to the house. . . . I remember I have always cooked from very little. We also had to clean the house, cook, do the wash, iron. We were never allowed to go outside or have friends over while our parents were gone." As Celia's comment earlier suggests, men were frequently exempted from chores and such responsibilities.

CONTRADICTIONS AND INCONSISTENCIES

Puerto Rican women promoted traditional gender norms, despite the fact that they were acutely conscious of the repression, conflicts, and power relations that made up home both in Puerto Rico and the United States. They saw little room for adventure, growth, or the creation of a place for themselves in their homelands. They desired to make significant contributions to their community, family, and home through meaningful work that did not require their deference and self-sacrifice. As one migrant woman put it, "I aspired to much more. I wanted much more." Migrant women's awareness that the homeland is not simply a utopia "politicizes and undercuts any psychic anchors" they "might use to construct a coherent notion of home or . . . [their] identity in relation to it" (Martin & Mohanty, 1986, p. 196).

Esmeralda Santiago's (1993) book, *When I Was Puerto Rican,* for example, highlights the realities of Puerto Rican women's lives in Puerto Rico during the industrialization period of the island's economy.

Mami was one of the first in Macun (Puerto Rico) to have a job outside the house. For extra money women in the barrio took in laundry or ironing or cooked for men with no wives. But Mami left our house every morning, primped and perfumed, for a job in a factory in Toa Baja. . . . The barrio looked at us with new eyes. . . . I got the message that my mother was breaking a taboo I'd never heard about. The women in the neighborhood turned their back on her when they saw her coming or, when they talked to her, they scanned the horizon, as if looking at her would infect them with whatever had made her go out and get a job. . . . Even tio Candido's wife, Meri, made us feel as if Mami was a bad woman for leaving us alone. I was confused by the effect my mother's absence caused in other people—"why Mami?" (pp. 122–123)

In Chicago, we found a number of contradictions and inconsistencies between the parents' gender ideologies and actual practices. For example, in contrast with the ideology of marianismo and the expectation that women stay home and engage only in caring work, the first-generation Puerto Rican women in our sample carried out both productive and subsistence work. In addition, although women were expected to be "feminine," they often performed heavy work both inside and outside the home, on farms and as part of paid work. In short, in both Puerto Rican and U.S. communities, Puerto Rican gender relations are paradoxical—a domestic ideology coexists with the reality that women engage in productive work (Momsen, 1993).

Similar to the Puerto Rican colonial context, the economic reality Puerto Ricans faced in the United States forced Puerto Rican women into wage labor. Thus, second- and third-generation Puerto Rican migrants observed how their mothers challenged traditional gender norms at the same time that they tried to uphold them. While Rosa's mother fulfilled all the traditional gender roles and responsibilities expected of her, she also challenged her husband's wishes that she not work outside the home.

> She worked for a very short period of time in a factory. She had to work nights because, as said, my father did not want her out of the house. So, she had to do everything, she had to do it all. My mother was brilliant. I think she had a real good head on her shoulders. My father was like as long as we eat today, there's no problem even though he did, you know, have money. Given the race and class oppression we endured, my mother too had to work outside the home, but she tried to do this, at times, while still preserving traditional gender roles, and yet other times she also challenged traditional roles—not just by taking a job outside the home.

Daughters admired how their mothers struggled to juggle work and family responsibilities. In the following, Rosa describes her mother's typical working day:

> This lady would get up, and, it actually started at night. When we were sleeping you would hear her mopping and doing the last dishes. When you got up in the morning everything was clean. She would wake up before everybody. She fixed breakfast and continued cleaning. We would come home from school for lunch and she had everything ready. I enjoyed my life!! When we would come home from school she had us a snack and then when my dad came we were all cleaned up. When she worked at the factory he would come home at a certain hour but when he opened up his printing shop he didn't come home for dinner. My mother is a terrific cook. We could sit down at the table and each of us would have our favorite foods at the same time. She cleaned and cleaned. I just remember having clean clothes all the time.

Similarly, Celia was aware of the struggles her mother faced as a single mother.

> I've learned the hard way, I think, to some degree, about hardships and to make it on my own because of the environment that I have been raised in. Also, because my mother was such a strong woman, and to go by herself to raise six children is just phe-

nomenal. I doubt if I could ever be like her. I doubt that I could have the same tolerance and patience that she has.

Thus, second- and third-generation Puerto Ricans witnessed a mismatch between the traditional gender responsibilities they were expected to carry out and the realities of their mothers' lived experiences. They observed their mothers' fierce independence and ability to provide for themselves and their children. Rosa, for example, shared with us how her mother purchased a home without her husband's knowledge. Sylvia describes her mother as "very independent" and "does not depend on nobody but herself right now." Another third-generation Puerto Rican described his grandmother and the ways she challenged traditional gender norms:

> My grandmother worked very hard. She was a promoter. She had very little education. She had a lot of ambition and a lot of guts and she had a lot of luck. She saved money and bought a home in Long Island. Right behind the house that she owned, there was a large potato farm. And a lot of migrants from Puerto Rico used to go there. A lot of them were not treated well. What she did was that she opened her home to these migrant farmworkers and she rented them rooms. She started expanding the home and she rented them rooms. Sometimes, I used to go over there on weekend and I used to have to jump over the people sleeping on the living room floor. She started promoting cultural activities for them because there was no cultural activities "para Puertoriqueños" in that area. I used to see her doing all these things and, ah, the bug rubbed off. As I grew older, I did the same. I used to involve myself in different activities.

While seemingly contradictory, Puerto Rican parents socialized their daughters to uphold traditional gender expectations while at the same time encouraging them to pursue an education and learn how to "take care of themselves." In the colonial, neocolonial, and disadvantaged conditions that Puerto Ricans have to confront both in Puerto Rico and the United States, and now within this transnational social field, contradictory values are promoted. Puerto Rican women encourage traditional values despite the fact that they are aware of and resistant to gender inequities. They promote gender values and traditional roles, but their lives in ways defy these expectations. For example, Puerto Rican women encourage their daughters to be good housewives and teach them that the household is their domain, but the reality is that they themselves had to work outside the household. Puerto Rican parents encourage their daughters to fulfill traditional gender expectations as a way to define a cultural space that is pure and pristine and that challenges belittling definitions of their race, but they also encourage their daughters to pursue an education.

Men also observed the contradictions and inconsistencies between traditional Puerto Rican values and their fathers' behavior. For example, Rico's father, on the one hand, warned his son against falling into the negative patterns of machismo by marrying very young, having children, and feeling that he has to assume the sole provider role of the family and in the process sacrifice his dreams. On the other hand, his very words reproduced the machismo ideology that encourages freedom and independence and a "macho" identity in which individual desires are not to be compromised.

> Since I was young, you know, my dad would talk about sex, you know, about how to treat a woman. What kind of shit not to take from a woman. [Like what?] Like controlling your freedom, your expression, your dream of what you want to be. Don't compromise that for anybody. It's not gunna make you happy. It's not gunna make your wife happy. It's not gunna make your children happy. Just be aware of that, be cautious of that. Make sure you choose the right woman. Dad was always like that, choose the right woman. Or you are gunna be screwed. You're gunna have kids . . . don't have kids. . . . Dad was big on that. That's why, you know, since we were young we talked about sex and relationships.

Parents operated out of these seemingly contradictory sets of values because they recognized that it was essential to their children's survival. Given the myriad of power relations and "cartographies of struggles" that make up the borderlands, it is no wonder that Puerto Ricans promote contradictory sets of values and strategies. It is part of the process of navigating through and negotiating these complex power relations. For Puerto Rican immigrants and second and third generations, to live simultaneously out of these "contradictory" sets of values is to live a contradictory life.

NEGOTIATING GENDERED NOTIONS OF HOME

Puerto Rican daughters and sons resisted and negotiated these gendered notions of home. In Chicago we found that daughters resented their parents' overprotectiveness. Some daughters sought to wrest freedom from their parents by getting married at a young age. Others did not openly challenge these gendered rules, but instead found ways to negotiate them. Second- and third-generation Puerto Ricans took advantage of the fissures and cracks within and between the many systems of oppression in which they lived (Davis & Fisher, 1993, p. 16). For example, Puerto Rican parents frowned upon letting children move away from home, but valued education as a means of social mobility. Consequently, daughters used education as a way to leave home. For example, in the following passage Irene explains how she negotiated moving away to attend Catholic school.

> My mom was like, "Oh my goodness, she is out of my sight. My daughter was out of my sight." My mom was very protective. And I think more so with me. And she still is now that I am 30 years old. She just worries about me so much. She's like "I'm so worried about you." I'm like "Mom, I'm 30, please just let me go." . . . I went to Catholic school and lived with my cousin. It was good for me, but I think it was the worst thing for my mom. Because my mother raised me to be very traditional Latino, very traditional. . . . When I came back home . . . she couldn't control me.

This was a critical point in Irene's life. She was able to challenge traditional gender norms within immigrant-based expectations of social mobility. As she reflects upon her choices, she recognizes in retrospect the social consequences of her behavior.

> But I remember thinking that if I would have kept on that path, you know, how would my life have been. Would I be a barefoot pregnant woman staying at home waiting for my husband to come home? You know the type of Latina, or would I be where I am now? [She is currently a residence hall coordinator in a state university.]

Jean Peterman's (1998) life history of a second-generation Puerto Rican woman, Marisol, who gets an abortion shows a woman struggling to reconcile the way she was raised with her own experiences.

> I don't agree that the woman doesn't need an education anymore. What about death or divorce? The family says they will be there for you but that is not true. They can help some but not enough. A woman needs an education. I have worked since I was twelve years old. I don't think my working hurts my daughters. I make our time together count . . . my opinions about these things have changed. (p. 174)

According to Peterman (1998), Marisol's narrative allows her to create an oppositional story through which she can give voice to the more conflictive aspects of her upbringing. As a mother herself, she now wants to create a different environment for her daughters.

> My mom doesn't agree with me about how I am raising my children. After the divorce, I was living with my parents. When I moved away, she was totally against it. She wondered why I was moving so far away [to the suburbs], why I was taking my daughters away from them, and why did I put them in a certain school. Actually, she didn't ask "why"; she said "don't." It took her a year to come and say to me, "You did the right thing." For a Puerto Rican mother—I was amazed. If they are wrong and they know it, they still don't admit it. So I hugged her, for the third time in my life.

Peterman concludes that "Marisol's narrative provides an example of a Puerto Rican woman who is trying to figure out how to continue to embrace her family and her culture while rejecting the gender inequality within it" (1998, p. 176).

While the men in our sample often embraced the ideology of machismo because it confers power, dominance, and privilege, we also found that they at times openly challenged it in the process of forming their own values about sexuality. Eduardo, for example, connected the macho ideology in his family to his grandfather's ideas about the proper role of women, and described how he and his father sought to reject it.

> I took everything with being a Puerto Rican, I guess. There is things I don't like though, all the Latin biases like "Bien macho, bien macho." I didn't take that because I have respect for the female, for all women. That's a United States custom that was given to me. My father got that as well from the United States. But my grandfather, his idea of a woman is to cook, clean and that's all she does. My dad, his opinion of

a woman is equality, where they share jobs, she can work too. I got that from my father, he got that from the United States. He said no thank you to my grandpa's way
of being with my grandmother. I said thank you to my dad when I received that as a
United States custom, but not a Puerto Rican custom. I don't want to be a macho
with my wife, like "You've gotta stay here and do this and that. That's all."

Rico evaluated and reassessed the dominant cultural story of sexuality by jux-
taposing himself with the men that he had met in Puerto Rico. He took the opportunity during the interview to place himself and his Chicago friends in a different category—more sensitive—thus reconstructing Puerto Rico not as a pristine
sexual place, but as a dangerous place in terms of sexual and personal relationships. Ironically, later on in the interview Rico admitted that he could not have a
girlfriend or be committed while in Puerto Rico because, as he put it, "temptation
was high, it's like in your face."

> I went to Puerto Rico and even in the neighborhood I see it a lot in my friends. They
> can be married and they have a woman on the side and I am like Wow!!! They are
> like "well my wife does not make me happy" or whatever. "She's getting fat, she is
> not taking care of herself." So, "yeah I'm gunna have another woman on the side"
> . . . but the majority of my Puerto Rican friends that I know and even Latinos for
> that matter they value the same thing that I do. But a lot like myself and my Puerto
> Rican friends who are male, who a lot of them are born in Chicago. Yeah we value,
> we value the fact that we want a good relationship. And there is nothing wrong with
> that. There is nothing wrong to have a sensitive side to yourself.

When the well-known second-generation Nuyorican poet Martín Espada became a father, he worried about the cultural legacy of machismo. In his essay "The
Puerto Rican Dummy and the Merciful Son" (1996), he writes:

> How do I think of my son as a Latino male? How do I teach him to disappoint and
> disorient the bigots everywhere around him, all of whom have bought tickets to see
> the macho pantomime? At the same time, how do I teach him to inoculate himself
> against the very real diseases of violence and sexism and homophobia infecting our
> community? How do I teach Clemente to be "Clemente"?[2]

He recognizes that his son's identity as a Puerto Rican male has been shaped by a
number of experiences that he himself did not have while growing up in New York.
For example, the son has witnessed his father engage in the "decidedly non-
stereotypical business" of giving poetry readings. Espada wishes to teach his son
that violence against women is not acceptable. The best way he can communicate
this message is by the way he treats his wife. As he puts it, "how else will he know
that jealousy is not love, that a lover is not property?" (1996, p. 81). Espada recognizes that the behavior associated with being "macho" has deep historical roots in
colonialism and is triggered by a profound sense of insecurity. He states: "My evolving manhood was defined by how well I could take punishment, and paradoxically I punished myself for not being man enough to end my own humiliation"

(1996, p. 79). In his struggle to rid himself of this legacy, Espada and his wife wish to provide Clemente with a secure and identity-affirming environment. At the age of 4 he has already spent time in Puerto Rico, something Espada didn't get to do until he was 10 years old.

CONCLUSION

In this study we found that in an effort to resist racial and class inequality in Puerto Rican communities, migrant parents shared with their children images and stories of the island that affirmed their identities as Puerto Ricans but tended to obscure gender inequality. Parents communicated to their children that Puerto Rican culture is fixed and that Puerto Ricans should work to preserve it. In addition, Puerto Rican parents socialized their daughters and sons to uphold traditional gender values. Daughters, in particular, felt the brunt of parents' efforts to construct home as pure and pristine. As shown, parents attempted to control women's sexuality, encouraged their daughters to be good wives and mothers, and, in some cases, limited their educational and career choices.

Second- and third-generation Puerto Rican sons and daughters struggled with accepting these views because it entailed submission and conformity to rules and codes of behavior that many saw as oppressive. The process of both challenging and embracing aspects of ethnic/racial and gendered identities is not a linear, unidimensional process for the second- and third-generation Puerto Ricans we interviewed. In fact, we found that as second- and third-generation Puerto Ricans try to define a place for themselves, at times they fall into a dualistic way of thinking by perceiving U.S. society as being more egalitarian than their homeland and U.S. Puerto Rican communities.

We interpret this dualistic thinking as part of the distortions of the borderlands, or as Anzaldúa (1990) puts it, an invention of the Anglo society. Although U.S. society is perceived as more egalitarian when compared with less industrialized nations, this notion fails to capture ways in which women are exposed to other forms of exploitation and domination in the U.S. context. For example, research has shown that U.S. employers prefer to hire immigrant women over men because of patriarchal and racist assumptions that these women can afford to work for less and are suited physiologically for routine work and work that requires good hand-eye coordination. In short, perceiving host societies as more egalitarian than homeland communities tends to obscure gender inequalities that women experience in the host society. It also fails to recognize the distorted representations of Latino men in U.S. popular culture and the media.

We also found that for second- and third-generation Puerto Ricans, life on the borderlands is difficult because they struggle to survive in the midst of a myriad of power relations. One can hear the tentativeness in their voices as they try to create a place for themselves. For example, aware that they could not totally reject their culture and identity, daughters learned, as one respondent put it, "to talk properly" when questioning their families. Sons and daughters remain flexible, and open, but they feel tenuous in their steps as they try to devise strategies and a language of "mestizaje" (Anzaldúa, 1987).

Life on the borders presents new challenges not just because second- and third-generation Puerto Ricans are trying to be a part of the process of an evolving culture, but because the process of creation is one that takes time. It is a process that first involves gaining a sense of awareness, then an acceptance that can lead to action. Like many of us, they struggle with the reality that change and integrating new aspects of their identity take time. That is, they are aware that they must shed old cultural baggage and surrender safety and familiarity in order to create a new place of security. The second- and third-generation immigrants that we interviewed nevertheless forge ahead to create a space for themselves.

NOTES

1. Our definition of home encompasses both Puerto Rico and U.S. Puerto Rican communities. In this essay, however, we have made a conceptual distinction between homeland (Puerto Rico) and home (U.S. Puerto Rican communities).

2. *Clemente* translates from Spanish as "merciful."

REFERENCES

Acosta-Belen, Edna. (1986). *The Puerto Rican woman: Perspectives on culture, history, and society.* New York: Praeger.

Alicea, Marixsa. (1990, September). Dual home bases: A reconceptualization of Puerto Rican migration. *Latino Studies Journal,* 78–98.

Alicea, Marixsa. (1997). A chambered nautilus: The contradictory nature of Puerto Rican women's role in the social construction of a transnational community. *Gender and Society,* *11*(5), 597–626.

Anzaldúa, Gloria. (1987). *Borderlands/La frontera: The new mestiza.* San Francisco: Aunt Lute Books.

Anzaldúa, Gloria. (1990). La consciencia de la mestiza: Towards a new consciousness. In Gloria Anzaldúa (Ed.), *Making face, making soul/Haciendo caras: Creative and critical perspectives by feminists of color.* San Francisco: Aunt Lute Books.

Bourgois, Philippe. (1996). In search of masculinity: Violence, respect, and sexuality among Puerto Rican crack dealers in East Harlem. *British Journal of Criminology, 36*(3), 412–427.

Brow, James. (1990). Notes on community, hegemony, and the uses of the past. *Anthropological Quarterly, 63,* 1–6.

Canino, Ian. A. (1994). The psychological effects of migration on the Puerto Rican child. In Carlos Antonio Torre, Hugo Rodríguez Vecchini, & William Burgos (Eds.), *The commuter nation: Perspectives on Puerto Rican migration.* Rio Piedras, Puerto Rico: Editorial de la Universidad de Puerto Rico.

Cintron-Velez, Aixa N. (1999). Generational paths into and out of work: Personal narratives of Puerto Rican women in New York. In Irene Browne (Ed.), *Latinas and African American women at work: Race, gender, and economic inequality.* New York: Russell Sage Foundation.

Cofresí, Norma I. (1999). Gender roles in transition among professional Puerto Rican women. *Frontiers, 20*(1), 161–178.

Colberg E. M., & Burgos, Nilsa M. (1988). Female-headed single parent families in Puerto Rico: An exploratory study of work and family conditions. *Journal of Social Behavior and Personality, 3*(4), 373–387.

Daponte, Beth. (1996). Race and ethnicity during an economic transition: The withdrawal of Puerto Rican women from New York City labour force, 1960–1980. *Regional Studies, 30*(2), 151–161.

DasGupta, Monisha. (1997). "What is Indian about you?" A gendered transnational approach to ethnicity. *Gender and Society, 11*(5), 572–596.

Davis, Kathy, & Fisher, Sue. (1993). Power and the female subject. In Sue Fisher & Kathy Davis (Eds.), *Negotiating at the margins: The gendered discourses of power and resistance.* New Brunswick, NJ: Rutgers University Press.

Dietz, James L. (1986). *Economic history of Puerto Rico: Institutional change and capitalist development.* Princeton, NJ: Princeton University Press.

Duany, Jorge. (1999). Imagining the Puerto Rican nation: Recent works on cultural identity. *Latin American Research Review, 31*(3), 248–267.

Duany, Jorge. (2000). Nation on the move: The construction of cultural identities in Puerto Rico and the diaspora. *American Ethnologist, 27*(1), 5–30.

Espada, Martín. (1996). The Puerto Rican dummy and the merciful son. In Ray González (Ed.), *Muy macho: Latino men confront their manhood* (p. 75–90). New York: Anchor Books.

Espiritu, Yen. (1999). *Family, culture, and gender in Filipino American life.* Paper presented at the annual meeting of the American Sociological Association, Chicago.

Falcon, Luis M., Gurak, Douglas T., & Powers, Mary G. (1990). Labor force participation of Puerto Rican women in greater New York City. *Sociology and Social Research, 74*(2), 110–117.

Gupta, Akhil, & Ferguson, James. (1992). Beyond culture: Space, identity, and the politics of difference. *Cultural Anthropology, 7,* 6–23.

Gurak, Douglas, & Kritz, Mary M. (1985). The Caribbean communities in the United States. *Migration Today, 12*(2), 6–12.

History Task Force. (1979). *Labor migration under capitalism: The Puerto Rican experience.* New York: Monthly Review Press.

Martin, Biddy, & Mohanty, Chandra Talpade. (1986). Feminist politics: What's home got to do with it? In Teresa de Laurentis (Ed.), *Feminist studies, critical studies.* Bloomington: Indiana University Press.

Mohanty, Chandra Talpade. (1991). Introduction: Cartographies of struggle. In Chandra Talpade Mohanty, Ann Russo, & Lourdes Torres (Eds.), *Third World women and the politics of feminism.* Bloomington: Indiana University Press.

Mohr, Nicholasa. (1986). *Nilda* (2nd ed.). Houston, TX: Arte Público Press.

Momsen, Janet. (1993). Introduction. In Janet Momsen (Ed.), *Women and change in the Caribbean.* Bloomington: Indiana University Press.

Ortiz, Altagracia. (1996). *Puerto Rican women and work: Bridges in transnational labor.* Philadelphia: Temple University Press.

Ortiz Cofer, Judith. (1990). *Silent dancing: A partial remembrance of a Puerto Rican childhood.* Houston, TX: Arte Público Press.

Padilla. Felix. (1987). *Puerto Rican Chicago.* Notre Dame, IN: University of Notre Dame Press.

Padilla Felix, & Santiago, Esmeralda. (1993). *Outside the wall: A Puerto Rican woman's struggle*. New Brunswick, NJ: Rutgers University Press.

Pantojas Garcia, Emilio. (1990). *Development strategies as ideology: Puerto Rico's export-led industrialization experience*. Boulder, CO: Lynne Rienner.

Perez, Gina. (1998). *"La Tierra's always perceived as woman": Imagining urban communities in Chicago's Puerto Rican community*. Paper presented at the annual meeting of the Latin American Studies Association (LASA), Chicago.

Perez, Gina. (2000). *The near northwest side story: Gender, migration, and everyday life in Chicago and San Sebastian, Puerto Rico*. Unpublished doctoral dissertation, Northwestern University.

Peterman, Jean. (1998). Marisol's story: Culture, family, and self, and the decision to get an abortion. *Applied Behavioral Science Review, 6*(2), 167–177.

Portes, Alejandro (Ed.). (1996). *The new second generation*. New York: Russell Sage Foundation.

Portes, Alejandro, & Zhou, Min. (1993, November). The new second generation: Segmented assimilation and its variants among post-immigrant youth. *Annual of the American Academy of Political and Social Sciences, 530,* 74–96.

Ramírez, Rafael L. (1999). *What it means to be a man: Reflections on Puerto Rican masculinity*. New Brunswick, NJ: Rutgers University Press.

Rodriguez, Clara. (1989). *Puerto Ricans: Born in the U.S.A.* Boston: Unwin Hyman.

Rogler, Lloyd H., & Santana-Cooney, Rosemary. (1984). *Puerto Rican families in New York City: Intergenerational processes*. Maplewood, NJ: Waterfront Press.

Rogler Lloyd H., & Santana-Cooney, Rosemary. (1994). From Puerto Rico to New York City. In Carlos Antonio Torre, Hugo Rodríguez Vecchini, & William Burgos (Eds.), *The commuter nation: Perspectives on Puerto Rican migration*. Rio Piedras, Puerto Rico: Editorial de la Universidad de Puerto Rico.

Roschelle, Anne R. (1997). Declining networks of care: Ethnicity, migration, and poverty in a Puerto Rican community. *Race, Gender, and Class, 4*(2), 107–125.

Rouse, Roger. (1992). Making sense of settlement: Class transformation, cultural struggle, and transnationalism among Mexican migrants in the United States. *Annals of the New York Academy of Sciences, 45,* 965–974.

Rumbaut, Rubén G. (1996). The crucible within: Ethnic identity, self-esteem, and segmented assimilation among children of immigrants. In Alejandro Portes (Ed.), *The new second generation*. New York: Russell Sage Foundation.

Sanchez-Ayendez, Melba. (1986). Puerto Rican elderly women: Shared meanings and informal supportive networks. In Jonetta Cole (Ed.), *All-American women: Lines that divide, ties that bind*. New York: Free Press.

Sánchez Korrol, Virginia. (1983). *From colonia to community: The history of Puerto Ricans in New York City, 1917–1948*. Westport, CT: Greenwood Press.

Sánchez Korrol, Virginia. (1986). The forgotten migrant: Educated Puerto Rican women in New York City, 1920–1940. In Edna Acosta-Belen (Ed.), *The Puerto Rican woman: Perspectives on culture, history, and society*. New York: Praeger.

Santana-Cooney, Rosemary, & Ortiz, Vilma. (1983). Nativity, national origin, and hispanic female participation in the labor force. *Social Science Quarterly, 64*(3), 510–523.

Santana-Cooney, & Colón-Warren, Alice. (1979). Declining female participation among Puerto Rican New Yorkers: Comparison with native white non-Spanish New Yorkers. *Ethnicity, 6*(3), 281–297.

Santiago, Esmeralda. (1993). *When I was Puerto Rican*. Reading, MA: Addison-Wesley.

Toro-Morn, Maura I. (1995). Gender, class, family, and migration: Puerto Rican women in Chicago. *Gender and Society, 9*(6), 706–720.

Toro-Morn, Maura I. (1999, June). Género, trabajo y migración: Las empleadas domésticas puertoriqueñas en Chicago. *Revista de Ciencias Sociales, 7,* 102–125.

Whalen, Carmen. (1998). Labor migrants or submissive wives: Competing narratives of Puerto Rican women in the post–World War II era. In Félix V. Matos Rodríguez & Linda C. Delgado (Eds.), *Puerto Rican women's history: New perspectives.* Armonk, NY: M. E. Sharpe.

Wiltshire, Rosina. (1992). Implications of transnational migration for nationalism: The Caribbean example. *Annals of the New York Academy of Sciences, 645,* 175–188.

Zhou, Min. (1997). Growing up American: The challenge confronting immigrant children and children of immigrants. *Annual Review of Sociology, 23,* 63–97.

PART FOUR

Gender, Generation, and Immigration

CHAPTER 11

De madres a hijas

Gendered Lessons on Virginity across Generations of Mexican Immigrant Women

Gloria González-López

This essay examines the content of what Mexican immigrant women teach their daughters about sexuality, and specifically, about premarital virginity. Using data collected from in-depth interviews with Mexican immigrant women living in Los Angeles, I analyze how Mexican women provide sex education for their daughters in the United States. My thesis is that what these mothers teach their daughters about sexuality and virginity reflects generational relations, regional patriarchies *(machismos regionales)*, and immigration experiences.

Virginity has long been a focus among those analyzing Mexican women's sexuality. In the extant scholarship, the practice of *mexicanas* preserving premarital virginity is largely attributed to compliance with Catholic sexual morality, religion, or sacred beliefs. These analyses underscore the strong role of the Catholic Church and its insistence on virginity for women (e.g., Guerrero-Pavich, 1986; Reid & Bing, 2000; Zavella, 1997). According to this view, the church allies with a patriarchal society to disparage women who cannot or will not maintain virginity (Espín, 1986; Twinam, 1989); the social mechanisms of moral control define a woman's virginity as *sagrada y pura* (sacred and pure) while portraying her sexual activity as *profana e impura* (profane and impure) (Amuchástegui, 1998).[1] However, in this essay I suggest that the moral standards of Catholicism are only one variable influencing mexicanas' ideas about virginity. I propose an alternative paradigm in which gender dynamics in Mexican society and mexicanas' experiences as immigrant women in the United States also shape women's perceptions of premarital virginity.

Even though Latin American Catholicism and culture place great value on female premarital virginity, Mexican immigrant women do not automatically advocate premarital virginity for their daughters (and when they do, this practice has no direct association with the cult of virginity in Mexican Catholic and cultural ideologies). As they educate their daughters regarding sexuality, mothers actively challenge the dynamics of gender and sexual oppression that they were exposed to as heterosexual women within family and couple relationships. For them, motherhood is an opportunity to resolve some of their unfinished issues as women. And for them, the issue of *protection* from gender and sexual oppression is central to the sex education of their daughters.

IMMIGRATION STUDIES AND MEXICANA SEXUALITIES

How and why do mexicanas transform their perceptions of virginity as they provide a sex education to their daughters in the new country? Mexican immigration studies have just recently begun to position sexuality in the center of their analyses.[2] In this chapter, I propose bridging the immigration and gender and sexuality fields to examine the fluid sexual reinventions mexicanas create in the United States as immigrant women. I propose a paradigm based on recent scholarship on the interlocking dynamics of gender, sexuality, and migration.

Sexuality, according to Cantú (1997), is "a dimension of power that—similarly to gender—shapes and organizes processes of migration and modes of incorporation." The interplay among gender, sexuality, and migration to the United States is equally central in studies that examine Mexican immigration experiences as a window to specific aspects of immigrants' sex lives (e.g., Bronfman & López-Moreno, 1996; Carrier, 1995; Hirsch, 1999). In particular, the migration-related spread of HIV/AIDS in communities on both sides of the border has generated extensive research based on the gender/sexuality/migration paradigm (e.g., Magis-Rodríguez, Del Río Zolezzi, Valdespino-Gómez, & García-García, 1995; Mena, 2000; Mishra, Conner, & Magaña, 1996; Salgado de Snyder, Acevedo, Díaz-Pérez, & Saldívar-Garduño, 2000; Salgado de Snyder, Díaz-Pérez, & Maldonado, 1996). This framework has also explained how migration is a door Latinas use to escape heterosexist oppression (Argüelles & Rivero, 1993) and to experience lesbian and heterosexual transformations in the United States (Espín, 1999).

The metaphor of sexuality luggage illustrates these processes. *De madres a hijas,* from mothers to daughters, mexicanas reconstruct the meaning of virginity as they unpack their gendered sexuality luggage within their U.S. communities as part of their immigration experience. As this process takes place, a mother's treatment of premarital virginity within the mother-daughter relationship is informed by three gender dynamics: generation, regional patriarchal differences, and immigration experiences.

Generation

Mothers wish to enhance their daughters' life opportunities, while safeguarding them from the many risks and dangers associated with female sexuality (e.g., pregnancy out of wedlock, sexually transmitted diseases, casual sex, promiscuity, marital unhappiness, discord and/or conflict in marriage). Across generations, mothers transform the ethic of *respeto a la familia* (family respect), symbolized by the *sexual abstinence* that used to govern their own sex lives, into an ethic of *protección y cuidado personal* (protection and care), represented by the *sexual moderation* they hope for a new generation of Mexican American women.

Regional Patriarchal Differences

Mexican culture is not one homogeneous entity. Mothers decide whether to advocate premarital virginity for their daughters based on the gender inequalities they themselves experienced as women raised in particular social contexts. I introduce the concept of *machismos regionales,* or regional patriarchies, to explain the different expressions of sexism in rural and urban Mexico.

Immigration Experiences

Mexican mothers who are exposed to culturally different sexual moralities in the United States may transform their perceptions of their daughters' sexuality. Regardless of the cultural context, however, a woman's sexuality is still defined by women's gendered assumptions of men's standards about female sexuality. In addition, socioeconomics, sexuality workshops or *pláticas sobre la sexualidad,* the media, and networking in the immigrant community prompt redefinitions of sexuality via motherhood.

RESEARCH METHODS

This essay is based on individual in-depth tape-recorded interviews with 40 heterosexual Mexican immigrant women living in the Los Angeles area. Study participants included women from a variety of educational, socioeconomic, and marital status backgrounds. All of the study participants identified themselves as heterosexual during the interview. As a native speaker, I conducted all of the interviews in Spanish.[3]

Study participants were women who migrated to the United States at the age of 20 or older. At the interview, they were between the ages of 25 and 45; the average age of study participants was 35. Half of the sample consisted of women born and raised in the state of Jalisco; the other half had been born and raised in Mexico City. With the exception of two Jalisco informants who have lived in the United States for 20 and 25 years, all participants have lived permanently in the United States between 5 and 15 years.[4] Three elementary schools and four community-based clinics located in inner-city Latino immigrant barrios in Los Angeles were the primary sites where I identified my final study sample of 40 participants.

Jalisco and Mexico City are two of the main regions of origin for Mexican immigrant women who enter the United States through Tijuana (Woo Morales, 1995). Socioeconomic differences between the two regions offer contrasting social sce-

Premarital loss of virginity is associated with...

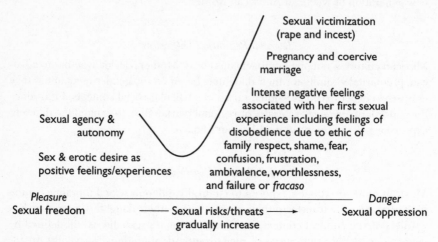

FIGURE II.I. Participants' Pleasure-Danger Continuum

narios influencing female sexuality in distinctive ways. Mexico City is the capital and the largest industrialized and modern city of the nation. Jalisco encompasses the city of Guadalajara (the second largest city in Mexico and the state capital) but also includes pre- and semi-industrialized rural areas consisting of *pueblos* (small towns) and *ranchos* (ranches). Jalisco is the birthplace of tequila, mariachi music, and *charro* culture, all dominant folklore images central to the creation of a national masculinist identity. Jalisco lies adjacent to Michoacán, a state where *el rapto* or *el robo* (literally, "kidnapping" or "stealing" of a woman) and *la violación* (rape) prevailed in the 1950s and 1970s (Wilson, 1990, pp. 78–80).

BETWEEN PLEASURE AND DANGER:
VIRGINITY AND THE MOTHER-DAUGHTER RELATIONSHIP

Mexican immigrant women socially construct virginity as a principal life-enhancing resource. For this reason, the women in this study viewed premarital loss of virginity more as a danger than as pleasure. Sexual activity before marriage is seen as dangerous because of two dynamics. In the first dynamic women's sexuality is the basis for an ethic of *respeto a la familia*, or family respect. Women fear premarital sex will lead to pregnancy, which would damage family honor. In Mexico, some families attempt to repair the moral damage to family honor caused by premarital pregnancy by forcing their daughters to marry. In extreme cases, daughters must marry their rapists. Other women fear premarital sex will lead to a deep sense of family betrayal, shame, and guilt because of an ethic of family respect safeguarded mainly by the mother figure.[5] Some Mexican women prefer to preserve their virginity until marriage in order to protect themselves from these negative consequences.

The second dynamic is connected to women's socially learned fear that engaging in premarital sex will lead to exacerbated machismo, or sexism in marriage. This sentiment was exemplified by many women who said: "*Los esposos te lo echan en cara cuando no eres virgen*" ("Husbands throw it in your face when you are not a virgin"). Even women who were nonvirgins at marriage as a result of sexual violence (e.g., incest, rape) report that their husbands blamed them.

Figure 11.1 illustrates how the Mexican women in this study construct premarital sexual activity along a *pleasure-danger* continuum.[6] The pleasure extreme represents the sexual experiences of the women who described premarital loss of virginity in terms of positive feelings of personal agency, autonomy, and satisfaction. The continuum progressively moves to the right to represent the gradually increasing danger women expressed regarding their first premarital sexual encounters. In the least dangerous situation, the women's premarital sexual activity was followed by negative feelings, such as a sense of family disobedience, shame, fear, confusion, a sense of failure, or *fracaso*. Then, the continuum identifies the testimonies of women who reported being subject to coercive marriage by their families because they became pregnant out of wedlock. And lastly, the most severe manifestation of danger is represented by the experiences of women whose sexual initiation occurred through rape and incest.[7]

My most stunning finding is this: Across generations and through immigration, the mother-daughter relationship begins to invert the dynamics of this image. As the generation of Mexican immigrant women in the study become mothers, they develop a concern about protecting their daughters from sexual oppression. To do this, they challenge the definition of sexual danger. All of the women interviewed were determined to improve the life opportunities of their daughters, and all of them wanted their daughters to have a healthy sex life. They have different and contrasting views, however, on how their daughters can accomplish these goals. They explore the various ways in which they can safeguard a new generation of women while challenging and/or protecting them from the forms of sexual and gender inequality that they themselves experienced (e.g., ethics of respeto a la familia, feelings of guilt after having sex). Some of them promote sexual emancipation, autonomy, and personal agency in terms of sexuality through sexual literacy and education. Some of them also empower their daughters by imposing less restrictive sexual moralities. However, the presence of sexism (machismo) and mainly Protestant religious values regarding virginity permeate some of these mothers' ideas about virginity.[8] As illustrated in Figure 11.2, over time, loss of virginity becomes associated with the pleasures of sex; and the dangers associated with premarital sex are greatly reduced but still alive.

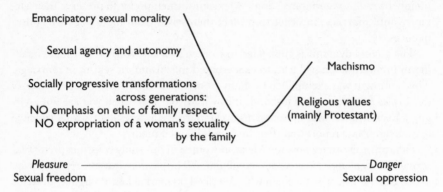

A daughter's premarital loss of virginity is associated with...

Emancipatory sexual morality

Sexual agency and autonomy

Machismo

Socially progressive transformations
across generations:
NO emphasis on ethic of family respect
NO expropriation of a woman's sexuality
by the family

Religious values
(mainly Protestant)

Pleasure ———————————————————————— *Danger*
Sexual freedom   Sexual oppression

FIGURE 11.2. Mother-Daughter Pleasure-Danger Continuum

VIRGINITY AS *CAPITAL FEMENINO:* MOTHERS' GENDERED LESSONS ABOUT VIRGINITY

Mexican women and the society in which they live commodify virginity as a form of capital that possesses a social exchange value. These women construct premarital virginity as a commodity that can be traded in a patriarchal society for financial stability and happiness via marriage. For many mexicanas—especially those with little access to higher education and opportunities for financial independence—marriage is a fundamental social institution of economic survival (Szasz & Figueroa, 1997). Lorena Márquez, 34, and from a small town in Jalisco, described to me how, for her and her sisters, maintaining premarital virginity had translated into a reassurance of obtaining a higher socioeconomic status and the promise of marital stability and happiness:

> In my family all of the women were virgins when we got married, *todas nos casamos bien* [all of us got married the right way]. Now all of us are living well with our husbands and we all have our own homes, independent and everything.

Lorena's testimony resonates with the experience of other mexicanas from rural Mexico. Research on the sexual initiation experiences of a group of young Mexican women and men from Mexico City, Oaxaca, and Guanajuato identified rural women as those who perceive premarital virginity as an asset that can be exchanged for financial support via marriage (Amuchástegui, 1994).

Hymen reconstruction conducted by a physician in Northern Mexico *para reparar la virginidad* (to "repair" virginity) explicitly confirms how women have strategically attempted to reverse, to this day, the depreciated exchange value of a damaged vaginal membrane. In the late 1960s, Dr. Guadalupe Irma Solís started to conduct *himenoplastia*—plastic surgery to restore a ruptured hymen—after witnessing the despair of mothers living in *ejidos* (rural communal lands) who expressed their concerns to her about the future of their raped young daughters. According to Dr. Solís, after being "repaired" with himenoplastia women are guaranteed to bleed after the hymen is reruptured.[9]

Based on these dynamics, I use the concept of *capital femenino* to identify virginity as a form of social capital, expanding on scholars' examinations of virginity's social exchange value (Amuchástegui, 1994, 1998; Córdova Plaza, 1998; Szasz & Figueroa, 1997; Tostado Gutiérrez, 1991; Twinam, 1989; Zavella, 1997). Premarital virginity, as *capital femenino,* possesses the following characteristics: (1) Virginity is a form of capital only women possess in the context of *el mercado matrimonial* (marriage market) in a patriarchal society. (2) Women, not just men, actively participate in socially constructing virginity as a life-enhancing resource. Women, as a subordinated social group in a patriarchal society, utilize this to improve and maximize their life conditions and opportunities. (3) These dynamics have their historical roots in Mexican colonial society, which linked female sexuality with a woman's moral virtue (i.e., virginity), socioeconomic status, and family honor.[10] (4) Virginity functions as a transaction commodity, and, depending on the social context, it may acquire a higher or lower social value: the more emphasized the gender inequalities and/or sexual moralities in a given social context (e.g., pueblos), the higher the value of virginity as capital femenino.

The women interviewed in this study engaged in these dynamics first as single women and later on as mothers. Via motherhood, they see premarital virginity as collateral that will enhance their daughter's opportunities in the marriage market. As mothers educate their daughters, they strive to protect their daughters from the gendered inequalities they themselves experienced.

PREVENTING LOSS OF VIRGINITY ACROSS GENERATIONS: A MAJOR PROTECTION AGAINST GENDER OPPRESSION

The mothers who advocated premarital virginity came primarily from Jalisco, not Mexico City. Most of them had themselves preserved their virginity until marriage in order to avoid potential recrimination from their future husbands. Similarly, many of the women who lost their virginity through rape promoted the same belief. Accordingly, these Jalisco mothers later repeated this gender pattern as mothers in an attempt to protect their daughters from the socially learned fear that future husbands would disrespect them.

For these mothers, preserving their daughters' virginity is a strategy to protect their daughters from machismo. They believe that virginity at marriage increases the likelihood that a newly married wife will be respected by her husband. Hortencia Ibarra, a 33-year-old mother of two daughters, reflected on how virginity had protected her from her husband's potential complaints, and she faithfully promotes this belief as she educates her daughters.

> I already told her that I want her to preserve her virginity until the day she gets married ... so, I would like for my daughter, well, for both of them, to be that way, to be

virgins at marriage so their husbands do not reproach them and they feel good about themselves. My husband, he cannot complain about it.

Similarly, Juanita Loreto expressed that virginity represented a guarantee that her daughters would be respected in marriage and, therefore, have a healthy marital relationship.

When a girl is not a virgin anymore, a man . . . even when she becomes his wife, is not going to treat her right because he would treat her like *una puta* [a whore]. He would say, "You were with other men before." That is an excuse to fight, to argue, or to get divorced, if not worse than that.

Some women from the more sexually liberal Mexico City also held these views. For instance, Azalea Zapata preserved her virginity until marriage, and she strongly believed that virginity would protect her daughters from the recriminations of a macho husband:

Men would always tell them things, that "you were not a virgin," that "who knows with whom you were with before." And they would complain about it a lot. That is why I think that my daughters would be able to have a better marriage, so nobody would tell them anything.

According to Oliva M. Espín, for Latina women, "To enjoy sexual pleasure, even in marriage, may indicate lack of virtue" (1986, p. 279).[11] During our interview, Azalea talked about her difficulties while having sex with her first husband. She reported that he complained about indicators of her normal arousal during their sexual encounters, such as vaginal lubrication. For men such as her husband, vaginal lubrication during intercourse represented a woman's lack of moral integrity and goodness: a virginal vagina is not only one that has never been penetrated, but one that does not yet know how to respond to any type of erotic pleasure or physical sensation. Because of this painful experience, Azalea firmly believed that virginity was crucial for the protection of her daughters from potential accusations from future husbands. Hortencia, Juanita, and Azalea preserved their virginity until marriage and felt it protected them. They promoted the same sexual behavior pattern while educating their daughters.

Mothers who were not virgins at marriage believed that lack of virginity created marital conflict for them, and they hoped their daughters would be protected from these problems by preserving their virginity until marriage. Candelaria de la Rosa, Tomasita Uribe, and Victoria Yáñez were survivors of premarital sexual violence. Rape was the first sexual experience for all of them. Candelaria was raped by a neighbor many times when she was very young. Tomasita was sexually abused by her uncle when she was 5 or 6. And Victoria was a victim of rapto and violación by a stranger in her small town.

Even though their loss of virginity was forced, not voluntary after marriage, these women's husbands reproached them at some point in their marital lives for not being virgins. Shame, guilt, or their husbands' refusal to listen kept them from revealing the truth about their rapes to their partners, as shown in this testimony from Candelaria de la Rosa.

> No, I did not tell him, I just told him that I was not a virgin but I did not tell him about it because he did not want me to tell him about it. When I was going to tell him, he said, "If you don't want, do not tell me about it. If you feel bad to tell me, do not tell me about it. After all, these days is kind of difficult to find a virgin woman anyway."

Lack of virginity at marriage haunted the marital conflicts of these three women. Their husbands' abuse of alcohol aggravated some of their personal difficulties.

> Aha! It is good to be a señorita at marriage because men complain, they say, "No, that is what you say, that you did it with one man, but only God knows with how many you were with that I did not know about." And it's just a reason for them to start drinking to offend you. (Tomasita Uribe)

> Well, before my husband used to drink a lot and when he got home drunk he always complained about me not being a virgin at marriage. He always yelled at me and he said that I was always thinking about someone else. (Candelaria de la Rosa)

> When we get angry at each other, he complains to me about it a lot and I ask him "Why?" and he says that it is because he was upset. But when he gets upset, he always brings it up. He has never complained about the child but he has told me he is upset because I was with another man. (Victoria Yáñez)

Exploring issues regarding sexuality, virginity, and a daughter's sex education was very painful for these three mothers. While reflecting on the sex education that they would like to offer to their daughters, they began to anticipate machismo in their daughters' future lives. This provoked anxiety.

> What if they end up with a *machista* man like it happened to me? "Well, you were not even a virgin. God knows who was the first man, or how many touched you," and they do not say, "The first one," but "How many touched you," even if it had happened only with one man! That is why I do not want for my daughters to suffer. That is why I want them to preserve their virginity until the day they get married. (Tomasita Uribe)

> But what if some day they have a fight, and I don't know . . . when you fight with your husband it always comes out . . . and then I think that probably some day he would say, "Why do you complain about it? If you were not even a señorita when we got married! How do I know with how many men you were with?" I imagine that he would say something like that to her. (Victoria Yáñez)

The testimonies offered by Candelaria, Tomasita, and Victoria are echoed by the accounts of other Mexican parents educating adolescent girls in different regions of the U.S. Southwest. According to research on families from New Mexico and Texas, young Mexican American girls who "secretly date older boys" prompt a family reaction. That is, "In the opinion of some parents, these older males are seeking a young virgin to ultimately marry as part of the machismo profile" (Barkley & Salazar-Mosher, 1995, p. 262). Thus, when a mexicana educates a daughter in the United States, her perception of premarital virginity is defined by the gender inequalities she has experienced as a woman. And as I will discuss next, these gendered disparities are shaped by the particular regional and geographic socioeconomic context in which a woman is raised in Mexico.

VIRGINITY AND GEOGRAPHIC DIFFERENCES: THE SOCIAL REPRODUCTION OF REGIONAL PATRIARCHIES

In general, Mexican immigrant women who migrated from Mexico City were more likely than those who migrated from Jalisco to promote sexual autonomy and activity for their daughters. This included both mothers who preserved their virginity until marriage and those who did not. Most of the women who preserved their virginity until marriage identified themselves with this belief. These mothers have specific characteristics. First, they expressed an interest in protecting their children from many risks (i.e., pregnancy out of wedlock, sexually transmitted diseases, promiscuity) while promoting practices of sexual autonomy. Second, they created and promoted a sexual morality regarding virginity based on what some of them perceived as a "contemporary and well-informed" perception of sexuality, that is, information received from professional sex educators and counselors teaching parenting and sex education classes at inner-city schools and clinics. And, third, they disregarded the importance of religious sexual morality, traditional values of family morality, and machismo.

In contrast, the majority of mothers promoting a preservation of premarital virginity were from Jalisco. They also disregarded both religious sexual morality and traditional ethics of family morality linking a woman's sexuality to family honor and respect. However, they still expressed a strong conviction that virginity would protect their daughters from the dangers of machismo. Yet, they challenged old patterns that force a pregnant daughter to marry and to tolerate an unhappy marital relationship.

Mexican immigrant women who were survivors of sexual violence were more likely to promote premarital virginity than those who were not. In this study, most of these mothers were from Jalisco. As indicated, exposure to recriminations from their husbands for their alleged lack of virtue was their main reason for wanting to preserve their daughters' virginity.

These sexual narratives are not isolated; they echo the gender inequalities reported by AIDS research. A major study conducted with 300 women from rural Jalisco (living in either Los Angeles or their respective sending communities) discovered a lack of negotiating power in these women's heterosexual encounters, and a perception of sexual intercourse not as a voluntary act but as an apparent marital obligation (Salgado de Snyder et al., 2000). Confirming this, another study concluded that urban women are less disadvantaged in negotiating preventive sexual practices compared with their rural counterparts (Del Río Zolezzi, Luguori, Magis-Rodríguez, Valdespino-Gómez, García-García, & Sepúlveda-Amor, 1995).

Mexicanas are more likely to be exposed to intensified expressions of sexually oppressive practices in rural or provincial places than in large and modernized ones.

Mexican women living in rural areas are subjected to more severe and accentuated gender inequalities than women living in urban social contexts (Barrios & Pons, 1994), and women who live in urbanized places have potentially less exposure to rigid sexual regulations (Amuchástegui, 1996, 1998; Szasz & Figueroa, 1997).

Thus, Mexican women are exposed to various types of socially constructed patriarchies. Each one of these patriarchies promotes multiple forms and various levels of gender inequality. I use the concept of machismos regionales, or regional patriarchies, to identify these gender patterns in Mexican society, based on Belinda Bozzoli's examinations of the "patchwork quilt of patriarchies" in South Africa (Bozzoli, 1983, p. 149) and R. W. Connell's analyses of gender and multiple masculinities as social constructions (Connell, 1987, 1995). Gender relations and representations of masculinity are not the same across historical, social, and cultural contexts. They are fluid and reproduced in social interaction, through social practice, and in particular social and geographic situations (Connell, 1987).[12]

Machismos regionales are reproduced in Mexico. The more intense expressions of machismo and gender inequalities appear in small provincial locations, or pueblos. I refer to these as *machismo rural*. Disguised or de-emphasized machismo, more common in larger urban metropolises, such as Mexico City, is identified as *machismo urbano*. In urban social contexts, multiple opportunities for education, paid work, well-informed sex education and training, and organized women's organizations may expose women to social circumstances that enable them to challenge gender inequalities (Figueroa Perea, 1997). Similarly, young heterosexual men from Mexico City are more likely than rural men to perceive their female counterparts as more equal in their sexual encounters and heterosexual experiences (Amuchástegui, 1994).

Both types of machismos regionales are fluid and may be contested or emphasized, weakened or strengthened, depending on socioeconomic and political contexts. For instance, as mothers educated in small locations become aware of gender inequalities, they may challenge many forms of rural machismo while educating their daughters and sons. In contrast, as mothers living in larger cities are exposed to rigid forms of urban machismo, they may still promote many gender inequalities. Regardless of the geographic region, the social reproduction of machismo is closely associated with *la doble moral*, or double standards of morality. In this study, mothers who were educating both daughters and sons reported not having the same need to "protect" their sons. Because of the special privileges granted to men by a patriarchal society, these mothers believe that their sons do not encounter the same social and moral risks women do.

PROMOTING FEMALE SEXUAL AUTONOMY VIA
MOTHERHOOD: REGIONAL DIFFERENCES

The majority of the Mexican immigrant women who expressed a more liberal attitude toward premarital sex for their daughters were from Mexico City. Rather than emphasizing premarital virginity, Mexican immigrant mothers from Mexico

City provided their daughters with what they considered a contemporary and well-informed perception of sexuality and sexual education. Azucena Bermúdez offers the best example of this type of sexuality transition across generations and international borders.

> I have changed. . . . For example, I was educated by my mother in one way and now I am trying to educate my daughter to become more free, more liberal but not to the point of *el libertinaje* [lack of moral restraint]. In other words, to explain things to her without making her feel that the loss of virginity is bad for a woman. Back then, if you were not a virgin at marriage, you were bad, you were dirty, inside and outside. But what I am trying to say is . . . that was the old tradition. Perhaps these days mothers are better educated with regard to this issue and that is what we want to transmit to our children and to our daughters.

Azucena Bermúdez is a 43-year-old mother of three children, one daughter and two sons. She was trained as a preschool teacher in Mexico City, and she currently works as a health educator for an inner-city community organization serving Latino immigrant families in Los Angeles. During our interview, she attributed the transition of her sexual morality to the many *pláticas* (informal presentations) on sexuality she had attended as part of her training as a school volunteer and as a community educator. Azucena displayed a keen awareness of the problems faced by the Mexican immigrant community in Los Angeles: drugs, gang activity, sexually transmitted diseases, and a high incidence of Latina adolescent pregnancy. She said that she is educating her children while exploring ways to protect them from these dangerous situations. Regarding her daughter, who is attending elementary school, she emphasized a need to promote sexual autonomy and personal responsibility. "She is the one who finally decides what to do with regard to sex," Azucena firmly stated. Then, she added, "Like I said, it is completely up to her. I talk with her about the pros and cons, the good and bad of experiencing premarital sex."

Other mothers from Mexico City addressed the importance of respecting a daughter's sexual autonomy. They believe that once their daughters reach maturity, the daughters should decide whether or not to be sexually active. When I asked Rosalía Silva and Norma Ortega how they felt about their daughters experiencing premarital sex, they replied,

> I would like for them to wait to have sex. Because you know, they are my little angels and I would not like for them to experience any risk, you know, to have sex that young. Here in the United States by the time they are 13, 14, they are already having sex. But when they get older, there is nothing I can do about it because she will be a young lady who will be completely aware of what she does. (Rosalía Silva)

> With regard to contraceptives and all that, I would not allow her to use them at an early age. But I know that at some point in her life she will have her first sexual relation, and I will not impose my will to keep her from doing it. On the contrary, I would like her to trust me so we can talk about it. (Norma Ortega)

For these women, preserving virginity is no longer the most important concern; rather, avoiding promiscuity becomes most crucial. Sexual activity before marriage is appropriate only if specific conditions are observed, such as well-informed sex education and sex within mutually exclusive and monogamous relationships. Both mothers, fearing their daughters will have more than one sexual partner, expressed concern about how to protect their daughters from promiscuity.

Similarly, other mothers now worry about unwanted premarital pregnancy and sexually transmitted diseases. For these women, openly communicating about sex took priority. As with Azucena Bermúdez, talking about "the good and the bad" of premarital sexual relations becomes an essential component of their daughters' sex education:

> Well, virginity is not that important, like I said, it is secondary. I really do not care if she is a virgin or not when she gets married, it is up to her. But I want to talk openly with her about everything . . . sex, you know, about the type of person she is sleeping with, and all the risks she is taking. (Soledad Torres)

> With regard to my daughter . . . , it is okay with me if she wants to preserve her virginity until marriage, but in case she decides to have sexual relations before she gets married, I have to teach her everything about sexually transmitted diseases. (Graciela Hurtado)

> I have told her already, "Look, you know what? It's not a matter of just going to sleep with anybody," I tell her. . . . "Because from there you find out there are many consequences, diseases, and you could also get pregnant and all that. And these days it is not only one disease, there are many diseases." (Jimena Lombardo)

In the past, for many mexicanas sexuality was shrouded in secrecy and silence. Many of these mothers, however, strive to develop a trusting mother-daughter relationship within which they can communicate openly about sexuality. When I asked Trinidad Urbina, "Would you like for your daughter to preserve her virginity until the day she gets married?" she replied, "No, to me it's the same. The only thing is that I really have to talk with her about it."

Few mothers from Jalisco promote sexual autonomy and emancipation. However, they have four things in common. First, they had all experienced premarital sexual relations. Second, they experienced negative feelings because of premarital sex. Third, they became aware of gender inequalities they themselves experienced earlier in life. And fourth, they were concerned about protecting their daughters in regard to sexual practices (e.g., pregnancy, sexually transmitted diseases, promiscuity) and in terms of their daughters' experiences as women in potential heterosexual relationships (i.e., intimacy, respect, healthy marital life). The testimonies of Idalia Jiménez, Xóchitl Arteaga, and Deyanira Estévez reveal these sex education narratives.

> What I have in mind to tell them is that when they have their first sexual relation, this is not something bad because it is something that their bodies desire, but that they

have to take care of themselves, not only because of pregnancy, but because of the many diseases that we have now. That is what concerns me the most, not sex itself that much, but the many diseases that we have these days. (Idalia Jiménez)

Well, that is her decision. She is the one who will decide about it. I have actually talked to my husband about it. I told him, "What if she gets pregnant or anything happened to her?" And he said, "She is my daughter and I am here to respond to her any time she needs me." Because, yes, she is sexually precocious . . . too much! (Xóchitl Arteaga)

I have to teach her in a way so she becomes more alert, so she knows about what is good and what is bad. For example, if some day she has sexual relations, she has to think about it and make her own decision. If she wants to do it some day, it is completely up to her. (Deyanira Estévez)

Lastly, for a couple of mothers from two small towns, their daughters' sexual activity before marriage is not as important as their daughters being genuinely in love and there being the potential for a permanent relationship. Oralia Pacheco and Romelia Sánchez promote these values while educating their adolescent daughters.

In case they had sexual relations before marriage, I would like for them to do it with a person they really love and with the one they are thinking about spending the rest of their lives with. I would like for them to be sure of that. I feel like they are more likely to be respected that way. (Oralia Pacheco)

I tell them, "Take care of yourselves, respect yourselves, respect your bodies, and the only thing I am going to ask you is that when you decide to have sexual relations do it because of love. Do not do it because you want to impress your friends. No! Do not do it to satisfy nobody else's needs but only if you feel like you are deeply in love." (Romelia Sánchez)

Like some of the Mexico City mothers, they still wish to protect their daughters from promiscuous sexual practices. Being in love or in a permanent relationship is a way to protect themselves from this risk. As Romelia stated:

Well . . . I have talked with my daughters and I have told them that when they have sexual relations I would like for them to have one partner, right? That I would not like for them to go here and there experimenting. I would like for them to have one boyfriend, someone perhaps whom you love so deeply and with whom you make love, and if they get married . . . well, that is my daughters' problem. But my ideal is that they have one boyfriend, that they fall in love with him, and then they either cohabit or get married.

Across generations, this group of Jalisco mothers promotes sexuality transitions. Within the context of the family, additional transformations take place as mothers actively disrupt the ethics linking a daughter's sexual activity with values of respect for the family.

IMMIGRATION AND THE GENDER MAZE:
GENDER TRAPS BEYOND BORDERS

For the Mexican immigrant women in this study, an important sexuality transition emerges out of their awareness of cultural differences in the United States—*"A los hombres de aquí no les importa si son vírgenes o no"* (Men over here do not care if they are virgins or not). Amparo Bárcenas and Patricia Quezada offered clear examples of this awareness. Even though they preferred that their daughters preserve virginity until marriage, both mothers expressed some flexibility because of cultural differences. For Amparo Bárcenas, who had lived in the United States for more than 20 years, giving up her beliefs about virginity was still a personal struggle. However, seeing the cultural differences and the way men living in the United States perceived virginity helped her to reexamine her own beliefs while raising her daughters.

> Those are the ideas that I have and they are so well rooted and there is no way that I can get rid of them. But, yes, I would like for my daughters to preserve their virginity until the day they get married. . . . But, it is different here, that's also something I have noticed here, that men do not care if a woman has had sexual relations.

Looking back upon her life, Amparo realized that as a result of the sexual difficulties she experienced with her husband, she developed strong prejudices against Mexican men. These prejudices intensified after listening to the many stories by her Mexican women friends about the limits on their sexuality. To Amparo, it was comforting to know that living in the United States would provide her daughters with alternatives. Her daughters, she reasoned, might become involved with men from different ethnic groups and perhaps experience a more satisfying sexual life.

> I have always thought that Mexican men do not care about lovemaking. They don't make sure the woman gets satisfied. I have a very bad image of Mexican men, and I shouldn't, because I have never been with a man from a different race. But, yes, I have always told my daughter Marisa not to marry a Mexican man.

For Patricia Quezada, educating her three daughters in the United States also offered alternatives in sex education. In Los Angeles, California, her daughters were exposed both to sexist men who would reproach them if they were not virgins at marriage and to men raised in the United States who displayed more tolerant attitudes. When I asked Patricia if she would like her daughters to have premarital sexual relations, she replied:

> I would say no . . . but then it depends because we are in this country . . . and it seems like it is no longer important if the woman is a señorita or not. It depends. If they marry a man who is very machista, he will always throw it in their face. But if they marry a man who was raised here and everything, I think that he will have a very different way of thinking about it.

Similarly, Diamantina Estrada and Yadira Vélez perceive differences in men's opinions about virginity and sexuality. Diamantina believes in promoting virginity when her two daughters reach adolescence. For her, the risk of sexual oppression depends on the "type" of man her daughters choose for a husband, as she expresses in this exchange:

How would your daughters' lives be different if they preserve their virginity until the day they get married?

No, it would be the same . . . but, it depends on what type of men they end up with, because there are good and bad men.

So, who are the bad men?

Pues . . . los machistas [Well . . . the sexist men]

Diamantina's awareness was based on her personal experience and her own perception of gender relations. Her consciousness about sexism was based on a "bad men/good men" dichotomy. She felt her daughters needed to preserve their virginity in case they ended up with the undesirable type of man. Similarly, Yadira Vélez was raising her adolescent daughter to preserve her virginity until marriage. But unlike Diamantina, she emphasized that the differences among men were based on ethnic or cultural backgrounds.

Yes . . . I am teaching her to preserve her virginity until marriage but it is difficult for many young girls to comply with that these days. Los latinos are the ones who value virginity in a woman. And many of them perhaps do not value it, but many of them have it within them because their parents teach them about it, so that way they teach it to the men and also to the women.

In our interviews, these mothers expressed a desire to help their daughters become emancipated. At the same time, as we can see, their narratives reflect women's complicity with men's expectations. The preservation of virginity is conditioned by women's gendered assumptions of what men think about it either *over here* in the United States or *over there* in Mexico. A woman's sexual destiny depends either on the "type of man" she will end up with ("good" versus "bad"), or on the man's sexual morality, which is influenced by his ethnic/cultural background. Thus, Mexican mothers who are exposed to culturally different sexual moralities may educate their daughters in ways that reflect transformations in their perceptions of a woman's sexuality. However, women adapt or accommodate to their socially learned perceptions of male standards, which are either restrictive or more flexible.

MEXICANAS' SEXUAL LANDSCAPE IN CALIFORNIA

Mexican immigrant women experience sexuality transformations after migrating and establishing a permanent life in the United States. For the women participating in this study, women's sexuality and sex life are transformed not through acculturation, but by additional and more complex socially constructed dynamics such as socioeconomic factors, immigrant community life, and social networking.

These women expressed their keen awareness of the increased employment and educational opportunities the U.S. economy offers to both their daughters and sons. Most of these Mexican immigrant women want their daughters to climb up the education ladder, develop a professional career, and obtain a well-paid job. Regardless of their places of origin, many of the informants asked me at the end of our interviews about my own mother's secret for making me stay in high school, go to college, and become a never-married professional. They praised single mexicanas who are able to become *"independientes, educadas y profesionistas."*

As these Mexican immigrant mothers replace marriage with career goals for their daughters, their ideas about appropriate sexual behavior also change. Virginity depreciates as a form of social capital. Education and employment opportunities emerge as new goods.

Mexican immigrant women also experienced transformations in their sex lives as a consequence of their exposure to sex education presentations, or *pláticas sobre la sexualidad,* and Spanish-language talk shows within their immigrant communities. Las pláticas are formal presentations on sexuality conducted by Spanish-speaking professionally trained health educators, most of whom are Latina/o immigrants themselves. During an interview with a Latina sex educator currently supervising these pláticas at a well-known community-based agency in Los Angeles, I discovered the feminist philosophy they promote in their sexuality workshops. An immigrant herself, this sex educator reported that during the summer of 1999, the agency issued certificates of completion to 165 Latina immigrants who attended its 12-week sex education program. Some of my informants who had attended las pláticas sobre la sexualidad at this agency talked about the ways in which they felt empowered and better equipped to help their daughters and sons have a healthy personal life. Lastly, women who attended similar workshops at their children's schools reported like experiences and feelings, explaining that they had noticed more ready access to sexuality-related school programs and educational materials here in the United States when compared with Mexico.

Spanish-language talk shows such as *Cristina, Sevcec,* and *El y Ella* regularly discuss controversial topics previously forbidden or considered taboo in Spanish-language media. Sexuality issues are their main fare. During my interviews, I learned about the ways in which mexicanas use *Cristina* to explore and create change in their sex lives. Talk shows were also utilized by some of the women in the study to facilitate sexuality-related conversations with their daughters and sons. Some mothers reported that they took advantage of talk show discussions of teenage pregnancy to involve their children, watch the shows with them, and have important conversations with their sons and daughters about this particular topic.

As they converse with one another within their immigrant communities, Mexican women experience sexuality transitions and establish new social metrics regarding sexual morality and sexuality. Via networking, they create a sexual discourse while helping each other to cope with their sexual difficulties and concerns. All the women in this study reported that conversing about sex while exchanging information about their sex lives with other immigrant women (e.g., friends, neighbors, coworkers, sisters, sisters-in-law, aunts) provided them with the means to exchange advice, personal support, and information about sex. For instance, some women from rural areas in Jalisco reported that they conversed about sex with *amigas educadas* from Mexico City or from other urban areas in Mexico and Latin America. Via networking, they reported, they had developed an emancipatory perspective about female sexuality. Thus, these Mexican immigrant women may provide a sex education that is more egalitarian for both their daughters and sons.

FINAL THOUGHTS

So, what was the role of Catholic teachings on sexuality in the lives of these women? The overwhelming majority of the women in this study were educated in the Catholic faith. By no means did they deny the punishing nature of Catholic sexual morality. Premarital loss of virginity was accompanied by Catholic guilt, shame, and remorse. However, these women experience Catholic religious guilt and shame a posteriori and as an internalized (personal, private) expression of control over their sex lives. In contrast, women's subjective interpretations identify family patriarchal morality (e.g., coercive marriage) and a socially learned fear of male-defined ideologies and practices (e.g., "Men throw it in your face when you are not a virgin") as externalized social and pragmatic forms of sexual control. The statement by Olga Ponce, "I did not follow them [religious teachings regarding virginity] because of religion. . . . I followed them because of fear of my mother!" represents the subjective interpretation women offered to explain that only a parent could enforce coercive marriage in case of pregnancy out of wedlock, but never God or a priest.

Thus, in *theory*, the Catholic Church formulates moral values that are sexually controlling to heterosexual mexicanas. But in *practice*, family and male-defined codes of sexual conduct establish and enforce gender politics linked to a mexicana's need to preserve her premarital virginity. It is a Mexican immigrant mother's job to decipher, contest, and redefine these gendered dynamics as she formulates new ethics to educate her daughter on virginity within immigration-related social and economic contexts and experiences.

To what extent are generation and regional patriarchies, on the one hand, and immigration and U.S. life, on the other, responsible for sexuality transitions across generations? These seem to be mutually interlocking forces. A mother's individual gendered sexual history experienced within specific socioeconomic contexts and regional patriarchies interacts with the particular changes she experiences in the United States. These include, but are not limited to, the following: learning more about sex via education received from community-based agencies; networking with other Latinas; employment, control over her income, and financial independence; and exposure to media within the immigrant community. The migration- and gender-related transformations across generations experienced by the women in this study parallel those Hirsch found in her ethnographic work with immigrants from Jalisco living in Atlanta. While comparing two family generations living in both receiving and sending communities, Hirsch found that younger women transform the functions of sexuality within marriage (i.e., from procreation purposes to emotional intimacy and sexual pleasure) and the nature of their marital relationships across generations (i.e., "from an ideal of *respeto* [respect] to one of *confianza* [trust])" (Hirsch, 1999, p. 1332).

Our research into and knowledge of Mexican women's and men's sexualities within the context of all these social complexities is virginal. Exploring the mother-daughter relationship is a first step to a sociological understanding of Mexican immigrant women's sexuality. As the research suggests, Mexican immigrant women enter the United States with particular gendered sexual ideologies and practices regarding virginity. Women socially construct these beliefs and behaviors within family and couple relationships, and through regionally defined social processes and economic conditions in their places of origin. But these normative ideals regarding premarital virginity are not set in stone—they shift across generations, time, and national borders. After migration to and settlement in the United States, mexicanas unload, revisit, and redefine these female heterosexuality prescriptions within their social and economic conditions as immigrants. As they educate their daughters about virginity, these women continue to articulate their own subjective interpretations of loss or preservation of premarital virginity within the contexts of couple and family relationships. Via motherhood, they unfold their sexual histories and resolve the gender inequalities they themselves have experienced in their personal lives. That is, across generations they replace an ethic of *respeto a la familia* that enforces premarital sexual abstinence with a new ethic of *protección y cuidado personal* that promotes sexual-moderation for their daughters. Through their exposure to pláticas, Spanish-language media, informal social networks, immigrant culture, and employment, mexicanas are reinventing new heterosexual norms for themselves and for a new generation of Mexican American women.

NOTES

This chapter represents a part of my completed dissertation work at the University of Southern California. I want to express my gratitude to the 40 women who trusted me with their personal lives and sexual stories. I am profoundly grateful to the Social Science Research Council for the generous dissertation fellowship I received through its Sexuality Research Fellowship Program. I want to thank (by alphabetical order) Professors R. W. Connell, María Patricia Fernández-Kelly, and Denise Segura for their recommendations on earlier versions of this text. I am especially grateful to Professor Pierrette Hondagneu-Sotelo for her consistent guidance and feedback from beginning to end of this chapter.

My dissertation research project was conducted in accordance with human subjects protocol; I obtained research approval from the Institutional Review Board at the University of Southern California. I utilize pseudonyms in order to assure the confidentiality and privacy of my respondents.

1. The Council of Trent (1545–1563), or El Concilio de Trento, established the Catholic Church's teachings with regard to sexuality and how the decrees were to be used as the basis for indoctrinating the indigenous population (Rubio, 1997). During the Council of Trent, virginity was defined as an idealized condition. Accordingly, virginity was socially defined in Mexico as the best "certificate" a woman had to prove her decency and honorability: "*la virginidad era un estado mas perfecto que el matrimonio*" (virginity was a state more perfect than marriage) (Tostado Gutiérrez, 1991, p. 197).

2. Recent scholarship on immigration and sexuality includes dissertation works by Jennifer S. Hirsch (1998) and Lionel Cantú (1999).

Studies on the Mexican mother-daughter relationship and sexuality have been mainly conducted in the behavioral sciences. To my knowledge, virginity-related themes between this dyad have not been qualitatively examined in these analyses. See references section for studies on mother-daughter communication, sexual initiation, and the sexual lives of adolescents—in U.S. Latinas in general (O'Sullivan, Jaramillo, Moreau, & Meyer-Bahlburg, 1999), in Mexican American teenagers (Hovell, Sipan, Blumberg, Atkins, Hofstetter, & Kreitner, 1994; Liebowitz, Calderon-Castellano, & Cuellar, 1999), and in adolescents from Mexico in particular (Pick & Andrade Palos, 1995).

3. Only the excerpts used in my analysis were translated into English. Since a person's first language is the one in which emotions and feelings are imprinted (Espín, 1987), much of the nuance, emotional meaning, and tone of the participants' stories was lost in the translation process. I have attempted to salvage this meaning by inserting expressions in Spanish.

4. The lowest level of formal education for both groups was *educación primaria*, which is equivalent to completion of sixth grade; the highest level was a *licenciatura*, or a bachelor's degree. However, women from Jalisco were more likely to have a lower level of formal education (average = 7.1 years) than their Mexico City counterparts (average = 10.15 years). Accordingly, Jalisco women were less likely to have paid employment (9 out of 20) and more likely to be full-time homemakers (11 out of 20) when compared with the Mexico City informants. Most women from Mexico City reported having paid jobs (15 out of 20); a few of them reported they were full-time homemakers (5 out of 20). Interestingly, women from Jalisco had longer permanent residence in the United States (average = 11.68 years) than the Mexico City group (average = 8.85 years). Most of them reported that they were raised in the Catholic faith (39 out of 40); 3 became Protestant in the United States. At the time of the interview, many participants were married ($n = 27$), and other women were cohabiting ($n = 7$). Other participants were legally divorced ($n = 1$) or separated after having been married ($n = 2$) or after cohabiting ($n = 1$). Only two of the women had never been married, and neither of these had any children. Many of them ($n = 33$) reported that they were raising daughters in the United States.

5. Latina mothers have been perceived as those "expected to mediate conflicts between family members and to prevent confrontations." (Boyd-Franklin & Garcia-Preto, 1994, p. 251). Also, in her work with Mexican families, Annelou Ypeij (1998) has identified the maternal figure as the one who is to blame for her daughter's immoral behavior, or "*conducta indecorosa.*" Ypeij examines three central aspects of the maternal figure for a better understanding of the mother-daughter relationship. First, the mother is *la figura de confianza,*

that is, she inspires intimacy, sensibility, and trust in her daughter. Second, the mother, responsible for the education of her daughter, becomes *la mediadora,* or a mediator in the father-daughter relationship. That is, gender arrangements within the family context make the mother responsible for the education of her children, while the father works outside the home to comply with his obligations as a family provider. As part of this dynamic, the maternal figure may protect the daughter from her father. And third, the mother is in charge of protecting *"el honor y la reputación de la hija"* (her daughter's honor and reputation) while controlling her daughter's behavior. For in-depth analysis of these dynamics, see Ypeij, 1998.

6. I use this paradigm inspired by Carol S. Vance's examinations of women's sexuality (1984).

7. About 70% of the women in this study were not virgins when they were married; only 12 out of the 40 women in the study remained virgins until marriage. One third of the women who lost their virginity before marriage did so through rape and/or incest.

8. Conversion to a new religion after migration and settlement did not occur frequently among the women of this study. Only 3 of the 39 Catholic women converted to a Protestant denomination after living in the United States: Belén Carrera, Fernanda Galindo, and Erendira Fuentes. Of the 40 study participants, only Diamantina Estrada was raised Protestant in Mexico. Even though the incidence of conversion to a new church is not striking, it is important to mention that two out of the three women who became Protestant (Belén Carrera and Fernanda Galindo) became more fundamentalist in their attitudes about sexual morality, especially while educating their daughters. Based on their religious values, both women hope their daughters will refrain from premarital sex.

9. See Solís, 1998. Journalist Silvana Paternostro identified a clinic that charges $1,800 to $2,000 for the "reconstrucción del hímen" services they offer to Latina immigrants living in Queens and Brooklyn, New York. For Paternostro's feminist reflections on this subject, see Paternostro, 1998, pp. 270–289.

10. Oliva M. Espín, Ann Twinam, and Marcela Tostado Gutiérrez examine the links between Latina women's sexuality, family respect, and socioeconomic status. Espín (1986) observes that "the honor of Latin families is strongly tied to the sexual purity of women" (p. 277). Twinam (1989) offers an analysis of the historical and elitist roots of a link between a woman's virginity, family honor and respect, socioeconomic status, and decency in colonial Latin America. As Twinam states: "Illegitimate women not only found their pool of potential marriage partners restricted, but their illegitimacy could adversely affect the occupational choices of their sons and the marriage potential of their daughters. Absence of honor could thus limit the social mobility of both sexes, as well as the future of succeeding generations" (p. 124). And Tostado Gutiérrez (1991) illustrates the experiences of Mexican women in colonial society with regard to virginity and its social exchange value. As she states, "In this way, the law recognized the importance of the woman's preservation of her sexual virtue, a condition upon which her possibilities of getting married and of maintaining family honor and social status depended" (p. 200, my translation).

11. See Manuel Peña's 1991 article for illustrations of the social construction of Mexican folklore and its multiple interactions with machismo and the dehumanization and sexual objectification of women.

12. Bozzoli (1983) contests the belief that one uniform patriarchy rules South Africa. She explains how and why capitalism did not establish itself uniformly in this region but irregularly, as local and previously established domestic economies survived as precapitalist systems. This dynamic produced, in turn, multiple economic patterns and contrasting multiple patriarchies coexisting in the area.

REFERENCES

Amuchástegui, Ana. (1994). *La primera vez. El significado de la virginidad y la iniciación sexual para jóvenes mexicanos* (Research report). México, DF: The Population Council.

Amuchástegui, Ana. (1996). El significado de la virginidad y la iniciación sexual. Un relato de investigación. In Ivonne Szasz & Susana Lerner (Eds.), *Para comprender la subjetividad: Investigación cualitativa en salud reproductiva y sexualidad* (pp. 137–172). México, DF: El Colegio de México.

Amuchástegui, Ana. (1998, Spring). La dimensión moral de la sexualidad y de la virginidad en las culturas híbridas mexicanas. *Relaciones, XIX*(74), 101–133.

Argüelles, Lourdes, & Rivero, Anne M. (1993). Gender/sexual orientation violence and transnational migration: Conversations with some Latinas we think we know. *Urban Anthropology, 22*(3–4), 259–275.

Barkley, B. H., & Salazar-Mosher, Enedina. (1995). Sexuality and Hispanic culture: Counseling with children and their parents. *Journal of Sex Education and Therapy, 21*(4), 255–267.

Barrios, W., & Pons, L. (1994). *Sexualidad y religión en Los Altos de Chiapas.* Cited in *Sexuality, gender relations, and female empowerment.* Paper presented by Ivonne Szasz and Juan Guillermo Figueroa Perea at the Seminar on Female Empowerment and Demographic Processes: Moving Beyond Cairo, Lund, Sweden, April 21–24, 1997.

Boyd-Franklin, Nancy, & Garcia-Preto, Nydia. (1994). Family therapy: A closer look at African American and Hispanic women. In Lillian Comas-Díaz & Beverly Greene (Eds.), *Women of color: Integrating ethnic and gender identities in psychotherapy* (pp. 239–264). New York: Guilford Press.

Bozzoli, Belinda. (1983). Marxism, feminism, and South African studies. *Journal of Southern African Studies, 2*(2), 139–171.

Bronfman, Mario, & López-Moreno, Sergio. (1996). Perspectives on HIV/AIDS prevention among immigrants on the U.S.-Mexico border. In Shiraz Mishra, Ross F. Conner, & Raul Magaña (Eds.), *AIDS crossing borders* (pp. 49–76). Boulder, CO: Westview Press.

Cantú, Lionel. (1997, April 17–20). *Sexuality and migration: Research implications.* Paper presented at the Pacific Sociological Association Conference, San Diego, CA.

Cantú, Lionel. (1999). *Border crossings: Mexican men and the sexuality of migration.* Unpublished doctoral dissertation, University of California, Irvine.

Carrier, Joseph M. (1995). *De los otros: Intimacy and homosexuality among Mexican men.* New York: Columbia University Press.

Connell, R. W. (1987). *Gender and power.* Stanford, CA: Stanford University Press.

Connell, R. W. (1995). *Masculinities.* Berkeley & Los Angeles: University of California Press.

Córdova Plaza, Rosío. (1998, September 24–26). *Sexualidad y Orden Moral: De las concepciones corporales al control social en una comunidad campesina en México.* Paper presented at the 1998 Latin American Studies Association Conference, Chicago.

Del Río Zolezzi, Aurora, Luguori, Ana Luisa, Magis-Rodríguez, Carlos, Valdespino-Gómez, José Luis, García-García, María de Lourdes, and Sepúlveda-Amor, Jaime. (1995, November–December). La epidemia de VIH/SIDA y la mujer en México. *Salud Pública de México, 37*(6), 581–591.

Espín, Oliva M. (1986). Cultural and historical influences on sexuality in Hispanic/Latin women. In J. B. Cole (Ed.), *All American women: Lines that divide, ties that bind* (pp. 272–284). New York: Free Press.

Espín, Oliva M. (1987). Psychological impact of migration on Latinas: Implications for psychotherapeutic practice. *Psychology of Women Quarterly, 11,* 489–503.

Espín, Oliva M. (1999). *Women crossing boundaries: The psychology of immigration and the transformations of sexuality.* New York: Routledge.

Figueroa Perea, Juan Guillermo. (1997). Algunas reflexiones sobre el enfoque de género y la representación de la sexualidad. *Estudios Demográficos y Urbanos, 12*(1–2), 201–244.

Guerrero-Pavich, Emma. (1986). A Chicana perspective on Mexican culture and sexuality. *Journal of Social Work and Human Sexuality, 4*(3), 47–65.

Hirsch, Jennifer S. (1998). *Migration, modernity, and Mexican marriage: A comparative study of gender, sexuality, and reproductive health in a transnational community.* Unpublished doctoral dissertation, Johns Hopkins University.

Hirsch, Jennifer S. (1999, June–July). En el norte la mujer manda: Gender, generation, and geography in a Mexican transnational community. *American Behavioral Scientist, 42*(9), 1332–1349.

Hovell, Mel, Sipan, Carol, Blumberg, Elaine, Atkins, Cathie, Hofstetter, C. Richard, & Kreitner, Susan. (1994, November). Family influences on Latino and Anglo adolescents' sexual behavior. *Journal of Marriage and the Family, 56,* 973–986.

Liebowitz, Stephen W., Calderon-Castellano, Dolores, & Cuellar, Israel. (1999). Factors that predict sexual behaviors among young Mexican American adolescents: An exploratory study. *Hispanic Journal of Behavioral Sciences, 21,* 470–479.

Magis-Rodríguez, Carlos, Del Río Zolezzi, Aurora, Valdespino-Gómez, José Luis, & García-García, María de Lourdes. (1995, November–December). Casos de sida en el área rural de México. *Salud Pública de México, 37*(6), 615–623.

Mena, Jennifer. (2000, September 29). Cruel memento: Mexican immigrant workers come back from the North with HIV. *San Francisco Chronicle,* pp. A18–19.

Mishra, Shiraz, Conner, Ross F., & Magaña, J. Raul (Eds.). (1996). *AIDS crossing borders.* Boulder, CO: Westview Press.

O'Sullivan, Lucia F., Jaramillo, Beatriz M. S., Moreau, Donna, & Meyer-Bahlburg, Heino F. L. (1999). Mother-daughter communication about sexuality in a clinical sample of Hispanic adolescent girls. *Hispanic Journal of Behavioral Sciences, 21*(4), 447–469.

Paternostro, Silvana. (1998). *In the land of God and man: Confronting our sexual culture.* New York: Dutton.

Peña, Manuel. (1991, March). Class, gender, and machismo: The "treacherous woman" folklore of Mexican male workers. *Gender and Society, 5*(1), 30–46.

Pick, Susan, & Andrade Palos, Patricia. (1995). Impact of the family on the sex lives of adolescents. *Adolescence, 30,* 667–675.

Reid, Pamela Trotman, & Bing, Vanessa M. (2000). Sexual roles of girls and women: An ethnocultural lifespan perspective. In Cheryl B. Travis & Jacquelyn W. White (Eds.), *Sexuality, society, and feminism* (pp. 141–166). Washington, DC: American Psychological Association.

Rubio, Eusebio. (1997). México: Estados Unidos mexicanos. In Robert T. Francoeur (Ed.), *The international encyclopedia of sexuality* (Vol. 2, pp. 869–894). New York: Continuum.

Salgado de Snyder, V. Nelly, Acevedo, Aurora, Díaz-Pérez, María de Jesús, & Saldívar-Garduño, Alicia. (2000). Understanding the sexuality of Mexican-born women and their risk for HIV/AIDS. *Psychology of Women Quarterly, 24,* 100–109.

Salgado de Snyder, V. Nelly, Díaz-Pérez, María de Jesús, & Maldonado, Margarita. (1996). AIDS: Risk behaviors among rural Mexican women married to migrant workers in the United States. *AIDS Education and Prevention, 8*(2), 134–142.

Solís, Guadalupe Irma. (1998, January 3). Interview by author. Tape recording. Ciudad Valles, San Luis Potosí.

Szasz, Ivonne, & Figueroa Perea, Juan Guillermo. (1997, April 21–24). *Sexuality, gender relations, and female empowerment.* Paper presented at the Seminar on Female Empowerment and Demographic Processes: Moving Beyond Cairo, Lund, Sweden.

Tostado Gutiérrez, Marcela. (1991). *El álbum de la mujer: Antología ilustrada de las mexicanas* (Vol. II). México: Instituto Nacional de Antropología e Historia.

Twinam, Ann. (1989). Honor, sexuality, and illegitimacy in colonial Spanish America. In Asuncion Lavrin (Ed.), *Sexuality and marriage in Latin America* (pp. 118–155). Lincoln: University of Nebraska Press.

Vance, Carol S. (Ed.). (1984). *Pleasure and danger: Exploring female sexuality.* Boston: Routledge & Kegan Paul.

Wilson, Fiona. (1990). *De la casa al taller: Mujeres, trabajo y clase social en la industria textil y del vestido, Santiago Tangamandapio.* Zamora: El Colegio de Michoacán.

Woo Morales, Ofelia. (1995). Las mujeres mexicanas indocumentadas en la migración internacional y la movilidad transfronteriza. In Soledad González, Olivia Ruiz, Laura Velasco, & Ofelia Woo (Eds.), *Mujeres, migración y maquila en la frontera norte* (pp. 65–87). Tijuana, México: El Colegio de la Frontera Norte.

Ypeij, Annelou. (1998). Las hijas "buenas" y las empacadoras zamoranas. In Gail Mummert & Luis Alfonso Ramírez Carrillo (Eds.), *Rehaciendo las diferencias: Identidades de género en Michoacán y Yucatán* (pp. 179–209). Zamora: El Colegio de Michoacán and la Universidad Autónoma de Yucatán.

Zavella, Patricia. (1997). Playing with fire: The gendered construction of Chicana/Mexicana sexuality. In Roger N. Lancaster & Micaela Di Leonardo (Eds.), *The gender-sexuality reader: Culture, history, political economy* (pp. 392–408). New York: Routledge.

CHAPTER 12

Raising Children, and Growing Up, across National Borders

Comparative Perspectives on Age, Gender, and Migration

Barrie Thorne, Marjorie Faulstich Orellana, Wan Shun Eva Lam, and Anna Chee

The participation of children in processes of migration came to the world's attention in 1999 through the widely reported saga of Elián González, a 5-year-old Cuban boy who became the focus of a child-custody struggle among members of a transnational family. Elián was rescued from the ocean off the coast of Florida after his mother and stepfather drowned when their boat capsized on the way to the United States. He was taken to the Miami home of his great-uncle, a Cuban émigré, who assumed temporary custody of the "unaccompanied minor" (the 5-year-old's classification under U.S. immigration law). Claiming that Elián would face "imminent and irreparable harm" if he were returned to Castro's "island prison," the great-uncle petitioned the Immigration and Naturalization Service (INS) to grant the boy political asylum. But the boy's father, Juan Miguel González, demanded that his son be returned to Cuba, where, he said, Elián "does not lack anything" and "has his health care and education free."

The INS and the Justice Department agreed that giving custody to the Cuban-based father would be in accord with U.S. laws as well as "in the best interests of the child," although several members of Congress actively supported the great-uncle's efforts to retain custody. The great-uncle and his supporters in the Miami Cuban enclave defied a Justice Department order to return the boy to his father, who eventually flew to the United States with his second wife and infant son to retrieve Elián. Federal agents seized Elián and reunited him with his father, and in June 2000, after a federal appeals court gave legal clearance, they returned to live in Cuba.

The unfolding story of Elián González highlights the experiences of families whose members sustain relationships, including those involving the raising of children, across national borders. As Elián's situation makes clear, state-defined age categories, such as "unaccompanied minor," figure centrally in the regulation of migration, as do negotiations of "social age," or perceptions of an individual's relative dependence or maturity (Solberg, 1997). The González story points to the relevance of child-rearing practices, ideas about the "nature" and needs of children, and comparisons of growing up "here" versus "there" in the shaping and uses of transnational social fields.[1] It also reveals complex relationships of age to nationality, racialized ethnicity, and gender.

What if Elián had been Haitian instead of Cuban? That question was posed by a number of news commentators who were alert to the racist and anti-communist double standards of U.S. immigration laws and public opinion. If he were Haitian, the rescued boy would have been thrown into the legal limbo and degraded circumstances of over 4,000 "unaccompanied alien minors," some of them in juvenile jails, who await deportation from the United States. Racial-ethnic, national, and political positioning clearly entered into the sentimentalized constructions and relatively privileged alternatives that framed the experiences of Elián González.

There is another question that no one, to our knowledge, has posed: What if Elián had been a girl? The category of "5-year-old child" conveys images of physical, emotional, economic, and legal dependence that mute the salience of gender. Whether Elián or Eliana, a 5-year old's legal position as a citizen of Cuba and as a potential applicant for asylum in the United States would remain the same. However, like, and in conjunction with, racialized ethnicity, gender may enter into judgments about maturity and competence, perceived manipulability and dependence, emotional needs, assessments of risk and opportunities, and positioning in family dynamics—all of which affect interpretations of a child's social age and enter into decisions about where and how a child should be raised.

INTERSECTIONS OF AGE AND GENDER IN THE STUDY OF MIGRATION

This essay examines the intersecting significance of age, national origin, citizenship status, and gender in shaping the back-and-forth migration of transnational family members. Our central focus is on *children* (an age group), with the goal of bringing their presence, participation, and relationships with adults more fully into research on migration. Before the transformative work of contemporary feminist scholars, research on migration was mostly organized around the lives and actions of adult men (Daniels, 1990). Recurring phrases like "the immigrants sent for their wives and children" portrayed women and children essentially as luggage—brought, left behind, or sent for by men, the central actors and decision makers.

Over the last two decades, as exemplified by the essays in this volume, feminist scholars have challenged this passive and marginalized image by documenting women's participation in processes of migration and settlement, and by unraveling the gendered dynamics of a range of transnational social practices. But children remain in a peripheral and luggage-like conceptual space, mostly framed as a source of contingency in decisions to migrate, stay, or return. Furthermore, compared with the attention given to social divisions of racialized ethnicity and gender, *age* as an organizing dimension of migration has been relatively neglected (significant exceptions include Kibria, 1993; Levitt, 2001; Menjívar, in press; Olwig, 1999; Soto, 1987; Stack & Cromartie, 1992).[2] Since gender and age are basic axes of kinship, more attention to their intersecting dynamics would be especially fruitful for the study of families and migration.[3]

In this essay we highlight the presence and participation of children in the transnational practices of families who have migrated to California, but who also sustain close ties with their places of origin. We compare the intersecting dynamics of age and gender in the construction and uses of two transnational social fields, one linking the Pico Union area of Los Angeles with parts of El Salvador, Guatemala, and Mexico; and the other bridging Oakland and Yemen. Two conceptual strands weave through our analysis of age, gender, and processes of family migration:

1. Legal constructions of age and gender.   Although transnationalism is often equated with the diminishing significance of national boundaries, state practices loom large in the regulation of family life, the constitution of childhoods, and in the shaping of patterns of family migration (Hondagneu-Sotelo & Avila, 1997; Mayer & Schoepflin, 1989). The U.S. government confers citizenship upon all individuals born in the United States, regardless of gender; thus a child may have rights, such as access to a passport and to social services, that are different from those of a sibling or parent born in another country. A study based on 1998 census data found that in Los Angeles County the rate of children living in families with mixed citizenship status was nearly five times the national average, partly because of the large number of undocumented migrants from Mexico and Central America living in Southern California. In the late 1990s, when the U.S. government ruled that noncitizen parents could no longer receive food stamps, the food was also denied to children who were U.S. citizens (McDonnell, 1999).

Families who organize their lives across national boundaries may have to negotiate different legal definitions of "child" and "adult." For example, according to the laws of Yemen, a "child" of either gender legally becomes an "adult" at age 15, but U.S. laws set the formal transition at 18. Gender, as well as age, may be embedded in the legal practices that govern movement across national borders. In the United States and in Mexico, gender does not bear on the formal right of adult citizens to apply for a passport, but women who are citizens of Yemen must have signed permission from either a husband or father, which limits options for migrating on their own. Laws that govern the allocation of child custody after divorce also vary. In some Latin American countries, mothers either have full custody or share it with their former husband; in other countries, the father is automatically given full custody, and it is illegal for a divorced mother to transport a child across national borders (Guy, 2000).

2. Gendered constructions of childhood and of processes of growing up and raising children.   Our analysis of the daily lives and practices of transnational families draws upon insights from the sociology and anthropology of childhoods (for reviews, see James, Jenks, & Prout, 1997; Stephens, 1995). These fields were invigorated by the argument of Philippe Ariès (1962) that the immaturity and dependence of infants and children, and processes of maturation toward adulthood, have been perceived and organized in historically changing ways. Building on this insight, Viviana Zelizer (1985) documented a striking transition in dominant American constructions of childhood that consolidated at the turn of the century through laws that excluded children from paid labor and required them to attend school. (Note that these laws tended to mute the salience of both gender and social class in the formal organization of children's daily lives and activities.)

The image of childhood as a set-apart and protected time of life, situated in families and schools and defined by (increasingly commercialized) play, has been exported by the media and by the circulation of commodities produced by corporations like Disney and Mattel (Stephens, 1995). But the media also circulate other images that unsettle conceptions of childhood as a protected and sentimentalized space, such as reports about child soldiers (mostly boys) fighting in Colombia or Rwanda, about children who live on the streets and manage to survive more or less on their own (both genders, although boys are more visible), and stories about girls and boys who make significant contributions to the economic survival of their families. While most of these reports come from nonindustrialized countries, some, such as stories of homeless children, child workers, and sexualized images that undermine traditional notions of child innocence, also come from the United States. American childhoods have always been more diverse than conveyed by dominant images, and widening income gaps and high rates of immigration have added to the diversity.

The concept of "childhood," a term with structural and discursive valence, refers to the positioning of an age-defined group. Terms like "growing older" and "child rearing" put the matter of age into motion, within contexts of dependence and guided movements toward adulthood. Metaphors such as "rearing," "raising," and "bringing up" children convey the purposive, caring, and controlling orientation of the adults (disproportionately women) who assume this responsibility. Children also exercise agency in the process; they see themselves, sometimes ambivalently, as "growing older," and they may variously cooperate with, negotiate, or resist adult efforts to guide and control.[4] Growing up/bringing up is a guided but open-ended and highly contingent process, involving conflicts of will and desire and struggles over autonomy and control (Allat, 1996; Brannen, 1996; Solberg, 1997). Gender, social class, ethnicity, religion, and other socially constructed differences may inflect this process in a variety of ways.

How do age-related processes unfold when children are raised, and grow up, in family and school contexts that extend across divides of geography, political economy, and culture? Transnational family arrangements provide alternative, gendered

ways of being and becoming, which adults and children may consider as they negotiate decisions about living or visiting "here" versus "there." As processes of
transmigration unfold over time, they may alter the social relations of adults and
children, as well as men and women. We will return to these analytic issues after a
brief discussion of our research sites and methods.

THE CALIFORNIA CHILDHOODS PROJECT:
RESEARCH SITES AND METHODS OF STUDY

The cases we will analyze, in a comparative and theory-generating spirit, are drawn
from a larger ethnographic study of childhoods in contemporary California. We
began this project with a local focus, trying to grasp the effects of rapid social
change, such as extensive immigration and widening income gaps, on the daily lives
of children and families living in two urban areas. In 1995 Marjorie Orellana began three years of fieldwork in the Pico Union area of Los Angeles, a low-income
urban enclave consisting mostly of migrants (some legal; many undocumented)
from Mexico, Guatemala, and El Salvador; Anna Chee gathered information about
Korean families living in that area and elsewhere in Los Angeles (see Orellana,
Thorne, Chee, & Lam, 2001). In 1996 Barrie Thorne, Wan Shun Eva Lam, and
others began fieldwork in our second site, a public elementary school located in a
mixed-income area of Oakland whose student body was about half African American and 20% Cantonese-speaking Chinese Americans (mostly families from China
and Hong Kong), with smaller numbers of European Americans and children of
immigrants from Mexico, Central America, Yemen, Cambodia, Vietnam, Laos,
and several other countries.

We used multiple methods to map the contours of children's daily lives across
lines of social class and ethnicity, including extensive fieldwork in the public school
that anchors each research site, and in neighborhoods, households, after-school programs, public libraries, and other child-related contexts. We also interviewed parents and children from the range of economic and cultural groups in each area;
where relevant, we asked about histories and experiences of migration. In order to
more fully grasp children's perspectives, we invited them to draw and write about
their lives, and we gave some of them disposable cameras to take pictures in California, as well as on trips to their home countries (Orellana, 2000). All of these data
inform our analysis of growing up and raising children in transnational families.

We have organized this discussion of children, age and gender relations, and
transmigration by selecting two empirical cases that seem especially good to think
with. One is a case study of Spanish-speaking families who are raising children in
transnational social fields that extend between Pico Union (where the children come
together in a large public elementary school) and various parts of Mexico,
Guatemala, and El Salvador. The other case, with fewer numbers, involves immigrant families from Yemen who live in Oakland, with various members going back
and forth, sometimes for extended periods, to stay with kin who are based in a city

and in several villages "back home" in the Middle East. Yemenis are a small minority of the children who attend the ethnically diverse public school that we studied in Oakland, but their cultural difference is highly visible because some of the girls wear headscarves, leggings, and long dresses to school.

After briefly sketching the historical and economic contexts of these two case studies, we will examine the significance of age and gender in patterns of initial migration, in movements back and forth, and in the deliberate use of transnational networks in the raising of children.

Migrants in Los Angeles: Close Ties to Mexico and Central America

In the 1980s the number of Central Americans migrating to Pico Union dramatically increased when Salvadorans and Guatemalans began to flee civil wars in their home countries (Chinchilla & Hamilton, 1992). Los Angeles is now home to more Mexicans, Salvadorans, and Guatemalans than any city outside of the capitals of those nations. The sheer numbers of migrants, as well as comparatively close geographic distances and local infrastructures for the movement of goods (such as overnight courier services), information (Spanish-language television and radio stations), and people, make it relatively easy for families to sustain active ties "back home."

There is no single story to tell about the transnational patterns of Pico Union residents, nor about the contexts they left behind when they initially migrated. Some come from rural areas, others from small towns or cities; levels of education vary widely. Some are from indigenous communities and speak Spanish as their second language. Some individuals and families frequently travel back and forth between Los Angeles and their country of origin, while others travel more rarely; many stay in touch through letters, telephone calls, e-mail, and the exchange of home videos (Orellana et al., 2001). Although extended kin figure centrally in family arrangements that cross national boundaries, a substantial number of nuclear families are divided, with some members living in Pico Union and others living "back home." In one first-grade classroom where Orellana observed, more than half of the children said they had a sibling in their country of origin. During fieldwork in an after-school program at the same school, Orellana invited children to draw maps of places where they spend time. Eleven-year-old Guayo drew his "casa" and nearby sites in Los Angeles, Guatemala (where he was born and where "nearly all" of his relatives live), and four other places in the United States where members of his extended family have moved seeking jobs.

In order to manage the high costs of living in Los Angeles, Central American and Mexican immigrants often crowd into small apartments, with frequent changes in household composition. Many adults are able to find work only in the informal economy. Women are often employed in garment factories or as paid domestic workers, and men more often work as day laborers in construction or as gardeners. Most of the families in Pico Union live on the economic margins; according to Los Angeles School District records, in the late 1990s over 98% of children in the large public elementary school qualified for free or reduced lunch.

Yemeni Families Who Live in Oakland and Sustain Active Ties "Back Home"

Migration from Yemen to the United States began in the 1960s when impoverished conditions led as many as one fourth of adult men to seek employment in other Middle Eastern countries and eventually in places further away (Swanson, 1988). Following a sojourning pattern that involved sending regular remittances to their families back in Yemen, the men who sought work in the United States clustered in two niches: industrial jobs in Detroit and migrant farmwork in the West. After 1975, when prices rose in Yemen and it became more difficult to acquire land and property there, more of the itinerant workers settled in the United States, and other family members joined them, which began to even out the sex ratio. Some men went into business, mostly through the labor-intensive work of running small grocery stores or newsstands; others continued in factory or migrant farmwork. Women have relatively low rates of formal employment in Yemen and among Yemenis living in the United States; and, unlike a growing number of women from Mexico and Central America, they virtually never take the lead in migration or migrate on their own.

Children from three large extended families, whose households expand and contract as visitors from "back home" come and go, attend the public elementary school in our Oakland research site. They are part of a larger network of East Bay Yemenis who participate in the activities of several mosques in Oakland, including one with an Arabic school attended by over 100 children for 3 hours on Saturday and Sunday. (Some parents and children refer to public school as "English school" to differentiate it from Arabic school.) This geographically dispersed network of Yemeni migrants includes families from a range of economic circumstances. Some are extremely poor; others, like the families we have gotten to know, are solidly middle class, with property (homes, land, small businesses) in the Bay Area and back in Yemen.

Yemen has one of the highest fertility rates in the world—an average of 7.2 children per woman (Population Resource Center, 2002). Yemeni families in Oakland also tend to be large, with extensive contact among extended kin. References to "cousins" and "aunties" pepper children's accounts of their activities and patterns of friendship, as they do descriptions of large gatherings to celebrate marriages and birthdays. Some of these families have satellite television, and they watch programs in both Arabic and English. The families in our study have thick ties to kin and fellow villagers back in Yemen, with some (but not all) family members occasionally traveling back and forth and sometimes staying in one or the other place for several years at a time. Relative affluence, high rates of citizenship, and extensive cross-national networks of kin facilitate these patterns of movement.

In the public school that anchors our Oakland field site, the teacher of a third-grade "sheltered English" class asked students to draw themselves as a growing tree, with "roots" reaching to the things that give their lives meaning. Nine-year-old Arwa, who was born in Oakland and whose parents migrated from Yemen, drew herself connected to a row of neighborhood places. At the end of the local urban landscape she sketched an apartment building that she labeled "Yemen." In a classroom essay, Arwa wrote, "Yemen is kind of fun but when you get on a plane it's really scary."

Unlike the transmigrants who live in Pico Union, the Yemeni families in Oakland do not live in an ethnic residential enclave, but many of them, even in the second and third generation, are determined to retain some of their religious and ethnic traditions. They mix these practices with those of American culture as they go about rearing children, and growing up as children—sometimes with considerable conflict. We will now turn to a more detailed analysis and comparison of these two case studies, highlighting the dynamics of age and gender in patterns of transmigration.

AGE AND GENDER MEDIATE TRANSMIGRATION BETWEEN CENTRAL AMERICA, MEXICO, AND LOS ANGELES

When it comes to adult decisions to migrate, the construction of children as "luggage" holds some truth. Children's economic and legal dependence and need for care, as well as bonds of love and attachment, indeed tend to constrain the movements of otherwise mobile adults, especially the mothers of infants and young children. However, various combinations of necessity, such as dire poverty, and of opportunity, such as the availability of jobs doing paid domestic work in the United States, have drawn a growing number of mothers into the migration streams that lead from Mexico and Central America to California (Hondagneu-Sotelo, 1994; Hondagneu-Sotelo & Avila, 1997). When mothers and/or fathers migrate, decisions about whether to bring young children or to leave them behind are largely shaped by the availability of resources here or there for the daily care of children, with little distinction made between the needs of girls or boys. As children grow older, gender weighs more heavily in decisions about whether they should come with parents, stay behind, or be sent for.

Parents may leave young children behind to protect them from the uncertainties of life during the transition or from the dangers they might encounter traveling by land or crossing the U.S. border without legal documents. One mother in Pico Union told us about a 5-year-old boy she knew who had come from El Salvador by plane. It took five days for "coyotes" to pass him through Texas and into Los Angeles (for a fee of $3000), but the dangers of land were avoided. Among teenagers, more boys than girls make journeys north unaccompanied by parents, both because boys are more likely to claim and be granted autonomy of movement and because girls are perceived as more vulnerable to dangers en route.[5]

In a focus group discussion among Pico Union parents who had "left children behind," in Mexico or Central America, there was animated discussion of whether,

when, and how to send for children. The parents mentioned a range of considerations, such as having money to pay for the journey, the needs and circumstances
of family members here and at home, the expressed desires of the children themselves, and parents' views of what is safe, appropriate, possible, or good for children
of different ages and genders. The word "freedom" comes up repeatedly when immigrant parents and children, especially those from rural areas, compare life "here"
and "there." They contrast the spatial freedom of children who live in safe physical and social circumstances "back home" where they can move about on their
own, with the spatial confinement associated with the danger of living in urban
areas in the United States.

When Alma Martínez and her husband came to the United States to seek work,
they left their son with his paternal grandmother back in Guatemala. They had a
second child a year after they arrived in the United States. In the focus group discussion, Sra. Martínez contrasted her 7-year-old son's freedom of movement in the
Guatemalan countryside with the spatial confinement, but material advantages,
experienced by the 6-year-old daughter who lived with them in Pico Union:

> The ones that are over there don't have material things, but they have freedom. . . .
> My son has his grandparents, his cousins, his uncles and aunts, and all. And my daugh-
> ter here is alone, closed up in an apartment filled with toys. Even if she has a closet
> overflowing with toys, she's stuck inside.

Parents worry about the children they "left behind," fearing that they will not
be well fed, clothed, or cared for, that they will feel abandoned or unloved, or that
something bad will happen to them while they are out of parental reach. But the
parents believe that working here and sending money home is the only way they
can provide for their children and offer possibilities for their futures. Elsa Fuentes
explained (in Spanish), "It's just something we have to do now. Even if we don't
want to. Nobody wants to leave their kids." Sra. Martínez talked frankly about the
terrible emotional costs of leaving a child behind:

> Look, something happens. Beyond the fact that they stop loving you, and all, let me
> also tell you that what also happens is that you lose your love for them. Because, look,
> I tell you that I love this girl [in LA] a lot, and I won't be separated from her. Because
> the other one, I did leave. And with time, you start losing your children's love, and
> also losing *your* love as a mother.

The parents' discussion touched on children's dependence and on their developing capacities to assume responsibility—and to get into varied kinds of trouble.
The parents also spoke of conflicts between taking care of children's present needs
and securing opportunities for their children's futures. And they described complex
patterns of cooperation and reciprocity that tied them to caregivers back home.
Because Central American and Mexican conceptions of family include extended
kin, taking care of "other mothers' children" (Dill, 1994) may not be seen as a problem, especially if the parents send remittances. However, when money is short, ex-

tra children may be experienced as a burden. Sra. Martínez spoke of strained relationships with her mother-in-law back in Guatemala:

> Sometimes, like right now it has been four months since we've sent a penny to my
> mother-in-law. And it's a little difficult. Because my mother-in-law gets really mad.
> She tells me, "You left me with a grandson, not a son." She says, "Remember to at
> least send the money."

As children who have been left behind grow older, they become more self-
sufficient, thus lessening the amount of hands-on care required from adults. With
increasing age, children are also able to contribute to systems of household labor.
Both in Pico Union and "back home" in Mexico or Central America, girls help
with housework and sibling care; boys are more likely to help fathers who work in
the fields "back home" or as gardeners hired by homeowners in suburbs of Los Angeles. Children's work, done alongside school and periods of play, is shaped both
by necessity and by beliefs about what children of different ages and genders are
capable of doing and should be expected to do (Schildraut, 1980). Negotiations of
social age (Solberg, 1997) occur during assessments about whether a child should
migrate, stay, or return. An older girl may be left behind, for example, because she
will be able to help care for her aunt's younger children. The contexts and phases
of growing up shape trajectories into adulthood, and when children reach school
age, parents may arrange their migration to the United States to facilitate access
to long-term educational and occupational opportunities in this country.

Transmigration between Yemen and the Bay Area

Yemen is much further away than Mexico or Central America, and the full journey cannot be made by land, which increases the cost of travel and amplifies the
risk of trying to enter without documentation. The mobility of Yemeni women is
more constrained than that of women from Mexico, Guatemala, or El Salvador.
While women in Yemen have the right to vote and are employed in some sectors
of the economy, Islamic culture defines them first and foremost as wives and mothers. Signed consent from a husband or father is required before a woman can get
a passport for international travel, and there are strictures against women interacting with men to whom they are not formally connected by marriage or descent.

Afrah Assad, a Yemeni-born woman who is active in the Oakland mosque, told
us that she had never heard of a woman who migrated on her own from Yemen,
nor had she ever heard of both parents migrating and leaving children behind. She
generalized, "The father comes first, then he sends for the eldest son to help the
dad in the business. Later they help the rest of the family to come." The rest of
the family—wives, parents, sons and daughters, brothers, cousins—may migrate,
or not, as opportunities, resources, and contingencies permit; but the migration of
married women is closely tied to the migration of their unmarried daughters and
younger children.

This gendered pattern of chain migration began for the Assad family in the 1960s when Hussein Assad (Afrah's father-in-law) left impoverished circumstances in rural Yemen to work in the oil fields of Bahrain. He migrated from there to the Central Valley of California, where he did migrant farmwork and continued to send regular remittances to his wife and child back in Yemen while also saving enough money to buy a small grocery store. His teenage son migrated to help him build the business, and his wife followed. They moved to Oakland and had three more sons, who got to know life in Yemen through occasional visits back home. Eventually Hussein Assad and his sons acquired a farm and other property back in Yemen as well as several liquor stores in the East Bay. Their transnational arrangements have a strong material as well as kinship base.

THE ORGANIZATION OF LABOR
IN TRANSNATIONAL FAMILIES

The migration streams from Mexico and Central America to and from Los Angeles and between Yemen and Oakland include many families from rural farms and villages whose relationships have developed within essentially preindustrial, household-based systems of production. Patterns of interdependence extend beyond smaller units like the nuclear family or single-mother households to encompass grandparents, aunts, uncles, and cousins. Adult divisions of labor tend to divide by gender, with Mexican, Central American, and Yemeni women assuming major responsibility for the daily care of children and families. In addition, many Mexican and Central American immigrant women are employed, primarily in female-dominated parts of the economy such as paid domestic work. Rates of female employment are much lower among Yemeni immigrants, although some women help out in family businesses and a few have paid jobs. After her children were raised, one of Afrah Assad's older sisters-in-law obtained her GED (high school equivalence degree) and began working as a real estate agent. This trajectory into employment inspired another sister-in-law, Khalid (who married another of the Assad brothers when they were both 15), to obtain a part-time clerical job in the real estate company and enroll in classes to prepare for the GED exam.

Immigrant parents who are raising children in Pico Union assume, as they did when they lived in Guatemala or Mexico, that children will be contributing members of the household (Orellana, 2001). One mother told her children, "You have a family, and if we're a family, we work together." Some children pitch in without questioning, such as 7-year-old Eva Morales, who, when we got to know her, lived with her parents, an uncle, two younger brothers, and occasional rent-paying lodgers in a one-bedroom apartment in Pico Union. Her father worked as a day laborer in construction, and her mother was employed off and on in a garment factory. In various visits to the household, Orellana saw Eva unpack the grocery bags her mother brought home and put the food away (without being asked to do so); answer the phone and take a message for her father; get her youngest brother out of a bath, toweled, and dressed; and read to her two brothers and teach them English rhymes she had learned in school. When asked how she helps at home, Eva animatedly replied (in Spanish): "I wash dishes, vacuum, arrange my clothes, every time we go to do the laundry my mom tells me, 'Eva, why don't you help me to fold.'" One of Eva's brothers is a year younger, but he did far less housework; during our field visits it was always Eva who was attentive to the guests and to the needs of her younger siblings. Our interviews with parents and children in California provide further evidence, across ethnic groups, that girls, like women, do a disproportionate share of housework (Goodnow, 1988).

Children in Pico Union participate not only in the activities of housework, but also in the informal economy, for example, by selling food, clothes, or other merchandise alongside adult street vendors. They also help their parents with paid work such as cleaning houses, doing child care, mowing lawns, or clearing tables in a restaurant. "Outside," like "inside," tasks are skewed by gender—boys more often help fathers; girls more often help mothers. Some parents and children do piecework at home; for example, the parents and five children (ages 4 to 12) of the Rodriguez family gathered in the evening at their kitchen table to put price stickers on Barbie sunglasses that were sold, they said, at Toys "R" Us.

When families move from rural areas or small towns to inner-city Los Angeles, the labor contributions of children change and may diminish. Instead of hunting in the mountains, raising chickens, or planting rice and corn, children may be sent to corner markets to buy groceries. But the need for children to care for siblings and assume other household chores may increase when families are detached from the support networks of extended kin and when parents work long hours at some distance from Pico Union. Since they go to school, children of immigrants acquire essential skills that their parents do not possess, especially knowledge of English. Translating for parents and other adults, sometimes in freighted contexts like medical appointments or job-related negotiations, is a major way in which children contribute to their households in Pico Union (Orellana, 2001). Girls more often than boys serve as the designated family translators, although birth order and level of skill also enter into the allocation of this work (a pattern also reported in Valenzuela, 1999).

Because the Yemeni immigrant parents we have gotten to know have lived in the United States for some years and work in family businesses like liquor stores or mini-marts, most of them know English, and their children do not regularly serve as translators. But children are expected to contribute to family labor systems in other ways. Back in Yemen, as Afrah Assad explained, "the boys do the work outside—pick fruit, carry grass. The girls work inside, doing the dishes, cleaning." An outside/inside gender division also organizes the work of the Assad siblings and cousins in Oakland. Starting at age 7, on weekends and sometimes after school, the boys stock shelves and help out in other ways in the family's stores; their responsibilities increase as they grow older.

Girls also start helping, with sibling care and household labor, between the ages of 5 and 7. When Thorne interviewed Afrah at her home, with four of the children quietly listening and sometimes chiming in, the mother praised Nadia, the oldest daughter (then 11) for doing "all the work at home. Today there's no school; Nadia cleaned the dishes, vacuumed, took the clothes to the washer. She did it on her own." During the interview, Nadia initiated activities that showed that she, like 7-year-old Eva in Pico Union, had assumed the responsibilities of a regular care-giver. Nadia leaned over to wipe mucus from her 2-year-old sister's nose, and, without any directive from her mother, took the toddler into the hall and changed her diaper. Afrah said that the 2-year-old was so attached to her older sister that she called out for Nadia as soon as she awoke each morning.

When they describe their weekly routines, Yemeni parents and children frequently use narratives of gender difference, emphasizing the duty and suitability of boys to work in the stores and of girls to do housework and child care at home. But in conversations about what actually took place during a particular day or week, girls sometimes talked about helping out at the store after Arabic school, and boys told about helping with the dishes at home. In the allocation and negotiation of labor, considerations of need, convenience, and ability (which is partly linked to age) may override gender (Goodnow, 1988).

THE DELIBERATE USE OF TRANSNATIONAL
PRACTICES IN RAISING CHILDREN

Since Yemeni families in Oakland live in homes and work in small businesses scattered across the city, they regularly interact with neighbors, customers, and schoolmates who know little about Islamic or Yemeni culture. But the parents (and some, but not all, of the children) are emphatic about wanting to retain at least some of their "traditions." As Afrah Assad said in an interview, "We don't want to lose what we came from and who we are. We want to keep both things." Back in Yemen, she said, most people are very poor, and she considers her family lucky to be living an essentially middle-class life in the United States with "medicine, doctors, good home, education." But Afrah and her husband also want their children to grow up as Muslims, devoted to their extended family, and sustaining strong cultural and personal ties to Yemen. They also want them to experience the contrast with "back there" so they will appreciate what they have here.

Saying that "kids will be kids," Afrah is flexible about some of the ways her children engage with American culture. She and the other Yemeni adult women we got to know during our fieldwork always wore headscarves when they went out in public. Afrah's daughters and nieces wore headscarves when they went to Arabic School, but didn't wear them to "English school" until fourth or fifth grade. When she was in fifth grade, Nadia dressed in hybrid ways, mixing assorted bits of culture. At a family math night she wore a headscarf of soft white fabric, the ends wrapped around her neck, a white sweatshirt with "Birthday Blast, Discovery Zone" in bright pink letters on the front, Nike shoes, jeans, and chipped-off silver-blue nail polish; a bulky gray and black Oakland Raiders jacket hung on the back of her chair. Women and girls (including those as young as 5) from another of the Yemeni families whose children attend the Oakland public school were not so eclectic; they dressed as they did when they were in Yemen, with headscarves, long dresses, and leggings. In this ethnic group, adherence to traditional culture is marked in the dress and comportment of girls and women much more than in the visible embodiment of boys and men.

Both of the Yemeni extended families make a point of taking their U.S.-born children back to the home country so that they will get to know their relatives, come to appreciate Yemeni traditions, become more fluent in Arabic (spoken, along with English, in their Oakland households), and appreciate what they have in the United States. Entire families journey back to Yemen for occasional summer vacations and sometimes for longer periods of time. Afrah Assad has a stock of before-and-after stories about the transformative effects of taking children back to Yemen; for example:

> My nieces [ages 15, 13, 12, 10] went last summer, and you should see the difference. Before they went, they didn't want to listen to Arabic music and they didn't know the words. They only wanted to hear English music. When they went back home they got in touch with what we're talkin' about. It's like you tell a story about back home, but they don't know the place. But if they go there then they appreciate it.

However, trips back home don't always work out as parents intend. Twenty-seven-year-old Khalid Assad, who was born in the United States, has been to Yemen once, when she was 6 years old. The family was supposed to stay during all of summer vacation, but they got sick and returned to the United States after a few weeks. Khalid now has no interest in visiting Yemen, although she and her husband "try to keep our religion"; "cultures and religions are different," she explained in an interview. She wears a headscarf, goes to mosque, and wants her children to grow up as practicing Muslims. But she and her husband agree that their three daughters should be able to choose whether, and whom, to marry. Khalid likes going to school and to her part-time job because "nobody tells me what I'm doing or where I'm going. It's a lot better." She wants her daughters to "make something of themselves," and she identifies with Yemeni women who are doctors and teachers.

Sending Kids Back

Few families in Pico Union have lived in the United States as long as the Assads: nor are they as well established. Indeed, Pico Union often functions as a "first stop area" before migrants move out to other places. They live in a Spanish-speaking enclave near others with similar food and customs, and they aren't as intent as some Yemeni immigrants on "going back home" for cultural replenishment (visiting relatives is another matter, of great importance to travelers in both transnational fields). Most of the Pico Union parents want their children to speak both English and Spanish (Orellana, Ek, & Hernández, 1999), partly because they anticipate that, given the unsettled nature of economies and politics, the next generation may continue to navigate between the United States and Mexico or Central America.

When asked about the goals and hopes that guide the ways they bring up children, parents in the Pico Union focus group said that they want their children to do well in school, to secure decent jobs as adults, and to live in a moral way. When children seem to be going off track, for example, with behavioral problems at school, parents sometimes threaten to send them back to live with relatives in Central America or Mexico. More parents threaten "sending back" than actually carry through, in part because children actively resist, some by lording their own citizenship rights over their parents or by threatening to call "911." Struggles about whether to stay or move back are a recurring theme in the generational conflicts of these families.

Parents' anxieties about younger children (who are defined by dependence, vulnerability, and innocence) focus on questions of physical safety, with minimal differentiation by gender. As children grow older and more independent, especially as they make the transition to middle school and into the heterosexualized positioning of "pre-teens" and "teens," parents' fears for their sons and for their daughters tend to diverge. While drugs are a general specter, parents believe that their sons are especially at risk of being drawn into gangs and violence. Fears about daughters focus more on the dangers of sexuality, especially the possibility that they will get pregnant or become promiscuous. This may also be a risk "back home"; one Mexican immigrant mother observed that girls back there get pregnant very young, and that keeping a daughter here, under the watchful eyes of her parents, may be the better strategy. As they go about the difficult task of trying to keep teenagers out of serious trouble, parents actively weigh what might happen there compared with what might happen here, although the specifics of "here" and "there" vary widely.

The worries of Yemeni parents also become more gendered as their children move into middle school and especially high school. The parents are vigilant about the dangers not only of gangs, violence, and drugs, but also of alcohol (while some own liquor stores, Yemenis who consider themselves good Muslims do not drink or allow their children to drink) and any hint of teenage romance (the line is drawn far short of actual sex, for both boys and girls). Sending back is a more practiced option for more affluent Yemenis than for the lower-income parents in Pico Union. Since most of the Yemeni teenagers are U.S. citizens, they can be more easily retrieved, and rural Yemen (the "back" in this case) is quite different, and distant, from Oakland. One of the Yemeni fathers told the story of a 15-year-old nephew who "wasn't listening" and was getting into trouble; "he was having girlfriends and staying out all night and saying 'It's America, I can do anything I want.'" So they sent him back to live on the family farm and work in the orchards under the watchful eye and discipline of his grandfather. After a few years he returned "a different person," married a young woman from the Bay Area Yemeni community, and now has his own store.

When Yemeni girls get into trouble—these stories mostly focus on trouble as being interested in boys—parents arrange marriages for them (girls have the option of refusing a particular groom). Khalid explained the philosophy:

> It's the culture. When they see a girl reach her puberty, instead of going out there and getting in trouble, in our culture, they like to keep them married. If something goes wrong, they have somebody to support them.

In recent years several of Nadia's cousins in the Bay Area married at ages as young as 14. Nadia attended a large public middle school in Oakland and went on to high school, but after a few months she and her parents decided that she should switch to a home-study program run by the school system that provided three hours of teacher assistance twice a week. They made the switch because boys were "touching her." Nadia's mother, Afrah Assad, believes that home schooling is not an option for her boys, one of whom had been beaten up at school, because "if you tell them to do it, they won't finish it. They have to be in school." The raising and disciplining of boys extends beyond the family; girls, to varying and sometimes contested degrees, are more spatially confined.

When they talk about the risks of raising children in the United States, especially during the teenage years, immigrant parents from Yemen, Central America, and Mexico refer to a kind of "freedom" quite different from the spatial freedom of younger children growing up in safe rural areas. This dangerous kind of freedom, which they associate with American culture and especially with American teens, is the freedom to "do whatever you want," to claim independence from family and parental authority, and to engage in age-graded activities like going out with friends, dating, and participating in conmmercialized youth culture. External forces like the media, and life in and around large urban middle schools and high schools (where youth, who are outside parental surveillance, may be drawn into drugs, gangs, sex), compound the risks of raising children in the United States. This is especially true for immigrant parents who want to sustain beliefs and values they have brought from "there" to "here."

CONCLUSION

Families who raise children across national borders often compare life "here" with life "back home," a split orientation that brings perspective on and pressure to negotiate different ways of organizing labor, rearing children and differences in the process of growing older, and—embedded in all of these domains of family life—relations of gender and generation. As Hirsch (1999) and Pessar (1999) have observed, the renegotiation of the authority of husbands over wives has been a central theme in feminist research on gender and migration. This literature highlights the horizontal or, as it is often called, *gender*, axis of patriarchal kinship, but it has been relatively inattentive to the vertical, or *age*, dimension of family structure, which is also gendered. In this essay we have examined the intersecting dynamics of age and gender in shaping the back-and-forth lives of migrants who are raising children, and growing up, in transnational families. We conclude by asking how patterns of transmigration, viewed from the perspective of migrants' U.S.-based lives, may, in turn, reconfigure their experiences of age and gender.

The immigrant parents we have gotten to know through fieldwork in California tend to be ambivalent about the Americanization of their children. Many of these families migrated to the United States in search of educational and employment opportunities unavailable in their countries of origin, and they want their children to learn English, do well in school, and engage with life in this country. But immigrant parents also fear that their children will pull away from family obligations and cultural roots and succumb to the individualized excesses of "doing what you want," which many immigrants regard as a central feature of life in America. This ambivalence, as previously discussed, may mobilize efforts to "take children back" and "send them back" to countries of origin.

American individualism is embedded in patterns of child rearing that emphasize the self-development of children and that frame the process of growing up as the negotiation of increased autonomy, the lessening of overt parental control, and the eventual shaping of one's own pathway through life. Families who come from rural ways of life in Mexico, Central America, or Yemen frame growing up not in terms of increased autonomy but as a process of assuming greater *responsibility* within family systems of labor (Brannen, 1996). Thus, Nadia Assad and Eva Morales experienced themselves as growing older, and were validated by their families as growing older, in a gendered way when they began to care for younger siblings and help with housework. The Assad boys grew older, also in a gender-marked way, when they began regular stints of helping in the family stores. Within these households, family-organized labor functions as a gendered "domain to grow by" (Haavind, in press). Because these unpaid forms of work are organized and controlled by adult kin, partly under the guise of parental teaching, they do not become a basis for claiming individual autonomy or resources apart from the family. (This contrasts with immigrant women's movement into paid labor, which provides spatial and material autonomy from the authority of husbands.)

Adult authority may be undermined rather than reaffirmed in family labor systems when immigrant parents depend on their children for help with tasks they cannot do themselves, like translating into English and dealing with U.S. bureaucracies. Children gain resources, and thus some autonomy from parental control, not only by attending school, but also through the U.S. discourse of children's rights. Patterns of physical discipline that may be acceptable back home may be unacceptable in the United States, and children of immigrants sometimes threaten to phone "911" to report what they regard as abusive behavior by their parents or other adults. The power and authority of parents over children, which has physical, economic, legal, and emotional dimensons, is double edged. When infused with an ethic of care, it may operate as the power to get things done—to protect, attend to needs, and help a child flourish. But adult power and authority may also shade into domination and exploitation. Which form of power is being exercised is partly in the eye of the beholder, and in situations of sharp cultural difference, those from marginalized groups may be especially suspect.

The equating of growing up with increased autonomy to "do what you want" is amplified by commercialized youth cultures and styles of dress, music, language, and behavior that distance youth from their families. In the age-graded cultures of U.S. schools, the transition to middle school is also a transition into social worlds that are organized around heterosexual dating and sexualized identities, making gender far more salient than it is in the official curriculum of schools (Thorne, 1993). This world, which troubles parents from many different cultural and social class backgrounds, is sharply at odds with Yemeni prescriptions against casual heterosexualized contact. Mexican and Central American parents are less prohibitive in the domain of teen romance, but they keep an especially watchful eye on their daughters. In both our Los Angeles and Oakland field sites, girls from immigrant families tend to be more spatially confined than boys (a pattern also reported by Kibria, 1993; Olsen, 1997; Zhou & Bankston, 1998), although there is no shortage of worry about the dangers (drugs, gangs, violence) that boys may encounter as they grow up in U.S. urban areas. Children and youth, as well as adults, are active participants in negotiating cultures, in shaping pathways through childhood and adolescence, and in the short- and long-term reconfiguring of family relations.

NOTES

The research for this paper was funded by a grant from the John D. and Catherine T. MacArthur Foundation Research Network on Successful Pathways Through Middle Childhood. We also received support from the Institute for Human Development and from the Center for Working Families at the University of California, Berkeley. We would like to thank the other researchers who helped us gather data and think about contemporary childhoods, including Lucila Ek and Arcelia Hernández in the Pico Union site, and Hung Thai, Nadine Chabrier, Ana González, Eileen Mears, Gladys Ocampo, and Allison Pugh in the Oakland site. We have also benefited from conversations with and comments from Pierrette Hondagneu-Sotelo, Nery Orellana, Hanne Haavind, Arlie Hochschild, Catherine Cooper, Jill Denner, Nazli Kibria, Eithne Luibhéid, Sarah Mahler, Judy Stacey, Diane Wolfe, Marjorie DeVault, and Mary Romero. Finally, we are grateful to the parents, children, teachers, school personnel, and community program leaders for their cooperation with this project.

1. Basch, Schiller, and Szanton Blanc (1994) introduced the concept of "transnational social fields" to refer to "multi-stranded social relations" developed through processes of migration across national borders, linking places of origin and of settlement. The transnational social fields that we discuss, which variously span between part of the United States and parts of Central America, Mexico, and Yemen, are well established, and for the families we

describe, transnational practices are a habitual part of life as in the situations analyzed by Georges (1992), Guarnizo and Smith (1998), Mahler (1998), and Rouse (1991).

2. Research on the dynamics of age and migration has been conducted mostly under the rubric of "generation," as in studies of assimilation that are framed by the distinction between first, second, and third generations. This usage, as Kertzer (1983) demonstrates, tends to confuse "generation" as kinship (relations of grandparents, parents, and children— a theme central to this paper); age cohort (a succession of people moving together through time); and "generation" in the sense of people who live in the same historical period. The latter two meanings are evoked by recent research on "the new second generation," a term used to refer to the children of contemporary immigrants, although it also extends to children who migrated along with their parents (Rumbaut [1994] calls the latter group the "1.5 generation"). Researchers who have studied "the new second generation" have primarily focused on contexts of reception, patterns of adaptation, modes of incorporation, and prospects for mobility of this cohort of children growing up in the United States (Portes & Zhou, 1996; Zhou, 1997). This essay explores dimensions of age that come to the fore when one highlights the presence and participation of children in processes of transmigration, such as the negotiation of age divisions and of shifting relations between adults and children as families move across space and through time.

3. The familiar assertion that age (in the relational sense of descent and generation) and gender (defined by heterosexuality) are axes basic to kinship and family structure has been unsettled by the deconstructive work of feminist and queer theorists such as Weston (1991). The empirical cases discussed in this essay encompass varied constructions of "family," both in the cultural and experiential sense of "who counts" and in the material sense of household dynamics. Our focus is not on reified conceptions of "family," but rather on beliefs, relations, and social practices connected with child rearing.

4. The Norwegian feminist psychologist Hanne Haavind (Haavind, in press; Haavind & Andenaes, 1997) describes this relational process with the metaphor of a "running wheel" that turns in the minds of mothers and other engaged caregivers as they mentally record how a child is doing, both now and with an eye to the future, and as they adjust their daily practices in accord with these assessments as well as other pressures and obligations. Children, in turn, monitor their own changing capacities, sometimes refusing to "go forward" or trying to accelerate the pace, and they may head in directions other than those mapped out by parents, teachers, or other adults who are raising them.

5. Our colleague Hung Thai took a close look at data from the U.S. Immigration and Naturalization Service (2000) and found striking intersections by age and gender. Of all legal immigrants entering the United States in 1998, 53.5% were females and 45.4% were males. But there were skews by age groupings. Women predominated among legal migrants between the ages of 20 and 39 and ages 55 and above. Men predominated among all migrants between the ages of 40 and 54. There were also more males than females among legal migrants between ages 5 and 19. Among adult legal migrants from Mexico, 57% were women and 42.9% were men; but among children and youth (ages 5–19) migrating from Mexico to the United States, 52% were boys and 48% were girls. Statistics for Salvadoran immigrants fell into a similar pattern. Only 1,859 legal migrants from Yemen entered the United States in 1998 (compared with a total of 167,254 from Mexico or Central America— 25% of the total).

REFERENCES

Allatt, Pat. (1996). Conceptualizing parenting from the standpoint of children: Relationship and transition in the life course. In J. Brannen & M. O'Brien (Eds.), *Children in families* (pp. 130–144). London: Falmer Press.

Ariès, Philippe. (1962). *Centuries of childhood: A social history of family life.* New York: Vintage Books.

Basch, Linda, Schiller, Nina Glick, & Szanton Blanc, Cristina. (1994). *Nations unbound: Transnational projects, postcolonial predicaments, and deterritorialized nation-states.* Amsterdam: Gordon & Breach.

Brannen, Julia. (1996). Discourses of adolescence: Young people's independence and autonomy within families. In J. Brannen & M. O'Brien (Eds.), *Children in families* (pp. 114–129). London: Falmer Press.

Chinchilla, Norma, & Nora Hamilton. (1992). Seeking refuge in the city of angels: The Central American community. In G. Reposa & C. Dersch (Eds.), *City of angels* (pp. 84–100). Dubuque, IA: Kendall/Hunt.

Daniels, Roger. (1990). *Coming to America.* New York: HarperCollins.

Dill, Bonnie Thornton. (1994). Fictive kin, paper sons, and *compadrazgo:* Women of color and the struggle for family survival. In M. B. Zinn & B. T. Dill (Eds.), *Women of color in U.S. Society* (pp. 149–169). Philadelphia: Temple University Press.

Georges, Eugenia. (1992). Gender, class, and migration in the Dominican Republic: Women's experiences in a transnational community. *Annals of the New York Academy of Sciences, 645,* 81–100.

Goodnow, Jacqueline J. (1988). Children's household work: Its nature and function. *Psychological Bulletin, 103,* 5–26.

Guarnizo, Luis E., & Michael P. Smith. (1998). The locations of transnationalism. In M. P. Smith & L. E. Guarnizo (Eds.), *Transnationalism from below* (pp. 3–34). New Brunswick, NJ: Transaction.

Guy, Donna. (2000). Women, children, and borders (No. 7 in Working Paper Series on Historical Systems, Peoples, and Cultures). Bowling Green, OH: Department of Ethnic Studies, Bowling Green State University.

Haavind, Hanne. (in press). Contesting and recognizing historical changes and selves in development—Methodological challenges. In Thomas Weisner (Ed.), *Discovering successful pathways in children's development: Mixed methods in the study of childhood and family life.*

Haavind, Hanne, & Andenaes, Agnes. (1997). *Care and responsibilities for children: Creating the life of women creating themselves.* Unpublished manuscript, Department of Psychology, University of Oslo.

Hirsch, Jennifer S. (1999). En el norte la mujer manda: Gender, generation, and geography in a Mexican transnational community. *American Behavioral Scientist, 42,* 1332–1349.

Hondagneu-Sotelo, Pierrette. (1994). *Gendered transitions: Mexican experiences of immigration.* Berkeley & Los Angeles: University of California Press.

Hondagneu-Sotelo, Pierrette, & Avila, Ernestine. (1997). "I'm here, but I'm there": The meanings of Latina transnational motherhood. *Gender and Society, 11,* 548–571.

James, Allison, Jenks, Chris, & Prout, Alan. (1997). *Theorizing childhood.* London: Polity Press.

Kertzer, David I. (1983). Generation as a sociological problem. *Annual Review of Sociology, 9,* 125–149.

Kibria, Nazli. (1993). *Family tightrope: The changing lives of Vietnamese Americans.* Princeton, NJ: Princeton University Press.

Levitt, Peggy. (2001). *The transnational villagers.* Berkeley & Los Angeles: University of California Press.

Mahler, Sarah J. (1998). Theoretical and empirical contributions toward a research agenda for transnationalism. In M. P. Smith & L. E. Guarnizo (Eds.), *Transnationalism from below* (pp. 64–99). New Brunswick, NJ: Transaction.

Mayer, Karl Ulrich, & Schoepflin, Urs. (1989). The state and the life course. *Annual Review of Sociology, 15,* 187–209.

McDonnell, Patrick J. (1999, June 28). Mixed citizenship in many families. *Los Angeles Times,* p. B-1.

Menjívar, Cecelia. (in press). Living in two worlds? Guatemalan-origin children and emerging transnationalism. In Mary C. Waters & Peggy Levitt (Eds.), *Transnationalism and second-generation immigrants.*

Olsen, Laurie. (1997). *Made in America: Immigrant students in our public schools.* New York: New Press.

Olwig, Karen Fog. (1999). Narratives of the children left behind: Home and identity in globalised Caribbean families. *Journal of Ethnic and Migration Studies, 25*(2), 267–284.

Orellana, Marjorie Faulstich. (1999). Space and place in an urban landscape: Learning from children's views of their social worlds. *Visual Sociology, 14,* 73–89.

Orellana, Marjorie Faulstich. (2001). The work kids do: Mexican and Central American immigrant children's contributions to households and schools in California. *Harvard Educational Review, 71,* 366–389.

Orellana, Marjorie Faulstich, Ek, Lucila, & Hernández, Arcelia. (1999). Bilingual education in an immigrant community: Proposition 227 in California. *International Journal of Bilingualism and Bilingual Education, 2*(2), 114–130.

Orellana, Marjorie Faulstich, Thorne, Barrie, Chee, Anna, & Lam, Wan Shun Eva. (2001). Transnational childhoods: The participation of children in processes of family migration. *Social Problems, 48,* 572–591.

Pessar, Patricia R. (1999). The case of new immigrants in the United States. *American Behavioral Scientist, 42,* 577–601.

Population Resource Center. (2003) *Executive summary: the Middle East* [On-line]. Available: http://www.prcdc.org/summaries/middleeast/middleeast.html (accessed on March 16, 2003).

Portes, Alejandro, & Zhou, Min. (1996). The new second generation: Segmented assimilation and its variants. *Annals of the American Academy of Political and Social Sciences, 530,* 74–96.

Rouse, Roger. (1991). Mexican migration and the social space of postmodernism. *Diaspora, 1,* 8–23.

Rumbaut, Rubén G. (1994). The crucible within: Ethnic identity, self-esteem, and segmented assimilation among children of immigrants. *International Migration Review, 28,* 748–794.

Schildraut, Enid. (1980). Children's work reconsidered. *International Social Science Journal, 12*(3), 479–489.

Solberg, Anne. (1997). Negotiating childhood: Changing constructions of age for Norwegian children. In A. James & A. Prout (Eds.), *Constructing and reconstructing childhood* (2nd ed., pp. 126–144). London: Falmer Press.

Soto, Isa Maria. (1987). West Indian child fostering: Its role in migrant exchanges. In C. R. Sutton & E. J. Chaney (Eds.), *Caribbean life in New York City.* New York: Center for Migration Studies of New York.

Stack, Carol B., & Cromartie, John B. (1992). The journeys of Black children: An intergenerational perspective. In P. C. Jobes, W. F. Stinner, & J. W. Wardwell (Eds.), *Community, society, and migration: Noneconomic migration in America* (pp. 363–383). Lanham, MD: University Press of the Americas.

Stephens, Sharon. (1995). Children and the politics of culture in late capitalism. In S. Stephens (Ed.), *Children and the politics of culture* (pp. 3–48). Princeton, NJ: Princeton University Press.

Swanson, Jon C. (1988). Sojourners and settlers in Yemen and America. In J. Friedlander (Ed.), *Sojourners and settlers: The Yemeni immigration experience* (pp. 49–67). Salt Lake City: University of Utah Press.

Thorne, Barrie. (1993). *Gender play: Girls and boys in school.* New Brunswick, NJ: Rutgers University Press.

U.S. Immigration and Naturalization Service. (2000). *Statistical yearbook of the immigration and naturalization service, 1998.* Washington, DC: U.S. Government Printing Office.

Valenzuela, Abel, Jr. (1999). Gender roles and settlement activities among children and their immigrant families. *American Behavioral Scientist, 42,* 720–742.

Weston, Kathleen M. (1991). *Families we choose: Lesbians, gays, kinship.* New York: Columbia University Press.

Zelizer, Viviana A. (1985). *Pricing the priceless child: The social value of children.* New York: Basic Books.

Zhou, Min. (1997). Growing up American: The challenge confronting immigrant children and children of immigrants. *Annual Review of Sociology, 23,* 62–95.

Zhou, Min, & Bankston, Carl L., III. (1998). *Growing up American: How Vietnamese children adapt to life in the United States.* New York: Russell Sage Foundation.

CHAPTER 13

"We Don't Sleep Around Like White Girls Do"

Family, Culture, and Gender in Filipina American Lives

Yen Le Espiritu

I want my daughters to be Filipino especially on sex. I always emphasize to them that they should not participate in sex if they are not married. We are also Catholic. We are raised so that we don't engage in going out with men while we are not married. And I don't like it to happen to my daughters as if they have no values. I don't like them to grow up that way, like the American girls.

FILIPINA IMMIGRANT MOTHER

I found that a lot of the Asian American friends of mine, we don't date like White girls date. We don't sleep around like White girls do. Everyone is really mellow at dating because your parents were constraining and restrictive.

SECOND-GENERATION FILIPINA DAUGHTER

Focusing on the relationship between Filipino immigrant parents and their daughters, this essay argues that gender is a key to immigrant identity and a vehicle for racialized immigrants to assert cultural superiority over the dominant group. In immigrant communities, culture takes on a special significance: it forms not only a lifeline to the home country and a basis for group identity in a new country but also a base from which immigrants stake their political and sociocultural claims on their new country (Eastmond, 1993, p. 40). For Filipino immigrants, who come from a homeland that was once a U.S. colony, cultural reconstruction has been especially critical in the assertion of their presence in the United States—a way to counter the cultural Americanization of the Philippines, to resist the assimilative and alienating demands of U.S. society, and to reaffirm to themselves their self-worth in the face of colonial, racial, class, and gendered subordination. Before World War II, Filipinos were barred from becoming U.S. citizens, owning property, and marrying Whites. They also encountered discriminatory housing policies, unfair labor practices, violent physical encounters, and racist as well as anti-immigrant discourse (Cordova, 1983; Jung, 1999; Scharlin & Villanueva, 1992; Sharma, 1984). While blatant legal discrimination against Filipino Americans is largely a matter of the past, Filipinos continue to encounter many barriers that prevent full participation in the economic, social, and political institutions of the United States (Azores-Gunter, 1986–87; Cabezas, Shinagawa, & Kawaguchi, 1986–87; Okamura & Agbayani, 1997). Moreover, the economic mobility and cultural assimilation that enables White ethnics to become "unhyphenated Whites" is seldom extended to Filipino Americans (Espiritu, 1994). Like other Asians, the Filipino is "always seen as an immigrant, as the 'foreigner-within'; even when born in the United States" (Lowe, 1996, p. 5). Finally, although Filipinos have been in the United States since the middle of the 1700s and Americans have been in the Philippines since at least the late 1800s, U.S. Filipinos—as racialized nationals, immigrants, and citizens—are "still practically an invisible and silent minority" (San Juan, 1991, p. 117). Drawing from my research on Filipino American families in San Diego, California, I explore in this essay the ways racialized immigrants claim through gender the power denied them by racism.

My epigraphs, statements by a Filipina immigrant mother and a second-generation Filipina daughter, suggest that the virtuous Filipina daughter is partially constructed on the conceptualization of White women as sexually immoral. This juxtaposition underscores the fact that femininity is a relational category, one that is co-constructed with other racial and cultural categories. These narratives also reveal that women's sexuality and their enforced "morality" are fundamental to the structuring of social inequalities. Historically, the sexuality of racialized women has been systematically demonized and disparaged by dominant or oppressor groups to justify and bolster nationalist movements, colonialism, and/or racism. But as these narratives indicate, racialized groups also criticize the morality of White women as a strategy of resistance—a means of asserting a morally superior public face to the dominant society.

By exploring how Filipino immigrants characterize White families and White women, I hope to contribute to a neglected area of research: how the "margins" imagine and construct the "mainstream" in order to assert superiority over it. But this strategy is not without costs. The elevation of Filipina chastity (particularly that of young women) has the effect of reinforcing masculinist and patriarchal power in the name of a greater ideal of national/ethnic self-respect. Because the control of women is one of the principal means of asserting moral superiority, young women in immigrant families face numerous restrictions on their autonomy, mobility, and personal decision making. Although this essay addresses the experiences and attitudes of both parents and children, here I am more concerned with understanding the actions of immigrant parents than the reactions of their second-generation daughters.

STUDYING FILIPINOS IN SAN DIEGO

San Diego, California, has long been a favored area of settlement for Filipinos and is today the third largest U.S. destination for Filipino immigrants (Rumbaut, 1991, p. 220).[1] As the site of the largest U.S. naval base and the navy's primary West

Coast training facility, San Diego has been a primary area of settlement for Filipino navy personnel and their families since the early 1900s. As in other Filipino communities along the Pacific Coast, the San Diego community grew dramatically in the 25 years following passage of the 1965 Immigration Act. New immigration contributed greatly to the tripling of San Diego County's Filipino American population from 1970 to 1980 and its doubling from 1980 to 1990. In 1990, nearly 96,000 Filipinos resided in the county. Although they made up only 4% of the county's general population, they constituted close to 50% of the Asian American population (Espiritu, 1995). Many post-1965 Filipino immigrants have come to San Diego as professionals—most conspicuously as health care workers. A 1992 analysis of the socioeconomic characteristics of recent Filipino immigrants in San Diego indicated that they were predominantly middle-class, college-educated, and English-speaking professionals who were more likely to own their own homes than to rent (Rumbaut, 1994). At the same time, about two thirds of the Filipinos surveyed indicated that they had experienced racial and ethnic discrimination (Espiritu & Wolf, 2001).

The information on which this essay is based comes mostly from in-depth interviews that I conducted with almost 100 Filipinos in San Diego.[2] Using the snowball sampling technique, I started by interviewing Filipino Americans whom I knew and then asking them to refer me to others who might be willing to be interviewed. In other words, I chose participants not randomly but through a network of Filipino American contacts whom the first group of respondents trusted. To capture the diversity within the Filipino American community, I sought and selected respondents of different backgrounds and with diverse viewpoints. The sample is about equally divided between first-generation immigrants (those who came to the United States as adults) and Filipinas/os who were born and/or raised in the United States. It is more difficult to pinpoint the class status of the people I interviewed. To be sure, they included poor working-class immigrants who barely eked out a living, as well as educated professionals who thrived in middle- and upper-class suburban neighborhoods. However, the class status of most was much more ambiguous. I met Filipinos/as who toiled as assembly workers but who, through the pooling of income and finances, owned homes in middle-class communities. I also discovered that class status was transnational, determined as much by one's economic position in the Philippines as by that in the United States. For example, I encountered individuals who struggled economically in the United States but owned sizable properties in the Philippines. And I interviewed immigrants who continued to view themselves as "upper class" even while living in dire conditions in the United States. These examples suggest that the upper/middle/working-class typology, while useful, does not capture the complexity of immigrant lives. Reflecting the prominence of the U.S. Navy in San Diego, more than half of my respondents were affiliated with or had relatives affiliated with the navy.

My tape-recorded interviews, conducted in English, ranged from 3 to 10 hours each and took place in offices, coffee shops, and homes. My questions were open-ended and covered three general areas: family and immigration history, ethnic identity and practices, and community development among San Diego's Filipinos. The interviewing process varied widely: some respondents needed to be prompted with specific questions, while others spoke at great length on their own. Some chose to cover the span of their lives; others focused on specific events that were particularly important to them. The initial impetus for this essay on the relationship between immigrant parents and their daughters came from my observation that the dynamics of gender emerged more clearly in the interviews with women than in those with men. Because gender has been a marked category for women, the mothers and daughters I interviewed rarely told their life stories without reference to the dynamics of gender (see Personal Narratives Group, 1989, pp. 4–5). Even without prompting, young Filipinas almost always recounted stories of restrictive gender roles and gender expectations, particularly of parental control over their whereabouts and sexuality.

I believe that my own personal and social characteristics influenced the actual process of data collection, the quality of the materials that I gathered, and my analysis of them. As a Vietnam-born woman who immigrated to the United States at the age of 12, I came to the research project not as an "objective" outsider but as a fellow Asian immigrant who shared some of the life experiences of my respondents. During the fieldwork process, I did not remain detached but actively shared with my informants my own experiences of being an Asian immigrant woman: of being perceived as an outsider in U.S. society, of speaking English as a second language, of being a woman of color in a racialized patriarchal society, and of negotiating intergenerational tensions within my own family. I do not claim that these shared struggles grant me "insider status" in respect to the Filipino American community; the differences in our histories, cultures, languages, and, at times, class backgrounds remain important. But I do claim that these shared experiences enable me to bring to the work a comparative perspective that is implicit, intuitive, and informed by my own identities and positionalities—and with it a commitment to approach these subjects with both sensitivity and rigor. In a cogent call for scholars of color to expand on the premise of studying "our own" by studying other "others," Ruby Tapia argues that such implicitly comparative projects are important because they permit us to "highlight the different and *differentiating* functional forces of racialization" (1997, p. 2). It is with this deep interest in discovering—and forging—commonalities out of our specific and disparate experiences that I began this study on Filipino Americans in San Diego.

"AMERICAN" AND WHITENESS:
"TO ME, AMERICAN MEANS WHITE"

In U.S. racial discourse and practices, unless otherwise specified, "Americans" means "Whites" (Lipsitz, 1998, p. 1). In the case of Asian Americans, U.S. exclusion acts, naturalization laws, and national culture have simultaneously marked Asians as the unassimilable aliens and Whites as the quintessential Americans (Lowe, 1996). Excluded from the collective memory of who constitutes a "real" American, Asians in the United States, even as citizens, remain "foreigners-within"—"non-Americans." In a study of third- and later-generation Chinese and Japanese Americans, Mia Tuan (1998) concludes that, despite being longtime Americans, Asians—as racialized ethnics—are often assumed to be foreign unless proven otherwise. In the case of Filipinos, who emigrated from a former U.S. colony, their formation as racialized minorities does not begin in the United States but rather in a "homeland" already affected by U.S. economic, social, and cultural influences (Lowe, 1996, p. 8).

Cognizant of this racialized history, my Filipino respondents seldom identify themselves as American. As will be evident in the discussion below, they equate "American" with "White" and often use these two terms interchangeably. For example, a Filipina who is married to a White American refers to her husband as "American" but to her African American and Filipino American brothers-in-law as "Black" and "Filipino," respectively. Others speak about "American ways," "American culture," or "American lifestyle" when they really mean *White* American ways, culture, and lifestyle. A Filipino man who has lived in the United States for 30 years explains why he still does not identify himself as American: "I don't see myself just as an American because I cannot hide the fact that my skin is brown. To me, American means White." A second-generation Filipina recounted the following story when asked whether she defined herself as American:

> I went to an all-White school. I knew I was different. I wasn't American. See, you are not taught that you're American because you are not White. When I was in the tenth grade, our English teacher asked us what our nationality was, and she goes how many of you are Mexican, how many of you are Filipino, and how many of you are Samoan and things like that. And when she asked how many of you are American, just the White people raised their hands.

Other Asian Americans also conflate *American* and White. In an ethnographic study of Asian American high school students, Stacey Lee reports that Korean immigrant parents often instructed their children to socialize only with Koreans and "Americans." When asked to define the term *American,* the Korean students responded in unison with "White! Korean parents like white" (Lee, 1996, p. 24). Tuan (1998) found the same practice among later-generation Chinese and Japanese Americans: the majority use the term *American* to refer to Whites.

CONSTRUCTING THE DOMINANT GROUP: THE MORAL FLAWS OF WHITE AMERICANS

Given the centrality of moral themes in popular discussions on racial differences, Michele Lamont (1997) has suggested that morality is a crucial site to study the cultural mechanisms of reproduction of racial inequality. While much has been written on how Whites have represented the (im)morality of people of color (Collins, 1991; Hamamoto, 1994; Marchetti, 1993), there has been less critical attention to how people of color have represented Whites.[3] Shifting attention from the otherness of the subordinate group (as dictated by the "mainstream") to the otherness of the dominant group (as constructed by the "margins"), this section focuses on the alternative frames of meaning that racially subordinate groups mobilize to (re)define their status in relation to the dominant group. I argue that female morality—defined as women's dedication to their families and sexual restraint—is one of the few sites where economically and politically dominated groups can construct the dominant group as other and themselves as superior. Because womanhood is idealized as the repository of tradition, the norms that regulate women's behaviors become a means of determining and defining group status and boundaries. As a consequence, the burdens and complexities of cultural representation fall most heavily on immigrant women and their daughters. Below, I show that Filipino immigrants claim moral distinctiveness for their community by representing "Americans" as morally flawed, themselves as family-oriented model minorities, and their wives and daughters as paragons of morality.

FAMILY-ORIENTED MODEL MINORITIES: "WHITE WOMEN WILL LEAVE YOU"

In his work on Italian immigrant parents and children in the 1930s, Robert Anthony Orsi (1985) reports that parents invented a virtuous Italy (based on memories of their childhood) that they then used to castigate the morality of the United States and their U.S.-born or -raised children. In a similar way, many of my respondents constructed their "ethnic" culture as principled and "American" culture as deviant. Most often, this morality narrative revolves around family life and family relations. When asked what sets Filipinos apart from other Americans, my respondents—of all ages and class backgrounds—repeatedly contrasted close-knit Filipino families with what they perceived to be the more impersonal quality of U.S. family relations.[4] In the following narratives, "Americans" are characterized as lacking in strong family ties and collective identity, less willing to do the work of family and cultural maintenance, and less willing to abide by patriarchal norms in husband/wife relations:

> American society lacks caring. The American way of life is more individual rather than collective. The American way is to say I want to have my own way. (Filipina immigrant, 54 years old)
>
> Our [Filipino] culture is different. We are more close-knit. We tend to help one another. Americans, ya know, they are all right, but they don't help each other that much. As a matter of fact, if the parents are old, they take them to a convalescent home and let them rot there. We would never do that in our culture. We would nurse them; we would help them until the very end. (Filipino immigrant, 60 years old)

Our [Filipino] culture is very communal. You know that your family will always be there, that you don't have to work when you turn eighteen, you don't have to pay rent when you are eighteen, which is the American way of thinking. You also know that if things don't work out in the outside world, you can always come home and mommy and daddy will always take you and your children in. (Second-generation Filipina, 33 years old)

Asian parents take care of their children. Americans have a different attitude. They leave their children to their own resources. They get baby-sitters to take care of their children or leave them in day care. That's why when they get old, their children don't even care about them. (Filipina immigrant, 46 years old)

Implicit in negative depictions of U.S. families as uncaring, selfish, and distant is the allegation that White women are not as dedicated to their families as Filipina women are to theirs. Several Filipino men who married White women recalled being warned by their parents and relatives that "White women will leave you." As one man related, "My mother said to me, 'Well, you know, don't marry a White person because they would take everything that you own and leave you.'" For some Filipino men, perceived differences in attitudes about women's roles between Filipina and non-Filipina women influenced their marital choice. A Filipino American navy man explained why he went back to the Philippines to look for a wife:

My goal was to marry a Filipina. I requested to be stationed in the Philippines to get married to a Filipina. I'd seen the women here and basically they are spoiled. They have a tendency of not going along together with their husband. They behave differently. They chase the male, instead of the male, the normal way or the traditional way is for the male to go after the female. They have sex without marrying. They want to do their own things. So my idea was to go back home and marry somebody who has never been here. I tell my son the same thing: if he does what I did and finds himself a good lady there, he will be in good hands.

Another man who had dated mostly White women in high school recounted that when it came time to marry, he "looked for the kind of women" he met while stationed in the Philippines: "I hate to sound chauvinistic about marriages, but Filipinas have a way of making you feel like you are a king. They also have that tenderness, that elegance. And we share the same values about family, education, religion, and raising children."

The claims of family closeness are not unique to Filipino immigrants. For example, when asked what makes their group distinctive, Italian Americans (di Leonardo, 1984), Vietnamese Americans (Kibria, 1993), South Asian Americans (Hickey, 1996), and African Americans (Lamont, 1997) all point proudly to the close-knit character of their family life. Although it is difficult to know whether these claims are actual perceptions or favored self-legitimating answers, it is nevertheless important to note the gender implications of these claims. That is, while both men and women identify the family system as a tremendous source of cultural pride, it is women—through their unpaid housework and kin work who shoulder the primary responsibility for maintaining family closeness. As the organizers of family rituals, transmitters of homeland folklores, and socializers of young children, women have been crucial for the maintenance of family ties and cultural traditions. In a study of kinship, class, and gender among California Italian Americans, di Leonardo argues that women's kin work, "the work of knitting households together into close, extended family ties," maintains the family networks that give ethnicity meaning (1984, p. 229).

Because the moral status of the community rests on women's labor, women, as wives and daughters, are expected to dedicate themselves to the family. Writing on the constructed image of ethnic family and gender, di Leonardo argues that "a large part of stressing ethnic identity amounts to burdening women with increased responsibilities for preparing special foods, planning rituals, and enforcing "ethnic" socialization of children" (1984, p. 222). A 23-year-old Filipina spoke about the reproductive work that her mother performed and expected her to learn:

> In my family, I was the only girl, so my mom expected a lot from me. She wanted me to help her to take care of the household. I felt like there was a lot of pressure on me. It's very important to my mom to have the house in order: to wash the dishes, to keep the kitchen in order, vacuuming, and dusting and things like that. She wants me to be a perfect housewife. It's difficult. I have been married now for about four months and my mother asks me every now and then what have I cooked for my husband. My mom is also very strict about families getting together on holidays, and I would always help her to organize that. Each holiday, I would try to decorate the house for her, to make it more special.

The burden of unpaid reproductive and kin work is particularly stressful for women who work outside the home. In the following narrative, a Filipina wife and mother described the pulls of family and work that she experienced when she went back to school to pursue a doctoral degree in nursing:

> The Filipinos, we are very collective, very connected. Going through the doctoral program, sometimes I think it is better just to forget about my relatives and just concentrate on school. All that connectedness, it steals parts of myself because all of my energies are devoted to my family. And that is the reason why I think Americans are successful. The majority of the American people they can do what they want. They don't feel guilty because they only have a few people to relate to. For us Filipinos, it's like roots under the tree, you have all these connections. The Americans are more like the trunk. I am still trying to go up to the trunk of the tree but it is too hard. I want to be more independent, more like the Americans. I want to be good to my family but what about me? And all the things that I am doing. It's hard. It's always a struggle.

It is important to note that this Filipina interprets her exclusion and added responsibilities as only racial when they are also gendered. For example, when she says, "the American people they can do what they want," she ignores the differences in the lives of White men and White women—the fact that most White women experience similar competing pulls of family, education, and work.

RACIALIZED SEXUALITY AND (IM)MORALITY:
"IN AMERICA . . . SEX IS NOTHING"

Sexuality, as a core aspect of social identity, is fundamental to the structuring of gender inequality (Millett, 1970). Sexuality is also a salient marker of otherness and has figured prominently in racist and imperialist ideologies (Gilman, 1985; Stoler, 1991). Historically, the sexuality of subordinate groups—particularly that of racialized women—has been systematically stereotyped by the dominant groups.[5] At stake in these stereotypes is the construction of women of color as morally lacking in the areas of sexual restraint and traditional morality. Asian women—both in Asia and in the United States—have been racialized as sexually immoral, and the "Orient"— and its women—has long served as a site of European male-power fantasies, replete with lurid images of sexual license, gynecological aberrations, and general perversion (Gilman, 1985, p. 89). In colonial Asia in the 19th and early 20th centuries, for example, female sexuality was a site for colonial rulers to assert their moral superiority and thus their supposed natural and legitimate right to rule. The colonial rhetoric of moral superiority was based on the construction of colonized Asian women as subjects of sexual desire and fulfillment and European colonial women as the paragons of virtue and the bearers of a redefined colonial morality (Stoler, 1991). The discourse of morality has also been used to mark the "unassimilability" of Asians in the United States. At the turn of the 20th century, the public perception of Chinese women as disease-ridden, drug-addicted prostitutes served to underline the depravity of "Orientals" and played a decisive role in the eventual passage of exclusion laws against all Asians (Mazumdar, 1989, pp. 3–4). The stereotypical view that all Asian women were prostitutes, first formed in the 1850s, persisted. Contemporary American popular culture continues to endow Asian women with an excess of "womanhood," sexualizing them but also impugning their sexuality (Espiritu, 1997, p. 93).

Filipinas—both in the Philippines and in the United States—have been marked as desirable but dangerous "prostitutes" and/or submissive "mail-order brides" (Egan, 1996; Halualani, 1995). These stereotypes emerged out of the colonial process, especially the extensive U.S. military presence in the Philippines. Until the early 1990s, the Philippines, at times unwillingly, housed some of the United States' largest overseas air force and naval bases (Espiritu, 1995, p. 14). Many Filipino nationalists have charged that "the prostitution problem" in the Philippines stemmed from U.S. and Philippine government policies that promoted a sex industry—brothels, bars, and massage parlors—for servicemen stationed or on leave in the Philippines. During the Vietnam War, the Philippines was known as the "rest and recreation" center of Asia, hosting approximately 10,000 U.S. servicemen daily (Coronel & Rosca, 1993; Warren, 1993). In this context, all Filipinas were racialized as sexual commodities, usable and expendable. A U.S.-born Filipina recounted the sexual harassment she faced while visiting Subic Bay Naval Station in Olongapo City:

> One day, I went to the base dispensary. . . . I was dressed nicely, and as I walked by the fire station, I heard catcalls and snide remarks being made by some of the firemen.

... I was fuming inside. The next thing I heard was, "How much do you charge?" I kept on walking. "Hey, are you deaf or something? How much do you charge? You have a good body." That was an incident that I will never forget.   (Quoted in Espiritu, 1995, p. 77)

The sexualized racialization of Filipina women is also captured in Marianne Villanueva's short story "Opportunity" (1991). As the protagonist, a "mail-order bride" from the Philippines, enters a hotel lobby to meet her American fiancé, the bellboys snicker and whisper *puta* (whore)—a reminder that U.S. economic and cultural colonization in the Philippines always forms a backdrop to any relations between Filipinos and Americans (Wong, 1993, p. 53).

Cognizant of the pervasive hypersexualization of Filipina women, my respondents, especially women who grew up near military bases, were quick to denounce prostitution, to condemn sex laborers, and to declare (unasked) that they themselves did not frequent "that part of town." As one Filipina immigrant said,

Growing up [in the Philippines], I could never date an American because my dad's concept of a friendship with an American is with a GI. The only reason why my dad wouldn't let us date an American is that people will think that the only way you met was because of the base. I have never seen the inside of any of the bases because we were just forbidden to go there.

Many of my respondents also distanced themselves culturally from the Filipinas who serviced U.S. soldiers by branding them "more Americanized" and "more Westernized." In other words, these women were sexually promiscuous because they had assumed the sexual mores of White women. This characterization allows my respondents to symbolically disown the Filipina "bad girl" and, in so doing, to uphold the narrative of Filipina sexual virtuousness and White female sexual promiscuity. In the following narrative, a mother who came to the United States in her 30s contrasted the controlled sexuality of women in the Philippines with the perceived promiscuity of White women in the United States:

In the Philippines, we always have chaperons when we go out. When we go to dances, we have our uncle, our grandfather, and auntie all behind us to make sure that we behave in the dance hall. Nobody goes necking outside. You don't even let a man put his hand on your shoulders. When you were brought up in a conservative country, it is hard to come here and see that it is all freedom of speech and freedom of action. Sex was never mentioned in our generation. I was 30 already when I learned about sex. But to the young generation in America, sex is nothing.

Similarly, another immigrant woman criticized the way young American women are raised: "Americans are so liberated. They allow their children, their girls, to go out even when they are still so young." In contrast, she stated that, in "the Filipino way, it is very important, the value of the woman, that she is a virgin when she gets married."

The ideal "Filipina," then, is partially constructed on the community's conceptualization of White women. She is everything that they are not: she is sexually modest and dedicated to her family; they are sexually promiscuous and uncaring. Within the context of the dominant culture's pervasive hypersexualization of Filipinas, the construction of the "ideal" Filipina as family oriented and chaste can be read as an effort to reclaim the morality of the community. This effort erases the Filipina "bad girl," ignores competing sexual practices in the Filipino communities, and uncritically embraces the myth of "Oriental femininity." Cast as the embodiment of perfect womanhood and exotic femininity, Filipinas (and other Asian women) in recent years have been idealized in U.S. popular culture as more truly "feminine" (i.e., devoted, dependent, domestic) and therefore more desirable than their more modern, emancipated sisters (Espiritu, 1997, p. 113). Capitalizing on this image of the "superfemme," mail-order bride agencies market Filipina women as "'exotic, subservient wife imports' for sale and as alternatives for men sick of independent 'liberal' Western women" (Halualani, 1995, p. 49; see also Ordonez, 1997, p. 122).

Embodying the moral integrity of the idealized ethnic community, immigrant women, particularly young daughters, are expected to comply with male-defined criteria of what constitute "ideal" feminine virtues. While the sexual behavior of adult women is confined to a monogamous, heterosexual context, that of young women is denied completely (see Dasgupta & DasGupta, 1996, pp. 229–231). In the next section, I detail the ways Filipino immigrant parents, under the rubric of "cultural preservation," police their daughters' behaviors in order to safeguard their sexual innocence and virginity. These attempts at policing generate hierarchies and tensions within immigrant families—between parents and children and between brothers and sisters.

THE CONSTRUCTION(S) OF THE "IDEAL" FILIPINA: "BOYS ARE BOYS AND GIRLS ARE DIFFERENT"

As the designated "keepers of the culture" (Billson, 1995), immigrant women and their behavior come under intense scrutiny both from men and women of their own groups and from U.S.-born Americans (Gabaccia, 1994, p. xi). In a study of the Italian Harlem community from 1880 to 1950, Orsi reports that "all the community's fears for the reputation and integrity of the homes came to focus on the behavior of young women" (1985, p. 135). Because women's moral and sexual loyalties were deemed central to the maintenance of group status, changes in female behavior, especially that of growing daughters, were interpreted as sins of moral decay and ethnic suicide and were carefully monitored and sanctioned (Gabaccia, 1994, p. 113).

Although details vary, young women of various groups and across space and time—for example, second-generation Chinese women in San Francisco in the 1920s (Yung, 1995), U.S.-born Italian women in East Harlem in the 1930s (Orsi, 1985), young Mexican women in the Southwest during the interwar years (Ruiz, 1992), and daughters of Caribbean and Asian Indian immigrants on the East Coast in the 1990s (Dasgupta & DasGupta, 1996; Waters, 1996)—have identified strict parental control on their activities and movements as the primary source of inter-generational conflict. Recent studies of immigrant families also identify gender as a significant determinant of parent-child conflict, with daughters more likely than sons to be involved in such conflicts and instances of parental derogation (Gibson, 1995; Matute-Bianchi, 1991; Rumbaut & Ima, 1988; Woldemikael, 1989).

Although immigrant families have always been preoccupied with passing on their native culture, language, and traditions to both male and female children, it is daughters who have the primary burden of protecting and preserving the family. Because sons do not have to conform to the same image of an "ideal" ethnic subject as daughters do, they often receive special daily privileges denied to daughters (Haddad & Smith, 1996, pp. 22–24; Waters, 1996, pp. 75–76). This is not to say that immigrant parents do not place undue expectations on their sons; rather, these expectations do not pivot around the sons' sexuality or dating choices.[6] In contrast, parental control over the movement and action of daughters begins the moment they are perceived as young adults and sexually vulnerable. It regularly consists of monitoring their whereabouts and forbidding dating (Wolf, 1997). For example, the immigrant parents I interviewed seldom allowed their daughters to date, to stay out late, to spend the night at a friend's house, or to take an out-of-town trip.

Many of the second-generation women I spoke to complained bitterly about these parental restrictions. They particularly resented what they saw as gender in-equity in their families: the fact that their parents placed far more restrictions on their activities and movements than on those of their brothers. Some decried the fact that even their younger brothers had more freedom than they did: "It was really hard growing up because my parents would let my younger brothers do what they wanted but I didn't get to do what I wanted even though I was the oldest. I had a curfew and my brothers didn't. I had to ask if I could go places and they didn't. My parents never even asked my brothers when they were coming home." As indicated in the following excerpt, many Filipino males are cognizant of this double standard in their families:

My sister would always say to me, "It's not fair, just because you are a guy, you can go wherever you want." I think my parents do treat me and my sister differently. Like in high school, maybe 10:30 at night, which is pretty late on a school night, and I say I have to go pick up some notes at my friend's house, my parents wouldn't say anything. But if my sister were to do that, there would be no way. Even now when my sister is in college already, if she wants to leave at midnight to go to a friend's house, they would tell her that she shouldn't do it.

When questioned about this double standard, parents generally responded by explaining that "girls are different":

I have that Filipino mentality that boys are boys and girls are different. Girls are supposed to be protected, to be clean. In the early years, my daughters have to have chaperons and curfews. And they know that they have to be virgins until they get married. The girls always say that is not fair. What is the difference between their brothers and them? And my answer always is, "In the Philippines, you know, we don't do that. The girls stay home. The boys go out." It was the way that I was raised. I still want to have part of that culture instilled in my children. And I want them to have that to pass on to their children.

Even among self-described Western-educated and "tolerant" parents, many continue to ascribe to "the Filipino way" when it comes to raising daughters. As one college-educated father explains,

Because of my Western education, I don't raise my children the way my parents raised me. I tended to be a little more tolerant. But at times, especially in certain issues like dating, I find myself more towards the Filipino way in the sense that I have only one daughter so I tended to be a little bit stricter. So the double standard kind of operates: it's all right for the boys to explore the field but I tended to be overly protective of my daughter. My wife feels the same way because the boys will not lose anything, but the daughter will lose something, her virginity, and it can be also a question of losing face, that kind of thing.

Although many parents discourage or forbid dating for daughters, they still fully expect these young women to fulfill their traditional roles as women: to marry and have children. A young Filipina recounted the mixed messages she received from her parents:

This is the way it is supposed to work: Okay, you go to school. You go to college. You graduate. You find a job. *Then* you find your husband, and you have children. That's the whole time line. But my question is, if you are not allowed to date, how are you supposed to find your husband? They say "no" to the whole dating scene because that is secondary to your education, secondary to your family. They do push marriage, but at a later date. So basically my parents are telling me that I should get married and I should have children but that I should not date.

In a study of second-generation Filipino Americans in Northern California, Diane Wolf (1997) reports the same pattern of parental pressures: Parents expect daughters to remain virgins until marriage, to have a career, and to combine their work lives with marriage and children.

The restrictions on girls' movement sometimes spill over to the realm of academics. Dasgupta and DasGupta (1996, p. 230) recount that in the Indian American community, while young men were expected to attend faraway competitive colleges, many of their female peers were encouraged by their parents to go to the local colleges so that they could live at or close to home. Similarly, Wolf (1997, p. 467) reports that some Filipino parents pursued contradictory tactics with their children, particularly their daughters, by pushing them to achieve academic excellence in high school but then "pulling the emergency brake" when they contemplated college by expecting them to stay at home, even if it meant going to a less competitive college or not going at all. In the following account, a young Filipina relates that her parents' desire to "protect" her surpassed their concerns for her academic preparation:

> My brother [was] given a lot more opportunity educationally. He was given the opportunity to go to Miller High School that has a renowned college preparatory program but [for] which you have to be bussed out of our area. I've come from a college prep program in junior high and I was asked to apply for the program at Miller. But my parents said "No, absolutely not." This was even during the time, too, when Southside [the neighborhood high school] had one of the lowest test scores in the state of California. So it was like, "You know, mom, I'll get a better chance at Miller." "No, no, you're going to Southside. There is no ifs, ands, or buts. Miller is too far. What if something happens to you?" But two years later, when my brother got ready to go on to high school, he was allowed to go to Miller. My sister and I were like, "Obviously, whose education do you value more? If you're telling us that education is important, why do we see a double standard?"[7]

The above narratives suggest that the process of parenting is gendered in that immigrant parents tend to restrict the autonomy, mobility, and personal decision making of their daughters more than that of their sons. I argue that these parental restrictions are attempts to construct a model of Filipina womanhood that is chaste, modest, nurturing, and family oriented. Women are seen as responsible for holding the cultural line, maintaining racial boundaries, and marking cultural difference. This is not to say that parent-daughter conflicts exist in all Filipino immigrant families. Certainly, Filipino parents do not respond in a uniform way to the challenges of being racial-ethnic minorities, and I met parents who have had to change some of their ideas and practices in response to their inability to control their children's movements and choices:

> I have three girls and one boy. I used to think that I wouldn't allow my daughters to go dating and things like that, but there is no way I could do that. I can't stop it. It's the way of life here in America. Sometimes you kind of question yourself, if you are doing what is right. It is hard to accept but you got to accept it. That's the way they are here. (Professional Filipino immigrant father)

> My children are born and raised here, so they do pretty much what they want. They think they know everything. I can only do so much as a parent. . . . When I try to teach my kids things, they tell me that I sound like an old record. They even talk back to me sometimes. . . . The first time my daughter brought her boyfriend to the house, she was eighteen years old. I almost passed away, knocked out. Lord, tell me what to do? (Working-class Filipina immigrant mother)

These narratives call attention to the shifts in the generational power caused by the migration process and to the possible gap between what parents say they want for their children and their ability to control the young. However, the interview data do suggest that intergenerational conflicts are socially recognized occurrences in Filipino communities. Even when respondents themselves had not experienced intergenerational tensions, they could always recall a cousin, a girlfriend, or a friend's daughter who had.

SANCTIONS AND REACTIONS: "THAT IS NOT WHAT A DECENT FILIPINO GIRL SHOULD DO"

I do not wish to suggest that immigrant communities are the only ones in which parents regulate their daughters' mobility and sexuality. Feminist scholars have long documented the construction, containment, and exploitation of women's sexuality in various societies (Maglin & Perry, 1996). We also know that the cultural anxiety over unbounded female sexuality is most apparent with regard to adolescent girls (Tolman & Higgins, 1996, p. 206). The difference is in the ways immigrant and nonimmigrant families sanction girls' sexuality. To control sexually assertive girls, nonimmigrant parents rely on the gender-based good girl/bad girl dichotomy in which "good girls" are passive, threatened sexual objects, while "bad girls" are active, desiring sexual agents (Tolman & Higgins, 1996). As Dasgupta and DasGupta write, "the two most pervasive images of women across cultures are the goddess and whore, the good and bad women" (1996, p. 236). This good girl/bad girl cultural story conflates femininity with sexuality, increases women's vulnerability to sexual coercion, and justifies women's containment in the domestic sphere.

Immigrant families, though, have an additional strategy: they can discipline their daughters as racial/national subjects as well as gendered ones. That is, as self-appointed guardians of "authentic" cultural memory, immigrant parents can attempt to regulate their daughters' independent choices by linking them to cultural ignorance or betrayal. As both parents and children recounted, young women who disobeyed parental strictures were often branded "nonethnic," "untraditional," "radical," "selfish," and "not caring about the family." Female sexual choices were also linked to moral degeneracy, defined in relation to a narrative of a hegemonic White norm. Parents were quick to warn their daughters about "bad" Filipinas who had become pregnant outside marriage.[8] As in the case of "bar girls" in the Philippines, Filipina Americans who veered from acceptable behaviors were deemed "Americanized"—as women who have adopted the sexual mores and practices of White women. As one Filipino immigrant father described "Americanized" Filipinas: "They are spoiled because they have seen the American way. They go out at night. Late at night. They go out on dates. Smoking. They have sex without marrying."

From the perspective of the second-generation daughters, these charges are stinging. The young women I interviewed were visibly pained—with many breaking down and crying—when they recounted their parents' charges. This deep pain, stemming in part from their desire to be validated as Filipina, existed even among the more "rebellious" daughters. One 24-year-old daughter explained:

> My mom is very traditional. She wants to follow Filipino customs, just really adhere to them, like what is proper for a girl, what she can and can't do, and what other peo-

ple are going to think of her if she doesn't follow that way. When I pushed these restrictions, when I rebelled and stayed out later than allowed, my mom would always say, "That is not what a decent Filipino girl should do. You should come home at a decent hour. What are people going to think of you?" And that would get me really upset, you know, because I think that my character is very much the way it should be for a Filipina. I wear my hair long, I wear decent makeup. I dress properly, conservative. I am family oriented. It hurts me that she doesn't see that I am decent, that I am proper, and that I am not going to bring shame to the family or anything like that.

This narrative suggests that even when parents are unable to control the behaviors of their children, their (dis)approval remains powerful in shaping the emotional lives of their daughters (see Wolf, 1997). Although better-off parents can and do exert greater controls over their children's behaviors than do poorer parents (Kibria, 1993; Wolf, 1992), I would argue that all immigrant parents—regardless of class background—possess this emotional hold on their children. Therein lies the source of their power: As immigrant parents, they have the authority to determine if their daughters are "authentic" members of their racial-ethnic community. Largely unacquainted with the "home" country, U.S.-born children depend on their parents' tutelage to craft and affirm their ethnic self and thus are particularly vulnerable to charges of cultural ignorance and/or betrayal (Espiritu, 1994). Despite these emotional pains, many young Filipinas I interviewed contest and negotiate parental restrictions in their daily lives. Faced with parental restrictions on their mobility, young Filipinas struggle to gain some control over their own social lives, particularly over dating. In many cases, daughters simply misinform their parents of their whereabouts or date without their parents' knowledge. They also rebel by vowing to create more egalitarian relationships with their own husbands and children. A 30-year-old Filipina who is married to a White American explained why she chose to marry outside her culture:

In high school, I dated mostly Mexican and Filipino. It never occurred to me to date a White or Black guy. I was not attracted to them. But as I kept growing up and my father and I were having all these conflicts, I knew that if I married a Mexican or a Filipino, [he] would be exactly like my father. And so I tried to date anyone that would not remind me of my dad. A lot of my Filipina friends that I grew up with had similar experiences. So I knew that it wasn't only me. I was determined to marry a White person because he would treat me as an individual.

The few available studies on Filipino American intermarriage indicate a high rate relative to other Asian groups. In 1980, Filipino men in California recorded the highest intermarriage rate among all Asian groups, and Filipina women had the second-highest rate among Asian American women, after Japanese American women (Agbayani-Siewert & Revilla, 1995, p. 156).

Another Filipina who was labeled "radical" by her parents indicated that she would be more open-minded in raising her own children: "I see myself as very traditional in upbringing but I don't see myself as constricting on my children one day and I wouldn't put the gender roles on them. I wouldn't lock them into any particular way of behaving." It is important to note that even as these Filipinas desired new gender norms and practices for their own families, the majority hoped that their children would remain connected to Filipino culture.

My respondents also reported more serious reactions to parental restrictions, recalling incidents of someone they knew who had run away, joined a gang, or attempted suicide. A Filipina high-school counselor relates that most of the Filipinas she worked with "are really scared because a lot of them know friends that are pregnant and they all pretty much know girls who have attempted suicide." A 1995 random survey of San Diego public high schools conducted by the Federal Centers for Disease Control and Prevention (CDC) found that, in comparison with other ethnic groups, female Filipino students had the highest rates of seriously considering suicide (45.6%) as well as the highest rates of actually attempting suicide (23%) in the year preceding the survey. In comparison, 33.4% of Latinas, 26.2% of White women, and 25.3% of Black women surveyed said they had suicidal thoughts (Lau, 1995).

CONCLUSION

Mainstream American society defines White middle-class culture as the norm and whiteness as the unmarked marker of others' difference (Frankenberg, 1993). In this essay, I have shown that many Filipino immigrants use the largely gendered discourse of morality as one strategy to decenter whiteness and to locate themselves above the dominant group, demonizing it in the process. Like other immigrant groups, Filipinos praise the United States as a land of significant economic opportunity but simultaneously denounce it as a country inhabited by corrupted and individualistic people of questionable morals. In particular, they criticize American family life, American individualism, and American women (see Gabaccia, 1994, p. 113). Enforced by distorting powers of memory and nostalgia, this rhetoric of moral superiority often leads to patriarchal calls for a cultural "authenticity" that locates family honor and national integrity in the group's female members. Because the policing of women's bodies is one of the main means of asserting moral superiority, young women face numerous restrictions on their autonomy, mobility, and personal decision making. This practice of cultural (re)construction reveals how deeply the conduct of private life can be tied to larger social structures.

The construction of White Americans as the "other" and American culture as deviant serves a dual purpose: It allows immigrant communities both to reinforce patriarchy through the sanctioning of women's (mis)behavior and to present an unblemished, if not morally superior, public face to the dominant society. Strong in family values, heterosexual morality, and a hierarchical family structure, this public face erases the Filipina "bad girl" and ignores competing immoral practices in the Filipino communities. Through the oppression of Filipina women and the denunciation of White women's morality, the immigrant community attempts to exert its moral superiority over the dominant Western culture and to reaffirm to itself its self-worth in the face of economic, social, political, and legal subordination. In other words, the immigrant community uses restrictions on women's lives as one form of resistance to racism. This form of cultural resistance, however, severely restricts the lives of women, particularly those of the second generation, and it casts the family as a potential site of intense conflict and oppressive demands in immigrant lives.

NOTES

I gratefully acknowledge the many useful suggestions and comments of George Lipsitz, Vince Rafael, Lisa Lowe, Joane Nagel, Diane Wolf, Karen Pyke, and two anonymous reviewers for *Signs*. I also would like to thank all those Filipinos/as who participated in this study for their time, help, and insights into immigrant lives.

1. Filipino settlement in San Diego dates back to 1903, when a group of young Filipino *pensionados* enrolled at the State Normal School (now San Diego State University).

2. My understanding of Filipino American lives is also based on the many conversations I have had with my Filipino American students at the University of California, San Diego, and with Filipino American friends in the San Diego area and elsewhere.

3. A few studies have documented the ways racialized communities have represented White Americans. For example, in his anthropological work on Chicano joking, José Limón (1982) reports that young Mexican Americans elevate themselves over Whites through the telling of "Stupid-American" jokes in which an Anglo American is consistently duped by a Mexican character. In her interviews with African American working-class men, Michele Lamont (1997) finds that these men tend to perceive Euro Americans as immoral, sneaky, and not to be trusted. Although these studies provide an interesting and compelling window into racialized communities' views of White Americans, they do not analyze how the rhetoric of moral superiority often depends on gender categories.

4. Indeed, people around the world often believe that Americans have no real family ties. For example, on a visit to my family in Vietnam, my cousin asked me earnestly if it was true that American children put their elderly parents in nursing homes instead of caring for them at home. She was horrified at this practice and proclaimed that, because they care for their elders, Vietnamese families are morally superior to American families.

5. Writing on the objectification of Black women, Patricia Hill Collins (1991) argues that popular representations of Black females—mammy, welfare queen, and jezebel—all pivot around their sexuality, either desexualizing or hypersexualizing than. Along the same line, Native American women have been portrayed as sexually excessive (Green, 1975), Chicana women as "exotic and erotic" (Mirande, 1980), and Puerto Rican and Cuban women as "tropical bombshells . . . sexy, sexed and interested" (Tafolla, 1985, p. 39).

6. The relationship between immigrant parents and their sons deserves an essay of its own. According to Gabaccia, "Immigrant parents fought with sons, too, but over different issues: parents' complaints about rebellious sons focused more on criminal activity than on male sexuality or independent courtship" (1994, p. 70). Moreover, because of their mobility, young men have more means to escape—at least temporarily—the pressures of the family than young women. In his study of Italian American families, Orsi reports that young men

rebelled by sleeping in cars or joining the army, but young women did not have such opportunities (1985, p. 143).

7. The names of the two high schools in this excerpt are fictitious.

8. According to a 1992 health assessment report of Filipinos in San Francisco, Filipino teens have the highest pregnancy rates among all Asian groups and, in 1991, the highest rate of increase in the number of births as compared with all other racial or ethnic groups (Tiongson, 1997, p. 257).

REFERENCES

Agbayani-Siewert, Pauline, & Revilla, Linda. (1995). Filipino Americans. In Pyong Gap Min (Ed.), *Asian Americans: Contemporary trends and issues* (pp. 134–68). Thousand Oaks, CA: Sage.

Azores-Gunter, Tania Fortunate M. (1986–87). Educational attainment and upward mobility: Prospects for Filipino Americans. *Amerasia Journal, 13*(1), 39–52.

Billson, Janet Mancini. (1995). *Keepers of the culture: The power of tradition in women's lives.* New York: Lexington Books.

Cabezas, Amado, Shinagawa, Larry H., & Kawaguchi, Gary. (1986–87). New inquiries into the socioeconomic status of Pilipino Americans in California. *Amerasia Journal, 13*(1), 1–21.

Collins, Patricia Hill. (1991). *Black feminist thought: Knowledge, consciousness, and the politics of empowerment.* New York: Routledge

Cordova, Fred. (1983). *Filipinos: Forgotten Asian Americans, a pictorial essay, 1763–circa 1963.* Dubuque, IA: Kendall/Hunt.

Coronel, Sheila, & Rosca, Ninotchka. (1993, November–December). For the boys: Filipinas expose years of sexual slavery by the U.S. and Japan. *Ms.,* 10–15.

Dasgupta, Shamita Das, & DasGupta, Sayantani. (1996). Public face, private space: Asian Indian women and sexuality. In Nan Bauer Maglin & Donna Perry (Eds.), *"Bad girls"/"good girls": Women, sex, and power in the nineties* (pp. 226–43). New Brunswick, NJ: Rutgers University Press.

Di Leonardo, Micaela. (1984). *The varieties of ethnic experience: Kinship, class, and gender among California Italian Americans.* Ithaca, NY: Cornell University Press.

Eastmond, Marita. (1993). Reconstructing life: Chilean refugee women and the dilemmas of exile. In Gina Buijs (Ed.), *Migrant women: Crossing boundaries and changing identities.* Oxford, England: Berg.

Egan, Timothy. (1996, May 26). Mail-order marriage, immigrant dreams, and death. *New York Times,* p. A12.

Espiritu, Yen Le. (1994). The intersection of race, ethnicity, and class: The multiple identities of second-generation Filipinos. *Identities, 1*(2–3), 249–73.

Espiritu, Yen Le. (1995). *Filipino American lives.* Philadelphia: Temple University Press.

Espiritu, Yen Le. (1997). *Asian American women and men: Labor, laws, and love.* Thousand Oaks, CA: Sage.

Espiritu, Yen Le, & Wolf, Diane L. (2001). The paradox of assimilation children of Filipino immigrants in San Diego. In Rubén Rumbaut & Alejandro Portes (Eds.), *Ethnicities: Children of immigrants in America.* Berkeley & Los Angeles: University of California Press; New York: Russell Sage Foundation.

Frankenberg, Ruth. (1993). *White women, race matters: The social construction of whiteness.* Minneapolis: University of Minnesota Press.

Gabaccia, Donna. (1994). *From the other side: Women, gender, and immigrant life in the U.S., 1820–1990.* Bloomington: Indiana University Press.

Gibson, Margaret A. (1995). Additive acculturation as a strategy for school improvement. In Rubén Rumbaut & Wayne A. Cornelius (Eds.), *California's immigrant children: Theory, research, and implications for educational policy,* 77–105. La Jolla: Center for U.S.-Mexican Studies, University of California, San Diego.

Gilman, Sander L. (1985). *Difference and pathology: Stereotypes of sexuality, race, and madness.* Ithaca, NY: Cornell University Press.

Green, Rayna. (1975). The Pocahontas perplex: The image of Indian women in American culture. *Massachusetts Review, 16*(4), 698–714.

Haddad, Yvonne Y., & Jane I. Smith. (1996). Islamic values among American Muslims. In Barbara C. Aswad & Barbara Bilge (Eds.), *Family and gender among American Muslims: Issues facing Middle Eastern immigrants and their descendants* (pp. 19–40). Philadelphia: Temple University Press.

Halualani, Rona Tamiko. (1995). The intersecting hegemonic discourses of an Asian mail-order bride catalog: Pilipina "oriental butterfly" dolls for sale. *Women's Studies in Communication, 18*(1), 45–64.

Hamamoto, Darrell Y. (1994). *Monitored peril: Asian Americans and the politics of representation.* Minneapolis: University of Minnesota Press.

Hickey, M. Gail. (1996). "'Go to college, get a job, and don't leave the house without your brother": Oral histories with immigrant women and their daughters. *Oral History, 23*(2), 63–92.

Jung, Moon-Kie. (1999). No whites, no Asians: Race, Marxism and Hawaii's pre-emergent working class. *Social Science History, 23*(3), 357–393.

Kibria, Nazli. (1993). *Family tightrope: The changing lives of Vietnamese Americans.* Princeton, NJ: Princeton University Press.

Lamont, Michele. (1997). Colliding moralities between black and white workers. In Elisabeth Long (Ed.), *From sociology to cultural studies: New perspectives* (pp. 263–285). New York: Blackwell.

Lau, Angela. (1995, February 11). Filipino girls think suicide at number one rate. *San Diego Union-Tribune,* p. A1.

Lee, Stacey J. (1996). *Unraveling the "model minority" stereotype: Listening to Asian American youth.* New York: Teachers College Press.

Limón, José E. (1982). History, Chicano joking, and the varieties of higher education: Tradition and performance as critical symbolic action. *Journal of the Folklore Institute, 19*(2/3), 141–166.

Lipsitz, George. (1998). *The possessive investment in whiteness: How white people profit from identity politics.* Philadelphia: Temple University Press.

Lowe, Lisa. (1996). *Immigrant acts: On Asian American cultural politics.* Durham, NC: Duke University Press.

Maglin, Nan Bauer, & Perry, Donna. (1996). Introduction. In Nan Bauer Maglin & Donna Perry (Eds.), *"Bad girls"/"good girls": Women, sex, and power in the nineties* (pp. xiii–xxvi). New Brunswick, NJ: Rutgers University Press.

Marchetti, Gina. (1993). *Romance and the "Yellow Peril": Race, sex, and discursive strategies in Hollywood fiction.* Berkeley & Los Angeles: University of California Press.

Matute-Bianchi, Maria Eugenia. (1991). Situational ethnicity and patterns of school performance among immigrant and nonimmigrant Mexican-descent students. In Margaret

A. Gibson & John U. Ogbu (Eds.), *Minority status and schooling: A comparative study of immigrant and involuntary minorities* (pp. 205–247). New York: Garland.

Mazumdar, Suchetta. (1989). General introduction: A woman-centered perspective on Asian American history. In Asian Women United of California (Ed.), *Making waves: An anthology by and about Asian American women* (pp. 1–22). Boston: Beacon.

Millett, Kate. (1970). *Sexual politics.* Garden City, NY: Doubleday.

Mirande, Alfredo. (1980). The Chicano family: A reanalysis of conflicting views. In Arlene S. Skolnick & Jerome H. Skolnick (Eds.), *Rethinking marriage, child rearing, and family organization* (pp. 479–493). Berkeley & Los Angeles: University of California Press.

Okamura, Jonathan, & Agbayani, Amefil. (1997). *Pamantasan:* Filipino American higher education. In Maria P. P. Root (Ed.), *Filipino Americans: Transformation and identity* (pp. 183–197). Thousand Oaks, CA: Sage.

Ordonez, Raquel Z. (1997). Mail-order brides: An emerging community. In Maria P. P. Root (Ed.), *Filipino Americans: Transformation and identity* (pp. 121–142). Thousand Oaks, CA: Sage.

Orsi, Robert Anthony. (1985). *The Madonna of 115th Street: Faith and community in Italian Harlem, 1880–1950.* New Haven, CT: Yale University Press.

Personal Narratives Group. (1989). Origins. In Personal Narratives Group (Ed.), *Interpreting women's lives: Feminist theory and personal narratives* (pp. 3–15). Bloomington: Indiana University Press.

Ruíz, Vicki L. (1992). The flapper and the chaperone: Historical memory among Mexican-American women. In Donna Gabaccia (Ed.), *Seeking common ground: Multidisciplinary studies.* Westport, CT: Greenwood.

Rumbaut, Rubén. (1991). Passages to America: Perspectives on the new immigration. In Alan Wolfe (Ed.), *America at century's end* (pp. 208–244). Berkeley & Los Angeles: University of California Press.

Rumbaut, Rubén. (1994). The crucible within: Ethnic identity, self-esteem, and segmented assimilation among children of immigrants. *International Migration Review, 28*(4), 748–794.

Rumbaut, Rubén, & Ima, Kenji. (1988). *The adaptation of Southeast Asian refugee youth: A comparative study.* Washington, DC: U.S. Office of Refugee Resettlement.

San Juan, E., Jr. (1991). Mapping the boundaries: The Filipino writer in the U.S. *Journal of Ethnic Studies, 19*(1), 117–131.

Scharlin, Craig, & Villanueva, Lilia V. (1992). *Philip Vera Cruz: A personal history of Filipino immigrants and the farmworkers movement.* Los Angeles: UCLA Labor Center, Institute of Industrial Relations, and UCLA Asian American Studies Center.

Sharma, Miriam. (1984). Labor migration and class formation among the Filipinos in Hawaii, 1906–46. In Lucie Cheng & Edna Bonacich (Eds.), *Labor immigration under capitalism: Asian workers in the United States before World War II* (pp. 579–611). Berkeley & Los Angeles: University of California Press.

Stoler, Ann Laura. (1991). Carnal knowledge and imperial power: Gender, race, and morality in colonial Asia. In Micaela di Leonardo (Ed.), *Gender at the crossroads of knowledge: Feminist anthropology in the postmodern era* (pp. 51–104). Berkeley & Los Angeles: University of California Press.

Tafolla, Carmen. (1985). *To split a human: Mitos, machos y la mujer Chicana.* San Antonio, TX: Mexican American Cultural Center.

Tapia, Ruby. (1997, May 24). *Studying other "others."* Paper presented at the Association of Pacific Americans in Higher Education, San Diego, CA.

Tiongson, Antonio T., Jr. (1997). Throwing the baby out with the bath water. In Maria P. P. Root (Ed.), *Filipino Americans: Transformation and identity* (pp. 257–271). Thousand Oaks, CA: Sage.

Tolman, Deborah L., & Higgins, Tracy E. (1996). How being a good girl can be bad for girls. In Nan Bauer Maglin & Donna Perry (Eds.), *"Bad girls"/"good girls": Women, sex, and power in the nineties* (pp. 205–225). New Brunswick, NJ: Rutgers University Press.

Tuan, Mia. (1998). *Forever foreigners or honorary whites? The Asian ethnic experience today.* New Brunswick, NJ: Rutgers University Press.

Villanueva, Marianne. (1991). *Ginseng and other tales from Manila.* Corvallis, OR: Calyx

Warren, Jennifer. (1993, March 5). Suit asks Navy to aid children left in Philippines. *Los Angeles Times*, p. A3.

Waters, Mary C. (1996). The intersection of gender, race, and ethnicity in identity development of Caribbean American teens. In Bonnie J. Ross Leadbeater & Niobe Way (Eds.), *Urban girls: Resisting stereotypes, creating identities* (pp. 65–81). New York: New York University Press.

Woldemikael, T. M. (1989). *Becoming Black American: Haitians and American institutions in Evanston, Illinois.* New York: AMS Press.

Wolf, Diane L. (1992). *Factory daughters: Gender, household dynamics, and rural industrialization in Java.* Berkeley & Los Angeles: University of California Press.

Wolf, Diane L. (1997). Family secrets: Transnational struggles among children of Filipino immigrants. *Sociological Perspectives, 40*(3), 457–482.

Wong, Sau-ling. (1993). *Reading Asian American literature: From necessity to extravagance.* Princeton, NJ: Princeton University Press.

Yung, Judy. (1995). *Unbound feet: A social history of Chinese women in San Francisco.* Berkeley & Los Angeles: University of California Press.

PART FIVE

Gender, Citizenship, and the Transnational

CHAPTER 14

Engendering Transnational Migration

A Case Study of Salvadorans

Sarah J. Mahler

Over the past two decades, a northeastern section of El Salvador (northern La Unión department) has become tightly networked transnationally to towns on Long Island, a New York City suburban region. The principal stimulus behind this unlikely connection was the Salvadoran civil war (1979–1992). Northern La Unión experienced repeated guerrilla-military combat during the war owing largely to its location in a remote, rural, mountainous, and arid region of the country. The area's populace, largely peasant, was victimized by both sides—including forcible recruitment, rape, and pillage. Thousands fled the terror, the majority moving to Long Island and Houston. In the United States, refugees from the war (estimated at close to one million overall) were rarely accorded safe haven; rather, their petitions for political asylum were systematically denied throughout the 1980s. As "illegal aliens," most could find only poorly paying jobs, and they lived on society's margins. Poverty, undocumented status, and the prolonged civil war precluded the vast majority from returning to El Salvador, and hundreds of thousands still lack the documents necessary for returning legally to visit relatives and friends (for details, see Mahler, 1996).

Salvadoran migrants' restricted mobility could be suggestive of the classic bipolar model of immigration—of peoples who migrate to a new land, settle, assimilate, and ultimately forsake ties to their homelands. I will argue in this article that such an assumption for the Salvadoran case is incorrect. There certainly are Salvadoran migrants who have settled in the United States and who express no desire to return to their homeland, but most retain some ties there, and some travel back and forth quite frequently. Many scholars studying quite different migrations are similarly critical of the bipolar model, arguing that it misrepresents migrations historically (e.g., Foner, 1997; Guarnizo & Smith, 1998) and in contemporary contexts (e.g., Basch, Schiller, & Szanton Blanc, 1994; Rouse, 1992). These scholars, including myself, have been sculpting an alternative model of migration called *transnational migration.* The project, as discussed below, is far from completed and is highly contested. At a minimum, however, and in my reading of the literature, most adherents to the transnational perspective would agree with its basic definition as "the processes by which immigrants build social fields that link together their country of origin and their country of settlement" (Schiller, Basch, & Blanc-Szanton, 1992, p. 1).

In this essay, I will argue that the Salvadoran migration described above is most certainly transnational. But my main focus will not be to substantiate the transnational model against the classic model of migration. Rather, I aim to push transnational migration analysis forward in its examination of how transnational practices and discourses affect existing social identities and power relationships (see Guarnizo & Smith, 1998, p. 27; Mahler, 1998). More specifically, I will focus on if and how gender relations have been transformed in northern La Unión. I will identify various practices, discourses, and processes that influence gender relations and argue that transnational influences are a significant but not singular agent for change. Conversely, I have found that multiple agents and agencies at the local, regional, and transnational levels affect gender relations. At times, they work in tandem and at other times in opposition, but no one holds a monopoly on either the social reproduction or transformation of gender. This textured portraiture communicates mixed messages to the youthful population in this region who represent the next generation of likely migrants. In the conclusion, I address girls' and boys' attitudes in northern La Unión toward migration and speculate how they have been shaped by transnational processes and as part of the process of negotiating and renegotiating gender in this region.

TRANSNATIONAL MIGRATION THEORY: STRENGTHS AND AREAS NEEDING ATTENTION

The term *transnational* long predates its coupling with migration, and this historical fact has been at the root of much confusion with regard to the definition of *transnationalism.* For example, *transnational* is often interpreted as a synonym for *global.* Here, Kearney's (1995) review of the literature is helpful. He subtly distills the two: "Transnationalism overlaps globalization but typically has a more limited purview. Whereas global processes are largely decentered from specific national territories and take place in global space, transnational processes are anchored in and transcend one or more nation-states" (p. 548). Kearney's use of the anchor metaphor is critical here. It implies that national territories and identities continue to be important and are not entirely superseded. Contradistinctively, global processes are often viewed as "largely decentered from specific national territories and [taking] place in global space" (p. 548). "Transnational practices do not take place in an imaginary 'third space' abstractly located 'in between' national territories," argue Guarnizo and Smith (1998, p. 9). Moreover, they cannot be construed as if they were free from the constraints and opportunities that contextuality imposes. Transnational practices, while connecting collectivities located in more than one national territory, are embodied in specific social relations established between specific people, situated in unequivocal localities, at historically determined times. (p. 9)

In short, it has become fashionable to speak of the global economy, transnational corporations, and globalized mass media as if they operated in the stratosphere and never touched down on the earth in tangible ways. Such discourse nurtures the prevailing paradigm of macrolevel social change: that the global is dynamic, and the local is static. Additionally, these terms gloss over and thereby obfuscate the fact that they signify human activities conducted in historical and spatial contexts that have real consequences. In this article, I will illustrate that these contexts indeed are important.

To my mind, the term *transnational* should communicate the fact that people's activities may span borders, while acknowledging that borders, nation-states, and national identities still exist and are of consequence. Transnational also implies macrolevel processes, while not dismissing the existence of micro- and mesolevel processes as well. Guarnizo (1997), for example, is careful to distinguish between levels of practices in his definition of transnationalism:

At the group level, transnationalism is understood as a series of economic, socio-cultural, and political practical and discursive relations that transcend the territorially bounded jurisdiction of the nation-state. At the individual level, transnational practices and discourses are those which are an *habitual* part of the *normal* lives of those involved. Transnational relations are considered to be part of the normal life of an individual when their absence will impede or drastically disrupt her/his habitual pattern of activities, whether social, economic, cultural, or political. (p. 9)

Guarnizo's choice of "group level" dodges distinguishing between macro- and mesolevel analyses, but in his written introduction to *Transnationalism from Below*, coauthored with M. P. Smith, he suggests explicitly that transnational research "should start from a meso-structural vantage point, the point at which institutions interact with structural and instrumental processes" to facilitate linkages to data on macro- and microlevel structures and practices (Guarnizo & Smith, 1998, p. 23).

Transnational migration should be viewed as a specific area within the broad field of transnationalism, one that focuses on "the social process in which migrants establish social fields that cross geographic, cultural, and political borders" (Schiller et al., 1992, p. ix). Transnational migration theory is maturing as scholars wrestle with issues of terminology and analytical apertures. Work has also been hampered by methodological issues, leading to few case studies that can be usefully compared and contrasted. Ideally, scholars of transnational migration should employ methods that can detect and comprehend complex and vast activities and processes by conducting fieldwork simultaneously in several sites with different subject groups and over long time periods. The notion of conducting multisite investigations to document transnational relations is logistically and financially daunting; field-workers have been trained—and to a large degree continue to be trained—to stay in one place over a long period. An alternative, more feasible though less satisfy-ing methodology is to conduct research that spans the subject group's transnational social field sequentially, not simultaneously. This is the research strategy I employed, as described in detail below.

Theories: Short on Gender and Youth

For most of the 20th century, migrant women were consistently excluded as subjects in migration research overall (e.g., Berger & Mohr, 1975; Piore, 1979; Portes & Bach, 1985). In the 1970s, a corrective began to be applied, and female migrants were added as subjects of scholarly inquiry. In the past two decades, a multitude of studies have been published that focus on women's migratory experiences (cf. Donato, 1992; Mo-rokvasic, 1984; Ong, 1991). Yet overall, few empirical studies have treated gender as a central theoretical principle; rather, issues relating to gender—if considered at all—tended to be handled merely by adding sex as a variable (see Pedraza, 1991, p. 314). Recent scholarship has been careful to problematize gender as a central orga-nizing principle of migration, a focus long overdue (e.g., Georges, 1990, 1992; Gras-muck & Pessar, 1991; Guarnizo, 1997; Hagan, 1994; Hondagneu-Sotelo, 1994; Kib-ria, 1993).

In many ways, the emergence of transnationalism as a critical optic for con-ceptualizing migration mirrors the emergence of gender. Migration was (and con-tinues to be) gendered long before scholars perceived it as a fundamental axis; sim-ilarly, transnationalism itself is not completely new (see Foner, 1997; Guarnizo & Smith, 1998; Haus, 1995), yet the predominant doctrine of bipolar migration de-terred its detection and investigation. Now, with the benefit of hindsight, we can see how disregarding these approaches seriously weakened our comprehension of migration. Moreover, gender and transnationalism grow in importance as central theoretical principles in migration scholarship and as key characteristics of mi-gration change: for example, the rising magnitude and multitude of migrations, the increasing proportion of women migrating, and the access migrants have to rapid transportation, telecommunications, and other technologies that facilitate transnational processes.

Although the gender bias in migration studies has been identified and is being addressed in the transnational literature, very little attention has been given to the fact that research has overwhelmingly focused on adult migrants, with little regard paid to children and youth. There is an abundant literature on migrant children who are viewed as resettled in a second country (e.g., work on school achievement and second-generation identity) but not about children whose lives are transna-tional. Reference is often made to transnational households and the fact that chil-dren born in one country may be sent to their parents' homeland for vacation or even during childhood (e.g., Guarnizo, 1997; Ong, 1993; Wiltshire, 1992), but the parents' voices are reflected, not the children's. Smith's (1994) work on identity among Mexican youth in New York is a good start; however, much more effort needs to be poured into studying younger populations of migrants through a transnational lens. For example, what does it mean when a "local" beauty pageant is won in a town in El Salvador by a girl raised in Washington, D.C., and flown "home" for the occasion? This has occurred repeatedly in El Salvador, and such pageants are key rituals of small-town life. Children and youth are pelted by mass media images and sounds as they develop their identities and aspirations for the future. To my mind, they are the groups most likely to contemplate what Appadurai (1997) has termed "imagined worlds." Appadurai does not equate imagination with fantasy but sees the "imagination [as] central to all forms of agency" and as "the key component of the new global order" (p. 33). The question these assertions raise in my mind is how well does this model of imagination and imagining fit ethnography in sites where media and other transnational influences are readily evident? Recognizing that Salvadoran youth in northern La Unión are enveloped in such a site, I made them a focus of my most recent research. What transnational influences are shaping their understanding of gender? Moreover, do these children actively pursue imagined worlds, and if so, does this (and/or other forces) propel them into the migrant stream?

BACKGROUND AND RESEARCH METHOD

Since 1989, I have been researching this transnational social field, beginning with the first phase from 1989 to 1992 when I worked exclusively with migrants on Long Island, although I collected information about life in El Salvador, migrants' relations with their communities of origin, and detailed histories of their actual trips through Guatemala and Mexico and into the United States. A study of migrants' desires to return to El Salvador was conducted in 1993 shortly after the Salvadoran civil war ceased, and follow-up research with many migrants interviewed from 1989 to 1992 was conducted from 1994 to 1995; all work was performed on Long Island. Much of this research has already been published, detailing the demographics of this predominantly peasant migration, their reasons for migrating, incorporation into the suburban Long Island economy, daily life, and distinctiveness from other Salvadoran migrations to other regions of the United States (see Mahler, 1995a, 1995b).

Salvadorans living on Long Island are estimated to number 60,000 to 100,000, although the 1990 census enumerated only 19,000.[1] This group represents less than 10% of the total Salvadoran population in the United States; 50% is concentrated in the Los Angeles area alone (Wisberg, 1994). Salvadorans on Long Island are best characterized as a group distinct from the overall population. They hail largely from the eastern provinces of La Unión and Morazán, which are predominantly rural and agricultural; Salvadoran communities in other cities tend to be more representative of El Salvador's regions, social classes, and occupations (Chinchilla, Hamilton, & Loucky, 1993; Funkhouser, 1992; Hamilton & Chinchilla, 1991, p. 94; Rodríguez, 1987; see also Chavez, 1994; Lopez, Popkin, & Telles, 1996; Menjívar, 1993; Montes Mozo & Garcia Vásquez, 1988). The Salvadorans who now live on Long Island typically labored in their homeland as poor peasants, as day or permanent laborers on large farms, as seasonal laborers harvesting export commodities such as coffee, or as street vendors, or they performed a combination of these subsistence and wage labor strategies. Even when landless, the majority owned their own modest homes located in *caseríos*—small hamlets constituting several dozen households of kin related through blood or marriage. During the civil war, scorched-earth policies, forced recruitment, terror and torture, and the appropriation of crops and livestock by both the military and the insurgents destroyed people's livelihoods and forced many to flee for their lives to neighboring countries and to the United States (Mahler, 1995a). The vast majority of all Salvadorans, including those on Long Island, entered the United States illegally and were denied political asylum. Consequently, most have lived as illegal immigrants, and for many, their legal status remains tenuous.[2]

Oral histories of early migrants to Long Island indicate that Salvadorans first arrived there in a trickle during the 1960s when factory and domestic work was abundant. Although these earliest migrants hailed from El Salvador's middle classes, they sent word of economic opportunities on Long Island back to their communities of origin and provided key assistance to poorer peasant refugees fleeing the war years later. Long Island in the 1970s and 1980s enjoyed a robust economy with a growing manufacturing sector (as opposed to New York City's shrinking manufacturing base), as well as an expanding demand for low-cost service sector labor. In light of their low levels of formal education and few marketable skills owing to their peasant backgrounds, as well as their problematic legal status, Salvadorans have proven to be a vulnerable workforce yet one well suited to certain sectors of the Long Island economy. Men have found work as landscapers, dishwashers, busboys, and assistant cooks and jobs in light manufacturing and commercial cleaning; women work almost exclusively as domestics (child care and housecleaning) and alongside men in the factories. The recession of the late 1980s and early 1990s shrank the island's job market for the first time, but the economy rebounded in the mid-1990s. Regardless, according to my follow-up research, the employment picture of Salvadorans on Long Island has not changed dramatically. They constitute a large proportion of the island's poor, working class.

Transnational Ties: The View from Rural El Salvador

After the decade-long civil war ended, I began research within El Salvador. Following two preliminary trips, I decided to do concentrated research during the third trip in northern La Unión, owing to the fact that many migrants from this region had lived in two towns on Long Island that I had studied in depth. This facilitated entrée and access; indeed, I often encountered people I knew. Men frequently would walk up to me or drive by and beep their horns, stop, and say, "I remember you from Long Island. You used to hang out with us at the deli!" referring to a famous day labor shape-up point where men are informally recruited for jobs.

The area is rural, mountainous, and accessible from the rest of the country only by one rutted dirt road some 30 miles long that requires 3 to 4 hours to navigate. Only four telephone lines (two in each municipal seat) operated by the national telephone company serve a population of approximately 25,000. Electric service during the war was regularly cut; since the cease-fire in 1992, service has improved, though it is intermittent and limited to homesteads located within a half-mile radius of the road. The region is widely acknowledged by local as well as national leaders as forgotten by the Salvadoran state. Few government officials ever visit the area, Salvadorans from other regions consider it a backwater, and merchants from the nearest cities do not even deliver goods to the region, citing the horrible condition of the roads and concerns for general security. Needless to say, foreigners visiting the area are scarce; with the exception of a group of international evangelist puppeteers, a visit by Honduran teachers, and some U.S. Agency for International Development personnel, I and my research team (two women and one man) constituted the only international presence.

Given its rudimentary technological and transportation infrastructure and geopolitical marginalization, northern La Unión would seem as remote from the world economy as any place could be. But as one's transnational gaze comes into focus, the area teems with ties to the outside, to the United States, and to Long Island in particular: Couriers arrive from and depart to the United States daily with remittances and letters, visiting migrants and returnees drive around in vehicles with U.S. license plates, people sport T-shirts given to them by migrant relatives that read everything from "New York: The Big Apple" to "I scored a goal at Jeremy's Bar Mitzvah party."[3] The telephone company office is constantly jammed with customers calling overseas; workers stated that 95% of all calls made were to the United States. And although television is just arriving along with electricity after years of limited service during the civil war, almost everyone has a radio, and teenagers dance to a polyphonic mix of local *ranchera* (country), imported techno, and bilingual rap. Moreover, a survey we took of a random sample of the region's sixth to ninth graders revealed that 95% had relatives living in the United States—on average, six apiece—and nearly 70% of the students reported some family members living in New York State, which is by far the most traveled network. One third of these students' fathers were living in the United States and 10% of their mothers.

The most striking indicator of this migration, however, is the construction of new and brightly painted homes made of concrete block and tiled floors, as contrasted with those made of wattle and daub or adobe with dirt floors and that have no electricity. Such homes are telltale markers of migrant relatives and remittances. Detailed interviews with long-term residents of northern La Unión as well as with migrants document unequivocally that these transformations are financed with migrants' remittances. Prior to the civil war, the population in the region interfaced with the global economy only as marginal seasonal workers harvesting export crops such as coffee and cotton (Mahler, 1995a).

In the summer of 1997, my research team conducted intensive fieldwork in northern La Unión designed precisely to investigate and comprehend the importance and impact of transnational migration, practices, and processes on this area. It was the first time anyone had conducted research in this area. The investigative team lived in one town and observed daily life in the region for 2 months, making frequent visits to homesteads, markets, churches, community meetings, and festivals. Moreover, the research was designed to take a baseline snapshot of the region's youth, a cohort that would be followed longitudinally to study future migration (transnational as well as internal or regional). Data were collected from students attending the highest grades readily available in the area (few enjoy access to high school). Students' lives at school, at home, and in the community were observed daily over the course of 6 weeks. Interviews with teachers, school and local officials, and parents were also conducted during this stage. Subsequently, a random sample of one third of the student population in these grades was surveyed, yielding 229 interviews, including 105 boys and 124 girls. This "ethnosurvey" (see Mines, 1981) research was intended to identify and measure forces impinging on these youths' lives, forces that might incline them toward or away from migrating to the United States.

REPRODUCING AND TRANSFORMING GENDER

Data collected during the different phases of research cover a wide array of topics, but the focus of this article is an investigation of if and how gender relations have been affected by transnational factors. As cited above, Guarnizo and Smith (1998) argue that a "main concern guiding transnational research should be the study of the causes of transnationalism and the *effects that transnational practices and discourses have on preexisting power structures, identities, and social organization* [italics added]" (p. 27). I support this approach, particularly when transnational analysis is applied on multiple levels, for it offers a more nuanced and textured analysis of multiple agencies involved in social change. My research, however, has uncovered a problem likely to affect the implementation of this approach. The problem is that this comparative method requires a baseline, an understanding of preexisting power structures and so on. This can be a relatively low hurdle if a historical and/or ethnographic record exists and the principal question revolves around its accuracy. A higher hurdle is confronted when such a baseline is lacking—precisely the situation I encountered and one I speculate will shackle many scholars who wish to employ this historical comparative approach.

Attempting to Reconstruct a Baseline for Salvadoran Gender Relations

For many years while observing Salvadoran migrants and interviewing them about their work and family lives in El Salvador, I wondered if they felt gender relations had shifted in the United States and, if so, why. What I have found over the course of nearly a decade of research is that this question is dicey precisely because I lack an adequate baseline for comparison and because reconstructing a baseline ex post facto yields suggestive but far from conclusive data.

During my early research among Salvadorans on Long Island from 1989 to 1992, and particularly as I asked informants to compare their lives in El Salvador with life in the United States, I hypothesized that this group's near instantaneous insertion into a postindustrial suburban economy—given their rural, peasant origins—would most likely affect gender relations. More specifically, I suspected that the constellation of gender relations operative in these migrants' region in El Salvador would be reconfigured on Long Island. Central to this hypothesis was work histories. Men in the region, although principally small-time farmers, typically had worked as seasonal laborers to earn cash, or they sold some crops to buy fertilizers, health care, clothes, and other necessities. Most of the women I interviewed, on the other hand, had not worked for wages in El Salvador, although some had worked intermittently as vendors. For the majority, their first experiences as compensated workers occurred in the United States. Moreover, in El Salvador, they depended on their husbands to supply them with funds for household expenditures, and now they commanded their own. Overall, they expressed marked differences between their lives in El Salvador and life on Long Island. Margarita Flores's[4] response is characteristic of others' responses. "In El Salvador only the husband works," she explained to me.

> There the man is in charge and the wife has to do what her husband says. Even today this is the custom. Here [in the United States] no. Here I work, I earn money, and I help him pay the expenses as much as I can, but I do with my money what I want. I administer my money, not [my husband]. We help each other and share the expenses. But I administer my own money. It's different in El Salvador because there the husband gives the wife the money. And if the husband says it's okay to buy a dress then [the wife] buys it, but if it is too expensive then he won't let her. Here women are different. They're more liberal.

Margarita's words reflect her empowerment both as a productive worker and as a principal player in the disbursal of her wages.

When I interviewed men from the same region, their responses also highlighted the women's enhanced economic status and independence in the United States as compared with life in El Salvador. For example, Gilberto Canales explained that in the northern La Unión department where he lived, the wife "makes the food and she washes the laundry and does that by hand. . . . In El Salvador, the man works and he knows what's needed in the house. He knows what has to be bought in the market on Sundays." He then explained that men will buy what is needed or give enough money to their wives to buy goods but that he administers the finances. When I asked him whether this was also customary among Salvadorans in the United States, he said no.

If I had a wife here then she'd have to work here like me. Here the woman earns her money, and her husband has his money. That's convenient for each. If you have your money in your pocket then you're the owner. It's not the same if I'm waiting for you to give me money.

Although the information I gathered via exhaustive interviews with dozens of Salvadorans on Long Island yielded similar replies to my questions regarding gender relations in El Salvador and on Long Island, my sample size was neither large nor representative enough to be conclusive. I then turned to search the literature on El Salvador for information on traditional gender relations with the anticipation that this would aid my understanding of preexisting relations. Against this general baseline (i.e., not specific to northern La Unión), I could then evaluate the migrants' accounts and speculate on whether transnational migration had affected life in northern La Unión in gendered ways. What I found is that there is a paucity of information about gender relations in El Salvador, particularly from the prewar era—the time frame most pertinent to my study.[5] This fact severely encumbered my objective, for it is counterintuitive to believe that the war did not alter Salvadoran gender relations, and I had little data from my research that could help establish the effects of the war on gender relations in the region.

After several unsuccessful attempts to overcome the obstacles to an evaluation of transnational practices and discourses on preexisting gender relations for my case study, I decided to abandon the problematic historical approach to the issue in favor of a more synchronic view—but one that can become the baseline for future analyses. What follows is an examination of life in northern La Unión with a focus on gender relations and how they are reproduced, reconfigured, and contested by the practices and discourses of local, regional, and transnational agents. I will begin by sketching gender relations as they appear in daily life and then continue with details from the fieldwork regarding their negotiation.

Gender in Everyday Life in Northern La Unión

In this region, work, time, and space are profoundly gendered. Among the peasantry in the countryside, men with older boys plant and harvest corn and bean fields; they also tend livestock in the fields. Women remain at home most of the day preparing food, caring for the children, and tending the chickens and pigs that inhabit spaces around the home. Wives and older girls rise before everyone else to stoke the fire in the kitchen area of the home—usually a corner of the one- or two-room adobe structures characteristic of the area. They grind corn and make stacks of tortillas for the morning meal. The male workers rise about a half hour later and prepare themselves, the tools, and the horses or mules (if any) for their day in the fields. When ready, they are served breakfast and leave for most of the day, returning in the afternoon to be served lunch by the womenfolk. During a typical day, a woman will not venture more than 100 yards from her home unless she must go into town to buy goods or take a child to the health clinic. When traveling, women tend to walk in groups, almost always accompanied by other women and children; in contrast, men are more frequently observed traveling alone.

In the small towns where commercial and administrative life abounds, men and women appear to move about with equal freedom. But beneath this veneer, relations remain deeply gendered. The mayors[6] and their principal assistants (or *secretarios*) are men, whereas typists are women, and janitors are men. Indeed, men occupy all the official public positions of authority and represent the towns in most regional and national forums.

Public as well as private spaces in this region are deeply segregated along gender lines. I attended numerous religious services in Catholic and Evangelical churches. In each case, men and women sat apart to some degree. In the Catholic services, some men would sit with their families, but there was always a protective blanket of men hugging the walls on the sides or lining the pews and open spaces in the back near the entrance. Priests and laymen performed most of the masses, but women occasionally were permitted to read scripture or make announcements. Evangelical services were marked by even starker divisions. Men and women sat separately, period. Men preached; women did not. Men removed their hats on entering the sanctuary, whereas women covered their heads with white kerchiefs.

Gendered space was also the rule in most other public forums I attended, including those addressing civic matters and at schools. This division of space along gender lines extends into the marketplace as well. Men own the formal stores that sell comestibles, hardware, and pharmaceuticals (although tended by male and female kin), whereas women sell from makeshift stalls or from a spot on the ground. The men offer a variety of goods in their stores; the women *vendedoras* sell only one commodity—for example, tortillas, avocados, cheese, or freshly made *atol* (a corn-based beverage customary for breakfast). The men never made what they sold, and the women only sold what they had made.

Finally, the student survey revealed a striking disparity by sex in the region's migrant population. In each category of kinship, from parents to siblings to aunts and uncles, males significantly outnumber females. Overall, two thirds of the total population of migrants was male (917 of the 1,434 migrants). Records from the 1992 population census (República de El Salvador, Ministerio de Economia, 1995) substantiate the survey findings as they reveal a disproportionately low number of working-age men in the populace. And on Long Island, I found more Salvadoran men than women (Mahler, 1995a). These last statistics leave little room for doubt that in northern La Unión, far more men than women have emigrated, at least to the United States. Table 14.1 summarizes the survey figures.

The high level of male emigration in northern La Unión fits the profile of migration in the region driven by the civil-war-forced recruitment of males in particular—but differs from other studies on Salvadoran migration that have reported higher rates of female rather than male migrants.[7]

TABLE 14.1. Students' Reported Relatives in the United States

Relationship	Valid Cases	Missing Cases	Total	% of Total
Fathers	229	0	77	5
Brothers	224	5	225	16
Uncles	229	0	615	43
TOTAL males			917	64
Mothers	229	0	23	2
Sisters	229	0	77	5
Aunts	224	5	417	29
TOTAL females			517	36
TOTAL all relatives			1,434	100

The marked absence of men in northern La Unión has not translated, however, into many visible opportunities for women. Rather, women almost always occupy positions and statuses that are marginal to existing power structures. Indeed, what emerges most notably in this sketch of everyday life is profound gender segregation that mirrors migrants' recollections of gender relations years ago. Does this mean that gender relations have remained static in the intervening years (acknowledging the weaknesses of inferring from migrants' accounts)? No. Fieldwork from 1997 provides ample evidence that gender relations are being negotiated constantly. Certainly there are forces working toward continuity. At the same time, however, and often in the same spaces, traditional gender relations are being contested and perhaps reconfigured. What strikes me the most and what I shall detail in the pages to come is that local, regional (or national), and transnational forces are at work in both reproducing and reconfiguring these relations. Sometimes, two will operate in tandem, while the third will crosscut the others, yielding conflicting messages. I will provide three examples that should be viewed as illustrative and not exhaustive. These are (a) activities and structures in the schools, (b) return migrants and transnational families and households, and (c) transnational couriers.

Reproducing and Contesting Gender Relations in the Schools

The educational system is deeply gendered and promotes gendered ideologies via its institutional practices, yet it also serves as an agent of change. Teachers in the schools studied are overwhelmingly female, whereas the two superintendents and most of principals of the region's larger schools are male. Women become principals only in small, rural schools located in remote hamlets that are often an hour or more walking distance from the towns. For the most part, classes are coeducational, but during physical education hour, girls are sent off to play softball while the boys play soccer. In social studies discussions about gender, boys and girls agree that women should place motherhood first over careers and that men should be the principal providers for their families. Many textbook images reinforce these ideas.[8] Taken as a whole, these observations show that school is a key institution for reproducing gender relations as described above. Moreover, on Mondays students are required by national policy to spend their first hour of school reciting the national creed, singing the national anthem, and listening to the principals and fellow students speak about proper social and moral conduct—activities designated as Moral Hour. Moral Hour was instituted by the Salvadoran government in the postwar epoch to promote national unity, patriotism, and good citizenship. But the ritualized assemblies convey more than national identity. Gender is a prominent subtext. For example, during Moral Hour, students were observed standing at attention segregated by grade and by sex. Moreover, the creed they recite states, "I believe in God" and "I believe in the mother," but makes no reference to fathers or fatherhood.

At the same time that local schools and the school system as a whole appear to promote gender segregation, they also play activist roles in promoting change in their communities and in the nation, much of it with regard to gender relations. A case in point is the instructional and occupational structure of the school system. In the rural areas, students usually only have ready access to a few years of elementary school. If they complete these grades, they must travel longer and longer distances to larger hamlets and then to towns or cities to continue their education, particularly past ninth grade. Likewise, pedagogy is predicated on migration, particularly female migration. Teaching is one of the few professions numerically dominated by women, and in the countryside, as in northern La Unión, women are more likely than in the cities to constitute the schools' leadership as well. They become role models to students, so much so that most of the girls surveyed indicated they hoped to become schoolteachers. The teachers' impact is more complex, however. Training teachers requires migration and, inadvertently or not, promotes social change. That is, legions of schoolteachers hail from the countryside but are educated in the cities (where the only universities are). This transforms them into urban subjects who are then sent to the deepest backwaters, the only places where jobs are available, and rarely to the areas where they are from. Sporting high-heeled shoes and makeup, these women symbolize modernity to their pupils, and the children long for the imagined worlds their teachers—regional, not transnational, migrants—bring to their doorsteps. The teachers are very cognizant of their "civilizing" influence, as I learned by lunching with them regularly. I often heard them disparaging the small towns and their students as "backward," and I learned that these teachers saw preparing their students to live "cultured" lives as one of their principal responsibilities.

Perhaps their desires to bring El Salvador into the 21st century lay behind the zeal with which they prepared for and celebrated special days in the calendar such as Father's Day. National educational regulations dictate to the schools that they must observe Father's Day (as well as many other occasions, including Mother's Day and Independence Day), but the exact celebrations are prepared several days beforehand by teachers and students. In one school, fathers were invited to attend a special presentation. A small proportion of the total (about 40 fathers) arrived a few hours after the scheduled start, and I heard many of the teachers complain that this was "typical" of the fathers in the area—that they did not give much attention to school activities. The attendees were seated in the center of the open-air auditorium—the only time I saw men surrounded by women and children in a public forum. Once the program began, the audience of some 200 was entertained by several skits and lip-synched songs performed by students. The performers were overwhelmingly female; the male roles were almost invariably played by older girls dressed as men. The skits and songs generally dealt with the subject of fathers, most often depicting them as not being good providers for their children and often abandoning them. In a couple of the skits, absentee migrant fathers living in New York and Texas were the focus. Students sporting new jeans, baseball caps, and T-shirts sang about missing their fathers and the troubles of teens who have no one to discipline them. Punctuating the student performances were oral exhortations by the principal and teachers against the fathers, chastising them for paying too little attention to their children and entreating them not to abandon them. A large vertical banner placed at the front of the auditorium read, "Father: Thank you for giving me part of your time." The transnational image on the banner accentuated the ambiguity of the day: The promotional ad for Steve Martin's film *Parenthood* had been clipped from the newspaper and glued on. It featured Martin being kissed by wife and child—a positive image of fatherhood and of fathers as central to families. At the end of the celebration, teachers and students—all female—served the attendees lunch.

When I asked a few of the fathers how they had felt about the celebration, I invariably received the same answer, "It was good," with no further embellishment of opinion and no apparent rankling. The students and teachers expressed greater delight. With hindsight, it is easier to disentangle the various agents and levels of agency at work in this scenario, but the effects of their activities on gender relations in the region are not easily distilled. For instance, teachers and students interwove local, national, and transnational images of and discourses on fatherhood and especially absentee fathers into their performances but with no singular message. Migrant fathers were at once portrayed as good providers and poor disciplinarians. Local fathers were depicted as just as absent as the migrants but to an audience of nonabsentee fathers. What strikes me most in retrospect is how the event, despite its layered ambiguity, still managed to invert deeply seated gender relations simply by providing a forum in which the men were overwhelmingly cast as passive spectators, while children, especially females, were the actors.

A few days later, another school provided a forum for negotiating gender relations, but in this case the men would not remain passive. The setting was a large parent-teacher forum in a remote hamlet, which was called to discuss elements of the educational reform being implemented on a national level. Approximately 200 parents attended this meeting in July 1997; they were seated in a covered outdoor amphitheater. Of the 20 to 30 men present, all but the one male teacher clustered tightly against one side. The meeting was emceed by the school principal, a highly regarded woman from the region, and assisted by the mostly female faculty. As a preamble to the school meeting, two social workers from the Salvadoran equivalent of the Family Welfare Bureau made a presentation about new national legislation protecting children and wives from domestic abuse and the regional resources available to victims. As their presentation proceeded, the men remained silent but grew increasingly restless, until one burst out saying, "But women can abuse men too!" and was immediately greeted with a chorus of agreement from surrounding men. The social workers and this man debated briefly, after which some men began leaving but were cut off by a major rainstorm. The roar of the rain deafened the rest of the meeting, and there were no further outbursts. Afterward, several women told me how pleased they were with the event, particularly the social workers' presentation, because they had no prior information about their rights and recourses if abused. On the other hand, the men left the distinct impression that they were disgruntled with the day's events and probably less likely to attend the next meeting.

I address this scenario, as well as the Father's Day forum, because it illustrates how gender is being renegotiated in the absence of any observable transnational practices or discourses. I say "observable" because it is very possible that the Family Welfare Bureau receives funding and direction from abroad and because the region where this event took place is one profoundly linked to the United States transnationally. Regardless, the principal agencies represented in this event are local and national, not transnational. The example serves to illustrate the local as dynamic terrain, thereby underscoring other scholars' criticisms of theories that cast the local as static and the global as dynamic (see Guarnizo & Smith, 1998, p. 9). Furthermore, a key piece of the local dynamism lies within the structure of the school system itself—the ways in which students pursuing their education and teachers their profession promote migration and urbanization.

Return Migrants and Transnational Families and Households

If schools provide ambiguous messages about gender to youth growing up in northern La Unión—and schools are generally construed to be primary institutions of socialization—then the fact that transnational migration has opened up new spaces where gender relations are also not renegotiated uniformly may not come as a surprise. To begin this discussion, I will address one of the most striking facts emerging from research in El Salvador: Far more men than women return from the United States. Each day of field notes brims with examples of men who have returned, often repeatedly and even without permission to reenter the United States. Some of these men have stayed for years and claim they never wish to return to the United States. They can be termed, with some reservation, *permanent returnees*. But most others either travel back and forth with some regularity or desire to keep a

foothold in the United States at the very least. These individuals are better characterized as *recurrent migrants*. Conversely, in more than 2 months of field research,
I encountered only a half dozen documented cases of women who had returned
to El Salvador after a period of living in the United States and who were not returning for vacation. There is one exception to this rule, which is discussed in detail below; this exception is several women who work as remittance couriers, known
locally as *viajeros*. Notwithstanding the small corps of viajeras, return migration
appears deeply gendered at first blush. Was the ethnographic data biased against
returning women? Was there a sampling problem? Perhaps fewer women returnees
were being found merely because there were many fewer women who had migrated
in the first place. Still, the student survey indicated that hundreds of women had
gone, and I could find fewer than a dozen returnees.

The conundrum of the "missing" female return migrants led to explicit attempts
to find more by asking everyone if they knew of any other cases and also by asking if women did not return as often as the men. This approach resulted in identifying few new returnees, but it yielded very similar responses to the question. A
case in point is the conversation I had with two older men in town one day. Both
have several children in the United States. They responded to my inquiry by stat-
ing that women who migrated tended to be single; they marry in the United States
and have children. The men added, however, that women who already had children in the El Salvador were much more reluctant to leave them to migrate. This
latter point is substantiated by the student survey: Mothers are more than three
times less likely than fathers to have migrated. This figure, coupled with the ethnographic data collected on gender ideologies, imputes that women are socialized to
feel that their primary responsibility is to their children, wherever they may be.

Once again, the consistency of informants' responses still left me wondering if
other explanations had not been uncovered. Moreover, the student survey yielded
some information that might contradict the ethnographic suggestion that mothers
would stay close to their children. Data were collected among parents, siblings, and
other relatives on how frequently migrant relatives returned, but most consistently
from the first group. The responses were then coded as *never, few,* and *several.* The
survey sample of migrant mothers is small ($n = 23$), and no data on return migration was available for one mother, but still there is a marked difference in the *never*
responses between fathers and mothers. Of 77 migrant fathers, 39% had never returned versus 57% of the mothers. Why would mothers be less likely than fathers
to return if they were principally concerned with family welfare? The answer may
be located within the survey data itself. That is, of the 13 mothers who had never
returned, only one left her family with her husband: the others left their families
with grandparents or other relatives. Additionally, 8 of these 13 women's husbands
or *compañeros*[9] were also migrants, and most lived together in the United States. In
short, migrant women probably were discouraged against returning because they
either (a) had established new families in the United States with attendant responsibilities or (b) were principal breadwinners whose families depended too much on

their remittances for them to return. The latter point is supported by research among Salvadoran migrants in Los Angeles (Hondagneu-Sotelo & Avila, 1997).

Another factor deterring women from returning emerged from interviews with Salvadorans conducted in 1993 regarding the prospect that they would return following the end of the civil war. Continued danger and the likelihood of returning to economic dependence characterized the responses of these women. They feared returning to a precarious life in El Salvador, a country that has become the second most dangerous society in the world owing to a massive postwar crime wave ("Civil War Over," 1997). They also expressed fear about visiting El Salvador without permission to return legally to the United States.[10] Many had suffered tremendously during their first trips overland and would not repeat the experience (see Mahler, 1995a). Finally, some of these women expressed concerns about returning to El Salvador without means of supporting themselves, which they enjoyed in the United States. In contrast, men frequently stated they longed to return home to resume their occupations as small-time farmers. They added that during their absences their fields often lay fallow and became overgrown; their wives were not deemed strong enough to handle this work, and they were too busy raising the children. In other words, men can return to productive, highly self-sufficient lives, but there are few economic opportunities for women except vending food. Studies of other migrant groups support the hypothesis that women prefer settling in the United States and work toward that goal for several reasons, most notably because they fear they will become dependent on husbands if they return (e.g., Goldring, 1996; Hondagneu-Sotelo, 1994, 1995; Pessar, 1986).

How can the paucity of returning women versus the abundance of returning men be interpreted? Moreover, does this fact affect gender relations? If it does, then how? And particularly, how are youth in the area affected? My analysis of these questions is still preliminary, but there are several highly apparent trends that can be identified. First of all, returnees enjoy an exaggerated presence in northern La Unión. Although they could never be invisible in an area so tightly linked by kinship, they generally try to distinguish themselves from the rest by sporting U.S.-style clothing and building new homes equipped with the consumer adornments symbolizing migrant status: televisions, large radios, vehicles, and even microwave ovens. The fact that more men command these symbols and, moreover, are available to verbalize life in the United States to local audiences must have gendered impacts. To date, the greatest impact of the returnees that I have found is that boys experience more pressure from their relatives and friends to emigrate than girls do. This fact emerges from the survey data (given in the conclusion to the essay) and from informal conversations with students. Indeed, I have discovered that returnee men often correlate with emigrating boys. As a man prepares to return, he first sponsors the (legal or illegal) entry of at least one child—usually a son—who assumes the responsibility of remitting dollars to El Salvador in the father's absence.

The absence of hundreds of fathers/husbands in the region has had other measurable effects. In northern La Unión, department tradition dictates that in formal marriage or common-law unions (*acompañarse*), the wife is expected to move to the hamlet where the husband's family resides and, often, into her in-laws' home. An exception to this rule of patrilocal postmarital residence applies to youngest daughters, for they are expected to be the primary caretakers of their parents as the parents age. Consequently, when men migrate alone (the predominant pattern in this region), their wives are most often left behind in the company of the men's relatives. There are several benefits to the men's families that accompany this relationship. First of all, the wives bring their labor power with them. Women in this region spend several hours each day grinding and cooking corn to make tortillas. Girls begin to assume this and other chores before puberty, but when they marry, they move out, and their labor is lost. Daughters-in-law substitute but may prove fickle. A case in point is the Acevedo family. This aging couple had two daughters and four sons. All of the sons and the older daughter live in the United States. One of their sons is a courier. As these sons married, their spouses came to live in the Acevedo household, and each acquired a different reputation with Señora de Acevedo. This matriarch confided in me that her first son married a fine woman who worked hard and never complained. But she left several years ago when she obtained a green card and joined her husband. The next daughter-in-law arrived just when the first was leaving and still lives there. She is characterized as lazy. Whenever I visited the household, Antonia, the daughter-in-law, was always occupied in the kitchen, and when we took a short walk one day, she told me it was the first time she had left the house in weeks except to go to church services. Antonia was a big help to the Acevedos' younger daughter who lived nearby but had seven children of her own and a migrant spouse. Still, Antonia's mother- and sister-in-law complained that she was unworthy. Finally, when the Acevedos' courier son had a relationship resulting in a pregnancy, his "wife" joined the household. After only a few months, she returned with the baby to her parents' home a few miles away. This woman was deeply criticized by all the Acevedo women, who claimed that she never lifted a finger and, conversely, that she demanded to be served.

In a kinship system where mothers eventually "lose" their daughters and "gain" daughters-in-law, the latter's willingness to lighten the mother's workload is valued. There is yet another benefit when husbands are migrants—they leave with a great deal of confidence that their wives will be watched over by the migrants' kin. The term *watched over* is deliberately ambiguous. I intend to imply that both concern for the wives' welfare and vigilance over their sexual fidelity and adherence to other gender relations can be achieved this way. Several scholars who have studied families spanning other transnational social fields have published similar findings—that women stay-behinds are kept under the vigilant eye of their husbands' kin, reinforcing traditional gender relations (e.g., Alvarez, 1991; Georges, 1990, 1992; Goldring, 1996). These studies do not discuss rules of postmarital residence. When it is patrilocal, such as in the Salvadoran case, the effect appears to be accentuated. Aihwa Ong's (1993, 1995) research among transnational Chinese entrepreneurs and their families substantiates this claim. Male transmigrant capitalists, referred to as "astronauts," are constantly in orbit doing business, while their wives, who refer to themselves as "widows," live patrilocally but in foreign countries. These wives are expected to attend to their children's education and are forbidden from most income-generating activities that would take them away from their primary activities as wives and mothers. The women that Ong studied find themselves extremely isolated, in the sole company of their spouses' relatives, and sometimes abused without recourse.

Postmarital residence rules, like most cultural customs, are not always obeyed, and in my research I uncovered several such cases. Moreover, regardless of whether wives were left behind in the company of their spouses' kin, they were left with greater responsibilities. The Rios family's experience is common. The father, Bernardo Rios, fled the region during the civil war and went to Long Island, leaving his wife and 10 children behind. A year later, he aided his eldest son's migration, and 6 years later his second son arrived. At this point, there were no male kin remaining in the household, and Bernardo's wife, Maria, and her daughters planted some corn and beans but lived primarily from the remittances the men sent back from the United States. In 1995, Maria finally convinced Bernardo to return from the United States because the responsibilities of handling home and *milpa* (cornfield) were too taxing. He returned, but the family's economic situation deteriorated, so after a year he went back to the United States, leaving Maria in charge but with several grown daughters to help with the younger children. When I asked Maria and her elder daughters how they felt about the men leaving, they giggled at first and admitted that the transition was very hard in the beginning. However, after a time alone, they added, they grew accustomed to assuming "male" activities such as planting and harvesting and sometimes even enjoyed crossing gender lines. I received numerous similar responses from women with migrant husbands who were left managing households. These examples corroborate findings from comparative transnational research among Ecuadorans (Kyle, 1995) and Mexicans (Goldring, 1996), suggesting that in the long run abandonment can be empowering to at least some women. They may even translate this sense of autosufficiency into wider arenas of agency, such as deciding to migrate themselves and developing the necessary networks to do so even if unassisted by their spouses (e.g., Hondagneu-Sotelo, 1994). Conversely, women who migrate abroad do not saddle their husbands with domestic duties. Rather, survey data show that migrant women almost always leave their children with female kin.

Transnational Couriers

To this point, my discussion of the effects of transnational migration on existing gender relations in northern La Unión offers no uniform outcomes. As in the examination of the school system, different actors and levels of agency appear to operate in tandem to reproduce existing gender relations yet also complement each other to push gender along new trajectories. What strikes me as critical is to recognize the importance of the local context and not merely focus on the transnational. For example, transnational migration has not destroyed local customs of patrilocality but, in many instances, has reinforced them and the female subordination inherent in them. Where custom is disjunctive for whatever reason, and most likely for locally produced reasons, transnational migration can, but does not necessarily, produce quite the opposite outcome. Such is the case cited above of the households in which, over time, absentee fathers/husbands promoted greater autonomy among the women left behind. Each of these possibilities engages transnational migration as a player in the negotiation of gender in historically established spaces, namely, family and household structures. What happens when transnational migration creates new spaces?

Transnational migration has created multiple new spaces that offer a unique vantage point for addressing the effects of transnationalism on existent social relations and power structures. The space I am most familiar with is that occupied by transnational couriers, or viajeros. As relatively few Salvadorans have historically enjoyed the legal status to permit them to travel freely between El Salvador and the United States, those with legal status could step into a new and growing entrepreneurial space as couriers. Of the lucky few on Long Island, many have taken advantage of the opportunity and become couriers. They travel usually at least once a month, delivering remittances, letters, packages, and even larger items such as cars and televisions to recipients—often door-to-door. For their services, they receive a fee: normally 5% of the money they handle and $5 per pound for packages. They have carved their niche by satisfying migrants' needs but also as the fortuitous outcome of factors specific to El Salvador. That is, formal remittance agencies have operated for some time, providing similar services, but—at least until very recently—they did not provide services to small towns, owing to the riskiness of such deliveries during the civil war and the postwar crime wave. Consequently, recipients would have to travel long distances to large towns to receive their remittances, and they were often targeted by thieves. Couriers, in contrast, targeted the rural market, assuming the risk of theft and charging slightly more for their services than the formal agencies did.

Courier work is quite risky not only because large amounts of money are transported but also owing to conditions in El Salvador. During the decade-long civil war, the armed forces and antigovernment guerrillas routinely set up roadblocks and intercepted all ground traffic. Detained individuals were frequently recruited against their will, forced to pay bribes, or even kidnapped or killed. Following the war, a notorious crime wave hit, and couriers became choice targets for thieves. The work performed by couriers is demanding as well. Individuals travel by land or by air back and forth between countries, carrying hundreds of pounds of merchandise. Furthermore, they travel widely at each pole to serve their clients. Travel takes time away from families in both countries and can be physically exhausting.

The characteristics of the courier trade—constant travel away from home, financial and personal risks, physical stress, and so on—are traits that I associated with traditionally male occupations in El Salvador. Consequently, when I first began studying couriers and encountered only men, I was not surprised. However, when I received consistent reports from male and female couriers that at least one third, if not one half, of all viajeros are women, I began to explore this space as a possible site of gender relations transformation.

What I have discovered is that although the viajero space is gendered, evidence is ambiguous regarding an inherent transformative process. For example, there is a distinct gendered division of labor among couriers: women travel almost exclusively by plane and handle cash and small transactions (such as hand-carried packages), whereas men dominate the terrestrial side of the business, traveling from the United States through the isthmus with large cargoes of cars, equipment, and so on. However, I found that regardless of the sex of the courier, he or she is always supported by a complement of opposite-sex assistants. For example, until recently, Don Leopoldo Cáceres traveled to El Salvador from Long Island one and a half times per month, on average. Meanwhile, Don Leo's wife, son,[11] and female secretary would remain in El Salvador overseeing the office. Couriers usually return to the United States with Salvadoran products for sale, the most important of which is cheese. And when Leo was in El Salvador, his daughter remained on Long Island overseeing that office. On the other hand, when Doña Felicidad Menjívar travels, she is always met at the airport by male relatives who safeguard her arrival and help her deliver her wares. Felicidad's domestic responsibilities, however, are covered for her by her female kin while she is away. Felicidad's mother and aunt live with her on Long Island and oversee her household while she is away in El Salvador.

As I researched the courier business more ardently, I found that above and beyond the obvious building blocks of the trade—having the legal, financial, and social wherewithal to travel—there is a more important foundation: being perceived as trustworthy and enjoying extensive social ties. These are necessary to the building up of a clientele and to keeping it satisfied. These additional traits favor women. Over and over again I have been told that the best couriers are those who are trustworthy, who take their responsibilities seriously by delivering remittances immediately on arrival, and who do not place themselves in situations that might jeopardize the remittances that so many people depend on. More specifically, I am told that people trust older couriers and women in particular because they are less likely to get drunk on the plane or go out and party on arrival. Moreover, when I observed couriers interacting with clients, I paid keen attention to the intimate conversations I often heard—conversations about a client's mother or brother or about the most recent crop of corn. Female couriers likened their job to a social worker's, where much of their time is spent allaying clients' fears and buoying their spirits regarding family members whom they have not seen for years. It began to make sense to me that older women, generally past childbearing age or at least with older children, would have nurtured extensive networks of reciprocity for decades and that quite unintentionally these people later became an optimal clientele.

What effects, if any, have this new transnational space and the people who occupy it had on gender relations in northern La Unión? Is the transnational space one in which established gender relations are supplanted in favor of relations more characteristic of those in the places these couriers travel to? That is, are they transnational agents of change? Do they not affect gender at all? Or do they have some transformative effects but ones largely interfaced with and contingent on local relations? What I see to date is the latter; that is, couriers are key transnational institutions in this area precisely because they personalize the transnational. People on Long Island and in northern La Unión depend on couriers for their transnational ties, tangible and intangible. Their importance is accentuated by the lack of hometown associations, transnational political organizations, and adequate telecommunications services in this region. Courier work, thus, is a linchpin of this transnational social field—a relationship evident in the intensity of courier-client discourse.

The fact that the courier domain is shared nearly equally by men and women—given the extent of gender segregation elsewhere—marks a significant divergence from "normality" in northern La Unión. For a girl growing up in this region, the viajera represents the antithesis of most women's marginal lives. Moreover, viajeras represent a role model that the girl can aspire to, for they come from the same roots. Other role models, such as schoolteachers, are rarely indigenous. Nevertheless, viajeras achieve success largely by following quite traditional gender relations: by cultivating close personal relationships with networks of kin and friends and by working in tandem with a protective complement of males. Finally, these courier women exercise their profession at least in part because they enjoy adequate support systems to cover their familial responsibilities while they are away. Here, local customs of extended family households or at least networks of kin propinquity are enabling to the entrepreneurs. Similarly, Wiltshire (1992) has found many West Indian women working as transmigrant entrepreneurs, traveling back and forth to the United States bringing wares such as clothing to sell, who enjoy this liberty because they have female kin at home whom they can entrust with their domestic duties. In sum, the courier illustration indicates that transnational processes may produce new spaces, but this does not mean that actors within these spaces are set completely loose from their social moorings. The tether may be loosened, redirected, and perhaps frayed but not lost into an imaginary "third space" (Bhabha, 1990).

CONCLUSION

In this essay, I have examined the social reproduction and transformation of gender relations in the context of transnational ties linking Salvadorans on Long Island with several of their communities of origin. What I have found is that people's lives in northern La Unión are deeply segregated by gender and that, although I cannot prove it owing to an inadequate baseline for comparison, this segregation appears to be historically continuous. Simultaneously, they live enmeshed in a tight web of transnational ties that dazzle the observer: smugglers who advertise their trade unabashedly and continually on the airwaves, money changers who carry wads of dollars, return migrants who drive new pickups with Texas plates to their newly built homes, and children who shed their school uniforms for "I Love New York" and "Ocean Pacific" T-shirts. Can it possibly be that this mass migration and its evolution into a transnational social field transformed the landscape yet left a key component of local social organization intact? The answer to this question is most certainly no. As I have argued above, there are many sites where gender is being negotiated and contested. Obviously, the list discussed is not comprehensive, the work far from done.[12] What I have attempted to do is to push the transnational gaze deeper into the "stuff" of everyday life—into the dynamics of families and schools and meetings—to see if and how the transnational is affecting the processes of reproducing locality, with a particular eye to gender relations. I have found that transnational activities, discourses, and actors can be agents of change but so too can local and regional ones. And they often complement or crosscut each other; that is, change is not likely to be a univariate function. Furthermore, at the same time or in the same spaces that transnational forces can promote change, they also can help reproduce local, historically constructed social customs and power hierarchies. In the age of the global, the local is not superseded. Rather, I agree with Guarnizo and Smith (1998) when they argue that "the social construction of 'place' is still a process of local meaning-making, territorial specificity, juridical control, and economic development, however complexly articulated these localities become in transnational economic, political, and cultural flows" (p. 10).

If, despite global economic interdependence and mass media, among other large-scale forces, the world is not becoming one people with a singular global culture (e.g., Appadurai, 1997; Hannerz, 1987), then a key task for social scientists is to examine how people retain or construct distinctiveness in an interrelated world. Gupta and Ferguson (1992) characterize this as "exploring the processes of *production* of difference in a world of culturally, socially, and economically interconnected and interdependent spaces" (p. 14). I have employed this optic in this essay. The data I marshal to support the interplay of the transnational with other levels of social agency is one of highly synchronic, albeit thick, description. In lieu of a historical baseline, I began one by surveying the youth, a group that has grown up with transnationalism. To what degree, I wondered, will the future life trajectories of these youth reflect, fortify, transform, and/or disregard these ties? And what other axes, such as gender, will be important? Students were asked a variety of questions regarding their future aspirations, including whether they wished to migrate to the United States, which social and capital resources they and their families enjoyed, and what obstacles to realizing their aspirations that they anticipated. At this time, data analysis is not complete, but the portraits painted by answers to several basic questions are striking, particularly with regard to issues of gender.

For example, students selected at random[13] were asked, "Are you considering or have you ever considered emigrating to the United States?" Chi-square analyses by sex showed no significant differences in responses ($p = .203$). For both groups, the proportions were approximately two thirds contemplating emigration and one third not. Furthermore, there was no significant change in these proportions by grade. From the sixth through the ninth grade, students held similar ideas. These findings are striking despite their similarity. Although the findings do not report a gendered effect, they are still provocative. Girls express as much eagerness as boys do despite the fact that they have many fewer female migrant role models (i.e., migrant female kin). Furthermore, the fact that the vast majority contemplate emigration, despite the fact that the civil war has been over for many years and the national economy as a whole has been quite stable, indicates that migration may have become a way of life in less than a generation. Formal and informal discussions with the youth indicate that they see little opportunity for themselves in their local areas unless they aspire only to peasant life. Even then, many conceded that they would have to migrate to earn enough money to buy land and build homes— the essential components for this lifestyle and ones they generally lacked. Most of these students had little or no access to television and the media images of faraway places, but they were surrounded by the trappings of transnational migration: return migrants, remittance-funded homes, flashy cars, and so on. Their imagined worlds were not telecommunicated but incarnate. To "keep up with the Joneses," they knew they had to migrate—at least to the cities, if not abroad.

Boys and girls overwhelmingly contemplate emigration, but will they emigrate in equal numbers? The answer will not be forthcoming for many years and is likely to involve a complicated algorithm. However, there are two indicators available in the survey that may help predict the answer. The students were asked about how many relatives they had in the United States and if they had ever been encouraged by anyone to migrate to the United States. The latter question was statistically significant by sex. Boys were almost equally split between those who had been offered aid and those who had not. Contrarily, only one third of girls expressed having been offered aid. Chi-square tests between the two groups in this case proved significant ($\chi^2 = 4.334$, $df = 1$, $p = .037$). However, when an analysis of their migrant kin was performed, boys and girls enjoyed similarly sized networks. The average number of migrant kin for boys was 6.58 ($SD = 5.26$) versus 6.08 ($SD = 4.34$) for girls. When compared, these means did not prove statistically different ($t = .789$, $df = 227$, $p = .431$).

To summarize these findings and their relationship to future migration, I can state the following: Northern La Unión is likely to continue its legacy of emigration to the United States. Most teenagers—regardless of sex—who are attending school in the area express a desire to emigrate and have access to networks of migrant kin who might assist them. Boys appear to receive more pressure than girls to emigrate, but this difference does not seem to have translated into more desire. If many students act according to their stated desires, the profile of the region's emigrant population is likely to shift toward a more even distribution of migrants by sex. Moreover, even if students do not emigrate, they are likely, really forced, to migrate to the more urban areas to pursue education and jobs—moves financed in large part by remittances. In sum, this region of El Salvador is in the process of shifting demographics that undoubtedly will have an impact. Will all this affect traditional gender relations in the region? I have little doubt, but I am not sure how. If much of the area's educated youth leave and few return—especially females—then gender segregation and male dominance seem likely to continue and perhaps become more pronounced. If many return, I predict a greater transformation. The future will tell.

NOTES

1. This estimate is based on information received from local service organizations. The 1990 census counted 19,152 Salvadorans. In an alternate enumeration that I conducted in a Salvadoran neighborhood on Long Island, I found an extremely high undercount on the order of 80% (see Mahler, 1993) due largely to unusual housing arrangements. In my opinion, more than 20,000 Salvadorans are resident on Long Island, but there is no way of obtaining an exact number, so I have selected the low-end estimate of those often cited by organizations.

2. For political and historical reasons, Salvadorans have had a difficult time securing legal status in the United States. That is, although nearly all Salvadorans migrated to the United States during El Salvador's civil war, they were systematically denied refugee or asylum status by the U.S. government through the 1980s. During 1987–1988, close to 150,000 obtained legal status (green cards) through a legalization program (only 4,000 on Long Island received these, however). During the 1980s and 1990s, approximately another 150,000 obtained green cards through other legal channels, but the majority continued to live precariously throughout the nation as undocumented immigrants (lacking authorization to work) until at least 1991. In that year and under considerable pressure from litigation, the U.S. government allowed Salvadorans to apply for temporary protected status, which permitted applicants to stay and work for a limited time period, ending in September of 1995. At this point, they were permitted several more months to file political asylum applications under a more equitable asylum system—but with little chance of winning their petitions owing to the fact that the civil war had ceased years ago. In 1996, the Immigration and Naturalization Service began to adjudicate these applications, resulting in denials and orders for repatriation. Finally, in November of 1997, the U.S. government agreed to allow certain Salvadorans (residency requirements applied) to obtain green cards via a procedure that had been restricted for them. Many still remain in legal limbo, however.

3. The information on this T-shirt has been slightly altered to protect the identity of the celebrants.

4. All informants' names have been changed to protect their identities.

5. Of the few studies published in the United States (e.g., Carter, Insko, Loeb, & Tobias, 1989; Nieves, 1979), the research focused on women in urban areas. These studies report high numbers of urban households as headed by women. Nieves (1979) studied urban households in the country's capital during the mid-1970s, just before the onset of the war. She found that 20% of the households were headed by women and had "no regularly present male in the role of husband/father" (p. 137). One third of women in the sample earned income, a figure that contrasts with a government report on rural women citing only 10%. Carter and colleagues (1989) argue that during the civil war many men fled the country such that the number of female-headed families in San Salvador, the nation's capital, surpassed

the 40% figure cited in a 1978 United Nations study (p. 27). Hoping to supplement the dearth of publications available in the United States that contained information relevant to Salvadoran gender relations, I canvassed women's organizations and universities in El Salvador, searching for additional information. Fortunately, a comprehensive bibliography of publications on women in El Salvador from 1902 to 1994 was published in 1995 (Herrera, 1995). Unfortunately, only a small percentage of these materials were published before the war, and of those, few were obtainable and contained useful information. One treatise documents the history of Salvadoran law regarding men's, women's, and children's rights; marital issues; infidelity; abortion; and other family law matters. This document is quite revealing. For example, in the constitution of 1860, Article 162 reads, "The husband must protect his wife and the wife must obey her husband" (Cisneros, 1976, p. 55). Moreover, from 1904 through 1973, a man who murdered his wife if he caught her in an adulterous relationship would receive a prison sentence of only 6 months, whereas in the reverse case, the wife would receive at least the minimum sentence for homicide, 25 years (Cisneros, 1976, p. 71). There have been changes in Salvadoran law nullifying this statute, but it serves as a clear indicator of patriarchy in prewar El Salvador. One report published during the war provides eight interviews with rural women in several departments (PNUD/FAO/MAG, 1989). The interviews document varying economic strategies employed by women who must generate income for their households. They also show that despite earning some income, a very strong gendered division of labor was the norm. One quotation from a woman named Rosa from Morazán is particularly exemplary: "Women are weaker than men because they don't work outside in the sun like the men do [a reference to agricultural work]. They only work inside. Men work harder and are stronger" (interview 2.9; my translation). This quotation is consistent with the other information available that has been published in El Salvador and the United States, with the exception of numerous publications regarding women's involvement as combatants with the guerrillas during the war (cf. Herrera, 1995). These latter publications suggest that major transformations in gender relations occurred during the war at least among the guerrillas and that these have had effects in the wider society.

6. Both towns have had women mayors over the years, but, to my knowledge, only one per town, so that the standard pattern is one of male governance.

7. For example, in their study of a town in Usulatán department, Lungo, Eckhoff, and Baires (1996) report more emigrant women than men. Repak (1995) highlights the high number of women migrants in her study of Salvadorans in Washington, D.C. U.S. census data on the Salvadoran population nationally in 1990 found nearly equal numbers of men and women. And in a study conducted in San Francisco, figures for males and females were also nearly identical (Menjívar, 1993).

8. A new kindergarten series funded by the U.S. Agency for International Development was developed to counter the prevailing images of domestic females and working males in existing national texts. Similar texts for other grade levels are in production.

9. Consensual unions (acompañarse) are as common as formal marriages, especially among younger and poor couples (see United Nations Population Fund, 1994, p. 13). (This is not true among evangelical Christians, at least in the study area.) So it is inaccurate to assume that these men are the married spouses of the migrant women. However, they are the fathers of the children who reported their mothers as migrants who have never returned.

10. Lack of legal status as a variable influencing return migration is supported by the survey data. All 13 mothers who had never returned to El Salvador lacked green cards.

11. Don Leo's son began traveling himself in the 1990s to learn the business and to relieve his father. At the end of 1996, however, his commercial visa was canceled.

12. I readily acknowledge that this article does not engage similar questions in the context of Long Island. In other publications (cf. Mahler, 1995a, 1995b), I have at least addressed these questions, although not in the same detail. However, such a project would far exceed the scope of this essay and remains for another day.

13. The male student population was slightly oversampled to correct for their higher attrition in some schools. In one case, only 2 boys were present in a class of more than 20 students. Both boys were included in the sample. Also, samples were drawn from each grade according to its percentage of the entire population.

REFERENCES

Alvarez, J. (1991). *How the Garcia girls lost their accents*. Chapel Hill, NC: Algonquin.

Appadurai, A. (1997). *Modernity at large: Cultural dimensions of globalization*. Minneapolis: University of Minnesota Press.

Basch, L., Schiller, N. G., & Szanton Blanc, C. (1994). *Nations unbound: Transnational projects, postcolonial predicaments, and deterritorialized nation-states*. Amsterdam: Gordon & Breach.

Berger, J., & Mohr, J. (1975). *A seventh man: The story of a migrant worker in Europe*. Harmondsworth, UK: Penguin.

Bhabha, H. K. (1990). DissemiNation: Time, narrative, and the margins of the modern nation. In H. K. Bhabha (Ed.), *Nation and narration* (pp. 291–322). New York: Routledge.

Carter, B., Insko, K., Loeb, D., & Tobias, M. (1989). *A dream compels us: Voices of Salvadoran women*. Boston: South End.

Chavez, L. R. (1994). The power of the imagined community: The settlement of undocumented Mexicans and Central Americans in the United States. *American Anthropologist, 96*(1), 52–73.

Chinchilla, N., Hamilton, N., & Loucky, J. (1993). Central Americans in Los Angeles: An immigrant community in transition. In J. Moore & R. Pinderhughes (Eds.), *The barrios: Latinos and the underclass debate* (pp. 51–78). New York: Russell Sage Foundation.

Cisneros, R. J. (1976). *Condición jurídica de la mujer Salvadoreña* [The legal predicament of Salvadoran women] (Monograph prepared for the Law and Population School of the Fletcher School of Law and Diplomacy, Harvard University and Tufts University). San Salvador, El Salvador: Salvadoran Demographic Association.

Civil war over, but violence goes on. (1997, August 4). *Miami Herald*, p. 1.

Donato, K. M. (1992). Understanding U.S. immigration: Why some countries send women and others send men. In D. Gabaccia (Ed.), *Seeking common ground: Multidisciplinary studies of immigrant women in the United States*. Westport, CT: Greenwood.

Foner, N. (1997, February). *What's new about transnationalism? New York immigrants today and at the turn of the century*. Paper presented at the Transnational Communities and the Political Economy of New York in the 1990s conference, New School for Social Research, New York.

Funkhouser, E. (1992). Mass emigration, remittances, and economic adjustment: The case of El Salvador in the 1980s. In G. J. Borjas & R. B. Freeman (Eds.), *Immigration and the work force*. Chicago: Chicago University Press.

Georges, E. (1990). *The making of a transnational community: Migration, development, and cultural change in the Dominican Republic.* New York: Columbia University Press.

Georges, E. (1992). Gender, class, and migration in the Dominican Republic: Women's experiences in a transnational community. In N. Glick Schiller, L. Basch, & C. Blanc-Szanton (Eds.), *Towards a transnational perspective on migration: Race, class, ethnicity, and nationalism reconsidered* (Annals of the New York Academy of Sciences, Vol. 645, pp. 81–99). New York: New York Academy of Sciences.

Goldring, L. (1996). Gendered memory: Constructions of rurality among Mexican transnational migrants. In E. M. DuPuis & P. Vandergeest (Eds.), *Creating the countryside: The politics of rural and environmental discourse* (pp. 303–329). Philadelphia: Temple University Press.

Grasmuck, S., & Pessar, P. (1991). *Between two islands: Dominican international migration.* Berkeley & Los Angeles: University of California Press.

Guarnizo, L. E. (1997). Social transformation and the mirage of return migration among Dominican transmigrants. *Identities, 4*(2), 281–322.

Guarnizo, L. E., & Smith, M. P. (1998). The locations of transnationalism. In M. P. Smith & L. E. Guarnizo (Eds.), *Transnationalism from below: Social transformation and the mirage of return immigration among Dominican transmigrants* (pp. 3–34). New Brunswick, NJ: Transaction Publishers.

Gupta, A., & Ferguson, J. (1992). Beyond "culture": Space, identity, and the politics of difference. *Cultural Anthropology, 7*(1), 6–23.

Hagan, J. M. (1994). *Deciding to be legal: A Maya community in Houston.* Philadelphia: Temple University Press.

Hamilton, N., & Chinchilla, N. S. (1991). Central American migration: A framework for analysis. *Latin American Research Review, 26*(1), 75–110.

Hannerz, U. (1987). The world Creolisation. *Africa, 57*(4), 546–558.

Haus, L. (1995, May). *Integrated issues: Migration and international economic dependence.* Paper presented at the Transnational Realities and Nation States: Trends in Migration and Immigration Policy in the Americas conference, the North/South Center, University of Miami, FL.

Herrera, M. (1995). *Bibliografía sobre mujer en El Salvador (1902–1994)* [Bibliography of women in El Salvador from 1902–1994]. San Salvador, El Salvador: Colección CEMUJER.

Hondagneu-Sotelo, P. (1994). *Gendered transitions: Mexican experiences of immigration.* Berkeley & Los Angeles: University of California Press.

Hondagneu-Sotelo, P. (1995). Beyond "the longer they stay" (and say they will stay): Women and Mexican immigrant settlement. *Qualitative Sociology, 18*(1), 21–42.

Hondagneu-Sotelo, P., & Avila, E. (1997). "I'm here, but I'm there": The meanings of Latina transnational motherhood. *Gender and Society, 11*(5), 548–571.

Kearney, M. (1995). The local and the global: The anthropology of globalization and transnationalism. *Annual Review of Anthropology, 24,* 547–565.

Kibria, N. (1993). *Family tightrope: The changing lives of Vietnamese Americans.* Princeton, NJ: Princeton University Press.

Kyle, D. (1995). *The transnational peasant: The social structures of economic migration from the Ecuadoran Andes.* Unpublished doctoral dissertation, Department of Sociology, Johns Hopkins University.

Lopez, D. E., Popkin, E., & Telles, E. (1996). Central Americans: At the bottom, struggling to get ahead. In R. Waldinger & M. Bozorgmehr (Eds.), *Ethnic Los Angeles* (pp. 279–304). New York: Russell Sage Foundation.

Lungo, M., Eckhoff, K., & Baires, S. (1996). *Migración internacional y desarrollo local en El Salvador* [International migration and local development in El Salvador]. San Salvador, El Salvador: FUNDE.

Mahler, S. J. (1993). *Alternative enumeration of undocumented Salvadorans on Long Island* (Final Report for the Joint Statistical Agreement 89–46). Washington, DC: U.S. Bureau of the Census.

Mahler, S. J. (1995a). *American dreaming: Immigrant life on the margins.* Princeton, NJ: Princeton University Press.

Mahler, S. J. (1995b). *Salvadorans in suburbia: Symbiosis and conflict.* Boston: Allyn & Bacon.

Mahler, S. J. (1996). *Bringing gender to a transnational focus: Theoretical and empirical ideas.* Unpublished manuscript, Department of Anthropology, University of Vermont, Burlington.

Mahler, S. J. (1998). Theoretical and empirical contributions toward a research agenda for transnationalism. In L. E. Guarnizo & M. P. Smith (Eds.), *Transnationalism from below* (pp. 64–100). New Brunswick, NJ: Transaction Publishers.

Menjívar, C. (1993). History, economy, and politics: Macro and micro-level factors in recent Salvadorean migration to the US. *Journal of Refugee Studies, 6*(4), 350–371.

Mines, R. (1981). *Developing a community tradition of migration: A field study in rural Zacatecas, Mexico, and California settlement areas* (Research Monograph No. 3). La Jolla: Center for U.S.-Mexico Studies, University of California at San Diego.

Montes Mozo, S., & Garcia Vásquez, J. (1988). *Salvadoran migration to the United States: An exploratory study.* Washington, DC: Hemispheric Migration Project, Center for Immigration Policy and Refugee Assistance, Georgetown University.

Morokvasic. M. (1984). Birds of passage are also women. *International Migration Review, 18*(4), 886–907.

Nieves, I. (1979). Household arrangements and multiple jobs in San Salvador. *Signs, 5*(1), 134–142.

Ong, A. (1991). The gender of labor politics and postmodernity. *Annual Review of Anthropology, 20,* 279–309.

Ong, A. (1993). On the edge of empires: Flexible citizenship among Chinese in diaspora. *Positions, 1*(3), 745–778.

Ong, A. (1995). Introduction. In A. Ong & M. G. Peletz (Eds.), *Bewitching women, pious men: Gender and body politics in Southeast Asia.* Berkeley & Los Angeles: University of California Press.

Pedraza, S. (1991). Women and migration: The social consequences of gender. *Annual Review of Sociology, 17,* 303–325.

Pessar, P. (1986). The role of gender in Dominican settlement in the United States. In J. Nash & H. Safa (Eds.), *Women and change in Latin America* (pp. 173–194). South Hadley, MA: Bergin & Garvey.

Piore, M. J. (1979). *Birds of passage: Migrant labor and industrial societies.* Cambridge, UK: Cambridge University Press.

PNUD/FAO/MAG. (1989). *Ocho entrevistas a mujeres campesinas* [Eight interviews with peasant women]. (Working Document, Project ELS/86/007, Incorporacion de la Mujer Campesina al Desarrollo de Pequeños Proyectos Productivos). San Salvador, El Salvador: Author.

Portes, A., & Bach, R. (1985). *Latin journey: Cuban and Mexican immigrants in the United States.* Berkeley & Los Angeles: University of California Press.

Repak, T. (1995). *Waiting on Washington: Central American workers in the nation's capital.* Philadelphia: Temple University Press.

República de El Salvador, Ministerio de Economia. (1995). *Censos nacionales V de poblacion y IV de vivienda 1992* [1992 Census of Population and Housing] (Vol. 14). San Salvador, El Salvador: Direccion General de Estadistica y Censos.

Rodríguez, N. P. (1987). Undocumented Central Americans in Houston: Diverse populations. *International Migration Review, 21*(1), 4–26.

Rouse, R. (1992). Making sense of settlement: Class transformation, cultural struggle, and transnationalism among Mexican migrants in the United States. In N. Glick Schiller, L. Basch, & C. Blanc-Szanton (Eds.), *Towards a transnational perspective on migration: Race, class, ethnicity, and nationalism reconsidered* (Annals of the New York Academy of Sciences, Vol. 645, pp. 25–52). New York: New York Academy of Sciences.

Schiller, N. Glick, Basch, L., & Blanc-Szanton, C. (Eds.). (1992). *Towards a transnational perspective on migration: Race, class, ethnicity, and nationalism reconsidered* (Annals of the New York Academy of Sciences, Vol. 645). New York: New York Academy of Sciences.

Smith, R. C. (1994). *Los ausentes siempre presentes: The imaging, making, and politics of transnational communities between the U.S. and Mexico.* Unpublished doctoral dissertation, Department of Political Science, Columbia University.

United Nations Population Fund. (1994). *Investigación diagnóstico sobre la situación de la mujer de los sectores populares, urbano y rural* [Diagnostic investigation of the situation of women of the popular sectors, urban and rural]. San Salvador, El Salvador: Author.

Wiltshire, R. (1992). Implications of transnational migration for nationalism: The Caribbean example. In N. Glick Schiller, L. Basch, & C. Blanc-Szanton (Eds.), *Towards a transnational perspective on migration: Race, class, ethnicity, and nationalism reconsidered* (Annals of the New York Academy of Sciences, Vol. 645, pp. 175–187). New York: New York Academy of Sciences.

Wisberg, M. (1994, February). Specific Hispanics. *American Demographics,* pp. 44–49.

CHAPTER 15

"I'm Here, but I'm There"

The Meanings of Latina Transnational Motherhood

Pierrette Hondagneu-Sotelo and Ernestine Avila

While mothering is generally understood as practice that involves the preservation, nurturance, and training of children for adult life (Ruddick, 1989), there are many contemporary variants distinguished by race, class, and culture (Collins, 1994; Dill, 1988, 1994; Glenn, 1994). Latina immigrant women who work and reside in the United States while their children remain in their countries of origin constitute one variation in the organizational arrangements, meanings, and priorities of motherhood. We call this arrangement "transnational motherhood," and we explore how the meanings of motherhood are rearranged to accommodate these spatial and temporal separations. In the United States, there is a long legacy of Caribbean women and African American women from the South leaving their children "back home" to seek work in the North. Since the early 1980s, thousands of Central American women and increasing numbers of Mexican women have migrated to the United States in search of jobs, many of them leaving their children behind with grandmothers, with other female kin, with the children's fathers, and sometimes with paid caregivers. In some cases, the separations of time and distance are substantial; 10 years may elapse before women are reunited with their children. In this chapter we confine our analysis to Latina transnational mothers currently employed in Los Angeles in paid domestic work, one of the most gendered and racialized occupations.[1] We examine how their meanings of motherhood shift in relation to the structures of late 20th-century global capitalism.

Motherhood is not biologically predetermined in any fixed way but is historically and socially constructed. Many factors set the stage for transnational motherhood. These factors include labor demand for Latina immigrant women in the United States, particularly in paid domestic work; civil war, national economic crises, and particular development strategies, along with tenuous and scarce job opportunities for women and men in Mexico and Central America; and the subsequent increasing numbers of female-headed households (although many transnational mothers are married). More

317

interesting to us than the macro determinants of transnational motherhood, however, is the forging of new arrangements and meanings of motherhood.

Central American and Mexican women who leave their young children "back home" and come to the United States in search of employment are in the process of actively, if not voluntarily, building alternative constructions of motherhood. Transnational motherhood contradicts both dominant U.S., White, middle-class models of motherhood and most Latina ideological notions of motherhood. At the beginning of the 21st century, transnational mothers and their families are blazing new terrain, spanning national borders, and improvising strategies for mothering. It is a brave odyssey, but one with deep costs.

IMMIGRATION: GENDERING TRANSNATIONAL PERSPECTIVES

We pursue this project by drawing from, and engaging in, dialogue with literature on immigration and transnational frameworks; family and motherhood; and women's work, place, and space. The last decade has witnessed the emergence of transnational perspectives of migration. Emerging primarily from postcolonial, postmodern-inspired anthropology, and explicitly challenging the linear, bipolar model of "old country" and "new world," of "sojourner" and "settler" that is typical of assimilationist models and other well-established immigration paradigms, transnationalist proponents argue that the international circulation of people, goods, and ideas creates new transnational cultures, identities, and community spheres (Basch, Schiller, & Szanton Blanc, 1994; Kearney, 1995; Rouse, 1991). Accordingly, these fluid entities become semiautonomous spheres in their own right, transcending national borders. The new emergent cultures and hybrid ways of life resemble neither those in the place of origin nor the place of destination.

Although we welcome these insights, we raise three objections to the transnational perspective. First, we object to transnationalism's emphasis on circulation and the indeterminance of settlement. While significant segments of foreign-born Latinos regularly return to their countries for annual fiestas or to visit family members, most Latino immigrants are here to stay, regardless of their initial migration intentions. Most Latina/o immigrant workers in California are not working in industries with seasonal labor demand—agriculture employs only a small fraction of Mexicans, for example—but in urban-based jobs requiring stability of employment.[2] A glance at cities, suburbs, and rural areas around California testifies to the demographic transformation, as new Latina/o communities have emerged in neighborhoods that were previously African American or White. While some of the Latina/o residents in these diaspora communities are involved in transnational political organizations and hometown associations, many more are involved in activities and organizations firmly rooted in the United States—with local Catholic parishes or storefront Evangelical churches, parent-teacher associations (PTAs) and schools, or workplace associations. Transnationalism emphasizes the ephemeral circuits and understates the permanency of Latina/o settlement.

The celebratory nature of the transnational perspective merits caution. In some of the writings, it is almost as if "resistance" is suggested merely through movement across borders and by the formation of circuits, which enhance the possibility of survival in places full of uncertainty. In these renditions, the power of the nation-state is often underestimated, and the costs—financial, social, and emotional—to the individuals involved in transnational migration may be overlooked.

A final objection to the transnational perspective is the assumption of genderless transnational migrants. In recent years, literature on women and migration has flourished (Pedraza, 1991; Tienda & Booth, 1991), but many studies that do look at women in migration—especially those informed by demography—examine gender as a variable rather than as a construct that organizes social life. With the exception of Mahler's (1996) recent work, transnationalism, like the assimilationist models that it counters, ignores gender altogether. Examining transnational motherhood, defined not as physical circuits of migration but as the circuits of affection, caring, and financial support that transcend national borders, provides an opportunity to gender views of transnationalism and immigration.

RETHINKING MOTHERHOOD

Feminist scholarship has long challenged monolithic notions of family and motherhood that relegate women to the domestic arena of private/public dichotomies and that rely on the ideological conflation of family, woman, reproduction, and nurturance (Collier & Yanagisako, 1987, p. 36).[3] "Rethinking the family" prompts the rethinking of motherhood (Glenn, 1994; Thorne & Yalom, 1992), allowing us to see that the glorification and exaltation of isolationist, privatized mothering is historically and culturally specific.

The "cult of domesticity" is a cultural variant of motherhood, one made possible by the industrial revolution, by breadwinner husbands who have access to employers who pay a "family wage," and by particular configurations of global and national socioeconomic and racial inequalities. Working-class women of color in the United States have rarely had access to the economic security that permits a biological mother to be the only one exclusively involved with mothering during the children's early years (Collins, 1994; Dill, 1988, 1994; Glenn, 1994). As Evelyn Nakano Glenn puts it, "Mothering is not just gendered, but also racialized" (1994, p. 7) and differentiated by class. Both historically and in the contemporary period, women lacking the resources that allow for exclusive, full-time, round-the-clock mothering rely on various arrangements to care for children. Sharing mothering responsibilities with female kin and friends as "other mothers" (Collins, 1991), by "kin-scription" (Stack & Burton, 1994), or by hiring child care (Uttal, 1996) are widely used alternatives.

Women of color have always worked. Yet, many working women, including Latina women, hold the cultural prescription of solo mothering in the home as an ideal. We believe this ideal is disseminated through cultural institutions of industrialization and urbanization, as well as from preindustrial, rural peasant arrangements that allow for women to work while tending to their children. It is not only White, middle-class ideology but also strong Latina/o traditions, cultural practices, and ideals—Catholicism, and the Virgin Madonna figure—that cast employment as oppositional to mothering. Cultural symbols that model maternal femininity, such as the Virgen de Guadalupe, and negative femininity, such as La Llorona and La Malinche, serve to control Mexican and Chicana women's conduct by prescribing idealized visions of motherhood.[4]

Culture, however, does not deterministically dictate what people do. Many Latina women must work for pay, and many Latinas innovate income-earning strategies that allow them to simultaneously earn money and care for their children.[5] They sew garments on industrial sewing machines at home (Fernández-Kelly & García, 1990) and incorporate their children into informal vending to friends and neighbors, at swap meets, or on the sidewalks (Chinchilla & Hamilton, 1996). They may perform agricultural work alongside their children or engage in seasonal work (Zavella, 1987); or they may clean houses when their children are at school or, alternatively, incorporate their daughters into paid house cleaning (Romero, 1992, 1997). Engagement in "invisible employment" allows for urgently needed income and the maintenance of the ideal of privatized mothering. The middle-class model of mothering is predicated on mother-child isolation in the home, while women of color have often worked with their children in close proximity (Collins, 1994), as in some of the examples listed above. In both cases, however, mothers are with their children. The long distances of time and space that separate transnational mothers from their children contrast sharply with both mother-child isolation in the home and mother-child integration in the workplace.

TRANSNATIONAL MOTHERS' WORK, PLACE, AND SPACE

Feminist geographers have focused on how gendered orientations to space influence the way we organize our daily work lives. While sociologists have tended to explain occupational segregation as rooted either in family or individual characteristics (human capital theory) or in the workplace (labor market segmentation), feminist geographers observe that women tend to take jobs close to home so that they can fulfill child rearing and domestic duties (Hanson & Pratt, 1995; Massey, 1994). Transnational mothers, on the other hand, congregate in paid domestic work, an occupation that is relentlessly segregated not only by gender but also by race, class, and nationality/citizenship. To perform child rearing and domestic duties for others, they radically break with deeply gendered spatial and temporal boundaries of family and work.

Performing domestic work for pay, especially in a live-in job, is often incompatible with providing primary care for one's own family and home (Glenn, 1986; Rollins, 1985; Romero, 1992, 1997). Transnational mothering, however, is not exclusive to live-in domestic workers or to single mothers. Many women continue with transnational mothering after they move into live-out paid domestic work, or into other jobs. Women with income-earning husbands may also become transnational mothers.[6] The women we interviewed do not necessarily divert their mothering to the children and homes of their employers but instead reformulate their own mothering to accommodate spatial and temporal gulfs.

Like other immigrant workers, most transnational mothers came to the United States intending to stay for a finite period of time. But as time passes and economic need remains, prolonged stays evolve. Marxist-informed theory maintains that the separation of work life and family life constitutes the separation of labor maintenance costs from the labor reproduction costs (Burawoy, 1976; Glenn, 1986). According to this framework, Latina transnational mothers work to maintain themselves in the United States and to support their children—and reproduce the next generation of workers—in Mexico or Central America. One precursor to these arrangements is the mid-20th-century Bracero Program, which in effect legislatively mandated Mexican "absentee fathers" who came to work as contracted agricultural laborers in the United States. Other precursors, going back further in history, include the coercive systems of labor of the 18th and 19th centuries whereby African American slaves and Chinese sojourner laborers were denied the right to form residentially intact families (Dill, 1988, 1994).

Transnational mothering is different from some of these other arrangements in that now women with young children are recruited for U.S. jobs that pay far less than a "family wage." When men come north and leave their families in Mexico— as they did during the Bracero Program and as many continue to do today—they are fulfilling familial obligations defined as breadwinning for the family. When women do so, they are embarking not only on an immigration journey but on a more radical gender-transformative odyssey. They are initiating separations of space and time from their communities of origin, homes, children, and, sometimes, husbands. In doing so, they must cope with stigma, guilt, and criticism from others. A second difference is that these women work primarily not in production of agricultural products or manufacturing but in reproductive labor, in paid domestic work, and/or vending. Performing paid reproductive work for pay—especially caring for other people's children—is not always compatible with taking daily care of one's own family. All of this raises questions about the meanings and variations of motherhood in the late 21st century.

DESCRIPTION OF RESEARCH

Materials for this article draw from a larger study of paid domestic work in Los Angeles County and from interviews conducted in adjacent Riverside County. The materials include in-depth interviews, a survey, and ethnographic fieldwork. We had not initially anticipated studying women who live and work apart from their children but serendipitously stumbled on this theme in the course of our research.

For this article, we draw primarily on tape-recorded and fully transcribed interviews with 26 women who work as house cleaners and as live-out or live-in nanny-housekeepers. Of these 26 women, 8 lived apart from their children to accommodate their migration and work arrangements, but other respondents also spoke poignantly about their views and experiences with mothering, and we draw on these materials as well. We also draw, to a lesser extent, on in-depth, fully transcribed interviews with domestic agency personnel. All of the interview respondents were located through informal snowball sampling. The domestic workers interviewed are all from Mexico, El Salvador, and Guatemala, but they are diverse in terms of demographic characteristics (such as education, civil status, and children), immigration (length of time in the United States, access to legal papers), and other job-related characteristics (English language skills, driver's license, cardiopulmonary resuscitation [CPR] training).

While the interviews provide close-up information about women's experiences and views of mothering, a survey administered to 153 paid domestic workers in Los Angeles provides some indication of how widespread these transnational arrangements are among paid domestic workers. Because no one knows the total universe of paid domestic workers—many of whom lack legal papers and work in the informal sector where census data are not reliable—we drew a nonrandom sample in three types of sites located in or near affluent areas spanning from the west side of Los Angeles to the Hollywood area. We solicited respondents at evening ESL (English as a second language) classes, at public parks where nannies and housekeepers congregate with the children they care for in the midmorning hours, and we went to bus kiosks on Mondays and Tuesdays during the early morning hours (7:00 A.M. to 9:00 A.M.) when many domestic workers, including live-in workers, are traveling to their places of employment. While we refrained from conducting the survey in places where only certain types of domestic workers might be found (the employment agencies or organizations of domestic workers), going to the bus stops, public parks, and ESL classes meant that we undersampled domestic workers with access to private cars, driver's licenses, and good English skills. In short, we undersampled women who are earning at the higher end of the occupation.

The study also draws on ethnographic field research conducted in public parks, buses, private homes, a domestic workers' association, and the waiting room of a domestic employment agency. A tape-recorded group discussion with about 15 women—including several who had their children in their countries of origin—in the employment agency waiting room also informs the study. Nearly all of the in-depth interviews, structured survey interviews, and fieldwork were conducted in Spanish. The climate of fear produced by California voters' passage of anti-immigrant legislation in November 1994 perhaps dissuaded some potential respondents from participating in the study, but more important in shaping the interviews is the deeply felt pain expressed by the respondents. The interview transcripts include tearful segments in which the women recount the daily indignities of their jobs and the raw pain provoked by the forced separation from their young children.

TRANSNATIONAL MOTHERHOOD
AND PAID DOMESTIC WORK

Just how widespread are transnational motherhood arrangements in paid domestic work? Of the 153 domestic workers surveyed, 75% had children. Contrary to the images of Latina immigrant women as breeders with large families—a dominant image used in the campaign to pass California's Proposition 187—about half (47%) of these women have only one or two children. More significant for our purposes is this finding: 40% of the women with children have at least one of their children "back home" in their country of origin.[7]

Transnational motherhood arrangements are not exclusive to paid domestic work, but there are particular features of the organization of domestic work that encourage temporal and spatial separations of a mother-employee and her children. Historically and in the contemporary period, paid domestic workers have had to limit or forfeit primary care of their families and homes to earn income by providing primary care to the families and homes of employers, who are privileged by race and class (Glenn, 1986; Rollins, 1985; Romero, 1992). Paid domestic work is organized in various ways, and there is a clear relationship between the type of job arrangement women have and the likelihood of experiencing transnational family arrangements with their children. To understand the variations, it is necessary to explain how the employment is organized. Although there are variations within categories, we find it useful to employ a tripartite taxonomy of paid domestic work arrangements. This includes live-in and live-out nanny-housekeeper jobs and weekly housecleaning jobs.

Weekly house cleaners clean different houses on different days according to what Romero (1992) calls modernized "job work" arrangements. These contractual-like employee-employer relations often resemble those between customer and vendor, and they allow employees a degree of autonomy and scheduling flexibility. Weekly employees are generally paid a flat fee, and they work shorter hours and earn considerably higher hourly rates than do live-in or live-out domestic workers. By contrast, live-in domestic workers work and live in isolation from their own families and communities, sometimes in arrangements with feudal remnants (Glenn, 1986). There are often no hourly parameters to their jobs, and as our survey results show, most live-in workers in Los Angeles earn below minimum wage. Live-out domestic workers also usually work as combination nanny-housekeepers, generally for one household, but, in contrast to live-ins, they enter daily and return to their own home in the evening. Because of this, live-out workers better resemble industrial wage workers (Glenn, 1986).

Live-in jobs are the least compatible with conventional mothering responsibilities. Only about half (16 out of 30) of live-ins surveyed have children, while 83% (53 out of 64) of live-outs and 77% (45 out of 59) of house cleaners do. As Table 15.1 shows, 82% of live-ins with children have at least one of their children in their country of origin. It is very difficult to work a live-in job when your children are in

TABLE 15.1. Domestic Workers: Wages, Hours Worked,
and Children's Country of Residence

	Live-ins (n = 30)	Live-outs (n = 64)	House Cleaners (n = 59)
Mean hourly wage	$3.79	$5.90	$9.40
Mean hours worked per week	64	35	23
Domestic workers with children	(n = 516)	(n = 553)	(n = 545)
All children in the United States (%)	18	58	76
At least one child "back home"	82	42	24

the United States. Employers who hire live-in workers do so because they generally want employees for jobs that may require round-the-clock service. As one owner of a domestic employment agency put it,

> They (employers) want a live-in to have somebody at their beck and call. They want the hours that are most difficult for them covered, which is like six thirty in the morning till eight when the kids go to school, and four to seven when the kids are home, and it's homework, bath, and dinner.

According to our survey, live-ins work an average of 64 hours per week. The best live-in worker, from an employer's perspective, is one without daily family obligations of her own. The workweek may consist of six very long workdays. These may span from dawn to midnight and may include overnight responsibilities with sleepless or sick children, making it virtually impossible for live-in workers to sustain daily contact with their own families. Although some employers do allow for their employees' children to live in as well (Romero, 1996), this is rare. When it does occur, it is often fraught with special problems, and we discuss these in a subsequent section of this essay. In fact, minimal family and mothering obligations are an informal job placement criterion for live-in workers. Many of the agencies specializing in the placement of live-in nanny-housekeepers will not even refer a woman who has children in Los Angeles to interviews for live-in jobs. As one agency owner explained, "As a policy here, we will not knowingly place a nanny in a live-in job if she has young kids here." A job seeker in an employment agency waiting room acknowledged that she understood this job criterion more broadly, "You can't have a family, you can't have anyone [if you want a live-in job]."

The subminimum pay and the long hours for live-in workers also make it very difficult for these workers to have their children in the United States. Some live-in workers who have children in the same city as their place of employment hire their own nanny-housekeeper—often a much younger female relative—to provide daily care for their children, as did Patricia, one of the interview respondents whom we discuss later in this essay. Most live-ins, however, cannot afford this alternative; 93% of the live-ins surveyed earn below minimum wage (then $4.25 per hour). Many live-in workers cannot afford to bring their children to Los Angeles, but once their children are in the same city, most women try to leave live-in work to live with their children.

At the other end of the spectrum are the house cleaners that we surveyed, who earn substantially higher wages than live-ins (averaging $9.46 per hour, as opposed to $3.79) and who work fewer hours per week than live-ins (23 as opposed to 64). We suspect that many house cleaners in Los Angeles make even higher earnings and work more hours per week, because we know that the survey undersampled women who drive their own cars to work and who speak English. The survey suggests that house cleaners are the least likely to experience transnational spatial and temporal separations from their children.

Financial resources and job terms enhance house cleaners' abilities to bring their children to the United States. Weekly housecleaning is not a bottom-of-the-barrel job but rather an achievement. Breaking into housecleaning work is difficult because an employee needs to locate and secure several different employers. For this reason, relatively well-established women with more years of experience in the United States, who speak some English, who have a car, and who have job references predominate in weekly housecleaning. Women who are better established in the United States are also more likely to have their children here. The terms of weekly housecleaning employment—particularly the relatively fewer hours worked per week, scheduling flexibility, and relatively higher wages—allow them to live with, and care for, their children. So, it is not surprising that 76% of house cleaners who are mothers have their children in the United States.

Compared with live-ins and weekly cleaners, live-out nanny-housekeepers are at an intermediate level with respect to the likelihood of transnational motherhood. Of the live-out nanny-housekeepers who are mothers, 42% reported having at least one of their children in their country of origin. Live-out domestic workers, according to the survey, earn $5.90 per hour and work an average of 35 hours per week. Their lower earnings, more regimented schedules, and longer workweeks than house cleaners, but higher earnings, shorter hours, and more scheduling flexibility than live-ins explain their intermediate incidence of transnational motherhood.

The Meanings of Transnational Motherhood

How do women transform the meaning of motherhood to fit immigration and employment? Being a transnational mother means more than being the mother to children raised in another country. It means forsaking deeply felt beliefs that biological mothers should raise their own children and replacing that belief with new definitions of motherhood. The ideal of biological mothers raising their own children is widely held but is also widely broken at both ends of the class spectrum. Wealthy elites have always relied on others—nannies, governesses, and boarding schools—to raise their children (Wrigley, 1995), while poor, urban families often rely on kin and "other mothers" (Collins, 1991).

In Latin America, in large peasant families, the eldest daughters are often in charge of the daily care of the younger children, and in situations of extreme poverty children as young as five or six may be loaned or hired out to well-to-do families as "child-servants," sometimes called *criadas* (Gill, 1994).[8] A middle-aged Mexican woman that we interviewed, now a weekly house cleaner, homeowner, and mother of five children, recalled her own experience as a child-servant in Mexico: "I started working in a house when I was 8 . . . they hardly let me eat any food. . . . It was terrible, but I had to work to help my mother with the rent." This recollection reminds us how our contemporary notions of motherhood are historically and socially circumscribed, and also correspond to the meanings we assign to childhood (Zelizer, 1994).

This example also underlines how the expectation on the child to help financially support her mother required daily spatial and temporal separations of mother and child. There are, in fact, many transgressions of the mother-child symbiosis in practice—large families where older daughters care for younger siblings, child-servants who at an early age leave their mothers, children raised by paid nannies and other caregivers, and mothers who leave young children to seek employment—but these are fluid enough to sustain ideological adherence to the prescription that children should be raised exclusively by biological mothers. Long-term physical and temporal separation disrupts this notion. Transnational mothering radically rearranges mother-child interactions and requires a concomitant radical reshaping of the meanings and definitions of appropriate mothering.

Transnational mothers distinguish their version of motherhood from estrangement, child abandonment, or disowning. A youthful Salvadoran woman at the domestic employment waiting room reported that she had not seen her two eldest boys, now ages 14 and 15 and under the care of her own mother in El Salvador, since they were toddlers. Yet, she made it clear that this was different from putting a child up for adoption, a practice that she viewed negatively, as a form of child abandonment. Although she had been physically separated from her boys for more than a decade, she maintained her mothering ties and financial obligations to them by regularly sending home money. The exchange of letters, photos, and phone calls also helped to sustain the connection. Her physical absence did not signify emotional absence from her children. Another woman who remains intimately involved in the lives of her two daughters, now ages 17 and 21 in El Salvador, succinctly summed up this stance when she said, "I'm here, but I'm there." Over the phone, and through letters, she regularly reminds her daughters to take their vitamins, to never go to bed or to school on an empty stomach, and to use protection against pregnancy and sexually transmitted diseases if they engage in sexual relations with their boyfriends.

Transnational mothers fully understand and explain the conditions that prompt their situations. In particular, many Central American women recognize that the gendered employment demand in Los Angeles has produced transnational motherhood arrangements. These new mothering arrangements, they acknowledge, take shape despite strong beliefs that biological mothers should care for their own children. Emelia, a 49-year-old woman who left her five children in Guatemala 9 years ago to join her husband in Los Angeles, explained this changing relationship between family arrangements, migration, and job demand:

> One supposes that the mother must care for the children. A mother cannot so easily throw her children aside. So, in all families, the decision is that the man comes (to the U.S.) first. But now, since the man cannot find work here so easily, the woman comes first. Recently, women have been coming and the men staying.

A steady demand for live-in housekeepers means that Central American women may arrive in Los Angeles on a Friday and begin working Monday at a live-in job that provides at least some minimal accommodations. Meanwhile, her male counterpart may spend weeks or months before securing even casual day laborer jobs. While Emelia, formerly a homemaker who previously earned income in Guatemala by baking cakes and pastries in her home, expressed pain and sadness at not being with her children as they grew, she was also proud of her accomplishments. "My children," she stated, "recognize what I have been able to do for them."

Most transnational mothers, like many other immigrant workers, come to the United States with the intention of staying for a finite period of time, until they can pay off bills or raise the money for an investment in a house, their children's education, or a small business. Some of these women return to their countries of origin, but many stay. As time passes, and as their stays grow longer, some of the women eventually bring some or all of their children. Other women who stay at their U.S. jobs are adamant that they do not wish for their children to traverse the multiple hazards of adolescence in U.S. cities or to repeat the job experiences they themselves have had in the United States. One Salvadoran woman in the waiting room at the domestic employment agency—whose children had been raised on earnings predicated on her separation from them—put it this way:

> I've been here 19 years. I've got my legal papers and everything. But I'd have to be crazy to bring my children here. All of them have studied for a career, so why would I bring them here? To bus tables and earn minimum wage? So they won't have enough money for bus fare or food?

Who Is Taking Care of the Nanny's Children?

Transnational Central American and Mexican mothers may rely on various people to care for their children's daily, round-the-clock needs, but they prefer a close relative. The "other mothers" on which Latinas rely include their own mothers, *comadres* (co-godmothers) and other female kin, the children's fathers, and paid caregivers. Reliance on grandmothers and comadres for shared mothering is well established in Latina culture, and it is a practice that signifies a more collectivist, shared approach to mothering in contrast to a more individualistic, Anglo-

American approach (Griswold del Castillo, 1984; Segura & Pierce, 1993). Perhaps this cultural legacy facilitates the emergence of transnational motherhood. Transnational mothers express a strong preference for their own biological mother to serve as the primary caregiver. Here, the violation of the cultural preference for the biological mother is rehabilitated by reliance on the biological grandmother or by reliance on the ceremonially bound comadres. Clemencia, for example, left her three young children behind in Mexico, each with their respective *madrina*, or godmother.

Emelia left her five children, then ranging in age from 6 to 16, under the care of her mother and sister in Guatemala. As she spoke of the hardships faced by transnational mothers, she counted herself among the fortunate ones who did not need to leave the children alone with paid caregivers:

> One's mother is the only one who can really and truly care for your children. No one else can.... Women who aren't able to leave their children with their mother or with someone very special, they'll wire money to Guatemala and the people (caregivers) don't feed the children well. They don't buy the children clothes the mother would want. They take the money and the children suffer a lot.

Both Central American and Mexican women stated preferences for grandmothers as the ideal caregivers in situations that required the absence of the children's biological mother. These preferences seem to grow out of strategic availability, but these preferences assume cultural mandates. Velia, a Mexicana who hailed from the border town of Mexicali, improvised an employment strategy whereby she annually sent her three elementary school-age children to her mother in Mexicali for the summer vacation months. This allowed Velia, a single mother, to intensify her housecleaning jobs and save money on day care. But she also insisted that "If my children were with the woman next door [who baby-sits], I'd worry if they were eating well, or about men [coming to harass the girls]. Having them with my mother allows me to work in peace." Another woman specified more narrowly, insisting that only maternal grandmothers could provide adequate caregiving. In a conversation in a park, a Salvadoran woman offered that a biological mother's mother was the one best suited to truly love and care for a child in the biological mother's absence. According to her, not even the paternal grandmother could be trusted to provide proper nurturance and care. Another Salvadoran woman, Maria, left her two daughters, then 14 and 17, at their paternal grandmother's home, but before departing for the United States, she trained her daughters to become self-sufficient in cooking, marketing, and budgeting money. Although she believes the paternal grandmother loves the girls, she did not trust the paternal grandmother enough to cook or administer the money that she would send her daughters.

Another variation in the preference for a biological relative as a caregiver is captured by the arrangement of Patricia, a 30-year-old Mexicana who came to the United States as a child and was working as a live-in, caring for an infant in one of

Southern California's affluent coastal residential areas. Her arrangement was different, as her daughters were all born, raised, and residing in the United States, but she lived apart from them during weekdays because of her live-in job. Her three daughters, ages 1 ½, 6, and 11, stayed at their apartment near downtown Los Angeles under the care of their father and a paid nanny-housekeeper, Patricia's teenage cousin. Her paid caregiver was not an especially close relative, but she rationalized this arrangement by emphasizing that her husband, the girls' father, and therefore a biological relative, was with them during the week.

> Whenever I've worked like this, I've always had a person in charge of them also working as a live-in. She sleeps here the five days, but when my husband arrives he takes responsibility for them. . . . When my husband arrives (from work) she (cousin/paid caregiver) goes to English class and he takes charge of the girls.

And another woman who did not have children of her own but who had worked as a nanny for her aunt stated that "as Hispanas, we don't believe in bringing someone else in to care for our children." Again, the biological ties help sanction the shared child-care arrangement.

New family fissures emerge for the transnational mother as she negotiates various aspects of the arrangement with her children, and with the "other mother" who provides daily care and supervision for the children. Any impulse to romanticize transnational motherhood is tempered by the sadness with which the women related their experiences and by the problems they sometimes encounter with their children and caregivers. A primary worry among transnational mothers is that their children are being neglected or abused in their absence. While there is a long legacy of child-servants being mistreated and physically beaten in Latin America, transnational mothers also worry that their own paid caregivers will harm or neglect their children. They worry that their children may not receive proper nourishment, schooling and educational support, and moral guidance. They may remain unsure as to whether their children are receiving the full financial support they send home. In some cases, their concerns are intensified by the eldest child or a nearby relative who is able to monitor and report the caregiver's transgression to the transnational mother.

Transnational mothers engage in emotion work and financial compensation to maintain a smoothly functioning relationship with the children's daily caregiver. Their efforts are not always successful, and when problems arise they may return to visit if they can afford to do so. After not seeing her four children for 7 years, Carolina abruptly quit her nanny job and returned to Guatemala in the spring of 1996 because she was concerned about one adolescent daughter's rebelliousness and about her mother-in-law's failing health. Carolina's husband remained in Los Angeles, and she was expected to return. Emelia, whose children were cared for by her mother and sister, with the assistance of paid caregivers, regularly responded to her sister's reminders to send gifts, clothing, and small amounts of money to the paid caregivers. "If they are taking care of my children," she explained, "then I have to show my gratitude."

Some of these actions are instrumental. Transnational mothers know that they may increase the likelihood of their children receiving adequate care if they appropriately remunerate the caregivers and treat them with consideration. In fact, they often express astonishment that their own Anglo employers fail to show such consideration. Some of the expressions of gratitude and gifts that they send to their children's caregivers appear to be genuinely disinterested and enhanced by the transnational mothers' empathy arising out of their own similar job circumstances. A Honduran woman, a former biology teacher, who had left her four sons with a paid caregiver, maintained that the treatment of nannies and housekeepers was much better in Honduras than in the United States, in part, because of different approaches to mothering:

> We're very different back there. . . . We treat them [domestic workers] with a lot of affection and respect, and when they are taking care of our kids, even more so. The Americana, she is very egotistical. When the nanny loves her children, she gets jealous. Not us. We are appreciative when someone loves our children, and bathes, dresses, and feeds them as though they were their own.

These comments are clearly informed by the respondent's prior class status, as well as her simultaneous position as the employer of a paid nanny-housekeeper in Honduras and as a temporarily unemployed nanny-housekeeper in the United States. (She had been fired from her nanny-housekeeper job for not showing up on Memorial Day, which she erroneously believed was a work holiday.) Still, her comments underline the importance of showing appreciation and gratitude to the caregiver, in part, for the sake of the children's well-being.

Transnational mothers also worry about whether their children will get into trouble during adolescence and whether they will transfer their allegiance and affection to the "other mother." In general, transnational mothers, like African American mothers who leave their children in the South to work up North (Stack & Burton, 1994), believe that the person who cares for the children has the right to discipline. But when adolescent youths are paired with elderly grandmothers or ineffective disciplinary figures, the mothers may need to intervene. Preadolescent and adolescent children who show signs of rebelliousness may be brought north because they are deemed unmanageable by their grandmothers or paid caregivers. Alternatively, teens who are in California may be sent back to the home country in hope that it will straighten them out, a practice that has resulted in the migration of Los Angeles-based delinquent youth gangs to Mexican and Central American towns. Another danger is that the child who has grown up without the transnational mother's presence may no longer respond to her authority. One woman at the domestic employment agency, who had recently brought her adolescent son to join her in California, reported that she had seen him at a bus stop, headed for the beach. When she demanded to know where he was going, he said something to the effect of "and who are you to tell me what to do?" After a verbal confrontation at the bus kiosk, she handed him $10. Perhaps the mother hoped the money would be a way to show caring and to advance a claim to parental authority.

Motherhood and Breadwinning

Milk, shoes, and schooling—these are the currency of transnational motherhood. Providing for children's sustenance, protecting their current well-being, and preparing them for the future are widely shared concerns of motherhood. Central American and Mexican women involved in transnational mothering attempt to ensure the present and future well-being of their children through U.S. wage earning, and, as we have seen, this requires long-term physical separation from their children.

For these women, the meanings of motherhood do not appear to be in a liminal stage. That is, they do not appear to be making a linear progression from a way of motherhood that involves daily, face-to-face caregiving toward one that is defined primarily through breadwinning. Rather than replacing caregiving with breadwinning definitions of motherhood, they appear to be expanding their definitions of motherhood to encompass breadwinning that may require long-term physical separations. Among these women, a core belief is that they can best fulfill traditional caregiving responsibilities through income earning in the United States while their children remain "back home."

Transnational mothers continue to state that caregiving is a defining feature of their mothering experiences. They wish to provide their children with better nutrition, clothing, and schooling, and most of them are able to purchase these items with dollars earned in the United States. They recognize, however, that their transnational relationships incur painful costs. Transnational mothers worry about some of the negative effects on their children, but they also experience the absence of domestic family life as a deeply personal loss. Transnational mothers who were primarily homemakers before coming to the United States identified the loss of daily contact with family as a sacrifice made to financially support the children. As Emelia, who had previously earned some income by baking pastries and doing catering from her home in Guatemala, reflected,

> The money (earned in the U.S.) is worth five times more in Guatemala. My oldest daughter was then 16, and my youngest was 6 [when I left]. Ay, it's terrible, terrible, but that's what happens to most women [transnational mothers] who are here. You sacrifice your family life [for labor migration].

Similarly, Carolina used the word *sacrifice* when discussing her family arrangement, claiming that her children "tell me that they appreciate us [parents], and the sacrifice that their papa and mama make for them. That is what they say."

Paid domestic work carries with it daily indignities—low pay, subtle humiliations, not enough food to eat, invisibility (Glenn, 1986; Rollins, 1985; Romero, 1992). So by leaving their children behind, transnational mothers are not only stretching their U.S.-earned dollars further by sending the money back home but by providing special protection from the discrimination the children might receive in the United States. Gladys, who had four of her five children in El Salvador, acknowledged that her U.S. dollars went further in El Salvador. Although she missed seeing those four children grow up, she felt that in some ways she had spared them the indignities to which she had exposed her youngest daughter, whom she brought to the United States at age 4 in 1988. Although her live-in employer had allowed the 4-year-old to join the family residence, Gladys tearfully recalled how that employer had initially quarantined her daughter, insisting on seeing vaccination papers before allowing the girl to play with the employer's children. "I had to battle, really struggle," she recalled, "just to get enough food for her [to eat]." For Gladys, being together with her youngest daughter in the employer's home had entailed new emotional costs.

Patricia, the mother who was apart from her children only during the weekdays when she lived in with her employer, put forth an elastic definition of motherhood, one that included both meeting financial obligations and spending time with the children. Although her job involves different scheduling than most employed mothers, she has similar views:

> It's something you have to do, because you can't just stay seated at home because the bills accumulate and you have to find a way. . . . I applied at many different places for work, like hospitals, as a receptionist—due to the experience I've had with computers working in shipping and receiving, things like that, but they never called me. . . . One person can't pay all the bills.

Patricia emphasized that she believes motherhood also involves making an effort to spend time with the children. According to this criterion, she explained, most employers were deficient, while she was compliant. During the middle of the week, she explained, "I invent something, some excuse for her [the employer] to let me come home, even if I have to bring the [employer's] baby here with me . . . just to spend time with my kids."

Transnational mothers echoed these sentiments. Maria Elena, for example, whose 13-year-old son resided with his father in Mexico after she lost a custody battle, insisted that motherhood did not consist of only breadwinning: "You can't give love through money." According to Maria Elena, motherhood requires an emotional presence and communication with a child. Like other transnational mothers, she explained how she maintained this connection despite the long-term geographic distance: "I came here, but we're not apart. We talk [by telephone]. . . . I know [through telephone conversations] when my son is fine. I can tell when he is sad by the way he speaks." Like employed mothers everywhere, she insisted on a definition of motherhood that emphasizes quality rather than quantity of time spent with the child: "I don't think that a good mother is one who is with her children at all times. . . . It's the quality of time spent with the child." She spoke these words tearfully, reflecting the trauma of losing a custody battle with her former husband. Gladys also stated that being a mother involves both breadwinning and providing direction and guidance. "It's not just feeding them, or buying clothes for them. It's also educating them, preparing them to make good choices so they'll have a better future."

Transnational mothers seek to mesh caregiving and guidance with breadwinning. While breadwinning may require long-term and long-distance separations from their children, they attempt to sustain family connections by showing emotional ties through letters, phone calls, and money sent home. If at all financially and logistically possible, they travel home to visit their children. They maintain their mothering responsibilities not only by earning money for their children's upbringing but also by communicating and advising across national borders, and across the boundaries that separate their children's place of residence from their own places of employment and residence.

Bonding with the Employers' Kids and Critiques of "Americana" Mothers

Some nanny-housekeepers develop very strong ties of affection with the children they care for during long workweeks. It is not unusual for nanny-housekeepers to be alone with these children during the workweek, with no one else with whom to talk or interact. The nannies, however, develop close emotional ties selectively, with some children but not with others. For nanny-housekeepers who are transnational mothers, the loving daily caregiving that they cannot express for their own children is sometimes transferred to their employers' children. Carolina, a Guatemalan woman with four children between the ages of 10 and 14 back home, maintained that she tried to treat the employers' children with the same affection that she had for her own children "because if you do not feel affection for children, you are not able to care for them well." When interviewed, she was caring for 2-year-old triplets for whom she expressed very little affection, but she recalled very longingly her fond feelings for a child at her last job, a child who vividly reminded her of her daughter, who was about the same age:

> When I saw that the young girl was lacking in affection. I began to get close to her and I saw that she appreciated that I would touch her, give her a kiss on the cheek. . . . And then I felt consoled too, because I had someone to give love to. But, I would imagine that she was my daughter, ah? And then I would give pure love to her, and that brought her closer to me.

Another nanny-housekeeper recalled a little girl for whom she had developed strong bonds of affection, laughingly imitating how the preschooler, who could not pronounce the *f* sound, would say "you hurt my peelings, but I don't want to pight."

Other nanny-housekeepers reflected that painful experiences with abrupt job terminations had taught them not to transfer mother love to the children of their employers. Some of these women reported that they now remained very measured and guarded in their emotional closeness with the employers' children, so that they could protect themselves for the moment when that relationship might be abruptly severed.

> I love these children, but now I stop myself from becoming too close. Before, when my own children weren't here [in the United States], I gave all my love to the children I cared for [then toddler twins]. That was my recompensation [for not being with my children]. When the job ended, I hurt so much. I can't let that happen again. I love them, but not like they were my own children because they are not! They are not my kids! Because if I get to love them, and then I go, then I'm going to suffer like I did the last time. I don't want that.

Not all nanny-housekeepers bond tightly with the employers' children, but most of them are critical of what they perceive as the employers' neglectful parenting and mothering. Typically, they blame biological mothers (their employers) for substandard parenting. Carolina recalled advising the mother of the abovementioned little girl, who reminded her of her own child, that the girl needed to receive more affection from her mother, whom she perceived as self-absorbed with physical fitness regimes. Carolina had also advised other employers on disciplining their children. Patricia also spoke adamantly on this topic, and she recalled with satisfaction that when she had advised her current employer to spend more than 15 minutes a day with the baby, the employer had been reduced to tears. By comparison with her employer's mothering, Patricia cited her own perseverance in going out of her way to visit her children during the week:

> If you really love your kids, you look for the time, you make time to spend with your kids. . . . I work all week and for some reason I make excuses for her [employer] to let me come [home] . . . just to spend time with my kids.

Similarly, many nanny-housekeepers criticize female employers who, though out of the labor force, employ nannies and hence do not spend time with their children.

> I love my kids, they don't. It's just like, excuse the word, shitting kids. . . . What they prefer is to go to the salon, get their nails done, you know, go shopping, things like that. Even if they're home all day, they don't want to spend time with the kids because they're paying somebody to do that for them.

Curiously, she spoke as though her female employer is a wealthy woman of leisure, but in fact both her current and past female employers are wealthy business executives who work long hours. Perhaps at this distance on the class spectrum, all class- and racially privileged mothers look alike. "I work my butt off to get what I have," she observed, "and they don't have to work that much."

In some ways, transnational mothers who work as nanny-housekeepers cling to a more sentimental view of the employers' children than of their own. This strategy allows them to criticize their employers, especially homemakers of privilege who are occupied with neither employment nor daily caregiving for their children. The Latina nannies appear to endorse motherhood as a full-time vocation in contexts of sufficient financial resources, but in contexts of financial hardship such as their own they advocate more elastic definitions of motherhood, including forms that may include long spatial and temporal separations between mother and children.

As observers of late 20th-century U.S. families (Skolnick, 1991; Stacey, 1996) have noted, we live in an era in which no one normative family arrangement predominates. Just as no one type of mothering unequivocally prevails in the White middle class, no singular mothering arrangement prevails among Latina immigrant women. In fact, the exigencies of contemporary immigration seem to multiply the variety of mothering arrangements. Through our research with Latina immigrant women who work as nannies, housekeepers, and house cleaners, we have encountered a broad range of mothering arrangements. Some Latinas migrate to the United States without their children to establish employment; after some stability has been achieved, they send for their children or they work for a while to save money and then return to their countries of origin. Other Latinas migrate and postpone having children until they are financially established. Still others arrive with their children and search for employment that allows them to live together with their children. While yet other Latinas have sufficient financial support—from their husbands or kin—to stay home full-time with their children.

In the absence of a universal or at least widely shared mothering arrangement, there is tremendous uncertainty about what constitutes "good mothering," and transnational mothers must work hard to defend their choices. Some Latina nannies who have their children with them in the United States condemn transnational mothers as "bad women." One interview respondent, who was able to take her young daughter to work with her, claimed that she could never leave her daughter. For this woman, transnational mothers were not only bad mothers but also nannies who could not be trusted to adequately care for other people's children. As she said of an acquaintance, "This woman left her children [in Honduras] ... she was taking care [of other people's children], and I said, 'Lord, who are they [the employers] leaving their children with if she did that with her own children!' "

Given the uncertainty of what constitutes "good mothering," and to defend their integrity as mothers when others criticize them, transnational mothers construct new scales for gauging the quality of mothering. By favorably contrasting their own behavior with models of mothering that they see in others—especially those that they are able to scrutinize in their employers' homes—transnational mothers create new definitions of good mothering. At the same time, selectively developing motherlike ties with other people's children allows them to enjoy affectionate, face-to-face interactions that they cannot experience daily with their own children.

DISCUSSION: TRANSNATIONAL MOTHERHOOD

In California, with few exceptions, paid domestic work has become a Latina immigrant women's job. One observer has referred to these Latinas as "the new employable mothers" (Chang, 1994). But these wage labor duties often require Latina workers to expand the frontiers of motherhood by leaving their own children for several years. While today there is a greater openness to accepting a plurality of mothering arrangements—single mothers, employed mothers, stay-at home mothers, lesbian mothers, surrogate mothers, to name a few—even feminist discussions generally assume that mothers, by definition, reside with their children.

Transnational mothering situations disrupt the notion of family in one place and break distinctively with what some commentators have referred to as the "epoxy glue" view of motherhood (Blum & Deussen, 1996; Scheper-Hughes, 1992). Latina transnational mothers are improvising new mothering arrangements that are borne out of women's financial struggles, played out in a new global arena, to provide the best future for themselves and their children. Like many other women of color and employed mothers, transnational mothers rely on an expanded and sometimes fluid number of family members and paid caregivers. Their caring circuits, however, span stretches of geography and time that are much wider than in typical joint custody or "other mother" arrangements.

The transnational perspective in immigration studies is useful in conceptualizing how relationships across borders are important. Yet, an examination of transnational motherhood suggests that transnationalism is a contradictory process of the early 21st century. It is an achievement, but one accompanied by numerous costs and attained in a context of extremely scarce options. The alienation and anxiety of mothering organized by long temporal and spatial distances should give pause to the celebratory impulses of transnational perspectives of immigration. Although not addressed directly in this essay, the experiences of these mothers resonate with current major political issues. For example, transnational mothering resembles precisely what immigration restrictionists have advocated through California's Proposition 187 (Hondagneu-Sotelo, 1995).[9] While proponents of Proposition 187 have never questioned California's reliance on low-wage Latino immigrant workers, this restrictionist policy calls for fully dehumanized immigrant workers, not workers with families and family needs (such as education and health services for children). In this respect, transnational mothering's externalization of the cost of labor reproduction to Mexico and Central America is a dream come true for the proponents of Proposition 187.

Contemporary transnational motherhood continues a long historical legacy of people of color being incorporated into the United States through coercive systems of labor that do not recognize family rights. As Bonnie Thornton Dill (1988), Evelyn Nakano Glenn (1986), and others have pointed out, slavery and contract labor systems were organized to maximize economic productivity and offered few supports to sustain family life. The job characteristics of paid domestic work, especially live-in work, virtually impose transnational motherhood on many Mexican and Central American women who have children of their own.

The ties of transnational motherhood suggest, simultaneously, the relative permeability of borders, as shown by the maintenance of family ties and the new meanings of motherhood, and the impermeability of nation-state borders. Ironi-

cally, just at the moment when free trade proponents and pundits celebrate globalization and transnationalism, and when "borderlands" and "border crossings"
have become the metaphors of preference for describing a mind-boggling range of
conditions, nation-state borders prove to be very real obstacles for many Mexican
and Central American women who work in the United States and who, given the
appropriate circumstances, wish to be with their children. While demanding the
right of women workers to live with their children may provoke critiques of sentimentality, essentialism, and the glorification of motherhood, demanding the right
of women workers to choose their own motherhood arrangements would be the
beginning of truly just family and work policies, policies that address not only inequalities of gender but also inequalities of race, class, and citizenship status.

NOTES

1. No one knows the precise figures on the prevalence of transnational motherhood, just
as no one knows the myriad consequences for both mothers and their children. However,
one indicator that hints at both the complex outcomes and the frequencies of these arrangements is that teachers and social workers in Los Angeles are becoming increasingly concerned about some of the deleterious effects of these mother-child separations and reunions.
Many Central American women who made their way to Los Angeles in the early 1980s, fleeing civil wars and economic upheaval, pioneered transnational mothering, and some of them
are now financially able to bring the children they left behind. These children, now in their
early teen years, are confronting the triple trauma of simultaneously entering adolescence,
with its own psychological upheavals; entering a new society, often in an inner-city environment that requires learning to navigate a new language, place, and culture; and entering
families that do not look like the ones they knew before their mother's departure, families
with new siblings born in the United States and new stepfathers or the mother's boyfriends.

2. Even among Mexican farmworkers, researchers have found a large and growing segment who settle permanently with their families in rural California (Palerm, 1994).

3. Acknowledgment of the varieties of family and mothering has been fueled, in part,
by research on the growing numbers of women-headed families, involving families of all
races and socioeconomic levels—including Latina families in the United States and elsewhere (Fernández-Kelly & García, 1990; Zinn, 1989)—and by recognition that biological
ties do not necessarily constitute family (Weston, 1991).

4. La Virgen de Guadalupe, the indigenous virgin who appeared in 1531 to a young Indian boy and for whom a major basilica was built, provides the exemplary maternal model,
la mujer abnezada (the self-effacing woman), who sacrifices all for her children and religious
faith. La Malinche, the Aztec woman that served Cortes as a translator, a diplomat, and a
mistress, and La Llorona (the weeping one), a legendary solitary, ghostlike figure reputed
either to have been violently murdered by a jealous husband or to have herself murdered
her children by drowning them, are the negative and despised models of femininity. Both
are failed women because they have failed at motherhood. La Malinche is stigmatized as a
traitor and a whore who collaborated with the Spanish conquerors, and La Llorona is the
archetypal evil woman condemned to eternally suffer and weep for violating her role as a
wife and a mother (Soto, 1986).

5. A study comparing Mexicanas and Chicanas found that the latter are more favorably disposed to homemaker ideals. This difference is explained by Chicanas' greater exposure to U.S. ideology that promotes the opposition of mothering and employment and to Mexicanas' integration of household and economy in Mexico (Segura, 1994). While this dynamic may be partially responsible for this pattern, we suspect that Mexicanas have higher rates of labor force participation because they are also a self-selected group of Latinas; by and large, they come to the United States to work.

6. See Romero (1997) for a study focusing on the perspective of domestic workers' children. Although most respondents in this particular study were children of day workers, and none appear to have been children of transnational mothers, they still recall significant costs stemming from their mothers' occupation.

7. Central American women may be more likely than Mexican women to have their children in their country of origin, even if their husbands are living with them in the United States, because of the multiple dangers and costs associated with undocumented travel from Central America to the United States. The civil wars of the 1980s, continuing violence and economic uncertainty, greater difficulties and costs associated with crossing multiple national borders, and stronger cultural legacies of socially sanctioned consensual unions may also contribute to this pattern for Central Americans.

8. According to interviews conducted with domestic workers in La Paz, Bolivia, in the late 1980s, 41% got their first job between the ages of 11 and 15, and one third got their first job between the ages of 6 and 10. Some parents received half of the child-servant's salary (Gill, 1994, p. 64). Similar arrangements prevailed in preindustrial rural areas of the United States and Europe.

9. In November 1994, California voters passed Proposition 187, which legislates the denial of public school education, health care, and other public benefits to undocumented immigrants and their children. Although it was never implemented because it was rejected by the courts, the ease with which Proposition 187 passed in the California ballots rejuvenated anti-immigrant politics at a national level. It opened the doors to new legislative measures in 1997 to deny public assistance to legal immigrants.

REFERENCES

Basch, Linda, Schiller, Nina Glick, & Szanton Blanc, Cristina. (1994). *Nations unbound: Transnational projects, postcolonial predicaments, and deterritorialized nation-states.* Amsterdam: Gordon & Breach.

Blum, Linda, & Deussen, Theresa. (1996). Negotiating independent motherhood: Working-class African American women talk about marriage and motherhood. *Gender and Society, 10,* 199–211.

Burawoy, Michael. (1976). The functions and reproduction of migrant labor: Comparative material from Southern Africa and the United States. *American Journal of Sociology, 81,* 1050–1087.

Chang, Grace. (1994). Undocumented Latinas: Welfare burdens or beasts of burden? *Socialist Review, 23,* 151–185.

Chinchilla, Norma Stoltz, & Hamilton, Nora. (1996). Negotiating urban space: Latina workers in domestic work and street vending in Los Angeles. *Humbolt Journal of Social Relations, 22,* 25–35.

Collier, Jane Fishburne, & Yanagisako, Sylvia Junko. (1987). *Gender and kinship: Essays toward a unified analysis.* Stanford, CA: Stanford University Press.

Collins, Patricia Hill. (1991). *Black feminist thought: Knowledge, consciousness, and the politics of empowerment.* New York: Routledge.

Collins, Patricia Hill. (1994). Shifting the center. Race, class, and feminist theorizing about motherhood. In Evelyn Nakano Glenn, Grace Chang, & Linda Rennie Forcey (Eds.), *Mothering: Ideology, experience, and agency.* New York: Routledge.

Dill, Bonnie Thornton. (1988). Our mothers' grief: Racial-ethnic women and the maintenance of families. *Journal of Family History, 13,* 415–431.

Dill, Bonnie Thornton. (1994). Fictive kin, paper sons, and *compadrazgo*: Women of color and the struggle for family survival. In Maxine Baca Zinn & Bonnie Thornton Dill (Eds.), *Women of color in U.S. society* (pp. 149–169). Philadelphia: Temple University Press.

Fernández-Kelly, M. Patricia, & García, Anna. (1990). Power surrendered, power restored: The politics of work and family among Hispanic garment workers in California and Florida. In Louise A. Tilly & Patricia Gurin (Eds.), *Women, politics, and change* (pp. 130–149). New York: Russell Sage Foundation.

Gill, Lesley. (1994). *Precarious dependencies: Gender, class, and domestic service in Bolivia.* New York: Columbia University Press.

Glenn, Evelyn Nakano. (1986). *Issei, Nisei, warbride: Three generations of Japanese American women in domestic service.* Philadelphia: Temple University Press.

Glenn, Evelyn Nakano. (1994). Social constructions of mothering: A thematic overview. In Evelyn Nakano Glenn, Grace Chang, & Linda Rennie Forcey (Eds.), *Mothering: Ideology, experience, and agency.* New York: Routledge

Griswold del Castillo, Richard. (1984). *La Familia: Chicano families in the urban Southwest, 1848 to the present.* Notre Dame, IN: University of Notre Dame Press.

Hanson, Susan, & Pratt, Geraldine. (1995). *Gender, work, and space.* New York: Routledge.

Hondagneu-Sotelo, Pierrette. (1995). Women and children first: New directions in anti-immigrant politics. *Socialist Review, 25,* 169–190.

Kearney, Michael. (1995). The effects of transnational culture, economy, and migration on Mixtec identity in Oaxacalifornia. In Michael Peter Smith & Joe R. Feagin (Eds.), *The bubbling cauldron: Race, ethnicity, and the urban crisis.* Minneapolis: University of Minnesota Press.

Mahler, Sarah J. (1996). *Bringing gender to a transnational focus: Theoretical and empirical ideas.* Unpublished manuscript, Department of Anthropology, University of Vermont.

Massey, Doreen. (1994). *Space, place, and gender.* Minneapolis: University of Minnesota Press.

Palerm, J.-V. (1994). *Immigrant and migrant farmworkers in the Santa Maria Valley of California* (Report for Center for Survey Methods Research, Bureau of Census). Washington, DC: U.S. Government Printing Office.

Pedraza, Silvia. (1991). Women and migration: The social consequences of gender. *Annual Review of Sociology, 17,* 303–325.

Rollins, Judith. (1985). *Between women: Domestics and their employers.* Philadelphia: Temple University Press.

Romero, Mary. (1992). *Maid in the U.S.A.* New York: Routledge.

Romero, Mary. (1996). Life as the maid's daughter. An exploration of the everyday boundaries of race, class, and gender. In Abigail J. Steward & Donna Station (Eds.), *Feminisms in the academy: Rethinking the disciplines.* Ann Arbor: University of Michigan Press.

Romero, Mary. (1997). Who takes care of the maid's children? Exploring the costs of domestic service. In Hilde L. Nelson (Ed.), *Feminism and families.* New York: Routledge.

Rouse, Roger. (1991). Mexican migration and the social space of postmodernism. *Diaspora, 1*, 8–23.

Ruddick, Sara. (1989). *Maternal thinking: Toward a politics of peace.* Boston: Beacon.

Scheper-Hughes, Nancy. (1992). *Death without weeping: The violence of everyday life in Brazil.* Berkeley & Los Angeles: University of California Press.

Segura, Denise A. (1994). Working at motherhood: Chicana and Mexican immigrant mothers and employment. In Evelyn Nakano Glenn, Grace Chang, & Linda Rennie Forcey (Eds.), *Mothering: Ideology, experience, and agency.* New York: Routledge.

Segura, Denise A., & Pierce, Jennifer L. (1993). Chicana/o family structure and gender personality: Chodorow, familism, and psychoanalytic sociology revisited. *Signs: Journal of Women in Culture and Society, 19*, 62–79.

Skolnick, Arlene S. (1991). *Embattled paradise: The American family in an age of uncertainty.* New York: Basic Books.

Soto, Shirlene. (1986). Tres modelos culturales: La Virgen de Guadalupe, la Malinche, y la Llorona. *Fem* (Mexico City), no. 48, 13–16.

Stacey, Judith. (1996). *In the name of the family: Rethinking family values in the postmodern age.* Boston: Beacon.

Stack, Carol B., & Burton, Linda M. (1994). Kinscripts: Reflections on family, generation, and culture. In Evelyn Nakano Glenn, Grace Chang, & Linda Rennie Forcey (Eds.), *Mothering: Ideology, experience, and agency.* New York: Routledge.

Thorne, Barrie, & Yalom, Marilyn. (1992). *Rethinking the family: Some feminist questions.* Boston: Northeastern University Press.

Tienda, Marta, & Booth, Karen. (1991). Gender, migration, and social change. *International Sociology, 6*, 51–72.

Uttal, Lynet. (1996). Custodial care, surrogate care, and coordinated care: Employed mothers and the meaning of child care. *Gender and Society, 10*, 291–311.

Weston, Kathleen M. (1991). *Families we choose: Lesbians, gays, kinship.* New York: Columbia University Press.

Wrigley, Julia. (1995). *Other people's children.* New York: Basic Books.

Zavella, Patricia. (1987). *Women's work and Chicano families: Cannery workers of the Santa Clara Valley.* Ithaca, NY: Cornell University Press.

Zelizer, Viviana. (1994). *Pricing the priceless child: The social value of children.* Princeton, NJ: Princeton University Press.

Zinn, Maxine Baca. (1989). Family, race, and poverty in the eighties. *Signs: Journal of Women in Culture and Society, 14*, 856–869.

CHAPTER 16

Gender, Status, and the State in Transnational Spaces

The Gendering of Political Participation and Mexican Hometown Associations

Luin Goldring

INTRODUCTION

This essay examines the gendering of Mexican transmigrant[1] political participation[2] in the context of hometown associations. I argue that the politics of Mexicans in the United States, whether oriented toward Mexico or the United States, are not gender neutral. On the whole, hometown organizations represent a privileged arena for men's homeland-oriented political activity. This masculine gendered project works for several reasons. Mexican men tend to experience a relatively greater loss of gender and social status in the United States. Consequently, Mexico-oriented activities, such as the community-oriented projects carried out through these organizations, provide an important vehicle for gaining status and deploying political power. Going beyond the individual and family levels, I argue that the Mexican state's outreach programs, including a provincial matching funds program, reinforce this gendered project through programs aimed at cultivating and maintaining ties with Mexicans abroad. When hometown associations scale up in the form of umbrella organizations, they offer a context for exercising substantive citizenship that enhances immigrant men's status and citizenship vis-à-vis the Mexican state while marginalizing women by excluding them from positions of agency and power. Mexican women, however, are far from politically inactive. A robust literature documenting their U.S.-based activism indicates that Mexican women (and other Latinas) are more likely to engage with organizations and institutions in the United States.

THEORETICAL BACKGROUND

An analysis of the gendering of political participation or substantive citizenship among Mexican transmigrants should draw on several literatures, including work on immigrant politics, Latino political participation, gender and migration, and transnationalism. Portes and Rumbaut, in their 1990 survey of the literature on immigrants and politics, document the vital role played by earlier immigrants in homeland politics and, in certain cases, in U.S. mobilizations. They propose that most contemporary first-generation immigrants orient their political activities toward their homeland, especially if they come from a nearby country, are relatively less educated, and are sojourners or immigrants who can reverse the direction of their migration (Portes & Rumbaut, 1990, p. 124). It is only the second and subsequent generations that Portes and Rumbaut expect to become involved in U.S.-based social movements and politics. In a section on Mexicans, these authors argue that the experience of Mexicans is consistent with this model.

At the same time, there is a literature that points to the *U.S.* participation of Latinos, including first-generation immigrant women and men. This activity involves a variety of issues and organizations, including union organizing (Delgado, 1993; Rose, 1988; Ruíz, 1987), nontraditional labor organizing (Cranford, 2000; Hondagneu-Sotelo & Riegos, 1997), a bus rider's union (Burgos & Pulido, 1998), environmental justice (Pardo, 1999), community organizations (Pardo, 1999), and local electoral politics (Hardy-Fanta, 1993). Much of this work has highlighted the activism of immigrant women and U.S.-born Latinas, who emerge as key players in mobilizing their communities. Indeed, scholars of Latino political participation in the United States have begun to use gender as a key analytic category, arguing that it shapes definitions of "politics" as well as ways of doing politics (Hardy-Fanta, 1993; Jones-Correa, 1998; Pardo, 1999). This work suggests that Latino men tend to focus on enhancing their status, gaining in the realm of political positions and electoral politics. Latina women may also work in electoral politics, yet their definition of "politics" is more likely to include personal consciousness-raising and neighborhood and community issues and organizations (Hardy-Fanta, 1993; Pardo, 1999).

The apparent inconsistency between the thesis that first-generation immigrants focus on homeland politics and the work documenting the political participation of Latino immigrants in the United States need not be read as an inconsistency if we make two theoretical moves. First, we need to look at opportunities in and barriers to transmigrant political participation from a transnational perspective (Basch et al., 1994), in which the analysis takes into account the relationship between social conditions and opportunities for participation in the countries of origin and destination. Second, we can pay more attention to processes that lead to variation within national-origin groups. For example, looking more closely at how gender, class, legal status, home-country policies, and the context of reception at the regional and national levels may contribute to our understanding of why segments of the Mexican immigrant population exhibit different patterns of political participation.

My concern in this essay is the relationship between gender, Mexican state policies, and transmigrant citizenship practices. Unfortunately, studies of contemporary homeland-oriented politics rarely address how and why gender shapes these activities. In one of the few exceptions, in this case based on research on Latinos in New York City, Jones-Correa (1998) argues that men are more likely to engage in homeland-oriented politics, particularly the quest for dual citizenship. This is due to an inconsistency between their former social status, framed mainly in terms of occupational status, and their current status in the United States. On the other hand, activist Latinas are more involved in U.S.-based political issues, largely because their status inconsistency is not as significant. Jones-Correa's findings are consistent with mine, despite the fact that he was working with a Latino population dominated by Dominicans, Colombians, and Puerto Ricans. These groups seemed to experience more occupational status loss than the Mexicans I spoke with, who were generally from relatively humble backgrounds and had in many cases experienced occupational mobility while still experiencing a loss of gender status.

The next section outlines the research methods used in gathering the information on which this essay is based. The following section provides background on Mexican migrant- and state-led transnationalism. It is followed by a section in which I analyze the gendering of migrant political practice and organizations, focusing on Zacatecan hometown associations and a matching funds program for community projects in Mexico. The final section discusses the implications of the analysis and offers conclusions and suggestions for further research.

METHODS

The paper is based on fieldwork initiated in Mexico in the summer of 1995, eight months of fieldwork in Mexico and California during 1996–1997, and follow-up work carried out less systematically in 1998 and 1999.[3] The project was designed to study relations between the Mexican state and transmigrants, with a focus on hometown organizations in the Los Angeles area. Data were collected through open-ended interviews, observation of meetings and relevant events, and secondary sources that included federal and municipal documents. The fieldwork in Mexico included interviews with staff in the Ministry of Foreign Affairs responsible for programs aimed at migrants and provincial government staff responsible for maintaining ties with migrants (for seven of the eight provinces that had active programs at the time). I visited projects and spoke with municipal staff in two provinces, Zacatecas and Jalisco. In Zacatecas, I spoke with representatives of U.S.-based clubs. In the Los Angeles area, I interviewed leaders of umbrella or hometown organizations from 12 provinces, but focused on Zacatecas[4] because of interesting developments taking place in relations between the Federation of Zacatecan Clubs and the provincial government (Goldring, 1998a, 1998b). I observed federation meetings and attended fund-raising events and meetings of several other groups. At the Mexican consulate, I interviewed several staff members responsible for migrant outreach. I was able to see many people several times over the course of the research. This allowed me to establish rapport, build on previous information, and compare notes, both from different people and perspectives at any one time and from individuals over time.

MIGRANT-LED AND STATE-LED TRANSNATIONALISM IN THE MEXICO-U.S. CONTEXT

Transnational social spaces or social formations are constituted through the practices of various actors and institutions with varying degrees of power, from "above" and from "below" (Basch et al., 1994; Guarnizo & Smith, 1998). In the Mexican case, migrant-led transnational practices predate state responses, but both are crucial in generating and maintaining transnational spaces.

Migrant-Led Transnationalism

Mexican migrant- or transmigrant-led transnationalism involves two important forms of organization: kin- or family-based transnationalism, and broader transnational collectivities such as mutual-aid societies and hometown organizations. Kin-based transnationalism has its roots in the expansion (or fragmentation) of family, social, and community networks across the border through the processes of nation building and international migration. The Mexico-U.S. migration literature documents the key role of family and social networks in contributing to the cumulative causation, or self-feeding process, of migration (Massey et al., 1988).

Mexican transmigrants also have a long history of organizing to raise funds and carry out collective projects in their places of origin (González Gutiérrez, 1995; Goldring, 1992b, 1996, 1998a, 1999a, 1999b; Moctezuma, 1998; Smith, 1995, 1998). Collective projects include church renovations and construction, cemetery improvements, transportation infrastructure (e.g., road construction and paving, bridges), sanitation infrastructure (drainage, sewage, potable water, washing areas, public restrooms), electrification, school buildings, clinics, education and health equipment (e.g., computers, textbooks, ambulances), "urban" beautification (e.g., plazas, benches), recreational infrastructure (e.g., playing fields, rodeo rings), community halls, social welfare projects (e.g., old-age homes, allowances for the elderly and/or needy, Christmas presents for poor children), and, less frequently, productive infrastructure (e.g., irrigation) and small businesses (Goldring, various; Smith, 1995, 1998; cf. Levitt, 1997).

The groups carrying out these projects represent a migrant-led form of transnational organization that I refer to as collective migrant-led transnationalism. The "clubs" that work on these projects are made up of people from the same locality or municipality of origin, who, though they may be related, generally claim to be working "for the good of the community." Hometown clubs may work with local religious or political authorities in Mexico, or on their own. Many hometown organizations have worked informally, coming together for particular projects, dissolving, and coming together again for another project, perhaps with new membership. Since 1993, largely as a result of Mexican state-led outreach programs, the number of hometown clubs and provincial-level umbrella organizations has grown, and many are registered with Mexican consulates in various U.S. cities.[5] Some of the larger and more established groups are also registered as nonprofit organizations in the United States. Some have worked with U.S.-based politicians and community organizations on sister-city programs and, more recently, on the campaign against Proposition 187 and on citizenship drives (cf. Zabin & Escala Rabadan, 1998).

This analysis focuses on transmigrant organizations for several reasons. While there have been significant advances in gendering migration research, there is little work on how gender operates at the level of these organizations. It is important to address this gap because these organizations' activities are a form of increasingly institutionalized substantive citizenship practice (cf. Goldring, 2001; Guarnizo, 1998). Starting in the 1990s, hometown clubs and umbrella transmigrant organizations became one of the main targets of the Mexican state's efforts to court Mexicans abroad. As a result, these groups are becoming identified as political actors in several provincial and many municipal contexts (Goldring, 1998b). Transmigrant organizations are key interlocutors vis-à-vis Mexican state policies, programs, and political authorities, and they represent an important arena for transmigrant Mexico-oriented political activity.

State-Mediated Transnationalism

A dramatic shift in Mexican government policy toward Mexicans residing outside the national territory began to occur in the late 1980s. After years of ad hoc government initiatives and consular protection going back as far as 1848, the government began to reach out to Mexicans abroad in an effort to establish a new relationship with the diaspora (González Gutiérrez, 1995). This was prompted by several related processes, including challenges to the hegemony of the Partido Revolucionario Institutional and the support Cuahutémoc Cárdenas received during his "campaign" tours in the United States prior to the 1988 presidential elections; the government's desire to build a pro-NAFTA and pro-Mexico lobby among the Mexican-origin population in the United States; and an interest in fostering closer economic as well as political ties with Mexicans and people of Mexican origin in the United States (Goldring, 1999a; González Gutiérrez, 1993; Guarnizo, 1998; Smith, 1998).[6]

The Program for Mexican Communities Abroad (Programa para las Comunidades Mexicanas en el Exterior, or PCME), established in 1991, was one of the most concrete elements of the state's efforts to redefine its relationship with Mexicans abroad.[7] The PCME is organized around a variety of thematic program areas aimed at different sectors of the Mexican and Mexican origin population in the United States. The communities program within the PCME carried out the mandate of fostering closer ties between Mexicans in the United States and their localities of origin. It followed and expanded the existing structure of hometown clubs and capitalized on their members' interest in carrying out projects to improve their hometowns through a matching funds program established in 1993 (Goldring, 1998a, 1999a; Smith, 1998). Under the program, which became known as the "2 for 1 program," the federal and provincial governments contributed two dollars for every dollar raised by a club for a community project. The "2 for 1" operated as a federal program in six provinces until 1995, when it folded. Zacatecas was the only province where it continued in an institutionalized manner, through special agreements between provincial governors, the federal government, and the Federation of Zacatecan Clubs.

Under the Zedillo administration (1994–2000), the PCME and related outreach programs aimed at Mexicans in the United States continued. The government also engaged in a historic redefinition and expansion of membership in the Mexican nation so as to officially include and reincorporate Mexicans abroad (Goldring, 1998b, 1999a; Guarnizo, 1998; Smith, 1998). In 1998, constitutional changes established the non-loss of Mexican *nationality* (not citizenship) for nationals who obtained another citizenship, and permitted the recovery of Mexican nationality by the foreign-born children of Mexicans living abroad. These changes, however, also reaffirmed a distinction between citizenship and nationality, reserving citizenship—and voting rights—for those living within the national territory. The laws went into effect in 1998.[8] Clearly, the non-loss of nationality was aimed at granting a largely symbolic form of membership in the nation, one that would affirm Mexican identity and nationalism and officially extend property rights, without granting formal political citizenship to Mexicans abroad (Goldring, 1999a; Ross, 1998).[9] While in theory universalistic and thus presumably gender neutral, the government's programs and policies aimed at migrants have contributed to the gendering of transmigrants' citizenship practices.

THE GENDERING OF POLITICAL PRACTICE
IN TRANSNATIONAL SOCIAL SPACES

Gender- and Kin-Based Transnationalism

At the level of kin-based transnationalism, gender relations are more variable, flexible, and contested than in the male-dominated, institutionalized, and public transmigrant organizations.[10] Contemporary research suggests that while stereotypes of "macho" Mexican men continue to prevail in the popular imagination, the meaning(s) of this concept in everyday life in Mexico may be more nuanced and can run counter to the stereotype (Gutmann, 1996). Migration may augment the variability and contradictions in already contested gender roles and relations. Women "left behind" in Mexico may gain limited arenas of authority while their spouses are absent (Hondagneu-Sotelo, 1992), although they may also come under increasing supervision by their husbands' relatives (Goldring, 1996; Malkin, 1998). These women often draw on other women to facilitate their own migration (Hondagneu-Sotelo, 1994). In the United States, women may be isolated at home and very dependent on their spouses. Alternatively, they may work outside the home or become increasingly familiar with social services and other institutions, which may increase their autonomy (Hondagneu-Sotelo, 1994; Malkin, 1998). Women who have migrated more recently may find more opportunities for "overcoming patriarchal constraints" (Hondagneu-Sotelo, 1992). Younger male partners may also be more amenable to more egalitarian gender relations (Hirsch, 1999).

Research on gender and Mexico-U.S.migration shows that women and men tend to have divergent interests and plans regarding settlement in the United States: men tend to be more interested in returning to Mexico to live (Espinosa, 1998; Goldring, 1996; Hondagneu-Sotelo, 1994; Malkin, 1998).[11] Part of the explanation for this has to do with the ways in which gender intersects with class and racialization to restrict the use of public space for Mexicans (and other immigrants) in the United States, especially men (Goldring, 1996; Hondagneu-Sotelo, 1994; Malkin, 1998; Rouse, 1990). Another important reason is that men experience a greater relative loss of gender-related status and authority in the process of migration (Espinosa, 1998; Goldring, 1996; Hondagneu-Sotelo, 1994). Mexican immigrant men are usually in a subordinate position in the United States compared with their situation in Mexico, whether it is framed in terms of social status or patriarchal privilege—despite possible improvements in their standard of living. And they are certainly in a subordinate class and ethno-racial position vis-à-vis White men. Hondagneu-Sotelo and Messner (1994) argue that this structural marginalization is accompanied by the erosion of patriarchal privilege within the family. In addition to reduced spatial mobility, men lose authority in family decision-making processes and control over household labor (Goldring, 1996; Hondagneu-Sotelo & Messner, 1994, p. 210).

In contrast, women are often less interested in returning to Mexico on a long-term basis because they tend to experience either a relative gain in status in the United States, or not as great a loss. Working outside the home for wages can improve women's ability to negotiate gender relations within the parameters of patriarchy (Hondagneu-Sotelo & Messner, 1994; Kandiyoti, 1988). Returning to Mexico might involve the reassertion of stronger patriarchal authority and a return to the premigration gender division of labor in a setting where household work is often more taxing. It might also involve separation from children settled in the United States (Goldring, 1996).

A substantial body of research suggests that interest in, and reasons for, maintaining transnational social spaces may differ significantly for men and women. At the level of kin-based transnationalism and social networks, men and women are both active in constructing the cross-border social fields that constitute transnational spaces. While they may continue to keep in touch with relatives and send money back home, women usually have a greater interest in settling in the United States than their male partners (Espinosa, 1998; Goldring, 1996; Hondagneu-Sotelo, 1994). Over time, and especially if their families are in the United States, women may lose interest in maintaining transnational spaces. This difference may manifest itself in gendered conflicts over where to invest resources (e.g., building or buying a home in Mexico versus the United States) (Goldring, 1992a, 1996; Grasmuck & Pessar, 1991). It may also contribute to differing interest in participating in the collective transnationalism of hometown organizations.

Gender and State-Mediated Collective Transnationalism

In this section I show how transmigrant citizenship and transmigrant-state relations are gendered in the context of the Federation of Zacatecan Clubs. Through programs like the "2 for 1," transmigrant men broaden the social citizenship benefits and social standing of their places of origin. In so doing, they may also expand their substantive political citizenship (Goldring, 1998b, 1999a). This male-dominated process is structured by the intersection of dominant gender ideologies with the ways in which outreach programs work and how transmigrant organizations are accustomed to operate.

In Mexico, public formal political citizenship remains a predominantly male arena despite the fact that, starting in the early 1980s, the panorama of women's formal and informal participation in politics began to change dramatically. The number of women elected to political office increased; women's participation became more visible in urban grassroots movements (Bennett, 1998), NGOs (Tarrés, 1998), and local opposition movements (Nelson, 1998); and women have played a key role in the Zapatista movement (Stephen, 1998). Despite such gains, significant constraints continue to prevent women from coming close to achieving gender parity in electoral politics (Camp, 1998). At the municipal level, few women are elected as mayors, alderwomen, or municipal trustees (Massolo, 1998). In 1998, only one out of the 56 municipalities in Zacatecas was governed by a woman. In the same year, other provinces with high rates of U.S.-bound migration had similarly low rates of women in municipal leadership positions: In Guanajuato one out of 46 municipalities was governed by a woman; for Michoacán and Jalisco the figures were 3 out of 113 and 2 out of 124, respectively. Again, in the same year, 9 of the country's states had no women mayors. Veracruz, the state with the largest number of municipalities governed by women, had 9 women mayors out of 207 municipalities (Massolo, 1998, p. 201). It follows that the political culture that most transmigrants are familiar with in Mexico does not present many opportunities for, or models of, women's participation in formal politics.[12]

This aspect of political culture appears to extend to transmigrant organizations in the United States. The Federation of Zacatecan Clubs of Southern California is one of the oldest, largest, and strongest umbrella organizations in the United States (Goldring, 1998a, 1998b, 1999a; González Gutiérrez, 1995; Zabin & Escala Rabadan, 1989). It is also, as previously noted, a male-dominated organization, as are most of these umbrella organizations. My argument is that substantive citizenship practices exercised through the federation are practically synonymous with male citizenship. This results from the interplay between the ways in which gender works through state policies and programs, such as the "2 for 1"; from how gender relations structure participation in organizations like the Federation of Zacatecan Clubs; and from Mexican men's relatively greater loss of status in the United States. I will illustrate these by discussing "2 for 1" projects and how they operate, what it takes to participate in federation activities, and the "benefits" associated with participation.

Reproducing male privilege through the "2 for 1."   Plans for "2 for 1" projects develop in various ways. Some are one or a few people's pet projects, while others have broader backing and management. They may stem from requests from people in the locality in Mexico, from the club members in the United States, or from discussions between the two. In any case, they often emerge in discussions among men and women. However, afterward, carrying out projects is men's business. Women help in fund-raising and attend public functions, but rarely implement projects. This both reflects and contributes to the dominance of men's citizenship practice in hometown organizations. How and why does this take place? One explanation lies in how the federation is organized and how gender structures participation in organizations like the federation. Another lies in the gendered quality of both political culture and the networks of power that are mobilized in order to get things done in Zacatecas.

Gender, organizational structure and participation, and scaling up.   Women participate in many hometown clubs, attend meetings, have a say in decisions, and also play more traditionally feminine roles in fund-raising activities (preparing and selling food, etc.). However, it is men who represent the club at federation meetings. The executive committee *(mesa directiva)* has been made up almost exclusively of men since the federation was established, although there have been women secretaries (usually young unmarried women, accompanied by a relative).[13] Three reasons for the absence of women in federation leadership positions stand out. First, once a club scales up by joining an umbrella organization like the federation, club activities no longer involve simply families who know each other working together. Instead, citizenship practice shifts from the familial and community arena to an explicitly public sphere of meetings, official events, and negotiations with Mexican political authorities and consular staff. While no federation rule bars women, the accepted fact is that positions of power are for men. While men sit at the negotiation table in meetings with consular staff, the governor, or mayors, women sit in the audience or meet separately with the governor or mayors' wives. Prevailing gender relations do not facilitate women's participation in this more public arena of citizenship practice. Women may support particular projects, but they will not be the ones pushing them through (see below). Women, particularly those with children, find it difficult to attend meetings—not necessarily because their husbands "don't let them," but because everyone knows that the family comes first. Meetings, which are usually held on weekday evenings, run quite late and involve a long drive for most participants. If women with young children attend, it would imply they are neglecting their families. Men's active participation both depends upon and reproduces gender relations that involve women staying home to care for children. During my fieldwork, only a few older women whose children were grown attended meetings regularly, and they did so with their husbands.

Second, women who try to promote a different agenda within the federation are usually marginalized. The wife of one club leader told me how a number of years ago, she and a group of women had tried to form their own club, paid their federation dues, and wanted to promote educational and cultural exchange projects. They attended meetings for nearly a year, but finally lost interest because they always felt ignored. There is also the case of "Rita," a young woman born in Zacatecas but who has lived in the United States most of her life. Since her university student days, she has been involved in a number of Latino community organizations and she decided to form a hometown club a few years ago (after I completed most of my fieldwork). As president of her club, Rita attended federation meetings and was not afraid to speak her mind. However, her interventions often met with disapproval. She was considered loud, opinionated, and "not familiar with the way things are done." Although she continued to participate, she expressed doubts about her long-term participation in the organization.

Gender and the politics of project implementation.   Implementing a project through the "2 for 1" required negotiations at many stages: for example, to be approved, initiated, funded on time, and completed properly. Club leaders engaged in these negotiations lobbied their mayor, relevant municipal staff, the governor, and the governor's liaison. They did this by traveling to Mexico themselves, during the U.S. visits of these Mexican authorities, or by phone. This process is gendered in several ways. First, as discussed above, there are very few women in positions of power in the clubs or federation, which means that the process of project implementation is also male dominated. Furthermore, women's domestic roles limit their non-family-related cross-border travel. Finally, these negotiations often rely on gendered, masculine networks of friendship, *compadrazgo*, student cohorts, former jobs, and so forth. For example, if a problem occurred during a meeting that might threaten a project's approval, local representatives would usually contact the club leaders, who would apply pressure through their networks to resolve it. If club leaders, club representatives in Mexico, or municipal presidents wanted to negotiate better terms for any aspect of a project, they relied on their networks. Projects also required considerable follow-up. A club leader might have to make several calls and perhaps some trips to Mexico to make sure that work was carried out satisfactorily. In the process, he would again be likely to draw on contacts to make sure things went well. Club representatives in Mexico did much of this follow-up work, but both they and club leaders in California told me that authorities in Mexico paid more attention to transmigrants. These men's involvement in the process of project implementation helped to reproduce a male-dominated form of substantive citizenship.

Gender and incentives to participation.   Women may approve of and benefit from projects carried out in their home communities, but they rarely work on implementing projects. Women encounter limits on their participation in leadership positions in umbrella organizations in the United States and would face similar difficulties negotiating the labyrinths of power in Mexico. Men usually have an easier time mobilizing the resources and time such activities require. What we see, as a result, is men actively exercising substantive citizenship in relation to provincial, municipal, and, in some cases, federal authorities in Mexico. This citizenship practice expands the social citizenship benefits of the communities where projects are carried out (Goldring, 1998a, 1999a), which often contributes some degree of power or leverage in negotiations with Mexican authorities. It also provides transmigrant leaders with a space for performing gendered citizenship and a particular form of masculinity. Together, these reproduce male privilege in ways that are either not available in the United States for some men or which complement relatively high status in the United States for others.[14] In sum, the political culture that surrounds the organization of, and participation in, the federation and the way "2 for 1" projects are carried out are extremely gendered processes. They depend on male privilege and reproduce it. Women may decorate the federation's annual magazine, but they do not occupy positions of power in the organization.

The state's outreach programs and the ways they are implemented at the subnational level are not designed with the purpose of perpetuating male privilege, but they end up doing just that. They build on existing gender relations, ideologies, divisions of labor, and hierarchies and facilitate the reproduction of a political culture in which gendered networks of power contribute to leaving women out of positions of power. While many hometown organizations existed before the state began to take a systematic interest in Mexicans abroad, state policies and programs have increased the number and strength of the organizations and contributed to their becoming political actors vis-à-vis the Mexican nation. The state plays a key role in the process of gendering political participation in transnational spaces by promoting programs such as the "2 for 1" that involve bringing transmigrants into the sphere of influence of Mexican political authorities. The willingness of provincial and municipal political authorities in Mexico to court and engage with transmigrants as part of their own political agenda expands the opportunities of male transmigrant leaders to overcome any marginalization they may experience in the United States (cf. Hondagneu-Sotelo & Messner, 1994) and to exercise a form of citizenship that raises their social status, increases their social capital, and expands their social citizenship as well as that of their communities of origin. By building on existing forms of male-dominated organizations and not taking steps to alter women's patterns of participation, the state's efforts to reincorporate Mexicans offers men a version of citizenship, limited as it may be, that is largely unavailable to women. It is in this sense that Mexican state policies contribute to the gendering of citizenship practices in transnational spaces.

CONCLUDING REMARKS ON GENDER
AND POLITICAL PARTICIPATION

First-generation Mexican hometown associations provide an important context for socializing, constructing and affirming ethnic and/or national identity, for carrying out community projects in Mexico, and in some cases, for political action. Most of their activities are oriented toward the towns, municipalities, and states of origin. In recent years, however, anti-immigrant legislation in the United States, rising rates of naturalization, and increasing contact with Latino and other politicians in the United States have contributed to broadening the opportunities for these im/migrants[15] to participate in Mexico as well as the United States. However, this increasingly transnationalized arena of transmigrant political participation is very gendered: it provides a privileged arena of participation for the overwhelmingly male leadership of hometown clubs and umbrella associations.

Transmigrant men and women are both active in constructing and maintaining kinship and compadrazgo ties in transnational social spaces. However, when it comes to participation in suprafamilial, collective, and more institutionalized transnational organizations such as hometown and umbrella organizations, women remain in the picture but in subordinate roles rather than in positions of power. For Mexican men, who experience a relatively greater loss of gender status compared with women, these organizations provide a special context for valorizing male status. Thanks to the Mexican government's outreach programs for Mexicans abroad, they are also a key arena for engaging with political authorities. State-mediated transnational spaces, in which transmigrant organizations operate, thus provide a special context for valorizing male status and deploying political power.

My work thus supports a conclusion reached by authors such as Hardy-Fanta (1993) and Jones-Correa (1998): namely, that opportunity structures for exercising citizenship for women and men lead to different patterns of participation for women and men and to gender differences in the geographic orientation of political activity. However, my research focused on the hometown organizations and their male leadership. As such, it did not examine men who were active in other, U.S.-based political institutions, nor did it investigate women's political participation directly. However, it is clear from the literature that Mexican and other Latino men do engage in U.S.-based organizing, and that Mexican and other Latina women are quite politically engaged, but in the United States. Not all Mexican men who engage in some form of political activity do so in the context of these organizations. While men may be able to exercise more choice about the geographic orientation of their participation, most women find that their way to work for change is through U.S.-based organizations.

This essay highlights three points that have broader theoretical relevance. First, it is important to conceptualize and analyze citizenship as a practice that potentially takes place in transnational contexts, vis-à-vis more than one nation-state. Second, analyzing the political participation of any ethnic or national group should include attention to within-group differences. In this case, I showed that participation in homeland-oriented politics through hometown organizations is extremely gendered. Key decision-making positions are dominated by men, while women play more "traditional" roles that do not involve negotiations with Mexican political authorities. Third, state policies and programs can contribute to the reproduction of male privilege in transmigrant organizations. In this case, state policies and programs, Mexican political culture, the structure and organization of the Federation of Zacatecan Clubs, and gender ideologies as they play out at the domestic level come together in a way that promotes active male citizenship while relegating women's participation to traditional roles as cooks, mothers, or beauty queens. This contributes to women having little opportunity or incentive to exercise active substantive political citizenship through the federation or in this transnational arena.

It is clear from the literature that Mexican and other Latina women are far from passive or politically uninvolved. On the contrary, they are, and have a history of being, active in a range of nonelectoral political activity in the United States. Without combined attention to the gender and geography of citizenship in transnational contexts, one could miss important aspects of men's or women's citizenship practices. For example, focusing on transmigrant citizenship practices toward Mexico without looking at the United States could suggest that transmigrant women are not politically involved. Conversely, studying Latina participation in environmental grassroots organizations might lead one to wonder where the men are.

Transmigrant or immigrant women who find their practice of citizenship limited in home-state-mediated transnational social spaces are more likely to engage in substantive citizenship oriented toward expanding social citizenship for their families in the United States. This tendency may be shaped by conformity to "traditional" gender norms, in that women's adherence to elements of patriarchal gender relations contributes to their focusing on issues related to children and family, such as schooling, health, the local environment, and labor. At the domestic level, their involvement may lead to tension as women's U.S.-oriented substantive citizenship and men's Mexico-oriented citizenship contribute to divergent long-term settlement plans. At a broader level, the gendering of citizenship in transnational spaces may contribute to differences in feelings of membership and belonging in the relevant nations and thus to the gender of membership in the nation (cf. Yuval-Davis & Anthias, 1989).

The specific mechanisms that contribute to the gendering of citizenship in transnational spaces deserve further comparative research (e.g., Levitt, 1998). My own research has emphasized the interaction between gender relations, men's relatively greater loss of gender and social status through migration, and home-state policies and programs. However, comparative research on different transmigrant groups and sending states, and the ways their policies contribute to the gendering of transmigrant citizenship practices, can tell us more about the implications for women's and men's citizenship practices in the United States and "at home." The role of class and rural/urban background also deserve attention. This kind of work may improve our theorization of transnational social spaces, citizenship, and transmigrant women's and men's participation in multiple settings.

NOTES

This chapter is a based on a paper presented at the conference on Engendering Theories of Transnational Migration held at Yale University, February 5–6, 1999. It is also a shorter and revised version of an article published in *Identities* (Goldring, 2001). I am grateful to Pierrette Hondagneu-Sotelo, Peter Vandergeest, and Kathy Bischoping for comments on this version.

1. I am following Basch, Schiller, and Szanton Blanc's (1994) use of "transmigrants" to refer to immigrants and migrants who maintain strong attachments to their places of origin, as expressed by active cultural, social, political, and economic ties and flows. Transmigrants build transnational social fields or social spaces, linking their places of origin and settlement.

2. I use "political activity," "political participation," and "citizenship practice" almost interchangeably to refer to collective activities aimed at claiming or expanding rights and entitlements that derive from membership in a political community. This usage is intended to capture a broad range of "politics," from electoral politics carried out by citizens, to non-electoral activities, including participation in voluntary associations by citizens and noncitizens. My emphasis is on substantive citizenship, or citizenship-like *practices*. This conception of citizenship does not rest on formal legal status and includes practices oriented toward one's homeland. See section on the gendering of citizenship and transmigrant-state relations in Goldring, 2001.

3. The research was supported through a postdoctoral fellowship from the Social Science Research Council. I am also grateful to the North American Integration and Development Center at UCLA, where I was affiliated.

4. Umbrella organizations existed for some but not all provinces. While there is no consistent relationship between the estimated number of people from a given province and the number of hometown clubs from that political unit, Zacatecas and Jalisco have consistently had the largest number of clubs (45 and 30, respectively, in 1996) and are among the top "sending" states (see discussions in Goldring, 1999a; González Gutiérrez, 1995; Zabin & Escala Rabadan, 1998).

5. In 1998 there were over 170 hometown clubs from 18 Mexican states in the greater Los Angeles area (Zabin & Escala Rabadan, 1998). For background on Mexican hometown organizations, see Espinosa (1998), González Gutiérrez (1995), Goldring (1992a, 1992b, 1996, 1998b, 1999a), Imaz (1995), Moctezuma (1998), Rivera (1998), Smith (1995, 1998), and Zabin and Escala Rabadan (1998).

6. Growing anti-immigrant hysteria and legislation in the United States, particularly California, would later add to the rationale for increasing the profile of Mexican consuls and consulates and for the new policy of encouraging naturalization as a way for Mexicans to defend their rights in the United States (Guarnizo, 1998; Martínez, 1998a, 1998b).

7. For more on the PCME, see Smith (1995, 1998), Guarnizo (1998), González Gutiérrez (1993, 1995), and Goldring (1998a, 1998b, 1999a).

8. In 1996 a more significant modification was made to the electoral law, allowing citizens to vote for president from outside their home districts. This established the possibility for Mexicans in the United States to vote in the 2000 Mexican presidential elections. However, in July 1999, the ruling party (PRI) blocked any possibility of the vote.

9. Since then, coalitions of Mexicans in Mexico and the United States and various groups in the United States affiliated with opposition parties in Mexico have continued to lobby in favor of extraterritorial voting rights.

10. This is especially true with respect to Zacatecan organizations. Women play important roles in some organizations from San Luis Potosí, Nayarit, and Guanajuato, but they are the exception. While this analysis of Zacatecan organizations is not meant to apply to all state-transmigrant organization relations, it raises questions that may be relevant to other contexts.

11. See Grasmuck and Pessar (1991) for similar discussions with respect to Dominican-U.S. migration, and Mahler (1996) on El Salvador.

12. I do not wish to imply that women as a group are not interested in politics, or that they have no experience in local organizations or politics. Women involved in grassroots activism would obviously be an exception to this generalization. I also want to guard against making essentializing statements about "political culture." However, I am referring to an overall "chilly climate" for women in politics in Mexico, one shaped by the understanding that women do not belong in the public realm of *la política*.

13. A woman from Michoacán headed the federation for one term (1983–1985), before the matching funds program was established. This was also during a period when the federation was not exclusively Zacatecan, but included clubs from other provinces.

14. Class interacts with gender in the process of exercising substantive citizenship through hometown clubs and umbrella organizations. Men in leadership positions in the federation tend to be self-employed business owners or professionals with flexible work schedules, rather than hourly workers. However, club leaders often include wageworkers.

15. I use im/migrants to draw attention to the potential difficulty of classifying people as *either* migrants *or* immigrants.

REFERENCES

Basch, Linda, Schiller, Nina Glick, & Szanton Blanc, Cristina. (1994). *Nations unbound: Transnational projects, postcolonial predicaments, and deterritorialized nation-states.* Amsterdam: Gordon & Breach.

Bennett, Vivienne. (1998). Everyday struggles: Women in urban popular movements and territorially based protest in Mexico. In Victoria E. Rodríguez (Ed.), *Women's participation in Mexican political life* (pp. 116–130). Boulder, CO: Westview Press.

Burgos, Rita, & Pulido, Laura. (1998). The politics of gender in the Bus Riders' Union/Sindicato de Pasajeros. *Capitalism, Nature, Socialism, 9*(3), 75–82.

Camp, Roderic Ai. (1998). Women and men, men and women: Gender patterns in Mexican politics. In Victoria E. Rodríguez (Ed.), *Women's participation in Mexican political life* (pp. 167–178). Boulder, CO: Westview Press.

Cranford, Cynthia. (2000). *Labor, gender, and the politics of immigration: Organizing justice for janitors in Los Angeles.* Unpublished doctoral dissertation, Department of Sociology, University of Southern California.

Delgado, Hector. (1993). *New immigrants, old unions: Organizing undocumented workers in Los Angeles.* Philadelphia: Temple University Press.

Espinosa, Victor M. (1998). *El dilema del retorno: Migración, género y pertenencia en un contexto transnacional.* Zamora, México: El Colegio de Michoacán; Zapopan, México: El Colegio de Jalisco.

Foner, Nancy. (1997). What's new about transnationalism? New York immigrants today and at the turn of the century. *Diaspora, 6*(3), 355–375.

Goldring, Luin. (1992a). *Diversity and community in transnational migration: A comparative study of two Mexico-U.S. migrant circuits.* Unpublished doctoral dissertation, Department of Rural Sociology, Cornell University.

Goldring, Luin. (1992b). La migración México-EUA y la transnacionalización del espacio político y social: Perspectivas desde el México rural. *Estudios Sociológicos, 10*(29), 315–340.

Goldring, Luin. (1996). Gendered memory: Reconstructions of the village by Mexican transnational migrants. In Melanie DuPuis & Peter Vandergeest (Eds.), *Creating the countryside: The politics of rural and environmental discourse* (pp. 303–329). Philadelphia: Temple University Press.

Goldring, Luin. (1998a). The power of status in transnational social spaces. *Comparative Urban and Community Research, 6,* 165–195.

Goldring, Luin. (1998b, July–December). From market membership to transnational citizenship: The changing politicization of transnational spaces. *L'Ordinaire Latino-Américain* (Toulouse, France), *173-174,* 167–172.

Goldring, Luin. (1999a). El estado mexicano y las organizaciones transmigrantes: Reconfigurando la nación y las relaciones entre estado y sociedad civil? In Gail Mummert (Ed.), *Fronteras fragmentadas* (pp. 297–316). Zamora, México: El Colegio de Michoacán.

Goldring, Luin. (1999b). *The Mexican state and transmigrant organizations: Negotiating the boundaries of membership and participation in the Mexican nation.* Unpublished manuscript.

Goldring, Luin. (2001). The gender and geography of citizenship in Mexico-U.S. transnational spaces. *Identities: Global Studies in Gender and Power, 7,* 501–537.

González Gutiérrez, Carlos. (1993). The Mexican diaspora in California: The limits and possibilities of the Mexican government. In Abraham Lowenthal & Katrina Burgess (Eds.), *The California-Mexico connection* (pp. 221–235). Stanford, CA: Stanford University Press.

González Gutiérrez, Carlos. (1995). La organización de los inmigrantes mexicanos en Los Angeles: La lealtad de los oriundos. *Revista Mexicana de Política Exterior, 46,* 59–101.

Grasmuck, Sherri, & Pessar, Patricia. (1991). *Between two islands: Dominican international migration.* Berkeley & Los Angeles: University of California Press.

Guarnizo, Luis Eduardo. (1998). The rise of transnational social formations: Mexican and Dominican state responses to transnational migration. *Political Power and Social Theory, 12,* 45–94.

Guarnizo, Luis Eduardo, & Smith, Michael Peter. (1998). The locations of transnationalism. In Michael Peter Smith & Luis Eduardo Guarnizo (Eds.), *Transnationalism from below.* New Brunswick, NJ: Transaction.

Gutmann, Matthew. (1996). *The meanings of macho: Being a man in Mexico City.* Berkeley & Los Angeles: University of California Press.

Hardy-Fanta, Carol. (1993). *Latina politics, Latino politics: Gender, culture, and political participation in Boston.* Philadelphia: Temple University Press.

Hirsch, Jennifer. (1999, February 5–6). *"Hay que saber lo que tienes en la casa": Notes toward a transnational political economy of masculinity.* Presented at the conference on Engendering Theories of Transnational Migration, Yale University, New Haven, CT.

Hondagneu-Sotelo, Pierrette. (1992). Overcoming patriarchal constraints: The reconstruction of gender relations among Mexican immigrant women and men. *Gender and Society,* *6*(3), 393–415.

Hondagneu-Sotelo, Pierrette. (1994). *Gendered transitions: Mexican experiences of immigration.* Berkeley & Los Angeles: University of California Press.

Hondagneu-Sotelo, Pierrette, & Messner, Michael A. (1994). Gender displays and men's power: The "new man" and Mexican immigrant man. In Harry Brod & Michael Kaufman (Eds.), *Theorizing masculinities* (pp. 200–218). Thousand Oaks, CA: Sage.

Hondagneu-Sotelo, Pierrette, & Riegos, Cristina. (1997). Sin organización no hay solución: Latina domestic workers and non-traditional labor organizing. *Latino Studies Journal, 8*(3), 54–81.

Imaz, Cecilia. (1995, October 1–5). *Las organizaciones por lugar de origen de los mexicanos en Estados Unidos (California, Illinois y Nueva York).* Paper presented at the XX Congreso de la Asociación Latinoamericana de Sociología, Mexico City.

Jones-Correa, Michael. (1998). *Between two nations: The political predicament of Latinos in New York City.* Ithaca, NY: Cornell University Press.

Kandiyoti, Denise. (1988). Bargaining with patriarchy. *Gender and Society, 2,* 274–290.

Levitt, Peggy. (1997). Transnationalizing community development: The case of migration between Boston and the Dominican Republic. *Nonprofit and Voluntary Sector Quarterly, 26*(4), 509–526.

Levitt, Peggy. (1998, June 11–14). *Forms of transnational community and their implications for immigrant incorporation: Preliminary findings.* Social Science Research Council International Migration Program Workshop on Transformations: Immigration and Immigration Research in the United States. Columbia University.

Mahler, Sarah J. (1996). *Bringing gender to a transnational focus: Theoretical and empirical ideas.* Unpublished manuscript, Department of Anthropology, University of Vermont.

Malkin, Victoria. (1998). Migration, Modernity and Respect. In *The Family and Gender in Transmigrant Circuits: A Case Study of Migration Between Western Mexico and New Rochelle, New York.* Unpublished doctoral dissertation, University College of London, England.

Martínez Saldaña, Jesus. (1998a). *Las instituciones para la democración México: Su fracaso ante la emigración.* Unpublished manuscript.

Martínez Saldaña, Jesus. (1998b). In search of our lost citizenship: Mexican immigrants, the right to vote, and the transition to democracy in Mexico. *L'Ordinaire Latino-Américain* (Toulouse, France), *173–174,* 152–162.

Massey, Douglas, Alarcón, Rafael, Durand, Jorge, & González, Humberto. (1987). *Return to Aztlan: The social process of international migration from western Mexico.* Berkeley & Los Angeles: University of California Press.

Massolo, Alejandra. (1998). Women in the local arena and municipal power. In Victoria E. Rodríguez (Ed.), *Women's participation in Mexican political life* (pp. 193–203). Boulder, CO: Westview Press.

Moctezuma, Miguel. (1998). *Redes sociales, comunidades y familias de migrantes. Sain Alto, Zac. en Oakland, Ca.* Draft of doctoral dissertation, Tijuana, México, El Colegio de la Frontera Norte.

Nelson, Lise. (1998, September 24–26). *Las que defienden el pueblo: Emerging discourses and practices of citizenship in Cherán, Michoacán.* Paper presented at the annual meeting of the Latin American Studies Association, Chicago.

Pardo, Mary. (1999). Gendered citizenship: Mexican American women and grassroots activism in East Los Angeles, 1986–1992. In David Montejano (Ed.), *Chicano politics and society in the late twentieth century* (pp. 58–79). Austin: University of Texas Press.

Portes, Alejandro, & Rumbaut, Rubén. (1990). *Immigrant America: A portrait.* Berkeley & Los Angeles: University of California.

Rivera Salgado, Gaspar. (1998, August 9). Radiografia de Oaxacalifornia. *Masiosare, La Jornada,* pp.3–8.

Rose, Margaret Eleanor. (1988). *Women in the United Farm Workers: A study of Chicana and Mexicana participation in a labor union, 1950–1980.* Unpublished doctoral dissertation, University of California, Los Angeles.

Rouse, Roger. (1990). *Men in space: Power and the appropriation of urban form among Mexican migrants in the United States.* Unpublished manuscript, Department of Anthropology, University of Michigan.

Ruíz, Vicki L. (1987). *Cannery women, cannery lives: Mexican women, unionization, and the California food processing industry, 1930–1950.* Albuquerque: University of New Mexico Press.

Smith, Robert C. (1995). *Los ausentes siempre presentes: The imagining, making, and politics of a transnational community between New York and Ticuani, Puebla.* Unpublished doctoral dissertation, Department of Political Science, Columbia University.

Smith, Robert C. (1998). Transnational localities: Community, technology, and the politics of membership within the context of Mexico and U.S. migration. *Comparative Urban and Community Research, 6,* 196–238.

Stephen, Lynn. (1998). Gender and grass-roots organizing: Lessons from Chiapas. In Victoria E. Rodríguez (Ed.), *Women's participation in Mexican political life* (pp. 146–163). Boulder, CO: Westview Press.

Tarrés, Maria Luisa. (1998). The role of women's nongovernmental organizations in Mexico. In Victoria E. Rodríguez (Ed.), *Women's participation in Mexican political life* (pp. 131–145). Boulder, CO: Westview Press.

Yuval-Davis, Nira, & Anthias, Floya (Eds.). (1989). *Women, nation, state.* London: MacMillan Press.

Zabin, Carol, & Escala Rabadan, Luis. (1998). *Mexican hometown associations and Mexican immigrant political empowerment in Los Angeles* (Nonprofit Sector Research Fund Working Paper Series). Washington, DC: Aspen Institute.

CHAPTER 17

"The Blue Passport"

Gender and the Social Process of Naturalization among Dominican Immigrants in New York City

Audrey Singer and Greta Gilbertson

INTRODUCTION

The formal acquisition of citizenship through naturalization has received little attention in the migration literature. In this research we look at the process of how immigrants become citizens, focusing on how they act and perceive citizenship rather than evaluating their actions from the perspective of the dominant group's perceptions and interpretations. How immigrants understand the process of "becoming" and "being"[1] a citizen is important because it illuminates issues relevant to a broader constitution of citizenship, both formal and social.

In this discussion, we focus on how gender influences the social process of naturalization. Gender relations are central to any understanding of how and why men and women experience changing social, economic, and cultural practices (Sorenson, 1998). Gender has played an important role in shaping citizenship practices and discourses (Bredbenner, 1998; Knop, 2001; Werbner & Yuval-Davis, 1999). Attention to how gender influences whether immigrants become citizens recognizes both the processes that antedate formal citizenship, such as migration and settlement, and those that follow it.

Despite the increase in attention to citizenship, few studies have examined the naturalization process, and we do not know of any that focus specifically on the gendered dimensions of naturalization. The social science literature has traditionally viewed the acquisition of citizenship as a signifier of the assimilation of immigrants into the host society. This view corresponds to a national model of citizenship, which sees immigrants as incorporating as full members into a single nation-state and national political community (Joppke, 2000; Smith, 1998). This model is problematic, because it assumes that immigrants become full members of the host society while severing ties with the country of origin. This optic is remedied in part by a transnational citizenship model (Brubaker, 1989; Faist, 2000;

Joppke, 2000). This perspective on citizenship recognizes numerous features of contemporary immigration that are given short shrift by the national citizenship model: the retention of strong ties to the country of origin by immigrants and the growth of transnational structures; the multiple allegiances and identities of immigrants; and the growth of large noncitizen immigrant populations. The growth of dual citizenship can be accounted for by a transnational citizenship model. Sending states, once thought irrelevant, are promoting the preservation of their national culture as well as the flow of resources from immigrants abroad (Guarnizo & Smith, 1998). These developments are significant for their implications for citizenship and membership, underscoring the contested and more contingent nature of integration and citizenship.

While the transnational model of citizenship is more descriptive of the experiences of immigrants today than the national citizenship model, both overlook the gendered nature of citizenship. While the national citizenship model uses an androcentric perspective and posits the experience of dominant-group men as central, the transnational model is only beginning to explore how gender intersects with other forces to shape a variety of citizenship practices and discourses (Pessar, this volume).

A growing body of research on the gendered nature of migration and settlement, though, is relevant to our thinking about citizenship acquisition as well as broader issues of membership and belonging. We know that migration and settlement experiences, including return migration and transnational migration, differ for men and women. For example, numerous studies suggest that gains in gender equity are critical to women's desire to settle in the United States (Grasmuck & Pessar, 1991; Hagan, 1994; Hondagneu-Sotelo, 1994). Conversely, men are more likely than women to return to their country of origin, in part to recoup some of the losses in power and status they experience in the United States (Guarnizo, 1997; Pessar, 1986; Rouse, 1992). The different migration and settlement experiences of men and women highlight the importance of considering how gendered structures and practices constitute citizenship and the process of citizenship acquisition.

We examine the naturalization process within the contemporary political, social, and policy context of the 1990s. Following the passage of Proposition 187, the 1994 California proposal that sought to deny social and medical services to undocumented immigrants, an increasingly antagonistic climate toward immigrants continued to build and reached national scope in the culmination of three laws passed within months of each other in 1996: the Illegal Immigration Reform and Immigrant Responsibility Act (the "Immigration Act"), the Antiterrorism and Effective Death Penalty Act (the "Anti-Terrorist Act") and the Personal Responsibility and Work Opportunity Reconciliation Act (the "Welfare Act"). The Anti-Terrorist Act was the most pernicious because it resulted in the detention of supposed "criminal" immigrants upon reentry into the United States after travel abroad. The detention of long-residing U.S. residents upon reentry into the United

States criminalized the immigrant population and heightened immigrants' sense of vulnerability to the arbitrary actions of state officials.

It was the welfare law, however, that gave rise to the most widespread repercussions and fear, even though by the late 1990s many of the original provisions had been modified and some benefits restored. The welfare law made sweeping changes to the structure of and access to public benefits for all residents of the United States; however, changes affecting the immigrant population were at the outset the most dramatic and the most draconian. It required U.S. citizenship status to receive means-tested public assistance and broadened restrictions on public benefits for undocumented immigrants. It also required the Immigration and Naturalization Service (INS) to verify an immigrant's status in order for him or her to receive benefits.

Changing legislation, particularly welfare reform, also demonstrated the state's gendered construction of the immigrant population, particularly immigrant women, as welfare burdens (Collins, 1999). In the wake of these reforms, a conservative discourse developed around the issue of the large and growing numbers of immigrants, presumably responding to punitive legislation, who were naturalizing. Immigrants were uniformly construed as bad citizens: those who naturalized were doing so for the wrong reasons (to secure benefits), while those who "resisted" were punished by legislative reforms that made their status more tentative (Singer & Gilbertson, 1999).

As of yet, few studies focus on how gender structures the entry into formal citizenship in the contemporary period that is characterized by anti-immigrant sentiment. To explore these issues, we use a qualitative case study to examine the naturalization decisions and behavior of an extended family of Dominican immigrants who reside in New York City.

THE CONTEXT OF U.S. CITIZEN ACQUISITION: WASHINGTON HEIGHTS

The Dominican Republic (DR) is currently the fourth largest source of immigrants to the United States (U.S. Immigration and Naturalization Service, 1997). In New York City, Dominicans form the largest immigrant group and the second largest group of Hispanics after Puerto Ricans. The primary destination of Dominican immigrants in New York is the Washington Heights area in northern Manhattan. More than 80% of immigrants arriving in Washington Heights in the 1990s were Dominican (NYC Department of Planning, 1996).

Historically, Dominicans have had low rates of naturalization; however, the proportion of naturalized women in New York City is higher than that of men (NYC Department of City Planning, 1996). The INS estimates that 28.6% of the Dominicans who entered the United States as legal permanent residents in 1977 have naturalized. This contrasts with an average rate of 45.9% for immigrants of all national origins.

Several factors account for the low levels of naturalization among Dominicans, including high levels of residential concentration in immigrant neighborhoods, low rates of English-language usage, low levels of education (Hernández & Rivera-Batiz, 1997), and high rates of sojourning and return migration (Duany, 1994). The growth of transnational ties and linkages between the United States and the Do-minican Republic (Itzigsohn, Cabral, Medina, & Vásquez, 1999; Levitt, 2001) con-tributes to immigrants' sense that they may neither need nor desire U.S. citizenship (see Jones-Correa, 1998). Finally, the fact that there was little difference between le-gal residency and citizenship status prior to the 1996 welfare reform probably con-tributed to the growth in the noncitizen immigrant population among Dominicans (Aleinikoff, 1998).

Despite low rates of naturalization, more Dominican immigrants—along with other groups of immigrants—made the decision to naturalize in the late 1990s. Our earlier research describes the local responses to the anti-immigrant climate and leg-islation. We argued that Washington Heights changed from an insular immigrant enclave that de facto discouraged naturalization to an environment where natu-ralization was strongly encouraged (Gilbertson & Singer, 2000).

Underlying the efforts of various groups, individuals, and structures to help im-migrants to naturalize was the linking of formal citizenship to recent legislative changes. In effect, immigrants were encouraged to naturalize as a way to protect themselves from the harsh consequences of recent legislative changes. Four broad factors help to account for the mobilization of large numbers of immigrants—not only Dominican immigrants—to naturalize: legislative changes, elite encourage-ment (CBOs, community advocates, and politicians), media promotion, and the in-creased pool of eligible immigrants, particularly due to Immigration Reform and Control Act (IRCA) program participants.[2] In Washington Heights, this was par-ticularly evident as community organizations, advocacy groups, and local activists turned their efforts toward naturalization, and the public's awareness grew espe-cially in the period immediately after the welfare law passed. Even the city of New York established a new citywide program (Citizenship NYC) that was explicitly designed to help immigrants to naturalize, targeting those who were most vulner-able in terms of losing welfare benefits. In tandem with the efforts of community organizations to provide immigrants with information about naturalization, the Spanish-language media (television, newspapers, radio) helped to publicize events surrounding the anti-immigrant laws and naturalization.

Finally, it is likely that the advent of dual-citizenship laws also contributed to the shifting climate surrounding naturalization. A 1994 constitutional reform in the Do-minican Republic allowed Dominicans who become citizens of other countries to retain their rights as Dominican nationals (Graham, 1997). Many Dominicans be-came aware of the existence and meaning of dual nationality only when Leonel Fernandez, then president of the Dominican Republic, in a televised speech en-couraged Dominicans abroad to naturalize and assured them that they would not lose any of their rights as Dominican citizens. In his speech, Fernandez called for

Dominicans to become U.S. citizens in response to "the changes in North American society caused by the end of the welfare era" (see Graham, 1997). This message contributed to the notion of citizenship as a necessary accommodation in the context of multiple memberships and identities (see Bauböck, 1994).

METHODOLOGY AND DATA

The aim of our study is to learn more about how women and men think and act about naturalization and the meanings they attach to U.S. citizenship within a context of changing sentiment and legislation regarding immigrants. Our qualitative case study of an extended family group, the Castillo family, includes intensive interviews and participant observation during a period of 3 years (1995–1998). We have continued to informally collect data on the Castillo family 2 years following that period. Interviews and observations of the Castillo family were supplemented by interviews with community actors, including immigrant service providers and local leaders in Washington Heights and other New York City communities. In the course of this research, we also spoke with about 50 other immigrants in the Washington Heights community and observed naturalization patterns among several other families. This information corroborated and complemented much of what we found in our more intensive study of the Castillos.

The Castillo family is a convenience sample. One of the authors (Gilbertson) resides in Washington Heights and as a result of ongoing participation in the community as a researcher and resident had extensive contact with several members of the Castillo family and another family group originating from the same town in the Dominican Republic. We chose to focus on the Castillo family because of its large size and complexity, both in terms of generations and number of family members, its concentration in the New York City area, and its cohesiveness, which facilitated the gathering of information from all family members. Another reason that we chose the Castillos was that most of the adult members residing in the United States were legal permanent residents and were eligible to become U.S. citizens (they had been living in the United States at least 5 years). The study of a family group facilitated the collection of qualitative data because it allowed us to better understand the immediate context of decision making about naturalization. Interviewing family members also ensured validity; in time we knew people well enough to collect multiple and ongoing accounts of events.

Although the extended family may be considered a single case, it is composed of a number of distinct nuclear and extended family households. Individuals in these households have a broad range of characteristics, including legal statuses, age, time in the United States, life-course stage, and labor force participation. On several socioeconomic indicators, the Castillos are similar to all Dominicans residing in New York City. Overall, 39% of all Dominicans aged 25 and over in New York City have a high school diploma or more compared with 53% of the Castillos in the same age range. In terms of occupation, the Castillo family members approximate the Dominican population residing in New York City. While about half (49%) of Dominicans in New York were employed as operatives, laborers, and personal service workers according to the 1990 census, 55% of the Castillos were in these occupational categories.

THE CASTILLO FAMILY

The Castillo family (excluding spouses) spans five generations and includes 65 members, 53 of whom "reside" in the United States (see Figure 17.1). The first sibling cohort comprises six sisters and two brothers between the ages of 39 and 64. They are the subject of this study together with their offspring, the second cohort, 14 men and 13 women ranging in age between 17 and 46. The majority of both cohorts have resided in the United States as legal permanent residents (LPRs) or U.S. citizens. The third cohort, the 31 children of the second cohort, ranged in age from infancy to 19 in the fall of 1997. Twenty-one members of the third cohort reside in the United States, and more than two thirds are U.S.-born citizens. One daughter of this cohort has a child, the first member of the fourth cohort.

The Castillos are originally from the city of Mao, located in the largely agricultural province of Valverde in the Dominican Republic. Mao is the largest urban area (population 68,000 in 1993) in the northwestern region of the Dominican Republic, which historically has been a major source of migration to the United States. In New York City, the majority of the Castillos live in Manhattan (31); others live in the Bronx and Brooklyn. Three members of the second cohort and their children reside in Connecticut, Massachusetts, and Florida.

Table 17.1 summarizes the migration and legal status of the Castillo family over a 27-year period, showing the growth of the family over the period as well as their migration to the United States. With the exception of the pioneer migrant, all members of the Castillo family were petitioned by family members and arrived in the United States with their legal permanent residency. The beginning of the migration chain was Zena, now 64 years old, who was the first of her extended family to migrate in 1969 when she was 28 years old. After ending her marriage, she entered the United States via Puerto Rico using a tourist visa; several years later she obtained legal permanent residency through an arranged marriage. By 1975, two members of the first cohort (Zena and Daniel), Zena's three children, and her mother, Julia, had acquired legal permanent residency and were living in the United States. Julia received her green card through her son Daniel's sponsorship and then subsequently petitioned five of her adult children. All except one of Julia's children obtained their legal permanent residency. Subsequently, all of Julia's offspring petitioned their own children.

By 1985 the number of Castillo family members in the United States had increased from 6 to 20 members and included 5 of the 8 members of the first cohort, 8 members of the second cohort, and 4 U.S.-born members of the third cohort. By 1997, the bulk of the family had migrated to the United States, including

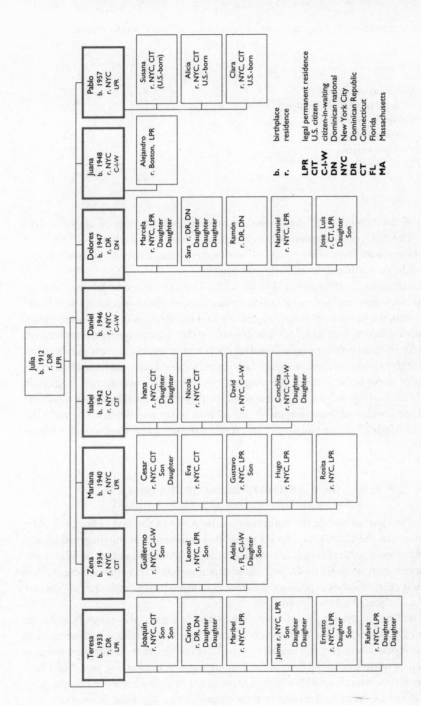

FIGURE 17.1. The Castillo Family

TABLE 17.1. Migration and Legal Status of the Castillo Family,
1975–1997

Legal Status	1975	1985	1997
Dominican national	27	24	12
U.S. legal permanent resident	6	15	20
"Citizen-in-waiting" or a			
naturalized citizen	—	1	13
U.S.-born citizen	—	4	20
Not yet born	32	21	—
TOTAL	65	65	65

7 out of the 8 members of the first cohort and the great majority of the second cohort. The U.S.-residing members of the second cohort have a mixture of U.S.-born
and Dominican-born children. As of late 1997, 13 members of the Castillo family
had either naturalized or applied to naturalize.

The Castillos' settlement in New York City is characterized by labor market incorporation into low-paying factory or service jobs, interaction in an extended family system, the practice of return migration, and residence in urban, working-class,
Spanish-speaking enclaves. Individuals manage the migration experience through
collectivist household strategies based on cooperation among nuclear family members and, to a lesser extent, extended family members. Changing household composition disrupts the abilities of individuals to collectively manage the household
and often corresponds to life-course changes, the arrival and departure of household members, and demographic events such as births and deaths. The most significant kinds of change involve children and parents establishing separate households.

"BUT NOW WITH THE PROBLEM OF THE CHECKS . . . ":
NATURALIZATION AND THE FIRST COHORT

In this section we look at the naturalization behavior of the first cohort, the older
members of the Castillo family. We argue that differences in the propensities and
approaches to naturalization are a function of the gendered nature of labor market incorporation and family/household organization. Life-course changes intersect with these factors to produce differences in immigrants' approach to "becoming" and "being" a U.S. citizen.

The first cohort consists of four women and two men who range in age from
their early 50s to late 60s. With the exception of one woman who has never worked
in the paid labor force, the remaining members of the first cohort have spent at
least part of their working lives in the United States in low-paying jobs. Most have
either independently or with a spouse maintained or built a home, or bought property in the Dominican Republic and have returned on a regular basis.

Although the older men and women of the first cohort both pursue U.S. citizenship as a way to facilitate a transnational lifestyle, we found that the meanings attached to U.S. citizenship differ for men and women. Given the first-cohort women's greater economic vulnerability, the new laws placed their livelihood in greater jeopardy and made U.S. citizenship more vital to their economic well-being. But as a result of their integration into family networks in ways that necessitate continued and intensive caretaking interactions and their more limited resources, women find a transnational residential pattern, rather than permanent return migration, more satisfactory. Men, on the other hand, tend to be less dependent on government assistance and are financially more independent than women. They are less integrated into family networks in ways that require sustained caretaking and seek out different ends to return migration. Return migration for men is envisioned as more permanent.

We now turn to the situations of several of the first-cohort migrants to illustrate gender differences in the pursuit and meaning of U.S. citizenship. As immigrants age and their children form their own families in the United States, they, like other elderly persons, are faced with the task of negotiating their retirement. As a result of the end of paid employment, the high cost of living in New York City, and their ties to the Dominican Republic, older immigrants often decide to move back to the Dominican Republic, although in actuality many take up a transnational residence pattern, spending time in both their country of origin and New York City. There are several reasons why immigrants live transnationally. The end of paid employment and the low incomes of these immigrants make permanent residence in the United States difficult—with the exception of those willing and able to live with their children or those with subsidized housing—particularly for aging, single women. Sixty-four-year-old Zena worked for 19 years and raised three children in the United States. She is single and cannot afford to maintain a household in New York on her own: her monthly social security check and Supplemental Security Income (SSI) stipend total about $500. Zena, who recently naturalized, does not feel comfortable living on a full-time basis in the households of any of her adult children, even though she stays in her married son's household for several months at a time when she is in New York. Currently, Zena lives most of the year in the Dominican Republic, in her own home, which is located next door to her mother's. Her home is paid off, so she does not need to worry about paying rent. Zena talked about how recent legislation threatened her only source of income and pushed her to naturalize:

> Well, I always said to my daughter-in-law, I'm going to become a citizen . . . but I never made the effort . . . but now with the problem of the checks . . . I know with social security I won't have a problem . . . but because they're giving me a supplemental disability check [SSI], I got scared. If they take that check away, I'm not going to have anything to live on. How am I going to maintain myself in my old age? So, I came back from the Dominican Republic with the objective of getting citizenship, not only because of the problem of the checks, but there are problems with everything, now you've got to become a citizen if you want to live in this country.

Fifty-year-old Juana is in a similar situation to that of her sister Zena. Juana worked for 8 years in a factory in the United States and then suffered a serious knee injury. She has been receiving disability payments (SSI) for a number of years and is not in the paid labor force. Juana, who is single, also has difficulty supporting herself in New York on her disability check. When she is the United States, she occasionally stays with her only son, who lives in Boston, but she does not want to live with him on a full-time basis. Like Zena, Juana owns a home in Mao and finds it easier to live with her knee injury there. Juana applied to become a U.S. citizen in 1997.

The desire to move back to the Dominican Republic is also fueled by the perception that certain conditions of old age such as infirmity and isolation (see Kurien, this volume; Menjívar, 2000) are alleviated in the Dominican Republic. Most of the women—and several of their husbands—of the first cohort suffer from a number of serious health problems that they find are aggravated in the United States. Many immigrants find that the warm Caribbean climate and slower-paced lifestyle are more conducive to their general physical and mental health.

Another reason why the first-cohort women move back and forth between the United States and the Dominican Republic is their ties to U.S.-residing children and grandchildren. Through unpaid housework and kin work, women bear the primary responsibility for maintaining close family ties (Espiritu, 2000). Several women of the first cohort stressed that the need to be with U.S.-residing children and grandchildren was the most crucial reason for maintaining their right to reenter the United States. A third sister, 58-year-old Mariana, who resides with her husband and several adult children, was ambivalent about return because of her role in caring for several of her children and grandchildren. But Mariana said that she will eventually return to the Dominican Republic. Her husband, who suffers from several health problems, including severe depression, wants to permanently settle in the Dominican Republic in the future. When asked why she was planning to naturalize, Mariana emphasized that it would allow her and her husband to remain in the Dominican Republic without fear of losing their right to return:

> Well, because now you go and you have problems when you spend six or seven months in the DR. And another is that the health of my husband is not very good now. . . . We think that we're going back to our country, and if you're not a citizen, you can't be coming and going every minute, because when you have family here, you're going to have to be coming back, but you can't be coming back every three months, every four months. This is one of the reasons.

Isabel, who lives with her husband, two adult daughters, a son, and two grandchildren in the United States, became a U.S. citizen in 1997. Isabel finds coresidence with her children difficult on a full-time, year-round basis. Not only is she responsible for most of the housework, but as a result of ongoing conflicts with her youngest daughter, Isabel has had to take legal custody of her daughter's two children. "Being" a U.S. citizen enables Isabel to flee her difficult family situation by allowing her to remain in the Dominican Republic without concern that she may lose her legal permanent residency. Indeed, Isabel threatened her children with her "blue passport" (U.S. passport), saying that she could now leave the country and never come back. While U.S. citizenship helps Isabel to periodically relieve herself of unwanted domestic responsibilities, both family obligations and economic factors compel her to continue to return to the United States. Isabel still heads the household in New York City, and her obligations and ties to her children and grandchildren invariably require that she be in New York. Also, when she can, Isabel often finds temporary factory employment while in New York.

U.S. citizenship also helps Isabel and Mariana, the two married women of the first cohort, to be with their husbands, both of whom suffer from a variety of serious health problems and prefer to live at least part of the year in the Dominican Republic. On different occasions, both women had to negotiate the conflicting demands of their U.S.-residing children and grandchildren and those of their husband. Although married women often feel obligated to follow their husbands to the Dominican Republic, many only reluctantly embrace the permanent return project. The task of maintaining transnational family ties was a concern to men as well; however, it was not mentioned as frequently as a motivating factor in either their migration or naturalization decisions.

A final dimension of "being" and "becoming" a U.S. citizen among the older immigrants concerns the gendered nature of reincorporating in the Dominican Republic. Although both men and women face the task of readapting to their communities of origin after many years abroad, reintegration appears more difficult for women than for men. First, family obligations—both real and fictive—are an important pull back to the United States for women, which disrupts their stay in the Dominican Republic. In addition, because older women are more likely to be receiving some form of state assistance, they are more likely to return in order to maintain an appearance of U.S. residence, as well as to fulfill various bureaucratic requirements associated with receiving state aid. Other dimensions of life in Mao propel women to return. Partly as a result of patriarchal structures and gendered socialization, women are less likely than men to find or create opportunities to engage in small or informal business ventures to generate income and occupy their time. Women are also more constrained in their spatial mobility (see Kurien, this volume). Thus, it is not uncommon to hear women express their desire to return to New York. This combined with some of the difficulties of daily life in Mao—including irregular if not absent social services, water and electricity shortages, and limited availability of consumer goods—propels women to return to the United States, enhancing the importance of U.S. citizenship (see Guarnizo, 1997).

Men's greater financial independence and weaker ties to family networks help to account for their different plans for the future. For the two *men* of the first cohort, fear of losing access to "benefits" was a concern, but their sense of vulnerability was less charged than that of the women. Both Daniel and Pablo were concerned about the possibility of losing access to their earned social security entitlements, while Pablo also mentioned the possibility of having to rely on Medicaid in the future. Unlike their sisters, both men anticipate permanent return migration with occasional reentry, rather than a sojourning pattern. Immigrants' subjective notions of personal fulfillment also encourage them to return to the Dominican Republic. For both men, retirement to the DR is seen as a "natural" end to their migrant career and represents an escape from the regimentation of urban, working-class life, particularly the disciplinary routines of wage labor.

Fifty-two-year-old Daniel has worked at a plastics factory for the last 26 years. He owns land in Mao and envisions retiring to the Dominican Republic when he stops working. He decided to naturalize earlier than he had anticipated due to changes in the laws. Daniel said:

> I think what made me rush my decision to become a citizen was the changing laws that we're seeing now . . . because in any case I was going to become a citizen, but I thought I'd do it when I was sixty, if I were alive . . . when I was ready to receive my pension. . . . It's one way to return to my country, and you know when you're a citizen, you don't have to come back every year like you do when you're a resident.

Forty-one-year-old Pablo, who has worked for several decades at the same plastics factory as his brother, views U.S. citizenship as guaranteeing the right to reenter the United States after permanent resettlement in the Dominican Republic. Pablo said,

> When I reach retirement age, sixty or sixty-two years old . . . if I want to go to the DR to live, it would be easy for me to say, I'm not going back to the U.S. for the time being. I'm going to stay five, three, four years. I have a friend who worked with me, he spent ten years without coming here, but then he got sick, and the treatment there was very expensive. . . . Here he had Medicaid because he had worked here for many years. It was easier to receive treatment here because over there it was very expensive. He was a citizen. I think it's an advantage.

Although men's independence allows them to envision return as permanent, married men must negotiate their "retirement" with their wives, many of whom do not want to return permanently. Both Pablo and Daniel expressed concern about whether their wives (and children) would want to go back.

"A MAN ALWAYS GOES BACK FROM WHERE HE CAME": NATURALIZATION AND THE SECOND COHORT

We now elaborate on the group of younger Castillo family members. As a result of their different migration and settlement experiences and their distinct life-course stage, this group warrants separate discussion. In an earlier article (Gilbertson & Singer, 2000), we discussed why the recently arrived members of the second cohort were less likely to have naturalized than their longer residing cousins. Here we focus on the longer residing members of the second cohort, many—but not all—of whom have applied to naturalize or have "become" U.S. citizens. Among this group, we found that women were more likely to have naturalized as a way to consolidate settlement. The younger men, on the other hand, approached naturalization more cautiously and defensively. They tended to chafe more at the requirements of the process, and when they undertook it, they were more likely to see U.S. citizenship opportunistically and as part of a transnational strategy.

The earlier arriving members of the second cohort came to the United States at a relatively young age and are better adapted to life in New York City than their parents (are more proficient in English, have higher levels of education, are more acculturated to New York City, etc.). This group consists of 14 offspring (8 men and 6 women) of the first cohort and arrived in the United States at an average age of 16. Most live in the Dominican enclave of Washington Heights.

Most of the second cohort have U.S.-born children; they tend to reside in two-earner nuclear family households and at times extended family households. Most members of the second cohort are intensively involved in family networks that provide both social and economic support. Women depend heavily on kin for help in caring for children. As a result of their primary responsibility for child care and because of gendered labor market opportunities, women tend to have had more sporadic, temporary, and part-time or informal employment experiences.

The second-cohort women are less likely than their mothers to emphasize the advantages of U.S. citizenship relative to a transnational vision. Instead, they were more likely to talk about U.S. citizenship from the vantage point of a long-term resident of the United States. Thus, Isabel's 33-year-old daughter Ivana said that she naturalized in the early 1990s to secure the rights of U.S. citizenship, including the right to vote. Ivana lives with her husband and two children, and she and her children recently moved from Washington Heights to Connecticut in search of a better quality of life. Ivana said that becoming a U.S. citizen made sense to her because she does not anticipate returning to the Dominican Republic: "I don't think I'll go back. . . . What is there in the Dominican Republic for me now? I don't even know most of the people when I go back. . . . My kids like to visit there, but they've been raised here. There are a lot of problems with living in New York City, but I can't see going back, except to visit."

Zena's 35-year-old daughter, Adela, said she was naturalizing because she has three "American" children and anticipates remaining in the United States. Adela, who lives in Tampa, works in a physician's office, owns a home with her Cuban husband, speaks fluent English, and has three children, two of whom speak only English. She said "I feel like an American, really I am American in certain ways. . . . There's a lot about Dominican culture that I don't like; I could never see going back to the Dominican Republic to live." Adela, who moved out of Washington Heights in search of a better environment for her children, said that prior to changes in laws she had never thought it was necessary to "be" a citizen to live in the United States. She applied to naturalize in 1998, prompted by the Green Card Replacement Program, which encouraged immigrants to naturalize instead of replacing their green cards.

Several of the single women of the second cohort were more attentive to the advantages of U.S. citizenship for the purpose of travel abroad, but these plans did not seem to revolve around their permanent relocation. Prior to the time they naturalized, both 30-year-old Nicola and her 31-year-old cousin Eva were romantically involved with Venezuelans and were traveling back and forth between the United States and Venezuela. They stated that they "became" U.S. citizens partly as a result of travel considerations, but they also said that U.S. citizenship was important to them because they anticipated living in the United States. Nicola, who is currently single, works in a factory and lives with her parents. She naturalized in 1994, prior to the changes in laws. She said: "Being a citizen helps . . . the ease of travel, for jobs—you're eligible for all kinds of employment, and you're more legal here, more secure." Although Nicola said that she wasn't sure whether she would reside permanently in the United States, she seemed comfortable with the idea of being a U.S. citizen, saying that she liked living in the United States. Eva, who also naturalized prior to the wave of anti-immigrant legislative changes, said that she became a U.S. citizen because "I live here, I feel good here, I like the United States." In fact, Eva said that "becoming" an American citizen has made her want to "be" more American: "In certain ways I appreciate the opportunity to become an American citizen; I see it as an opportunity; I want to learn more English and learn more about American culture."

These accounts of U.S. citizenship contrast with those of the men of the second cohort. The earlier arriving men of the second cohort were more likely than their female counterparts to say that they plan on returning to the Dominican Republic at some time, and their decisions to naturalize were seen as a way for them to facilitate travel and/or future transnational residence. As a result, naturalization was approached with greater ambivalence, and the naturalization outcomes of this group vary more than for the second-cohort women. While most of the younger women have naturalized or have applied to naturalize, the men are less likely to have naturalized; those who did apply to naturalize were more likely to have done so since the advent of anti-immigration laws.

Isabel's 28-year-old son, David, for example, lives in his parents' household in Washington Heights. He is single and works as a driver for an express mail delivery service. He arrived in the United States when he was 12 years old. David, who applied to naturalize in 1996, said that he had been interested in naturalizing for several years but had not because he was afraid of losing his Dominican citizenship. He said that he was concerned about this because he anticipates returning to the Dominican Republic to start a business. David "naturalized" his return to the Dominican Republic, saying, "A man always goes back from where he came." David was more at ease about becoming a U.S. citizen when he was certain that dual nationality protected his rights as a Dominican citizen.

Guillermo expressed a similar ambivalence toward U.S. citizenship. Guillermo, who is 45, arrived in the United States when he was 19 years old, is married, has a U.S.-born son, and has worked in a factory for over two decades. Guillermo owns a home in Mao, visits on a regular basis, and anticipates returning there when he retires. When asked why he was naturalizing, Guillermo said:

> I'm not doing it because I feel it in my heart. People say that being a legal permanent resident isn't worth anything now. And, to live here you have to become a citizen now, to get medical insurance, other things. They say you've got to become a citizen in order to retire, too. For me, I'm becoming a citizen so that I can travel with greater ease.

Part of the reluctance to naturalize for men may also be linked to their unwillingness or their inability to comply with the requirements of naturalization in the context of recent anti-immigration legislation. This context cast doubt on the motivations of immigrants who wanted to "be" citizens. The process of "becoming" a U.S. citizen required that immigrants submit to various types of testing procedures, open their lives and pasts to state surveillance, and renounce old-country allegiances. Ironically, in seeking relief from various forms of gender and class-related discipline in the United States, men had to submit to other forms of state-imposed discipline to "become" a U.S. citizen.

Several immigrant men told us they lacked the English skills and/or the time to study the English they believed necessary to pass the exam, while others mentioned that they were going to wait until the fever surrounding naturalization died down, so as not to appear that they were naturalizing "for the benefits." Other men found it difficult to naturalize due to changing laws. For example, 38-year-old Leonel, a fluent English speaker who has resided in the United States for over 20 years, was more adamant in his rejection of state-imposed constructions of U.S. citizenship due to his belief that he is going to return to the Dominican Republic to live. However, Leonel wants to naturalize, in part, out of fear that, because of a prior drug conviction, he may be restricted from reentering the United States if he were to leave. Leonel has been advised by several lawyers neither to leave the country nor to apply to naturalize at the present time. Pablo, a member of the first cohort who had not yet naturalized, told us that U.S. citizenship would also help him to resolve his concern that he might have problems reentering the country because of the advent of the Anti-Terrorist Act and the stricter screening of immigrants entering the United States. He had a prior problem with the local welfare bureaucracy that has since been resolved through paycheck deductions by his employer; however, these payments are often submitted late, leaving Pablo in a vulnerable state.

> If I travel now, for example, the way the laws are now, I could have problems when I return from there. They could check in the computer, and I could have problems. It's not that I'm afraid, because I have all the receipts, but it would be a hassle, I'd have to go to court, etc. I was going to go back, but now I'm not because of this, not until I resolve this problem. This is one of the reasons for me becoming a citizen, and for many immigrants who are here. If I were a U.S. citizen, I could go back to the Dominican Republic without fear, and even if there was a problem, they couldn't deport me because I'm a citizen. This is one of the main reasons for becoming a citizen.

Why are the men of the second cohort more likely than the women to see U.S. citizenship as a way to return to the Dominican Republic? In part because U.S. citizenship facilitates the possibility of a life that men see as more fulfilling and rewarding. Men's views are informed by a bifocal perspective (Rouse, 1992), which has been nurtured by transnational structures and is based on gendered assumptions. In the United States, their incorporation in low-status service and factory occupations, restricted spatial movement, and their racialization also shape their experiences. In seeking release from the conditions of their "immigrant" lives in the United States, most men engage in some sort of imagining, planning, and investing in a future where they can sustain themselves and their family in the Dominican Republic through entrepreneurial activities.

Forty-six-year-old Joaquín has returned to the Dominican Republic numerous times over the past decade, each time staying for as long as a year. Joaquín, the first Castillo family member to naturalize in 1985, said that when he became a citizen he was planning to stay in the United States. However, he now plans on returning permanently to the Dominican Republic, and to that end has built a large home in Mao. Joaquín is bitter about his experience in the United States: he feels that various forms of racialized discrimination have limited his and his family's opportunities. Joaquín's permanent resettlement plan, though, is complicated by the fact that he has not been able to earn enough income to support himself and his family in Mao and that his wife does not want to reside permanently in the Dominican Republic. Recently, Joaquín "moved back" to the Dominican Republic with his wife and youngest son and plans to establish a business there.

Men's dissatisfaction with changing gender relations also informs their desire to return. Like the Mexican immigrant men in Roger Rouse's study (1992), Dominican men often lament how women and children "change" once they have lived in the United States, and they complain frequently, as Rouse's respondents did, of the forces that challenge their authority at home—including the state, police, and schools. Return, or the "mirage of return" (Guarnizo, 1997), is a way for men to look for some sort of psychological alleviation from the domination they experience in the United States (Rouse, 1992).

Dominican men also seek enhanced status in their return to the Dominican Republic (see Basch, Schiller, & Szanton Blanc, 1994). This enhanced status has gender, class, racial, and sexual dimensions. As *retornados*, men bring resources from the United States that can translate into a more privileged class status—often as self-employed entrepreneurs or as members of a leisure class—in the local stratification scheme. Men—and women to a lesser extent—also make status and membership claims upon return through intensive and often conspicuous consumption. As Goldring states, "transnational social spaces and the locality of origin in particular, offer a special context for claiming and valorizing status" (1998, p. 167). Mexican men in Goldring's study make status and membership claims through spending U.S. earnings on consumer goods, a home, vehicles, land, cattle, or productive activities. These are among the activities that constitute being a sojourner or return migrant among the Castillos.

An additional—and overlooked—reason that return migration is attractive to men concerns men's greater opportunities for sexual relationships with women in the Dominican Republic. Men's enhanced status as retornados increases their ability to establish sexual relationships with other women. This gendered dimension of return migration also pressures men's wives to return with their husbands and reduces returning wives' bargaining power in their marriages.

A bifocal perspective also informs younger women's views of their experiences in the United States. Although they face challenges and problems similar to those of men in the process of settlement—low-paying, low-status employment, identification as members of a subordinate and inferior racial group—women perceive that they are better off in the United States than they would be in the Dominican Republic. Women's increased ability to find work and their access to other networks of support—both informal and state sponsored—facilitate independence and contribute to women's desire to remain in the United States. Women's primary responsibility for raising children and their closer ties to their children also account for their greater rootedness in the United States. U.S. citizenship, thus, is more likely to confirm and extend women's sense of place. This interpretation is in accord with research on gendered settlement that finds that women make greater gains in status, autonomy, and resources relative to men in the United States (Hondagneu-Sotelo, 1994; Kibria, 1993; Menjívar, 2000; Pessar, 1986). The benefits of life in the United States, though, belie the difficulties many immigrant women face, particularly those who are raising children in impoverished urban neighborhoods on low incomes (see Weyland, 1999). As Hirsch (2000) cautions, there is no one story to be told about women's migration to the United States.

CONCLUSION

The contemporary experiences of Dominican immigrants in New York City help us to decenter the "citizenship model of membership" narrative. Immigrants' multiple allegiances and identities, the retention of ties to their homeland, and their marginal status in the United States shape the acquisition and practice of citizenship, while the structures and meanings attached to U.S. citizenship also shape immigrants' experiences. Part of the experience of contemporary citizenship acquisition has been immigrants' insertion in a gendered, racialized, and national space where they were constructed as undeserving recipients of both citizenship and the rights of citizens.

Within this context, we hope to have clarified how gender contributes to the constitution of U.S. citizenship by seeing naturalization through an immigrant lens. Not only does gender influence the naturalization process, but it informs immigrants' understanding of what "being" a citizen means and the practice of citizenship. Citizenship practices, in turn, influence gender relations. The social process of "becoming" and "being" a U.S. citizen contributes to the reconstitution of traditional gender hierarchies by facilitating transnationalism, especially among men. However, these processes also contribute to the inversion of such hierarchies by facilitating women's independence and legitimating their relationship with the state. The recent context of anti-immigrant legislation, which restricted access to state benefits to U.S. citizens, pressured immigrants to confirm their allegiance to the United States through acquiring legal membership rights.

NOTES

1. Quotation marks are used to remind the reader of the difference between the process of "becoming" a U.S. citizen (naturalization, or the formal acquisition of citizenship) and "being" a U.S. citizen (i.e., the substantive dimensions of citizenship, or social, economic, cultural, and political experiences after naturalization).

2. In 1997 alone, 1.6 million applications for naturalization were filed with the Immigration and Naturalization Service (INS)—nearly five times those filed in 1992. This surge in naturalization represents a major departure from the stable rates of approximately 250,000 applications per year during the 1980s and early 1990s. Three federal programs contributed to the increase. Applications began a sustained rise in 1992, which coincides with the INS's Green Card Replacement Program, which required permanent residents to replace their green cards with new, more counterfeit-resistant cards. This program encouraged immigrants to naturalize rather than apply for a new green card. Secondly, in 1994 the first of approximately 3 million undocumented immigrants who changed status under the amnesty provisions of the 1986 Immigration Reform and Control Act became eligible to naturalize. It is expected that they will continue to contribute to the increase in applications in the coming years. A third program that encouraged immigrants to naturalize was the Citizenship USA initiative, which by one estimate encouraged nearly a million immigrants to apply for citizenship. This program was shut down, however, after Republicans charged that it was designed to increase the Democratic electorate and an investigation revealed that some people had made it through the naturalization process without proper FBI background checks.

REFERENCES

Aleinikoff, T. Alexander. (1998). *Between principles and politics: The direction of U.S. citizenship policy* (International Migration Policy Program 8). Washington, DC: Carnegie Endowment for International Peace.

Aleinikoff, T. Alexander, & Klusmeyer, Douglas. (2001). *Citizenship today: Global perspectives and practices*. Washington, DC: Carnegie Endowment for International Peace.

Basch, Linda, Schiller, Nina Glick, & Szanton Blanc, Cristina (Eds.). (1994). *Nations unbound: Transnational projects, postcolonial predicaments, and deterritorialized nation-states*. Amsterdam: Gordon & Breach.

Bauböck, Rainer (Ed.). (1994). *Transnational citizenship: Membership and rights in international migration*. Aldershot, England: Edward Elgar.

Bredbenner, Candice. (1998). *A nationality of her own: Women, marriage, and the law of citizenship.* Berkeley & Los Angeles: University of California Press.

Brubaker, W. Rogers. (1989). *Immigration and the politics of citizenship in Europe and North America.* Washington, DC: German Marshall Fund of the United States and University Press of America.

Collins, Patricia Hill. (1999). Producing the mothers of the nation: Race, class, and contemporary U.S. population policies. In Nira Yuval-Davis & Pnina Werbner (Eds.), *Women, citizenship, and difference.* London: Zed Books.

Duany, Jorge. (1994). *Quisqueya on the Hudson: The transnational identity of Dominicans in Washington Heights* (Dominican Research Monographs). New York: Dominican Studies Institute, City University of New York.

Espiritu, Yen Le. (2000). Americans have a different attitude: Family, sexuality, and gender in Filipina American lives. In Maxine Baca Zinn, Pierrette Hondagneu-Sotelo, & Michael Messner (Eds.), *Gender through the prism of difference* (2nd ed.). Boston: Allyn & Bacon.

Faist, Thomas. (2000). Transnationalization in international migration: Implications for the study of citizenship and culture. *Ethnic and Racial Studies, 23*(2), 189–122.

Gilbertson, Greta, & Singer, Audrey. (2000). Naturalization under changing conditions of membership: Dominicans in New York City. In Rubén Rumbaut, Nancy Foner, & Steven Gold (Eds.), *Immigrant research for a new century: Multidisciplinary perspectives.* New York: Russell Sage Foundation.

Goldring, Luin. (1998). The power of status in transnational social fields. In Michael Peter Smith & Luis Eduardo Guarnizo (Eds.), *Transnationalism from below.* New Brunswick, NJ: Transaction.

Grasmuck, Sherri, & Pessar, Patricia. (1991). *Between two islands: Dominican international migration.* Berkeley & Los Angeles: University of California Press.

Graham, Pamela. (1997). Reimagining the nation and defining the district: Dominican migration and transnational politics. In Patricia Pessar (Ed.), *Caribbean circuits: New directions in the study of Caribbean migration.* New York: Center for Migration Studies.

Guarnizo, Luis Eduardo. (1997). The emergence of a transnational social formation and the mirage of return migration among Dominican transmigrants. *Identities, 4,* 281–322.

Guarnizo, Luis Eduardo, & Smith, Michael Peter. (1998). The locations of transnationalism. In Michael Peter Smith & Luis Eduardo Guarnizo (Eds.), *Transnationalism from below.* New Brunswick, NJ: Transaction.

Hagan, Jacqueline Maria. (1994). *Deciding to be legal: A Maya community in Houston.* Philadelphia: Temple University Press.

Hernández, Ramona, & Rivera-Batiz, Francisco. (1997). *Dominican New Yorkers: A socioeconomic profile, 1997.* New York: CUNY Dominican Studies Institute.

Hirsch, Jennifer. (2000). En el norte la mujer manda: Gender, generation, and geography in a Mexican transnational community. *American Behavioral Scientist, 42*(9), 1332–1349.

Hondagneu-Sotelo, Pierrette. (1994). *Gendered transitions: Mexican experiences of immigration.* Berkeley & Los Angeles: University of California Press.

Itzigsohn, José, Cabral, Carlos Dore, Medina, Esther Hernández, & Vásquez, Obed. (1999). Mapping Dominican transnationalism: Narrow and broad transnational practices. *Ethnic and Racial Studies, 22,* 316–339.

Jones-Correa, Michael. (1998). *Between two nations: The political predicament of Latinos in New York City.* Ithaca, NY: Cornell University Press.

Joppke, Christian. (2000). How immigration is changing citizenship: A comparative view. *Racial and Ethnic Studies, 22,* 629–652.

Kibria, Nazli. (1993). *Family tightrope: The changing lives of Vietnamese Americans.* Princeton, NJ: Princeton University Press.

Knop, Karen. (2001). Relational nationalities: On gender and nationality in international law. In T. Alexander Aleinikoff & Douglas Klusmeyer (Eds.), *Citizenship today: Global perspectives and practices.* Washington, DC: Carnegie Endowment for International Peace.

Levitt, Peggy. (2001). *The transnational villagers.* Berkeley & Los Angeles: University of California Press.

Menjívar, Cecilia. (2000). *Fragmented ties: Salvadoran immigrant networks in America.* Berkeley & Los Angeles: University of California Press.

New York City Department of City Planning. (1996). *The newest New Yorkers, 1990–1994.* New York: Department of City Planning.

Pessar, Patricia. (1986). The role of gender in Dominican settlement in the United States. In June Nash & Helen Safa (Eds.), *Women and change in Latin America* (pp. 273–294). South Hadley, MA: Bergin & Garvey.

Pessar, Patricia. (1995). *Visa for a dream: Dominicans in the United States.* Boston: Allyn & Bacon.

Rouse, Roger. (1992). Making sense of settlement: Class transformation, cultural struggle, and transnationalism among Mexican migrants in the United States. *Annals of the New York Academy of Sciences, 64,* 25–52.

Singer, Audrey, & Gilbertson, Greta. (1999, June 7). Blurring the welcome to immigrants. *Washington Post,* p. A19.

Sorenson, Ninna Nyberg. (1998). Narrating identity across Dominican worlds. In Michael Peter Smith & Luis Eduardo Guarnizo (Eds.), *Transnationalism from below.* New Brunswick, NJ: Transaction.

Smith, Robert. (1998). Transnational localities: Community, technology, and the politics of membership within the context of Mexico and U.S. migration. In Michael Peter Smith & Luis Eduardo Guarnizo (Eds.), *Transnationalism from below.* New Brunswick, NJ: Transaction.

U.S. Immigration and Naturalization Service. (1997). *Statistical yearbook of the immigration and naturalization service, 1996.* Washington, DC: U.S. Government Printing Office.

Werbner, Pnina, & Yuval-Davis, Nira. (1999). Introduction: Women and the new discourse of citizenship. In Nira Yuval-Davis & Pnina Werbner (Eds.), *Women, citizenship, and difference.* London: Zed Books.

Weyland, Karin. (1999). *Dominican women con un pie aquí y el otro allá: International migration, class, gender, and cultural change.* Unpublished doctoral dissertation, New School for Social Research, New York.

CONTRIBUTORS

Marixsa Alicea is an associate professor at DePaul University in the School of New Learning and earned her PhD from Northwestern University in sociology. In addition to carrying out research in Puerto Rican studies, she does work on women and drug use and adult education issues. She has published articles concerning Puerto Rican women and their transnational migration experiences and is the coauthor of *Surviving Heroin: Interviews With Women in Methadone Clinics*, published by the University Press of Florida.

Ernestine Avila is a doctoral candidate in the Sociology Department at the University of Southern California. Her areas of interest include race, gender, and immigration. She is Social Science Research Council, International Migration fellow for the 2001–2002 academic year. She is currently researching and writing her dissertation on Mexican and Central American transnational mothers and fathers and their children.

Anna Chee is an assistant professor of education, language, and literacy development at California State University, Los Angeles. For the last ten years, her teaching and research have focused on the interdisciplinary study of the lives of immigrants and the children of immigrants and their processes of literacy development and educational achievements. As part of this research focus, the coauthored chapter in this book examines immigrant lives and their sociopolitical and economic contexts.

Yen Le Espiritu is professor of ethnic studies at the University of California, San Diego. She is the author of two award-winning books: *Asian American Panethnicity: Bridging Institutions and Identities* (Temple University Press, 1992) and *Asian American Women and Men: Labor, Laws, and Love* (Sage, 1997). Her forthcoming book, *Home Bound: Filipina American Lives across Cultures, Communities and Countries* (University of California Press, 2003), addresses the transnational and gendered lives of Filipino Americans.

Greta Gilbertson is associate professor in Fordham University's Department of Sociology and Anthropology, where she teaches courses on immigration, race, and ethnicity. She has published articles on the social and economic incorporation of immigrants, and she received an Open Society Institute Fellowship to study naturalization in the context of the 1996 welfare reforms.

Steven J. Gold is professor and associate chair in the Department of Sociology at Michigan State University. He has published articles on qualitative research methods, immigration, ethnic economies, and ethnic community development in numerous journals and edited volumes. He is coeditor of *Immigration Research for a New Century: Multidisciplinary Perspectives* (Russell Sage Foundation, 2000) (with Rubén G. Rumbaut and Nancy Foner) and the author of three books: *Refugee Communities: A Comparative Field Study* (Sage, 1992), *From the Worker's State to the Golden State: Jews from the Former Soviet Union in California* (Allyn & Bacon, 1995), and *Ethnic Economies* (with Ivan Light) (Academic Press, 2000).

Luin Goldring is an associate professor of sociology at York University and a fellow at York's Centre for Research on Latin America and the Caribbean. She has published articles on Mexican state-migrant relations and property rights reform. Her current research examines transnational practices among Latin American migrants in Toronto.

Gloria González-López is an assistant professor in the Department of Sociology at the University of Texas, Austin. Born and raised in Mexico, she received a PhD in sociology from the University of Southern California. She has worked with Latin American immigrants as a psychotherapist, teacher, and sex educator at different community-based agencies in Texas and California. Her book on Mexican immigrant women and sexuality is forthcoming from the University of California Press.

Pierrette Hondagneu-Sotelo is an associate professor in the Department of Sociology, and affiliated with the program in American studies and ethnicity, at the University of Southern California. She is author of *Gendered Transitions: Mexican Experiences of Immigration* (University of California Press, 1994) and *Domestica: Immigrant Workers Cleaning and Caring in the Shadows of Affluence* (University of California Press, 2001), which received the Pacific Sociological Association's Distinguished Scholarship Award, several awards from the American Sociological Association, and the C. W. Mills Award of the Society for the Study of Social Problems. Currently, she is researching various sites of the faith-based immigrant rights movement in California.

Prema Kurien is an assistant professor of sociology at the University of Southern California. Her work focuses on understanding the ways in which religious background and ethnicity shape and are shaped by international migration, settlement, and immigrant politics. She is author of *Kaleidoscopic Ethnicity: International Migration and the Reconstruction of Community Identities in India* (Rutgers University Press, 2002). She is completing a second book-length manuscript, "Multiculturalism and Immigrant Religion: The Development of an American Hinduism."

Wan Shun Eva Lam is a PhD candidate in the School of Education at the University of California, Berkeley. Her research examines literacy practices in informal learning environments and the intersection of language, culture, and identity in the education of immigrant students. She is writing a dissertation on how Chinese youngsters in the United States are socialized to use English in the global peer group networks on the Internet.

Nancy López is an assistant professor of sociology at the University of New Mexico, Albuquerque. Her book *Hopeful Girls, Troubled Boys: Race and Gender Disparity in Urban Education* (New York: Routledge, 2002) focuses on second-generation Dominicans, West Indians, and Haitians and explains why girls of color from these groups are succeeding at higher rates than their male counterparts. Her forthcoming coedited book, *Creating Alternative Discourses in Latino Education* (New York: Peter Lang Publishing) with Raul Ybarra, addresses the need for counterhegemonic discourses on how to improve educational opportunities among Latinos. Her current work includes research in the Albuquerque Public Schools.

Sarah J. Mahler is an associate professor of anthropology at Florida International University in Miami. Her research and publications focus primarily on Latin American and Caribbean migration to the United States and the development of transnational ties between migrants and their home communities. She is author of *American Dreaming: Immigrant Life on the Margins* (Princeton University Press, 1995) and *Symbiosis and Conflict: Salvadorans in Suburbia* (Allyn & Bacon, 1996), and she is also coeditor, with Patricia Pessar, of a special issue of the journal *Identities: Global Studies in Culture and Power* on gender relations in transnational spaces (2001).

Cecilia Menjívar is a sociologist and associate professor in the School of Justice Studies at Arizona State University. Her research on immigration focuses on the social processes embedded in population movements. She has written several articles and book chapters on social networks, gender relations, family dynamics, and religious communities and the church, mostly among Central Americans in the United States. She is also the author of *Fragmented Ties: Salvadoran Immigrant Networks in America* (University of California Press, 2000).

Marjorie Faulstich Orellana is an assistant professor of education and social policy at Northwestern University. Her research focuses on the experiences of Latino immigrant children in urban schools and communities, using language and literacy as a window into the construction of childhoods and children's identities. She has published in such journals as the *Harvard Educational Review, Anthropology and Education Quarterly, Visual Sociology, Social Problems,* and the *International Journal of Bilingualism and Bilingual Education.*

Patricia R. Pessar is an associate professor of American studies and anthropology at Yale University. She has conducted ethnographic research in Brazil, the Dominican Republic, the United States, and Guatemala. Her publications on international migration include *When Borders Don't Divide: Labor Migration and Refugee Movements in the Americas* (Center for Migration Studies, 1988), *Between Two Islands: Dominican International Migration* (coauthored with Sherri Grasmuck) (University of California Press, 1991), and *A Visa for a Dream: Dominicans in the United States* (Allyn & Bacon, 1995).

Saskia Sassen is the Ralph Lewis Professor of Sociology at the University of Chicago. She is the author of *The Global City: New York, London, and Tokyo* (Princeton University Press, 1991), *Guests and Aliens* (New Press, 2000), *Globalization and Its Discontents* (New Press, 1998), and editor of *Global Networks / Linked Cities* (Routledge, 2002). Her books have been translated into twelve languages. She is codirector of the Economy Section of the Global Chicago Project, a member of the National Academy of Sciences Panel on Urban Data Sets, and chair of the newly formed Information Technology, International Cooperation, and Global Security Committee of the SSRC.

Audrey Singer is a visiting fellow at the Center on Urban and Metropolitan Policy at the Brookings Institution. Her current research focuses on demographic issues in U.S. cities, including the economic, social, and political incorporation of immigrants. She received an Open Society Institute Fellowship and a Social Science Research Council Postdoctoral Fellowship for her research on naturalization.

Barrie Thorne is a professor of sociology and women's studies at the University of California, Berkeley. She is the author of *Gender Play: Girls and Boys in School* (Rutgers University Press, 1993) and coeditor of *Feminist Sociology: Life Histories of a Movement* (Rutgers University Press, 1997), *Rethinking the Family: Some Feminist Questions* (Northeastern University Press, 1992), and *Language, Gender, and Society* (Newbury House, 1983). She is currently working on a book about children growing up in Oakland that is situated in an analysis of the changing political economy and social construction of childhoods in contemporary California.

Maura I. Toro-Morn is an associate professor of sociology at Illinois State University, where she teaches about race, class, and gender inequality in the United States. She is the author of numerous articles on the class and gender dimensions of Puerto Rican migration to Chicago. She is currently completing a book on the gendered aspects of international migration.

James A. Tyner is an assistant professor of geography at Kent State University. His primary research areas involve gender and migration in Southeast Asia, especially in the Philippines. He has published over 30 articles and book chapters in journals such as *Society and Space, The Professional Geographer, Asian and Pacific Migration Journal,* and *Gender, Place, and Culture.*

INDEX

Compositor:	Impressions Book and Journal Services, Inc.
Text:	10/12 Baskerville
Display:	Baskerville
Printer and binder:	Maple-Vail Manufacturing Group